Globalisation and the Western Legal Tradition

What can 'globalisation' teach us about law in the Western tradition? This important new work seeks to explore that question by analysing key ideas and events in the Western legal tradition, including the Papal Revolution, the Protestant Reformations and the Enlightenment. Addressing the role of law, morality and politics, it looks at the creation of orders which offer the possibility for global harmony, in particular the United Nations and the European Union. It also considers the unification of international commercial laws in the attempt to understand Western law in a time of accelerating cultural interconnections. The title will appeal to scholars of legal history and globalisation as well as students of jurisprudence and all those trying to understand globalisation and the Western dynamic of law and authority.

Dr David B. Goldman is a Special Counsel at Deacons, Sydney, and an Honorary Affiliate, Julius Stone Institute of Jurisprudence, University of Sydney.

D1262468

The Law in Context Series

Editors: William Twining (University College London), Christopher McCrudden (Lincoln College, Oxford) and Bronwen Morgan (University of Bristol).

Since 1970 the Law in Context series has been in the forefront of the movement to broaden the study of law. It has been a vehicle for the publication of innovative scholarly books that treat law and legal phenomena critically in their social, political and economic contexts from a variety of perspectives. The series particularly aims to publish scholarly legal writing that brings fresh perspectives to bear on new and existing areas of law taught in universities. A contextual approach involves treating legal subjects broadly, using materials from other social sciences, and from any other discipline that helps to explain the operation in practice of the subject under discussion. It is hoped that this orientation is at once more stimulating and more realistic than the bare exposition of legal rules. The series includes original books that have a different emphasis from traditional legal textbooks, while maintaining the same high standards of scholarship. They are written primarily for undergraduate and graduate students of law and of other disciplines, but most also appeal to a wider readership. In the past, most books in the series have focused on English law, but recent publications include books on European law, globalisation, transnational legal processes, and comparative law.

Books in the Series

Anderson, Schum & Twining: *Analysis of Evidence*
Ashworth: *Sentencing and Criminal Justice*
Barton & Douglas: *Law and Parenthood*
Beecher-Monas: *Evaluating Scientific Evidence: An Interdisciplinary Framework for Intellectual Due Process*
Bell: *French Legal Cultures*
Bercusson: *European Labour Law*
Birkinshaw: *European Public Law*
Birkinshaw: *Freedom of Information: The Law, the Practice and the Ideal*
Cane: *Atiyah's Accidents, Compensation and the Law*
Clarke & Kohler: *Property Law: Commentary and Materials*
Collins: *The Law of Contract*
Cranston: *Legal Foundations of the Welfare State*
Davies: *Perspectives on Labour Law*
Dembour: *Who Believes in Human Rights?: The European Convention in Question*
de Sousa Santos: *Toward a New Legal Common Sense*
Diduck: *Law's Families*

Globalisation and the Western Legal Tradition

Recurring Patterns of Law and Authority

DAVID B. GOLDMAN

CAMBRIDGE
UNIVERSITY PRESS

CAMBRIDGE UNIVERSITY PRESS
Cambridge, New York, Melbourne, Madrid, Cape Town, Singapore, São Paulo, Delhi

Cambridge University Press
The Edinburgh Building, Cambridge CB2 8RU, UK

Published in the United States of America by Cambridge University Press, New York

www.cambridge.org
Information on this title: www.cambridge.org/9780521688499

First published 2007

Printed in the United Kingdom at the University Press, Cambridge

A catalogue record for this publication is available from the British Library

ISBN 978-0-521-68849-9   paperback

Contents

Preface

History shows that humans attempt, with some success, to control what was previously uncontrollable. Now more than ever, globalisation and its technological manifestations attest to humans surprising older generations by increasing their control over, for example, time and space, the atom, health and food production. Yet globalisation has a history with roots deeper than the topsoil of its late twentieth-century receipt into popular language. The roots penetrate to a core reservoir of philosophical, theological and legal aspirations. Thought about in this way, these aspirations appear never to leave us even though, technologically, humans can make such incredible advances over their physical constraints (with good and bad implications).

This book explores the recurring, deeper level problems of authority underlying law in 'the West', with a sense of hopefulness for the future, but also with some anxiety about the way law is conceived and used today. The conviction emerged during the composition of this book that a major theme of the Western legal tradition is that humans invest their constitutions and legal discourses with vital visions for the future which are too easily forgotten when revolutionary urgencies are perceived to have passed. Today, it seems important to be aware of this decadent potential of law. Rights can be proclaimed as 'global', 'fundamental' or 'universal' in the service of partisan objectives without thought for the bloody signposts of their evolution. If those historical signposts are forgotten or worse still ignored, what foundation can there be for the changes which must come in the future? In making choices, what confidence can be available?

These signposts come into focus, in chapter 2, with the exploration of dualities from globalisation literature such as universality and diversity, space and time, and state sovereignty and world society. A 'Space–Time Matrix' is offered as a comparative model for attempting to understand historical patterns of law and authority, by reference to interior moral and exterior political impulses, and versions of history and visions of the future, in chapter 3. This model is then applied to Western history in order to illuminate the development of the Western legal tradition and its usefulness for understanding globalisation and its challenges to the sovereign nation-state.

Chronological discussion begins with the unrest of the original European community, in chapter 4, culminating in the Papal Revolution and the birth of the Western legal tradition around 1100, in chapter 5. An expansive notion of a 'holy Roman empire' is adopted to describe the God-centred norms and government which grew amidst a universalist moral and political discourse maintained by a supranational Catholic church, constitutionally co-ordinated with feudal princes and their diverse realms. Territorial ideas of law and authority grew away from the Christian commonwealth, leading to the idea of the state, considered in chapter 6. Notwithstanding a universalist European legal science, states fostered their own particular legal orders after the Protestant Reformations, assisted by the 'legislative mentality', explored in chapter 7.

The emergence of a European public international law system of states in the seventeenth century was increasingly secular. Universalist moral and political authority decreased. By the eighteenth century, and the arrival of the liberal political economy, it becomes possible to see the God of the loosely defined Holy Roman empire being challenged by what might be thought of as a new god of Mammon. In the extreme, this may be associated with a 'wholly Mammon empire', although the picture is more complicated. Contemporary with the Enlightenment and the French Revolution, universal human rights and the 'codification mentality' have their origins, discussed in chapter 8, although constricted in operation to the nation-state and its particularistic notions of authority which are explored in chapter 9. The common human catastrophe of the twentieth-century 'World Revolution' of the two world wars, we see in chapter 10, has established human rights and free trade norms as morally and universally attractive although politically problematic as tenets of a pervasive new secular authority.

Two case studies of competing jurisdictions highlight, respectively, the recurring natures of public authority and private authority. Publicly, the European Union demonstrates the constitutional reversion from the European public international law model to a modernised version of the Christian commonwealth, centred less on God than on market values. This we see in chapter 11, where lessons of regional and global scope are drawn from European Union constitutionalism. Privately, international commercial law is traced historically to illustrate the change in the underlying god-concepts and to show the historical viability of law without the state, in chapter 12. The *lex mercatoria*, international arbitration and the codification of European contract law are evaluated for their elucidation of cross-border authority.

I have not been able to separate bookish tendencies from my practice as a lawyer and concern as a human being. (These latter two attributes are not necessarily mutually exclusive.) These pages endeavour to reflect more than a purely historical or conceptual approach to law. Recommendations are presented by way of conclusion, in chapter 13, for understanding and participating in law more meaningfully in our global era through a renewed historical consciousness.

Perhaps ironically, the space and time constraints inherent in writing a book have led to shortcomings in a work devoted to developing a legal theory which promotes the relevance of space and time. At the outset, I should respond to two obvious criticisms. A book about the Western legal tradition which is based upon sources appearing only in English commits an injustice by ignoring shelves of relevant Continental writings. For this I must plead personal linguistic limitations and practical experience of only the Anglo-Australian legal system. Fortunately there are some (but not enough) books in translation which I have considered. Also inviting criticism is this book's degree of generalisation in covering such vast spaces and times, a defence of which is offered in chapter 1. Because no discipline, profession or vocation alone tells the whole story about the creation, acceptance and maintenance of authority, I have trespassed outside my own experiences of legal education and practice. Whatever criticisms may be deserving, I do hope that they will be vindicated in some measure by provoking debate about the relationship of history, globalisation and law in the quest for meaningful and just social orders at all levels.

This book has benefited immensely from the support and encouragement of the persons and institutions below, to whom I extend my deepest gratitude (of course, without implicating them in any deficiencies which remain in my text). Momentum for the thoughts in this book was sprung from a stimulating undergraduate legal education at Macquarie University Law School in the early 1990s. The book began as a Ph.D. thesis at the University of Sydney Faculty of Law, supervised by Klaus A. Ziegert, later with indispensable co-supervision by Jeremy Webber and associate supervision from Patrick Kavanagh. The law firm Deacons accommodated my need at times for flexible employment arrangements. An Australian Postgraduate Award scholarship enabled me to undertake full-time research between 1999 and 2001. William Twining has generously commented on the revised manuscript of this book, amongst other kindnesses. I have also benefited greatly from comments and kind support at various stages from Harold J. Berman, H. Patrick Glenn, Ian Lee, Heidi Libesman and James Muldoon. Anonymous reviews from Cambridge University Press were also helpful. The Julius Stone Institute of Jurisprudence at the University of Sydney and its Law Library have extended vital research facilities and collegiality. Cambridge University Press, particularly Finola O'Sullivan and Sinéad Moloney, have been patiently supportive, and provided professional production by Richard Woodham and Wendy Gater with keen-eyed copy-editing by Sally McCann.

My mother, Rhonda, and sister, Jane, have been encouraging of this enterprise and tolerant of my distractedness; in addition to which my father, Alec, has assisted with current affairs observations from his many subscriptions. Especially to my wife Yvonne, and infant sons, Benjamin and Jeremy: thank you for your patience and for being a voice of measure for this book and in life – it is now time for an overdue holiday and much more play.

Christmas Eve 2006
Sydney, Australia

1

Introduction

Children often wonder why things are the way they are. Although a child appears to enjoy what can become a never-ending game of asking 'but why?' after every answer given by an adult, the child is innocent enough to be dissatisfied with what the adult is forced by experience to take for granted. Children are naturally curious and question what the adult has become accustomed not to question. The child's logic challenges the adult's custom. So might the curious social observer challenge the legal status quo. In this vein, I seek to investigate what globalisation can teach us about law in the Western tradition, and what the Western legal tradition can teach us about globalisation. The subtitle of this book anticipates my conclusion that globalisation demonstrates recurring patterns of law and authority. Recognising these patterns is crucial to advancing law in the third millennium. To appreciate these patterns requires the child's sustained wonder, and the uncommon sense that the world we see today began long, long before the adult's lifetime.

Philosophy has its origin in simple wonderment perhaps akin to that of the child. Such simple wonder at things being the way they are is captured in the Ancient Greek concept of *thaumazein*, for example in the dialogue of Socrates with the perceptive youth Theaetetus.[1] This curiosity is a 'playful looking about when one's quite immediate vital needs are satisfied', which, if unchecked, develops into the philosophy of philosophers.[2] An enquiry which proceeds explicitly under this banner may hazard being childish, especially when the enquirer has worked long enough in the legal profession to be considered an adult or at least a youth who knows his way about. I believe this risk to be worth taking. The prevailing, unquestioning acceptance of law as a tool of the state for achieving social goals with which one may or may not agree as a matter of

---

[1] Plato, *Theaetetus*, in B. Jowett (ed. and trans.), *The Dialogues of Plato*, 5 vols. (Oxford: Oxford University Press, 1892), vol. IV, 155c–d, p. 210: '[W]onder is the feeling of a philosopher, and philosophy begins in wonder. He was not a bad genealogist who said that Iris (the messenger of heaven) is the child of Thaumas (wonder).'

[2] Edmund Husserl, 'The Vienna Lecture: Philosophy and the Crisis of European Humanity' appearing as Appendix 2, in *The Crisis of European Sciences and Transcendental Phenomenology*, trans. David Carr (Evanston: Northwestern University Press, 1970), p. 285. Husserl was critical of this purely theoretical attitude. His criticism can be deflected if better questions can be formulated independently of staid answers.

convenience (as opposed to being a measure, say, of virtue or redemption with ethical significance) demands the asking of basic questions in the quest to shed light on what is happening to law today in this time of 'globalisation'.

Adopting the stance of the inquisitive and inadvertently philosophical child, enquiry about law might proceed with the adult as follows (and this is not so far from contemporary, mainstream jurisprudential thought):

Question 1:   Why is something law?
Answer 1:   Because the state says so.

Question 2:   Why does it say so?
Answer 2:   Because people must listen to the state.

Question 3:   Why must they listen to the state?
Answer 3:   Because the state has power over them.

Question 4:   Why does the state have power over them?
Answer 4:   Because the people gave it the power.

Question 5:   Why did the people give it the power?
Answer 5:   Because people want to live orderly lives.

Question 6:   Why is this orderly?
Answer 6:   Because the people said so.

Question 7:   Why did they say so?
Answer 7:   Because that's what's best for people.

Question 8:   Why is that best for people?
Answer 8:   Because they want to get on with their lives.

Question 9:   Why do they want to get on with their lives?
Answer 9:   Because they've got to earn money.

Question 10:   Why do they want to earn money?
Answer 10:   To feed children. You do want to eat, don't you?

In this context – and other paths of frustrating logic can be contemplated – the present book seeks to make a contribution. The 'how?' instead of 'why?' question will instead be asked in the hope that better questions should lead to better answers. 'How is something law?' is the better question. Although a little semantic at first glance, the 'why?' question assumes that there is a cause. Maybe there are causes or even one cause; however those causes would be so imbued with ideology and contention that there could never be widespread agreement as to those causes let alone one single cause. Rather, in asking 'how is something law?', the opportunity presents to examine the meaning underlying the social order. Social order and social change are, above all, testaments to meaning and humans' understandings of their relationships to their environment and ultimate reality and meaning. The 'how?' question provides greater scope to appreciate law throughout history (time) and across cultures (space) even within just one tradition – the Western tradition – enabling lessons to be learned from the social manifestations of changes in patterns of thought.[3] Enquiries into 'how?' changes occurred at different times, and in different places and spaces, yield more helpful answers than speculation merely as to 'why?' they occurred. 'How?' is linked to the processes of accomplishing change by reference to what can be argued to be legitimate; whereas 'why?' guesses at causation. By approaching the enquiry into the modern legal condition as a study in the achievement of authority, the temptation of a precocious child to answer the questions of the world with little life experience can be balanced with the answers dictated by the less critical experiences of an adult.

Detailed enquiry into the word 'globalisation' will proceed in chapter 2. For the time being, the simple definition of it as 'the accelerated interconnections amongst things that happen in the world' will suffice. Globalisation presents a timely opportunity to appreciate law for something it has always been, as the sovereign nation-state visibly declines as the monopoly law creator and maintainer. A major contention of this book is that law in the West has never come only from one place; it has never, for any extended period of time, been validated by only one system of doctrine and belief; and it has never required territorial exclusivity for its essence. Such recurring themes will be seen in the selective chronological analysis of the Western legal tradition. Chapter by chapter, a secular, economics-grounded authority, which might be caricatured as a 'wholly Mammon empire', emerged from the medieval Christian commonwealth, which can conveniently be thought of as a 'holy Roman empire'.[4]

1.1 The Western legal tradition

Before exploring 'globalisation' in the next chapter, in the detail befitting such a ubiquitous buzz word, the 'Western legal tradition' presents its own conceptual challenges. The phrase as it is used in this book derives from the subtitle of Harold J. Berman's first volume of *Law and Revolution* – '*The Formation of the Western Legal Tradition*'.[5] Arguably the term 'Western legal tradition' has a life of its own, popularised if not coined by that author.[6] The term has come to carry a set of specific attributes identified by Berman, which are considered below in

---

[3] For other approaches which take this question seriously, see Harold J. Berman, *Law and Revolution: The Formation of the Western Legal Tradition* (Cambridge, MA: Harvard University Press, 1983), pp. 336, 361; G. R. Elton, *English Law in the Sixteenth and Seventeenth Century: Reform in an Age of Change* (London: Selden Society, 1979), p. 4; and William Twining, *Globalisation and Legal Theory* (London: Butterworths, 2000), pp. 76–81 (proposing Karl Llewellyn as 'the jurist of the How'). See too chapter 3, section 3.2, pp. 58–9 below for reference to Husserl's philosophy of 'how'.

[4] On these nuanced notions, see chapter 4, section 4.1, pp. 80–1 below.

[5] Berman, *Law and Revolution*.

[6] John Witte Jr, 'From Homer to Hegel: Ideas of Law and Culture in the West' (1991) 89 *Michigan Law Review* 1618–36, 1619.

section 1.5. The components of the term do warrant some basic elaboration in the meantime: the words 'Western', 'legal' and 'tradition' may all mean different things to different people.

1.1.1 'Western'

The idea of the 'West' is used in this book to locate, culturally, multiplex legal phenomena occurring at a generalised level in Western Europe and in its colonial offspring (for example, Australia, Canada, New Zealand and the United States of America). Variations on the 'West' will be used alternately with 'Europe'. England, whilst geographically separated from the Continent, is undoubtedly part of this description, given its Romanist legal influences and reciprocal intellectual and religious contributions. R. C. van Caenegem's 'First Europe' of the eighth- and ninth-century Carolingian dynasty – present-day France, western Germany, Belgium, the Netherlands, Luxembourg, Switzerland, north-east Spain and northern and papal Italy – are clearly within the Western and European purview.[7] Ancient Greek philosophy, Jewish spirituality and Roman law, whilst outside this territory and time frame, made their way into the West of my concern, by way of adoption, transformation and reconciliation.[8]

Since the heartland of the 'Roman' Empire shifted to Byzantium in the fourth century, Greece and more eastern European countries have periodically parted ways with certain trends in the West (the main political significance of which was the 'Caesaropapism' of the Orthodox Church fusion with Empire, which was different from the Western constitutional separation of the spiritual and secular powers). Associated Eastern European legal history is therefore not included in my notion of the Western legal tradition. For the past 500 years, Russia has teetered on the verge of Europe, although more lately its twentieth-century Marxist Revolution was directly inspired by European thought,[9] and its main constitutional developments have taken place in the European part of its territory.[10] Distinctive features of Western civilisation, such as Catholicism, the fifteenth-century Renaissance, the Protestant Reformation and the Enlightenment are mostly absent from the Russian experience.[11] For lack of direct relevance to the task at hand, although not lack of importance to understanding law and globalisation (especially in respect of their movement to market economies), these territories have generally been omitted from my discussion.

There were Arabic influences on the West, particularly in philosophy (including Aristotelian natural law) and science in the early second millennium. The presence of Arab communities in the Mediterranean basin may have helped to

---

[7] R. C. van Caenegem, *An Historical Introduction to Western Constitutional Law* (Cambridge: Cambridge University Press, 1995), p. 43.   [8] Berman, *Law and Revolution*, p. 3.

[9] See Norman Davies, *Europe: A History* (London: Pimlico, 1997), pp. 11–13.

[10] van Caenegem, *Western Constitutional Law*, p. 6.

[11] See Samuel Huntington, *The Clash of Civilizations and the Remaking of World Order* (New York: Simon & Schuster, 1996), p. 139 and pp. 144–62 on Greece.

provoke the profound Western developments in law of the late eleventh century. The Western legal tradition may have been influenced doctrinally in a relatively minor way by Islam.[12] Constitutionally, nonetheless, the legal science and systematisation of legal doctrines associated with the emergence of the Western legal tradition appear to be a peculiarly Western phenomenon.

1.1.2 'Legal'

Enquiry into the meaning of 'legal' is to ask the question: 'what is law?' Books on the philosophy of law and conventional jurisprudence attempt to deal with this question. A brief statement from a number of schools of thought is all that is required for deriving an idea of 'legal' for present purposes. The popular, positivist definition of law by H. L. A. Hart holds law to be generally obeyed rules of behaviour, valid according to rules of recognition (such as a constitution) accepted by public officials.[13] Natural law exponent John Finnis might add to this definition the requirement that law aspire to practical reasonableness.[14] These positivist and naturalist theories are both somewhat dependent upon each other: Hart's rule of recognition (and the similar idea of Hans Kelsen's *Grundnorm*)[15] requires a naturalistic norm to establish the validity of the legal system; whilst Finnis's natural law is dependent upon a positive legal system being in place. Ronald Dworkin, responding to Hart, has maintained that legal authority comes from the history of the political community and the individual's rights against the state.[16] Roscoe Pound, a founder of sociological jurisprudence, viewed law as a social institution for satisfying social wants in a civilised society.[17] This latter definition of law seems to encompass the present, predominant legal mentality, as opposed to the more metaphysical and means-driven (as opposed to ends-driven) philosophy of Finnis.

Definitions of law – of what law is and is not – continue almost *ad infinitum*. As William Twining has argued, the continuities and discontinuities between law and different types of ordering can be obscured by trying to define law too precisely.[18] It is possible in this regard to have some sympathy with Richard

---

[12] See chapter 5, section 5.4, pp. 108–9 below.

[13] See H. L. A. Hart, *The Concept of Law* (Oxford: Clarendon Press, 2nd edn 1994), p. 116.

[14] See John Finnis, *Natural Law and Natural Rights* (Oxford: Clarendon Press, 1980 reprinted 1992), esp. pp. 276–7. 'Natural law' for Finnis can be conveyed in three 'rather bald assertions' encompassing: (1) practical principles for human flourishing used by all; (2) requirements of practical reasonableness leading to morally right and wrong acts; enabling (3) 'a set of general moral standards' (p. 23).

[15] There is though a significant difference between the positivisms of Hart and Kelsen: Kelsen is satisfied that there is a single global normative order, whereas Hart admits the possibility that different orders can overlap with fundamental validity depending upon point of view (e.g., as an English person or as an international diplomat). See Neil MacCormick, 'Beyond the Sovereign State' (1993) 56 *Modern Law Review* 1–18, 8–9.

[16] See generally Ronald Dworkin, *Taking Rights Seriously* (Cambridge, MA: Harvard University Press, 1977).

[17] See Roscoe Pound, *Introduction to the Philosophy of Law* (New Haven: Yale University Press, 1954), p. 47.   [18] Twining, *Globalization and Legal Theory*, p. 244.

Posner's criticism of enquiries in the manner of Hart and Dworkin, which have attempted to define what law 'is' rather than what law 'does'.[19] The pitfall should be avoided, however, of succumbing to what law 'does' as opposed to the richness of what law 'might be' in light of that which it 'has been', across cultures and through time. Legal authority may come from the state, the tribe, the international organisation or myriad other organisations. Usually there will be some manner of hierarchy for resolving conflicts where they occur amongst these legal systems, in a stable society. Sovereignty may then be said to reside in this hierarchy (rather than necessarily centrally), and it may be shared, for example, between church and state or between state and international bodies.

Bearing in mind the historical development of the Western legal tradition in later chapters, it should be accepted that law can be thought about as 'norms which, for one reason or another, achieve authority or receive allegiance', without the necessity for the centralised sovereign state of the theorists above. Every society has a constitution, not necessarily written. Not every society is a state. A neighbourhood association, tennis club, no less than the Group of Eight, has a constitution, because 'to be a society', as Philip Bobbitt observes, 'is to be constituted in some particular way'.[20] The model of law I advance in chapter 3 aims to progress beyond stereotypical and historically contingent ideas of law by showing the social construction of authoritative norms in terms of space and time. The resulting reliance of law upon intuitive moral and cultural allegiance together with more intellectual political and rational allegiance will then aid the exploration of authority which continues to be constructed in traditional ways in our time of globalisation.

1.1.3 'Tradition'

To have a tradition means to have a history and a framework for the future. That is not necessarily something grandiose, abstract or tautological, such as the satirical school motto, 'A Heritage of Tradition', appearing on an episode of the television cartoon 'The Simpsons'. According to H. Patrick Glenn, a tradition is composed of cultural information brought from the past into the present. A large and great tradition becomes so because it has 'an over-arching means of reconciling different views'.[21] Attempts to close traditions (especially legal traditions) from change fail. Witness God (believed to have been via Moses)[22] and others including Emperor Justinian, Frederick the Great and French

---

[19] See Richard Posner, *Law and Legal Theory in England and America* (Oxford: Clarendon Press, 1996), pp. 1–37.

[20] Philip Bobbitt, *The Shield of Achilles: War, Peace and the Course of History* (London: Penguin, 2003), p. xxiii.

[21] H. Patrick Glenn, *Legal Traditions of the World: Sustainable Diversity in Law* (Oxford: Oxford University Press, 2nd edn 2004), pp. 13, 50.

[22] Deuteronomy 4: 1–2. '. . . You shall not add to the word which I command you, nor take from it . . .' (New King James Version, NKJV).

revolutionaries trying to state the law in one place, for all time.[23] Tradition can also evoke emotion, pride and inspiration – for example, church historian Jaroslav Pelikan defines *tradition* as the living faith of the dead (as opposed to *traditionalism* being the dead faith of the living).[24] For present purposes, it is unnecessary to adopt such evocations. It suffices to note that legal if not textual traditions encompass both continuity and change.[25]

Eric Hobsbawm's essay 'Inventing Traditions'[26] is frequently deployed in the social sciences to undermine the notion of tradition. For example, he contends that nationalism has seen some traditions invented 'comparatively recently', typically involving anthems and images. To answer Hobsbawm's notions, the Western legal tradition is not 'recent'; it is not based upon an 'invariant' vision of social life with 'novel situations as anathema'; nor is it pragmatically invalid. 'Invented traditions' are different from 'genuine traditions', according to Hobsbawm, 'where the old ways are alive'.[27] On these criteria, the Western legal tradition is energetically alive, although not without the usual challenges for survival and influence which all traditions face.

1.1.4 A world legal tradition?

The above should not be taken to suggest that the Western legal tradition is the only tradition relevant to globalisation. Nor should it suggest that the Western social experience has not suffered famine, injustice, pestilence, absolutism and inhumanity, which still have the ability to reappear. The Western narrative has not been an inexorable journey of progress 'from Plato to NATO'.[28] On the contrary, exciting prospects arise for a plurality of legal traditions to exist side by side, to enrich each other through the sharing of information. The Western legal tradition as, in effect, the first legal tradition on the scene with a global reach if not grasp in some fields may have the constitutional resources to respond to this challenge through its historical emanation from competing legal systems in Europe. In mixing with the traditions of other cultures of greater difference, it may be transformed. In time it may then be possible and desirable to speak of a world legal tradition.[29] Any such tradition would be loose and, if at all possible,

[23] Martin Krygier, 'The Traditionality of Statutes' (1988) 1 *Ratio Juris* 20–39, section 7.

[24] Jaroslav Pelikan, *The Vindication of Tradition: The 1983 Jefferson Lecture in the Humanities* (New Haven: Yale University Press, 1984), p. 65.

[25] See Martin Krygier, 'Law as Tradition' (1986) 5 *Law and Philosophy* 137–62, 251–4. See too William Twining, 'Glenn on Tradition: An Overview' (2005) 1 *Journal of Comparative Law* 107–15.

[26] See Eric Hobsbawm, 'Introduction: Inventing Traditions' in Eric Hobsbawm and Terence Ranger (eds.), *The Invention of Tradition* (Cambridge: Cambridge University Press, 1983).

[27] Hobsbawm, 'Inventing Traditions', pp. 1–13.

[28] This is shown in David Gress, *From Plato to NATO: The Idea of the West and its Opponents* (New York: The Free Press, 1998).

[29] The major proponent of – if not founder of – the term 'Western legal tradition', welcomes this possibility: Harold J. Berman, 'The Western Legal Tradition in a Millennial Perspective: Past and Future' (2000) 60 *Louisiana Law Review* 739–63, Section II C, D.

something of a collection of approaches to the idea of tradition.[30] The Western heritage might still be visible, amidst valuable doctrines and ways of thinking about law from other traditions. It is to be hoped the result will be a richer conception of law, less reliant upon the normative monopoly of the state in the Western fashion of the past two or three centuries.

The prospect for something enduringly new to come from the melting pot of cultures and traditions heralded by globalisation is not without precedent from the Western legal tradition. Roman law, Hebrew theology and Greek philosophy are often thought to be hallmarks of the Western cultural achievement. Yet each in its historical time, taken in isolation, was antagonistic to the other. It was only in their adoption by a later culture we know as 'Western' that they became reconciled and merged in a way of living and thinking.[31] A global or world legal tradition may one day, with the appropriate attitudes, synthesise now disparate ideas and practices into a discourse which may maintain stability whilst accommodating change within manageable, consistent parameters of normativity and meaning. This may already be within the Western collective experience. Cultural relativism and understandable fears of Western imperialism must first be addressed with appropriate sensitivity, the pursuit of which is embarked upon in chapter 10.

1.2 Patterns of law and authority: from the celestial to the terrestrial

Whereas once the Judeo-Christian God was the source of meaning at the core of legality in the Western legal tradition, economics appears now to be emerging as the significant discourse. A universal discourse, be it of God or economics or human rights, or a mixture of such discourses, has been necessary to legitimate all Western constitutional law, including decisions of legislatures. Just how these *actual* sources of authority changed, yet the *patterns* of authority underlying Western constitutionalism have recurred, serves to plot the trajectory of my historical discussion and the questions to be asked.

As will be explored in more detail later in chapter 3, all law requires legitimacy from discourses of authority purporting to describe some manner of ultimate reality and meaning. By way of introduction and for conceptual ease, sources of legal authority may be illustrated by reference to the depiction of fundamental law in certain artworks.

In the ninth century, the Ten Commandments were portrayed, in an illustration in the Bible of Montier-Grandval,[32] as being literally handed to Moses from

---

[30] On traditions of traditions, see Krygier, 'Traditionality', section 7, referring to Karl Popper.

[31] See Berman, *Law and Revolution*, p. 3. This emergence was not smooth, contrary to what chauvinistic and perhaps nationalistic writers about the idea of 'the West' have sometimes propounded, as observes Gress in *Plato to NATO*.

[32] *Moses Receives the Tables of the Law; Moses Presents Them to the People*, from the Bible of Montier-Grandval, mid-ninth century, miniature on parchment, British Museum, London, in Sara Robbins (ed.), *Law: A Treasury of Art and Literature* (New York: Hugh Levin, 1990), p. 34.

a hand penetrating from a heavenly ceiling with two angelic beings hanging upside-down in the top of the scene. In the lower part of the drawing, in a separate scene, Moses is portrayed as presenting that law to the people. Papal authority was similarly thought to be directly, divinely ordained at that time, as will be seen in chapter 4.

In the seventeenth century, Rembrandt depicted the same biblical event very differently.[33] Pensively, Moses carries the Decalogue above his forehead. He stands in front of Mt Sinai, with realistically drawn cloud settled on the mountain. There is the hint in the Rembrandt that the seventeenth-century interpretation of Moses had him invested with more personal agency in the carriage of the laws; neither God nor the angels are to be seen. In chapter 7, we shall witness a coeval rise of a 'legislative mentality' possessed by less inhibited kings freed from papal law, with a differently conceived divine right and ability to create law.

A depiction of the authority of the Declaration of the Rights of Man and Citizen, in the late eighteenth century, features different symbols of authority.[34] Two tablets, slightly resembling those carried by Rembrandt's Moses, are set into a Romanesque sandstone monument. A capstone features the French title of the document, with a smaller reference attributing it to the human agency of the National Assembly. In keeping with this agency and coeval revolutionary ideals, a woman crouches, holding a broken shackle. Yet, to the right of the capstone, an angel sits leaning against it, pointing above towards the Enlightenment symbol of the all-seeing eye in the triangle – a (perhaps Trinitarian) symbol of God adopted on the United States Great Seal.

Further ambivalence towards the source of constitutional authority features in a nineteenth-century oil painting. J. B. Mauzaisse depicts the French Civil Code,[35] the Code Napoléon, held by Napoleon with his pen poised. Yet this human legal creation is surrounded with images of historical and divine authority. Floating on a cloud sitting only marginally higher than Napoleon, an angelic if not God-like figure representing Time sits over what looks like the Grim Reaper's scythe, crowning Napoleon with a Roman laurel. Napoleon's foot rests on the outstretched wing of an eagle. He sits over further Roman imperial imagery in the form of the senatorial mace at the top of which perches an ornamental gold eagle. Mauzaisse ascribes divine and deeply historical symbolism to Napoleon's law. The 'codification mentality' of this era, associated with the deistic belief that God had invented but abandoned the world, is explored in chapter 8.

---

[33] Rembrandt, *Moses with the Tables of the Law*, 1659, oil on canvas, Gemäldegalerie Staatilche Museen Preussischer Kulturbesitz, Berlin, in Robbins, *Law*, p. 35.

[34] *Declaration of the Rights of Man and Citizen*, c. 1789, Musée Carnavalet, Paris, in Robbins, *Law*, p. 139.

[35] J. B. Mauzaisse, *Le Code Napoléon Coronne par le Temps* (The Napoleonic Code Crowned by Time), 1833, oil on canvas, Le Musée National de Château de Malmaison, Rueil, France, in Robbins, *Law*, p. 201.

These are the observations of no art critic or *aficionado*. The selection is drawn from one book. No art in that book celebrates the tables of the United Nations Charter or the treaties of the European Union. If such art exists, it might not feature supernatural imagery. To reflect the new sources which inspire law, one might expect to find in this art an emphasis on human agency, industry and affluence, reflecting a fundamental transformation from celestial to terrestrial legal authority in the second millennium.[36]

Although the artworks described above do not amount to a scientific demonstration of the constitution of legal authority, they literally if not artistically illustrate the point that, at least according to these artists in their times, law is connected to sources of authority outside contemporary time and space, and these sources are open to change and reinterpretation. Whether law can continue to be inspired by the profoundest perceived sources of authority will depend upon the richness of the social philosophies which inspire and are relied upon by the legal imagination today. The conclusion to emerge in chapter 10 is that although sources of authority may have changed, the patterns of legal authority in the West have not. Law is dependent upon perceptions of ultimate reality and meaning.

1.3 Grand theory in the human sciences

Attempting to write about the Western legal tradition, in the qualified sense suggested, might appear ambitious enough. Yet globalisation must be brought into the analysis, too. This venture is not as overconfident as it might at first seem. The title is 'Globalisation *and* the Western Legal Tradition'. One might know something of the Western legal tradition or something of globalisation. The 'and' could cause some problems by introducing additional scope, although this conjunctive word can also add much needed refinement. This book is neither an exhaustive treatment of the Western legal tradition nor of globalisation. My concern is with the Western legal tradition as it can be elucidated by reference to globalisation, and vice versa. The Western legal tradition is explored by reference to the supra-territorial interconnections which suggest globalisation is a challenge less radical to the legal tradition than might otherwise be expected. Globalisation is explored for associated and recurring legal themes – namely, competing legal systems and jurisdictions, and universal patterns of authority comprising cultural and rational allegiances. This underlies my guiding aim: to investigate the phenomenon of law from my Western (specifically Australian) location and dawning third millennium time, and to enquire into its nature by reference to its history and perhaps its most obvious challenge, globalisation.

An aspiration of this book is to present, more generally, a meaningful framework for viewing the role of law in the social order, and the role of the social order in constructing law. The purpose behind doing so is to attempt to

---

[36] But see the background to the EU flag, in chapter 11, section 11.5, p. 270 below.

understand the reality of law and what constitutes law; to attempt to fathom, where possible, the limits and potentials of attitudes towards the social order and law; and to formulate a strategy for pursuing meaningful social order and law.

Each chapter and many sub-headings of this book could perhaps justify a dedicated Ph.D. or book from one of a number of social science and humanities disciplines. Analytical depth has been of particular concern to historians. Into how much depth should one delve? How many pages must be written, and how very many more pages read, about how many numerous topics, before one can make assertions about the discipline of study within which one writes? Norman Davies broaches this concern in the introduction to his book *Europe: A History*. He makes the critical remark that the magnification of historical detail into very short time periods 'is an example of the modern compulsion to know more and more about less and less'. Against this, the *Annales* school of history, from 1929, attempted to encourage 'specialists, whilst carefully tending to their own gardens, to take the trouble to study the work of their neighbours' in not only economics and sociology, but also psychology, demography, statistics, geography, climatology, anthropology, linguistics and medical science.[37]

Broad enquiry must be balanced with the potential to be too eclectic with insufficient supporting detail. A 'big-picture' approach must still, though, have its place in the attempt to make one's discipline relevant to contemporary developments and the wider community. In law, these connections are easy to make and difficult to contain. In the preface to his thoroughgoing theoretical investigation of, and recommendations for, world order, Philip Allott highlights this plight by remarking that his 400-page book required fifteen years of tenured academic appointment. It was

> difficult to sustain psychologically, as one area of study led on to another and there seemed no prospect of ever reaching an overall view of a kind which could be communicated to others. It is a ramshackle castle of self-reflection which the human mind has constructed over the last four or five thousand years . . . It is a place of interconnecting rooms, echoing with discordant voices, rooms with more or less arbitrary names on their half-open doors – Theology, Metaphysics, Epistemology, Moral Philosophy, Aesthetics, Philosophy of Science, Political Theory, Social Theory, Economic Philosophy, Legal Philosophy, Constitutional History, Economic History, Social History, Diplomatic History, and so on and strangely on.[38]

Specifically in the context of globalisation, after nearly ten years of research into globalisation and legal theory, William Twining felt able to provide only an 'interim report'. Fortunately, according to the job description he applies to the jurist, he is 'a licensed dilettante as well as a hired subversive'.[39] In making

[37] Davies, *Europe*, pp. 1, 955–6.
[38] Philip Allott, *Eunomia: New Order for a New World* (Oxford: Oxford University Press, 1990), p. xvi.   [39] Twining, *Globalisation and Legal Theory*, pp. 2–3, 90.

references to 'Grand Theory' or 'big-picture' approaches, not only the difficulties[40] but also the legitimacy attaching to such interdisciplinary study within the field of law may be appreciated.

More intuitively, the present age and that which is to come are overly concerned with particulars, at the cost of general themes which can bring understanding and fulfilment. The particularistic mentality was captured in Aldous Huxley's prophetically satirical *Brave New World*. 'For particulars, as every one knows, make for virtue and happiness; generalities are intellectually necessary evils. Not philosophers, but fret-sawyers and stamp collectors compose the backbone of society', according to Huxley's Director of Hatcheries and Conditioning.[41] For an unchallenged, strait-jacketed, predictable society, that may be alright. For our globally challenged society, excessive concentration upon particulars without reference to overall, general meanings and directions is seriously detrimental not only to personal fulfilment and self-awareness, but also to the economy which relies for efficiency upon individuals with a sense of purpose.

As such, the present book may well fall into the category of a renascent genre of legal scholarship, 'general jurisprudence'.

1.4 General jurisprudence

General jurisprudence is a notion which has been around for some time. It describes a 'big-picture' attempt to understand the nature of law in different social contexts or legal systems – that is, with some level of generality. The concern of Aristotle to separate universally held natural law propositions from particular positive laws varying from place to place (such as a goat and not two sheep shall be sacrificed)[42] was a type of general jurisprudence. The term developed currency in the eighteenth and nineteenth centuries. In this recent discourse, discussion begins with Jeremy Bentham.[43] In England (the Continental notion of 'general jurisprudence' was different),[44] perhaps surprisingly, in view of their fixation on sovereigns resembling states, John Austin[45]

---

[40] In addition to the scholarly difficulties of grand theory, many 'postmodernists' are cynical of the human ability to know and to generalise. According to Quentin Skinner, that very scepticism, when expanded, itself becomes a big picture view of the world, even if that picture is one of disorder or the need for enquiry into the concepts themselves: Quentin Skinner, 'Introduction: The Return of Grand Theory' in Quentin Skinner (ed.), *The Return of Grand Theory in the Human Sciences* (Cambridge: Cambridge University Press, 1985 reprinted 1997), p. 3.   [41] Aldous Huxley, *Brave New World* [1932] (Essex: Longman Group UK, 1989), p. 2.

[42] Aristotle, *The Nicomachean Ethics*, trans. David Ross (Oxford: Oxford University Press, reprinted 1980), V, 7, p. 124.   [43] See Twining, *Globalisation and Legal Theory*, ch. 3.

[44] A Continental sub-discipline of general jurisprudence sought to establish itself somewhere between the abstraction of legal philosophy and the practicality of legal dogmatics, in the first half of the twentieth century: William Twining, 'General Jurisprudence' in Manuel Escamilla and Modesto Savedra (eds.), *Law and Justice in a Global Society* (Granada: International Association for Philosophy of Law and Social Sociology, 2005), section IIb, referring to Van Hoecke.

[45] See John Austin, *The Uses of the Study of Jurisprudence* (London: Weidenfeld & Nicolson, 1954).

and H. L. A. Hart[46] considered themselves to be involved in the project of a general jurisprudence. That was so because they sought to lay down the principles of a theory of law which they believed was universally applicable to all law. In the global age, with these older concepts of centralised law muddied by jurisdictions of all shapes, sizes and locales, the need for attention to a general jurisprudence is returning to contemporary thought and legal practice.

Three contemporary theorists have taken the challenge of general jurisprudence seriously. William Twining and Brian Tamanaha use the specific phrase 'general jurisprudence' in their writings, and Harold J. Berman uses the term 'integrative jurisprudence' in similar terms and for the same goal of developing a general approach to law in the context of particular theories which do not singularly capture the complexity and diversity of law. Other authors implicitly suggest the need for a general jurisprudence, significant contenders perhaps being Boaventura de Sousa Santos,[47] Philip Allott,[48] H. Patrick Glenn[49] and Niklas Luhmann.[50] Tamanaha, Twining and Berman deal squarely with the concept of a general jurisprudence for our global era.

Tamanaha develops the notion of a general jurisprudence in what he calls a 'socio-legal positivist' fashion, reviewing law-type phenomena and reducing them to a universalist, 'core concept' of law – namely, 'whatever people identify and treat through their social practices as law'.[51] The excellence of his theory is to call for investigation of whatever people identify and treat through their social practices as law, in different 'social arenas',[52] by reversing the usual assumptions about law into questions which treat critically rather than take for granted the essence and function of law.[53] Arguably this answers only the 'what?'

---

[46] See Hart, *Concept of Law*. This view of the enterprise of general jurisprudence persists in Leslie Green, 'General Jurisprudence: A 25th Anniversary Essay' (2005) 25 *Oxford Journal of Legal Studies* 565–80.

[47] See Boaventura de Sousa Santos, *Toward a New Legal Common Sense: Law, Globalization and Emancipation* (London: Butterworths, 2nd edn 2002), esp. p. 371 for his map of capitalist law into domestic law, production law, exchange law, community law, territorial (state) law and systemic (world) law.

[48] See Philip Allott, *Eunomia: New Order for a New World* (Oxford: Oxford University Press, 1990), for his unreferenced attempt to construct, from first principles, a new theory of law for a peaceful and uniquely 'world' society; and his more orthodox *The Health of Nations: Society and Law Beyond the State* (Cambridge: Cambridge University Press, 2002).

[49] See Glenn, *Legal Traditions*, for an evaluation of structural aspects of the major legal traditions of the world and an attempt to appreciate comparative commonalities and diversity.

[50] See Niklas Luhmann, *Law as a Social System*, trans. K. A. Ziegert (Oxford: Oxford University Press, 2004), for perhaps the most advanced scientific attempt to describe and understand the phenomenon of law in modern societies.

[51] Brian Z. Tamanaha, *A General Jurisprudence of Law and Society* (Oxford: Oxford University Press, 2001), p. 166. Social systems specifically accepted by Tamanaha as law are state law, customary law, religious law, international law, transnational law, indigenous law and natural law (pp. 224–30).

[52] Tamanaha, *General Jurisprudence*, pp. 206–8. The social arena is used to identify boundaries for the study of a particular legal enquiry, such as a nation-state, a village, a local business community, the international merchant community, etc.

[53] Tamanaha, *General Jurisprudence*, p. 231.

question – that is, what law is. That approach may be useful for those theorists or practitioners who are happy to adopt a broad view of law and who feel challenged to compare the natures of different legal orders by reference to assumed qualities such as law's social mirroring[54] and social control functions. Tamanaha's theory does little, however, to illuminate how it is that the law achieves its authority and effectiveness through the changing tides of time.

Twining's notion of a general jurisprudence calls for a more open enquiry without the universalist ambition. Inviting a 'broader approach to law',[55] he is concerned 'about the health of the institutionalized discipline of law for the next ten to twenty years in the face of "globalization" '.[56] Twining seeks to 'enlarge the discipline'.[57] His general jurisprudence may be interpreted as a caution against the precipitate use of the term 'global jurisprudence' and 'global' especially. '[W]henever we hear a g-word we should pause and ask: is it being used precisely, or in this context is it exaggerated, superficial, misleading, simplistic, ethnocentric, false or just plain meaningless?'[58] Similarly, caution is required before using the word 'universal', which all too often will reflect a particular way of thinking, neither universally held nor applicable throughout the world. For present purposes, of further significance is Twining's call for a normative and historical jurisprudence to add to our understanding, inviting consideration of the construction of law and authority over time.

Berman's jurisprudence appears to offer a viable way forward in this latter respect, presciently responding to Twining's later call. Berman's notion of an integrative jurisprudence[59] infuses a normative agenda into the study and practice of law through the programme of 'historical jurisprudence', to be reconciled with the positive law and natural law schools which maintained a virtual duopoly over twentieth-century legal theory. Berman's suggestive model for a general jurisprudence is a corollary of his excursus into Western legal history.[60]

A purpose of the present book is to contribute to the current discourse of general jurisprudence by attempting to build a normatively and historically rich general jurisprudence relevant to the global age. That it purports to do so primarily by comparing cultures and orders within the Western legal tradition,

---

[54] That is, the way law reflects (or is supposed to reflect) the consensus of society.

[55] Twining, *Globalisation and Legal Theory*, p. 36; 'A Post-Westphalian Conception of Law' (2003) 37 *Law & Society Review* 199–257, 202.

[56] See William Twining, 'Reviving General Jurisprudence' in Michael Likosky (ed.), *Transnational Legal Processes* (London: Butterworths, 2002), p. 4; *Globalisation and Legal Theory*, pp. 175, 243.

[57] William Twining, *Law in Context: Enlarging a Discipline* (Oxford: Clarendon Press, 1997).

[58] Twining, 'General Jurisprudence', section IIa; and see his 'Globalisation and Comparative Law' in David Nelken and Elsin Orucu (eds.), *Comparative Law: A Hart Handbook* (Oxford: Hart Publishing, forthcoming).

[59] See Harold J. Berman, *Faith and Order: The Reconciliation of Law and Religion* (Atlanta: Scholars Press, 1993), ch. 13.

[60] See Berman, *Law and Revolution*; and more recently, his *Law and Revolution, II: the Impact of the Protestant Reformations on the Western Legal Tradition* (Cambridge, MA: Harvard University Press, 2003).

across time, still qualifies it as a work of general jurisprudence.[61] Marginalised and forgotten texts and ideas in the Western legal tradition have lessons to teach our globalist age and mentality.

Immediately, I must qualify my use of words such as 'global' and 'universal'. Twining's circumspection about using such words is justified. Often the word 'global' is used to describe processes which occur at multiple local or regional levels. Despite straddling territories if not continents, such allegedly 'global' processes may affect certain types of people in a society and leave other societies out completely. Literally, such processes are not 'global' in the sense of touching everyone or even nearly everyone on the globe. Similarly, 'universal' norms are often universal merely at regional levels or amongst particular peoples. Imprecision and exaggeration characteristically accompany these 'u-words' and 'g-words'. My own preference is to accept that, in popular parlance, these words are misused. A more readily comprehensible response requires using the words under dispute but using them more sensitively. With this intention, an '-ist' suffix is adopted in this book.[62] This is to suggest tendencies or purport rather than an absolute state of affairs connoted by the words 'global' and 'universal'. In each chapter, the prospects for 'universal*ist*' and 'global*ist*' norms are evaluated in different places and times. I believe it is helpful to consider these prospects, with appropriate sensitivity and realism. Provided that diversity and the possibilities for meaningful norm-making at the levels most affected by those norms are not precluded, improved peace and social flourishing are a prospect of learning to think along universalist and globalist lines. Looking in this manner beyond the immediacy of oneself and one's immediate society with a view to the 'welfare of the world' or 'humanity in general' is not foreign to Western social and legal history, as we shall see. There is much still to be done, to be pursued with alertness to the associated errors (at least to the modern mind) of the past such as those associated with imperialism, colonisation and intolerance. Heightened and new sensitivities are required. That is why this book resorts to terms such as 'global*ist*', 'universal*ist*' and '*purportedly* global', and dares only to venture a quest '*towards* a global*ist* jurisprudence' rather than to have the hubris to write of an unqualified 'global jurisprudence'.

So may one wonder what options there are for settling tensions between global concerns such as human rights, free trade, poverty, overproduction of consumer items, terrorism and American imperialism. Beholden to that wonder is the possibility that something bigger than we can imagine today will settle these tensions characteristic of the globalising society, through a reconciling

---

[61] On the permissibility of these criteria, see Twining, 'General Jurisprudence', sections IIb and III.

[62] Grammatically, I arrive at 'globalist' and 'universalist' as agent-nouns (used adjectivally) from the verbs 'globalise' and 'universalise', suggesting the attempt or purport of the act of globalising and universalising, falling short of the achievement of the actual end of this action. Such a use of the word 'globalist' is consistent with its definition in *The Shorter Oxford English Dictionary* (5th edn), as '*advocating* a global *approach* to economic etc. issues' [my italics].

discourse of world traditions and experiences.[63] That will not come through people thinking only of their current political and economic needs in the context of their current ethical and rational predilections towards what is right and wrong. It will come only through speaking about all of these things, with other peoples, in the context of a history which gives meaning to all of these precepts with the possibility for their reinterpretation to meet the present and future needs of our interconnected age.

1.5 Danger and opportunity

In 1983, Harold Berman wrote of his belief that the Western legal tradition was experiencing a crisis. In his opinion, only four out of the ten characteristics of the Western legal tradition remained:

1 law is different from politics and religion;
2 law is entrusted to a profession with its own discipline;
3 law is still systematised and conceptualised; and
4 this legal learning is something outside the laws on paper which allow the legal institutions and law to be understood.[64]

Despite these continuations, the other six characteristics of the tradition were no longer thought by Berman to remain:

5 the hierarchy of sources of law has been lost (that is, the conflict has been lost, for example, between feudal, royal, manorial, urban and canon law and with it the possibility of a constitutional synthesis of a solution for a given situation involving a plurality of jurisdictions), replaced by anti-formal techniques to justify rules and 'a new kind of cynicism' about legal discourse;
6 there has been a weakening in the belief that law is subject to ongoing development with the emergence of generations, such that the development of law is now seen as being simply ideological;
7 changes in the law, both historically and in the present, are thought to be due to pressure from forces outside the law;
8 in place of the distinction between law and politics, law is viewed as an instrument of the state and politics;
9 instead of a plurality of jurisdictions more recently including independent professions and trades but formerly including, for example, canon and urban law, there is a programme of swallowing up jurisdictions 'in a single central program of legislation and administrative regulation'; and
10 rather than law being reinterpreted and adapted to the future during times of revolution or great social change, there is the view that a new political regime spawned by revolution brings in a wholly new law, or old forms with new content.[65]

---

[63] Insights into this project, and the difficulties it faces, are to be found in Glenn, *Legal Traditions*.
[64] Berman, *Law and Revolution*, p. 37.   [65] Berman, *Law and Revolution*, pp. 38–9.

Perhaps this is overly pessimistic. In the attempt to find a way out of the present predicament, Berman confessed his existential need to look back on the fading Western legal tradition like a drowning man seeing his life flash before his eyes, whilst not bemoaning the changes. Somewhat ambivalently he admitted that the changes may even be 'a good thing', posing the question 'how do we go forward?'[66] In later publications his position is clearer. The 'crisis' of the Western legal tradition is a crisis in the true, translatable sense of the word. For the Greeks, *krisis* means a choosing, a time when choices must be made; in Chinese, 'crisis' is described as *wei-ji* – danger and opportunity.[67]

The choice for the individual is primarily one of attitude. How law is thought about and talked about will be crucial. The broad lesson I shall attempt to draw from the Western legal tradition for guidance value is the historical reliance of law upon logical and cultural allegiance for effectiveness and meaning amidst changing circumstances. My aim, perhaps similar to that of Berman, is to demonstrate that a consciousness of legal and social history is the only way to avoid relegating law to the anomie of faceless, ends-driven, majoritarian politics. Law should not just be thought of as a tool for getting things done – particularly during a time of great change.[68]

Many will argue over the particular lessons of history. In so doing, however, the belief in the guidance value of history must be conceded as a 'good thing', the more so if the context is the attempt to understand an analogous but uncharted present state of affairs. The present time is seeing to the performance of modern adaptations of scenes from medieval constitutional theatre which premiered at the formation of the Western legal tradition almost a millennium ago. Perhaps we can 'go forward' by revisiting some of the points of Berman's characterisation of the Western legal tradition.

5 & 9   It is now apparent that the number of viable jurisdictions is increasing, and the purported nation-state monopoly of authoritative norms is declining. The laws of the European Union, international trade laws including the World Trade Organization and human rights committees (both national and international) attest to this.

6   Arguably law has always been subject to criticism as an ideological institution, if 'ideology' is understood to mean the dominant, self-perpetuating social reality.[69] Those grounds in other times have been theological, philosophical and, perhaps characteristic of the twentieth century, political

---

[66] Ibid., pp. v–vi.   [67] Berman, 'Integrative Jurisprudence', p. 309.

[68] 'A social reality in which law is seen, not as the source, the limit and the judge of social power but as merely an incidental by-product of social power, is an illegitimate social reality': Allott, *Health of Nations*, [3.52]. An instrumentalist conception of law discredits law by associating it with special interests. It runs the risk of franchising judges to decide cases according to personally desired objectives, particularly in the US: see Brian Z. Tamanaha, *Law as a Means to an End: Threat to the Rule of Law* (Cambridge: Cambridge University Press, 2006).

[69] This notion of ideology is derived from Valerie Kerruish, *Jurisprudence as Ideology* (London: Routledge, 1991), pp. 34–42.

(liberalism versus communism). Western revolutionaries always attack the ideology of the predecessor. That law may now be thought to operate in the service of free trade or human rights may reflect, as is suggested later in this book, an emerging secular theology of our time with its own cultural resources and complexities. The challenge is to explore those complexities, and to keep attempting to reconcile them to an older legal discourse.

7 & 8   The perception that legal change occurs, for example, through politics as a result of pressure from outside the law, does indeed appear to underestimate the case-based innovation effected by judges in the common law fashion (sometimes referred to as judicial activism). Even judges are, though, responding to outside arguments about norms which are put to them. The outside arguments are filtered by advocates into legal terminology from their source in the outside world, in which change is ongoing. At revolutionary times, law is forced to take on the concerns which cannot be dissipated outside the filter of the court process or through remedial legislation. Nonetheless, there appears to be an increasing trend for law and legal process to be viewed by the government executive as a means to a political end, with traditional separation of powers doctrine under challenge.

10   The popular perception that laws are simply uprooted and replaced at times of revolution remains current. Although thoughts of revolution are far from the minds of most individuals born in common law countries, occasional remarks by professional colleagues to me about the topic of this book have drawn comments along the lines of 'I think we are headed for a world government with a world legal system'. The singularity of such a government and legal system should stretch the bounds of credulity for at least another two centuries. Such an overthrow of law appears unlikely.

Where they touch on globalisation, these themes will be explored in later chapters by reference to the historical precedents of interconnected and non-state societies with their underlying discourses of authority.

Returning to his question 'how do we go forward?', the solution proffered by Berman is to integrate the theories of positive law and natural law (mentioned above in section 1.1.2), and to add a third school: that of historical jurisprudence, which instils 'the national character, the culture, and the historical ideals and traditions of the people or society whose law it is'.[70] This consciousness need not be national, but it must be felt as a matter of group attachment to something outside oneself. Historical consciousness is crucial to the enterprise of maintaining and improving upon a sense of legality which attracts allegiance through, for example, an appreciation of parliamentary sovereignty as opposed to royal tyranny, or a common horror such as the World Revolution of the two world wars.

---

[70] Berman, 'Integrative Jurisprudence', p. 290.

In chapter 3, I will suggest a revised analytical scheme to apply to the task of understanding authority and formulating better law. Notions of positive law, natural law and historical jurisprudence will be considered in the more historically and socially transportable terms of 'custom' (*nomos*) and 'reason' (*logos*). Possibly these terms are transportable across traditions, too. To be effective, law must be able to appeal from these foundations to the individual, morally and culturally (*nomos*), as well as exert a more objective impulsion supported by reason, maintained politically (*logos*). This is the science of law, or 'nomology', as it is obscurely known. This 'Space–Time Matrix' will be used in the balance of the book to explore the patterns of law and authority in the millennium of the Western legal tradition.

1.6 Key issues in globalisation and legal theory

Although historical parallels do not prove anything of themselves, they will aid investigation into the extent to which jurisprudential thought needs to be amended to accommodate globalisation and the normative challenges of technology. To advance the general jurisprudence foreshadowed in the foregoing pages to understand law in the world today, the following signal themes will be employed to evaluate the recurring patterns of law and authority in the second millennium in the context of the historical changes.

- Paradigmatic aspects of the Western legal tradition, such as competing jurisdictions and transnational legal science, are recurring. Twentieth-century technology and industry have thrown the state back into the boxing ring with other jurisdictions. Law and legal authority have never, in the West, come from only one place, contrary to the popular fixation on the state as the only legitimate source of either.
- The modern fixation upon law as a political tool of the state for achieving present social goals, without necessarily and consciously deferring to deeper principles of ultimate reality and meaning, is a historically contingent trend. It is derivable particularly from the twentieth century and the focus on legislation which emerged. This instrumentalist tradition is a symptom of the modern fallacy in the point above (that law comes from one place – the state). For example, human rights and free-trade developments can be viewed as novel universalistic, natural law discourses with functional commonalities shared with medieval religious natural law. Reference to these discourses in law demonstrates the social requirement to ground law in an authority subject to sophisticated claims for legitimacy expressed in a legal science. Legal norms and social authority do not come from one place. Although a proposition may ultimately be 'legal' or 'illegal', it will be so by reference to different legal or normative systems which compete for priority in the prevailing discourse of authoritative norms.
- Commonly perceived themes in the globalisation literature, such as universality versus particularity and diversity, space and time, sovereignty versus

world society, and cultural forms of community versus political community, are manifested in the history of Western law and authority. These patterns may be said to be recurring. In older times, 'empire' was the preferred term or concept for purporting to maintain if not impose order of geographical magnitude amidst diversity. In more recent times, the idea of 'union' predominates. This is demonstrated, for example, by the appellations '*United* Kingdom of Great Britain and Northern Ireland', '*United* States of America' and, most recently, European *Union*. Easily forgotten, semantically, is that the oldest surviving Western political institution is the Roman *Catholic* (or *Universal*) Church.

- Thinking about the authority of law in terms of the Space–Time Matrix expounded in chapter 3 (interior, culturally acquired morality versus exterior, politically coerced rationality; and retrospection versus radicalism as horizons of social thought) enables us to contemplate, comparatively, the inadequacies and benefits of different approaches to the authority of law at different times. The chief pattern of authority is the requirement to have a core legitimating principle at the centre of the normative system. At the beginning of the Western legal tradition in the late eleventh century, God was at the centre of legitimacy (and markets dispersed), whereas today, markets are towards the centre of legitimacy (and spiritual communities dispersed). The inflexion of this pattern occurred about the time of the Protestant Reformations.

- Peace and co-operation at the national and international levels will not be accomplished by cold legal systems and formalities. Inquisitions and world wars bespeak the passions and shifting spiritualities and ultimate concerns which underlie fundamental legal challenges. Legal systems which ignore these allegiances do so at the peril of missing out on the increased effectiveness of laws which are believed in, rather than simply coerced.

- Western history shows that humans invest their constitutions with vital visions for the future which are all too easily forgotten when revolutionary urgencies are perceived to have passed. Treaties associated with globalisation, establishing the United Nations, the European Union, the Bretton Woods economics institutions and the International Criminal Court, should all be regarded as constitutional documents responding to the World Revolution of the two world wars in the twentieth century.[71]

At present, there is a widespread need to contemplate, deeply and critically, just what the challenges of globalisation mean to the way we think about law and social order in the West, and what are the historical continuities and discontinuities in the Western legal tradition which can be illuminated by globalisation studies. What is of value in the Western legal tradition? What should, or indeed can, be retained in a time of change? Answers to these questions may best be

---

[71] See ch. 10, section 10.3, pp. 220–6 below.

pursued by reference to the historical, philosophical and normative struggles of Western societies for the constitution of authoritative social orders.

These are not just matters for legal or social philosophers. Hopefully, in considering these questions, teachers and their students, writers, curious practitioners and policy-makers grappling with their own particular areas of legal doctrine in the face of globalisation, may ground their pedagogy, practice and research, both strategically and normatively. That is, strategically, they may contemplate what might be conceptually new about particular doctrinal and social challenges occupying their attention. Thoughts on legal strategies for dealing with these 'globalisation and law' challenges, such as legislative regulation, codification or encouragement of customary norms, may be stirred. Normatively, these teachers, writers, practitioners and policy-makers may appreciate the limits and the potential of law, by reference to the moral, political, conservative and radical dimensions inherent in the discourses of authority which have constituted the Western legal tradition.

The balance of this book attempts to address these key issues. For now, an exploration of the challenge of our time as it intersects with law – globalisation – can be postponed no longer.

Part 1
Towards a Globalist Jurisprudence

2

Globalisation and the World Revolution

Technology is a key element of globalisation. The effects of globalisation are frequently explored in the context of sovereignty. Technology therefore has constitutional implications. Perceived legal correlates to globalisation, such as the blurring divide between private and public international law through present constitutional issues associated with competing jurisdictions, legal pluralism, multinational enterprises and a 'world society', are related to the technological innovation associated with the World Revolution of the two world wars of the twentieth century. Yet it would be a mistake to assume that these legal developments are simple reactions to technological and economic forces of globalisation representing the latest political and economic goals. Far from today's legal responses being surface events, deeply layered sediments of legal and political philosophy and history underlie the topsoil intersections of law and globalisation. Globalisation and law cannot be understood without delving into the deeper sediments, pursued in later chapters. In this chapter, the topsoil formations are first surveyed in order to identify the sites of authority for later excavation.

The general notion of globalisation as 'the accelerated interconnections amongst things that happen in the world' will be maintained after some investigation. The terrorist events of 'September 11' 2001, in the United States, confirm this definition. (Within a fortnight, the world aviation industry was plunged into dire financial circumstances, international tourism reeled and the insurance industry faced massive losses.) After observing the profound associated challenges for social time and space in this chapter, a novel model will be proposed in chapter 3 to complete the outline for a globalist jurisprudence the subject of part 2. That will in turn enable, in the balance of this book, an appreciation of the nature of legal authority today by reference to the past millennium. Patterns of law and authority from the first half of the second millennium will be seen to be recurring today. Recognition of these patterns and the assessment of law in different locations and times will be essential to advancing a general, globalist jurisprudence.

2.1 Grappling with globalisation

2.1.1 Symbols and political change

Before being able to think about something, that thing must have its symbols in the world.[1] This insight will aid the attempt to define and understand globalisation. Michael Walzer has argued that the symbolic 'changes in the way men conceived the cosmological reference-world' made possible the political changes which occurred in the seventeenth century.[2] That is, when the earth was found not to be the centre of the universe, alternative political ideas emerged from these new symbols. The notion of a Godly, harmonious, hierarchical body politic was challenged by the socially contracted state comprising clashing individuals. What symbols of globalisation preceded the thoughts and ultimate incarnation of globalisation in our world?

Symbolically, the nation-state has, as its scientific correlates, order, precision and containment within manageable, territorial bounds, certain of time and space. That very type of Newtonian science was part of Walzer's example, in which territorial, parliamentary government became incipient. As the twentieth century unfolded, certain very different models from the natural sciences emerged. Einsteinian cosmology posited the relativity of time and space. According to Albert Einstein, there is no absolute measurement across space: clocks, for example, will vary according to the speed travelled. Measurement is localised.[3] Although this has only the most miniscule fractional significance for any activity on earth, it may have remarkable consequences for philosophy and, in a less direct way, society. It undermines certainty and increases relativity, particularly where judgements are concerned. That is, there may be other ways of looking at things. There may not be one divine set of norms to govern all people.

Chaos theory provides more useful symbolism. The study of natural phenomena in all their complexity is attempted by chaos theory, unlike classical science which tends to be reductionist and limiting of its variables. Chaos theory posits the significant interconnections amongst relatively distant, minute things that happen in the world.[4] In the common example now approaching a cliché, a butterfly fluttering its wings in one hemisphere of the world may have a significant effect in the other hemisphere, by way of snowballing weather effects which are initiated by the seemingly minor activity of the butterfly. Benoit Mandelbrot discovered a mathematical formula in fractal geometry which underlies chaos theory – positing that randomness produces

---

[1] Langer, *Philosophy in a New Key* cited in Michael Walzer, 'On the Role of Symbolism in Political Thought' (1967) 82 *Political Science Quarterly* 191–204, 194.

[2] Walzer, 'Role of Symbolism', 197.

[3] See Boaventura de Sousa Santos, *Toward a New Common Sense: Law, Science and Politics in the Paradigmatic Transition* (New York: Routledge, 1995), p. 18.

[4] See James Gleick, *Chaos: Making a New Science* (New York: Penguin, 1987).

recurring patterns, reflected in the related shapes of, for example, a tree, broc-coli or the coastline viewed from a distance. His formula, in plot form, pro-duces a psychedelic, paisley-like pattern which, when magnified, discloses at the edges of the pattern a further paisley-like pattern, within the edges of the first pattern which decrease in intricacy and complexity with magnifica-tion and further enquiry. Magnification may be repeated *ad infinitum*. The effect is that what appears to be, on the surface, a single unified pattern, con-tains underneath ever expanding, complex sub-patterns which, when mag-nified, stabilise into the single pattern, demonstrating complexity within the singularity.

The simple–complex, general–particular, identical–different paradox[5] of chaos theory is typical of globalisation studies, particularly by sociologists and cultural theorists. There is complexity behind the easy assumption that global-isation is a singular, domineering tendency in an emerging global society of cen-tralised norms. At the same time, there are universalist themes deriving from all sorts of social diversities, such as human rights. With this caution in mind, an attempt to define globalisation may proceed.

2.1.2 History

Literature which explores the notion of globalisation in any depth acknowl-edges that its origins go way back. Those historical origins and developments are not, however, globalisation itself – they are factual precursors which enable the concept of globalisation to be better understood.

Roland Robertson has proposed, in skeletal terms, the phases leading to glob-alisation. The 'germinal phase' lasted from the early fifteenth century to the mid-eighteenth century, featuring increasing individualism and awareness of humanity, with the spread of the Gregorian calendar and the heliocentric idea of the world. The 'incipient phase' began in the mid-eighteenth century and ended in the 1870s. The concept of the unitary state emerged, with standard citizens and formalised notions of international relations, although there were problems with non-European societies being admitted to 'international' society. The third phase, the 'take-off phase', from the 1870s until the mid-1920s, witnessed the increasing importance of national identity, the inclusion of some non-European societies in 'international' society, and, perhaps most significantly, the '[v]ery sharp increase in the number and speed of global forms of communication' and the development of global competitions such as the Olympics. From the early 1920s to the mid-1960s, the fourth 'struggle for hege-mony' phase saw disputes and wars about national ideals formalised from the previous phase. Humanity was confronted with the Holocaust, atomic bomb

---

[5] This is a theme of Fredric Jameson, 'Notes on Globalization as a Philosophical Issue' in Fredric Jameson and Masao Miyoshi (eds.), *The Cultures of Globalization* (Durham, NC: Duke University Press, 1998).

and United Nations.[6] Finally, there is the 'uncertainty phase' from the 1960s, which brings us to the present, discussed in the next section.

Commerce-led cultural interconnection has been a characteristic of world and not just Western history since very early times. In the eighteenth and early nineteenth centuries, it received a boost with the Industrial Revolution and the free thinking of British economists such as Adam Smith and David Ricardo. The separation at that time of the economic and political spheres, leaving the market more to its own devices, in effect *de*-moralised production.[7] The effect on productivity was tremendous, illustrated by the hegemonic success of England in the following century[8] as the premier exemplar of this approach to political economy. Here, most likely, are to be found the profound sources of what is today termed 'globalisation'. Although the world economy had been becoming noticeably more integrated from the sixteenth century onwards, it was not until the nineteenth century that world prices began to converge – a truer sign of interconnection, showing that opportunities for profits around the world were being exploited.[9] It was a significant century for economic interconnection. Migration back then was far greater,[10] moving people into new economies. Indeed, by 1996, world trade as a share of world production was not much bigger than it had been at the end of the nineteenth century.[11] Real time information sharing was occurring between financial markets,[12] although, of course, it was not popularly accessible as it is today via the internet. On balance, there is today, however, an undeniably heightened presence of interconnection in the market and cause and effect consequences, for example in interest rate responses, means of production, macroeconomic policies and growth in developing countries.

In the field of legal theory, international law is the most immediate place to look for the impact of globalisation, being concerned with 'inter-national' legal

---

[6] Roland Robertson, 'Mapping the Global Condition: Globalization as the Central Concept' in Mike Featherstone (ed.), *Global Culture: Nationalism, Globalization and Modernity* (London: Sage, 1990 reprinted 1996), pp. 26–7. Under a title which could have belonged to our time, the Fabian Society in 1926 sponsored a series of lectures called 'The Shrinking World: Dangers and Possibilities': see Arnold Toynbee, *Civilization on Trial* (Oxford: Oxford University Press, 1948), p. 97.   [7] See ch. 8, section 8.3, pp. 177–8 below.

[8] See Paul Kennedy, *The Rise and Fall of the Great Powers: Economic Change and Military Conflict from 1500 to 2000* (London: Unwin Hyman, 1988), pp. 151–8; Martin Daunton, 'Britain and Globalisation Since 1850: I. Creating a Global Order, 1850–1914' (2006) 16 *Transactions of the Royal Historical Society* 1–38.

[9] See Kevin O'Rourke and Jeffrey Williamson, 'After Columbus: Explaining the Global Trade Boom, 1500–1800' (March 2001) NBER Working Paper No. W8186.

[10] See David Held and Anthony McGrew, *Globalization/Anti-Globalization* (Cambridge: Polity Press, 2002), p. 39.

[11] Paul R. Krugman, *Pop Internationalism* (Cambridge, MA: MIT Press, 1996), p. 212.

[12] Paul Hirst and Grahame Thompson, *Globalization in Question: The International Economy and the Possibilities of Governance* (Cambridge: Polity Press, 2nd edn, 1999), p. 9. In 1910, 'international investment as a percentage of total investment was higher than at any other time': Samuel Huntington, *The Clash of Civilizations and the Remaking of World Order* (New York: Simon & Schuster, 1996), p. 52.

matters as the word, invented by Jeremy Bentham at the end of the eighteenth century, suggests. It was not until the mid-twentieth century that this notion began to be modified with persuasiveness.[13] Hans Kelsen was the only major legal positivist to see international law and national municipal law as part of a unity: he maintained that the basic foundational norm (*Grundnorm*) which gave all law its constitutional validity was from international law.[14] For Kelsen, the international capacity to invoke sanctions was becoming more centralised in the manner this capacity had developed centuries earlier in national legal systems.[15] In anticipation of the 'world society' (as opposed to the international society of sovereign states), Hersch Lauterpacht contended that international law had to modify the sovereignty of the state so that the sovereignty of the person could be re-established in situations of abuse.[16]

Sociology furthers the idea, in a more thoroughgoing way, that comparative studies of the nation-state are the appropriate places to look for the conceptual origins of globalisation. Indeed, sociology is perhaps the most illuminating discipline for locating the emergence of globalisation as a concept in human consciousness. For a century, critiques of modernisation, notably those of Karl Marx, had tended to deal with societies (more than just their law) by using a comparative, mainly national methodology, albeit in a way which sought to draw out universal principles. That is, comparisons were made between societies against a Western standard. Yet it was not until the 1970s that these societies began to be considered as part of an overall system,[17] clearing a path for concerns about globalisation to permeate and transcend national boundaries as they do now.

2.1.3 Definition and context

In the 1990s, globalisation entered popular culture, if usage of the word in a major Sydney tabloid is any guide. In 1987, the word 'globalisation' appeared four times, six times in 1988 and fewer than twenty times a year up to 1993;

---

[13] Numerous utopian proposals had nonetheless found their way into the history of international relations and law, surveyed where they occur in the chronological developments mapped in parts 2, 3 and 4 of this book.

[14] See Danilo Zolo, 'Hans Kelsen: International Peace Through International Law' (1998) 9 *European Journal of International Law* 306–24.

[15] See Hedley Bull, 'Hans Kelsen and International Law' in Richard Tur and William Twining (eds.), *Essays on Kelsen* (Oxford: Clarendon Press, 1986), p. 170.

[16] See Hersch Lauterpacht, *International Law and Human Rights* (London: Stevens & Sons, 1950). Other modern writings to this end, prior to consciousness of 'globalisation', include C. Wilfred Jenks, *The Common Law of Mankind* (London: Stevens, 1958); Julius Stone, *Of Law and Nations: Between Power Politics and Human Hopes* (Buffalo: W. S. Hein, 1974), ch. 1. On the late nineteenth-century capture of preliminary human rights in international law by Pasquale Fiore, see Martti Koskenniemi, *The Gentle Civilizer of Nations: The Rise and Fall of International Law 1870–1960* (Cambridge: Cambridge University Press, 2001), pp. 54–7.

[17] See Roland Robertson, *Globalization: Social Theory and Global Culture* (London: Sage Publications, 1992 reprinted 1998), pp. 12–15, discussing Wallerstein's 'world-systems theory'.

growing to 143 times in 1997, 260 in 1998, 280 in 1999, 355 in 2000 and 373 by early September 2001.[18]

Around 1996, William Twining ran searches for the words 'global' and 'globalization' in a library catalogue. After scanning some 250 titles, his synthesis of a definition of globalisation is useful. He uses the word 'globalization' 'to refer to those processes which tend to create and consolidate a *world* economy, a *single* ecological system, and a *complex* network of communications that covers the whole globe, even if it does not penetrate to every part of it'[19] [my italics]. Note the characterisation of this phenomenon as a *world* undertaking, *single* yet *complex*. This reinforces the paradoxical, chaos theory nature of the phenomenon, in less abstract terms than another pithy definition – 'the compression of the world and the intensification of consciousness of the world as a whole'[20] – by Roland Robertson. Anthony Giddens defines globalisation as 'the intensification of worldwide social relations which link distant localities in such a way that local happenings are shaped by events occurring many miles away and vice versa',[21] emphasising the technological feats of communications and travel. The more specific that definitions of globalisation are, the more simplistic and preclusive they become by virtue of their focus.[22]

A mosaic survey of associations will crystallise the most important of the many inputs which evoke the complex concept of globalisation. Robertson, continuing his sketch of historical phases of globalisation,[23] writes of the 'uncertainty phase' of globalisation, referring to technological, world society and individual issues. Technologically, he lists the moon landing, nuclear weapons and global media. More socially, he lists the heightening of global consciousness in the late 1960s and the inclusion of the Third World, civil rights, interest in world civil society and world citizenship, the increase in the number of global institutions and movements, social issues of multiculturality and polyethnicity, and individuals complicated by gender, ethnic and racial considerations.[24]

Sensitive to local diversities and identities, Boaventura de Sousa Santos writes that:

> the globalization process is connected to other transformations in the world system which are nonetheless irreducible to it, such as growing world-level inequality, population explosion, environmental catastrophe, proliferation of weapons of mass destruction, formal democracy as a political condition for international assistance to peripheral and semiperipheral countries and so on.[25]

---

[18] Vic Caroll, 'What if . . . free trade had won in 1901', *Sydney Morning Herald*, 5 September 2001.
[19] William Twining, 'Globalization and Legal Theory: Some Local Implications' (1996) 49 *Current Legal Problems* 1–42, 2.   [20] Robertson, *Globalization* p. 8.
[21] Anthony Giddens, *Sociology* cited in Boaventura de Sousa Santos, *Toward a New Legal Common Sense: Law, Globalization and Emancipation* (London: Butterworths, 2nd edn 2002), p. 165.
[22] Definitions abound, particularly in the social and cultural studies spheres: see generally, Frank Lechner and John Boli (eds.), *The Globalization Reader* (Oxford: Blackwell Publishers, 2nd edn 2004).   [23] His sketch to this point was outlined in section 2.1.2, pp. 27–8 above.
[24] Robertson, 'Mapping the Global Condition', p. 27.
[25] Santos, *New Legal Common Sense*, pp. 166–7.

Globalisation should be thought about in general terms to appreciate it as a process, not a thing, and to embrace the variety of events and occurrences which produce the concept of globalisation in our consciousness. Globalisation can be thought about as much more than just an economic concept. Former World Bank Chief Economist Joseph Stiglitz defines globalisation as 'the removal of barriers to free trade and the closer integration of national economies', brought about by 'the enormous reduction of costs of transportation and communication accompanied by new cross-border institutions'.[26] Whilst many writers treat globalisation in those economic terms, many including myself do not embrace such limitations. Such matters must be clarified at the outset of any conversation about globalisation, to avoid semantic misunderstandings.

2.1.4 Operation

Who is doing what to whom under conditions of globalisation? Take the worldwide American icon of jeans. The name 'jeans' comes from the French name for Genoa, 'Gènes'. They are made of denim, derived from a tough blue sailcloth, called *Serge de Nîmes*, woven in the French town. Levi Strauss, a Bavarian, emigrated to New York and supplied prospectors in the 1860s with jeans.[27] Who is doing what to whom may not always be clear, in terms of who is benefiting and who is being exploited. Is or are France, the United States, Italy and/or Germany the beneficiary or beneficiaries – or is the rest of the world? Do the durability and comfort of these upstart trousers justify flouting traditional or formal dress? Different answers may be possible and all may offer helpful distinctions.

The worldwide spread of, for example, Coca-Cola (sometimes described as 'Cocacolonisation'), demonstrates, on one view, a neat, uncomplicated picture of a global product. Looking deeper, Coca-Cola is an example of a local product, originating late in the nineteenth century, in Georgia, USA, as an inauspicious elixir among many such elixirs which have since fallen by the wayside. In his model of ideal-types of globalisation, Santos describes this phenomenon as one of 'globalized localism' – a local product turned global. Oppositely, the phenomenon of 'localized globalism' may be identified – where a global phenomenon has a uniquely local effect.[28] According to one of his examples, local society and environment may change in response to transnational influences such as tourism impacting on local crafts or wildlife. It can also be seen, for example, in the impact of 'Americanizing' films on Indian or French culture.[29] In a peasant Egyptian marriage, the Americanization of femininity, celebration, happiness, prestige and progress has been observed.[30]

---

[26] Joseph Stiglitz, *Globalization and its Discontents* (London: Penguin, 2002), pp. ix, 4–9.
[27] See Norman Davies, *Europe: A History* (London: Pimlico, 1997), p. 774.
[28] Santos, *New Legal Common Sense*, pp. 179–80.
[29] Fredric, 'Notes on Globalization', pp. 58, 62.
[30] Sherif Hetata, 'Dollarization, Fragmentation and God' in Jameson and Miyoshi (eds.), *Cultures of Globalization*, p. 278.

These two ideal-types of globalisation ('globalized localism' and 'localized globalism'), although they may be 'different dimensions of the same phenomena', ideally correlate as follows: globalized localism emanates from developed countries and may be linked with Santos's idea of 'hegemonic neo-liberal globalization'; and 'localized globalism' is felt in less developed countries and may inspire 'counter-hegemonic globalization'.[31] Such relationships of subordination and domination may not always be clear.[32] That is, some cultures, in some ways, appear to benefit from globalisation as well as suffer detriment. A number of examples can be given. In a developed country like Australia, the impact of international tourism on the indigenous way of life at a massive sacred rock, Uluru, is an example of localised globalism. It may be at once good (the indigenous community receives financial reward) and bad (traditional culture is being affected, particularly as some believe it is sacrilege for tourists to climb the rock). The Ainu of Japan (unlike Hawaiians) apparently thrive on sales and the sense of identity which comes of purchases by tourists passing through traditional villages. In a similar vein, the Sapeurs of the Congo have appropriated the global image of the white coat of the medical profession to bolster the prestige of the witch doctor.[33] These general patterns reveal a complexity of particularistic manifestations which are not the same shape everywhere. These chaotic manifestations are nonetheless helpful for isolating core themes of globalisation. Perhaps a better description is 'glocalization', to transcend the perceived global–local duality.[34]

Law manifests this complexity. The experience of imperialism from the West, featuring the imposition of Western legal systems on the new colonies, is a manifestation of 'globalized localism'. For example, state law as an emanation of Western imperialism has an almost 'alien presence' in Micronesia.[35] Yet colonialism – the response of a local community to imperialism, has resulted in peculiar local responses in local legal systems to more universally imposed rules – that is, 'localized globalism'. For example, a unique jurisprudence developed in early colonial New South Wales.[36] Such processes have been and are uneven in most jurisdictions.[37]

---

[31] Santos, *New Legal Common Sense*, pp. 458–61.

[32] See e.g. William Twining, *Globalisation and Legal Theory* (London: Butterworths, 2000), p. 222. International legal concepts characteristic of globalisation can be used in counter-hegemonic ways: José Manuel Pureza, 'Defensive and Oppositional Counter-Hegemonic Uses of International Law: From the International Criminal Court to the Common Heritage of Mankind' in Santos and Rodríguez-Garavito (eds.), *Law and Globalization from Below: Toward a Cosmopolitan Legality* (Cambridge: Cambridge University Press, 2005).

[33] See Jonathan Friedman, 'Being in the World: Globalization and Localization' in Featherstone (ed.), *Global Culture*.   [34] Robertson, *Globalization*, pp. 173–4.

[35] Brian Z. Tamanaha, *A General Jurisprudence of Law and Society* (Oxford: Oxford University Press, 2001), pp. xi, 112–17.

[36] Bruce Kercher, 'Resistance to Law Under Autocracy' (1997) 60 *Modern Law Review* 779–97.

[37] See William Twining, 'Diffusion of Law: A Global Perspective' (2004) 49 *Journal of Legal Pluralism and Unofficial Law* 1–45; M. B. Likosky, 'Cultural Imperialism in the Context of Transnational Commercial Collaboration' in Michael Likosky (ed.), *Transnational Legal*

Two other processes supplement Santos's theory of globalisation at the 'paradigmatic' level of 'current worldwide transformations', with more hopeful possibilities. 'Cosmopolitanism', for Santos, describes the real potential for 'subordinate nation-states, regions, classes or social groups and their allies to organize transnationally in defense of perceived common interests'; such cosmopolitan examples include human rights organisations, aid organisations and worldwide labour organisations.[38] Along this line, Twining has suggested a preference for thinking in terms of 'cosmopolitanism' over 'globalisation'. Cosmopolitanism generally implies an interest in, and loyalty to, humanity as a whole, rather than globalisation, which is more descriptive and theoretically dubious in terms of its exclusions, such as more localised issues (for example, the status of women under Islam) or causes amongst nation-states (for example, European Union law).[39] The concept of cosmopolitanism has, though, received much criticism from the left. It has been associated with 'overcom[ing] the limits of national sovereignty by constructing a global order that will govern important political as well as economic aspects of both the internal and external behaviour of states'.[40] It is associated with capitalist market forces, and American hegemony and hypocrisy. This would appear to be just one reading of the idea of cosmopolitanism – and a narrow one at that. The heritage of cosmopolitanism has a far richer lineage dating back to ancient times, when Diogenes proclaimed himself 'a citizen of the world', amplified later by Immanuel Kant in his pioneering enquiry into the conditions for a continuing world peace. It is not apparent that the Greek Stoics wished to establish a single world state; they did, however, insist on the individual human's standing in the world being viewed as 'fundamentally and deeply linked to humankind as a whole'.[41] This elucidates the core sense of cosmopolitanism: the notion of a world civil society, or a world society of interactive human beings, discussed below in section 2.3.4.

The 'common heritage of humankind' is the second of Santos's more hopeful paradigmatic processes. Certain issues make sense by reference to the whole globe, as truly global concerns. These include environmental issues such as ozone layer depletion, opposition to weapons of mass destruction, together with positive ventures such as the exploration of outer space. The concept of

---

Processes (London: Butterworths, 2002); H. Patrick Glenn, *On Common Laws* (Oxford: Oxford University Press, 2005), ch. 2; Lauren Benton, *Law and Colonial Cultures: Legal Regimes in World History, 1400–1900* (Cambridge: Cambridge University Press, 2002).

[38] Santos, *New Legal Common Sense*, pp. 180–2; Boaventura de Sousa Santos and César A. Rodríguez-Garavito, 'Law, Politics, and the Subaltern in Counter-Hegemonic Globalization' in Santos and Rodríguez-Garavito (eds.), *Law and Globalization*, p. 14.

[39] William Twining, 'The Province of Jurisprudence Re-examined: Problems of Generalization in a Global Context' in Catherine Dauvergne (ed.), *Jurisprudence for an Interconnected Globe* (Aldershot: Ashgate, 2003).

[40] Peter Gowan, 'Neoliberal Cosmopolitanism' (2001) 11 *New Left Review* 79–93, 79.

[41] See Martha C. Nussbaum, 'Kant and Cosmopolitanism' in James Bohman and Matthias Lutz-Bachmann, *Perpetual Peace: Essays on Kant's Cosmopolitan Ideal* (Cambridge, MA: MIT Press, 1997), pp. 29–30. See, too, ch. 9, section 9.4.2, pp. 209–10 below.

this common heritage contains particular legal responses to globalisation, which will be discussed below in section 2.4.2.

Our general definition of globalisation as 'the accelerated interconnections amongst things that happen in the world' fares well, considering the foregoing. It also recognises the unprecedented velocity, intensity and reach of the concept.[42] It is a way of maintaining the integrity of globalisation as a process and not as an event, suggesting that the various aspects of globalisation introduced above be considered holistically.[43] Delving beneath the surface, though, globalisation is found to be a highly normative phenomenon reliant in large measure, more so in developed countries, upon law. There, law maintains social stability and order and facilitates technological progress in these times. Although imperfect, the generalisations employed above go a good way to creating some sort of order from the chaos of globalisation (although lacking the beauty of one of Mandelbrot's fractal patterns). What does law contribute to, or reflect of, this pattern?

2.2 Globalisation and legal categories

No contemporary doctrinal legal textbook is untouched by globalisation. Whereas the first chapter of nearly every doctrinal textbook used to contain discussion of the related legal history (mostly ignored by students), an additional indirectly relevant chapter may now appear, discussing the international and global implications and sources of the subject. If such a chapter does not appear, the chances are that the global implications and sources are woven into the main text, in the form of treaty references and decisions from foreign jurisdictions. Books oriented towards practical legal training in areas such as conveyancing or municipal court procedure are perhaps the exception. Even in court procedure, in common law countries at least, there will be persuasive comparative references to authorities from fellow Commonwealth courts, if not direct references from times when ultimate appellate jurisdiction belonged to England. Court rules will refer to service of legal process outside the jurisdiction and the treatment of claims in foreign currencies. Even the most parochial conveyancing manual may contain references to domestic requirements for satisfying, for example in Australia, Foreign Investments Review Board regulations concerning the intrusion of foreign ownership capital into the jurisdiction. Understanding such intrusion requires identifying how the intruder is sifted through universal and particular laws into a category of person with imposed legal attributes, according to the authority underlying the status quo. The surface view is exposed in the next section, deferring

---

[42] See Andreas Wimmer, 'Globalizations *Avant la Lettre:* A Comparative View of Isomorphization and Heteromorphization in the Inter-Connecting World' (2001) 43 *Comparative Studies in Society and History* 435–66, 438.

[43] See Bruce Mazlish, 'A Tour of Globalization' (1999) 7 *Indiana Journal of Global Legal Studies* 5–16, esp. 10.

evaluation of the deeper history of that construction to parts 3 and 4 with the rise of the sovereign nation-state concept.

2.2.1 Private international law globalisation

When the words 'globalisation' and 'law' are run together in a phrase, the standard response (at least amongst commercial lawyers) is to agitate issues relating to the law of international transactions, global financial markets, cyberspace, environmental compliance and barriers to international transactions. These issues are all of exponentially increasing currency. For the most part, they are related to unprecedented advances in information technology, tending to be concerned with questions such as, 'can the law cope with the complexities of the technology?' – for example, privacy concerns and cross-border jurisdictional issues. Adopting the demarcation of law into public and private law categories, these technology issues sound of private international law in the international conflicts of laws sense; and also what might be termed *international private law* as domestic law seeks to regulate the interaction of private interests from outside the jurisdiction with internal private interests.

Traditionally, private international laws function as tools for getting things done – for pursuing economic objectives and redressing breaches of socio-economic norms. Globalisation has caused codification and harmonisation of law initiatives in this category of laws (see chapter 12) to assume a particular priority for lawyers acting for cross-border interests for the purpose of advancing client interests more efficiently.

2.2.2 Public international law globalisation

Globalisation and law may also evoke thoughts of, for example, human rights law, international war crimes and the proper domain of the United Nations. Many commentators write of the decline of the nation-state, in the face of the transference of national sovereignty to such structures as the UN, the World Trade Organization, the European Union and even international arbitration bodies. Traditional public international law faces other consequences of globalisation: nuclear weapons testing, cross-border environmental pollution, migration, citizenship and struggles for national self-determination and recognition. Public international law traditionally conceived has concentrated on regulating the contests for survival and prosperity of the state society as against other state societies, rather than being concerned with humans in their relationships with one another. Individual humans 'were nothing but spectators of the international scene'.[44]

Traditionally, such matters of sovereignty are of public international law significance or what might be termed *international public law*, with a more

---

[44] Philip Allott, *Eunomia: New Order for a New World* (Oxford: Oxford University Press, 1990), [15.48]–[15.49], [16.8].

explicitly moral ambition, loftier than the technological or industrial advances sought to be addressed by private international law and international private law (and indeed loftier than concerns individuals might have had about life within their state borders). Hunting and trying war criminals serves no direct productive purpose, exciting instead feelings of justice.

2.3 Globalisation as an integrative concept

Contemporary reality is rendering these hallowed distinctions inconvenient if not intrinsically problematic[45] and historically contingent (as parts 2, 3 and 4 of this book will evidence). Globalisation, thought about as the accelerated inter-connections amongst things that happen in the world, inherently transcends notions of public and private international law norms, and, indeed, the meaning of such words as public, private, domestic and local. For example, the public international law notion of war and the public national law of crime appear to be blurring.[46] Notoriety surrounding the detention in Guantanamo Bay of captives taken by the US in Afghanistan is partly attributable to the detainees not being afforded rights according to the laws of war, making them appear more like criminals – yet initially without the modern Western rights of a criminal to be arrested, charged and tried.

The traditional notion of sovereignty and international law is challenged in a manner which may be illustrated by four contemporary legal phenomena.

2.3.1 'Sovereign egg-shells' and the 'global community omelette'

Paul Vinogradoff appreciated the problematic and unrealistic claims of sovereignty as early as 1920 by comparing with King Canute's inability to control the tide the inability of a sovereign to direct and command society.[47] He noted in another essay that the basic Western categorisation of law is inadequate because it starts from forms of state organisation (politically established in an Aristotelian sense) rather than social organisation.[48]

A suitable metaphor for sovereignty in the interconnected legal order, devised by Ken Booth, is of 'an egg-box containing the shells of sovereignty, alongside which a global community omelet is cooking'.[49] The omelette is a

---

[45] See Alex Mills, 'The Private History of International Law' (2006) 55 *International and Comparative Law Quarterly* 1–49; Paul Schiff Berman, 'From International Law to Law and Globalization' (2005) 43 *Columbia Journal of Transnational Law* 485–556; and generally the essays in Paul Schiff Berman (ed.), *The Globalization of International Law* (Burlington: Ashgate, 2005).

[46] See Philip Bobbitt, *The Shield of Achilles: War, Peace and the Course of History* (London: Penguin, 2003), p. 354; Michael Sherry, 'Dead or Alive: American Vengeance Goes Global' (2005) 31 *Review of International Studies* 245–63.

[47] Paul Vinogradoff, *The Collected Papers of Paul Vinogradoff*, 2 vols. (Oxford: Clarendon Press, 1928), vol. II, p. 220.   [48] Paul Vinogradoff, *Collected Papers*, vol. II, p. 250.

[49] Ken Booth, 'Security in Anarchy: Utopian Realism, in Theory and Practice' (1991) 67 *International Affairs* 527–45, 542.

world society of human beings as an alternative or supplement to nation-state societies (see section 2.3.4 below). Yet the egg-shells – the sovereign nation-states – are not, of course, spent forces in their own right, and they too feature interconnections and channels of co-operation with other states (for example, networks of police, financial regulators and judiciaries of different states) constituting a new role for states in Anne-Marie Slaughter's view of the 'new world order' in which she identifies 'disaggregated sovereignty'.[50] The patterns of authority underlying the social construction of the egg-box – that is, the society of nation-states now symbolised by eggshells in the egg-box – are explored in detail in parts 2, 3 and 4.

2.3.2 Competing jurisdictions and legal pluralism

Legal pluralism is an alternative to absolutist conceptions of sovereignty which insist upon the state for legal validity. A discourse has grown from this critical insight,[51] pioneered by Eugen Ehrlich and his notion of the 'living law' of society.[52] Organised groups exist alongside and within the state, with their own autonomous 'legal' orderings which can call into play psychological and physical coercion (for example, an employer with the conditional power to terminate an employee's employment). Emerging global networks of jurisdictions and orders feature 'a multiplicity of diverse communicative processes in a given social field that observe social action under the binary code of legal/illegal'.[53] That is, the rules of states, the 'supranational' rules of regional entities such as the European Union, the rules of the world market, and rules of conduct amongst merchants, as often separate communication processes, become their own sources of the legal and the illegal, taking on the character of law.

This idea of legal pluralism is more than simply admitting 'multiple perspectives' of norms; rather, it represents 'the co-existence of multiple legal orders in the same context of time and space'.[54] A positivist jurist, Neil MacCormick, admits within the definition of law the species of international law, primitive

---

[50] Anne-Marie Slaughter, *A New World Order* (Princeton: Princeton University Press, 2004), p. 34.

[51] Space constraints disallow elaboration of the nuances. See generally John Griffiths, 'What is Legal Pluralism?' (1986) 24 *Journal of Legal Pluralism and Unofficial Law* 1–55; Sally Engle Merry, 'Legal Pluralism' (1988) 22 *Law & Society Review* 869–96; Santos, *New Legal Common Sense*, pp. 89–98; Tamanaha, *General Jurisprudence*, pp. 115–17, 172–3; Neil Walker, 'The Idea of Constitutional Pluralism' (2002) 65 *Modern Law Review* 317–59; Jeremy Webber, 'Legal Pluralism and Human Agency' (2006) 44 *Osgoode Hall Law Journal* 167–98. For an illustrative case study of the transnational toy industry, see Francis Snyder, 'Governing Globalisation' in Likosky (ed.), *Transnational Legal Processes*. *Contra* Simon Roberts, 'After Government? On Representing Law Without the State' (2005) 68 *Modern Law Review* 1–24, privileging centralism over 'negotiated understanding'.

[52] Eugen Ehrlich, *Fundamental Principles of the Sociology of Law*, trans. Walter L. Moll (Cambridge, MA: Harvard University Press, 1936).

[53] Gunther Teubner, ' "Global Bukowina": Legal Pluralism in the World Society' in Gunther Teubner (ed.), *Global Law Without a State* (Brookfield: Dartmouth Publishing Company Limited, 1997), p. 14.   [54] Twining, *Globalisation and Legal Theory*, p. 216.

law and church law, plus the living law of universities, firms and families, when law is considered by definition to be partly institutionalised normative order.[55]

Importantly, there is a historical connection between, and significance to, these more sociological approaches to recognising multiple legal systems and law in the evolution of the Western legal tradition. In medieval times, with diverse systems of ecclesiastical, feudal, manorial, royal, urban and mercantile law operating and sometimes competing in the same territory, legal and social sophistication ensued. Technical jurisdictional questions belied 'important political and economic considerations: church versus town, town versus lord, lord versus merchant, and so on'.[56]

The jurisdictional complexity or competing jurisdictions borne of increasing numbers of legal systems therefore has parallels with the medieval social condition as will be seen in parts 2 and 3 of this book, with promising indications that legal discourse is equipped with the intellectual resources to find authoritative answers in the process of fathoming important political and economic considerations. Presently, overlapping networks of national, regional and truly global tribunals are developing[57] beyond internationally contemplated hierarchies;[58] and 'functional, overlapping, and competing jurisdictions' has become a term of art for an economic evaluation of jurisdictions.[59] '[M]ultinational companies, NGOs, governments and ad hoc coalitions share overlapping authority within a framework of universal commercial law but regionalized political rules.'[60] If this is 'a key concept of a post-modern understanding of law',[61] it might well be the key to a medieval and modern understanding, too.

The 'race to the bottom' jurisdictional mentality, whereby some jurisdictions offer incentives to law consumers to take advantage of lax laws (for example, Third World labour laws, Delaware incorporation laws), may be understood in

---

[55] Neil MacCormick, 'Beyond the Sovereign State' (1993) 56 *Modern Law Review* 1–18, 14.

[56] See Harold J. Berman, *Law and Revolution: The Formation of the Western Legal Tradition* (Cambridge MA: Harvard University Press, 1983), p. 10. As late as the eighteenth century, Blackstone wrote that English law contained different systems – natural law, divine law, international law, ecclesiastical law, Roman law, law merchant, local customs, common law, statute law and equity. These systems were administered by different courts, such as church courts, admiralty courts, university courts, common law courts and courts of equity, although parliament and common law courts were by that time supreme (pp. 268–9). And now, see H. Patrick Glenn, 'Transnational Common Laws' (2006) 29 *Fordham International Law Journal* 457–71.

[57] See Laurence R. Helfer and Anne-Marie Slaughter, 'Toward a Theory of Effective Supranational Adjudication' (1997) 107 *Yale Law Journal* 273–391, 282; Yuval Shany, *The Competing Jurisdictions of International Courts and Tribunals* (Oxford: Oxford University Press, 2003).

[58] e.g. article 103, UN Charter; article 30, Vienna Convention on the Law of Treaties.

[59] See Bruno S. Frey and Reiner Eichenberger, *The New Democratic Federalism for Europe: Functional, Overlapping and Competing Jurisdictions* (Northampton, MA: Edward Elgar Publishing, 1999); Horatia Muir Watt, 'Choice of Law in Integrated and Interconnected Markets: A Matter of Political Economy' (2003) 9 *Columbia Journal of European Law* 383–409.

[60] Bobbitt, *Shield of Achilles*, p. 363.

[61] Jean-Philippe Robé, 'Multinational Enterprises: The Constitution of a Pluralistic Legal Order' in Gunther Teubner (ed.), *Global Law Without a State* (Brookfield: Dartmouth Publishing Company Limited, 1997), p. 56.

this process. It is not new. Informality and pragmatism in the fifteenth-century Chancery courts attracted business from the common law courts.[62] Similarly a 'race to the top' between jurisdictions can be positive – for example, today London and New York are popular commercial jurisdictions for their predictability and fairness, just as the emancipatory fairness of a medieval royal court might attract the vassal away from the feudal court. (Whether these are 'races to the top or bottom' may depend upon standpoint.) Tensions between laws of different jurisdictions can be creatively exploited to achieve gains for marginalised people – for example, Portuguese water laws versus European Union directives, the latter offering more protection to marginalised Portuguese.[63]

As a matter of legal science, globalisation makes it difficult to govern global spaces by traditional territorial means and laws. Legal rules are typically general in application. It is difficult for such rules to be uniformly applicable, given the diversity of the world. Two case studies in part 5, on the European Union (chapter 11) and international commercial law (chapter 12), respectively illuminate the public and private law aspects of the phenomenon of competing jurisdictions.

2.3.3 The multinational enterprise

Pertinently following a discussion of legal pluralism and its tendencies for normative integration or confrontation amongst different cultures or interests, the multinational enterprise or transnational corporation exists simultaneously under different state legal regimes. Such institutions include profit-seeking corporations (such as IBM or Toyota), as well as religious institutions, trade, industrial and sporting associations.[64] Despite not having its own legal category in either state or international law (although in a different national jurisdiction a branch of it can be recognised as a corporation or a foreign corporation), the multinational enterprise nonetheless constitutes 'an autonomous legal order' with its own coercive means, be they physical or psychological,[65] within the culture of the organisation (for example, the organisation's attitude to work hours, attention to detail).

Producing more than a third of the world's industrial output, multinationals feature a new international division of labour, characterised by worldwide sourcing, and low transportation costs allowing for consumption by developed countries and production in the poorer country.[66] Their political distribution is shifting from almost exclusive American–European origin, to almost two-fifths Japanese–Asian origin.[67] Although relying upon economic and cultural peculiarities of nation-states particularly in the area of property rights,[68] with their headquarters and assets often concentrated in one or a small number of

---

[62] J. H. Baker, *An Introduction to English Legal History* (London: Butterworths, 4th edn 2002), pp. 39–41.   [63] Santos and Rodríguez-Garavito, 'Law, Politics and the Subaltern', p. 17.
[64] See Allott, *Eunomia* [13.80].   [65] Robé, 'Multinational Enterprises', pp. 52–3.
[66] See Santos, *New Legal Common Sense*, pp. 167–8.   [67] Mazlish, 'Tour of Globalization', 12.
[68] Robé, 'Multinational Enterprises', p. 51.

states,[69] the economic effect of multinationals is powerful. Firms, and particularly global financial markets, may be said to have an 'economic citizenship' beyond the participation of individuals with respect to national governments[70] and an economic significance greater than many nation-states[71] without the democratic safeguards (although there is extensive constitutional regulation of corporations in most Western jurisdictions). To address this, increasing numbers of voluntary codes abound.[72] A recent draft UN code, *Norms on the Responsibilities of Transnational Corporations and other Business Enterprises with Regard to Human Rights*,[73] purports to transform transnational corporations. It proposes to divert them from the *raison d'être* of private, shareholder-value-maximisation into a style of entity with public, state-like functions to enforce labour, civil and political and human rights, challenging traditional domestic, international, public and private institutions of governance.[74]

In terms of brute political power, states still prevail according to the measures of tax levying and production of weapons of mass destruction.[75] Nonetheless, a theory of international law and society which ignores the multinational 'is not worthy to be a theory of the international society of the future'.[76]

What of the global community omelette?

2.3.4 World society

Martians might be able to look at the earth and see only one global culture, but for earth-bound humans, 'the idea of a "global culture" is a practical impossibility, except in interplanetary terms'.[77] So much would be suggested by the notion of legal pluralism. Yet, although the concept of a single global culture stretches the imagination, the ability to relate to other cultures and civilisations, past and present, is widespread. 'Always and everywhere, the struggle of human life and the response of socializing humanity have a family resemblance.'[78] Ethically, we need to ask ourselves whether it is better to continue to live or at least think within the boundaries of nation-states, or should we consider ourselves to be members of a world society?[79]

---

[69] See Hirst and Thompson, *Globalization in Question*, p. 272.

[70] Saskia Sassen, *Losing Control: Sovereignty in an Age of Globalization* (New York: Columbia University Press, 1996), pp. 38–58.

[71] Fifty-two multinationals were richer than 120–30 Member States of the UN, according to UN figures quoted in 1999 by Mazlish, 'Tour of Globalization', 12.

[72] See Ronan Shamir, 'Corporate Social Responsibility: A Case of Hegemony and Counter-Hegemony' in Santos and Rodríguez-Garavito (eds.), *Law and Globalization*, p. 102.

[73] UN Doc. E/CN.4/Sub.2/2003/L.8.

[74] See Larry Cata Backer, 'Multinational Corporations, Transnational Law: The United Nation's Norms on the Responsibilities of Transnational Corporations as Harbinger of Corporate Responsibility (2005) 37 *Columbia Human Rights Law Review* 287–389.

[75] See Held and McGrew, *Globalization/Anti-Globalization*, p. 9.   [76] Allott, *Eunomia*, [13.45].

[77] Anthony D. Smith, 'Towards a Global Culture?' in Featherstone (ed.), *Global Culture*, p. 171.

[78] Allott, *Eunomia*, [5.6].

[79] See Peter Singer, *One World: The Ethics of Globalisation* (Melbourne: Text Publishing, 2nd edn 2004), p. 187.

Present moral developments in public international law, such as human rights and free trade, are attracting personal allegiance to such traditionally public, meta-state laws previously the domain of states. In this process, international society is becoming more of a 'society' in the true sense of the word, comprised not only of states caring about narrowly defined state interests but also of citizens (sometimes mobilised at the transnational level, for example, through the diverse interests comprising the World Social Forum).[80] Such citizens may relate to the international order sometimes with more allegiance than they relate to the state and are able to effect change within the state. This is discussed in some detail in chapter 10, in the context of human rights, as is the problematic of normative universality. In some such cases, citizens can compel state behaviour according to public international law treaty standards. The continued development of these norms may be rendering 'the moral significance of the human race . . . available as a moral reality of international society, as the society of the whole human race and the society of all societies'.[81] Global (as distinguished from national) generations appear to be emerging, connected by technology.[82] Following from our legal pluralism insights, these developments do not suggest a single, all-encompassing society, but rather an alternate society – a global society in a dynamic conversation with powerful ideas and realities (for example, environmental issues) transcending more local societies.

The increasing numbers of international governmental and non-governmental organisations (IGOs and INGOs, respectively) also demonstrate the rise of a world society. At the beginning of the twentieth century there were only 37 IGOs and 176 INGOs, compared with, in the year 2000, 6,743 IGOs and 47,098 INGOs (less some 'inactive or dead' organisations). Highly active international policy formulators, such as the United Nations, G7, International Monetary Fund, World Trade Organization, Asia–Pacific Economic Co-operation and the World Social Forum, also evidence the emergence of a world society.[83]

This so-called 'transnational civil society' or world society suffers, like any agency of social order be it the family, incorporated association or state, from problems of authority such as delegated power and majority will. The particular problem of the world society is that those who participate in the life of the

---

[80] See Boaventura de Sousa Santos, 'Beyond Neoliberal Governance: The World Social Forum as Subaltern Cosmopolitan Politics and Legality' in Santos and Rodríguez-Garavito (eds.), *Law and Globalization*, p. 11.

[81] Allott, *Eunomia*, [6.60], [13.105]. See more generally John W. Meyer *et al.*, 'World Society and the Nation-State' in Lechner and Boli (eds.), *The Globalization Reader*; Alex Y. Seita, 'Globalization and the Convergence of Values' (1997) 30 *Cornell International Law Journal* 429–91; Thomas M. Franck, *The Empowered Self: Law and Society in the Age of Individualism* (Oxford: Oxford University Press, 1999), pp. 35–7, 196–223; Harold J. Berman, 'World Law' (1995) 18 *Fordham International Law Journal* 1617–22.

[82] June Edmunds and Bryan S. Turner, 'Global Generations: Social Change in the Twentieth Century' (2005) 56 *British Journal of Sociology* 559–78.

[83] Statistics from Union of International Associations, cited in Held and McGrew, *Globalization/Anti-Globalization*, pp. 18–19.

myriad non-governmental organisations may be politically fulfilled, however the association may be unaccountable to a sovereign, therefore instilling a lack of democratic legitimacy. For example, the World Trade Organization routinely makes decisions affecting states, with only the original delegated consent from those states which ratified the treaty. The United Nations Security Council has only five permanent members – the US, the UK, France, China and Russia – each with the power of veto. This 'democratic deficit' will be explored more in the context of the European Union in chapter 11.

Most importantly, if the world society is to flourish, it will need to become more conscious of its history.[84] That consciousness is required for a sense of purpose born of common historical debates and grievances upon which to develop and work for common visions for the future. The historical narrative in chapters 4–10 is a preliminary offering to that consciousness.

2.4 The sphere of containable disruption

Technology is the locomotive of globalisation thought about as interconnections. The accelerated interconnections of globalisation spurred by changing technologies bear significant responsibility for challenging the legal categories and underpinning the phenomena of globalisation identified in the previous sections. There is an obvious connection between technology and the changing nature of sovereignty which is so implicated in globalisation discourse, which has always been so. Technology will be managed and exploited by some form of government – or, more popularly in the discourse today, *governance*[85] – which exists to bring order to a realm or territory. That government manages to contain disruption. People have always required government of some sort. They have always lived in territorial 'survival units', initially dependent upon physical strength, collective fighting capacity and weapons, to prevent possible annihilation or enslavement by another survival unit.[86] These units may be thought of as spheres – what I term 'spheres of containable disruption'. Sovereignty or political power is exercised within these spheres and amongst other spheres or collective survival units. They are porous, overlapping, always changing and are key to understanding the geographical reach of legal and normative systems.

---

[84] See Philip Allott, *The Health of Nations: Society and Law Beyond the State* (Cambridge: Cambridge University Press, 2002), ch. 11. For recent initiatives, see Bruce Mazlish and Akira Iriye (eds.), *The Global History Reader* (New York: Routlege, 2005); Patrick O'Brien, 'Historiographical Traditions and Modern Imperatives for the Restoration of Global History' (2006) 1 *Journal of Global History* 3–39 inaugurating that journal; the *Journal of World History*; and edited collections of A. G. Hopkins (ed.), *Global History: Interactions Between the Universal and the Local* (Basingstoke: Palgrave Macmillan, 2006) and *Globalization in World History* (New York: W. W. Norton & Co., 2002).   [85] See ch. 12, section 12.3.2, pp. 291–2 below.

[86] The notion of the 'survival unit' comes from Norbert Elias, to which reference is made in Stephen Mennell, 'The Globalization of Human Society as a Very Long-term Social Process: Elias's Theory' in Featherstone (ed.), *Global Culture*, p. 360.

2.4.1 Technological influences on sovereignty

The size and reach of these spheres of containable disruption will vary according to historic and economic circumstances. A small territory may only have a small government and may become part of a big territory because it is easily taken over by another government. Weak states are weak because they lack technology.[87] A big territory will need a stronger, bigger government, in terms of a combination of human capital, economic power, military apparatus and/or perhaps tradition.

Government will be challenged to maintain peace on two fronts. First, peace will depend upon the government's capacity to maintain some differentiation of the realm from the outside space and to protect the realm from the outside forces which may be hostile to the realm, through war and defence. Secondly, the government will need to maintain peace within the realm by appealing to the various communal, political groups, typically as a last resort through policing, but ideally through less coercive notions of 'legitimacy' or 'authority' which receive allegiance. Technology is crucial to this function of government, and to the territorial reach of government – and the modern state with its notions of sovereignty. Strategic and constitutional innovations successfully pursued by one state tend to be copied by competing states such that new forms of legitimacy replace older ones[88] (for example, monarchy, parliamentary democracy, federalism, corporatism) rendering governments or 'governance' dynamic.

Technology is integral to the threat of invasion of the realm from within or without. That invasion may be military, economic or normative.[89] Military invasion speaks for itself. Economic invasion comes from the power to offer benefits from outside the sphere, principally through trade. Normative invasion may be in the form of new ideas, inevitably relating to justice, being spread by radical movements, internally; or from the outside, by customs of another realm or state (for example, communism or Protestantism), via cultural media technology such as the printing press or, more recently, the internet. At these 'contact zones', normative systems and jurisdictions meet and produce new meanings often amidst social dislocation and innovation, in the recognition and denial of rights to new subjects. This affects, for example, indigenous peoples, migrant communities, labour movements, as well as establishment individuals, communities, states and transnational institutions.[90] It is not possible 'to prevent the members of a society from recognizing what they share and

---

[87] See Martin van Creveld, *The Rise and Decline of the State* (Cambridge: Cambridge University Press, 1999), p. 378.

[88] See Bobbitt, *Shield of Achilles*, Book I Part II, for the constitutional movement he charts from princes to princely states to kingly states to territorial states to state-nations to nation-state and, in Part III and Book II Part III, from nation-states to market-states.

[89] See Johan Galtung, *The European Community: A Superpower in the Making* (London: George Allen & Unwin, Ltd, 1973), pp. 33–4; Gianfranco Poggi, *The State: Its Nature, Development and Prospects* (Stanford: Stanford University Press, 1990), p. 4.

[90] Santos, *New Legal Common Sense*, pp. 472–4.

do not share with the members of other societies';[91] societies and subcultures are prone to jealousy. Normative invasion may even use the vehicle of a permeating language such as English[92] or the Latin of the Holy Roman Empire.

A number of examples of the historical construction of the sphere of containable disruption, by reference to technology, illustrate the dependence of sovereignty on technology. Inadequate maps are said to have influenced Napoleon's retreat from Moscow.[93] The prior technology of 'precisely demarcated territories' made possible by developments in cartography was essential to the nation-state. This reflects what has been termed the 'territorialization of social relations'.[94] Similarly, the invention of the printing press, and its connection, in the sixteenth century, of fellow readers into particular language fields, fertilised the nationally imagined community.[95] With such technology may come increased strength inside the designated sphere of containable disruption, balanced by an external, opposing threat of military and normative invasion from other spheres.

Historical rights asserted over the sea also illustrate that political power is a correlate of technology. In the thirteenth century, Venice was the transient sovereign of the Adriatic Sea. In the fifteenth century, access to the Atlantic (and thus to the Americas) was papally divided between Spain and Portugal. In the eighteenth century, when the sun never set on the British Empire, England asserted sovereignty only over adjacent seas at a time when no state had the power or technological advantage to pretend to own the Atlantic, nor a city the impudence to claim the Adriatic. Beyond the nineteenth century, it became an acknowledged principle of international law that maritime sovereignty was limited largely to inland and territorial waters – defined (upon reflection, not surprisingly) in military–technological terms by the three-mile rule – the reach of the cannon ball from the shore,[96] this being the symbolic technological limit of the sphere of containable disruption. There appears to be a pattern: as soon as economics, military power and technology increase power and the ability to contain disruption within a sphere, an opposing force seems to increase the ability to disrupt that sphere. Arguably, spying from satellites in space has not been prohibited under international law because such espionage is outside any

---

[91] Allott, *Eunomia*, [5.23].

[92] See David Crystal, *English as a Global Language* (Cambridge: Cambridge University Press, 1997). English is native to only 8 percent of the world. Its importance derives from being a lingua franca, or language of wider communication, amongst people of different tongues: Huntington, *Clash of Civilizations*, p. 60.   [93] van Creveld, *Rise and Decline*, p. 144.

[94] 'Territorialization' reflects a trend from status to locus, accompanying Maine's model of the movement from aristocratic status to liberal contract-based society. That is, the strength of kinship and customary relationships grew into convenient contract-based relationships featuring a new, shared concept of territoriality: see Richard T. Ford, 'Law's Territory (A History of Jurisdiction)' (1999) 97 *Michigan Law Review* 843–930, 845, 872.

[95] See Benedict Anderson, *Imagined Communities: Reflections on the Origin and Spread of Nationalism* (London: Verso, 1991), p. 44.

[96] See James Muldoon, 'Who Owns the Sea?' in Bernhard Klein (ed.), *Fictions of the Sea: Critical Perspectives on the Ocean in British Literature and Culture* (Aldershot: Ashgate, 2002), pp. 14–17; Harvard Law Review Association, 'Note: National Sovereignty of Outer Space' (1961) 74 *Harvard Law Review* 1154–75, 1160–1.

realistic hope of containment, in a way that deployment of spy-planes under international law is not.[97]

The system of nation-states had evolved, by the twentieth century, as the paradigmatic unit of governance, for the ability of nation-states to be internally regulating and rigid enough externally on the territorial boundaries to protect the interior. Alas, later that century, the system of nation-states had collapsed as monopoly spheres of containable disruption, as part of the process of globalisation. The European Union provides a 'tangible expression' of the fact that the modern complexity of economic relationships occurs at a scale too large to be dealt with by the sphere of the territorial nation-state alone.[98] The relatively pluralist 'super-sphere' of the EU has been consolidated from some 150 independent political entities in Europe in 1500, to about 25 in 1900.[99] This has occurred apparently in recognition of the economic inefficiency of smaller, stronger spheres of containable disruption and their tendencies towards mutual annihilation.

2.4.2 Common heritage of humankind

Further illustrative of the technological construction of sovereignty is the doctrine of the common heritage of mankind now more regularly known as the common heritage of *humankind*. It also has significance as a more widely, potentially useful property concept for global times.

The 'common heritage of mankind' is taken from a speech in 1967 by the Maltese Ambassador, Arvid Pardo, in the UN. It is a term which has been given to areas beyond the traditional nation-state's sphere of containable disruption, such as the ocean floor, the moon and Antarctica – to 'common space areas . . . owned by no one, though hypothetically managed by everyone'.[100] Ownership as such is legally absent, reflecting, although it is arguable, the Roman law concept of *res communis*: that states have a right to enjoyment, but not ownership, of the property of the community.[101] Consequences attach: 'the entire area would be administered by the international community, so all people, excluding states or national governments, could be expected to share in its management; economic benefits should be shared according to management; and uses would have to be peaceful; and research would have to be shared'.[102]

---

[97] David B. Goldman, 'Historical Aspects of Globalization and Law' in Catherine Dauvergne (ed.), *Jurisprudence for an Interconnected Globe* (Aldershot: Ashgate, 2002), pp. 64–5.

[98] van Creveld, *Rise and Decline*, p. 385.   [99] Poggi, *The State*, p. 22.

[100] Christopher C. Joyner, 'Legal Implications of the Concept of the Common Heritage of Mankind' (1986) 35 *International and Comparative Law Quarterly* 190–9, 191.

[101] See Brian M. Hoffstadt, 'Moving the Heavens: Lunar Mining and the "Common Heritage of Mankind" in the Moon Treaty' (1994) 42 *UCLA Law Review* 575–621, 587. The possibility that states could own materials exploited from the moon, with specific obligations, does however undermine the *res communis* rule: see Michael E. Davis and Ricky J. Lee, 'Twenty Years After: The Moon Agreement and its Legal Controversies' (1999) *Australian International Law Journal* 9–33, 19–20.   [102] Joyner, 'Common Heritage of Mankind', 191–2.

Concerning the moon, article XI of the *Agreement Governing the Activities of States on the Moon and Other Celestial Bodies* (1979)[103] seeks to dispel any prospects of national appropriation by claim of sovereignty or occupation, requiring equal access to state parties (paragraph 4) and an international regime (paragraph 5) to govern exploitation. This would not, however, prevent the international regime from creating property rights and ownership, perhaps providing for leases and licences for exploitation in a similar way to Australian domestic mining leases.[104]

The concept of the common heritage of humankind carries the potential for the development of community interests at a global level, as opposed to the economic and dominant political interests hitherto associated with the international state system.[105]

2.4.3 New challenges and new spheres

Terrorism perhaps embodies the most feared challenge associated with globalisation. A spectre once again haunts the Western world, having taken the place of communism. Unlike communism, terrorism is not state sponsored, at least to any significant, currently discernible, extent in the wake of September 11 and apparently kindred attacks, for example, in Madrid and London since. Terrorism is the first major non-state initiative which threatens the global order in modern history. Sympathy has been shown by some anti-globalisation protestors for Islamic jihad terrorists. Both movements in fact rely upon globalism to gain adherents. The connection is quite plain: common hostility to Western technology and capitalistic decadence, which is thought to undermine traditional ways of life and increase economic inequality. Conventional political means to disrupt globalisation appear to be limited, as even states on their own are unable, economically, to stem the tide of globalisation and its free-trade economic ideology within and outside their territories.

To what extent are conventional twentieth-century spheres of containable disruption threatened? Territorially, jihad terrorism appears weak, but the world is yet to see the survival value of this 'global' terrorism. By contrast, the global anti-terrorism alliance appears very strong. The power of states, too, has been strengthened in the aftermath of September 11. The domestic policies, as well as foreign policies, of Western nations and some traditionally non-Western nations have become relatively unified in relation to the terrorist threat. The consequence appears to be greater state surveillance and the prospect of restrictions

---

[103] UN Doc.A/AC.105/L.113/Add.4 (1979).

[104] See Davis and Lee, 'Moon Agreement', 24–5. On other aspects, see Harminderpal Singh Rana, 'The "Common Heritage of Mankind" & the Final Frontier: A Revaluation of Values Constituting the International Legal Regime for Outer Space Activities' (1994) 26 *Rutgers Law Journal* 225–50; Bin Cheng, 'Outer Void Space: The Reason for this Neologism in Space Law' (1999) *Australian International Law Journal* 1–8.

[105] See José Manuel Pureza, 'Uses of International Law', p. 275.

on civil liberties, particularly for those whose appearances fit stereotypes. At the same time as there is increasing state and terrorist cell interconnection, there is an increase in state power. Although such paradoxes cannot be overcome, an understanding of this aspect of globalisation can perhaps be enhanced by regarding the traditional state spheres of containable disruption as being perforated and reduced to feudal spheres in search of an empire.

Other new spheres and challenges to old spheres abound. Cross-border risks in the finance industry demonstrate the difficulties of containing disruption within the sphere of the nation-state. For example, despite a state protecting privately owned domestic banks, it is difficult to stop those banks from incurring bad debts with banks of foreign nations, thereby creating the possibility for great domestic insecurity. The problem arises from tying laws to domestic actors whilst the risks are beyond those actors. '[T]ransnationally mobile civil society actors' are difficult to regulate.[106]

Major new spheres in the form of internet communities have appeared. They subvert territoriality and present challenging regulatory issues to the sphere of the nation-state. Intangible boundaries such as technological compatibility and language may compete with state borders,[107] together with more palpable jurisdictional obstacles. For example, a French court ordered American internet company Yahoo to prevent French internet users from accessing any site on Yahoo which might contest or apologise for the crimes of Nazism. Should enforcement of the judgment in the US be attempted, it will likely be refused there under the First Amendment free-speech protection, notwithstanding a failed attempt by Yahoo for a pre-emptive declaration.[108] A literature is developing surrounding the regulation of cyberspace including its effect upon democracy.[109]

It is worthy of note that the guarantee of peace – of the life and property of citizens – is falling to organisations other than the state. By 1972 in the USA, private security firms had twice as many employees and 1.5 times the budget of all local, state and federal police combined; and mercenary soldiers have been used relatively recently in the developing world, for example in New Guinea and Sierra Leone.[110] Nonetheless, mercenary forces are generally thought to be illegal as a matter of international law. For how long this will be the case is problematic, given the increasing reluctance of Western states to incur war casualties. Traditional state spheres of containable disruption may avoid disruption by importing the means of containment or privatising them.[111]

---

[106] See Jarrod Wiener, *Globalization and the Harmonization of Law* (London: Pinter, 1999), pp. 33–4, 188.   [107] See Bobbitt, *Shield of Achilles*, p. 354.

[108] *Yahoo! Inc. v La Ligue Contra le Racisme et l'Antisemitisme* 379 F.3D 1120 (9th Cir. 2004).

[109] See Paul Schiff Berman, 'The Globalization of Jurisdiction' (2002) 151 *University of Pennsylvania Law Review* 311–545; Neil Weinstock Netanel, 'Cyberspace Self-Governance: A Skeptical View from Democratic Theory' (2000) 88 *California Law Review* 395–498.

[110] van Creveld, *Rise and Decline*, pp. 404–5.

[111] See P. W. Singer, 'War, Profits, and the Vacuum of Law: Privatized Military Firms and International Law' (2004) 42 *Columbia Journal of Transnational Law* 521–49.

Our explorations of the notion of globalisation and subsequent look at how law has generally been affected might arouse the suspicion that what has gone on in the twentieth century is revolutionary, although, in the instance of law, not unprecedented. A globalist jurisprudence for the third millennium must take heed of this, if it is to respond effectively.

2.5 The 'World Revolution' and legal theory

A feeling that the end of the world is nigh – not just the apprehension of revolution – appears to be helpful in establishing a new legal order. It happened at the time of the birth of the Western legal tradition, beyond territorial boundaries, in the Papal Revolution of the late eleventh, early twelfth centuries, to be discussed in chapter 5. The sensation of apocalypse also occurred in the twentieth-century world wars, on the globalised Megiddo Plains of Europe and the Asia-Pacific. In spite of attempts by jurists in recent centuries 'to work out a law of nations, the sovereign states have turned modern Europe into a jungle, with disastrous consequences for that continent and the world'.[112] Globalisation as a process encompasses the unconscious reactions and the conscious responses to the cataclysm of this 'World Revolution'.

The years 1914–89 (the outbreak of World War I to the fall of the Berlin Wall) contain a period in which the accelerated, tentacular interconnections amongst things that happen in the world were accomplished from an almost global war. With associated political calamities, this period through its lethal technology resulted in 187 million people being killed in conditions of terror – 10 percent of the population of 1900.[113] Between just 1939 and 1945, 40–60 million people were killed.[114] This 'string of conflicts . . . destroyed more human beings than all past convulsions put together'[115] in Europe, 'consisting of two periods of unprecedented public mass murder punctuated by a period of economic and social anarchy',[116] together with global phenomena such as environmental degradation (an 'ecological holocaust').[117] (Judgements cast from the West about allegedly uncivilised peoples today, blaming their social problems or violence upon cultural backwardness, are delusional, given the abysmal failures of twentieth-century Westerners.)[118] To the extent that economic integration is

---

[112] R. C. van Caenegem, *An Historical Introduction to Western Constitutional Law* (Cambridge: Cambridge University Press, 1995), p. 30; see too MacCormick, 'Beyond the Sovereign State', 17; van Creveld, *Rise and Decline*, p. 224.

[113] Bobbitt, *Shield of Achilles*, p. 61, quoting Hobsbawm, *The Age of Extremes*.

[114] van Creveld, *Rise and Decline*, p. 257.   [115] Davies, *Europe*, p. 897.

[116] Allott, *Eunomia*, [18.44].

[117] Jim Chen, 'Globalization and Its Losers' (2000) 9 *Minnesota Journal of Global Trade* 157–218, 159.

[118] Because of the cultural interconnection, technology and luxurious levels of health, wealth and education of twentieth-century Westerners, it should be no consolation to them that the percentages of annual population deaths due to war in many tribal societies was greater than in Germany and Russia in the twentieth century (statistic from Singer, *One World*, p. 121, citing Keeley, *War Before Civilization*).

a key component of the globalisation concept, it must also be recognised as a conscious response to the human carnage. These events are entwined as both cause and effect with technological and industrial developments which have revolutionised the human relationship to time and space associated with 'globalisation'.

Is the word 'revolution' warranted to describe this twentieth-century movement? Historian Norman Davies, amongst others, suggests that the word 'Revolution' is overused, as for example 'the Industrial Revolution',[119] 'the Scientific Revolution', 'the Sexual Revolution' and the like. His idea of revolution is 'the complete overthrow of a system of government together with its social, economic and cultural foundations', resulting in an effect beyond the nation and 'far beyond mere politics'.[120] Such categorical statements risk being at semantic if not disciplinary cross-purposes just as 'globalisation' can be thought about as more than just economic globalisation.[121] Davies's definition seems to assume the French Revolution as a benchmark. Harold Berman, following Eugen Rosenstock-Huessy, convincingly suggests six great Western revolutions – the Papal, the Protestant, the English, the French, the American and the Russian – which appear to meet most of the criteria of Davies. These 'national' revolutions were of 'international' effect as their ideas spread across territories like nuclear fallout, yet their legal traditions survived with doctrinal modifications to reflect the new politics.[122] At the intuitive level, there was a World Revolution in the twentieth century. Even on Davies's stringent criteria, a World Revolution can be accepted – there was an overthrow of a system of government conceived in terms of exclusive sovereign statehood.

Still maintained, through this revolution, as through the great Western national revolutions, were patterns of law and authority seen since the twelfth century, grounding the legal order in fundamental concepts of ultimate reality and meaning with a professional science of law collection, exposition and application. Demonstrative of this ultimate reality and meaning is a concept of time and divinity which gives purpose to law. The Papal Revolution of Gregory VII was imbued with a Christian view of time, seeking to establish the

---

[119] That there has recently been an information technology revolution associated with globalisation seems justified if one accepts, as many historians do, that there were industrial revolutions in the eighteenth and nineteenth centuries: see Manuel Castells, *The Information Age: Economy, Society and Culture*, 3 vols. (Malden & Oxford: Blackwell Publishers, 1996), vol. I, *The Rise of the Network Society*, ch. 1.   [120] Davies, *Europe*, p. 675.   [121] See section 2.1.3, p. 31 above.

[122] See Berman, *Law and Revolution*, pp. 5, 24–5. Cf. H. Patrick Glenn, 'Law, Revolution and Rights' in Werner Maihofer and Gerhard Sprenger (eds.), *Revolution and Human Rights, Proceedings of the 14th IVR World Congress, Edinburgh, 1989* (Stuttgart: Franz Steiner Verlag, 1990), p. 11; Alan Watson, *The Evolution of Western Private Law* (Baltimore: The Johns Hopkins University Press, expanded edn 2001), pp. 226–30. The natural lawfulness of the innovation takes precedence over the political illegality of the revolution as part of a cyclical process which restores some aspects of pre-revolutionary life: see Eugen Rosenstock-Huessy, *Out of Revolution: Autobiography of Western Man* (Providence and Oxford: Berg, 1993), pp. 188, 342 ff. For the classic idea of revolution as a circular motion or return, see Polybius, *The Rise of the Roman Empire*, trans. Ian Scott Kilvert (Harmondsworth: Penguin, 1979), p. 350.

conditions for the millennial rule of Christ on earth,[123] with law a means to improve society, in effect to 'bring on the Messiah'. This was in the context of one God, and numerous dispersed markets throughout Europe, authorising law. In contrast, the conception of time and progress underlying the World Revolution was a belief in unlimited progress – a belief which, according to Ernst Kantorowicz, was cherished by the generations preceding the two world wars.[124] More cherished if not coveted than ever, time is now to be consumed, with more and more consuming activity to be packed into less and less time. This is in pursuit of a progress which seems intent upon the very achievement of more progress measured by speed and consumption, checked primarily by environmentalism, human rights discourses and community groups concerned about family life. Speed is the new virtue, discussed with relevant recommendations for contemporary legal education by way of conclusion in chapter 13. This occurs in the context of one market and many different types of gods and religions girding the authority of law today. Legal theory must evaluate this transformation and the optimum role for law in the new context.

That so many tens of millions of people have died not just in wars but at the hands of their societies in the twentieth century – through consciously articulated norms and laws (the two most populous nations of Europe killed more tens of millions of people through murderous political regimes than their wars did)[125] – invites urgent enquiry into the concepts behind those norms and laws which have created and legitimated such mass dehumanisation and carnage. Global counter-efforts aspire to entrench peace through new normative ideologies and interrelationships after the collapse of the ideologies of communism and fascism.[126] The preambles to the major international treaties of our age, characteristic of globalisation and law, are overflowing with moral exhortations to improve on what has been the most humanly destructive century ever, as we shall see in chapter 10. Like the blood sacrifices associated with the biblical covenants, the sacrifice of the soldiers and civilians of the twentieth-century World Revolution must give sanctity and memory to the important new transnational agreements, reflective of the survivors and their ultimate realities and meanings upon which the legal initiatives were founded.

A jurisprudence which seeks, first, to understand the impact of globalisation on the legal order,[127] and, secondly, to provoke attitudes to norms and law which might make difficult a repeat of the carnage of the World Revolution, will need to appreciate the construction of authority in terms of social space and historical time. In later chapters, that authority will be evaluated in different periods

---

[123] See Berman, *Law and Revolution*, pp. 25–8.

[124] Ernst Kantorowicz, *The King's Two Bodies: A Study in Medieval Political Theology* (New Jersey: Princeton University Press, 1957), p. 274.   [125] Davies, *Europe*, p. 897.

[126] For a view of the disaster of twentieth century Europe as an ideological product (and for polemical critique of current developments), see Robert Conquest, *Reflections on a Ravaged Century* (New York: Norton, 2000).

[127] On this necessity, see Walker, 'Constitutional Pluralism', 334–6.

of history to understand Western patterns of law and authority. Law, in the West, has never come only from one place. Never has it rested upon static beliefs about what constitutes 'law', nor has there been enduring, widespread acceptance that territorial boundaries must enclose a centrally declared legal system. As we shall see in the next chapter, law in the West requires deep-order legitimacy. It obtains that legitimacy, dynamically, from within the cultural, private societies of peoples and not just the public, external, political constitution of the state. These societies, with their diverse views of history and the future, are proliferating at all levels in association with globalisation, rendering appreciation of the construction of legal legitimacy and responsibility vital to a general, globalist jurisprudence.

3

Law and authority in space and time

At least so far as law is concerned, reality wears a mask in the shape of 'the here and the now'. Space (not just 'the here') and time (not just 'the now') must be explored to understand law and authority properly. In furtherance of the historical and normative general jurisprudence with which to evaluate patterns of law and authority relevant to globalisation, this chapter proposes a theory which contemplates the space and time dimensions of law and authority. I call this 'the Space–Time Matrix', drawing on writings of Eugen Rosenstock-Huessy. If there is a third dimension of human being, then it would be the spiritual or metaphysical dimension. That too is explored, under the heading of 'ultimate reality and meaning'. This dimension can only ever be revealed to humans at some spatial location in society (for example, to a loner on a mountain or in a room full of people) and at points in time. This is contemplated by the Space–Time Matrix.

Frequent references will be made to this model in the balance of this book. It grounds the way I attempt to make sense of law and authority, historically and normatively. Assertions in this chapter need not all be accepted, though, for the purpose of the historical jurisprudence proposed and the historical discussion which occupies the balance of the Parts of this book. It will suffice if the present chapter conveys law and authority as morally, culturally and politically constructed (that is, spatially on the 'Space Axis') by reference to experiences and expectations of the future (that is, temporally, on the 'Time Axis'). This chapter may, however, prove helpful, in and of itself, for developing a normative jurisprudence (that is, a principled approach to the consideration and deployment of law) in the face of the challenges of globalisation.

3.1 Normative foundations of a historical jurisprudence

Our observations in connection with globalisation forbid confinement to the state of a legal consideration of authority. Rather, resort must be had to the ultimate reality and meaning which underlies social authority and conceptions of right and wrong. With an appreciation of fundamental authority then in hand, we can move to a normative jurisprudence. This will proffer individual self-consciousness, expressed as an 'autobiographical attitude' (not to be

mistaken for individualism), to be an essential ingredient to successful constitutionalism.

3.1.1 Ultimate reality and meaning

Ignorance of the constitution of society by individuals and the reciprocal social
construction of the individual may have resulted in law being distant and, for the
most part, morally irrelevant to individuals in modern social history. That may be
one factor contributing to the World Revolution: a number of centuries of increasingly national, individualistic philosophy. Individual responsibility was alienated
from the domestic legal order. Individual responsibility and international law did
not go together because international law related to states, not individuals. Laws
were technical rules to be exploited. Generally, laws were not a part of one's moral
existence – they came only from the distant state. They had grown unrelated to the
individual's sense of ultimate reality and meaning. Human disenchantment with
the social world was reflected in Nietzsche's famous aphorism towards the end of
the nineteenth century, 'God is dead'.[1] In fact, Western perceptions of ultimate
reality and meaning were generally *changing*. Ultimate reality, or God, was generally not perceived to be connected to the nature of law at that time.

Some justification is required before asserting that God, gods or religions
change and resurface in societies where, and times when, reference to such
deities or ultimate reality and meaning is not commonly made. It is really a
matter, from the Western Judeo-Christian perspective, of equating 'God' with
'ultimate reality and meaning' and then noticing that every conscious person in
every culture has some sense of what the meaning of life is all about. The conscious person can therefore be said to acknowledge some sense of ultimate
reality and meaning. 'Ultimate Reality and Meaning' is actually a term of art
used by interdisciplinary and cross-cultural scholars interested in collectively
pursuing the idea in their studies. As such, 'URAM' has been described as 'that
to which the human mind reduces and relates everything: that which man
does not reduce to anything else'.[2] This notion is compatible with the Judeo-
Christian God. The Tetragammaton, the Hebrew 'YHWH' pronounced
'Yahweh', translates to such a notion, although personified.[3] It means 'I am who

---

[1] Friedrich Nietzsche, *Thus Spoke Zarathustra: A Book for None and All*, trans. Walter Kaufman
(Harmondsworth: Penguin Books, 1978), p. 259. Nietzsche's philosophy suggests that God
was never alive. Cf. 'death of God' theology since the 1960s which has emphasised the
hiddenness and mysteriousness of God: see Daniel J. Peterson, 'Speaking of God after the
Death of God' (2005) 44 *Dialog: A Journal of Theology* 207–26.

[2] Ronald Glasberg, 'The Evolution of the URAM Concept in the Journal: An Analytic Survey of
Key Articles' (1996) 19 *Ultimate Reality and Meaning* 69–77, 70 citing Tibor Horvath in the
first issue of the journal. My use of such deconstructed conceptualism is not intended to
eschew the richness of accounts of the personhood of God.

[3] See Exodus 3: 14–15: 'And God said to Moses, "I AM WHO I AM . . . Thus you shall say to the
children of Israel: 'The LORD God of your fathers, the God of Abraham, the God of Isaac,
and the God of Jacob, has sent you. This *is* My name forever, and this *is* My memorial to all
generations . . .' " ' [original italics, NKJV].

I will be' or 'I will be who I am' or 'I will be who I will be'.[4] As such, this is a Being whose essence is its existence, given that it is defined by reference only to its complete self – a perfect Be-ing. As St Thomas Aquinas wrote in the middle ages following from St Anselm, by the name God 'is signified that thing than which nothing greater can be conceived'.[5] As such, a notion of God or ultimate reality and meaning is a type of cultural default answer to questions which may be too hard to answer using conventional human logic: 'Because that's how God created the world'. Even with all of his science, in the seventeenth century when Newton had calculated the orbit of planets around the sun, he could not explain why the solar system was stable. His answer was to say 'God keeps watch over the system.'[6] Such phenomena are reducible no further, just as the final irreducible answer which could be given by the adult to our inquisitive child in chapter 1 was that law is obeyed to enable people to earn money to feed children,[7] implicitly perpetuating an economics- or Mammon-driven world as its functional equivalent of God. In earlier times, the answer might have been 'because God requires it'.

Any person who engages in activity aspiring to ultimate reality and meaning is being theological or philosophical. 'The power which makes the atheist fight for atheism is his God.'[8] As theologian Karl Barth has expressed the issue:

> For this reason, there are many kinds of theologies. There is no man who does not have his own god or gods as the object of his highest desire and trust, or as the basis of his deepest loyalty and commitment. There is no one who is not to this extent also a theologian. . . . There is no philosophy that is not to some extent also theology. Not only does this fact apply to philosophers who desire to affirm – or who, at least, are ready to admit – that divinity, in a positive sense, is the essence of truth and power of some kind of highest principle; but the same truth is valid even for thinkers denying such a divinity, for such a denial would in practice merely consist in transferring an identical dignity and function to another object. Such an alternative object might be 'nature', creativity or an unconscious and amorphous will to life. It might also be 'reason', progress, or even a redeeming nothingness into which man would be destined to disappear. Even such apparently 'godless' ideologies are theologies.[9]

---

[4] Karl Barth, 'The Place of Theology' reprinted in Ray S. Anderson (ed.), *Theological Foundations for Ministry: Selected Readings for a Theology of the Church in Ministry* (Edinburgh: T.&T. Clark Ltd, 1979), p. 33. In Taoism: 'Man takes his law from the Earth; the Earth takes its law from Heaven; Heaven takes its law from the Tâo. The law of the Tâo is its being what it is.' Tâo Téh King, cited in Philip Allott, *Eunomia: New Order for a New World* (Oxford: Oxford University Press, 1990), part 1 cover page.

[5] St Thomas Aquinas, *Summa Theologica*, in Anton C. Pegis (ed.), *Introduction to St Thomas Aquinas* (New York: The Modern Library, 1948), p. 21. See too generally Questions II ('The Existence of God') & III ('On the Simplicity of God'), pp. 21–33.

[6] Moshe Kaveh, 'Faith and Science in the Third Millennium' in *Eshkolot: Essays in Memory of Rabbi Ronald Lubofsky* (Melbourne: Hybrid Publishers, 2002), p. 313.

[7] See ch. 1, p. 2 above.

[8] Eugen Rosenstock-Huessy, *Out of Revolution: Autobiography of Western Man* [1938] (Oxford: Berg, 1993), p. 725.   [9] Barth, 'Place of Theology', pp. 22–3.

Whilst such thinking might be too essentialist for some who may take semantic objection to the employment and imposition of the nouns 'God', 'theology' or 'philosophy' on all humanity, it does not actually impose a belief or set down a single lifestyle for the pursuer of insight. That is, no single ontology is being imposed; rather, the inevitability of adopting an ontology is acknowledged. The way I am using such terms here is merely to suggest that concern with ultimate reality and meaning is a universal human tendency, upon which authority will be grounded and explained.

A constitution can be thought about as a manifestation of ideas formed by a society about the relationship of its social order to divine order, sovereignty of law, natural cosmic order and/or natural social order,[10] all of which are concepts which presuppose ultimate reality. It is from an individual's culturally developed conception of God, or ultimate reality and meaning, that notions of reality, justice, right and wrong will originate. God and functional equivalents have featured representations of specific human social ideals and characteristics, like the Thracian red-haired, blue-eyed God; the black, snub-nosed gods of the Ethiopians;[11] and drawings of a European-looking Jesus with long hair.[12] The history of Western Christianity, with its reformations, tells the story of changing perceptions of God and justice, with evolving human ideals. Authority changes in line with the evolution of notions of ultimate reality and meaning.

Thus written, this chapter and indeed this book will employ a general notion of God and ultimate reality and meaning in discussions about authority and allegiance, even in the context of secular societies in more recent times (arguably orientated towards a new god, being that of economic progress or Mammon). As Niklas Luhmann noted, law requires principles which give meaning to the 'right answers' which law produces: for example, this may take the form of 'the will of God' or 'the maximisation of welfare'.[13] With the notion of God and ultimate reality and meaning in place, we can now begin to analyse the way authority is constructed and might be improved in legal systems. Authority and allegiance are moral notions located in the socially constructed individual. Law is dependent upon tapping into ultimate reality and meaning as the moral, metaphysical *grundnorm* or foundation, if law is to be more than

---

[10] Philip Allott, *The Health of Nations: Society and Law Beyond the State* (Cambridge: Cambridge University Press, 2002), [12.30].

[11] Xenophanes, quoted in Robin Horton, *Patterns of Thought in Africa and the West: Essays on Magic, Religion and Science* (Cambridge: Cambridge University Press, 1995), p. 424. Xenophanes observed that 'if an ox could paint a picture, its god would look like an ox': Allott, *Health of Nations*, [12.49] n. 49, citing Dodds, *The Greeks and the Irrational*.

[12] Jesus was of course Jewish and was likely to have been swarthy in the manner at that time of the inhabitants of the Holy Land, almost certainly with the 'well trimmed' hair required by Ezekiel 45: 20. On the anthropomorphic projection of the Christian God from human ideals, see Ludwig Feuerbach, *The Essence of Christianity*, trans. George Eliot [1851] (Amherst: Prometheus Books, 1989).

[13] Niklas Luhmann, *Law as a Social System*, trans. K. A. Ziegert (Oxford: Oxford University Press, 2004), p. 429.

just the untrammelled exercise of power. The social construction of the individual is therefore vital to the enterprise of understanding law. As will be shown, the individual's activity in, or contemplation of, her or his social location in this world of norms is crucial to advancing law meaningfully.

3.1.2 Social activity as autobiography

It is the beginning of the World Revolution. Picture a German law professor fighting in the trenches of Verdun in 1917. Shells explode loudly and painfully. Corpses litter the landscape. European air is thick with the suffering of tens of millions of people. Eugen Rosenstock-Huessy is the name of this law professor. After World War I he confessed that he had to try to understand this episode in what he termed 'the Suicide of Europe'. Like a seed germinated by a bushfire, Rosenstock-Huessy could not stare at history as a spectator – not as a law professor at Breslau, then a lecturer in German art and culture at Harvard, nor as a teacher of social philosophy at Dartmouth College. The history of Europe was a short story – not more than twenty-seven generations when Rosenstock-Huessy wrote in the 1920s and 1930s.[14] When history and social life are thought about as a generational project – of our children, parents and grandparents and their parents and societies, the sub-title of Rosenstock-Huessy's work on European history, *Autobiography of Western Man*, makes sense. He felt compelled as a human being to try to work out his own role, and individuals' roles, as members of the warring societies, to attempt in the future to avoid the mass horror of war. This required conscious thought and examination of the historical construction of the authority and social norms which had failed European societies so badly.

We are all autobiographers.[15] We are all writing accounts of the lives we lead, whether or not we do so consciously. We all inadvertently present our stories to the world and invite judgement upon ourselves every time we, in the West, leave the front door. Speech and writing are implicated in this struggle for survival and significance, which is observed, biographically, and responded to by society. Our only references are the words of fellow humans in the present and words recorded from the past. Music, art and the performing arts contribute to this significance, but they are inarticulate unless they are lyrical – that is, unless they contain words with objective-orientated meaning. In her analysis of the alienation of social activity from human thought, Hannah Arendt observed that 'Men in the plural . . . can experience meaningfulness only because they can talk

---

[14] Rosenstock-Huessy, *Out of Revolution*, pp. 6–12.

[15] See Hannah Arendt, *The Human Condition* (Chicago: University of Chicago Press, 1958), p. 97: 'The chief characteristic of this specifically human life, whose appearance and disappearance constitute worldly events, is that it is itself always full of events which ultimately can be told as a story, establish a biography . . . For action and speech . . . are indeed the two activities whose end result will always be a story with enough coherence to be told, no matter how accidental or haphazard the single events and their causation may appear to be.'

with and make sense to each other and to themselves.'[16] At once speech and literacy become the only media for the conscious, articulate participation in significance. The unit of significance is the word, carried in speech.

Philip Allott emphasises the significance of words and speech uniquely amongst legal philosophers. 'We live and die for words; we create and kill for words; we build and destroy for words; wars and revolutions are made for words. *Sovereignty, the people, the faith, the law, the fatherland, self-determination, nationality, independence, security, land, freedom* . . .'[17] 'Everything in the world – the physical world and the world-of-consciousness – has, within moral reality, its own moral significance. Nothing is without moral significance – no word, no idea, no theory, no value, no willing, no acting.' Indeed, the printed page releases energy.[18] As we all crave significance, although by varied means, significance as a concept emerges as a focus for enquiry. In attempting such a study, investigation must be carried out into *how* right and wrong, good and bad, mean something through words and their use.

Of what relevance is this to law? Law is composed of norms in word form. Additionally, as soldiers are responsible for fighting wars, lawyers and their writings contribute to the starting of wars (that is, by theorising whether a state of affairs is illegitimate if not illegal) and to the ending of wars (that is, by facilitating settlement on normative terms). Similarly, lawyers are responsible in this fashion for starting and ending litigation or conveyances of property. That is not to say that lawyers are the *cause* of wars, or the authors of their conclusion, any more than soldiers keep them going. Politicians, governments and their constituencies bear that responsibility, just as clients cause litigation and conveyances. Lawyers, though, as the only social group expertly trained in authoritative norms, bear a responsibility for advancing the rules of conflict as a technology. Such special norms (which we recognise as 'laws') should make more difficult the waging of war and easier the possibility for creating peace, encouraging the pursuit of virtue independent of coercion.

Not just lawyers but everyone requires an autobiographical awakening and realisation of the moral power of personal action. Lawyers, especially, must be alert to the rules they work with. As Allott writes, '[t]he universe is altered for all time by the existence and acting of every human individual'.[19] *Everyone* is responsible for society through everything he or she says, does and thinks. This statement is as true for communism as it is for liberalism, given that the unit of

---

[16] Arendt, *Human Condition*, pp. 4, 50; see too Frank G. Kirkpatrick, *A Moral Ontology for a Theistic Ethic: Gathering the Nations in Love and Justice* (Aldershot: Ashgate, 2003), ch. 5.

[17] Allott, *Eunomia*, [1.10]; see too his *Health of Nations*, p. x and [3.17].

[18] Allott, *Eunomia*, [6.56], [8.21].

[19] Allott, *Eunomia*, [3.7]. Allott also writes of the possibility that there is no frontier between personal psychology and the social psychology of the nation: Allott, *Health of Nations*, [4.82], [5.3]. On the self-critical, autobiographical attitude required for these times, see Abdullahi A. An-Na'im, 'Globalization and Jurisprudence: An Islamic Law Perspective' (2005) 54 *Emory Law Journal* 25–51, 41; and, more popularly, Michelle P. Brown and Richard J. Kelly (eds.), *You're History: How People Make the Difference* (London: Continuum Press, 2006).

all human social order is the individual. Spraying deodorant with CFCs in New York may contribute to skin cancer deaths in Chile; driving a car may lead to lethal floods in Bangladesh through ozone layer depletion.[20] The need for the self-conscious exercise of individual responsibility for the world has never been more apparent than now in the increasingly interconnected world represented by globalisation. Especially is this so, if one accepts the frequent criticism that globalisation provides an excuse for state governments to abrogate economic management to treaty-based formulas which tend to reward free trade at the cost of other values.

Two propositions emerge, if law is to work meaningfully and effectively. First, law must appeal to the individual. Second, the individual must think outside individual interests. A normative jurisprudence must cultivate these propositions, now pursued.

3.2 The Space–Time Matrix

Conventional positivist jurisprudence assumes that law proceeds as an instrument which can be wielded with varying degrees of success to accomplish social goals. Law, on that understanding, comprises rules sanctified by bureaucracy which are legislated, judicially considered, enforced by the executive and/or applied by lawyers. Law is a tool of the arms of government, these being legislature, executive and judiciary (including lawyers who are officers of the court). Law in this scheme is assumed to have 'objective' qualities, beyond the influence of individuals other than through the democratic processes of government. Yet this is only one appearance of the reality of law, ignoring arbitration, voluntary codes, religious laws, employer policies, university regulations, indigenous laws and myriad other normative systems which radiate authority for constituents of those societies.

A project for understanding law more accurately, in such socially constructed terms with the individual as the basic unit, can borrow for its foundation the criticism of the claims to objectivity of modern science made by mathematician-turned-philosopher Edmund Husserl. Theory which attempts to go beyond mere technical mastery or use of a discipline such as law must admit and account for the multiplicity of subjective appearances of reality. As Husserl observed, this is most difficult for the mathematician or the natural scientist who is usually 'at best a highly brilliant technician of the method', totally immersed in the objectivity of the venture. The same may apply to the lawyer. The scientist of the world must, however, develop 'the ability to *inquire back* into the *original meaning* of

---

[20] Peter Singer, *One World: The Ethics of Globalisation* (Melbourne: Text Publishing, 2nd edn 2004), p. 22. On the challenges to the legal concept of proximity and negligence posed by globalisation, see William Twining, 'Globalization and Legal Theory: Some Local Implications' (1996) 49 *Current Legal Problems* 1–42, 32, 34; M. Galanter, 'Law's Elusive Promise: Learning from Bhopal' in Michael Likosky (ed.), *Transnational Legal Processes* (London: Butterworths, 2002).

all his meaning-structures and methods, i.e., into the *historical meaning of their primal establishment*, and especially into the meaning of all the *inherited meanings* taken over unnoticed in this primal establishment, as well as those taken over later on' – and this must not simply be rejected as 'metaphysical'[21] [original italics]. This is termed by Husserl 'a return to the naïveté of life – but in a reflection which rises above this naïveté . . . to overcome the "scientific" character of traditional objectivistic philosophy'.[22] This returns us to our 'how?' enquiry: that is, how is meaning bestowed in science,[23] or law.

Applying this scientific technique to law, the data for investigation are communications. Rosenstock-Huessy's 'grammatical method' or 'cross of reality' provides a key to understanding the human constitution of society and the society's constitution of the human. Essentially, humans are socially determined and society-determining creatures through their communications, which can be mapped according to four orientations on two axes. They are: close social relations (interior) versus distant social relations (exterior) on the Space Axis; and history versus the future on the Time Axis.[24]

Diagrammatically, these normative influences by which the individual is located in society can be expressed on the Space–Time Matrix; see figure 3.1.

Each axis will be elaborated below in some detail, beyond the suggestive model offered by Rosenstock-Huessy, to attempt to understand the bestowal of authority. In summary, the individual is caught between, on the Space Axis, extremes ranging from, at the interior end, an insane ability to relate only to oneself which is otherwise acceptable only in earliest childhood, moving along the axis to relating to one's parents, broader family, neighbourhood, moving outward to the exterior social realms such as, in the West, local community, school, bureaucracies, government and, possibly at the outmost exterior extreme, jail, where (assuming a just conviction) legal norms of sufficient gravity have failed to receive obedience from the individual. This is the interior construction of personal morality versus the exterior construction of politics.[25]

---

[21] Edmund Husserl, *The Crisis of European Sciences and Transcendental Phenomenology*, trans. David Carr (Evanston: Northwestern University Press, 1970), pp. 56–7.

[22] Husserl, *Crisis*, p. 59.

[23] Ibid., pp. 146–7: 'In opposition to all previously designed objective sciences, which are sciences on the ground of the world, this would be a science of the universal *how* of the pregivenness of the world, i.e., of what makes it a universal ground for any sort of objectivity. And included in this is the creation of a science of the ultimate grounds [*Gründe*] which supply the true force of all objective grounding, the force arising from its ultimate bestowal of meaning.' See too chapter 1, pp. 2–3 above.

[24] See Eugen Rosenstock-Huessy, *Speech and Reality* (Norwich: Argo Books Inc., 1970), pp. 18, 52; and his *The Christian Future; or, The Modern Mind Outrun* (New York: Harper Torch, 1966), ch. 7.

[25] See generally Immanuel Kant, 'Perpetual Peace: A Philosophical Sketch – Appendix 1: On the Disagreement Between Morals and Politics in Relation to Perpetual Peace' in Hans Reiss (ed.), *Kant: Political Writings*, trans. N. B. Nisbet (Cambridge: Cambridge University Press, 1970, 2nd edn 1991), pp. 116–25; Jerome Hall, *Foundations of Jurisprudence* (Indianapolis: Bobbs-Merrill Co., 1973), p. 117. See too Bikhu Parekh and R. N. Berki (eds.), *The Morality of Politics* (London: George Allen & Unwin Ltd, 1972).

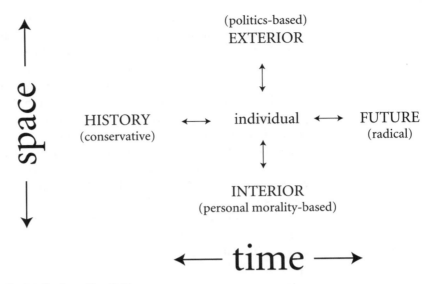

Fig. 3.1 The Space–Time Matrix.

This type of social conditioning *process* is arguably universal, concerned as it is, like Philip Allott's *Eunomia*, with emphasising 'the internal points of reference of each developing human mind', not the 'external points of reference of any particular culture'.[26] That is, the individual awakens to the society (the society does not awaken to the individual) in a universal social process. On the Time Axis, individuals can only measure or calculate activity by reference to norms derived from the past or hoped for in the future. The extreme conservative will look only to the past for norms, whilst the extreme radical will only look for norms in a vision of the future.

Social conflict and alienation from norms or laws occur when there is an imbalance in the orientation of norms on this matrix for the individual – for example, the norms break too radically from the past and do not have interior moral appeal. For widespread allegiance to norms and respect of authority, there must be widespread appeal to the individual in all four orientations. That will not necessarily make all law good, but it will make law more meaningful.

We have already noted Einstein's theory of the relativity of time and space as a symbol which may have helped to account for the emerging consciousness of globalisation as a concept.[27] Anthony Giddens has observed that globalisation is characterised by the radical transformation of space and time. Time and space have become 'disembedded'[28] from the social world. Time is now significantly abstracted from the life cycle as seasons and daylight matter increasingly less to

---

[26] Allott, *Eunomia*, p. xxii. See generally his ch. 8 ('The Dimensions of Reality') for an exposition of time and space as providing the basic normative orientation for consciousness.

[27] See ch. 2, section 2.1.1, p. 26 above.

[28] Anthony Giddens, *The Consequences of Modernity* (Stanford: Polity Press, 1990), pp. 17–21.

human activity; and in the age of jet travel and virtual video meetings, space has become abstracted from place. Communications technology has allowed intercourse to be quickened to the pace of spontaneous urgency, no matter the time or where one is in the world – at work, privately engaged, at home or abroad – from which there may once have been the solace of surface or even air mail delivery, and more patient social expectations. To understand the authority of any time, in any place, it is necessary to appreciate the constitution of that authority as a matter of its societal (space) dimension and its historical (time) dimension, including the actual attitude to, and utilisation of, time in the present.

It is perhaps a poetic coincidence that a focus on 'space and time' as a matter of jurisprudence just so happens to be relevant to globalisation in a way which is becoming established in the scholarly discourse on globalisation. This jurisprudential technique will be used in future chapters to attempt to understand normative authority in the past millennium, and, most importantly, now.

3.2.1 The Space Axis: personal morality versus politics

Enquiry into authority begins even earlier than with our inquisitive child in chapter 1. It begins with the baby. If Rousseau was correct to say 'the first tears of children are prayers', it was because babies have complete reliance on a power beyond themselves for their very survival.[29] Human babies are spectacularly underdeveloped compared with the babies of other higher mammals, both physiologically (a great deal of physical development occurs outside the womb compared with other mammals) and in terms of drives and instincts.[30] Many babies need to be taught to fall asleep! A distinctive attribute of being human is that conditioning and education are required by our very nature. The human condition cannot be separated from human conditioning. Crucially, that social conditioning begins with being called a name.

Naming is the fundamental normative act. It is in the act of naming a human that it first becomes a someone with a sense of identity and a consciousness of her or his own being.[31] Early on, ideally, the infant is made to feel secure in the world and is addressed by parents with the second person singular pronoun 'you' together with the name, in the imperative.[32] *Ben, show us how you walk; You wave goodbye to Aunty Jane;* or, *Don't pick your nose!* Parents, or perhaps

---

[29] Jean-Jacques Rousseau, *Émile; or, Treatise on Education* [1762], trans. William H. Payne (Amherst: Prometheus Books, 2003), p. 30.

[30] Peter Berger and Thomas Luckmann, *The Social Construction of Reality: A Treatise in the Sociology of Knowledge* (Harmondsworth: Penguin, 1966), p. 66. 'We are born weak; we have need of strength: we are born destitute of everything; we have need of assistance: we are born stupid; we have need of judgment': Rousseau, *Émile*, p. 2.

[31] This is recognised in Neil MacCormick, *Questioning Sovereignty: Law, State, and Nation in the European Commonwealth* (Oxford: Oxford University Press, 1999), p. 163.

[32] See Eugen Rosenstock-Huessy, *Practical Knowledge of the Soul*, trans. Mark Huessy and Freya von Moltke (Norwich: Argo Books, 1988), p. 16; and his *Christian Future*, p. 37.

extended families, depending upon the culture, are God (in the sense of 'ultimate reality and meaning') to the infants, defining as they do the expectations
of, and possibilities for, the normative world of the infant.[33] That is, there is
nothing capable of greater conceptual reduction for the child than the parents:
the world begins and stops with them. The first people and things we learn to
name are the most intimate, and the order of naming and hearing names generally coincides with the unfolding of the parameters of our social space on the
Space Axis. Infants begin by responding to their own names (as do some of the
more intelligent animals), then they learn to name their parents and family and
household, as well as some things like milk and food. In the construction of this
normative world, infants are addressed by figures naturally authoritative, being
parents. Parents' imperative commands earn allegiance for the fact, ideally, of
their capacity to nurture. The parents are absolute sovereigns in the household
sphere of containable disruption (although that 'sovereignty' is lost only too
soon, as most parents will vouch).

The origin of our humanity, in speech and the development of norms, is
therefore in the interior space. St Augustine elaborated this theme from an
(imaginatively extrapolated) account of his own childhood:

> For when I tried to express my meaning by crying out and making various sounds
> and movements, so that my wishes should be obeyed, I found that I could not
> convey all that I meant or make myself understood by everyone whom I wished
> to understand me. . . . I noticed that people would name some object and then
> turn towards whatever it was that they had named. I watched them and under-
> stood the sound they made . . . [s]o, by hearing words arranged in various
> phrases and constantly repeated, I gradually pieced together what they stood for.
> . . . I took a further step into the stormy life of human society[34]

Gradually we become conscious of a more exterior world outside the family
household, stepping beyond the neighbourhood, to shops, and beyond shops
to schools and bureaucracies which unfold at the exterior end of social space.

Classical Roman law, finalised in the sixth century CE and so influential on
the Western legal tradition, appears to have evolved in the manner suggested by
the Space–Time Matrix. Roman law reflected the blossoming of the human
consciousness from Greek thought into the concept of self and other. The progressive recognition by Roman law of persons, things and then actions corresponds to the movement from the more intimate to the less intimate (or, as we
saw with the help of St Augustine, the progressive recognition by the child of
the surrounding world). This tripartite Roman scheme represents the progressive evolution from persons to things and then to actions, which corresponds to

---

[33] This is a variation upon what Goethe wrote in *Pandora* ('A father is always a god'), according
to Rosenstock-Huessy, *Practical Knowledge*, p. 16. Furthermore, God's relationship with his
people is portrayed in this way, in Isaiah: 43: 1 (NKJV): 'Fear not, for I have redeemed you;
I have called you by your name; You are Mine.'

[34] Saint Augustine, *Confessions*, trans. R. S. Pine-Coffin (Harmondsworth: Penguin, 1961), p. 29.

the linguistic evolution from subject (person), object (thing) and verb (facilitating relations between person and thing – subject and object).[35] Possibly this reveals something of the structure of Christian theology too.[36]

The fundamental naming process and learning of speech occurs intimately in a moral world and within the reach of family and teachers. Often there will be a deep sense of moral commitment to that world, if only because the child is still 'innocent'. Under the gaze of the parent power-holder, that commitment will probably arise out of a sense of guilt at doing wrong[37] or pleasure at doing right.[38] Notwithstanding, an authentic existence requires orientation to norms, if only because there would otherwise ensue the individual's developmental dysfunction and ultimate rejection from society. Ideally, there is education into a critical, meaningful relationship with those norms. Far from lacking any legal quality, the norms which arise from this household and associational life are vital to the very substance of law.

Moving along the Space Axis to societal relationships, there is an inner order or 'living law', shaped by the 'living law of economics'[39] which creates mechanisms of human social survival – possession, private contracts, inheritance, corporate articles of association and family.[40] Meaning for that living law is still able to be generated by religion, education, art, science, social life and entertainment[41] – it is not simply economic. In the West, more external sources of law, chiefly from the state, do however come to supplant the economic, household normative foundations of law (in the Ancient Greek etymological sense of

---

[35] See Donald R. Kelley, *The Human Measure: Social Thought in the Western Legal Tradition* (Cambridge, MA: Harvard University Press, 1990), pp. 9, 52, 255–7.

[36] Kelley, *Human Measure*, pp. 118–19. *Contra* J. Witte, 'From Homer to Hegel: Ideas of Law and Culture in the West' (1991) 89 *Michigan Law Review* 1618–36, 1634. Cf. Harold J. Berman, 'Law and Logos' (1994) 44 *DePaul Law Review* 143–65, 150–3.

[37] See Sigmund Freud, *Civilization and its Discontents*, trans. James Strachey (New York: W. W. Norton & Co., Inc., 1961), pp. 70–86. 'Civilization, therefore, obtains its mastery over the individual's dangerous desire for aggression by weakening and disarming it and by setting up an agency within him to watch over it, like a garrison in a conquered city' (pp. 70–1).

[38] Foucault has deconstructed power into something not only repressive but possibly pleasurable, reproduced in all human interactions (e.g., schools or medical profession and not just law): Michel Foucault, *Power/Knowledge: Selected Interviews and Other Writings (1972–1977)*, ed. and trans. Colin Gordon *et al.* (New York: Pantheon, 1980), p. 119.

[39] Eugen Ehrlich, *Fundamental Principles of the Sociology of Law*, trans. Walter L. Moll [1913] (Cambridge, MA: Harvard University Press, 1936), p. 98. Ehrlich's classic notion of the 'living law' is the law to be found in the documents and practices attested by witnesses (p. 397).

[40] Ehrlich, *Fundamental Principles*, p. 46. On more recently published aspects of English unofficial sources of law in history, see J. H. Baker, *The Law's Two Bodies: Some Evidential Problems in English Legal History* (Oxford: Oxford University Press, 2003), Lecture Three; 'Why the History of English Law Has Not Been Finished' (2000) 59 *Cambridge Law Journal* 62–84, 78.

[41] See Ehrlich, *Fundamental Principles*, pp. 114–15. For example, the social forces at play in creating a duty to make a last will and testament were consideration for the family, church, institutions of public welfare and reverence for the dead. A similar sense of duty and reprehensibility at intestacy prevailed in ancient Roman society: Barry Nicholas, *An Introduction to Roman Law* (Oxford: Clarendon Press, 1991), p. 251.

economics as *oikos nomos* – norms of the household). The law court, as an association of persons not party to a legal controversy, marks the movement outwards on the Space Axis. Exterior principle[42] is imposed on more interior, personal, dutiful relationships, overtaking norms which feature less authoritatively in the hierarchy such as morals, religion, ethical custom, decorum, tact, etiquette and fashion.[43] This exterior space is the hub of the positivists' concept of the legal.[44]

Alienation and anomie[45] tend to occur as exposure increases to the world of bureaucracy and the state, and cold, hard facts and things, with estranged relationships based upon production and consumption, and formal, official letters addressed to surnames often as an adjunct of a file number. In the normal course, this is associated with the process of losing innocence, as the youngster becomes alienated from household normativity, to some extent, by political and bureaucratic matters which do not touch the heart of the youngster because they are outside his or her history, culture and realm of experience. Little wonder may it be that the state, exemplifying the '*depersonalisation* of power relations'[46] [original italics] and for Nietzsche 'the coldest of all cold monsters',[47] can produce law which the individual reflexively tries to 'keep on the right side of' or not get caught breaking.[48] That is the peril of bureaucratic law which does not engage the conscience,[49] exemplified in extreme form in totalitarian communist and fascist regimes of the twentieth century.[50]

Authority without coercion can only be achieved in a situation of respect. This begins for the individual with being addressed personally by name and being touched by communication within the normative system. It is difficult for the state to do this. In past times and situations it was easier. The Old and New Testaments are replete with names containing significance, and with people

---

[42] Ehrlich, *Fundamental Principles*, p. 122; Edward Jenks, *Law and Politics in the Middle Ages* (London: John Murray, 1898), p. 297.   [43] See Ehrlich, *Fundamental Principles*, p. 169.

[44] The introduction into the social equation of judges and legislators, in effect, to supervise social rules of duty, marks the step 'from the pre-legal into the legal world': H. L. A. Hart, *The Concept of Law* (Oxford: Clarendon Press, 2nd edn 1994), p. 42.

[45] The extreme of the notion of anomie derives from a categorisation of suicide in which limits are everywhere found without any value, resulting in a dissociation from the wider community: Emile Durkheim, *Suicide: A Study in Sociology*, trans. John A. Spaulding and George Simpson (London: Routledge & Kegan Paul, 1970), pp. 258, 285–9.

[46] Gianfranco Poggi, *The State: Its Nature, Development and Prospects* (Stanford: Stanford University Press, 1990), p. 18.   [47] Nietzsche, *Zarathustra*, p. 48.

[48] This sounds like Oliver Wendell Holmes's 'Bad Man' who only cares for what courts do in response to his own acts which might come before the court: see William Twining, *Globalisation and Legal Theory* (London: Butterworths, 2000), pp. 108–35.

[49] Perceptions of fairness will affect behaviour towards law: see e.g. Tom R. Tyler, *Why People Obey the Law* (Princeton: Princeton University Press, reprinted 2006).

[50] Martin van Creveld, *The Rise and Decline of the State* (Cambridge: Cambridge University Press, 1999), pp. 204, 375. See too Ehrlich, *Fundamental Principles*, p. 59, for his prescient remarks about how socialist societies would impose an 'omnipotent board of superhuman stature' over the 'law acting automatically and with such simple instrumentalities as the family order, possession, contract, and the law and right of inheritance'.

being renamed to mark new relationships.[51] A monk, until the late eighteenth century, formally renounced his birth name in a ceremony and received his monastic name upon entering into the new community.[52] Vestiges of importance being afforded to names can still be found in the conferment of titles, for example the creation of a life peerage in the House of Lords or knighthood. Along with other sirs and recipients of state honours, Sir Gerard Brennan, cited below, may since his award have felt a more personal relationship with the Commonwealth of Australia. Similarly, knighthood may also have some association with the softening anarchism of some ageing English pop stars. Such titles create something approaching a state–individual relationship which is richer than the modern state simply addressing a form to a tax file number connected to 'Ms J. Citizen' – a Jane Citizen who is likely to have only her immediate family and friends as a normative peer group. Alternatively, recipients of state awards have been known to reject them, signifying the alienation felt by some from the state. An individual (at least in common law countries)[53] may even change his or her birth name to express disaffection for the normative world of the state or the more general world.[54] On a more profound plane of this naming phenomenon are to be found various marginalised groups alienated from state institutions of norm generation and norm maintenance. In these situations, the state is challenged to be able to speak directly to such people in meaningful language by calling those people by a name to which they relate.[55]

Unfortunately, so often when the state intervenes in society, the state demonstrates the political, impersonal, objective aspect of speech. Characterised by imperative commands, such speech suffers from poor authority because there is only a weak allegiance between the individual and the political body. The individual is addressed in the third person plural with all the other third persons – for example, 'passengers will not stick their hands out of the train window'. The state and large corporate groups have difficulty addressing the individual personally because such entities cannot relate more intimately to the individual as may family, friends, teachers and religious or community leaders.

---

[51] E.g., Abram – Abraham (Genesis 17: 5); Sarai – Sarah (Genesis 17: 15); Jacob – Israel (Genesis 32: 28); Saul – Paul (Acts 9 cf. Acts 13).

[52] Harold Stahmer, 'Introduction' in Rosenstock-Huessy, *Christian Future*, p. xliii.

[53] Thomas M. Franck, *The Empowered Self: Law and Society in the Age of Individualism* (Oxford: Oxford University Press, 1999), p. 155. Many civil law countries are less liberal.

[54] On 10 June 1998, the Anti-Discrimination Tribunal heard an application by a man to change his name to Mr 'Prime Minister John Piss the Family Court and Legal Aid', according to his representative, Mr 'Justice Nevil Abolish Child Support and Family Court': *Australian Current Law News* (11 June 1998).

[55] See e.g. James Baldwin, *Nobody Knows My Name: More Notes of a Native Son* (New York: Vintage International, 1961 reprinted 1993), esp. pp. 75–7; Milner S. Ball, *The Word and the Law* (Chicago: University of Chicago Press, 1993), p. 86. Names have in times past occasionally been imposed by bureaucracies on ancient communities without any honour: e.g., the Gaels of Scotland and the Jews of Poland in the late eighteenth century (see Norman Davies, *Europe: A History* (London: Pimlico, 1997), p. 169) and the Jews in Nazi Germany being forced to assume Old Testament first names (Franck, *The Empowered Self*, p. 39).

The challenge is to move away from unquestioned imperatives – that is, from orders and rules which have lost their context.[56] An autobiographical approach to social activity stands the chance of recovering that context by critical and moral engagement with the norms – that is, through the forging of some sort of meaningful relationship with those norms, even if those norms are ultimately rejected. The meaningful engagement with norms requires, where possible, keeping political, exterior controls out of the moral, private realm of functional family and civic relationships,[57] where moral attitudes have greater potential to develop. Fortunately this principle is recognised, at least in theory, by the emerging European Union (if not global) doctrine of 'subsidiarity'. By this richly historical, constitutional principle, different levels of normative organisation are held to be appropriate for different types of social relationships.[58]

The exterior dimension is still relevant, nonetheless. Private, individualistic inklings of morality have contributed to the 'troublous storms' which have shaken the public world throughout history.[59] There must be some social mechanism for overcoming the whim of the individual – that is, exterior, objective standards are needed by which to reconcile subjective conflicts, particularly in multicultural societies. In fact, one of the virtues of legal systems is their objectivity. It is the history of Western legal systems that they have replaced magic and arbitrariness by the so-called 'rule of law', although this exterior orientation can sometimes be too extreme. Just as politics will work better when there is moral allegiance to the government, objectivity will work best when it is capable of subjective allegiance – for example, where the principles comprising the legal system are based upon community acceptance and practice. Religion has traditionally achieved this balance better than the legal system: that is, exterior bodies like the church can successfully advance their norms within their communities because there is an interior allegiance in the form of a moral attachment to the principles of the church as expressed in sacred writings such as the Bible.

3.2.2 The Time Axis: past versus future

Time is a deeply normative concept.[60] It is, in Niklas Luhmann's phrase, 'the unit of difference between the past and the future', when choices must be made.[61] 'Halfway between the ape that it was and the being that it could become,

---

[56] See Alasdair MacIntyre, *After Virtue: A Study in Moral Theory* (London: Duckworth, 2nd edn 1996), p. 60. We are all 'contextual individuals': MacCormick, *Questioning Sovereignty*, p. 186.

[57] See Sir Gerard Brennan, 'Principle and Independence: The Guardians of Freedom' (2000) 74 *Australian Law Journal* 749–59, 751.   [58] See ch. 11, section 11.2.5, pp. 263–4 below.

[59] See Edmund Burke, *Reflections on the Revolution in France* [1790] (Oxford: Oxford University Press, 1993), p. 141.

[60] A court in 1188 could not ascertain the time of day without 'discussion and enquiry': Marc Bloch, *Feudal Society*, trans. L. A. Manyon (London: Routlege & Kegan Paul, 1942), p. 74. See too Jacques Le Goff, *Time Work & Culture in the Middle Ages* (Chicago: University of Chicago Press, 1980); Rebecca R. French, 'Time in the Law' (2001) 72 *University of Colorado Law Review* 663–748.   [61] Luhmann, *Law as a Social System*, pp. 198, 283.

the human must each day choose its future.'[62] 'To live means to look backward as well as forward, and to decide, in every moment, between continuity and change.'[63]

Competing ideas of how the past should constitute the future have been at the heart of all of the major revolutions.[64] The Time Axis is the social field for attempting to resolve the relationship between the exterior and the interior dimensions of society – between individual and state, according to beliefs about history and the future. The Time Axis is a dimension for choosing between Utopia and more of the same, affecting the very functioning of society. Stability requires some degree of acceptance of what has come before in order to be able to move on.[65] This requires historical norms being maintained and invested with new content,[66] or, otherwise expressed, the past being reinterpreted to meet present and future challenges.[67] There is, then, an aspect to law of the dead ruling the living.[68]

Anyone who undertakes social activity is acting on personal experience or interpretation of other individuals' pasts, and acting to project an anticipated future. This involves wrestling with tradition: at extremes, the faithful seek to perpetuate cultural information and opponents seek to overcome it, with degrees of commitment in between.[69] Even those unconscious of their traditions may be motivated by an often mythical 'good old days' notion which they would like to see return in the future. Human history in any tradition, having been produced by humans, will contain much to be disappointed with, judged from the standpoint of the present. (No doubt there are things we accept today which will be regarded as cruel by generations in the future.) As such, the Western tradition contains more than its fair share of disappointments. Colonialism, ecological destruction, cultural, gender and religious arrogance, and regular internecine wars which have featured the worst feats of cruelty

---

[62] Allott, *Eunomia*, [19.1].   [63] Rosenstock-Huessy, *Speech and Reality*, p. 18.

[64] See Berman, *Law and Revolution*, pp. 15–18 and his *Law and Revolution, II: The Impact of the Protestant Reformations on the Western Legal Tradition* (Cambridge, MA: Harvard University Press, 2003), pp. 3–4. In the twentieth-century Russian Revolution, the Bolsheviks sought the classless society preceding the advent of property. In the eighteenth century, in the American Revolution, classical democracy was an aspiration of independence through a deistic ontology; and classical Greek and Roman liberty through philosophy was similarly an aspiration of the French Revolution. Government and ancient liberties under law were an aspiration of the English Glorious Revolution pursuant to a biblical vision, in the seventeenth century. In the German Revolution of the sixteenth century, Luther sought early Christianity untainted by the papacy. A return to scriptural authority was the aspiration of the Cluniacs of the Papal Revolution of the late eleventh century.

[65] See Allott, *Eunomia*, [5.16]–[5.17].   [66] See Ehrlich, *Fundamental Principles*, pp. 134–5.

[67] Berman, *Law and Revolution*, p. 9. This is a characteristic of the Western legal tradition.

[68] See Ehrlich, *Fundamental Principles*, p. 401, referring to Goethe. See too Ronald Dworkin, 'The Arduous Virtue of Fidelity: Originalism, Scalia, Tribe, and Nerve' (1997) 65 *Fordham Law Review* 1249–68, 1252; and *Re Wakim: Ex parte McNally* (1999) 163 ALR 270 per McHugh J at 283–6.

[69] See H. Patrick Glenn, *Legal Traditions of the World: Sustainable Diversity in Law* (Oxford: Oxford University Press, 2nd edn 2004), p. 20.

imaginable, are but a few examples – all, strangely enough, reflecting partial human visions of ultimate reality and meaning or God. Satisfaction with a tradition requires, at the same time, regret.[70] History gives a sense of achievement *and* wrongdoing.[71] Rather than treating history as either a field of rotting corpses to be buried in the attempt to become truly modern and enlightened, or seeing in history a beautiful garden being poisoned by the decadence of the present, history should be considered in all of its normative complexity on the Space–Time Matrix.

Traditions or communities of history and destiny, no matter how large, participate in the constitution of the individual's morality and normative consciousness.[72] Allegiance without coercion is dependent upon tapping into that sense of morality. This is difficult in a plural society and requires a commitment to communication. Attempting to appreciate normative motivations constructed historically with these past–future references is a significant step towards understanding law and authority as it has operated in the past and may be improved upon in the future.

Indeed, law is, in Robert Cover's words, 'the projection of an imagined future upon reality'.[73] Law is not, contrary to the archetypal natural law analysis, confined to what the present law of the state should or ought be in comparison to what the law actually is. Law, on Cover's view, embodies that tension at all times and by its very nature seeks a future different from the present, born of the debates and histories ('narratives') of a community which seeks to live according to a legal order. For example, when the Parliament of the Commonwealth of Australia enacted the 'misleading or deceptive conduct' provision of the Trade Practices Act in 1974, it was because Parliament imagined a world where misleading conduct would be minimised. Similarly, anti-discrimination law has been enacted because a world has been imagined where undesirable forms of discrimination will decrease. Law, no matter how black-letter, is someone's vision of a better world, even if it just means increasing government revenue through stamp duty.

Of course law can be changed, perhaps to what it *ought* be; although if it contains a moral aspiration, law will still probably never fulfil that aspiration all the time. (Unlike a vaccine being withdrawn upon eradication of the target disease, legislation is seldom, if ever, repealed for success.) Law, then, moderates the tension between visions from the imagination and the foundations of the old world. For this reason, Cover used the symbolism of the bridge to describe

---

[70] See Jeremy Webber, 'Beyond Regret: Mabo's Implications for Australian Constitutionalism' in Duncan Ivison *et al.* (eds.), *Political Theory and the Rights of Indigenous Peoples* (Cambridge: Cambridge University Press, 2000), p. 79, and the sources cited therein.

[71] Philip Bobbitt, *The Shield of Achilles: War, Peace and the Course of History* (London: Penguin, 2003), p. 332.

[72] See Anthony D. Smith, 'Towards a Global Culture?' in Mike Featherstone (ed.), *Global Culture: Nationalism, Globalization and Modernity* (London: Sage, 1990 reprinted 1996), p. 179.

[73] Robert M. Cover, 'Violence and the Word' (1986) 95 *Yale Law Journal* 1601–29, 1604.

law – a bridge to the future. He regarded all human efforts and understandings as being situated within two worlds: namely between memory and desire – or earth ('what is') and heaven (taken not necessarily as a supernatural place but simply a better place, chiefly 'what could be').[74] This idea of law as a bridge is compatible with the concluding view taken by Ronald Dworkin in *Law's Empire*, namely that law aims 'to show the best route to a better future, keeping the right faith with the past'.[75]

In addition to highlighting the imaginative nature of law, a critical awareness of time will also reveal the contingency of many norms and laws. Law is a craft concerned with what *is not* law. What *is* law may be considered to be the problematical and sometimes temporary triumph over what *is not* law.[76] Frequent overruling of trial courts by appellate courts, and even appellate courts being overruled by higher appeal courts, attest to this, not to mention the menagerie of dissenting judgments which do not make it into legal textbooks. Of the US Supreme Court, Joseph Vining has observed:

> Even a Supreme Court opinion on a matter is not the law. It is one more statement of law, and often one which some justices bringing the vote on it to a majority have signed all the while full of troubled reservations, and to which dissenting justices deny any lasting validity beyond settling the immediacies of the immediate case.[77]

A precedent is only a precedent because its principle was once in dispute,[78] sometimes fuelled by opposing senior counsel with judicial acumen who believed they could win the case for their clients. Well-funded clients may even run test cases – which they half-expect to lose – in the hope of advancing legal reasoning which might one day tip the scales of justice in their favour. Far from being disparaging, these examples of the contingency of law highlight the value-laden nature of law and the fact that beliefs and intellects are being brought to bear on scenarios which involve choices within the framework of a social science. 'At a given moment in time, law does not exist except as a possibility from the past, a possibility for the future',[79] albeit a possibility to be realised through a discourse with its own grammar and rules.

---

[74] Ronald R. Garet, 'Meaning and Ending' (1987) 96 *Yale Law Journal* 1801–24, 1808.

[75] Ronald Dworkin, *Law's Empire* [1986] (Oxford: Hart Publishing, 1998), p. 413, and ch. 7 on the idea of law as a chain novel. See too Allott, *Health of Nations*, [3.30], [5.7], [8.50] and [11.1].

[76] See e.g. David B. Goldman, 'Canon Law Origins of Common Law Defamation, the Hunne Whodunit and Western Legal Science: An Historical Challenge for Modern Lawyers' (1996) 2 *Australian Journal of Legal History* 79–94, 79, 92–3.

[77] Joseph Vining, *From Newton's Sleep* (Princeton: Princeton University Press, 1995), p. 112. See too Allott, *Health of Nations*, [2.16(4)].

[78] Stanley Fish, cited in Peter Fitzpatrick, *The Mythology of Modern Law* (London: Routledge, 1992), p. 208.

[79] Allott, *Eunomia*, [6.70]; see too John Finnis, *Natural Law and Natural Rights* (Oxford: Clarendon Press, 1980 reprinted 1992), p. 269; A. W. B. Simpson, *Legal Theory and Legal History: Essays on the Common Law* (London: The Hambledon Press, 1987), pp. 370–3.

In this way, Western law may be understood as a Zenonic paradox of motion.[80] Zeno of Elea, a contemporary of Plato and Aristotle, posited amongst other dialectical paradoxes of motion the paradox of the airborne arrow which appears, at a given moment – that is, in the snapshot of the present – to be still. Yet it cannot be still if it is in flight. Law does not exist in the present yet it is made in the present which no sooner comes than it is past. Husserl wrote that '[h]istorical past is a continuity of pasts which proceed one from another, each, as a past present, being a tradition producing tradition out of itself'.[81] Law is always past and it is always imagining its future from its tradition. 'Its many movements', applying to law what Aristotle wrote about motion, 'are incomplete and different in kind, since the whence and whither give them their form.'[82]

Law is therefore a normative practice dependent upon time.

3.3 Law as culture (*nomos*) and reason (*logos*)

For maximum allegiance, a programme of norms or law must seek to appeal to all orientations of the human on the Space–Time Matrix. That is, on the Time Axis, a proposition for the future must be located in a cultural history, and that culture's vision for the future. This history and this future will always be contested. Dialogue is suited to this contest. Dialogue works best if presuppositions, particularly about history, are not taken for granted. The best chance for a proposition to be received with allegiance on the Space Axis is for the proponents of the proposition to relate it to the individual at a personal moral level, to encourage the individual to recognise or at least grapple with the exterior legitimacy espoused by the proposition-maker or law-giver (typically government). According to 'the one indisputable principle of what may be called substantive natural law', formulated by Lon Fuller: 'Open up, maintain and preserve the integrity of the channels of communication by which men convey to one another what they perceive, feel, and desire.'[83]

Constitutional authority will usually appeal to some but not all four orientations (past, future, conservative, radical) of the human in society. Social and legal history can be analysed in these terms. Before doing so in the remainder of this book, a further, helpful distinction is necessary to fit the Space–Time Matrix into a historical evaluation of law and globalisation: *nomos* and *logos*. Put simply, these concepts can be thought about respectively as a matter of what one does and the reason one does it.

---

[80] Eric Voegelin, 'The Nature of the Law' in R. Pascal *et al.* (eds.), *The Collected Works of Eric Voegelin*, 34 vols. (Columbia: University of Missouri Press, 1991), vol. XXVII, pp. 16–20.

[81] Husserl, *Crisis*, 'Appendix 6: The Origin of Geometry', p. 374.

[82] Aristotle, *The Nicomachean Ethics*, trans. David Ross (Oxford: Oxford University Press, 1925 reprinted 1980) X.4, p. 255. Allott refers to law 'as a sort of probability-wave, transient but undetachable from the total reality': Allott, *Health of Nations*, [2.23].

[83] Lon Fuller, *The Morality of Law*, quoted in J. M. Kelly, *A Short History of Western Legal Theory* (Oxford University Press, 1992), pp. 421–2.

3.3.1 *Nomos* as cultural law

The moral world of right and wrong, good and bad, was law in the Ancient Greek sense of *nomos*. The word *nomos* connoted 'a normative way of life, as a proper way of conduct, or as a norm of sacrifice . . . as part of how the universe is constructed';[84] a human law 'compounded of custom and the exigencies of physical, psychological, political and social conditions'.[85] It was an idea of custom observed in practice, which was 'law' in the sense of binding society to an order.[86] *Nomos* is what comes as 'second nature', as opposed to *physis*, which is, at least in law, the pretence to natural, divine or rational authority. *Nomos* 'was the living force of human laws, customs, and cultural achievements'.[87] It is the connotation of this rich universe of norms which characterises Robert Cover's idea of law as a bridge from past to future. For Cover, a '*nomos* is a present world constituted by a system of tension between reality and vision'.[88] It can accommodate both reverence for history and messianic goals. *Nomos* is a lived law, entwined with ultimate reality and meaning, subject though to discourse and learning. As such, it tends to create a moral allegiance through dialogue with those open to it.

Herodotus well illustrated the value of *nomos*, reporting on a Persian War battle between the Persian king, Xerxes, and the exiled Spartan leader, Demaratus, in 480 BCE. Xerxes, who had despotically led his massive army across the Hellespont to Europe, ridiculed the reliance Demaratus said his weaker Greek forces placed upon courage and virtue which came of being a free people, although conditioned to obeying a law which required them to stay in the ranks and either win or die. Xerxes, on the other hand, relied upon despotic coercion. Xerxes' coerced forces were defeated by the free Greeks. The word which Herodotus used to describe the phenomenon which the Greeks obeyed willingly and courageously as a matter of law was *nomos*. It was stronger than the command of a despot like Xerxes. *Nomos* was both 'social and political' to the ancient Greeks. Such social or lived law works because it is believed in.[89]

The word *nomos* is readily translatable into language which will facilitate a journey through legal history to illuminate the present challenges of globalisation.

---

[84] That is, prior to the reign in the fifth century BCE of Cleisthenes, who used the word *nomos* to mean statute: see Martin Ostwald, *From Popular Sovereignty to the Sovereignty of Law: Law, Society and Politics in Fifth-Century Athens* (Berkeley: University of California Press, 1986), p. 88.

[85] Julius Stone, *Human Law and Human Justice* (Sydney: Maitland Publications Pty Ltd, 1965), p. 15.

[86] See Kelly, *Western Legal Theory*, pp. 8–9. Originally, it seems, *nomos* meant 'dwelling place', later signifying a province within which defined powers could be exercised; it was linked to *nemo*, meaning to apportion. See too Arendt, *Human Condition*, p. 63; Brian Z. Tamanaha, *A General Jurisprudence of Law and Society* (Oxford: Oxford University Press, 2001), pp. 5–6.

[87] Kelley, *Human Measure*, pp. 12–26.

[88] Robert M. Cover, 'The Supreme Court 1982 Term—Foreword: *Nomos* and Narrative' (1983) 97 *Harvard Law Review* 4–68, 9.

[89] See David Gress, *From Plato to NATO: The Idea of the West and its Opponents* (New York: The Free Press, 1998), pp. 52–4.

To avoid the jargon of *nomos*, the words 'culture' and 'custom' can be used. Although not quite capturing the complex relationship between the past and future in Cover's sense, cultural practice and custom do suggest an interior, moral connection to norms and law, manifesting allegiance from the mainstream individuals in the culture (although such norms can tend to be conservatively grounded in the past).

3.3.2 *Logos* as rational law

If *nomos* can be thought about as 'second nature', what of first nature, *physis*? *Logos* comprehends *physis*, as to a certain extent does *nomos*. Perceptions of nature (*physis*) will always be mediated by the rational (*logos*) and customary (*nomos*) context of nature as it is perceived by humans. Yet *logos* is distinguishable from *nomos*, and this (at times slightly overlapping) duality will feature in the historical approach to authority adopted in this book.

Relevantly, the Greek word *logos* has been defined as 'the rational, intelligible principle, structure, or order which pervades something'[90] and 'the universal methodical norms by which any knowledge of the world existing "in itself, objectively" must be bound'.[91] In Ancient Greece, the 'divine law, *logos*, is made by reason and expresses reason and not mere inscrutable fate'.[92] *Logos* is logic or method of reasoning, from which derives the suffix '-logy' found at the end of words such as psychology, biology, theology and sociology.[93] It also translates as 'the Word', as in the famous opening line of the Gospel according to John. 'In the beginning was the Word, and the Word was with God, and the Word was God . . .', dwelling in the world thereafter (through Christ) by which the Jewish scriptures would, in effect, make logical sense (through 'grace and truth').[94] From these definitions and the biblical example of *logos* comes the strong sense of *logos* as the continual advance of reason or knowledge in the world.[95]

To give the idea of *logos* a more contemporary feel in the context of legal theory, *logos* may be thought about as a more objective force of reason, as a basis for reforming, politically, what has emanated as a matter of culture and custom. Legislation is the typical manifestation of this concept. The danger is that it is imposed on the world, newly, but its virtue is that it can change what (at least in someone's view) needs to be changed.

---

[90] Nicholas Dent, 'Logos' in Ted Honderich (ed.), *The Oxford Companion to Philosophy* (Oxford: Oxford University Press, 1995), p. 511.   [91] Husserl, *Crisis*, p. 139.

[92] Stone, *Human Law*, p. 15.

[93] See Berman, 'Law and Logos', 145. Cf. Rosenstock-Huessy, *Out of Revolution*, pp. 743 ff, who argues that studies which are not helped by the subject–object dualism should actually employ the suffix '-nomy' (as in 'economy') rather than '-logy', because the ending '-logy' connotes the Newtonian, Cartesian conceptual world of the division of physics and metaphysics, object and subject. That is to appreciate the cultural location of these disciplines ('-nomy' being from *nomos*).

[94] See John 1: 1–18 (NKJV). The Old Testament Hebrew term for 'word' is *dabar*, meaning 'effective power', which differs from the New Testament Ancient Greek *logos*, meaning 'correct reasoning': Ball, *Word and the Law*, pp. 119–20.   [95] Finnis, *Natural Law*, p. 376.

3.3.3 Reconciling cultural and rational laws

Robert Cover has suggested, with specific illustrations from Judaism, that *nomos* can be subject to thoroughgoing intellectual enquiry and that it is future orientated[96] ('law as a bridge to the future'). So *nomos* or custom is not simply irrational and conservative. The sense of *nomos* as culture is maintained by the universe of meaning in which the norms reside. That is, everything makes sense by reference to authoritative texts, teachings and upbringing within the culture, which cultivates its own rationality. That meaning can be contested, but the universe makes sense, fundamentally, through the cultural way of examining the world. In the process of contesting this meaning, rationality plays a part.

To this extent, *nomos* and *logos*, culture (including moral sensibilities) and logic, can overlap, perhaps akin to the way in which emotion can be guided by *logos*, according to Aristotle.[97] Similarly, Plato could regard the *nomos* or decreed laws of the Ancient Greek polis as containing the rationality of *logismos*.[98] There are cultural, normative aspects to logic and also logical bounds for the unfolding of culture and norms. Generally, logic is elevated to objectivity, as with modern science, and culture is associated with more subjective relations and associations such as a religious or minority standpoint. Yet what is 'scientific' can be received into culture, such as economic rationalism or Darwinism; and, vice versa, what is cultural for some people can be received into objective legitimacy, such as state laws or the common law rights of Englishmen being received, on Blackstone's observation, into natural rights. Authority is conceivable in this double helix of logic and culture which exists interdependently with society. It is suggestive of the somewhat obscure word 'nomology' – the science of law.

A problem arises when cultural practices have become outmoded with respect to the rest of society and there needs to be change. Human attributes which create and maintain social norms such as 'physical strength, power, experience, personal prestige, age . . . wealth, birth, personal relations'[99] are, of course, problematic. Reason will from time to time dictate that such attributes should not determine aspects of social order. This may cause resentment among those with power in the association (characteristically they will be conservative). Legislation typically appears. Whilst legislation can be subject to interior allegiance (and it can also attempt to impose one person's interior allegiance or natural law on someone else),[100] legislation tends to be conceived by someone else's intellect, imposed from the exterior political dimension of the Space–Time Matrix, and orientated to the future. Reason is not something in

---

[96] See generally Cover, '*Nomos* and Narrative'.

[97] Aristotle, *Nicomachean Ethics*, I.13, p. 27; Martha C. Nussbaum, *Upheavals of Thought: The Intelligence of Emotions* (Cambridge: Cambridge University Press, 2001).

[98] See Finnis, *Natural Law*, p. 407.   [99] Ehrlich, *Fundamental Principles*, p. 86.

[100] Tamanaha, *General Jurisprudence*, pp. 5–6, and more extremely, his observation of Shari'a law in his 'The Contemporary Relevance of Legal Positivism' (2007) 32 *Australian Journal of Legal Philosophy* 1–38.

the world, but something which tends to be imposed on the world.[101] Such juridical reason therefore warrants scrutiny.

Another difficulty associated with interior, cultural norms can occur when some cultural practices may be incompatible or requiring of modification in a multicultural society, such as tribal punishments and forced marriages. Typically, the exterior norms of courts will be imposed and consideration may be given to mitigating sentences passed on offenders.[102] Dialogue between opposing groups on the Space Axis of the Space–Time Matrix will be desirable.

Notwithstanding some earlier correspondence noted between *nomos* and *logos*, religious and customary-based laws (*nomos*) will typically appeal to the moral and conservative orientations of the individual. Legislation and the secular laws of the state (*logos*) can be alienating or ignorant of the individual's allegiance, because they are external to the individual's personal existence and too future orientated with inadequate historical references; they are perceived to be political. Even the process of distilling state law from customs and prevailing attitudes can be difficult: cultural attitudes lose something when they are dressed in the legal vocabulary of the state.[103] The solution perhaps lies in encouraging attachments to norms which, although possessing specifically exterior-legal qualities, can demonstrate living, interactive interior-norm qualities. At the same time, a measure of learning to love and respect the outside, and to look for rational, universal principles, will also assist.[104] To this end, suggestions will be proffered in chapter 10, arising from the normative successes and failures discernible in the legal history to which attention will turn in the intervening chapters.

3.4 Law as autobiography in a global world

Moral allegiance is a style of allegiance which may be particular to one individual but not necessarily another. Political allegiance is of a kind which may not catch the scruples of all individuals, but which may be coerced as a matter of law by the state contrary to the individual's liking. Accepting the central theme of Rosenstock-Huessy's work – that everyone bears a moral responsibility for living meaningful and orderly existences at the risk of catastrophic consequences – this imperative must be related to law. The conclusion which will have emerged by the end of this book is that exterior political imperatives (signified by *logos*) and private moral allegiances (signified by *nomos*) have been in conflict for the millennium of the Western legal tradition. It culminated in the

---

[101] Christine Korsgaard, 'Prologue: Excellence and Obligation: A *Very* Concise History of Western Metaphysics 387 BC to 1887 AD' in Christine Korsgaard (ed.), *The Sources of Normativity* (Cambridge: Cambridge University Press, 1996), p. 5, referring to Kant.

[102] See Roger Cotterrell, 'Law in Culture' (2004) 17 *Ratio Juris* 1–14, 9–11.

[103] See Ball, *Word and the Law*, pp. 55–6.

[104] See Joseph Raz, *Value, Respect and Attachment* (Cambridge: Cambridge University Press, 2001), p. 14.

World Revolution, which has delivered globalisation as we popularly recognise it. That conflict must be recognised, and resolution pursued, through insights gained from the historical constitution of laws across societies. Essentially this requires reconciling law with individual moral allegiances.

Globalisation studies highlight the *contingency* of the authority of the state from the late twentieth century onwards, in the face of competing authorities both within the state (for example, indigenous communities, religious groups) and outside the state in the international and world societies. Repudiation of ideas of singular legal authority is then possible in the context of the norms and enforcement measures which exist independently of the state. As Max Weber observed, coercion in legal orders can exist outside political authority, 'wherever coercive means, of a physical or psychological kind, are available'.[105] Furthermore, Ehrlich, it could be said, discovered for the benefit of legal studies the 'numberless' associations in society which have legal effect without relying upon the state, obtaining cohesion from reciprocal rights and obligations which follow from membership.[106] Some of these culturally based constitutions will be considered as they occurred and continue to occur in the Western legal tradition, in contradistinction to politically imposed law characterised by modern legislation from the exterior of the Space Axis.

As such, the standard treatments of legal authority fall somewhat outside this analysis because they do not appreciate the complete social picture of law conceptually described by the Space–Time Matrix. They are generally premissed upon a monolithic state legal order (which is historically problematic) and the cold 'institutional', as opposed to community, aspect of law. For example, Joseph Raz, in his theory of law, does not admit the reciprocal relationship between law and individual. He assumes the irreconcilable character of law and individual by earlier assuming that 'law', properly so-called, issues only from the political, external extreme of the Space Axis. Even if there are moral reasons (such as reliance of impressionable people on one's community example) or prudential reasons (such as sanctions) to obey law, even 'good law' does not have to be obeyed, for law's sake, because obedience would not issue from the legal system's own standards, according to Raz. He does, though, acknowledge the need to assess each case on its own merits, conceding that it may be possible to have a ' "practical" respect for the law', 'in all but iniquitous societies'.[107]

No authority is ever justified in and of itself. Both the norm-giver and the norm-receiver owe an existential responsibility to each other to reconcile, through dialogue, competing expectations of each other. That is, the norm-giver must seek to avoid thinking about authority as 'the right to command, and

---

[105] Max Weber, *On Law in Economy and Society*, trans. Max Rheinstein and Edward Shils [1925] (New York: Simon & Schuster, 1954), p. 17. See too Jacques Derrida, 'Force of Law: The "Mystical Foundations of Authority" ' (1990) 11 *Cardozo Law Review* 921–1045, 925, 927.

[106] Ehrlich, *Fundamental Principles*, p. 63.

[107] See Joseph Raz, *The Authority of Law: Essays on Law and Morality* (Oxford: Clarendon Press, 1979), pp. 237–44, 258, 260.

correlatively, the right to be obeyed', and the norm-receiver must transcend the view that allegiance to law is 'purely sentimental and has no objective moral basis'.[108] All of the constitutional troubles in Western history arise from ignorance of this proposition. Such dialogue, however, is all very well in theory. In practice, a party subject to an adverse judicial decision may not feel consoled by the opportunity to examine the decision and search for ways to achieve reconciliation – particularly, for example, if false evidence has been accepted at trial or the party feels misunderstood by the judge. At that point, though, there may be the opportunity to campaign against or at least agitate the legal norms in various political and law-reform arenas – or to accept, regrettably, that no human social system will get things right every time.

Globalisation is adding to the sources of norms from within and without the state, provoking new laws and norms. With them comes the possibility of appealing to the individual at a moral level, often because of the common existential experience of the World Revolution and an emerging world society amongst other societies. Being able to tap into the history of such moral achievements and aspirations for the future will be crucial to the effectiveness of the new laws which appear to embody some of these moral aspirations.

The tensions on the Space–Time Matrix today between conservative/radical, moral/cultural and political/rational dimensions of authority can now be explored historically in the balance of this book, to illuminate the recurring patterns of Western law and authority in the second millennium. Those insights might then assist with a more effective reformulation of the idea of, and prospects for, law in an interconnected globe, as part of the proposed general, globalist jurisprudence. If law is to achieve its potential, all four dimensions of human social nature (past, future, interior, exterior) will need to be conceptually integrated, requiring cultivation of moral *and* political allegiance. Universalism will need to be reconciled with diversity. In that way, our normative jurisprudence will help law to appeal to the individual, and also help the individual to think outside individual interests. Coercive authority may then be minimised for societies of this most peculiar of creatures, the human, whose species makes and navigates rules like spiders with their webs.

---

[108] See Robert Paul Wolff, *In Defence of Anarchism* (New York: Harper, 1976), ch. 1. The two somewhat simplistic propositions quoted, that authority is the right to command and be obeyed (p. 4), and that allegiance to law is purely sentimental (p. 19), ground Wolff's advocacy of 'philosophical anarchism'.

Part 2
A Holy Roman Empire

4

The original European community

In this great intermingling at the time of Europe's birth, a salient feature, right
from the start, was the dialectic between unity and diversity, Christendom and
nations, which even today is still one of the fundamental characteristics of Europe.

Jacques Le Goff[1]

As unjust as it might seem for a historical discussion of European society to dispense with Greek and Roman antiquity, unjust we must be for present purposes.
(Reference will be made in later chapters, though, to reincarnations of Greek
philosophy and Roman law.) With the nightfall of the inaptly named 'dark ages'
heralded by raiding Germanic tribes, the 'high' classical culture and Roman
Empire receded in the fifth and sixth centuries, in the face of fragmented,
indigenous diversity. This was tempered by the emerging universalistic, moral
and political tentacles of the Roman Catholic Church. It was that style of diversity, after the fall of the Roman Empire, which was the original Europe. To the
extent there was then a medieval European union, membership depended not
upon the fulfilment of economic criteria required today, but the conversion of
people to Christianity.[2]

Just as the challenges faced by the European Union (EU) today are endemic
of many of the challenges of globalisation and law, so may the original European
community assist our enquiry. Especially will this aid the formulation of a normative jurisprudence concerned to take questions of allegiance and authority
seriously. The *diversity* of Europe in the time preceding and including the foundation of the Western legal tradition in the late eleventh century will be considered. Practical authority or sovereignty was extremely *particular* – there was
nothing like a state in the modern sense. Europe was made up of quasi-tribal
units, with the increasing legal formality of feudalism. Against that particularity, papal authority was projected onto a rich social tapestry as a *universalistic,
moral* concern, becoming important for justifying authority at all social levels.
The limited *political* power of the first millennium papacy was buttressed by the
considerably greater *political* power of the ephemeral Carolingian Empire and

---

[1] *The Birth of Europe*, trans. Janet Lloyd (Oxford: Blackwell Publishing, 2005), p. 19.
[2] Le Goff, *Europe*, p. 43.

secular powers which would follow. All of this should help to sketch a picture of the 'true European Community', the notion of which Philip Allott has contrasted to the inorganic, twentieth-century treaty version.[3]

4.1 A rhetorical 'holy Roman empire'

Chapter 3 proposed that a notion of ultimate reality and meaning or God underlies a constitution. To make sense in a book concerning itself with the Western legal tradition, reference must be made to God in association with legal institutions. A way to do this is to associate the Holy Roman Empire with the God of the Judeo-Christian tradition, and to reflect upon a vying if not potentially substitute concept of that ultimate reality, culminating in a competing twentieth-century god-concept, Mammon. Perhaps too whimsically, this movement can be thought about as a shift from the Holy Roman Empire to a 'wholly Mammon empire'. The conclusion will *not* emerge in chapter 10 that there is a *wholly* Mammon source of ultimate meaning legitimating Western law today (although Mammon appears to dominate the contest so far as free trade and human rights are concerned). To describe an extreme of a tendency, however, the term 'wholly Mammon empire' can be illuminating, if the pun can be excused. Implied in this shift is a functionally recurring authority (an ultimate principle of 'good' upon which to justify law), in an ethically different guise (that is, whereas material prosperity was not so important to the conception of God at the beginning of the second millennium, it was extremely important at the end of the second millennium and is so today).

Some flexibility is required in the use of the term 'Holy Roman Empire', inherent in the title. Introduction of the name 'Roman empire', centuries after the fall of its classical namesake, occurred by grant of the pope in the later part of the tenth century when German kings sought to make Rome the capital of the empire, in the quest for control over the kingdoms of Burgundy, Italy and Germany. It became 'holy' in the later twelfth century when Frederick I Barbarossa sought to establish the special nature of the empire, becoming formally entitled the Holy Roman Empire in 1254.[4] England never recognised in its own territorial realm the sovereignty of the emperor of the Holy Roman Empire or a German king. Rhetorically, and to avoid confusion with the primarily German association of the formal title, reference will be made descriptively but not titularly to 'a holy Roman empire', when contrast is to be drawn to a potential 'wholly Mammon empire', principally in part 4. This sense of '*a holy Roman empire*' is more akin to the Christian commonwealth than '*the*

---

[3] See Phillip Allott, 'The European Community is Not the True European Community' (1991) 100 *Yale Law Journal* 2485–500.

[4] See Hendrik Spruyt, *The Sovereign State and its Competitors: An Analysis of Systems Change* (Princeton: Princeton University Press, 1994), p. 235; Harold J. Berman, *Law and Revolution: The Formation of the Western Legal Tradition* (Cambridge, MA: Harvard University Press, 1983), p. 89.

Holy Roman Empire', as medieval rulers increasingly denied subordination to the emperor. It is used in contrast to 'a wholly Mammon empire' as a pithy attempt to capture the different ethics of functionally similar god-concepts authorising law at the beginning and end of the second millennium. The holy Roman empire evokes the contemporary notion of *governance* (not *government* in the sense of one state-like government).[5] Moral allegiance to its universalist norms was sought by the church through the authoritative normative text of the Bible in an increasingly objective manner, in a relationship (at times stretched) with local, particularistic political powers and ultimately the universalistic[6] Holy Roman Emperor himself. It represented a governmental alliance with high claims to moral allegiance and political power within a relatively common normative history and vision for the future.

4.2 Tribalism

With the eruption of the Germanic invasions from the fifth century onwards, the embrace of the classic Roman Empire gradually weakened.[7] The so-called dark ages (about 476–800) were characterised by the raiding Gothic, Teutonic and Viking tribes. Any functional equivalent of international law at that time was difficult to conceive between tribes. Most Germanic tribes revered Valhalla, the hall of the god Odin, who received the souls of warriors killed in battle.[8] The other tribes had no less bellicose veins. When life is not revered, and death for a cause praised within a culture, it becomes difficult to have law between such cultures (a fact to which modern times still attest). Ultimate reality and meaning in such societies inspires death and repulses a shared legal order.

A strong sense of normativity did, however, inhere within the Germanic tribes and there were interclan meetings. Constitutional elements, for example amongst the Visigoths, attempted to limit the autonomy of kings with respect to the church, although in practice the king's power was often unchecked.[9] The Lombards availed their administration of Roman centralism and city and diocesan structures. 'Vulgar' Roman law, a corrupted form of the original, survived,[10] although it is perhaps best regarded without deprecation as a point of

---

[5] On this distinction in today's globalisation discourse, see ch. 12, section 12.3.2, pp. 291–2 below.

[6] Frederick's death on crusade in 1190 demonstrates the universalism of the Holy Roman Empire inclusive of the papacy: Malcolm Barber, *The Two Cities: Medieval Europe 1050–1320* (London: Routledge, 1992), p. 212.

[7] On this gradual process, see Henry Chadwick, 'Envoi: On Taking Leave of Antiquity' in John Boardman *et al.*, *The Oxford History of the Classical World* (Oxford: Oxford University Press, 1986).

[8] T. A. Walker, *History of the Law of Nations* (Cambridge: Cambridge University Press, 1899), p. 64.

[9] O. F. Robinson, T. D. Fergus and W. M. Gordon, *European Legal History* (London: Butterworths, 1994), [1.7.3].

[10] See Franz Wieacker, 'Foundations of European Legal Culture' (1990) 38 *American Journal of Comparative Law* 1–29, 9–10; Berman, *Law and Revolution*, p. 53; R. C. van Caenegem, *An Historical Introduction to Private Law*, trans. D. E. L. Johnston (Cambridge: Cambridge University Press, 1988), pp. 17–18.

departure from Roman law on the way to the arrival of the later medieval European common law.[11] There was also a Christian influence, although superstition was rife in dispute resolution procedures such as trial by ordeal. An oral legal tradition and some unsystematic compilations of laws did not stop blood feuds, although there was a rationalisation of this process through emerging lists of penalties.[12] The ultimate reality and meaning in these societies was thought to reside in arbitrariness and fate.[13] On the Space-Time Matrix, there was a high degree of interior, moral allegiance in these legal processes, without exterior political power in the form of bureaucracy or decisions imposed by unknown individuals. Generally, these societies were traditional and conservative, without a radical vision for the future.

As Sir Henry Maine wrote, this time and place in history can be characterised by 'tribe-sovereignty'. Germanic tribes were 'masters' over their occupied territories, although 'they based no claim of right upon the fact of territorial possession, and indeed attached no importance to it whatever'.[14] Frontiers were more in the nature of meeting places than borders. Clashes at these meeting places, as well as trade and general intermingling, were characteristic, including the mixing of blood and ethnic regroupings.[15] Within this emerging, diverse feudal society, two political powers did attempt to fill the vacuum left by the Roman Empire. One would be relatively short-lived, and another the longest surviving normative institution in the Western world: the Carolingian Empire and the Roman Catholic Church, respectively.

4.3 Charlemagne's short-lived political universalism

If Europe appeared when the ancient Roman Empire fell, Charlemagne's empire first gave Europe its form.[16] The Merovingians had ruled over the Franks occupying transalpine Gaul and part of Germany as kings of the Franks, not kings of France as a territory (which lacked dignity). The only alternative would have been the ancient Roman imperial title of 'emperor' – a universalist claim to rulership of the whole world.[17] The term 'Europe' was revived in, and survived ephemerally with, the successor to the Merovingians, Charlemagne, who did style himself after the Roman emperors. He ruled what is now much of western Germany, France, northern Italy and part of northern Spain.[18] His aspirations

---

[11] Maurizio Lupoi, *The Origins of the European Legal Order*, trans. Adrian Belton (Cambridge: Cambridge University Press, 2000), p. 38.   [12] See van Caenegem, *Private Law*, pp. 18–19, 26.

[13] See generally Berman, *Law and Revolution*, ch. 1.

[14] Sir Henry Sumner Maine, *Ancient Law: Its Connection with the Early History of Society and its Relation to Modern Ideas* [1861] (reprinted Dorset Press, 1986), p. 86.

[15] Le Goff, *Europe*, pp. 4, 19.

[16] Alessandro Barbero, *Charlemagne: Father of a Continent*, trans. Allan Cameron (Berkeley: University of California Press, 2004), p. 3, quoting from Marc Bloch and Lucien Febvre.

[17] Maine, *Ancient Law*, pp. 86–7. Territorial sovereignty, upon which modern sovereignty is based, was to await the French Capetian dynasty (987–1328). See ch. 6 below.

[18] See Norman F. Cantor (ed.), *The Medieval Reader* (New York: HarperPerennial, 1995), p. 97.

were universalist, as opposed to the previously fragmented concerns of tribal chiefs, and wars were led against Lombards, Saxons, Gascons, Avars and Danes, amongst others.[19] The universalist moral authority was reliant upon the papacy. Either his father's or his own hands crowned Charlemagne emperor, using an unprecedented right assumed by pope Leo III on Christmas Day, 800. With the pope's immediate genuflection before Charlemagne in homage,[20] the theocratic powers of Charlemagne as Vicar of Christ bound his legitimacy to that of Rome and the futurist vision of the continuing Roman Empire as the final empire of all time, believed to have been prophesied by Daniel in the Old Testament.[21] Yet pagan Germanic rituals remained. Christianity was largely passive and used to garb pagan superstitions.[22] This is analogous, perhaps, to the 'glocalization' we have already seen of the Sapeurs of the Congo appropriating the Western, globally projected, image of the white coat of the medical profession to bolster the prestige of the witch doctor.[23]

Charlemagne's 'kingdom and empire were governed by an itinerant court that journeyed incessantly from one domain to the next; by a number of subordinate courts . . .; and by a network of perhaps 300 *comitates* or "counties" . . .',[24] each controlled by a pair of envoys, one lay and one clerical.[25] A *comitatus* was an assembly or general meeting of the population, where customs were stated, sometimes reduced to writing and sometimes even changed, and also where disputes might be settled. An imperial central court, the *Aula Regis,* was able to influence more local courts. Semi-professional judges (*scabini*) heard inquests, as sworn inquests sought to replace blood feuds and trial by ordeal.[26] The Christian church spanned the continent and its diverse ethnic identities and social ranks, providing 'a supplementary structure of communication and leadership', also seeing to some public needs such as welfare.[27]

An international executive class arose, as did centralised currency. Capitularies, or collected royal edicts (in today's terms, 'statutes, orders, directions and regulations'),[28] encouraged uniform rules for church and state, although local customs and leaders remained powerful. Previously unwritten customary laws were recorded in writing.[29] Johan Galtung has noted the similarity between the EU

---

[19] See Einhard, 'Life of Charlemagne' in Cantor, *Medieval Reader*, pp. 97–103.

[20] See Norman Davies, *Europe: A History* (London: Pimlico, 1997), pp. 301–2; Barbero, *Charlemagne*, pp. 93–4.

[21] See Spruyt, *Sovereign State*, pp. 43–4. On Charlemagne's priestly status, see Barbero, *Charlemagne*, pp. 141–4.   [22] Berman, *Law and Revolution*, pp. 66–7, 75.

[23] See ch. 2, section 2.1.4, p. 32 above.   [24] Davies, *Europe*, p. 302.

[25] Johan Galtung, *The European Community: A Superpower in the Making* (London: George Allen & Unwin Ltd, 1973), p. 118. See too Berman, *Law and Revolution*, p. 89; Barbero, *Charlemagne*, pp. 156–66.

[26] See Alan Harding, *Medieval Law and the Foundations of the State* (Oxford: Oxford University Press, 2002), pp. 33–8.

[27] See Gianfranco Poggi, *The State: Its Nature, Development and Prospects* (Stanford: Stanford University Press, 1990), p. 38.   [28] See van Caenegem, *Private Law*, pp. 21–4.

[29] See Robinson, *European Legal History*, [1.9.4]. On the justice system generally, see Barbero, *Charlemagne*, ch. 9.

technocrats and the Carolingian aristocracy, and the EU parliamentarians who represent the counterpart voice of God or authority as the Carolingian clerics had done.[30] Against this parallelism, the bureaucratic workings of the Carolingian Empire bore little kin, as such, to the decentralised supranationalism of the EU. Charlemagne sought to dominate Europe with only his own Frankish people, making his vision an 'anti-Europe', in effect.[31]

Amidst this purported universality, there were intractable political problems at the tribal and moral level, particularly at the hands of Viking plunderers. Carolingian strength declined soon after the demise of Charlemagne in 814. The papacy could not rule centrally and power shifted to local courts, bishops and dukes, which filled the vacuum left by Charlemagne. Administrative tasks were generally taken over by local counts, bishops and dukes, leaving behind four major kingdoms: Italy, the West-Frankish kingdom (now France), the East-Frankish kingdom (now Germany) and Burgundy.[32] '[U]nending strife' was to be the legacy of Charlemagne's succession to his three grandsons.[33]

4.4 Christian moral and political universalism

After Christianity had been made the official religion of the Roman Empire by imperial decree in 380, the papacy was given a legal complexion as a governmental institution. Authority was conceived as emanating from God in legal terms. An early theologian of Latin Christianity, a jurist named Tertullian, contributed to the framing of Christian dogma in the form of legal maxims and principles. The Latin translation in the late fourth and early fifth centuries of the Hebrew Old Testament and the ancient Greek New Testament (the Vulgate of St Jerome) – although linguistically correct – presented the Bible 'in a thoroughly juristic garb (that of the Roman law) as far as matters concerning government were affected'.[34] From this developed, between the early fifth and the late sixth centuries, what Walter Ullmann has termed the monarchic (or descending) theme of authority, which was wielded by the pope and emperor within their historically contested spheres.[35]

4.4.1 Peter's papal legacy

With a constitutional importance which would be contested regularly throughout the middle ages and finally by the Protestants, papal monarchy was justified

---

[30] Galtung, *European Community*, p. 118.   [31] Le Goff, *Europe*, p. 29.
[32] See Spruyt, *Sovereign State*, p. 135.   [33] Davies, *Europe*, pp. 306–8.
[34] Walter Ullmann, *Medieval Political Thought* (Harmondsworth: Penguin, 1975), p. 21 and his *Law and Politics in the Middle Ages* (London: Sources of History Ltd, 1975), pp. 119–20.
[35] See Ullmann, *Medieval Political Thought*, p. 22; and his 'The Medieval Papal Court as an International Tribunal' (1971) 11 *Virginia Journal of International Law* 356–71. The determinism of his model is problematic in light of medieval political complexity: see e.g. Antony Black, *Political Thought in Europe, 1250–1450* (Cambridge: Cambridge University Press, 1992), p. 201.

by appeal to a passage in the Gospel of Matthew, where Christ gave Peter the keys to the kingdom of heaven.

> Thou art Peter and upon this rock I will build my church; and the gates of hell shall not prevail against it. And I will give unto thee the keys of the kingdom of heaven: and whatsoever thou shalt bind on earth shall be bound in heaven: and whatsoever thou shalt loose on earth shall be loosed in heaven.[36]

The bequeathal to the papacy of Peter's keys to heaven was grounded in the *Epistola Clementis*, a dubious letter from the end of the second century, purportedly written by Pope Clement I to James, the brother of Christ. In the face of approaching death and in front of the Roman community, Peter handed over his powers to bind and loose to Clement; although this letter is problematic, as Pope Linus apparently followed Peter, not Clement. Nonetheless, the Roman law of inheritance could vindicate and elaborate the papal monarchy and its succession. The papal powers of binding and loosing were treated like assets and liabilities in Roman law, capable of transmission to an heir. The doctrine founded by Pope Leo (440–61) posited that 'no pope succeeded his immediate predecessor but succeeded St Peter directly . . .' From this, a separation of office and office-holder or person could be envisaged, and governmental action could still be valid no matter what the characteristics of the person who held the office, so long as the decree emanated validly from a properly elected office-holder.[37]

A political basis to government and authority was therefore conceived through law. It was not only theological, as Christ had given all of the disciples the power to bind and loose.[38] It also had Roman law legitimacy. Political church government therefore based its claims to legitimacy at the interior end of the Space Axis of the Space–Time Matrix, morally through the words of sacred theological texts appealing to individuals. The church also sought legitimacy at the exterior end of the Space Axis and conservative end of the Time Axis through historical and legal texts outside the experience and knowledge of most individuals. In this descending model of authority, there were no indigenous powers; all power was derived from the pope or law-giver, as a symbol for the divine order or the objective truth. The members of the church in this scheme had no power, and the authority of the church came from God. Paul's words, 'what I am, I am by the grace of God', promoted this view.[39]

4.4.2 'Two Swords' legal pluralism

The plural jurisdictions of emperor and pope were the subject of a constitution grounded in the ultimate reality and meaning expressed in theology. Papal authority in worldly affairs was derived from Christ's statement to Pontius Pilate: 'Thou couldest have no power at all against me, except it were given thee

---

[36] Matthew 16: 18–19 (KJV).   [37] Ullmann, *Medieval Political Thought*, pp. 23–7.
[38] Matthew 18: 18–20.   [39] See Ullmann, *Medieval Political Thought*, pp. 28–30.

from above.'[40] This power was conceded as a matter of grace by divinity to one worthy to wield power, not as of the recipient's right. Broader political significance attached to this theory of government. Power was thought to flow down from the king to those of lower governmental rank, conceded by the king by 'the exercise of God's will and pleasure', buttressed by Old Testament sources.[41]

Originating in papal–imperial constitutionalism, the 'Two Swords' constitutional theory of government developed and grew later in medieval Europe. The Two Swords theory was based upon chapter 22 of the Gospel of Luke. Just after a dialogue between Christ and the disciples in which Christ foretold of his imminent arrest, Christ was thought to have inferred that two swords were enough for the disciples to use in defence. (That interpretation is problematic and for the most part rejected by theologians today.)[42] Immediately following, whilst Christ was being arrested, Christ commanded a disciple (Peter no less, recorded in John 18: 11) to put the sword back after the disciple had cut off the ear of a slave. Christ then healed the slave's ear. This chapter was taken to be the foundation for two world forces, because not only could Christ make heavenly decrees but he had authority to command earthly forces too.

Constantine, in 325 at the council of Nicea, told the bishops that they were bishops for the *internal* matters, being matters of spirit and scriptural theology – the sacramental, charismatic and pneumatic. Constantine declared himself bishop of the *external*, by which he meant 'the legal, organizational, administrative, and purely external arrangements and management of Christianity'.[43] This political theology avowedly catered to both the *internal* and *external* social tendencies on the Space Axis of the Space–Time Matrix.

No small discourse developed about the jurisdictional impact of these concepts, which contained church and state posturing into the later middle ages. Bringing the future dimension of the Time Axis into the constitution, Pope Gelasius I (492–6) articulated his position to the Emperor Anastasius:

> There are two things, most august emperor, by which this world is chiefly ruled: the sacred authority of the priesthood and the royal power. Of these two, the

---

[40] John 19: 11 (KJV). See generally Lester L. Field, *Liberty, Dominion, and the Two Swords: On the Origins of Western Political Theology (180–398)* (Notre Dame: University of Notre Dame Press, 1998).

[41] Walter Ullmann, *The Church and the Law in the Earlier Middle Ages: Selected Essays* (London: Variorum Reprints, 1975), III, pp. 190–3.

[42] At the disciples' thoughts of physical resistance and their comment 'Lord, behold there are two swords', Christ responded 'It is enough.' Modern theological interpretation regards Christ's statement as an abrupt dismissal of the disciples' lack of immediate insight into the Christian message. Medieval commentators, however, sought in the style of their Latin fathers to uncover any mystical teachings which the text might be concealing – hence the justification for the constitutional theory of the two powers. See J. A. Watt, 'Spiritual and Temporal Powers' in J. H. Burns (ed.), *The Cambridge History of Medieval Political Thought c.350–c.1450* (Cambridge: Cambridge University Press, 1988), p. 370.

[43] Ullmann, *Medieval Political Thought*, p. 36.

priests carry the greater weight, because they will have to render account *in the divine judgment* even for the kings of men.[44] [italics added]

If the bishops obeyed the imperial laws, established by divine disposition of royal powers, how much more then, it was thought by the church, should the imperial order obey the bishops, who had been invested with administering the sacred mysteries of religion for preparation of the future world. Gelasius insisted on the pope's exclusive power, to bind and loose, and on the restriction of the emperor's power, which operated within the pope's superior authority.[45] This is sometimes referred to as the Gelasian doctrine. This did not stop the empire from making laws for exterior political aspects of the church, but it did leave the sacred mysteries of interior moral life, such as the sacrament of marriage or the eucharist (communion mass), to the clergy. This was satisfactory for Gelasius, as he 'had no intention of laying claim to a share in secular government', accepting as he was of the Augustinian gulf between heaven and earth. Essentially this policy remained until the eleventh century, despite deviations, supported by the Donation of Constantine.[46] Although not taken very seriously, this document, forged in the mid eighth century, purported to show that the Emperor Constantine had given Pope Sylvester I rule over Rome and its western possessions, authorising the papacy to crown emperors and make some claim to influence in secular life.[47]

Amidst this pluralism, Christian monotheism suggested that, just as there was only one God in heaven, there could only be one monarchical ruler on earth, in an 'imperial theology' of 'one God, one Empire, one church', the emperor being viewed as 'Christ's vicegerent on Earth'.[48] As the pope later was,[49] the emperor was regarded as the living law – a descending notion of living law.[50] Imperial laws would be read out to the subjects, who listened 'in sacred silence' with the same awe and reverence accorded to holy scripture.[51] Until the tenth and eleventh centuries, European royal powers interfered in religious doctrine as well, amidst a decline in papal prestige.[52] Even then, though, amidst the radical transformations of the Papal Revolution, the Two Swords theory was really just adjusted in order to deal with the corrupt, secular infiltration of the spiritual power. There were still dualistic constitutional, jurisdictional limits to both spiritual and secular powers until about the fourteenth century.[53] This is well expressed by A. J. Carlyle:

---

[44] Quoted in Gerd Tellenbach, *Church, State and Christian Society at the Time of the Investiture Contest*, trans. R. F. Bennett (Oxford: Basil Blackwell, 1948), p. 33.

[45] Ullmann, *Medieval Political Thought*, p. 41.   [46] Tellenbach, *Church*, pp. 36–7, 68–9.

[47] See Barber, *Two Cities*, pp. 102–3.   [48] Tellenbach, *Church*, p. 33.

[49] The pope was regarded as *lex animata* in Roman law, as was any monarch making the claim: see K. Pennington, 'Law, Legislative Authority, and Theories of Government, 1150–1300' in J. H. Burns (ed.), *The Cambridge History of Medieval Political Thought c.350–1450* (Cambridge: Cambridge University Press, 1988), p. 434.

[50] We might regard this as an inversion of what Eugen Ehrlich was to describe in his (ascending) notion of the 'living law' of nineteenth-century Western European communal relationships. See ch. 3, section 3.2.1, pp. 63–4 above.   [51] Ullmann, *Medieval Political Thought*, p. 33.

[52] Berman, *Law and Revolution*, pp. 92–3.   [53] Watt, 'Spiritual and Temporal Powers', p. 415.

To the Western Church it was in the main clear that there were two great authorities in the world, not one, that the Spiritual Power was in its own sphere independent of the temporal, while it did not doubt that the Temporal Power was
also independent and supreme in its sphere . . . This conception of the two
autonomous authorities existing in human society, each supreme, each obedient,
is the principle of society which the Fathers handed down to the Middle Ages, not
any conception of a unity founded upon the supremacy of one or other of the
powers.[54]

The spiritual–secular powers debate recognised the internal and external
construction of human normativity, highlighted in the discussion above,
within similar internal–external terms propounded of the Space Axis in our
Space–Time Matrix. Within the sphere of its alliances, which included kings
and emperors, the papacy had political influence. That influence was politically
unreliable and swayed with the political fortunes of medieval Europe. At the
interior level, that power was spawning a complex, culturally compelling morality which was grounded in a normative history with a salvationist vision for the
future, susceptible to intellectual (theological and legal) enquiry at the exterior
level. Whilst the papal and imperial ideas of authority were similar, the imperial authority was grounded more externally in historical sources and Roman
law, compared with the legally cloaked, biblical reliance of the papacy, which
was more aspiring to personal, moral allegiance. All four orientations of the
Space–Time Matrix were being called upon in this emerging universalism,
which would compete with the feudal diversity of Europe. In this sense, it is possible to consider Two Swords constitutionalism as a type of legal pluralism, featuring coexisting legal systems in the same territory.

4.5 Feudal moral and political diversity

Feudal diversity was extremely compelling in its own way. Important lessons for
legal authority are to be learned from the feudal constitution, especially in relation to the interior construction of moral attitudes to law through reciprocal
rights and duties which were lived and not just preached or claimed.

Feudal society inspired a more moral and cultural allegiance on the interior
orientation of the Space–Time Matrix. The paradigmatic form of political
organisation in the early middle ages was the Germanic kingdom, which was 'in
some ways the complete antithesis of a modern state'. The modern state is characteristically detached from moral allegiance and requires coercion to obtain
obedience to law. The very early Germanic kingdom, on the other hand, 'lacking
continuity in time and stability in space', was based on loyalties to persons, not
impersonal institutions. The medievals recognised the authority of a certain
man or family with hereditary claim to kingship to deal with emergencies, not
a legal or administrative system. Security came from family, neighbourhood

---

[54] Quoted in Watt, 'Spiritual and Temporal Powers', p. 367.

and lord, not from the king. Later, in the Frankish kingdom of the eighth and ninth centuries, and the Anglo-Saxon kingdom of the tenth and eleventh centuries, despite a general kingly duty to preserve peace and do justice through uniform systems of local courts, basic social and economic structures remained mainly local and familial, and royal officials 'tended to become leaders of autonomous local communities rather than agents of central authority'.[55]

4.5.1 Ritual, meaning and time

The ritual and meaning of homage demonstrates the nature of authority associated with feudalism and the source of its moral allegiance. Historian Marc Bloch provides examples of different types of ceremony establishing and reinforcing the personal nature of authority which permeated medieval relationships and the emerging notions of legal authority. The subordination of one individual to another, in turn subordinated to others – subinfeudation – permeated the whole life of society. The Germanic ritual of homage has been described by Bloch thus:

> Imagine two men face to face; one wishing to serve, the other willing or anxious to be served. The former puts his hands together and places them, thus joined, between the hands of the other man – a plain symbol of submission, the significance of which was sometimes further emphasized by a kneeling posture. At the same time, the person proffering his hands utters a few words – a very short declaration – by which he acknowledges himself to be the 'man' of the person facing him. Then chief and subordinate kiss each other on the mouth, symbolizing accord and friendship.[56]

The superior was known as the 'lord'; the subordinate known more commonly today as the 'vassal'. Fealty was later a superimposed Christian ritual in Carolingian times, a time in which promises could be scarcely valid unless God were guarantor. This second rite required the placing of hands on the Gospels or on relics. Homage was always performed first in the ceremony, establishing the relationship of vassalage and the connoted pledge of dependence and protection on each part. Fealty, often without a corresponding oath from the lord, could be repeated more than once without the rite of homage given in the first place.[57]

In the more contractual, existential society of today, individual mortality brings a finality with which medieval notions of individual afterlife and communal continuity were incompatible. Homage and fealty are to be distinguished from modern contractual relations which terminate upon death, or, as a matter

---

[55] Joseph R. Strayer, *On the Medieval Origins of the Modern State* (Princeton: Princeton University Press, 1970), pp. 13–15.

[56] Marc Bloch, *Feudal Society*, trans. L. A. Manyon (London: Routlege & Kegan Paul, 1942), pp. 145–6. For a French charter or written contract of fealty, see Cantor, *Medieval Reader*, pp. 21–2. A detailed chapter on the laws of 'private allegiance' at this time is to be found in Lupoi, *Origins*, pp. 321–67.   [57] Bloch, *Feudal Society*, p. 146.

of the English common law rule against perpetuities, within twenty-one years of the death of a 'life in being'. In practice, vassalage became mostly hereditary, although the ceremony would be conducted anew for the surviving son.[58] Medieval legal authority occurred within a fairly stationary view of time; a view of the future upon which was projected the present structure of social relationships, reflected in the rituals and laws described.

The interior, moral allegiance – the heartfelt allegiance – to this pattern of social relationship can scarcely be imagined today, in the industrialised world. To disregard the bond of vassalage was a terrible sin. The devotion of the vassal to his lord was the model upon which the Provençal poets 'based their conception of the fealty of the perfect lover' when they invented courtly love.[59] Excellent fictitious examples of such deep and loving relationships amongst men, with thematic historical reality,[60] are to be found for the modern reader (and now movie-goer) in *The Lord of the Rings*, by former Oxford Professor of Anglo-Saxon, J. R. R. Tolkien.[61] Although vassalage could become meaningless, 'the fealty of the vassal survived in all its freshness . . . [W]hen the old rites were finally outmoded, it was replaced . . . by other forms of personal dependence.'[62] Those other forms of dependence could later be found in the ties of the manor and villeinage.

The ceremony of making a knight – the process of 'dubbing' a knight – is interesting for the model it provides for the creation of moral allegiance and cultural significance.

> The ritual consisted of several acts. To the candidate, who as a rule was scarcely more than a boy, an older knight first of all handed over the arms symbolic of his future status; in particular, he girded on his sword. Then, almost invariably, this sponsor administered a heavy blow with the flat of his hand on the young man's neck or cheek.[63]

'Dubbing to knighthood' was connected with the mentality of the initiation ceremony practised in many different types of cultures, providing entry into adulthood and the assumption of responsibility. The blow to the head was either a test of strength and/or 'a method of making an impression on the memory, so that . . . the young man would remember his "promise" for the rest of his life'. It is likely to have been, whatever its origins, a device for maintaining memory;

---

[58] Ibid., p. 147.   [59] Ibid., pp. 232–3.
[60] See Norman F. Cantor, *Inventing the Middle Ages: The Lives, Works, and Ideas of the Great Medievalists of the Twentieth Century* (New York: Quill William Morrow, 1991), pp. 226–33. 'Tolkien is [F.W.] Maitland's successor as an archaeologist of medieval society' (p. 232).
[61] See J. R. R. Tolkien, *The Lord of the Rings* [1954] (London: HarperCollins Publishers, 1997), in particular part III, *The Return of the King*. Pippin pledges 'fealty and service to Gondor, and to the Lord and Steward of the realm' the Lord Denethor (pp. 739–40); and Merry, '[f]illed suddenly with love for this old man' laid his sword on the lap of Théoden King, and received the king's blessing (p. 760). The relationship between Frodo and Sam appears more in the nature of an inherited manorial relationship, still demonstrating a relationship of love more than mere friendship by today's standards.
[62] Bloch, *Feudal Society*, pp. 236–8.   [63] Ibid., p. 312.

'a box on the ear was one of the commonest methods, sanctioned by the legal customs of the time, of ensuring the recollection of certain legal acts – though it is true that it was inflicted on the witnesses and not on the parties themselves';[64] so too was dunking in a river or the giving of a 'resounding slap'.[65] Indubitably, this practice attracted a significance or allegiance to authority, rare by today's standards, and perhaps thankfully so.

If we can temporarily suspend our preconceptions of cruelty, the significance of the ritual should not be dismissed. It is a counter-model to the emerging globally projected consumer society, which seems to thrive on constant stimulation, short memory and legal and normative disenchantment – in other words, an absence of meaning. For its ability to foster individual allegiance, the feudal cultural model will be of value to a normative jurisprudence.

4.5.2 Parcellised sovereignty, economy and space

Land, comprising the fief which was from the lord's estate, or the allod which was independent, was not held in the modern form, the title to which transmits like a commodity. There could be 'multiple bearers of rights in the same land', and 'future interests' of land could be held by different people contingent, for example, upon the survivorship of fellow knights; various persons, born and unborn, could have 'rights of possession, use, disposition, and control of property'.[66] Ownership of land was therefore based very much upon personal relationships. In Perry Anderson's words, there was 'organic *unity* of economy and polity, paradoxically distributed in a chain of parcellized sovereignties throughout the social formation'.[67] That is, the economy and the political organisation of society were conceived as a naturally occurring phenomenon, governed by interwoven sources of authority. As such, land and labour were neither commodified nor traded at an objective market price.

The term 'parcellization of sovereignty' was coined specifically by Anderson in his analysis of the feudal mode of production. It describes the multifarious, interconnecting sources and networks of authority governing medieval European society. 'The consequence of such a system was that political sovereignty was never focused in a single centre. The functions of the State were disintegrated in a vertical allocation downwards, at each level of which political and economic relations were, on the other hand, integrated.'[68] The lord and ultimately the monarch were protectors and supervisors of production, the way of life, and religion, in social worlds which possessed inherent order,

---

[64] Ibid., p. 313.

[65] Martin van Creveld, *The Rise and Decline of the State* (Cambridge: Cambridge University Press, 1999), p. 143. A related ritual survived until recently in Catholic Church confirmation ceremonies, in which the bishop slapped confirmees on the cheek.

[66] Berman, *Law and Revolution*, pp. 312–13.

[67] Perry Anderson, *Lineages of the Absolutist State* (London: NLB, 1974), p. 19.

[68] Perry Anderson, *Passages from Antiquity to Feudalism* (London: NLB, 1974), p. 148.

maintained by law. Kings, although supposed in theory to be mightier than any of their subjects, were often vassals of other men for part of the royal lands, and 'a vassal might be caught in crosscutting obligations which are very difficult to comprehend within our understanding of "international" relations'.[69] Due also to the practice of intermarriage amongst foreign royal families, kings could possess land in geographically diverse and separate places.[70] There was a 'dispersal of coercion', for whereas the church in the classical Roman Empire had been integrated into the imperial machinery from Constantine onwards, the medieval church was an autonomous institution, along with other competing institutions such as manor, crown, feudal demesne and town. There was neither need nor place for an across-the-board executive (because authority was not unitary) or a legislature (law was anyway declared, not made or innovated).[71] Matters fell before one jurisdiction or another, although there could be conflict. Oral customs, together with old Roman law texts and treatises, provided the material for the finding of the law by induction (that is, by extracting a proposition from many supporting sources). Government therefore, rather than being something the authority of which touched every modern person like a computer attached to a network, instead radiated authority along branches of a tree to other lesser and then lesser lords who had to keep the smaller branches and leaves to their duty – superimposing the mass irrelevance of the peasantry which was under private control.

The term 'parcellized sovereignty', as used by Anderson, is posited in the context of an economy which he asserts was not parcellised. In a change of emphasis from his usage of the word 'parcellisation', which is valuable for its concision, it also does well to consider the medieval economy as parcellised. This is because actual medieval markets were fragmented, soil-based and territorial. Subsistence production for direct consumption and barter, not market exchange, predominated.[72] This is not to dispute Anderson's observation that, from a functional perspective, the economy relied upon serfdom as a universal mode of production in a regularly occurring political hierarchy. It is to say that the practical institution of economic activity was carried out across, for the most part, disunited, discriminating and parochial markets, where in fact they did occur. Spiritual belief in the Christian God was projected universally. 'The realm of faith is the only universal and unifying home for the scattered villages of the tenth century.'[73] This will be of utmost relevance to our later understanding of authority at the end of the second millennium, in the inverse context of a unified economy with its challenge of Mammon, and now parcellised notions of God and spirituality.[74]

---

[69] Spruyt, *Sovereign State*, p. 39.   [70] van Creveld, *Rise and Decline*, pp. 88–9.

[71] See Anderson, *Antiquity to Feudalism*, p. 153.

[72] Benno Teschke, 'Geopolitical Relations in the European Middle Ages: History and Theory' (1998) 52 *International Organization* 325–58, 339–42.

[73] Eugen Rosenstock-Huessy, *Out of Revolution: Autobiography of Western Man* [1938] (Providence and Oxford: Berg, 1993), p. 501.   [74] See ch. 10.6, pp. 247–51 below.

Explained in terms of our concept of the sphere of containable disruption,[75] the many small sovereignties were logically testament to the inability of one organisation to be able to maintain to its own design a single order in a large territory the likes of a modern state. Transport networks were poorly developed, and there were many local dialects and currencies (where they were even used, as opposed to barter) in, as we have seen, parcellised economies. In short, *interconnection* was poor. What violence could be mustered was localised beneath weak kings and above the abilities of freemen: military technology was chiefly to be found in expensive heavy-shock cavalry, limited to wealthy nobles who became rivals of central authority.[76]

Deserving of remark is the widespread disenfranchisement of the bulk of the medieval population. The serfs – agrarian peasants – had no input into political processes. Paternalistic political meaning was imposed upon them. Out-of-context beatitudes such as 'the meek shall inherit the earth' and the supposedly divinely ordained submission of the peasantry kept the serfs under the thumb of feudal society until the development of cities provided them with a release – which was to take many centuries. What is worth salvaging from this first medieval era is the legal meaning available to those who did, in effect, 'belong' to society, primarily the nobility, clergy and freemen.

4.6 Lessons for a globalist jurisprudence

In early medieval society, there were many different sovereignties and social groupings, with both particular and universalist norms. The original European community possessed a very rich normative atmosphere marked by personal relations rather than impersonal offices. In the absence of a medieval state as such, it is possible to speak of medieval public authority in modern terms as 'privatised'[77] (although that falsely presupposes the naturalness of state public authority). Competing jurisdictions, numerous legal systems in a given territorial space and universalist laws transcending particular territorial laws were not therefore new to the world at the end of the second millennium. As observed by Thomas M. Franck, rich and divided loyalties characterised the medieval social landscape in a manner similar to today's 'global system increasingly characterised by overlapping communities and multivariegated personal loyalties yielding more complex personal identities'.[78] The medieval epoch demonstrates the possibilities for internal allegiances to be forged across competing interests, so crucial for meaningful law.

Conceptually, 'empire' appears to be the closest medieval counterpart to the modern fixation upon political entities now 'united' or purporting to 'unite' in

---

[75] See ch. 2, section 2.4, pp. 42–8 above.   [76] See Spruyt, *Sovereign State*, p. 37.

[77] See Jan Zielonka, *Europe as Empire: The Nature of the Enlarged European Union* (Oxford: Oxford University Press, 2006), p. 10.

[78] Thomas M. Franck, *The Empowered Self: Law and Society in the Age of Individualism* (Oxford: Oxford University Press, 1999), p. 99; cf. Susan Reynolds, *Kingdoms and Communities in Western Europe, 900–1300* (Oxford: Clarendon Press, 2nd edn 1997), pp. 330–1.

their diversity, such as the *United* Kingdom of Great Britain and Northern Ireland, the *United* States of America, the *United* Nations and the European *Union*. At least eight different meanings can be attributed to the medieval idea of 'empire' of this time and forthcoming centuries, concerning the relationships amongst papal, imperial and kingly authorities with their business of peace, conquest, moral government, spirituality and eschatology.[79] Today's competing governmental structures inside, across and above territories share parallel political and welfare concerns to enable the perceived proper ordering of human societies across diverse, naturally occurring communities.[80]

At the beginning of the second millennium, open conflict grew between the church, empire and local rulers. Competing universalist papal and imperial aspirations would extend further over the diverse parcellised sovereignties of lords and kings, with their uncoordinated secular governance. The consequence would be a revolution not only in the political status quo, but also in the idea and practice of law and its potential for allegiance.

---

[79] See James Muldoon, *Empire and Order: The Concept of Empire, 800–1800* (New York: St Martin's Press, Inc., 1999), pp. 15–17.

[80] On modern imperial movements, see Jean L. Cohen, 'Whose Sovereignty?: Empire Versus International Law' and Jebediah Purdy, 'The New Liberal Imperialism: Assessing the Arguments', both in Christian Barry and Thomas W. Pogge (eds.), *Global Institutions and Responsibilities: Achieving Global Justice* (Malden: Blackwell Publishing, 2005).

5

Universal law and the Papal Revolution

> All authority in medieval Christendom was thought to derive ultimately from God . . . It might therefore seem fanciful to contemplate a return to the medieval model, but it is not fanciful to imagine that there might develop a modern and secular counterpart of it that embodies its central characteristics: a system of overlapping authority and multiple loyalty.
>
> Hedley Bull[1]

For the advancement of a general, globalist jurisprudence, the legal achievement of the Papal Revolution is pre-eminent. The Papal Revolution instituted a mode of law with the possibility for universal application yet subjective allegiance across diverse jurisdictions in Western Europe. That we might there discover the key to a globalist jurisprudence so rusted yet capable of opening new doors may not be surprising. '[I]n no other age, since the classical days of Roman law, has so large a part of the sum total of intellectual endeavour been devoted to jurisprudence.'[2]

Grand in scale, the new mode of law was conceived to coexist with other legal systems, in the context of a legal vision for world redemption. That is not to say that the everyday reality of canon and civil law met these ideals. Western legal science nonetheless evolved with that encoded facility. The crucial 'ultimate reality and meaning' which legitimated this social system was the Judeo-Christian God. Miracles and holiness demonstrated by leaders back then[3] occupied a similar status to politicians today justifying their worthiness by delivering economic prosperity, highlighting the nature of the two millennial authorities. Just as there was a World Revolution associated with twentieth-century universalist

---

[1] *The Anarchical Society: A Study of Order in World Politics* (London: Macmillan, 1977), p. 254. On the 'new medievalism', see Jörg Friedrichs, 'The Meaning of New Medievalism' (2001) 7 *European Journal of International Relations* 475–502.

[2] Pollock and Maitland, *History of English Law*, quoted in Charles Homer Haskins, *The Renaissance of the Twelfth Century* (Cambridge, MA: Harvard University Press, 1927 reprinted 1993), p. 194.

[3] See R. I. Moore, *The First European Revolution: 970–1215* (Oxford: Blackwell, 2000), ch. 1; Sofia Boesch Gajano, 'The Use and Abuse of Miracles in Early Medieval Culture' in Lester K. Little and Barbara H. Rosenwein (eds.), *Debating the Middle Ages: Issues and Readings* (Malden: Blackwell Publishers, 1998).

norms, so too was there a revolution of Western European compass with universalist norms in the late eleventh, early twelfth centuries.

5.1 Apocalypse

In the face of numerous collectives of allegiance at the beginning of the second millennium, political power was severely contested. The collapse of the Carolingian empire bifurcated the universalism of imperial constitutionalism. Emerging from the collapse was a purported papal universality inherited by the clans of the Roman aristocracy, and a purported imperial universality inherited by the fluid Italian nobility and ultimately, from 962, the German sovereigns.[4] So ended what is sometimes referred to as the first of the two feudal eras.

Profound social discord was characterised by the trust placed in the sword to cure social ills. In the original European Community of the middle ages, violence played an important role in the economy. Plunder provided an opportunity to prosper at a time when trade was elusive. The economy, as previously discussed, was fragmented and disorganised and subject to localised and idiosyncratic market controls – a far cry from a nationally organised economy let alone a global economy. Customary law could be used as a legal basis for 'almost every usurpation' and law was taken into private hands in the manner of the family blood feud. Men, quick as a point of honour to display animalistic strength, 'were emotionally insensitive to the spectacle of pain, and they had small regard for human life, which they saw only as a transitory state before Eternity'.[5] The end of the world appeared nigh for some Christians who had been waiting for heaven on earth since Christ when the early Christians had foretold relief from the evil empires in the first century.[6]

Beginning in the tenth century, the Peace Movement was an attempt by certain bishops 'to organise peasants and other non-combatants into a sort of vigilante association to repress the violence and pillaging of feudal lords', lacking, though, in success, because the lords were usually militarily superior. Fortunes of the Movement improved when powerful lords took up the cause for political stability. The church assumed a secondary role and simply sanctioned the lay rulers.[7] Civil war was, however, to rage sporadically throughout Europe from 1075. The premier European drama was unfolding in the wings. The high achievements which would follow gave rise to phrases such as 'The Twelfth-century Renaissance', 'The Making of the Middle Ages', 'The Rise of Europe', 'The Flowering of Medieval Civilisation' and 'The Intellectual Expansion of Europe'.[8]

---

[4] Marc Bloch, *Feudal Society*, trans. L. A. Manyon (London: Routlege & Kegan Paul, 1942), p. 390.   [5] Ibid., p. 411.

[6] See Richard Landes, 'The Fear of an Apocalyptic Year 1000: Augustinian Historiography, Medieval and Modern' (2000) 75 *Speculum* 97–145.

[7] Joseph R. Strayer, *On the Medieval Origins of the Modern State* (Princeton: Princeton University Press, 1970), pp. 19–20. See too Alan Harding, *Medieval Law and the Foundations of the State* (Oxford: Oxford University Press, 2002), ch. 4 and sources therein.

[8] Norman Cantor (ed.), *The Medieval Reader* (New York: HarperPerennial, 1995), p. 87.

5.2 The Papal Revolution

5.2.1 Space: the reconciliation of morality and politics

Amidst the extraordinary affliction of 'tribulations and difficulties' causing 'tranquillity and peace' to be 'wholly despaired of' (paraphrasing the Bishop of Cologne)[9] in this era, peace associations emerged, in meetings of bishops, led by the Cluniac monks. (The monastery at Cluny was perhaps the prototype multinational corporation, with branch monasteries throughout Europe[10] including England.) Certain ideological beliefs sought institutional expression in this chaotic society: for example, to kill a Christian is to kill Christ. Not only was there a duty on the part of the church to protect its own members but there was also a duty to protect the poor and wretched, who had been entrusted to the church. Belief in the state, remembered from imperial times, tended to oppose clerical interference in the temporal matter of peace, although, particularly in France, the powerlessness of the monarchy was evident.[11]

On the Space Axis of the Space–Time Matrix, interior, popular movements filled in for the imperial state. Special days in the calendar spread and drew prohibitions on blood feuds (Sundays) and bans on violence, for example, over the Easter period (known as the 'Truce of God');[12] protection was extended to church property, unarmed clerics, peasants' livestock and later, merchants, despite some exceptions in times of war (the 'Peace of God').[13] These restrictions were developments in the ideology of the 'Just War'.[14] Peace decrees from provincial church synods generally forbade, 'under pain of excommunication, any act of warfare or vengeance against clerics, pilgrims, merchants, Jews, women, and peasants, as well as against ecclesiastical and agricultural property'.[15] Collective oaths of reconciliation and good conduct were undertaken in the form of 'pacts', although these were not always voluntary, for the church might take hostages and enforce a pledge of peace (for example, in Le Puy, 990). These collective oaths played an important role in the later formation of cities, guilds and corporate groups. Some of these communities set up militia and appointed judges, arousing the jealousy of the temporal authorities and barons and earls, although gradually some kings and princes sought to establish themselves as 'great peacemakers' in their own spheres (for example, in Provence,

---

[9] Bishop of Cologne, 'The Truce of God' in Cantor (ed.), *Medieval Reader*, p. 89.

[10] Eugen Rosenstock-Huessy, *Out of Revolution: Autobiography of Western Man* [1938] (Providence and Oxford: Berg, 1993), p. 506.   [11] Strayer, *Medieval Origins*, p. 413.

[12] Bishop of Cologne, 'Truce of God', pp. 89–90.

[13] See Strayer, *Medieval Origins*, p. 414; Moore, *First European Revolution*, p. 8; and more specifically, e.g. Thomas Head, 'The Development of the Peace of God in Aquitaine (970–1005)' (1999) 74 *Speculum* 656–86.

[14] See O. F. Robinson, T. D. Fergus and W. F. Gordon, *European Legal History: Sources and Institutions* (London: Butterworths, 1994), [5.6.1].

[15] Harold J. Berman, *Law and Revolution: The Formation of the Western Legal Tradition* (Cambridge, MA: Harvard University Press, 1983), p. 90.

1226).[16] A common, universalist Christianity was used to imply a family relationship[17] at the moral, interior level of the Space Axis.

The institutional separation of the religious and political spheres had
declined. Gelasian doctrine, demarcating the 'Two Swords' constitutionalism of
separate spiritual and temporal spheres from centuries earlier,[18] had been whit-
tled away by expedience. Kings, who had been considered 'semi-religious
personages', had appointed abbots, bishops and often popes, and under
Charlemagne, matters of theological doctrine had received royal intervention.[19]
Ecclesiastical offices (benefices) were mostly appointed by secular authorities
(that is, by emperor, kings and feudal lords). These church offices had tended to
be tied to revenues and land services, which were lucrative and often assigned
by the secular powers to their relatives and friends, and bought and sold (the
practice of 'simony'). Furthermore, integration of church and state had been
aided through clerical marriages (a practice known as 'nicolaism'), whereby
priests married into secular rulers' families, and clerics became involved in
secular administration. The church could not extricate its clergy from the
secular powers, nor could the secular powers be extricated from the church.[20]

The emperors had supported the church reformers attacking the corruption
of feudal and local rulers, the emperors in turn taking from the Roman nobility the power to appoint the pope. As the eleventh century progressed, the spiritual power of the emperor became too much a part of the problem. The Papal
Revolution can be dated from 1075, when wayward priests were boycotted by
Pope Gregory VII and a charter of his emerging mindset,[21] the Dictates of the
Pope (*Dictatus Papae*), written. Followed by the 'Investiture Wars', it was not
until the Concordat of Worms (1122) in the German provinces and the
Concordat of Bec (1107) for England and Normandy, that the constitutional
spheres were recast between church and state in a compromise.[22] 'Peace' and
'concord' were key words in Gregory's vocabulary.[23]

In addition to the Cluniac achievement of clerical celibacy and the prohibition on sales of benefices, the political and legal supremacy of the papacy was
declared. The papacy wrested its right to elect bishops and abbots, and its
freedom from imperial investiture of the bishops and abbots with ring and staff
symbolising their power to care for souls. The papacy conceded imperial intervention in disputed elections (in effect giving both pope and emperor a power
of veto) and also conceded the homage of the prelate to the secular authority
prior to consecration. The 'supranational' jurisdiction claimed by the church

---

[16] Bloch, *Feudal Society*, pp. 415–17.   [17] Robinson, *European Legal History*, [5.6.3].
[18] See ch. 4, section 4.4.2, pp. 85–8 above.   [19] Strayer, *Medieval Origins*, p. 20.
[20] Berman, *Law and Revolution*, pp. 93–4.
[21] See H. E. J. Cowdrey, *Pope Gregory VII: 1073–1085* (Oxford: Clarendon Press, 1998), pp. 502–7.
[22] See Uta-Renate Blumenthal, *The Investiture Controversy: Church and Monarchy from the Ninth
to the Twelfth Century* (Philadelphia: University of Pennsylvania Press, 1988), pp. 142–59
(Bec), 167–73 (Worms); Berman, *Law and Revolution*, pp. 94–9.
[23] See Cowdrey, *Pope Gregory*, pp. 576–83.

was established, the pope being 'judge ordinary of all persons', and it came to exercise 'the legislative, administrative, and judicial powers of a modern state', although sacred and relatively unsecularised,[24] with shared jurisdiction. Papal supranationality will be considered later in this chapter.

In the wake of the revolution, the legal order of the church became subject to objective systematisation, in Gratian's *Concordance of Discordant Canons* (commonly called the *Decretum*). Exterior and rationally conceived though it was on the Space Axis, its interior, moral inspiration at the other end of the Space Axis is evidenced by its author's conception of it as *theologia practica externa* – that is, practical, external theology.[25] Published in 1140 and in use until 1917 in Catholic ecclesiastical courts, the *Decretum Gratiani* was the first modern systematisation of law characteristic of the Western legal tradition. Legal implications of distinctions amongst divine law (including biblical laws), natural law, human law, church law, princely law, enacted law and customary law were explored, and the sources of law arranged in hierarchical order.[26] These sources of laws covered the Space Axis of the Space–Time Matrix; a recent monograph has conveniently referred to Gratian's 'mastery of the *exterior, public* court of justice and the *interior, sacramental* court of the confessional' [italics added]. (This may be one reason why Gratian is apparently the only lawyer known to be in Paradise, according to Dante in *Paradiso*.)[27] That is, the systematisation of interior norms such as divine and natural laws with princely and enacted laws in effect reconciled morally felt laws with politically imposed laws. Systematisations spread from canon law to territorial laws, including English, French, Italian and German systems. Law and legal authority did not come from just one place, to be discussed in greater detail in chapter 6.

In political philosophy, the counterpart of Gratian was John of Salisbury. Exterior, rationalising tendencies of the time were captured and endued with momentum in his book *Policraticus* (1159), moderated by the interior, cultural resort to scripture. The new legal systems were conceived as components in a greater social system. This reflected a higher divine law (breach of which could in some circumstances permit tyrannicide).[28] It was at once international, constitutional and private, for it was binding on individuals and their associations.[29] Furthermore, his organic theory of government, whereby, for example,

---

[24] Berman, *Law and Revolution*, pp. 99, 113–14.

[25] See Franz Wieacker, *A History of Private Law in Europe, With Particular Reference to Germany*, trans. Tony Weir (Oxford: Oxford University Press, 1995), p. 49.

[26] See Berman, *Law and Revolution*, pp. 143–64.

[27] See Anders Winroth, *The Making of Gratian's Decretum* (Cambridge: Cambridge University Press, 2000), pp. 1–2. Which particular Gratian is in heaven is not clear, as Winroth convincingly suggests that the *Decretum* is not the product of one person, time and place (p. 193).

[28] See John of Salisbury, *Policraticus*, trans. Cary J. Nederman (Cambridge: Cambridge University Press, 1990), bk VIII, ch. XX.

[29] John Dickinson, 'Introduction: The Place of the Policraticus in the Development of Political Thought' in *Policraticus: The Statesman's Book of John of Salisbury* (New York: Russell & Russell, 1963), pp. xxix–xxx.

the prince is head, the priesthood soul, the senate the heart and financial officers the stomach and intestines, whilst avowing origins in a now doubted work of Plutarch, 'traces back in part no doubt to the Christian identification of the church with the body of Christ'.[30]

Girded by Christian notions of a community of believers and popular movements bringing peace, the church, especially through the Cluniacs, was able to repel secular infiltration into the spiritual arm of government through norms with appeal at the cultural, moral, interior end of the Space–Time Matrix. That spiritual arm, though a jurisdiction over souls, was to develop as a significant political power, with a sophisticated, objective legal science at the exterior end of the Space Axis, drawing on the permeating Western authority of the Bible to inspire interior, cultural allegiance.[31] To this extent it is possible to write of a reconciliation of morality and politics sought by the jurisprudence consequent to the Papal Revolution. Today, the relative freedom from tyranny enjoyed in the West, at the expense of excessive legalism, may be a consequence of the medieval facility for the conversion of exterior political and interior moral problems into legal issues.[32]

5.2.2 Time: the pursuit of heaven on earth

The reformed Catholic church introduced, in a serious philosophical fashion, a futurist, visionary aspect to exterior political authority. In Western Europe, to this point, the previously prevailing Augustinian notion of time, since the early fifth century, did not encompass a utopian role for the church in the here-and-now other than to facilitate the social conditions for the faithful to engage in an interior, privatised, moral striving for the better world of the City of God.[33] St Augustine had maintained that the church had to forgo its present physical location in the (evil) times or *saeculum* (from which derived the pejorative terms 'temporal' and 'secular'), concentrating instead upon the heavenly City of God.[34] In a change of emphasis, the aim of the church under Pope Gregory VII became to instigate this divine city on earth, through law.

> The church set out to reform both itself and the world by law. It established itself as a visible, corporate, legal entity, independent of imperial, royal, feudal, and urban authorities. Autonomous bodies of law were articulated, first within the ecclesiastical polity and then within the various secular polities, in part to maintain the cohesion of each polity, in part to achieve the reform of each, in part to keep an equilibrium among them all.[35]

[30] Dickinson, 'Introduction', p. xx.; cf. 1 Corinthians 12.
[31] See Susan Reynolds, *Kingdoms and Communities in Western Europe, 900–1300* (Oxford: Clarendon Press, 2nd edn 1997), pp. 5–7.
[32] See Berman, *Law and Revolution*, pp. 223–4; Wieacker, *History of Private Law*, p. 7.
[33] See St Augustine, *City of God*, trans. Henry Bettenson (London: Penguin, 1984).
[34] See Berman, *Law and Revolution*, p. 110.   [35] Ibid., p. 83.

Innovation was no longer condemned *per se*. 'History no longer mapped a decline toward the end of the world but an ascent to the point at which time would have run its course', essential to the development of the concept of Europe, according to Jacques Le Goff.[36] The reformers sought, no less, 'the Kingdom of God in the here and now', based upon a return to the primitive church.[37] Amidst this millennial futurism on the Time Axis, history had also provided law of a 'timeless standard' in the form of the recently rediscovered text of Justinian's *Corpus Iuris Civilis* – a 'revelation of law' authoritative for all legal thinkers by virtue of its 'sacred origin in the Empire'.[38]

The spiritual precursor to universal human equality arose in this milieu. All Souls' Day was programmed into the church calendar on 2 November probably sometime between 1024 and 1033, by St Odilo of Cluny in his 'Statute Concerning the Dead'.[39] Associated with the future vision of the Last Judgement, earthly diversities were united in the universal subjection to death and judgement which all humans face. This new day of prayer for the souls of the dead to qualify for heaven can be contrasted with the celebration of the Saints on All Saints' Day, 1 November – that is, of God's elect and chosen people who found heaven, to whom the faithful sent their prayers. The timing of the two rituals brought saints and sinners conceptually closer in the imagination. A new acceptance of tombs in the town and village brought the dead closer to the living.[40] According to Eugen Rosentock-Huessy, 'All Souls' established the solidarity of all souls from the beginning of the world to the end of time'. This new celebration recognised that 'everyone is a comrade in the army of death, on equal terms with all souls'; it was 'the Christian democracy of the Last Judgement'.[41] All souls faced doing penance for their sins – their breaches of the law – after death, according to the new, temporal doctrine of purgatory, whilst awaiting the Last Judgement.[42] This new day of commemoration suggested 'an empathic union between all sinners – i.e., everyone – living and dead'[43] including the excommunicated;[44] connected to 'a *global*, meaningful structure of time . . . with its *universalist* protection of the dead . . .' [italics added].[45]

---

[36] Jacques Le Goff, *The Birth of Europe*, trans. Janet Lloyd (Oxford: Blackwell Publishing, 2005), pp. 150–1.

[37] Blumenthal, *Investiture Controversy*, p. 65; Berman, *Law and Revolution*, p. 118. See too H. E. J. Cowdrey, *The Cluniacs and the Gregorian Reform* (Oxford: Clarendon Press, 1970), pp. 135–41; Gerd Tellenbach, *Church, State and Christian Society at the Time of the Investiture Contest*, trans. R. F. Bennett (Oxford: Basil Blackwell, 1948).

[38] Wieacker, *History of Private Law*, pp. 30–1.

[39] See Michael E. Hoenicke Moore, 'Demons and the Battle for Souls at Cluny' (2003) 32 *Studies in Religion/Sciences Religieuses* 485–98, 487.   [40] See Le Goff, *Europe*, pp. 51–2.

[41] Rosenstock-Huessy, *Out of Revolution*, pp. 506–8.

[42] See Berman, *Law and Revolution*, pp. 166–73.

[43] Andrew Skotnicki, 'God's Prisoners: Penal Confinement and the Creation of Purgatory' (2006) 22 *Modern Theology* 85–110, 104.

[44] Dominique Iogna-Prat, 'The Dead in the Celestial Bookkeeping of the Cluniac Monks Around the Year 1000' in Little and Rosenwein, *Debating the Middle Ages*, p. 349.

[45] Moore, 'Battle for Souls', 492.

The origins of the modern state reside in this religious and constitutional endeavour – an undertaking sown with the seeds of its own secularisation. Earth became important in and of itself, as a matter of ultimate reality and meaning, with politics and law to be taken seriously as a matter of religious commitment. Sociological literature has generally regarded the studious pursuit of Christianity and, in particular, Protestantism, as stimulants of secularisation.[46] This is premised upon the assumption that there are more 'mystical' and irrational traditions than Christianity. Christianity, especially when scholasticism was encountered, attempted to ground faith in reason and earthly perceptions. Protestantism went even further, as shall be seen in chapter 7, marking a turning point in the ultimate reality and meaning used to legitimate law in the Western legal tradition.

Emerging from this revolution of European proportions, the church claimed to represent an idealistic and universal notion of politics authorised by God and scripture, appealing to interior legitimacy. Inspirational, universalist religious ideology challenged, with the promise of peace and salvation, an unstable, particularistic war of the worlds. Law, universally conceived, was to be used for peace and the pursuit of ultimate reality and meaning, after revolution. Conceptually, this will be juxtaposed in chapter 10 to the universalism of modern human rights and free-trade laws challenging the sovereignty of the diverse, unstable nation-states and societies associated with the apocalyptic World Revolution.

5.3 Papal supranationality

The Roman Catholic church of the time possessed broadly accustomed constitutional competences which attracted jurisdiction throughout Western Europe. The basis of the church's political power is worth noting, to understand its jurisdictional power. As Bishop of Rome, the pope had the right to considerable property in Italy. Payments were received from monasteries in consideration of support against secular (as opposed to monastic) clergy; the pope could receive annates (for example: one-third of the first year's revenue of a new benefice given to a bishop); clergy might contribute subsidies; and the papacy might impose taxes on laity and clergy. Militarily, armed retainers were often in the service of monasteries and bishops.[47] Importantly, the papacy also exercised a virtual monopoly on literacy, rendering its services vital to secular rulers who required laws and some degree of bureaucratic efficiency beyond that of chiefdoms or feudal fiefs.[48] Interdiction and excommunication were very real

---

[46] See e.g. Reid Mortensen, 'The Theory Behind Secularisation' (1993) 18 *Bulletin of the Australasian Society of Legal Philosophy* 19–42, 23.

[47] Hendrik Spruyt, *The Sovereign State and its Competitors: An Analysis of Systems Change* (Princeton: Princeton University Press, 1994), pp. 45, 213.

[48] See Haskins, *Renaissance of the Twelfth Century*, pp. 212–13; Martin van Creveld, *The Rise and Decline of the State* (Cambridge: Cambridge University Press, 1999), p. 60.

coercive church powers which had the effect of depriving an individual from associating with Christians and from receiving the services of the clergy – serious secular and spiritual impediments.[49] The papacy could therefore enjoy a relatively large sphere of containable disruption within which to regulate normative and social concerns, although that sphere was not territorially absolute and it was contested.[50] The jurisdictional power of the papacy is best understood as 'supranational'.

Supranationality is a term used most commonly in connection with the European Union (see chapter 11 below). It stands for a constitutional division of powers by which the supranational EU can issue a variety of styles of norms, within its constitutional competence, which become laws within the Member States. At an essential level, the concept is not new to Europe. There were no nation-states as such in the Europe of the Papal Revolution, but there were principalities and kingdoms which were to evolve into them. Leaving aside, for the moment, significant differences in legal technology and competences, the Papal Revolution offers a viable precedent for understanding the obvious global relevance of supranationality as the centralised administration of universalist legal norms in competition with more localised legal norms.

5.3.1 Non-territorially defined jurisdiction

Innocent IV (pope from 1243 to 1254) claimed that popes could judge not only Christians but Jews who had violated the Old Testament where they had not been punished by their own leaders. (He in fact ordered the burning of the Talmud.) He also claimed the right to judge infidels who had breached natural law.[51] Papal jurisdiction was essentially a non-territorially defined jurisdiction over persons, exercised in relation to clergy and their households, students, crusaders, wretched persons, Jews in disputes involving Christians, and travellers and merchants. Similarly, a subject-matter jurisdiction was exercised by the church over spiritual matters, including administration of the sacraments, testaments, ecclesiastical benefices and tithes, oaths and sins. Consequently, family law (derived from the sacrament of marriage), wills and succession (from testaments), contract (from oaths), property law (from benefices) and criminal and tort law (from sins) could develop. Even a separate system of taxation was

---

[49] Malcolm Barber, *The Two Cities: Medieval Europe 1050–1320* (London: Routledge, 1992), p. 26; Paul Vinogradoff, 'Historical Types of International Law' reprinted in *The Collected Papers of Paul Vinogradoff*, 2 vols. (Oxford: Clarendon Press, 1928), vol. II, p. 287; R. H. Helmholz, 'Excommunication in Twelfth-century England' (1994–95) 11 *Journal of Law and Religion* 235–53 and his 'Excommunication and the Angevin Leap Forward' (1995) 7 *Haskins Society Journal* 133–50 on the secularisation of the process.

[50] See generally Walter Ullmann, 'The Medieval Papal Court as an International Tribunal' (1971) 11 *Virginia Journal of International Law* 356–71 (although exaggerating the harmony of the papal jurisdiction).

[51] James Muldoon, *Popes, Lawyers, and Infidels* (Philadelphia: University of Pennsylvania Press, 1979), pp. 10–11.

maintained by the church, as mentioned above, in the form of annates, subsidies and direct taxes.[52]

Choice of law clauses in contracts could nominate the civil jurisdiction of the church, through a procedure known as prorogation,[53] similar to choice of law clauses in modern contracts nominating an applicable legal system. A party could bring an action from secular jurisdictions to the ecclesiastical court, on 'default of secular justice'. Modern rival national, arbitral and EU jurisdictions echo, over the centuries, the medieval conflicts of jurisdictions which incited each legal system, including the papal canon law, to improve the science behind that legal system and the overall hierarchical harmony.

Non-territorial, universal rights, which would become human rights, have their origin in this time. They had, as we saw, a prior institutional manifestation by virtue of the recognition of fundamental equality in All Souls' Day. The Papal Revolution may have been 'the first great "human rights movement" of the West in the name of "freedom of the church" (*libertas ecclesiae*)'.[54] The autonomy of the church from the claims of provincial, feudal and imperial figures and institutions was established, as well as its subjection to the standards it sought to uphold. Gratian regarded the pope's freedom from judgement as being dependent on the pope's faithfulness, and Huguccio wrote that the pope was not immune from trial and judgement for crimes giving scandal to the church.[55] Much canon law was framed in terms of rights.[56]

Clergymen became involved in secular politics and used their training in Roman law to assist administration,[57] in what was a remarkable growth in the number of professional jurists in only one hundred years.[58] This was crucial to the development of a non-territorial Western legal science, propounded by a profession, if not a priesthood, of lawyers with an international presence.[59]

> [B]etween 1070 and 1170, the whole of educated Europe formed a single and undifferentiated cultural unit. In the lands between Edinburgh and Palermo,

---

[52] Berman, *Law and Revolution*, pp. 222–3.

[53] Ibid., p. 223. See too Charles J. Reid Jr and John Witte Jr, 'In the Steps of Gratian: Writing the History of Canon Law in the 1990s' (1999) 48 *Emory Law Journal* 647–88, 650–1.

[54] John Witte Jr, 'Law, Religion, and Human Rights' (1996) 28 *Columbia Human Rights Review* 1–31, 9. Human rights have been philosophically traced to ancient Rome, in particular to the concept of *humanitas*: see Richard Bauman, *Human Rights in Ancient Rome* (London: Routledge, 2000).   [55] See Berman, *Law and Revolution*, p. 214.

[56] See Charles J. Reid Jr, 'The Medieval Origins of the Western Natural Rights Tradition: The Achievement of Brian Tierney' (1998) 83 *Cornell Law Review* 437–63.

[57] See David S. Clark, 'The Medieval Origins of Modern Legal Education: Between Church and State' (1987) 35 *American Journal of Comparative Law* 653–719.

[58] See James A. Brundage, 'The Rise of the Professional Jurist in the Thirteenth Century' (1994) 20 *Syracuse Journal of International Law & Commerce* 185–90.

[59] See Donald R. Kelley, *The Human Measure: Social Thought in the Western Legal Tradition* (Cambridge, MA: Harvard University Press, 1990), pp. 130–1. According to Baldus, 'Professors of Law are called priests', 'they discharge the office of priesthood': Ernst Kantorowicz, *The King's Two Bodies: A Study in Medieval Political Theology* (New Jersey: Princeton University Press, 1957), p. 123.

Mainz or Lund and Toledo, a man of any city or village might go for education to any school, and become a prelate or an official in any church, court, or university (when these existed) from north to south, from east to west.[60]

'Many of the students at Bologna came from Northern France, Germany, Scandinavia, and the Western Slav countries, nations where in general secular Roman law was not applied at all.'[61] With their social and spatial mobility, the clergy were the equivalent of the modern managerial class.[62] The church taught that secular rulers were bound to create peace and stability and the church was influential through the educated bureaucrats who assisted royal administration.

By the thirteenth century, in almost every European government (including the papacy), courts, together with permanent financial institutions, were complemented by the chancery – an executive body co-ordinating special duties, issuing orders to revenue collectors and judges, and dealing directly with prelates and barons administering internal order and security against external threats.[63] Pope Boniface VIII's 1302 bull, *Unam Sanctam Ecclesiam*, resorted to the Old Testament book of Jeremiah: 'I have set thee over the nations and over the kingdoms.' Between the supranational papacy and the growing impotence of the Holy Roman Empire, 'the great monarchies' grew, from which would eventuate the states.[64]

5.3.2 Competing jurisdictions

In the gaps between the constitutional powers of the emperor, the pope, kings, and princes, there were other legal systems throughout Western Europe. Feudal law, manorial law, mercatorial law and urban law all comprised viable legal systems which existed alongside, although increasingly subordinate to, the royal law and the canon law. Problems of jurisdiction and an attendant emerging discourse about priority were endemic. Appeal mechanisms existed and as a matter of feudal law, 'reciprocity of rights between lords and vassals' (the principle of equal enforcement) demonstrates foundation hallmarks of the rule of law. Peasants might flee the manorial law of their lords and seek protection in a city under cover of the urban law, which occurred with the rise of commerce in the cities and the growth of the bourgeoisie at that time. So too might vassals seek to escape from the feudal law under which military service or taxes in lieu were owed to the liege lord. Although all of these systems were systems in the scientific sense, there were disparities in the quality of their implementation in terms of the professionalism and consistency of the court of hearing, the inferiority of feudal law as opposed to canon law being a case in point.[65]

---

[60] David Knowles, *The Evolution of Medieval Thought* (London: Longman, 2nd edn 1988), p. 73.
[61] Wieacker, *History of Private Law*, p. 54; and see too p. 85 for the diffusion of learned law in Germany.   [62] Jörg Friedrichs, 'New Medievalism', 490.
[63] See Strayer, *Medieval Origins*, pp. 32–3.   [64] See van Creveld, *Rise and Decline*, p. 61.
[65] Berman, *Law and Revolution*, pp. 308–15, and generally on medieval legal pluralism. See too Reynolds, *Kingdoms and Communities*; Harding, *Medieval Law*, pp. 61–8.

Philosophically, it is arguable that increased choice means increased freedom. Individuals with access to, or in possession of, legal knowledge had choices to make about which system of justice would suit their purposes. When people choose what might appear at an early time to be an unconventional jurisdiction, massive social transformations can be encouraged and eventually reflected when that jurisdiction later becomes conventional. Inevitably, systems were forced to confront their outdated customs (for example, inflexible status relationships on the manor) which were not compatible with new ideas of economy, morality, politics and rationality which could be better pursued in alternative jurisdictions. Still, the European legal order managed to retain cultural, interior references for allegiance, despite the agglomeration of external political references on the Space Axis. In addition to the interior, religious aspect of law based upon scriptures, a tradition of group adjudication prevailed, and in England the feudal right of a person to be tried by jury was increasingly recorded in the twelfth century.[66] This helped to popularise the king's justice, retaining the moral input of the people: the jury typically comprised neighbours who could pronounce on property ownership (asking the question 'who was last in peaceful possession?'); and almost the entire free population of the country was involved in the work of the law courts as either litigants or jurors.[67]

The martyrdom of Thomas Becket at the hands of Henry II in 1170,[68] the martyrdom of Sir Thomas More at the hands of Henry VIII in 1535,[69] and the Protestant reformations in Germany and England[70] are relatively popular historical events. They demonstrate the unsettled nature of the competing jurisdictions between the supranational church and the emerging state of England and the German principalities. Notably, this was a constitutional tension spanning some four hundred years of a superstructure relatively stable in its movements, perhaps analogous to, although much more dramatic than, modern contests between states in Western federal systems and their central governments. At the end of this time, in the sixteenth-century reformations, the constitutional cable snapped, illustrating, as will be seen in more detail later in chapter 7, the entwined moral and political complexity of medieval jurisprudence.

5.4 Legal education and practice in a universe of meaning

How is it that universalist legal norms could be propagated and exist relatively harmoniously amidst such diversity? To answer this, it is necessary to consider

---

[66] See R. C. van Caenegem, *The Birth of the English Common Law* (Cambridge: Cambridge University Press, 1973), ch. 3 (and appearances elsewhere in Europe, pp. 72–9).
[67] Strayer, *Medieval Origins*, pp. 40–1.
[68] See James J. Spigelman, *Becket and Henry: The Becket Lectures* (Sydney: St Thomas More Society, 2004); Berman, *Law and Revolution*, ch. 7.
[69] See ch. 7, section 7.5, p. 159 below.   [70] See ch. 7 generally, below.

the construction of the mature medieval world view. The establishment of anything social requires education in its ways.

> To give an educational curriculum a place in the Model of the universe may at first seem an absurdity; and it would be an absurdity if the medievals had felt about it as we feel about the 'subjects' in a syllabus today. But the syllabus was regarded as immutable; the number seven is numinous; the Liberal Arts, by long prescription, had achieved a status not unlike that of nature herself.[71]

C. S. Lewis is describing a universe. It is the normative universe of medieval education and the seven liberal arts: Greek-derived grammar, dialectic, rhetoric (the *Trivium*); and arithmetic, music, geometry and astronomy (the *Quadrivium*). The devices for exposition and conclusion from the *Trivium* were applied at law schools such as Bologna.[72] A universe is a collectivity of worlds in which everything is connected – there is a purpose or explanation for everything. This is not to describe an absolute constitution, but an absolute commitment to a process of living in the world, with a discoverable purpose. Historically, in the West, this purpose or explanation has been a Creator God with a plan for the world. The subset of disciplinary worlds or spheres of endeavour exist for, and give meaning to, the created universe in which the individual participates. In medieval times, these worlds of activity did not function solely for themselves. They interrelated harmoniously as part of a grand purpose which located the worlds and gave them meaning in the universe.

The high middle ages witnessed the origin of the university; and it is of little surprise to learn that education belonged to the spiritual[73] rather than the secular arm of government, given the church's preoccupation with ultimate reality and meaning. The liberal arts were a way of studying the universe: that is, the manner by which all the worlds fitted together and could be understood. The liberal arts prepared scholars for their approach to 'higher' professional faculties of theology, canon law and medicine. Theology, philosophy, the sciences and the arts were part of the hierarchical ordering for knowing God.[74] All sciences known to the pagan world contributed to understanding the Bible in the Christian curriculum, following Christ's exhortation in Matthew 10: 16: 'Be ye wise as serpents.'[75] Mysteries of the faith were subjected to reason.[76] Canon law, whilst dealing 'with contingencies and practical necessities rather than timeless

---

[71] C. S. Lewis, *The Discarded Image: An Introduction to Medieval and Renaissance Literature* (Cambridge: Cambridge University Press, 1964 reprinted 1994), pp. 185–6.

[72] Wieacker, *History of Private Law*, p. 33.

[73] See Jacques Le Goff, *Intellectuals in the Middle Ages*, trans. Teresa Lavender Fagan (Cambridge, MA: Blackwell, 1993), pp. 79–82.

[74] See G. R. Evans, *Philosophy and Theology in the Middle Ages* (London: Routlege, 1993), p. 9; Le Goff, *Birth of Europe*, p. 123; Barber, *Two Cities*, p. 442.

[75] R. W. Southern, *The Making of the Middle Ages* (New Haven: Yale University Press, 1953), p. 171.

[76] Joseph R. Strayer, *Western Europe in the Middle Ages* (New York: Appleton-Century-Crofts Inc., 1955), pp. 129–30.

truths, must not blind us to the grandeur of its purpose, which is the ordering of those contingencies in a coherent whole'.[77] According to Accursius, it was unnecessary for a lawyer to study theology because 'all that is found in the body of Law'.[78]

Rhetoric was defined in the sixth century as 'expertness in discourse in civil questions'.[79] It later encompassed the study of rudimentary Roman law and practical law training (*ars notaria* – the art of writing legal, business, church and government documents); and (dialectical) logic developed skills of argumentation for law.[80] These were devices which attempted to condense into law a way of life from an atmosphere humid with spiritual, natural and customary meaning. This 'law' was not something narrowly doctrinal in the sense of the law associated with lawyers today. Law was then closer to what we now call sociology.[81]

Through this process, canon law (ecclesiastical norms), and indeed the concept of law (as the hierarchy of norms in the universe), took on a more objective, less necessarily spiritual quality, as the canon law became differentiated from more socially abstract theology[82] and its disputable stories about the beginning and ending of humanity. This was a meaningful universe where different worlds fitted together. There was a coherence, through the synthetical concordance of seemingly discordant disciplinary canons in a universe which sought, after the Lord's Prayer, the establishment of the 'Kingdom come . . . on earth as it is in heaven'.[83]

Western legal science flourished after the rediscovery of Justinian's texts in about 1080, with the study of law in European universities such as that at Bologna shortly afterwards.[84] An Islamic contribution must be acknowledged. The intellectual environment had been inspired by Arabian contributions to mathematics (encompassing the importation of Hindu numerals from India), medicine, astronomy, botany, agronomy, alchemy and philosophy.[85] There may have been some Islamic doctrinal legal connections, although to suggest the new Western laws were a 'product' of Islam is implausible because of the location and references of the discourse.[86] Highly civilised Arab communities present in the Mediterranean basin may have acted as some impetus for

---

[77] Robinson, *European Legal History*, p. 73, citing Kuttner, 'Harmony from Dissonance'.

[78] Kantorowicz, *King's Two Bodies*, p. 123.　　[79] Kelley, *Human Measure*, p. 109.

[80] Clark, 'Medieval Origins', 671, 705.

[81] Walter Ullmann, cited in Kelley, *Human Measure*, p. 152.

[82] Clark, 'Medieval Origins', 678.

[83] See Berman, *Law and Revolution*, pp. 25–8; Tellenbach, *Church*, esp. pp. 47–56, 154; and pp. 100–1 above.

[84] See generally Manlio Bellomo, *The Common Legal Past of Europe 1000–1800* trans. Lydia G. Cochrane (Washington, DC: Catholic University of America Press, 1995) chs. 3, 5–6.

[85] Le Goff, *Birth of Europe*, p. 18.

[86] Cf. Joh A. Makdisi, 'The Islamic Origins of the Common Law' (1999) 77 *North Carolina Law Review* 1635–1739; see too P. G. Monateri, 'Black Gaius: A Quest for the Multicultural Origins of the "Western Legal Tradition" ' (2000) 51 *Hastings Law Journal* 479–555.

the profound Western developments in law of the late eleventh century.[87] Nonetheless, Western legal science as it emerged was to describe an evolution in the systematisation of legal doctrines centred in Western Europe.

This new legal science saw the fission of differences between the Hebrew culture which would not tolerate Greek philosophy or Roman law; the Greek culture which would not tolerate Roman law or Hebrew theology; and the Roman culture which would not tolerate Hebrew theology and resisted large parts of Greek philosophy.[88] Although Greek dialectics had been applied to Roman law in the republican period, resulting in a form of reasoning which could draw a conclusion from a problem or question as opposed to the apodictic conclusion drawn from true or false statements, Cicero was to argue unsuccessfully for a more complex systematisation of the law, 'with clear definitions and abstract legal rules'. The Romans had been suspicious of the application of more sophisticated Greek philosophy to their own practical mastery of adjudication.[89]

The scholastic jurists of the eleventh and twelfth centuries in Western Europe were not perturbed by perceived inconsistency between Roman pragmatism, Judeo-Christian theology and Greek conceptualism. Whereas the systematisation of the Roman law had been effected by drawing rules from common elements in particular species of cases, the new jurists sought to draw principles from the rules and these principles themselves into an entire system which could demonstrate what was true and just, thereby elevating the Roman pragmatic genius to the lofty heights of Greek philosophy.

Opening up the new contexts of theological texts using Greek metaphysics, interior cultural and moral norms could be rationalised if not transformed into purportedly universal laws. St Thomas Aquinas (1224/5–74), the father of scholasticism, turned Aristotle's notion of natural law (*Ius Naturale*) into a different type of natural law (*Lex Naturalis*) which was part of the Eternal Law of God, the creator of nature.[90] This Islamic derivative, Averroist doctrine separated the nature of man and his reason from the divine order, although this nature participated in the divine order. Thus a man could be a citizen in a state separate from ecclesiastical authority. The separation of what is now called positive law (predominantly custom but also enactment, for Aquinas) from the divine standard could then allow human law to develop from references outside theology and scripture. Law in general could develop according to its own imperatives and subject to human responsibility, although by reference to a transcendent framework and order (divine law as it had been revealed) which could serve as a foil. Aquinas' natural law of (what are today called) nations (*ius*

---

[87] See H. Patrick Glenn, *Legal Traditions of the World: Sustainable Diversity in Law* (Oxford: Oxford University Press, 2nd edn 2004), p. 133, and cf. pp. 225–7 and his *On Common Laws* (Oxford: Oxford University Press, 2005), p. 125.

[88] Berman, *Law and Revolution*, pp. 132–43.   [89] Ibid., pp. 134–9.

[90] Aquinas, *Summa Theologica*, I–II, q. 90–114. See generally John Finnis, *Aquinas: Moral, Political, and Legal Theory* (Oxford: Oxford University Press, 1998).

gentium) was separated from positive, humanly authorised law: the positive law for nations was to be deduced from the natural principles.[91] In Aquinas, there prevailed the exercise of exterior justification in the form of textual discourse, grounded in an accessible, interior morality perceivable from those texts – chiefly the Bible – which was at once the rational word of God and therefore also culturally compelling to a Christian society. Morally, law sought to induce the pursuit of virtue by individuals; it did not only exist politically to order the common good of society.[92] That society was at a juncture in the movement from local, customary, feudal ways of understanding order, to the more rational dominion of states with more universal claims on the peoples within them.

The Gregorian, Papal Revolution view of time, with its view of the necessary evil of the secular world on its way to the conversion of the faithful to the City of God on earth, blossomed with the Aristotelian belief in the eternity of the world. The doctrine of the eternity of the world 'captivated Western minds after the middle of the thirteenth century'. The world would get older. This view of time has been implicitly described by Ernst Kantorowicz as a 'decisive histori-cal factor' in 'the genesis of the modern state and of modern economy'.[93] Humanity was part of time, and this time would continue indefinitely until the last days, as part of the *tempus*. God belonged to the *aeternitas*. God was before time, and would be after time; though not part of time. Law had a cosmic rele-vance to this. '[T]he personified collectives of the jurists, which were juristically immortal creatures' were beyond the transitory *tempus* of man. That is, the lawyers, taken as a whole, corporately, had a transcendent significance. This immortal notion of the jurists – the expositors of Western legal science – existed in the *aevum* of the angels: angels were created by God, therefore they could not belong to the *aeternitas*; although they would outlast the Last Day unlike humans who were limited by the *tempus*.[94] Thus the political and legal world took on a 'sempiternal' character (that is, created at a beginning point in time but unending), analogous to 'the "spiritual bodies" of the celestial beings'.

> The de-individualised fictitious persons of the lawyers, therefore, necessarily resembled the angels, and the jurists themselves recognised that there was some similarity between their abstractions and the angelic beings. In this respect, then, it may be said that the political and legal world of thought of the later Middle Ages began to be populated by immaterial angelic bodies, large and small: they were invisible, ageless, sempiternal, immortal and sometimes even ubiquitous; and they were endowed with a *corpus intellectuale* or *mysticum* which could stand any comparison with the 'spiritual bodies' of the celestial beings.[95]

[91] See Alfred Verdross and Heribert Franz Koeck, 'Natural Law: The Tradition of Universal Reason and Authority' in R. St J. Macdonald and Douglas M. Johnston (eds.), *The Structure and Process of International Law: Essays in Legal Philosophy Doctrine and Theory* (The Hague: Martinus Nijhoff Publishers, 1983), pp. 19–20.

[92] J. M. Kelly, *A Short History of Western Legal Theory* (Oxford: Oxford University Press, 1992), p. 136.   [93] Kantorowicz, *King's Two Bodies*, pp. 273–4.

[94] Ibid., pp. 280–2.   [95] Ibid., p. 283.

That there could be such a cosmological significance attached to the collective enterprise of lawyers today could barely be taken seriously. More gravity might be accorded to a not inconceivable but related proposition. Lawyers today could become known for their sensitivity to their crucial technical role in the mediation of authority and the achievement of the moral and political purposes of authoritative norms with which they engage, intellectually, for a historical purpose. That this is required after the World Revolution should be taken seriously. Some preliminary propositions to this end are contained by way of conclusion to this book in chapter 13.

5.5 Threshold characteristics of the Western legal tradition

The indicia of the Western legal tradition, as identified by Harold Berman,[96] were established in the Western European legal order following the Papal Revolution. Islamic inputs into the scientific milieu must be acknowledged, although the legal science and its practical application were uniquely Western.[97] Law could be distinguished from other social institutions; it was largely organised and taught by specialists or professionals; and the institutions of law could be criticised by reference to the doctrines they produced (a rule of law principle). These qualities were possessed also by the ancient Roman law of Justinian. In addition, Western legal science from the twelfth century featured a sense of wholeness in the system which permitted the scholastic reconciliation of contradictions whilst not compromising the integrity of the system; law was believed to have the resources to develop organically into the future; law developed coherently by its internal logic to reinterpret the past 'to meet present and future needs'; systems of law were separate from political authorities; this supremacy of law was because of its embrace of the legal pluralism of diverse legal systems; and the ideals and realities of law were in a constant tension by which legal systems could periodically be overthrown by revolution, without destroying, in the longer term, the legal tradition which underlay these characteristics.[98]

So the Western legal tradition was established in the twelfth century, from the Papal Revolution.[99] Complexity from interconnections between many sub-societies could be contained in a relatively stable social order. This is the main legal challenge of globalisation which confronts third-millennium humanity.

---

[96] See ch. 1, section 1.5, pp. 16–18 above.   [97] See pp. 108–9 above.

[98] See Berman, *Law and Revolution*, pp. 7–10.

[99] On the significance of this period to legal history, with various interpretations, see Brian Tierney, *The Crisis of Church and State 1050–1300* (NJ: Englewood Cliffs, 1964) part III and his *Foundations of the Conciliar Theory: The Contribution of the Medieval Canonists From Gratian to the Great Schism* (Cambridge: The University Press, 1955 reprinted 1968). See too R. H. Helmholz, 'Harold Berman's Accomplishment as a Legal Historian' (1993) 42 *Emory Law Review* 475–96; Charles J. Reid Jr and John Witte Jr, 'Steps of Gratian'; Patrick Wormald, *The Making of English Law: King Alfred to the Twelfth Century* (Oxford: Blackwell, 1999), p. 471; Maurizio Lupoi, *The Origins of the European Legal Order*, trans. Adrian Belton (Cambridge: Cambridge University Press, 2000), pp. 3–4.

A general, globalist jurisprudence may today take heart that disparate interior, moral, cultural ideas and practices *can* be synthesised into an exterior, universalist political discourse on the Space Axis which may maintain stability whilst accommodating change within manageable, consistent parameters of normativity. Of course this exercise will not be without its challenges and controversies, especially amongst cultural sub-groups with varying interpretive commitments. Cultural and political openness, and textual rigour tempered with imagination, will be essential, some preliminary suggestions towards which are offered in chapter 10.

Attention must now turn to the decline of universality, including the loss of what might be termed the 'universe-concept' of ultimate reality and meaning through which medieval lawyers were so differently understood in comparison to their disciplinary descendants today. After 1300, things started to decline politically for the papacy. To the constitutional aspects of the decline of our rhetorical holy Roman empire and the rise of the concept of the state, attention will now turn. This is relevant to the perceived naturalness of the doctrine of state sovereignty, regarded by many to be threatened by globalisation.

Part 3
State Formation and Reformation

6

Territorial law and the rise of the state

About twenty generations or ten grandparents ago, the notion of the state as we know it was dawning. Before then, as we have seen, there was certainly law. University-trained lawyers, law books, rule of law, and courts with rules and procedures which (like today) left laypersons cold, were permeating Western Europe. They lubricated diverse social systems and their interconnections. Jurisprudence, of its nature, was general. Furthermore, jurisprudence was historical, in the sense that it was an evolving discourse which made reference to its past in a vision for the future. It was also normative, authorised by and serving an articulated ultimate reality and meaning, being God's creation, and the human's place in the world.

The supranational law of the papacy was to grow less universally effective, in tune with the emerging fortunes of the state and the decline in the political power of the papacy. A secular, selective universality would be advocated by theorists for an emerging international legal order of particularistic, self-determining states. Various theorists based this order in human consent and political will (positivism) and/or rational idealism (naturalism), without the former, universalistic, European political and moral discourse of allegiance. (Western legal science remained, nonetheless, conceptually universalistic in terms of the mechanics and institutions of Western legal systems.) Signified by the end of the Thirty Years War and the Peace of Westphalia in 1648, the continuing decline of the supranational papal authority made these new secular theories increasingly relevant.

This chapter will consider these universalistic and particularistic aspects of the Western legal tradition up until the early seventeenth century. (Investigation of the crucial transformation in the pattern of law and authority in the Protestant Reformations will be deferred until chapter 7.) Diverse state forms, exemplified by the different English and German legal systems, were permeated by a common, universalistic legal science, continuing the globalisation theme of universality versus particularity and diversity.

6.1 The birth of the state

The word 'state' assumed its current meaning after the establishment of the Western legal tradition. Earlier, medieval charters had referred to 'the welfare of the kingdom' (*status regni*) – 'state' was used as one would use the word 'situation'. Justinian's *Corpus* had addressed the 'state' or 'situation' of the Roman republic (*status rei Romanae*). In the early thirteenth century, Accursius pioneered the modern usage, by writing of 'the state', of itself, as in 'to preserve the state so that it shall not perish' (*ad statum conservandum ne pereat*).[1] By 1300, Accursius' idea of the state was gaining acceptance and overtones of patriotism were emerging.[2] Not until the fifteenth century did states develop the fiction of corporate legal personality separate from the civil society.[3]

The significance of the medieval town to constitutional thought and law generation is often overlooked. In the eleventh and twelfth centuries, towns were a major innovation in sovereignty, unevenly embedding frames of economic, political and cultural interconnection in the emergence of sovereign polities.[4] As such, they are not totally devoid of analogy to the 'urban geography' of cities today being physical sites 're-territorializing' industries and markets and re-negotiating authority and allegiances.[5] The cities which emerged were the first secular polities, in the sense of being controlled by laity. Nonetheless, much of their 'spirit and character' came from the church, displayed through 'religious values and rituals, including religious oaths'.[6] In addition to religious commonality, there was also a strong sense of social solidarity, brotherhood, friendship and mutual aid in corporate guild and craft groups to protect economic livelihood,[7] although freedom and equality did not reign supreme.[8]

Parliaments have significant origins around this time in the representative assembly, reflecting the 'general climate of opinion'. Writings emerged on feudal, customary and of course revived Roman law. This juristic discourse advanced the rule of law ideal that 'important decisions should be made publicly, that customs should not be changed without general agreement, that consent was necessary when the superior needed extraordinary additions to his

---

[1] See R. C. van Caenegem, *An Historical Introduction to Western Constitutional Law* (Cambridge: Cambridge University Press, 1995), pp. 5–6. Aquinas used the word 'state' similarly in the sense of the 'state of the people of the Jews': Alan Harding, *Medieval Law and the Foundations of the State* (Oxford: Oxford University Press, 2002).

[2] See Joseph R. Strayer, *On the Medieval Origins of the Modern State* (Princeton: Princeton University Press, 1970), p. 57; see too Ernst Kantorowicz, *The King's Two Bodies: A Study in Medieval Political Theology* (New Jersey: Princeton University Press, 1957), pp. 232–62.

[3] Philip Bobbitt, *The Shield of Achilles: War, Peace and the Course of History* (London: Penguin, 2003), p. 214. On the jurists' fictions of the king's two bodies – his office and his person – and the perpetuity of 'the People' as a body politic, see Kantorowicz, *King's Two Bodies*.

[4] On the varying relationships of towns and cities to the emerging states, see Hendrik Spruyt, *The Sovereign State and Competitors: An Analysis of Systems Change* (Princeton: Princeton University Press, 1994) and p. 126 below.

[5] See Saskia Sassen (ed.), *Global Networks, Linked Cities* (New York: Routledge, 2002).

[6] Harold J. Berman, *Law and Revolution: The Formation of the Western Legal Tradition* (Cambridge, MA: Harvard University Press, 1983), p. 362.

[7] Antony Black, *Guilds and Civil Society in European Political Thought from the Twelfth Century to the Present* (London: Methuen, 1984), pp. 12–17.

[8] See Malcolm Barber, *The Two Cities: Medieval Europe 1050–1320* (London: Routledge, 1992), p. 52.

income, that "what touches all should be approved by all" '.[9] The latter, fundamental proposition grew from the Romano-canonical maxim, *Quod omnes tangit ab omnibus approbetur*.[10] Parliaments adapted to these historical legal visions over time, although not always without challenge.

The sovereign state emerged from a variety of prototypical forms with varying diversities of currency, weights, measures and military and administrative organisation. In different ways, the prototypical states settled issues of independence from outside powers and asserted final authority over populations within geographical boundaries or spheres of containable disruption. Evidently these prototypical states were the most expedient political form for coping with internal stresses and external threats, in effect 'de-parcellising' sovereignty, over centuries, into larger, self-contained and homogeneous spheres of containable disruption. England and France were to emerge as the two most centralised and sovereign of states, after fighting strongly for fringe territories along frontiers; whilst German principalities and Italian cities showed lesser signs of modern sovereignty.[11]

6.2 Legal diversity and universality in the emerging European states

In today's parlance, the later medieval lawyers sought to marry the global with the local. The 'Glossators' were the post Papal Revolution jurists who revived Roman law and assimilated it into the medieval legal systems. The glosses which they produced were in the form of explanatory comments concerning Roman law words, phrases and texts, including accepted usages and interpretations, and answers to questions not settled by the texts.[12] The later 'Commentators' of the fourteenth century onwards brought about the reception of Roman law into Western Europe particularly with respect to the plurality of jurisdictions and legal systems, transforming Justinian's *Corpus* into 'a common law for the whole of Europe' – '*ius commune*'.[13] The *ius commune* was the name given to the legal science[14] – not necessarily doctrinal law – which was common to Germany, France, Italy, Scotland and even England around the time of Bracton in the thirteenth century. R. H. Helmholz propounds the *ius commune* as an amalgam of

---

[9] Strayer, *Medieval Origins*, pp. 65–6.
[10] See Gaines Post, *Studies in Medieval Legal Thought: Public Law and the State 1100–1322* (Princeton: Princeton University Press, 1964), ch. 4.
[11] Strayer, *Medieval Origins*, pp. 58–60.
[12] See generally O. F. Robinson, T. D. Fergus, W. M. Gordon, *European Legal History* (London: Butterworths, 1994), ch. 3.
[13] Franz Wieacker, *A History of Private Law in Europe, with Particular Reference to Germany*, trans. Tony Weir (Oxford: Oxford University Press, 1995), pp. 56–7.
[14] 'Legal science' refers to 'every vocational occupation with the law' according to Fritz Schulz, *A History of Roman Legal Science* (London: Oxford University Press, 1967) and represents 'an institutionalization of the process of resolving conflicts in authoritative texts' according to Berman, *Law and Revolution*, p. 160. See too Harold J. Berman and Charles J. Reid Jr, 'Roman Law in Europe and the Jus Commune: A Historical Overview with Emphasis on the New Legal Science at the End of the Sixteenth Century' (1994) 20 *Syracuse Journal of International Law & Commerce* 1–31.

Roman law and canon law with feudal law occupying a secondary role.[15] James Brundage observes five meanings from the historical writings: natural law, *ius gentium*, Justinian's *Corpus*, the canons of the Western church and, from the thirteenth century, the Romano-canonical law of the universities.[16]

The opposite of *ius commune* or common law was *ius proprium* or particular law – the norms of local institutions such as the kingdom, principality, free city, feudality, corporation or confraternity.[17] Uniquely balanced between historical custom (particularity) and intellectual reason (universality grounded in Roman law), the *ius commune* was something of a universalist way of dealing with diversity. As Manlio Bellomo has written:

> Plurality was thus part of the 'system', and the system itself was inconceivable and would never have existed without the innumerable *iura propria* linked to the unity of the *ius commune*. The greater imperfection of men's laws (the *ius proprium*) was related to the lesser imperfection of the laws of the rulers of the earth (the *ius commune*), but both laws, in varying measure, contained and divulged only a tenuous glimmer of the Justice that was absolute, divine, hence eternal.[18]

Patrick Glenn has recently captured the complexity of this 'common law' notion. There was not just one *ius commune* system, but 'multiple, interactive common laws; each radiating out from major centers', being 'law common in relation to law that was particular'.[19] The *ius commune* was part of a 'relational common law', coexisting with, for example, the English common law, the German *gemeine Recht*, the French *droit commun coutumier* and Italianate regional common laws.[20] The value to a general, globalist jurisprudence is apparent, given the interaction exposed in medieval jurisprudence between universalistic and diverse human tendencies in the *diffusion* across Europe of Romanist law and Western legal science.[21] A relatively common legal science arose organically from diverse political organisations, prompted by the universalism of the church and its canon law model. Legal pluralism flourished.

The emerging state systems of Germany and England prior to the Reformations are briefly investigated to demonstrate this viable model for legal pluralism and also the diverse paths but common origin of law in the interior, personal dimension of the Space–Time Matrix – not the exterior, bureaucratic,

---

15 R. H. Helmholz, *The* ius commune *in England: Four Studies* (Oxford: Oxford University Press, 2001), pp. 3, 10.

16 James A. Brundage, *The Profession and Practice of Medieval Canon Law* (Aldershot: Ashgate Variorum, 2004), VIII, pp. 238–9.

17 See Manlio Bellomo, *The Common Legal Past of Europe 1000–1800*, trans. Lydia G. Cochrane (Washington, DC: Catholic University of America Press, 1995), p. xi, ch. 4.

18 Bellomo, *Common Legal Past*, p. xii.

19 H. Patrick Glenn, *On Common Laws* (Oxford: Oxford University Press, 2005), p. 19.

20 Glenn, *Common Laws*, pp. 42–3.

21 On the relevance of diffusion to globalisation, see William Twining, 'Diffusion of Law: A Global Perspective' (2005) 49 *Journal of Legal Pluralism and Unofficial Law* 1–45; and more relevantly for present purposes, William Twining, 'Social Science and Diffusion of Law' (2005) 32 *Journal of Law and Society* 203–40, 208–13.

political dimension. Space constraints prevent investigation of, for example, France (centralised early, like England) and Italy (not united until the nineteenth century, like Germany). Neither of these two exclusions deviates from the axiom that their later states originated, in terms of the Space–Time Matrix, in the interior, cultural dimension of custom.[22] At once less bureaucratic and more interior in origin on the Space Axis, exterior legitimacy also attached to the laws of these emerging states through a Western legal science.

6.2.1 Germany

Germany has been a fragmented, decentralised state, perhaps more akin to a federation of political communities, for most of its history. Centralisation was not to succeed, even by the time of the demise of the Holy Roman Empire in 1806 (the real and spiritual power of which had been declining since the latter thirteenth century).[23] Unlike the alliance which the French kings had forged with the towns, the German kings had allied themselves with the lords, at the expense of the towns. German kings, in their efforts to achieve the aspirations of the Holy Roman Empire, had also sought control over Italy. This also required the support of the dukes and ecclesiastical lords to grant them control over the towns, at the expense of obtaining any real authority over the lords.[24] In effect, the German kings alienated the towns and were indebted to the lords in a bargain honoured by none of the parties.

In opposition to the feudal governmental structures and the imperial pretensions of the papacy and the Holy Roman Empire, the German free towns formed the city-league. From this grew a federation of towns, the Hanseatic League, in the thirteenth century, peaking in the fourteenth and fifteenth centuries. As a major economically unifying force in Europe embodying emerging ideas for good government, the Hansa was not merely 'an economic association'; 'like states it waged wars, and on occasion it could make or break kings'; and it could 'send emissaries, sign treaties, collect revenue, enforce Hansetag decisions . . . raise an army, conduct foreign policy, decree laws, engage in social regulation, and collect revenue'.[25]

Hendrick Spruyt maintains that the Hanseatic League provides evidence for 'a viable way of organizing economic and political activity in the absence of a central authority',[26] in contrast to the state model. Nonetheless, if sovereignty is considered in the modern sense to encompass a final decision-making structure with a monopoly on violence and justice within broad territorial boundaries, city-leagues failed this measure. They were small islands of containable disruption in the tempestuous seas of other rulers. Furthermore, the Hansa

---

[22] See generally Spruyt, *Sovereign State;* and Glenn, *Common Laws.*

[23] Martin van Creveld, *The Rise and Decline of the State* (Cambridge: Cambridge University Press, 1999), p. 100.   [24] Spruyt, *Sovereign State*, p. 109.

[25] Ibid., pp. 123–6. See too Wilhelm G. Grewe, *The Epochs of International Law*, trans. Michael Byers (Berlin: Walter de Gruyter, 2000), p. 58.   [26] Spruyt, *Sovereign State*, pp. 126–8.

could not manage to provide standard weights, measures and coinage, nor to enforce centralised justice or revenue raising. The Hanseatic League also faced difficulties obtaining recognition in international politics, for example, at the Peace of Westphalia (to which we shall come later in this chapter), because the League could not bind all members to the agreements.[27]

Despite the loose empire of Germany – some 350 principalities – there was a strong German 'common law'. This comprised the canon law common to the whole of Western Europe and its universities and bishops' courts, which included Roman law and its revival scholarship, as well as German customs worked into this system. The proportion of Roman law was low relative to custom, because of the diffusion of customary laws. Particular custom or *ius proprium* was, however, accommodated by the universalistic method. Courts of leading cities provided guidance to the other cities, fostering a common approach. The very large territories (*Länder*), in developing their legal institutions, borrowed extensively from one another.[28] Contrary to the impression perhaps created by its political fragmentation, Germany featured a legal sophistication and coherence. The customary law, which operated at the secular level, was administered by a lay (as opposed to university-trained legal professional) staff, *Schöffen*, which systematised the custom in 'mirrors' reflecting the territorial customs of the people. The authority of the *Schöffen* was grounded not in university learning but 'on practical experience and familiarity with life, and perhaps even more on their social position'.[29] The *Schöffen* had to rely upon the learned clerk of the city to cope with the submissions of the legal professionals who practised the 'learned law' of the *ius commune*. This was a centralising, imperial phenomenon, which had begun earlier in Bavaria. The *Schöffen* of the larger cities had sometimes been merchants who were aware of other regimes, and they were often the subject of appeal for law (*responsa*) by 'daughter' towns. '[O]ne of the greatest of the tribal laws' or 'mirrors', premissed in the authority of Christian political theology, was the *Sachsenspiegel* (Mirror of the Saxons).[30] This was itself a transportable, common law.[31] There was, then, a strong historical, customary basis for the German secular positive law, attracting allegiance by virtue of its location towards the interior orientation of the Space Axis, whilst featuring an exterior rationality.

To cope with the increasing diversity of interconnections, in the absence of a legal profession as such practising customary law (as was the case in England), learned lawyers were imported from the law faculties in Italy and later their German offspring. Roman law and canon law had been applied to secular

---

[27] Ibid., pp. 163–70.
[28] See Harold J. Berman, *Faith and Order: The Reconciliation of Law and Religion* (Atlanta: Scholars Press, 1993), p. 92; Harding, *Medieval Law*, pp. 99–108.
[29] Wieacker, *Private Law*, p. 82.
[30] See Wieacker, *Private Law*, p. 78; see too Harold J. Berman, *Law and Revolution, II: The Impact of the Protestant Reformations on the Western Legal Tradition* (Cambridge, MA: Harvard University Press, 2003), p. 34.   [31] Glenn, *Common Laws*, pp. 37–9.

litigation in ecclesiastical courts since the thirteenth century. In the second half of the fifteenth century, the *ius commune* was applied regularly in the secular courts by learned judges.[32] A formal reception of Roman law occurred in Germany and its Holy Roman Empire in 1495, amidst an established movement for public peace, with the establishment of the *Reichskammergericht* as a refurbished imperial supreme court of justice. Together with other new courts of justice staffed by Romanist jurists, the German princes, it is widely accepted, were attempting to create a rational government order to suppress violence.[33] (This violence, we shall see in the next chapter, inspired Luther and his juristic cofactor, Phillip Melanchthon, in their reforming efforts.) Written procedure was emphasised. Although restricted primarily to imperial courts, Romano-canonical procedure was used gradually to supersede the oral forms by 1505. Given that the court, as a court of appeal, could not be expected to have technical knowledge of the law and customs of the many different trial jurisdictions, Roman law was applied by default unless local law was specifically pleaded.[34] This reflected an older subsidiarity principle relevant especially to EU law today:[35] the most local of laws could receive the highest authority, in the absence of reasons to the contrary.[36]

Contrary to the private law in England,[37] the universities played an important role in the development of Romanist German jurisprudence, particularly after the reception of Roman law. At the end of the fifteenth century, the opinions of the law professors were obtained, by despatch of record to a university for consideration (*Aktenversendung*).[38] The *usus modernus Pandectarum* (the modern application of the *Pandects*, or, literally, Justinian's *Corpus*) was used by the faculties, transcending boundaries of princes and taking authority from the imperial source.[39] This is perhaps best considered 'an *intellectualisation* of German law and lawyers'[40] [original italics]. The universal tolerance of particularity and diversity therefore declined with the growth of prototypical German state institutions and the Roman law, whilst still drawing on a long Romanist legal tradition for authority. Movement towards the exterior orientation of the Space Axis was occurring.

6.2.2 England

In analysing the growth of the absolutist state, Perry Anderson, in passing, described the England relevant to the present enquiry as 'the strongest mediaeval

---

[32] See Wieacker, *Private Law*, pp. 83–90, 113–18.
[33] Whitman, *Legacy of Roman Law*, pp. 12–13.
[34] See Robinson, *European Legal History*, [11.3.3]; Bellomo, *Common Legal Past*, pp. 217–20.
[35] See ch. 11, section 11.2.5, p. 263 below.   [36] Glenn, *Common Laws*, p. 19.
[37] As will be seen (see ch. 7, section 7.2.1, pp. 148–50), the public law tradition in England did at times draw on Roman law for authority.
[38] See Robinson, *European Legal History*, [7.4.1]–[7.4.2]; Wieacker, *Private Law*, pp. 136–7; Whitman, *Legacy of Roman Law*, pp. 34–5.   [39] Robinson, *European Legal History*, [11.4.4].
[40] Wieacker, *Private Law*, p. 95.

monarchy in the West'.[41] Saxon kings had centralised the country efficiently. By the time of Norman feudalism in the later third of the eleventh century, England possessed an administrative centralisation which, when taken with the original conquest and modest size of the country, generated 'an unusually small and regionally unified noble class, without semi-independent territorial potentates comparable to those of the Continent'.[42] Towns were part of the royal estate as a consequence of the Norman conquest in 1066, when all land in England became held of the crown (a fiction which survives to this day even in Australian land law). Towns were never powerful enough to challenge their subordinate status; and the clergy was not so powerful either, comparatively. It will surprise some to learn that the English common law which arose at this time was essentially imported by the French conquerors.[43]

There was initially coexistence between royal courts and manorial, feudal and church courts. The royal courts were not, though, the 'regular professional justice'. Royal courts were extraordinary as there were no permanent administrative, legislative and judicial bodies operating on their own authority.[44] From an early stage, parliaments emerged as 'collective institutions of the feudal ruling class', coinciding with the boundaries of the country. From the time of Edward III (reigned 1327–77), barons and bishops in the English parliament were represented alongside knights and towns. The courts which emerged 'blended' the royal jurisdiction with surviving local customary courts. Courts 'retained vestiges of their original character as popular juridical assemblies in which the free men of the rural community appeared before their equals'; evolving into 'an unpaid aristocratic self-administration' in the counties, from which the then judicial role of the Justice of the Peace was to emerge.[45] Similarly to the German common law, the English common law had (and to a very limited extent still has today) an inherent subsidiarity principle, deferring to more locally established custom.[46]

The similarities between classical Roman and English legal science often go unnoticed. Both Roman law and English common law developed though a case-based discourse. In both systems, law 'developed' out of an assumption that the relevant law actually existed, although not yet articulated, and that the scope simply needed definition. The development of English law, like Roman law, was concentrated upon particular forms of action, such that legal discussion was concerned with remedies rather than with rules. This was exemplified by the formula granted by the *praetor* in Rome, published in his edict; and by the writ granted by the Chancellor in England, published in a register of writs. The classical procedure of English common law, like Roman law, divided legal actions

[41] Perry Anderson, *Lineages of the Absolutist State* (London: NLB, 1974), p. 113.

[42] Anderson, *Lineages*, pp. 113–14.

[43] R. C. van Caenegem, *European Law in the Past and the Future: Unity and Diversity over Two Millennia* (Cambridge: Cambridge University Press, 2002), pp. 2–3.

[44] See Berman, *Law and Revolution*, p. 441.   [45] Anderson, *Lineages*, pp. 114–16.

[46] See Glenn, *Common Laws*, pp. 25–32.

into two stages: at the first stage, the legal issue was identified; and the second stage concerned proof and the adjudication of the issue. In both systems, the second stage was assigned to laymen: the jury in England and the *iudex* in Rome. If the jury or *iudex* found the allegations proved, judgment would be ordered against the defendant.[47]

The laymen's decisions in fact replaced the judgment of God – which was supposed to have been channelled through nature, for example, by trial by ordeal or battle. The award of money damages was the only remedy the laymen could provide, 'probably because of the transitory nature of their office; once they had given their verdict, their office ceased to exist'. When remedies other than money came to be required, the first such remedies issued were the interdict by the *praetor* himself in ancient Roman times, and the injunction by the Chancellor in the English system, who restricted the common law judges to control of the writ system. This is how, in time, the systems evolved of the *ius honorarium* of the Roman *praetor* and the equity of the English Chancellor,[48] which in England was to develop in its own jurisdiction separate from the common law until 1875.[49]

There is a difference between a similar legal science as opposed to similarities in legal doctrines. That is, similar systems of procedure can exist with marked doctrinal differences. There can be similarities in legal science although much less in common, doctrinally. For example, there was no major English 'reception' of Roman law as there was on the Continent. That is, English law could not be derived as a matter of principle by practitioners from Roman jurisprudence. Yet the doctrinal similarities should not be dismissed: 'rather than speaking of conscious borrowings, one must speak instead of parallels, of similarities of language, of coincidences that seem too striking to be coincidental'.[50] It is perhaps going too far to suggest that commonalities may have arisen from the time of the withdrawal of Roman troops from England in the fifth century.[51] The Anglo-Saxon invaders knew nothing of Roman law or canon law, although after they converted to Christianity in the seventh century they began to write down their laws, probably with some trace of Roman law. King Ethelbert of Kent had compiled or codified the laws of his Kingdom (*c.*600 CE) in 'Roman fashion'.[52]

The Norman invasion in the mid-eleventh century had eschewed any relevance of Latin charters used to record conveyances of land until that point, and it was not until the first century after the conquest that the *Leis Willelmi* appeared with ten short extracts which seemed to be borrowed from the Digest. Like the

---

[47] Peter G. Stein, 'Roman Law, Common Law, and Civil Law' (1992) 66 *Tulane Law Review* 1591–1604, 1592–3.   [48] Ibid., 1593–4.

[49] See J. H. Baker, *An Introduction to English Legal History* (London: Butterworths, 4th edn 2002), pp. 114–15.

[50] Charles Donahue Jr, '*Ius Commune*, Canon Law, and Common Law in England' (1992) 66 *Tulane Law Review* 1745–80, 1748.

[51] Cf. Edward D. Re, 'The Roman Contribution to the Common Law' (1993) 39 *Loyola Law Review* 295–311, 300.

[52] Re, 'Roman Contribution', 302. Cf. Donahue, '*Ius Commune*', 1750.

efforts of Vacarius in England, they were intended to set down a few principles of Roman law that might be useful for practitioners.[53] The Treatise called Glanvill contained considerable knowledge of Roman law, effectively displayed in the classification of actions of debt and in the dialectical method.[54] No doubt this was because Glanvill was the student of Vacarius, the first law professor in England, who founded the civil law school at Oxford. (English common law was not taught in English universities in earnest until 1753 at Oxford.)[55] The second major treatise on the practice of the central royal courts, buoyant with Roman legal science, was *Bracton on the Laws and Customs of England*, arranged accord-ing to the tripartite persons, things and actions scheme of *Justinian's Institutes*, with extensive citation of the *Corpus Iuris Civilis* (the entire body of Justinian's texts, including the Institutes, Digest, Codes and Novels).[56] Sir Henry Maine ventured to call Bracton's work 'the plagiarisms of Bracton'.[57]

Indubitably, the private law doctrinal development of the common law and the civil law took on considerable differences,[58] to the point suggested by Alan Watson that 'the stress on similarities in these two approaches is . . . funda-mentally misplaced, and leads to serious misunderstandings of the two systems, and of legal development in general'.[59] Obviously there were differences in the systems. Yet a categorical acceptance of Watson's assertion would be to overlook 'the essential kinship, not of the Roman and the English law, but rather of the Roman and the English lawyer';[60] and the similar constitutional development of European kingdoms[61] and the common legal science.[62]

By the end of the fifteenth century, the King's Council, which had come to handle more of the judicial business of the type which had previously been pre-sented to parliament, generated a separate court, the Court of Requests, 'which had a distinctly Romano-canonical form of procedure, and which for this reason had a number of civil lawyers among its personnel'. In the sixteenth century, the Court of Star Chamber was also born of King's Council, which fol-lowed the Continental inquisitorial form of procedure used by the council.[63] The doctrines and procedures of the Chancellor's court, eventually the Court of

---

[53] Re, 'Roman Contribution', 302.   [54] Donahue, '*Ius Commune*', 1751–2.

[55] See Baker, *English Legal History*, p. 170.   [56] Donahue, '*Ius Commune*', 1752.

[57] Sir Henry Sumner Maine, *Ancient Law: Its Connection with the Early History of Society and its Relation to Modern Ideas* [1861] (reprinted Dorset Press, 1986), p. 67.

[58] See van Caenegem, *Western Constitutional Law*, p. 7.

[59] Alan Watson, 'Roman Law and English Law: Two Patterns of Legal Development' (1990) 36 *Loyola Law Review* 247–74, 248.   [60] W.W. Buckland cited in Watson, 'Roman Law', 248.

[61] van Caenegem, *Western Constitutional Law*, p. 7.

[62] After the notable continental codification initiatives from the late eighteenth century onwards, modern civil lawyers attempting to understand 'the true nature of Roman law' may even have been disadvantaged compared to common lawyers: Obrad Stanojevic, 'Roman Law and Common Law – A Different View' (1990) 36 *Loyola Law Review* 269–74, 274; Eugen Ehrlich, *Fundamental Principles of the Sociology of Law*, trans. Walter L. Moll [1913] (Cambridge, MA: Harvard University Press, 1936), pp. 254–95.

[63] The Star Chamber procedure was part of the controversy which contributed in the following century to the English civil war.

Equity, showed considerable influence from the *ius commune*, and for some time civil lawyers practised before it. The church courts, from the middle of the thirteenth century, followed the substantive canon law and Romano-canonical procedure, and the High Court of Chivalry, emerging from the fourteenth century, also followed the Continental procedure.[64]

Whilst common law lawyers were not required to have training in the *ius commune* of the Continent, some of the common law lawyers were learned in it. Early on, the university at Bologna had trained many English ecclesiastics in canon law, which inspired a familiarity with Roman law which re-entered England in the student's intellectual baggage.[65] Many lawyers practising in England before the English revolution possessed polymathic qualifications including civil law training,[66] and many English judges tended to be quite learned in the *ius commune*. Before 1600, references by common law practitioners and judges to Continental law increased markedly. This included resort to Roman legal classifications such as 'public and private, criminal and civil, real and personal, property and possession, contract and delict, among other examples', borrowed from Roman civil law and canon law taught in European universities. Between 1300 and 1600, more than 200 cases contained propositions from canon law or civil law, excluding the many mentions of Latin maxims derivable from Continental sources.[67] Indeed, 'England was never entirely cut off from continental legal culture.'[68]

At no point, however, in the absence of English local law, was reference made to the *ius commune* for an authoritative statement of the law, as was the practice on the Continent.[69] Why was there not a more profound reception of Roman law doctrine in England? A number of suggestions have been made. Perhaps it represented a historical rejection by the English of papal and imperial influence.[70] Perhaps, too, the uniquely feudal landholding law fundamental to English law (comprising 'convoluted' estates doctrine) was simply incongruous with Roman law.[71] Perhaps most significantly and uniquely, England had

---

[64] Donahue, '*Ius Commune*', 1754–5; see too Helmholz, *Ius Commune*, p. 3; Berman, *Law and Revolution II*, pp. 212–13; van Caenegem, *European Law*, pp. 19–21.

[65] Charles Homer Haskins, *The Renaissance of the Twelfth Century* (Cambridge MA: Harvard University Press, 1927 reprinted 1993), p. 211.

[66] See David J. Ibbetson, 'Common Lawyers and the Law Before the Civil War' (1988) 8 *Oxford Journal of Legal Studies* 142–53, 147, on the disproportionate contribution of English lawyers to the renaissance; Brian Levack, *The Civil Lawyers in England 1603–1641* (Oxford: Clarendon Press, 1973).

[67] David J. Seipp, 'The Reception of Canon Law and Civil Law in English Common Law Courts Before 1600' (1993) 13 *Oxford Journal of Legal Studies* 388–420, 388–91.

[68] See Reinhard Zimmermann, 'Savigny's Legacy: Legal History, Comparative Law, and the Emergence of a European Legal Science' (1996) 112 *Law Quarterly Review* 576–605, 588.

[69] Donahue, '*Ius Commune*', 1747.

[70] See James Muldoon, *Empire and Order: The Concept of Empire, 800–1800* (New York: St Martin's Press, Inc., 1999), p. 96.

[71] See Alan Watson, *The Evolution of Western Private Law* (Baltimore: The Johns Hopkins University Press, expanded ed. 2001), pp. 244–7.

schools of customary law, the inns of court, unlike nations on the Continent where only 'the learned' law (*ius commune* and Roman law) was studied in the universities.[72] Furthermore, the very fact of the grounding of early royal judges in Roman law may have 'immunised' English law from the need for a more radical reception. In this respect, the strength of English law may have been its latent Romanist influence which carried English law into the future.[73]

6.2.3 The diffusion of European common law

Today, the diffusion of a cultural product, be it law or technology, may be bad for some people, for example, if operating in an imperial-colonial fashion; or it could be good, if it advances values perceived to be universally or regionally beneficial, such as human rights or uniform contract rules. Consensus from such debates may be elusive. What might be hoped for is debate based upon all material facts, which requires appreciating the historical globalisation and law precedents such as the interaction of European common laws and more local particular laws. Lawyers are instrumental in achieving the diffusion of law, with different cultural effects depending upon the arguments they employ. For example, lawyers encouraged a centralised discourse of *ius commune* in Western Europe, except in Germany. Fragmented German legal systems and principalities received the support of legal authority marshalled by the lawyers.[74] Today, lawyers play a part in diffusion depending upon the jurisdictions and discourses they cite in submissions and base judgments upon, and the terms they deploy in the agreements they draft.

France, Germany, Italy and England, on their ways to becoming states, were all organised differently, politically. On the Continent, in France, there was an alliance between centralist kings and towns. Conversely, German principalities, loosely united under the Holy Roman Empire, harboured an opposition between the centralist Empire and towns, some of which were organised in the sovereign-like Hanseatic League. Italy never looked like being united, and developed strong city-states through commerce. Across the Channel, England was relatively centralised very early on in the second millennium. All of these nascent states, although differently constituted, featured different laws but shared a familial legal science. England, we have seen, was something of an odd beneficiary.

More than just four different systems of municipal law, or *iura propria*, there were actually many competing systems within those municipalities grounded in custom, together with a pervading legal science and a constitutionally bounded, supranational ecclesiastical law. On the Continent, much of that customary law came to be subject to the systematic discipline of Roman law under the

---

[72] J. H. Baker, *Oxford History of the Laws of England, Volume VI: 1483–1558* (Oxford: Oxford University Press, 2003), p. 12.
[73] See Baker, *English Legal History*, p. 28; Wieacker, *Private Law*, p. 82, n. 10.
[74] See Wieacker, *Private Law*, pp. 66–7.

scientifically similar but doctrinally different systems of *ius commune* of the various sovereign territories, using a Romano-canonical legal science. Early on, the English too used this Western legal science for categorising laws as they related to persons, things and actions. In all of these systems, the legal science was primarily inductive in nature. Law was gathered from cases and commentaries – as opposed to the deductive nature of working from all-important codes or statutes characteristic of the nineteenth-century Continent. It must be stressed that this commonality between England and the Continent operated not *particularly* at the level of secular doctrinal law but at the *general* level of a universalistic legal science – a common Western legal science. It was a rational practice, typified by 'glosses on glosses of glosses' of legal texts[75] – albeit a rationality deeply rooted in culture and custom. It could be traced back to Roman law and the Western experience of its revival and conversion into a science which emanated from universities such as Bologna in the eleventh century.

Perhaps, to employ globalisation parlance, and at the risk of oversimplification inherent in the terminology,[76] these domestically sustained commonalities are demonstrations of 'globalised localisms'. That is, the globalised localism of the papacy (which had state-like attributes) and the Romanist *ius commune* were diffused throughout Western Europe. Equally, there were localised globalisms in this history, given that the Italian, French, German and English legal and political systems all evolved differently. Like today, Western Europe was a normatively complex and rich place at this time. On the Time Axis, historical references in Roman law and custom, and visions for a Christian future, abounded in these legal systems. On the Space Axis, at nearly every level, there were systems of norms, ideally, to guide conduct. The Space–Time Matrix was relatively full of legal references and allegiances for the medieval human. Today, however, legal references are commonly perceived only to come from the exterior, political dimension of the Space Axis, not the cultural, morally engaged interior. That law does, or that it should, in addition to the interior, moral dimension, have references to history and the future for its vitality is a proposition of limited concern for most Westerners.

Of course, no human system is ever set solidly. Centralising tendencies were in operation, territorially. The increase in commerce played a significant role in this political tendency. As territorial rulers were gaining control over larger spheres of containable disruption, the need became more urgent to close legal systems from outside influences, and to centralise, for administrative efficiency, those systems operating at different levels within the sphere. Territorial scale was important because of the increasing military costs, as was centralised taxation. As such, the sovereign state was emerging with a programme for its own particular rather than universal law. To grasp these tendencies, it will be helpful to examine the 'international' legal thought evolving during this period (not that it was known by this name) for an understanding of the regulation of interconnection

---

[75] Kelley, *Human Measure*, p. 114.   [76] See ch. 2, section 2.1.4, pp. 31–2 above.

amongst political bodies in Europe and their constitution. This will also assist an understanding of the role of God, and beliefs in ultimate reality and meaning, in the construction of legal authority and order. God, as maintained by the papacy and its universalistic canon law, was on the way out of international legal theory.

6.3 The decline of the Christian commonwealth

What were to become particular state legal systems had been, in the case of each state or principality, a system of royal law in a plurality of legal systems constituting the universalistic legal pluralism of later medieval Europe. The other systems such as feudal, urban, mercatorial and manorial law were tempered by the increasing territorial centralisation of this state royal law, and the papacy's universalistic canon law at a supranational level. When that purportedly universal papal law began to lose authority, state legal particularity, in the form of the royal law, was left with no real check. The emerging state law was authorised mainly by new theories of political representation and consent, alongside older notions of theologically justified right to rule. An idealistic, universalistic trend for the emerging international law was now to be observed, theoretically reliant upon human will mediated by states, signifying a secular rather than Christian political approach to world order. This was to be known as the movement from the Christian commonwealth towards European public law (*ius publicum Europaeum*). This also symbolised the longer term move from our rhetorical holy Roman empire and the real Holy Roman Empire (representing European unity in a more than symbolic fashion in the fourteenth century)[77] to a paradigm more driven by a secular and economic universalism.

Thus followed a contest between particular, political ways of conceiving authority (positivism) versus purportedly universal (naturalist) ways. Although initially grounded in theology, this political approach catered to a self-referencing normativity which tended to delegate normative power to political, institutional authorities on the exterior orientation of the Space Axis. Onwards from the twelfth century, writings grew in sophistication and compellability about the power of the church including popes, and secular authorities including emperors, kings and the rights of subjects, amongst and between themselves.[78] Not simply academic musings, social theories are of utmost importance in these circumstances. The structure of legal orders is determined by 'the particular intellectual and political style of the leader of the time', according to Wilhelm Grewe.[79] As Philip Allott has written, '[t]he total social process of every society contains a struggle to control the commanding heights of theory. The

---

[77] Jacques Le Goff, *The Birth of Europe*, trans. Janet Lloyd (Oxford: Blackwell Publishing, 2005), p. 183.

[78] See generally Pennington, *The Prince and the Law, 1200–1600: Sovereignty and Rights in the Western Legal Tradition* (Berkeley: University of California Press, 1993), pp. 4, 37, 46 ff.

[79] See Grewe, *Epochs of International Law*, p. 23, writing about the Spanish, British and French periods of paramountcy in European international law.

history of every society is also a history of that society's theories.'[80] The theories of positive and natural law, and the decreasing role for Christendom, are therefore crucial for understanding what was happening at the level of legal authority as state societies collected on fragmented territorial lines.

6.3.1 The post-scholastic period

Shortly after Aquinas, Dante (1265–1321), in *De Monarchia*, contended that the temporal power came directly from God (although subject to the pope in certain church matters which connected earthly and eternal life).[81] This was part of a vision for a single world state.[82] Most original and relevant for present purposes was Dante's conception of human unity, *humana civilitas*.[83]

The break of jurisprudence into factual positive laws which could be derived from abstract natural laws (which were hypothesised) was set in train by Marsiglio of Padua (1280–1342). He proposed, in *Defender of the Peace* (1324), a primordial theory of popular sovereignty which bridged medieval imperial and modern republican thought.[84] This he based upon his personal experience of the communal dynamic of Italian city-states, which had to that time been relatively free from public clerical interference, now requiring defence.[85]

Marsiglio argued that the church comprised the whole church community, and not just the priesthood. The priesthood, he submitted, was a human construct for the benefit of the civil community. The civil community assumed an importance hitherto unrecognised. Because Christ judges in the future world, and it is the temporal ruler who maintains the peace for the priesthood to do their work which is primarily of importance only in encouraging civil obedience, the ruler alone is essential to the well-being of society.[86] That is to say, the church, and Christ, were too far in the future to be relevant, politically, to the present. The well-being of society depended upon the rational agreement of citizens to the standards of the executors of justice. According to Marsiglio, the social order should not be paternalistic along the lines of the family either, because, as Aristotle wrote in the *Ethics*, there is no relationship of civil justice between father and son.[87] There had to be a human reason – a civil

---

[80] Philip Allott, *Eunomia: New Order for a New World* (Oxford: Oxford University Press, 1990), [12.41].   [81] Barber, *Two Cities*, p. 433.

[82] David Gress, *From Plato to NATO: The Idea of the West and its Opponents* (New York: The Free Press, 1998), pp. 223, 363.   [83] Muldoon, *Empire and Order*, p. 93.

[84] Cary J. Nederman, 'Empire and the Historiography of European Political Thought: Marsiglio of Padua, Nicholas of Cusa, and the Medieval/Modern Divide' (2005) 66 *Journal of the History of Ideas* 1–15.

[85] See Quentin Skinner, *The Foundations of Modern Political Thought*, 2 vols. (Cambridge: Cambridge University Press, 1978), vol. I, pp. 18–22; Antony Black, 'Communal Democracy and its History' (1997) 45 *Political Studies* 5–20, 13.

[86] Joan Lockwood O'Donovan, *Theology of Law and Authority in the English Reformation* (Atlanta: Scholars Press, 1991), pp. 22–6.

[87] Cary J. Nederman, 'Private Will, Public Justice: Household, Community and Consent in Marsiglio of Padua's *Defensor Pacis*' (1990) 43 *Western Political Science Quarterly* 699–717, 703–5.

justice – behind legal relationships, not simply a law based in habit or custom for the sake of custom. Therefore the rigid authoritarianism of the papacy could not be legitimate, in his view. Distinguished from Aquinas,[88] law for Marsiglio was concerned with the exterior dimension of social welfare, not the interior dimension of individual salvation on the Space Axis.[89]

Secularisation of law and authority are apparent in this thinking. That is, the mystery of the biblical, legal texts, guarded by a papacy with a custody theologically grounded in the words of Christ himself to St Peter,[90] was being dislodged as the binding source of authority which attracted the interior, moral, religious allegiance to its political authority. The church was being conceived more in terms of a civil institution, not properly the domain of the mysteries and political vagaries of Catholic political theology being played out in real life. Yet, for this proposed realism, there was a cost. If authority was to come from the people (although still a privileged few from the nobility and royal households), that authority could not be hung upon the same universalistic moral hooks of mysterious, sacred canon law and Roman law. This style of terrestrial authority from the people was similar to, but heretically overshot, the conciliarist notion[91] of God's will being mediated through the people's election. Marsiglio also modelled not only a direct sovereignty but a delegated authority[92] – by analogy, what Rousseau was later to call 'the general will' – by which individuals delegated some autonomy to elected or hereditary representatives. That could also attract moral allegiance because, after all, individuals were being self-propelling of their own norms. Interior norm generation and allegiance, however, can be alienated in this process by virtue of the delegation of that human capacity to a representative body making decisions without recourse. This occurred over many centuries, arguably to the detriment of the twentieth-century concept of law.

The fourteenth century featured the germination of discontent with the purportedly universal power and its guise of the holy, imperial norms which sought to bind Western Europe through Christianity. A constitutional discourse developed around the projected universality of the emperor and papacy and the more local constituencies within the empire. Bartolus (1310–52) reached a conclusion about authority similar to that of Marsiglio on juristic grounds. In Roman law, the citizen transferred all power to the emperor although maintained the power to make customary law, tacitly.[93] Bartolus and Marsiglio advocated

---

[88] See ch. 5, section 5.4, pp. 109–10 above.

[89] J. M. Kelly, *A Short History of Western Legal Theory* (Oxford: Oxford University Press, 1992), p. 136.   [90] See ch. 4, section 4.4.1, pp. 84–5 above.

[91] Skinner, *Foundations*, vol. II, p. 37. See generally Brian Tierney, *Foundations of the Conciliar Theory: The Contribution of the Medieval Canonists From Gratian to the Great Schism* (Cambridge: The University Press, 1955 reprinted 1968).

[92] Skinner, *Foundations*, vol. I, p. 62.

[93] Floriano Jonas Cesar, 'Popular Autonomy and Imperial Power in Bartolus of Saxoferrato: An Intrinsic Connection' (2004) 65 *Journal of the History of Ideas* 369–81.

city rule by 'the people as a whole'. Monarchs are best elected openly (and not in fear) rather than inherited, with limited discretion. Government should be answerable through administrative checks between magistrates and ruling councils.[94]

William of Ockham (1285–1347), in this vein, advocated a meritocratic intellectualism. By questioning scholasticism, and 'the Anselmian concept of "faith itself seeking understanding" ',[95] a sceptical rift was rent in the balance between faith in the given order and reason. This was radical. The given order was not necessarily rational. The positive law from earthly rulers and natural law became more distinguishable. Ockham maintained that the law of nations (*ius gentium*), which purported to regulate relations between peoples by reference to their rulers according to custom, could not be derived from the natural law, although this law of nations could be equal with natural law if natural law were considered as divine positive law – that is, as willed law. This distinction between reason and will led to the breakthrough that, 'for a precept to be normative, it must be commanded, either by God or human authority'[96] – therefore not simply found in natural law or reason without human consent. God's will, revealed in the Bible, could authorise divine positive law; consent, not reason alone, became the key device for legitimating human law.

Even though papal supremacy came from God, under this new humanist approach, the electors of the pope were the 'ministers of God's ordination', involving human agency in the constitution of papal authority. Furthermore, Ockham argued against the universalism of church hierarchy if it contravened human insight. The implication for the papacy was negative, for those best qualified to correct errors were those most capable of demonstrating them. Erudite theologians who ranked more highly than the more lowly educated prelates should wield authority in the church, for they possessed the intelligence to point out errors. That is not to say that Ockham thought the pope did not have spiritual authority over the emperor: he thought the pope did have that power, in spiritual matters involving the correction of sin.[97] Nonetheless, the pope should rule with the knowledge and consent of the church, confining papal government to those things relevant to eschatology (the futurist doctrine of the end times). Ockham also made a valuable contribution to human rights in support of the Franciscan monks' renunciation of property, by holding that they still had natural rights to the necessities of life derived from nature, without any human law grant.[98]

---

[94] Skinner, *Foundations*, vol. I, pp. 62–5.

[95] Jaques Le Goff, *Intellectuals in the Middle Ages*, trans. T. L. Fagan (Cambridge, MA: Blackwell, 1992), p. 130.

[96] See Francis Stephen Ruddy, *International Law in the Enlightenment: The Background of Emmerich de Vattel's Le Droit des Gens* (New York: Oceana Publications, 1975), p. 11, citing Daniel O'Connell.   [97] See O'Donovan, *Theology of Law*, pp. 15–19.

[98] Brian Tierney, 'The Idea of Natural Rights – Origins and Persistence' (2004) 2 *Northwestern University Journal of International Human Rights* 1–33, 21–2.

6.3.2 The renaissance

To facilitate interconnection amongst this political diversity, international law began to take shape in the early renaissance period. Permanent embassies started being established abroad.[99] Less reliance continued to be placed in universalistic, ecclesiastical ideas of authority, as the spiritual and moral authority of the Catholic church was increasingly displaced by the political authority of the centralising states.

The developing discipline of international law was stimulated by the tremendous overseas discoveries that were made about that time. During this period also, broadly speaking, modern notions of consent and custom raised the profile of state positivism and particularistic state law over the interior, moral operation of faith, reason and ideals in the universalistic Christian natural law. This marked a major milestone in the secularisation of Western law. Orthodox nineteenth- and twentieth-century jurisprudence rarely ventured beyond the givenness of this split. The imperialistic and culturally arrogant idea of law as exclusively a product of a modern civilised state (exterior and political), separate from witch-doctors, churches and religion (interior, cultural sources of norms), was to become so entrenched.

The 'inter' nature of laws of states, as in '*inter*national law', was an ambiguous achievement of world relations on the way to globalisation as the increased interconnections amongst things that happen in the world. On the one hand, the very thought, in a systematic manner, of 'inter' relations suggests a framework within which increasing interconnections can take place. Yet, on the other hand, the fact that this 'inter' was being worked out between increasingly strong territorial powers suggests demarcation and insulation which, to be sure, erected hurdles to the smooth traffic of these 'inter' relations at the level of human interaction. The 'world society' observations in respect of globalisation suggest those hurdles are now being dismantled.[100] Emerging territorial powers were, however, consolidating a plethora of parcellised sovereignties: taking the example of the Habsburg Holy Roman Empire, 900 units were reduced to 300.[101] Furthermore, this consolidation of sovereignty made possible the standardisation of weights and currencies which had to occur before the type of capitalism upon which globalisation depends could take hold. Therefore *international* law had to develop, as a matter of practice and also of logic, before there could be an increasing *inter*connection amongst things that happen in the world, today, with less dependence on the state. Despite parallels between medieval society and global society, global society would not have succeeded medieval society without the intercession of the Western territorial state and public international law.

---

[99] Davies, *Europe*, p. 523.   [100] See ch. 2, section 2.3.4, pp. 40–2 above.
[101] See Leo Gross, 'The Peace of Westphalia, 1648–1948' (1948) 42 *American Journal of International Law* 20–41, 27.

The work of Francisco Vitoria (1480–1546) marked a major move towards the 'inter' or intercourse aspect of the law between states as it was to develop. He saw the perfection of political communities in their ability to act independently of each other, with their own laws, councils and bureaucracies. In the absence of a society of states, the papacy was otherwise the appropriate arbiter of the lawfulness of state conduct *vis-à-vis* other states.[102] He attempted 'to set up rules of conduct *inter gentes*, between peoples', denying imperial and papal claims to supremacy and favouring, for example, the sovereignty of Indian princes in the face of European colonialism.[103] This appearance of enlightenment was, though, conditional on certain terms which effectively required the Indians to accept Spanish commerce and exploitation of the soil.[104] Vitoria reflects a humanistic recognition of a universal humanity in all races. His contemporary, Vasquez, articulated this in terms of a law between *the rulers* of free peoples, not between the free peoples themselves. So marked the arrival of a *public* conception of international law involving a society which belonged to *rulers* rather than *free peoples*. No doubt it was a goodly thing to have appreciated the universality of humanity in all peoples. Problematic by today's political standards was Vitoria's intention to achieve the conversion of the heathen to Christianity, notwithstanding his apparent tolerance of other races,[105] which imperial powers deployed to justify colonisation. Papal justification of colonial jurisdiction, in addition to the controversial use of 'discovery' as a means for colonial ownership, was based upon the universalistic non-territorially defined power to take care of Christian missionaries. Arguably this was a prescription for the missionaries to disguise territorial jurisdiction in religion with a desire to break the Islamic domination of trade and commerce in the Indian Ocean.[106] This was no original *ius gentium*.

In classical Roman law, the *ius gentium* had been the law thought common to all peoples and applied by all governments (such as laws against murder), as opposed to the particular laws of a people (such as particular penalties),[107] ideas to be found earlier in Aristotle's natural law thought.[108] It developed from the generalisation of principles from various peoples such as the Greeks and Egyptians.[109] Less well known is the war aspect. Gods were invoked in ceremonies accompanying the conclusion of treaties, administered by the *fetiales* (Roman

---

[102] Bobbitt, *Shield of Achilles*, p. 490.   [103] Ruddy, *International Law*, p. 12.

[104] Bobbitt, *Shield of Achilles*, p. 491. See too James Thuo Gathii, 'Commerce, Conquest and Wartime Confiscation' (2006) 31 *Brooklyn Journal of International Law* 709–39, 730–4; and generally Antony Anghie, *Imperialism, Sovereignty and the Making of International Law* (Cambridge: Cambridge University Press, 2006), ch. 1.

[105] Grewe, *Epochs of International Law*, pp. 25, 147.   [106] Ibid., pp. 257–60.

[107] See Barry Nicholas, *An Introduction to Roman Law* (Oxford: Clarendon Press, 1962 reprinted 1991), p. 54, quoting Gaius. Whilst *ius gentium* and *ius naturale* represent the same idea, the *ius naturale* is concerned with natural reason whilst the *ius gentium* looks to the universal application of reason to real situations.

[108] Aristotle, *The Nicomachean Ethics* (Oxford: Oxford University Press, 1925 reprinted 1980), V.7, p. 124.

[109] Paul Vinogradoff, 'Historical Types of International Law' in *The Collected Papers of Paul Vinogradoff*, 2 vols. (Oxford: Clarendon Press, 1928) vol. II, p. 267.

herals) in the *collegium fetialium*. In them originated the formality of the 'just war'. Under oath before the Roman gods, an assertion could be made by a *fetialis* that a nation had violated its duties towards the Romans. Delegates of the *fetiales* 'would demand satisfaction of the foreign nation'.[110] Here the ambiguity of the renaissance idea of *ius gentium* crystallises. The Roman war herald or *fetialis* idea of the *ius gentium* was seized upon by renaissance thinkers, not the alternative notion of it as a true, comparative law of peoples. The war herald idea was to become the prevailing idea of public international law, entrenched by Aquinas and originally advanced by Isidore of Seville (560–636). It pertained to laws of wars, captivity, slavery, treaties and the like.[111]

The *ius inter gentes* of Vitoria and Vasquez was more in the nature of this public international law notion of the *ius gentium*. Vitoria nonetheless appeared to foresee a world community not grounded in treaties, because the people of the world community comprised that community and happened only incidentally to be constituted politically as states.[112] Vitoria further entrenched the difference between positive law and natural law, echoing the dictum of the classical Roman jurist Ulpian, that although slavery could be contrary to the *ius naturale*, as an offence to natural equality, the consent of all peoples reflected in the *ius gentium* could allow the tolerance of slavery as a matter of law.[113] Therefore the positivism of human will could not always be reconciled with the naturalism of reason and indeed did not have to be.

The continued relocation of authority from divinity to human consent is starkly apparent in the notorious work of Niccolò Machiavelli (1469–1527), *The Prince*. Disavowing the Christian commonwealth for the political virtues of the ancients, his work is famed for its advocacy of political expediency. A contemporary of Martin Luther, Machiavelli led a 'Secular Reformation' of the state which sought the subordination of religion to politics through a universalist, civic humanism.[114] By extolling fear as a better political tool than love,[115] Machievelli's political philosophy epitomises the excesses of state law. In appropriate circumstances, law should be coercive from the exterior dimension of the Space Axis of the Space–Time Matrix (through 'fear'), as opposed to being compelling at an interior, personal level (through 'love').

---

[110] Arthur Nussbaum, *A Concise History of the Law of Nations* (New York. The Macmillan Company, 1947), p. 16. If the thirty or thirty-three days of deliberation time allowed to the transgressor passed without satisfaction, in the Republican days, 'the *fetiales* would certify to the senate the existence of just cause of war'; if declared, the war 'would then be "just" as well as "pious"' (p. 17). See generally Alan Watson, *International Law in Archaic Rome: War and Religion* (Baltimore: Johns Hopkins University Press, 1993).

[111] Grewe, *Epochs of International Law*, p. 83.   [112] Ibid., p. 146.

[113] See Percy E. Corbett, *Law and Society in the Relations of States* (New York: Harcourt, Brace and Company, 1951), p. 21.

[114] Graham Maddox, 'The Secular Reformation and the Influence of Machiavelli' (2002) 82 *Journal of Religion* 539–62; J. G. A. Pocock, *The Machiavellian Moment: Florentine Political Thought and the Republican Tradition* (Princeton: Princeton University Press, 2nd edn 2003).

[115] See Niccolò Machiavelli, *The Prince*, trans. N. H. Thompson [1513] (Toronto: Dover Publications, Inc., 1992), VIII, p. 23, XVII, p. 43.

The Six Books of the Commonwealth, by Jean Bodin (1530–96) responded to the crisis of authority in the French religious wars with an absolutist prescription. Sharing some of the social contract absolutism of Thomas Hobbes (1588–1679), Bodin defined sovereignty as 'the absolute and perpetual power of a commonwealth'. This sovereignty was indivisible in nature and reposing in the king (in France), subject to fundamental laws not generally employable against the king,[116] who was answerable only to God. Bodin rejected the Roman notions of *ius naturale* and *ius gentium* for being unable to guide relations between sovereign states. Bodin seems implicitly to have regarded the Roman war herald idea of international law encompassing war, peace and treaties (*ius belli ac pacis*) as being the closest Roman law idea relevant to laws between states.[117] Bodin also refuted the all-too-convenient justifications for universalist Christian rulership which had been based upon the imperial imagery of the four kingdoms prophesied in the Book of Daniel.[118] He showed that certain overlooked (including non-Western) empires were more deserving of count than the Roman Empire, especially as it had come to be represented by Germany.[119]

Amongst other accomplishments, Gentili (1552–1608) assisted the decline of the Christian universe of meaning[120] by separating theology from jurisprudence. Theology should be left to theologians and legal matters should be left to those who study jurisprudence. This was in keeping with the difference between those laws of the Ten Commandments which dealt with God's relation to humans (*ius divinum* – the first table) and those other commandments (*ius hominum* – the second table) which dealt with human relationships with each other. International law, according to Gentili, was of the *ius hominum*, contrary to the insight of Aquinas, centuries before, which had linked universal human law (natural law) to participation in the Eternal Law.[121] Yet there was still in Gentili a naturalist distance from positivism and an aversion to associating law from naturalistic norms with cold, hard, posited facts of social life. As he wrote: 'We are not seeking out facts, nor do we establish law from facts. On the contrary, we examine facts in the light of the law and forejudge what is to be done.'[122] He regarded international law as a universal order 'in which things

---

[116] Drawing upon medieval canonists, Bodin excluded from sovereign absolutism the arbitrary deprivation of a subject's property and the sovereign being judge in his own cause: see Pennington, *Prince*, pp. 280–1.

[117] Jean Bodin, *On Sovereignty:* Four Chapters from *The Six Books of the Commonwealth*, trans. and ed. Julian H. Franklin [1583] (Cambridge: Cambridge University Press, 1992), pp. 1, 31–4, 45, 59–63, 100–2.

[118] Cf. the deployment of this political theology to justify Charlemagne's Roman Empire (ch. 4, section 4.3, p. 83 above) and Roman law in the Lutheran Reformation (ch. 7, section 7.4.1, p. 153 below).

[119] See John Bodin, *Method for the Easy Comprehension of History*, trans. Beatrice Reynolds [1565] (New York: Columbia University Press, 1945), ch. 7.

[120] See Ch. 5, section 5.4, pp. 106–11 above.   [121] Ruddy, *International Law*, p. 17.

[122] Gentili, cited in Corbett, *Law and Society*, p. 24.

divine and human are included . . . and we are members of a great body'.[123] As such, there is the semblance in Gentili of a world society for which humanity bears a universalistic responsibility.

Francisco Suárez (1548–1617) supported the distinction between divine law and human law, regarding the law of nations as a voluntary product of the human will and therefore in the human positive law category.[124] With a 'what's good for the goose is good for the gander' style of secularised universal approach, he criticised the Spaniards for seizing territories from 'barbarous peoples', writing that the discovery of such territory by Spaniards 'gives no support to a seizure of the abororgines [*sic*] any more than if it had been they who had discovered Spain'; 'barbarous peoples can be "true owners in public and private law" '.[125] This continued the train of thought from Vitoria on the distinction between the laws of actual people in states and not just the rulers (*ius gentium intra se*) as opposed to the international law of states and rulers (*ius gentium inter se*).[126] He recognised the interdependent and interconnected nature of human communal existence. It was up to a universal jurisprudence to fill the vacuum left by the departure of the universal jurisdiction of the papal law.[127]

Hugo Grotius (1583–1645) is often called, perhaps unjustifiably[128] given the paragraphs evaluating the sophisticated authors above, 'the father of international law'. He began to refine a law among states, 'based ultimately on natural law, but more directly on custom, consent, and contract' which attempted 'to reconcile the doctrine of state sovereignty, as advocated by Bodin, and the medieval idea of the unity of Christendom'.[129] It was contemporary and connected with Hobbes's social contract thought,[130] although Grotius had a more optimistic view of the natural law.[131] Grotius derived his system of the *ius gentium voluntarium* (voluntary international law) from a public international law notion of *ius gentium* (the war herald as opposed to comparative law

---

[123] Gentili, *De Iure Belli Libri Tres* cited in Gross, 'Peace of Westphalia', 32.
[124] Gross, 'Peace of Westphalia', 34; Kelly, *Western Legal Theory*, p. 211.
[125] See Alfred Verdross and Heribert Franz Koeck, 'Natural Law: The Tradition of Universal Reason and Authority' in R. St J. Macdonald and Douglas M. Johnston (eds.), *The Structure and Process of International Law: Essays in Legal Philosophy Doctrine and Theory* (The Hague: Martinus Nijhoff Publishers, 1983), pp. 19–20.
[126] See Grewe, *International Law*, p. 26; Philip Allott, *The Health of Nations: Society and Law Beyond the State* (Cambridge: Cambridge University Press, 2002), [14.38].
[127] See Cornelius F. Murphy Jr, 'The Grotian Vision of World Order' (1982) 76 *American Journal of International Law* 477–98, 496–7.
[128] See Grewe, *Epochs of International Law*, p. 188. According to Grewe, Grotius's definition of natural law has been criticised as a combination of the definitions of Vasquez and Suárez and others (pp. 194–5). Grotius's work featured a 'simple lack of logical rigour which makes it difficult to clarify some of the contradictions and absurdities of his text' and he described an impossible relationship between the law of nature and the voluntary law of nations (p. 215).   [129] Ruddy, *International Law*, pp. 23–4.
[130] See Kelly, *Western Legal Theory*, p. 212.
[131] Grotius believed in human altruism and right reason, compared with the selfish and asocial tendencies of Hobbesian humans: see Murphy, 'Grotian Vision', 483–5.

notion)[132] which contained the multilateral law of nations grounded in a universalistic natural law,[133] not limited to Christendom. Natural law, for Grotius, was the essence of international commonality. This was, however, a different type of natural law, which could be complemented by positive law. Although positive law lay outside the realm of natural law and reason, in the free will of men,[134] positive law as a matter of will was capable of exterior, political allegiance, through participation in reason. The natural law was the timeless law grounded in reason. For Grotius, this could exist even without God, based upon 'man's natural desire for society', although not without entanglement in theological fictions which showed a thinker seemingly 'hedging his bets' between the power of his own discoveries and the old ways,[135] with a strong sense of the future and improvement. (Grotius, like the other progenitors of international law mentioned so far in this section, appealed amongst other things to the hope of salvation in the effort to obtain compliance with international law.)

A Protestant, Grotius was a stepping stone for the development of secular legal positivism.[136] As such, Grotius applied 'Roman law within the new nation-state system which, however, technically departed from traditional distinctions of the law', grounded instead upon 'brotherhood and universal love based on a natural law that was Stoic-Christian in origin but secular in expression'.[137] Exhibiting the tension between positive and natural law, Grotius does not appear to have been troubled by the paradox that consensus could override the natural law, for example, in the international law prohibition against killing male or female prisoners and hostages which the natural law allowed.[138] He affirmed the rule of law in international law and confirmed the legitimacy of treaties entered with infidels,[139] advancing the exterior, objective quality of international law on the Space Matrix. Unsurprisingly from all of this, Hersch Lauterpacht wrote that it was impossible to classify Grotius as belonging to any of the accepted schools of international jurisprudence.[140]

Samuel Pufendorf (1632–94) stands out, with Grotius, a little oddly in the pattern being established, as a Hobbesian and a naturalist. His naturalism was bold and perhaps retrograde for his time. Pufendorf accepted 'Hobbes' doctrine that nations live in a state of nature in relation to one another, not being subject

---

[132] See pp. 133–4 above.   [133] Ruddy, *International Law*, pp. 24–5.
[134] See Verdross, 'Natural Law', p. 25.
[135] Thus Grotius has been regarded as one who 'admitted that there is truth, denied that we could have knowledge of it, but agreed that many opinions of ours are probable': Thomas Mautner, 'Grotius and the Skeptics' (2005) 66 *Journal of the History of Ideas* 577–601, 579.
[136] See Hedley Bull, 'Natural law and International Relations' (1979) 5 *British Journal of International Studies* 171–81, 175.
[137] James A. R. Nafziger, 'The Functions of Religion in the International Legal System' in Mark W. Janis and Carolyn Evans (eds.), *The Influence of Religion on the Development of International Law* (Dordrecht: Martinus Nijhoff, 1991), pp. 155–6.
[138] Corbett, *Law and Society*, p. 23.
[139] H. Lauterpacht, 'The Grotian Tradition in International Law' in Falk, Krathochwil and Mendlovitz (eds.), *International Law: A Contemporary Perspective* (Boulder: Westview Press, 1985).   [140] Lauterpacht, 'Grotian Tradition', p. 12.

to any common human master'; but rather than holding that this state of nature was a war of all against all, Pufendorf claimed that the state of nature was one of friendship and peace motivated by self-preservation. The laws of nature derived their superiority from God, and natural law governed states in their mutual relations: custom could have no legal authority.[141] This was to prove overly narrow in his utopian vision of international law.

The confusion between natural law and positive law, but the new recognition of the political authority of consent grounded in positive law which was overtaking natural law, was another demystifying chapter in the secularisation of law. The Thirty Years War, to which we now turn, was prompting, in an apocalyptic manner, the concept of a guaranteed state and international order. Despite variations of emphasis amongst jurists in this process, international law (and law in general, as we shall see in the next chapter) was becoming more exterior to individual perceptions of morality, establishing itself as an institution and political instrument at a cross-cultural level (although it was still often disobeyed by emerging states). Interestingly, that political, exterior quality, although decreasing the moral allegiance inspired by a Christian empire and the mass adherence to that idea through a universe of meaning maintained, for example, by ritual churchgoing, could actually attract a new type of moral and cultural allegiance – the allegiance which can come from being able to relate to human consent. Such consent is easily alienable, though, from the norms created by the representative or delegated body.

6.4 The arrival of the state

Developments in technology associated with the military revolution were of great importance to the centralisation which took place and the reorganisation of spheres of containable disruption along state lines, in accordance with our observations about globalisation, technology and sovereignty.[142] From the sixteenth century, within Europe there developed improved musketeers and gunners; the infantry pike to counter cavalry charges; the disciplined professional army; the cannon; increased tonnage, range and manoeuvrability of ships; the improved science of navigation; and systems of trenches and entrapments. In addition, the sovereign model of territorial English and French states proved economically superior at this time for standardising measures and coinage, and establishing territorially organised legal systems. All of these factors required new sources of income for administration by the monarch, and the economies of scale deriving from the centralised government of broader territories.[143]

Despite the tyrannical behaviour of the papacy at times, the early twelfth century Papal Revolution demonstrated the possibilities for good which could arise from a centralised supranational power. Truces and peaces, prohibiting and

[141] Corbett, *Law and Society*, pp. 24–5. See too Murphy, 'Grotian Vision', 487.
[142] See ch. 3, pp. 25, 42–7 above.   [143] See Davies, *Europe*, pp. 578–9.

regulating private wars, were good examples. The papacy's abilities to compel compliance with canon law have already been noted, chiefly through interdiction and excommunication.[144] Excommunication often meant ostracism from one's community, with the prospect of eternal damnation. The papacy did, however, lack the ability to enforce its law in some significant areas. It could not prohibit treaties with non-Christian rulers.[145] Although church norms were articulated with all the political formality of modern law, such norms had become too abstract. All very well it might have been to reign over the hearts of a devout congregation, but it was another thing to be able to compel behaviour in persons wielding power over tremendously large territories with much at stake, economically and as a general matter of sovereign pride in the realm.

In chapter 4, we saw that in the ninth century, Charlemagne as 'emperor' had made the first universal claim to rulership since the Roman Empire; limited, however, to the Latin Christian West (although history does not tell us exactly what he thought the title entailed). The secular sword of government (as opposed to the spiritual sword of the Two Swords constitutional theory) was otherwise grounded in a 'tribe-sovereignty' which pertained to the persons of the tribe or nation and not the fact of territorial location. Territorial sovereignty, on the other hand, was a 'distinctly . . . tardy' offshoot of feudalism – of the personal rights attached to ownership of land. It was not until the Capetian dynasty in France (from the tenth to fourteenth centuries), that a king had the gall to call himself the King *of France* (the territory) and not the King *of the Franks* (the people). He then stood 'in the same relation to the soil of France as the baron to his estate, the tenant to his freehold'. This person who had started as 'the feudal prince of a limited territory surrounding Paris . . . uniting an unusual number of suzerainties in his own person', became King of France.[146]

If in the Capetians can be found the conception of modern nationally and territorially based sovereignty, then the gestation has been signified by the Thirty Years War of 1618–48, delivering the popularly accepted year zero of the sovereign state in the 1648 Peace of Westphalia. The Thirty Years War and its aftermath have been described as the first global war, considering the Dutch maritime expeditions striking at Spanish bastions in Brazil, Angola and Ceylon.[147] The peace settlement at Westphalia was, however, a profoundly Western experience.

6.4.1 The Peace of Westphalia

Leading up to the Westphalian reorganisation, in 1555, at the Peace of Augsburg, Catholics and Protestants had reached a compromise. Lutheranism

---

[144] See ch. 5, section 5.3, pp. 102–3 above.   [145] Nussbaum, *Law of Nations*, pp. 26–7.
[146] Maine, *Ancient Law*, pp. 88–9. See too van Caenegem, *Western Constitutional Law*, pp. 39, 76.
[147] Paul Kennedy, *The Rise and Fall of the Great Powers: Economic Change and Military Conflict from 1500 to 2000* (London: Unwin Hyman, 1988), p. 40.

was to be allowed as the only sanctioned Protestant Christianity, each prince being free to decide the religion of his subjects. In addition, Lutheranism was to be tolerated in Catholic states.[148] This compromise was shaky, as was to be expected from the fractured politics of Europe, in the face of the breakdown of the purportedly universal papal authority.

Two factors would lead to the Thirty Years War, applying Paul Kennedy's analysis of the Habsburg Holy Roman Empire's 'bid for mastery', 1519–1659. First, the Protestant Reformation and the Catholic Counter-Reformation divided Christendom into transnational struggles over Christian doctrine (such that 'Europe' became a more popular term than 'Christendom' for the political geography).[149] Secondly, the establishment Catholic Habsburg leaders, elected often to the position of Holy Roman Emperor, had expanded to lands noted for their 'sheer heterogeneity and diffusion', making rulership difficult.[150]

Following the 'Defenestration of Prague', when Protestants threw two Catholic members of the Bohemian Council from a window in 1618, the Bohemians revolted against their Habsburg ruler, Ferdinand II. The Bohemian crown passed to the Calvinist Elector Palatine, Frederick V. The Habsburgs then pursued German territories and lands lost to the Reformation from the church.[151] Christian IV of Denmark championed German resistance and was defeated in 1629. Into his place strode the Swedish Gustavus Adolphus II, with the aid of French allies. France, keen to break Habsburg domination, joined German Protestant princes and the Swedes, raising up enemies from within Italian city-states and Spain, and also from Dutch provinces. These forces weakened Austrian and Spanish Habsburg power, culminating in 1648 with the Peace of Westphalia.

Recognition was given, in the Peace, to French and Swedish territorial gains. The independence of German princes was guaranteed, as was the independence of Switzerland and the Dutch United Provinces (previously Catholic Spain's 'richest single asset').[152] For those subjects who had been denied freedom of religion outside the religion of their rulers, the component Treaty of Osnabrück granted:

> the right of conducting private worship, and of educating their children, at home or abroad . . . they were not to suffer in any civil capacity nor to be denied religious burial, but were to be at liberty to emigrate, selling their estates or leaving them to be managed by others . . .; [and] a majority of votes should no longer be held decisive at the Catholic and Protestant Diet . . . but should be settled by an amicable 'composition' between its two parts or *corpora*.[153]

The other component Treaty of Münster provided for:

> a moratorium of war, the settlement of disputes by peaceful means, and for individual and collective sanctions against the aggressor, after a delay of three years. . .

---

[148] See Davies, *Europe*, p. 504; Berman, *Law and Revolution II*, p. 51.
[149] Davies, *Europe*, p. 496.   [150] Kennedy, *Rise and Fall*, pp. 32–3.
[151] See van Creveld, *Rise and Decline*, p. 85.   [152] Davies, *Europe*, p. 534.
[153] A. W. Ward cited in Gross, 'Peace of Westphalia', 22.

[T]o facilitate reconstruction . . . two clauses were inserted . . . [O]ne aimed at restoring freedom of commerce by abolishing barriers to trade which had developed in the course of the war, and the other intended to provide a measure of free navigation on the Rhine.[154]

Importantly, this new constitutionalism contained the seeds of the secular, fundamental doctrines characteristic of globalisation in the twentieth century: human rights; and free trade. The Augsburg principle of *cuius regio eius religio* was also confirmed – that is, whoever rules has the right to determine religion.

It seems fair to conclude that these component treaties, collectively the Peace (or Treaty) of Westphalia, marked Western Europe's first effective written secular constitution. In violation of previous usage, these treaties did not even mention God.[155] The waned hopes for a universal Christendom were angrily expressed in the papal denunciation of the Westphalian settlement: Innocent X described it as 'null, void, invalid, iniquitous, unjust, damnable, reprobate, inane, and devoid of meaning for all time'.[156] The Christian commonwealth was now entering a second phase. Although Christianity remained the benchmark ideology in Western Europe, Christendom imploded in this second phase, associated with internal fights for the spoils of colonisation, contrary to the first phase in the eleventh century when there had been a united advance against Islam in the East. At one stage, France even joined forces with the Turks against the Habsburg/Spanish emperor, to the disgust even of the French people.[157]

6.4.2 Territorial consolidation and the decline of universality

The momentousness of the Westphalian settlement is difficult to comprehend, even though globalisation brings us so much change today. That momentousness was symbolic. There was no sudden revelation of a new political model. The Peace of Westphalia was more of a signpost along the long road of territorial consolidation.[158] Of moment is the fact that Two Swords legal pluralism had prevailed for over one thousand years in Europe and it was this undoing which was reflected in the Westphalian treaties. Today, the state which is so easily taken for granted has been around for less than four hundred years.[159] Although state sovereignty is often traced to this treaty, the Westphalian state system which it legitimated does not represent the polar opposite of globalisation, as suggested above.[160] That is because, in the scheme of things, the state was a step in the direction of globalisation. At least 600 parcels of sovereignty were reduced in

---

[154] Gross, 'Peace of Westphalia', 25–6.   [155] van Creveld, *Rise and Decline*, p. 86.
[156] Cited in Davies, *Europe*, p. 568.   [157] See Grewe, *Epochs of International Law*, p. 142.
[158] See Stéphane Beaulac, *The Power of Language in the Making of International Law: The Word Sovereignty in Bodin and Vattel and the Myth of Westphalia* (Leiden: Martinus Nijhoff Publishers, 2004).
[159] See Arthur Eyffinger, 'Europe in the Balance: An Appraisal of the Westphalian System' (1998) 45 *Netherlands International Law Review* 161–87, 165.
[160] See n. 101 and surrounding text above.

the Holy Roman Empire of the Habsburgs as a consequence. Europe, over centuries, was losing the Christian moral allegiance to the Two Swords constitutionalism required for its supranational legal science. The state-centred system of interconnection which we know as public international law is the result of the political failure of medieval spiritual and secular moral universality.[161] What Christian moral universality did survive was splitting along state lines. To be sure, a new mode of imperialism, which avoided that appellation for its medieval Romanist and anti-republican baggage, emerged as some states such as England and Spain acquired overseas territories.[162] Sovereignty, considered in modern times as 'near-absolute law-making power conferred by constitutional law', became, however, a source of certainty; metaphysical and moral questions could be assumed by the 'unquestionable word of the sovereign in the state'.[163] Moral allegiance from the people was not necessarily to follow.

6.5 Lessons for a globalist jurisprudence

Conventionally, the Peace of Westphalia is credited with delivering the modern notion of sovereignty and the European public law system – the *ius publicum Europaeum*. From the perspective of late twentieth-century globalisation and supranationalism, two important constitutional principles of interconnection emerged. First, freedom of religion and associated human rights emerged with free trade in response to war. A prototype 'most favoured nation' equal import tariff trading concept was related generally to the rights of merchants rather than macroeconomics.[164] The Treaty of Münster, we saw, explicitly sought to abolish trade barriers which had developed during the war. In a foreign country, a merchant could expect to be accorded the same status as his own country accorded a merchant from that foreign country. The second important principle of interconnection is that religion became a matter for territorial determination. The king (and later queen) became, in effect, emperor in his (or her) own realm. It symbolised the new gravitational force of the state to be able to propel its own ideologies within its territory or sphere of containable disruption.

The legal pluralism which had embraced Europe became less widespread and less plural as a result of state centralisation. A common Western legal science remained, though. There were still universalist principles of world order

---

[161] Josef L. Kunz, 'Pluralism of Legal and Value Systems and International Law' (1955) 49 *American Journal of International Law* 370–6, 371.

[162] Muldoon, *Empire and Order*, ch. 6 and pp. 144–9.

[163] See Neil MacCormick, 'Beyond the Sovereign State' (1993) 56 *Modern Law Review* 1–18, 12–15.

[164] Nussbaum, *Law of Nations*, pp. 30–1. An early example of such a clause occurred in a twelfth-century treaty between Henry II and the city of Cologne: see Berman, *Law and Revolution*, p. 344. On the origins of the most favoured nation concept in the middle ages and its subsequent development in international law, see H. Neufeld, *The International Protection of Private Creditors from the Treaties of Westphalia to the Congress of Vienna (1648–1815): A Contribution to the History of the Law of Nations* (Leiden: A. W. Sijthoff, 1991), pp. 110–12.

formulated in the naturalist theories of authors such as Grotius, and legal systems remained relatively similar in operation. The political theory of consent was also establishing itself. The historical diffusion of different legal systems in the Europe of this chapter is fertile with significance today, as codification, harmonisation and reform of local, regional and globalist laws are debated, to cope with the modern diversity of laws and interacting cultures amidst common ordering systems.

Something connected to the splintering universality of Christian ultimate reality and meaning is still missing, however, from our historical investigations of law and authority. Protestant political theology explains why there has, in the modern West, been an unwillingness on the part of many to accept that law can come other than from the state, given the ascendency of the 'legislative mentality' which the Protestant Reformations established. Understanding the Protestant Reformations is crucial for comprehending the authority of territorial law and parliament today – institutions directly involved in the mainstream debates about globalisation. Attention must now turn to this transformation of authority and the emerging focus of state law on the exterior dimension of the Space–Time Matrix.

7

The reformation of state authority

If today it is possible to speak of the 'globalisation of law', we might equally speak of the 'state-isation of law' which was occurring in the sixteenth century. Looking to that process shows the triumph of state and territorial constitutions over the universalist constitution of the Catholic church. The arrival of Protestantism receives less than its deserved acknowledgement for its contribution to territorial sovereignty as we know it. By effectively acknowledging the king as emperor in his realm and allowing him to use law as a policy tool through legislation, the Protestant Reformations transformed the universalist Two Swords legal pluralism which operated as a constitution of moderation between the Catholic church and the kingdoms. Capitalism and the rise of market values were to become readily justifiable by a new approach to ultimate reality and meaning which emphasised personal rather than church responsibility for salvation. As the Catholic church lost control of vital social institutions through the de-legitimatisation of its 'holy' doctrine, the state took over those institutions through doctrines more conducive to Mammon.

7.1 The neglect of the Protestant Reformations by legal theory

Neil MacCormick has, in passing, recognised the importance to modernity of 'the epoch of reformation and religious wars in sixteenth- and seventeenth-century Europe'.[1] 'The Reformation has not been investigated as an event in the history of the law',[2] wrote Sir Geoffrey Elton about the Henrician Reformation in England. The Reformations were largely responsible for the processes which made the sovereign state into the constitutional entity challenged by globalisation. The Protestant Reformations are an untapped resource for comprehending the diverse, particular authorities which were established in opposition to the universalism of our rhetorical holy Roman empire.

---

[1] Neil MacCormick, *Questioning Sovereignty: Law, State, and Nation in the European Commonwealth* (Oxford: Oxford University Press, 1999), p. 123.

[2] G. R. Elton, '*Lex Terrae Victrix:* The Triumph of Parliamentary Law in the Sixteenth Century', in D. M. Dean and N. L. Jones (eds.), *The Parliaments of Elizabethan England* (Oxford: Basil Blackwell, 1990), p. 16.

Marsiglio of Padua, whom we encountered in the context of the decline of the Christian commonwealth,[3] was important for laying the philosophical and juridical groundwork. He had maintained that the ruler has his primary origin in the legislator – the whole body of citizens – with the power to depose rulers and to make laws. For Marsiglio, civil law was characterised by its relationship to coercion, not by the verity of its content. The priesthood was relegated, in Marsiglio's thought, from significance in the exterior, political dimension of the Space–Time Matrix to the future orientation of the Time Axis – the future life or afterlife – by being allocated the role of teaching God's promises to men. The truth or falsity of resurrection or eternal reward or punishment was irrelevant; rather, the value was in the fear it struck in the human mind and the engendered social order. The evangelical law was to distribute reward or punishment in the future life in contrast to the worldliness of the civil law.[4] The priestly, other-worldly power was convenient for its use as a political tool for moral manipulation in the present by secular government.

A salient reason for the failure of the universalist moral authority by which the Catholic church had sought to regulate its body of believers was church corruption. Although the buying and selling of church offices (simony) and clerical marriage (nicolaism)[5] were no longer the vices of the day, the selling of indulgences reflected poorly upon the Catholic church. There was much diversity in the practice of the granting of indulgences. Alleged relics of holy personages such as fragments of their bones or associated antiques such as pieces of the Saviour's crucifix were made compulsory purchases for members of the church, to gain access to heaven. The Gregorian Reformation was failing: secular government and society could not look to the Roman church for ultimate moral guidance; the idea that grace and justice were concerns of a government inspired by the church could no longer be taken seriously.[6] Against this background, it became more difficult for the church to maintain its 'supranational' jurisdiction.

Of broad significance to the Western world is the origin in the Reformations of the state domination of law. A legacy of that presumptuous, ontological association of law with the state has been the presentation by contemporary legal theory of supranationality, and more notably the constitutional jurisprudence of the European Union, as threatening for its novelty. There was, in fact, an advanced medieval precedent in Europe.

7.2 Supranationality legislation prior to the Reformations

Medieval Europe had been generally governed, as we have seen, by the Two Swords constitutionalism of shared jurisdiction between the secular ruler and

---

[3] See ch. 6, section 6.3.1, pp. 129–30 above.
[4] Joan Lockwood O'Donovan, *Theology of Law and Authority in the English Reformation* (Atlanta: Scholars Press, 1991), pp. 23–5.   [5] See ch. 5, section 5.2.1, p. 98 above.
[6] See Harold J. Berman, *Faith and Order: The Reconciliation of Law and Religion* (Atlanta: Scholars Press, 1993), p. 87, citing Myron Gilmore.

the papacy, which had comprehended a widespread legal pluralism. Emperors, princes and kings had quarrelled for centuries with popes and bishops, within legal parameters, about the proper scope of their respective secular and spiritual jurisdictions. Other legal systems had subsisted, such as feudal, manorial, urban and mercatorial law.

In France, in the second half of the fifteenth century, Louis XI had insisted that judgments of ecclesiastical courts were subject to the review of the *Parlement* of Paris and priests required permission of the king to travel outside France.[7] Papal taxes, appeals to Rome and election of French bishops were regulated by the French Pragmatic Sanction of Bourges (1438) and the Concordat of Bologna (1516). The German-speaking polities of the Holy Roman Empire, of which there were 364, were subject to the jurisdiction of pope and canon law, emperor and imperial law, and local princes and rulers. German laws comparable to those in France and England (discussed below) were understandably more 'sporadic' in application.[8]

England had statutes of *praemunire*, first enacted in 1353 by Edward III (reigned 1327–77). They were intended to protect the royal courts from interference by foreign courts. They amplified a prohibitory procedure originally devised by Henry II (reigned 1154–89), staying proceedings in an ecclesiastical court until the crown had decided where jurisdiction lay. By suing on a writ of *praemunire*, an affected applicant could seek to prevent a respondent from having a matter heard in a court other than the king's court; ecclesiastical courts, in particular, were held to exceed their jurisdiction when there was a remedy at common law.[9]

7.3 From 'Two Swords' to single sword sovereignty

Henry VIII (reigned 1509–47) was to use parliament to achieve his ends with the result that exterior, political goals could be legislated in a manner which was abstracted from the interior, moral atmosphere of the individual. This is what I term 'the legislative mentality'. The English emergence is explored because it is paradigmatic of the mentality; and other European developments were not as sensational. The general Western experience will later be considered more briefly.

---

[7] See Martin van Creveld, *The Rise and Decline of the State* (Cambridge: Cambridge University Press, 1999), p. 66.

[8] John Witte Jr, *Law and Protestantism: The Legal Teachings of the Lutheran Reformation* (Cambridge: Cambridge University Press, 2002), p. 41, and ch. 1 more generally with respect to Germany.

[9] Sir William Blackstone, *Commentaries on the Laws of England*, 4 vols. [1783] (New York: Garland Publishing Inc., 1978), bk. IV, ch. 8; see too R. H. Helmholz, *The Oxford History of the Laws of England, Volume I: The Canon Law and Ecclesiastical Jurisdiction from 597 to the 1640s* (Oxford: Oxford University Press, 2004), pp. 175–81.

7.3.1 The English experience under Henry VIII

Henry's marriage to Catherine of Aragon had failed to produce a male heir. This failure was a failure to produce a monarch, despite the fact that they had already borne a daughter, Princess Mary. No woman had ever sat on the throne in England in her own right (as opposed to carrying the title 'queen' as an incident of being the wife of the king), and it was doubtful that the subjects would now submit to a queen so enthroned.[10] There was also a fear that Mary might be paired with a Continental ruler[11] (as eventually she was). Henry's bastard son, the Duke of Richmond, could only further confuse the royal succession.[12] King Henry required a son for the constitutional stability of the realm. He had to obtain a divorce from Catherine virtually at all costs. Pope Clement VII was not minded to grant the annulment of the marriage as a matter of theology and also, no doubt, because Catherine's nephew, Emperor Charles V of the Holy Roman Empire, at that time effectively controlled the papacy. Nor would Clement, in the political climate, have wished to undermine papal power by countermanding the dispensation his predecessor, Pope Julius II, had granted Henry to marry Catherine in the first place.[13]

The infertile seeds of Henry's seemingly private issue gestated into a grave constitutional problem at the most public of levels. The mechanism for usurping from the papacy the spiritual jurisdiction over the marriage was ingenious and also historically and legally grounded in Roman law and the logic of legal manipulation. Henry invoked Roman public law, even though it had never been received in England as positive law in any widespread doctrinal sense. Justinian's *Corpus* could be used to support the legal and political superiority of the secular sphere as against the spiritual sphere. Indeed, the Roman law had been used, in a less totalising way, for centuries in Europe for this purpose, in France, Germany, Sicily, Bohemia and even by Richard II in England, who reissued *praemunire* legislation in 1392. *Rex in regno suo est imperator*[14] – the king is emperor in his own realm. In effect, this condensed the power of the Roman 'lord of the world' concept of the emperor (*dominus*

---

[10] J. A. Froude, *The Divorce of Catherine of Aragon: The Story as Told by the Imperial Ambassadors Resident at the Court of Henry VIII* [1891] (New York: Ams Press, 1970), p. 22.

[11] J. J. Scarisbrick, *Henry VIII* (London: Methuen, 1976), p. 202.

[12] S. T. Bindoff, *Tudor England* (Harmondsworth: Penguin, 1964), p. 69.

[13] Catherine had originally been married to Henry's late brother, who had left Catherine a widow. Henry had then obtained dispensation to marry Catherine. At canon law, in order for Henry to have been able to have his marriage with Catherine annulled, there had to be some reason, such as an invalid dispensation being granted to Henry in the first place. On the theological arguments, see Scarisbrick, *Henry VIII*, pp. 219–29, for a discussion of the prohibition in Leviticus 18: 16 and 20: 21, which seems to oppose the prescription in Deuteronomy 25: 5 for the brother of a deceased man to marry the widow.

[14] Azo (1150–1230) had defined the independence of royal authority in this way: see K. Pennington, 'Law, Legislative Authority, and Theories of Government, 1150–1300' in J. H. Burns (ed.), *The Cambridge History of Medieval Political Thought c.350–1450* (Cambridge: Cambridge University Press, 1988), p. 433.

mundi)[15] into a neat territorial package. Henry VIII claimed to be emperor of his realm – of his sphere of containable disruption. The *Corpus* contained the role and function of the late Roman emperor: it 'conveyed the concept of properly understood monarchic government within the framework of that body of law which had always been considered to be the acme of jurisprudential achievement, *even if it had not been "received" as a positive legal system* . . .'[16] [italics added].

The fact that there had been no positive reception of this jurisprudence, yet that it could be regarded in the sixteenth century as an acme of jurisprudential achievement to which resort could be had for authoritative norms, illustrates the transcendent nature of Western legal science. This science could be constrained neither by time nor space. It also demonstrates the historical nature of Western law, in particular the strategy for legitimacy which the past may recursively provide for obtaining allegiance. The use of such fictions is 'a sign of change occurring and a means whereby it does occur' even though the fictions 'are legal rules which *deem* something to be so even though everyone knows it is not' [original emphasis].[17] Henry VIII was no Roman emperor. Secular monarchs had assumed the *plenitudo potestatis* – fullness of power – which derived from the papal vicarship of Christ and the constitutional position of the Roman emperor.[18]

It was an identification with terminology which enabled Henry to apply the formulation by Ulpian, glossed in the canon law by Gratian. This was notwithstanding the fact that Roman jurists 'had never analysed legislative authority, jurisdiction, or delegated power in any systematic way'.[19] The reasoning proceeded like this. Any government worth its name must have control of the public law.[20] 'Public law covers religious affairs, the priesthood, and offices of state': *Digest* 1.1.1.[21] Using this Roman public law theory, Henry was to attempt to do to the church and more what Constantine, the first Christian Roman emperor (reigned 306–37), had done in his time. Constantine, through the

---

[15] On the *dominus mundi* concept, see James Muldoon, *Empire and Order: The Concept of Empire, 800–1800* (New York: St Martin's Press Inc., 1999), ch. 4.

[16] Walter Ullmann, 'This Realm of England is an Empire' (1979) 30 *Journal of Ecclesiastical History* 175–203, 176. See too Franz Wieacker, *A History of Private Law in Europe, With Particular Reference to Germany*, trans. Tony Weir (Oxford: Oxford University Press, 1995), pp. 98–101.

[17] See Keith Mason, *Constancy and Change: Moral and Religious Values in the Australian Legal System* (Leichhardt: Federation Press, 1990), p. 68. It may be harsh to dismiss such archetypal legal reasoning as 'historical fabrications' as does van Creveld, *Rise and Decline*, p. 84. Law and constitutional development are invigorated by the finding of fictions and the making of assertions by analogy: for example, the church as the bride of Christ, the king as the head, the pope as the holder of the keys to heaven, the king's body personal and body politic, We the People of the United States etc.   [18] Pennington, 'Law, Legislative Authority', pp. 435–6.

[19] See Pennington, 'Law, Legislative Authority', p. 430.

[20] Ullmann, 'This Realm of England', 179–80.

[21] Theodor Mommsen and Paul Krueger (eds.), *The Digest of Justinian*, trans. Alan Watson (Philadelphia: University of Pennsylvania Press, 1985).

application of corporate status, had given legitimate constitutional status to the church whilst keeping it subordinate to the fully applicable public law. As a corollary, Constantine's imperial right to convoke church councils was conceived to be within the public law. But Constantine did not interfere with the 'complex christological matters': he was '"the overseer of the *external* matters" of the Church' [italics added]. This is very significant. Interior moral allegiance on the Space Axis was thought even then to come from the interior spiritual realm governed by the church. This important Constantinean distinction 'between internal and external matters was, as it were, canonised in no less a place than the crowning formula in most royal coronation orders of medieval Europe'. Ingenious prescience on the part of the young Prince Henry (or his advisors) was to give him even greater regal licence. The changes reserved the king's right to act within the terms of the Roman public law in his function as emperor of his realm. Secondly, by using the terms 'royal' and 'imperial' jurisdiction, and 'crown' and 'dignity' as interchangeable terms, Henry could be constituted within Roman public law the more boldly.[22]

The Act in Restraint of Appeals was the vehicle by which this constitutional innovation was implemented.

> Where by divers sundry old authentic histories and chronicles . . . this realm of England is an empire . . . governed by one supreme head and king . . . with plenary, whole and entire power . . . to render and yield justice to . . . all subjects within this realm, in all causes . . . without restraint or provocation to any foreign princes or potentates of the world.[23]

The 'divers . . . histories and chronicles' upon which the new political theory was founded made the Act in Restraint of Appeals the only act to call for the testimony of historians for legitimacy.[24] It was by this reasoning that the scope of the Act in Restraint of Appeals could be legitimate, and the course of English history altered: the monarch could have absolute authority in his own realm. The first base of this was the king's ancient personal sovereignty from which derived all judicial authority in the realm. The second base was the king's territorial sovereignty, which was derived from a decretal of Pope Clement V in 1313: from the *lex diocesana*, subjects of the bishop, and by extension the king, could not lawfully be cited to appear in court outside the territorially defined jurisdiction. For the king, this territorially restricted jurisdiction was in fact the kingdom – his newly expanded sphere of containable disruption. In delimiting the domain of the territorial sovereignty of bishops, the pope had made that domain inviolate. Henry could use this to his advantage: 'no jurisdiction could be exercised over the king by an organ *extra territorium*'. Furthermore, Henry cited more canon law against the pope: nobody should be cited to attend court

[22] See Ullmann, 'This Realm of England', 181–3.
[23] 'The Act in Restraint of Appeals': 1533: 24 Henry VIII, c. 12 extract in G. R. Elton, *The Tudor Constitution: Documents and Commentary* (Cambridge: Cambridge University Press, 1960), p. 344.   [24] Elton, '*Lex Terrae Victrix*', p. 21.

if involving a journey of more than two days.[25] The pope could not touch the king in the regnal empery. Specific spiritual (as opposed to Constantinean *external*, ecclesiastical) matters were engulfed by royal authority by virtue of Henry's coronation as *typus Christi* (figure of Christ) and the nomination of the king, centuries before by Bracton, as *vicarius Dei* (deputy of God).[26]

The authority of God had been the starting-point for the Henrician reformers, although the way this authority was accomplished, through parliament as the grand means of legitimacy, was radical. In England, in the Tudor period alone, as much bulk in legislation was enacted as had been in existence to that reign since the Magna Carta.[27] Theologically, Henry's headship of the church was owed to God, under new Church of England thought; however, 'the reality of his powers as supreme head he owed to the common law, enlarged for this purpose by the relevant legislative authority'.[28] In official statements, the royal supremacy was seen to originate not only with the *lex divina* but also with the *lex parliamentaria*; the church existed under the rule of parliament, and not just the king.[29]

The challenge to the social status of natural and divine laws by the king and his parliament opened up the king's law itself to challenge. The very resort Henry made to parliament for monarchical power would be the eventual undoing of monarchical power. Henry had unleashed 'the legislative mentality', which parliament was able to usurp from him and subsequent monarchs. Ultimately, this foreshadowed the parliamentary absolutism of modern times, and the monopoly which the state claims over law. Parliamentary sovereignty was set upon its trajectory, within a limited national territorial sphere of containable disruption.

Needless to say, Henry obtained his divorce, and several subsequent wives with fewer regulatory impediments.

7.3.2 The general Western experience

In Germany, Lutheranism authorised the territorial prince as the ultimate source of law.[30] At the level of Western generality, monarchical and then legislative absolutism was eventually to remove the moral attachments of ordinary people from the laws governing them. The most important institution of law creation was to become the territorial monarch acting with the royal council or parliament, which could declare or make good or bad laws mechanically with

---

[25] Ullmann, 'This Realm of England', 184–8.   [26] Ibid., 197.

[27] See J. H. Baker, *An Introduction to English Legal History* (London: Butterworths, 4th edn 2002), p. 207.

[28] Elton, '*Lex Terrae Victrix*', pp. 25, 27. '[W]ithout the cooperation of parliament it would . . . [have been] impossible to equip the royal supremacy with practical reality' (p. 23).

[29] Ibid., p. 31.

[30] Harold J. Berman, *Law and Revolution, II: The Impact of the Protestant Reformations on the Western Legal Tradition* (Cambridge, MA: Harvard University Press, 2003), p. 65.

the emerging state bureaucracy and associated coercive powers. Increasing popular participation in law could of course increase the allegiance of those involved in the creation of new laws or, much later, the election of politicians for a mandated purpose. That is, however, a very political idea of law. It is also particularistic, because it does not defer to ethical principles in the same way as religiously based, universalist justifications for law do. Although Western laws mainly fall within the principled bounds of rule of law (except in revolutionary times), the basis for legislated laws may be no more inherently just or moral than the political flavour of the month. The Western world was being fractured, and there were to be many different political worlds or states in the increasingly incoherent normative universe of Europe, continuing the demise of our rhetorical holy Roman empire.

Generally, in Western Europe, monasteries were dissolved and there was large-scale confiscation of church property – 25–30 percent of all land – in Scotland, the Scandinavian countries, England, Germany, Bohemia, Poland, Hungary, Switzerland, France and the Low Countries.[31] In the German principalities, Catholic institutions were secularised and populated by lay people, with doctrinal changes implemented by local magistrates.[32] The Habsburg Charles V, as Holy Roman Emperor, was unable to contain the spread of Lutheranism in Germany. Although defeating the Schmalkaldic League of Protestant rulers, he failed to prevent the disaffection in Germany which was encouraged by Henry II of France. When Charles finally abdicated in 1555, Protestant and Catholic rulers 'swept through the country like raging boars', secularising church property.[33] In Germany, secular courts took over 'the crimes of heresy, blasphemy, sumptuousness of dress'; marriage and divorce, wills and charities were also assumed, and cathedral schools, libraries and universities were all established and placed under the secular authorities, together with what we now consider to be the 'welfare' obligations of a government.[34]

In many respects, the changes to the institutions of government were minimal (apart from the new legislative facility). Ecclesiastical courts remained ecclesiastical courts. The hierarchy was, however, capped at a territorial level. In effect, the church became a department of the state and the territorial borders of the realm officially garrisoned the inhabitants.

7.4 Protestant legal authority

In chapter 6, because of space constraints, attention to particular legal systems was concentrated upon Germany and England. So too will attention now be confined to those territories for exploring the new legal philosophy. References

---

[31] van Creveld, *Rise and Decline*, pp. 67–8.
[32] See O. F. Robinson, T. D. Fergus and W. M. Gordon, *European Legal History* (London: Butterworths, 1994), [10.6.1]–[10.6.3].   [33] van Creveld, *Rise and Decline*, p. 101.
[34] Berman, *Faith and Order*, p. 99; and his *Law and Revolution II*, p. 64; Witte, *Law and Protestantism*, p. 84.

to legal authority can be broadly inferred to France and Switzerland when discussion refers to John Calvin in the balance of this chapter.

7.4.1 German legal philosophy

In 1517, Martin Luther famously nailed his Ninety-five Theses on the door of the church of the prince-elector of Saxony, in Wittenberg. The document called for the abolition of papal jurisdiction and attacked abuses of papal authority (including the sale of indulgences) and the interposition of the church between the human and God. Three years later, he fuelled a bonfire with writings including Gratian's *Decretum* and canon laws.

Lutheran legal philosophy was to preach the supremacy of the state given the otherworldliness of Christ's Kingdom. Philip Melanchthon posited this in the Protestant manifesto, the Confession of Augsburg (1530). By this emerging theory, the Catholic church, and the laws which it made and upheld, were unnecessary for the salvation of the soul. Sinful humans were justified by faith alone, not by works or actions (the theological doctrine of solifidianism). Sinners, according to Catholicism, relied upon the divine authority of the priesthood to hear the sinner's confession and to prescribe the works (penance) by which the sin could be purged. Church law, as the revelation of God, sought, in addition, to offer the standards by which humans could minimise sin. Only the Bible, for Luther, offered this possibility. Law, to him, was irrelevant to this process. Salvation could not be earned or mediated by the priesthood.[35]

With echoes of Marsiglio, Luther offered a 'two kingdom' approach to political theology, encapsulating, from the Augsburg Confession, the supremacy of the state over the otherworldliness of Christ's Kingdom. Humans were destined to live first in the earthly and then in the heavenly kingdom. The visible political regime of the secular authority should reign on earth. The spiritual regime of the true church, for him, was invisible and did not extend to law: its visibility could extend only to preaching the word of God and administering the sacraments.[36]

The Thomist tradition of (natural) law had taught that divine revelation was accessible to human reason; that is, in modern parlance, divine truth could be the aim of law. Lutheran law, however, was not interested in truth outside the already divinely posited Bible – law was simply to enforce obedience. For Luther, truth was of the second, heavenly kingdom, not a realistic concern for those inhabiting the temporal first kingdom of the earth. Law as an expression of human reason was 'inevitably corrupted by man's innate inclination to greed and power' and natural law was confined to the Bible,[37] making it difficult to

---

[35] Harold J. Berman and John Witte Jr, 'The Transformation of Western Legal Philosophy in Lutheran Germany' (1989) 62 *Southern California Law Review* 1575–1660, 1582; Berman, *Law and Revolution II*, p. 42; Witte, *Law and Protestantism*, pp. 55–9.

[36] See Berman and Witte, 'Transformation', 1586–90; Berman, *Law and Revolution II*, pp. 40–1; Witte, *Law and Protestantism*, ch. 3.   [37] See Berman and Witte, 'Transformation', 1617–21.

reconcile natural law with positive law.[38] People were unable, without coercion, it was thought, to avoid evil and do good by their own reason and will. An attempt to involve the soul with law or its advancement through interpretation was an incursion into God's power over the soul.[39] Consequently, the Ten Commandments (not scholastic reason) were posited as the basic natural law on Earth and used as a model for positive law.[40] Yet, the Christian conscience was the ultimate source for moral decisions and could disobey civil authorities as a matter of inward reflection with God's grace, although not as a matter of human reason.[41] Here we have a complicated recipe for civil disobedience; although the state could practically smash that disobedience with its political might. The trend to be identified is the written objectification of natural law from an interior morality and conscience into an exterior, more readily identifiable, standard to be administered by the state.

Roman law and the German *ius commune* which was perceived to embody the German spirit were to figure prominently in the thought of the Lutheran jurist Philip Melanchthon. Chiefly the attraction lay in the capacity for peace which the imperial protection of the Roman law offered in the face of the Peasant War of 1524–5. There was also the continued theological association of Rome with the last of the four monarchies of the Old Testament Book of Daniel – a monarchy which offered a universal empire of God-given peace.[42] Roman law was the law of peacemakers for four main reasons: it was written and offered certainty; equity was available if justice required the departure from legal inflexibility; arbitration was extensively described in two titles of Justinian's *Corpus* and equity was suited to arbitration; and, most importantly, according to James Whitman, choice of law technology was very advanced in the *ius commune*. That is, customary, parochial, interior territorial laws could be embraced, on our Space Axis, in the compelling legal science of the more exterior *ius commune*, provided proof could be adduced.[43] The prospects these factors offered, overall, for peace in a violent Germany, were immense. By 1530, this was reflected in Luther's recantation of his early denunciation of lawyers. He now referred to them as 'Angels of the Empire' and 'Apostles of the Kaiser'.[44]

---

[38] Wieacker, *Private Law*, p. 209; Witte, *Law and Protestantism*, pp. 124–5.

[39] Berman and Witte, 'Transformation', 1627.　　[40] Witte, *Law and Protestantism*, pp. 126–7.

[41] Berman and Witte, 'Transformation', 1647; Berman, *Law and Revolution II*, pp. 92–3; and in detail, Quentin Skinner, *The Foundations of Modern Political Thought*, 2 vols. (Cambridge: Cambridge University Press, 1978), vol. II, ch. 7.

[42] James Q. Whitman, *The Legacy of Roman Law in the German Romantic Era: Historical Vision and Legal Change* (Princeton: Princeton University Press, 1990), pp. 4, 21–3. Cf. ch. 4, section 4.3, p. 83 and ch. 6, section 6.3.2, p. 135 above. On the medieval political theology, see Muldoon, *Empire and Order*, ch. 5.

[43] Whitman, *Legacy of Roman Law*, pp. 7–8. On this aspect of the *ius commune*, see ch. 6, section 6.2.1, pp. 120–1 above.

[44] Whitman, *Legacy of Roman Law*, p. 23. On dismounting this antinomian platform of 'jurists are bad Christians' and 'I shit on the law of the emperor, and of the pope, and on the law of the jurists as well' to law as a blessing, see more fully Witte, *Law and Protestantism*, p. 4 and ch. 4.

According to Melanchthon, law was to be used coercively by the state, where necessary, to provide for an order of justice; to ensure safety; to make an example of those punished to remind the people of God's wrath; and to serve as a reminder of judgement for those who did not convert to God.[45] Melanchthon 'redirected the "basic thrust" of the Reformation from being an anti-law movement to a pro-law one'; the new Lutheran state paradoxically came to be administered by something approaching a police state,[46] authorised by prototypical statute as the legislative mentality took hold. This was a major precursor to legal positivism (although Lutheranism did have a place for conscience, properly exercised in faith).

A crucial, interior dimension of legal creativity was being drained from society. Law and its generation were strictly prescribed by the state. Although law was not of itself spiritual, in Luther's opinion, law could still be put to 'spiritual uses' to decrease evil in the world, to increase co-operation and to help fallen man 'to fulfil his calling'.[47] The magistrate was to serve the church, and establish and maintain true religion.[48] A paradox emerges. Whilst Luther sought to remove the layer of the church between God and humans through the catchcry 'every Christian a priest', at the level of law, Luther inserted the state – if not as a level – as an agent of normative intervention between humans and their ultimate reality and meaning. God and the pursuit of meaningful and better living through law were obscured. Superficially, this was a step in the direction of the separation of church and state – although, more accurately, it was a step in the concentration of absolute normative authority being that of the church and state in the hands of the state, leaving the church politically dependent if not impotent.

Equity was transformed, too, in a manner formally different from the English transformation discussed below, although with similar effect. Whereas in both pre-Reformation England and Germany, equity was administered by the chancellor's ecclesiastical court according to the Christian conscience, Johann Oldendorp saw a merger of law and equity. Earthly magistrates were charged with administering all laws equitably, because all rules essentially required flexibility.[49] Conscience was territorialised.

As Henry VIII in England had made the laws of marriage a major issue in the conflict between state and church, so had Luther in Germany. The Holy Roman Emperor, the Habsburg Charles V, endorsed the canon law of marriage, in tune with the pope. Luther maintained that the Roman heritage had passed to the secular rulers of the formerly Roman world, including the Holy Roman Empire

---

[45] Berman and Witte, 'Transformation', 1629; Berman, *Law and Revolution II*, pp. 80–1.

[46] Gottfried G. Krodel, 'Review Essay: The Opposition to Roman Law and the Reformation in Germany' (1993/94) 10 *Journal of Law and Religion* 221–66, 245.

[47] Berman, *Law and Revolution II*, pp. 44, 75–6.

[48] See James M. Estes, 'The Role of Godly Magistrates in the Church: Melanchthon as Luther's Interpreter and Collaborator' (1998) 67 *Church History* 463–83.

[49] Witte, *Law and Protestantism*, pp. 174–5.

of the German nation, entailing the Roman law of marriage as opposed to the canon law. Consequently the emperor was obliged to follow the Roman law.[50] 'The Reformation put an end to the universalist authority of the papal curia, and the Roman empire became a national, German monarchy.'[51] Although not officially to fall until 1806, the Holy Roman Empire came to a theological end with the German Reformation.

7.4.2 English legal philosophy

The English experience embraced aspects of Lutheran theology together with other Continental theologies such as those of Zwingli and Calvin, as part of a seamed 'garment' of 'various intellectual fabrics'. In the English Reformation, law was more infused with God's grace and less positivistic to that extent; God manifested 'His eternal will as law in the creation, preservation, redemption and sanctification of the world'; truth was knowledge of God's laws. The exhortation to righteous disobedience in the event of a ruler's command to violate God's law was similar,[52] whilst still recognising the obligation of subjects to submit to the ruler's will in the ordinary course. As with Lutheranism, this was a dual prescription which could be fraught with the timeless tension between personal morality and government politics.

Like Luther, major English theologians of the time, for example Tyndale and Cranmer, supported the 'every Christian a priest' credo with the aim of universal biblical literacy. The departure from Lutheranism by Erastianism – the English vision for secular control of ecclesiastical matters – was featured in the different function which the English ascribed to church law. Because God ' "withdraws His Hand" (of judgment) for His Son's sake, the civil magistrate should wield his so much the harder for the suppression of sin', representing the Calvinistic 'increased passion for a divinely legislated polity in the church if not in the commonwealth'.[53] Outward forms of religious practice were still important. The interior, personal significance of spiritual and moral belief was still somewhat connected to the exterior, political dimension of being a human in society (although this connection was to be stretched to severance with the development of the legislative mentality).

'The international world of Lutheranism' was present in the thought of Tyndale, who appreciated the opposition of law and gospel, although who, like his predecessors Wycliffe and Fortescue, thought that salvation through Christ and obedience to the law were not in opposition. The law showed up sin and death, whereas the gospel beheld a new life through belief in justification through faith in Christ. That belief – 'the Spirit of Christ' – caused one to

[50] Whitman, *Legacy of Roman Law*, pp. 24–5. On Lutheran marriage law, see more fully Witte, *Law and Protestantism*, ch. 6.

[51] R. C. van Caenegem, *An Historical Introduction to Western Constitutional Law* (Cambridge: Cambridge University Press, 1995), p. 9.   [52] See O'Donovan, *Theology of Law*, pp. 155–7.

[53] See O'Donovan, *Theology of Law*, pp. 159–60.

consent to the law. On the Space Axis, law seems to have captured the inwardness of personal moral allegiance and balanced it uneasily with the outwardness of politically necessary obedience to laws on the Space Axis: 'it gives *outward* form to the *inward* goodness bestowed by the Spirit of Christ' [italics added].[54]

In Thomas Starkey, the civil laws were modelled on natural law, which aimed to perfect civil life; although, as if an afterthought, 'the keeping of the natural law may be enough for salvation',[55] thus depriving civil law of sanctity. Starkey also advocated the transference of constitutional powers, pre-empting the creation of a cabinet from parliament, 'appointed by the assembled parliament and invested with its authority during the period of its dissolution'.[56] All of these theories could provide theological and political justification for the circumscription or expulsion of the activity of the Roman church in England, and the reception of the new Reformation attitude to law and the authority of legislation. Natural law as the law of reason was overtaking natural law as posited divine law. Reason was an increasingly secular *logos* or logic, which was being established as 'reasonable' by virtue of possessing an increasingly popular, territorial mandate.

The new relationship of the ecclesiastical and temporal spheres is well illustrated by the transformation of English equity. Prior to the Reformation, the chancellor of the equity jurisdiction had occupied an ecclesiastical office. The domain of the realm and the domain of the church had met in the chancellor, who could award justice based upon principles of fairness. In equity proceedings, it was the conscience of the defendant which was in question, which required comparison to some objective standard. The 'inner convictions of every Christian' or 'general conscience of the realm' was kept, as one justice put it.[57] Practically speaking, this had brought the representative Christian conscience of the chancellor to bear on the temporality of the realm, on behalf of the king. The equity of the Reformation, however, saw the king's territorial conscience replace that of the medieval chancellor, which was manifest in the new constitutional theory. This was nothing less than '[t]he reduction of conscience to *particularity*' [italics added], as Timothy Endicott writes of equity at this time. The projected *universality* of the chancellor's Christian conscience, following our globalisation theme, was circumscribed and individualised within a territory. No longer was there 'any external check on the law at all, but only an internal process of reconciling a rule to its rationale'.[58] The submission of equity to the common law was confirmed by the Statute of Uses in 1536.[59]

---

[54] Ibid., pp. 56–60.
[55] Thomas F. Mayer, 'Starkey and Melanchthon on Adiaphora: A Critique of W. Gordon Zeeveld' (1980) 11 *Sixteenth Century Journal* 39–49, 46.   [56] See O'Donovan, *Theology of Law*, p. 79.
[57] See Harold J. Berman, *Faith and Order: The Reconciliation of Law and Religion* (Atlanta: Scholars Press, 1993), pp. 71–7.
[58] Timothy A. O. Endicott, 'The Conscience of the King: Christopher St German and Thomas More and the Development of English Equity' (1989) 47 *University of Toronto Faculty of Law Review* 549–70, 562–3; see too Christopher St German, *Doctor and Student*, ed. T. F. T. Plucknett and J. L. Barton (London: Selden Society, 1974), pp. 13, 81–94.
[59] Elton, '*Lex Terrae Victrix*', p. 34.

What of this transformation? With the mechanisation of law and equity as answerable to something purportedly no higher than humans and their political association, parliament was to replace the historically constructed Christian conscience. Conscience lost its inherent transcendence over laws and degenerated into 'a tortuous system of precedent' characteristic of Western legal systems. This transformation was expressed in the new, secular constitution espoused by Christopher St German. With the fall of humans from God's grace in the Garden of Eden, property could be conceived as part of the law of man, because property had not been needed in the Garden of Eden. Human laws were necessary for the ordering of society after 'the Fall'. Positive law could be as important as the natural or divine law. The divine natural law of Exodus 20: 17, 'thou shalt not covet thy neighbour's house' required clarification by the positive law as to just when the house was thine or thy neighbour's.[60] That is, knowledge of nature did not necessarily speak for itself in everyday life. Sensitivity to such '*adiaphora*' – laws without necessarily universal significance,[61] indifferent to salvation[62] – was heightened by Protestantism. Positive law was required to provide the particular implementation of universalist propositions, assuming authority in and of itself.

7.5 Understanding the legislative mentality

The *innovative* as distinguishable from *declaratory* attributes of legislation which were emerging from Reformation political thought and practice were a Western experience. Previously, innovative legislation to address 'the needs of the moment' had been principally associated with the papacy, as a right recorded by Gregory VII in the *Dictatus Papae* in the Papal Revolution, to avenge the subordinate role custom had assigned to the papacy.[63] The innovative legislative mentality was a new or at least only recently emerging phenomenon in the secular realm and it was to increase in intensity in subsequent years.

In Germany, there being no unified state or effective central legislature, the instrument was that of the 'reformation ordinance' as literally a 'reforming' legal tool sometimes called a 'statute', which predated the Lutheran Reformation. Of different types and origins typically in cities and territories, they could be small or massive statements and restatements of varying authority. That they were

---

[60] Endicott, 'Conscience', 558–60, latterly quoting St German's *Doctor and Student*.

[61] Aristotle discusses this concept of *adiaphora*, or 'political justice', as natural justice versus legal justice: e.g., it may have been naturally obvious for a sacrifice to a god to be made in a given context, but the content of the sacrifice itself was a matter of legal, or particular justice: see Aristotle, *The Nicomachean Ethics* (Oxford: Oxford University Press, 1980), V.7, pp. 124–5.

[62] See Skinner, *Foundations*, vol. II, pp. 103–5.

[63] R. C. van Caenegem, *An Historical Introduction to Private Law*, trans. D. E. L. Johnston (Cambridge: Cambridge University Press, 1988), pp. 86–7. As Gregory VII recalled from Tertullian and St Cyprian, Christ said ' "I am the truth". He did not say "I am the custom" ': Harold J. Berman, *Law and Revolution: The Formation of the Western Legal Tradition* (Cambridge, MA: Harvard University Press, 1983), pp. 112, 258.

innovative is demonstrated by the adoption of the new Lutheran doctrines blended with Catholic theology, canonical and civilian law.[64] In France, codification of customs had occurred in the early sixteenth century. Reform was inherent in this process because to establish the correct custom could be a matter of choosing the better of two or more competing customs, although the purpose was not innovation. That there were twelve independent territorial jurisdictions with their own *parlements* meant that even the relatively centralised France made England the most paradigmatic and trailblazing of the modern legislative attitude.[65]

Parliament in England was originally conceived as a court with both legislative and judicial powers, from the time of the Norman conquest in the late eleventh century. Judicial or curial powers were demonstrated by parliament's concern to dispense justice to individual petitioners (a practice which was declining in 1327), although legislative, or in modern terms, executive powers, were exercised in the areas of diplomacy, taxation and public affairs.[66] Medieval enactments, or acts, which we associate by evolution with modern legislation and parliaments, were, though, very different species. Indeed, in the late fourteenth century, the word 'act' was used of a parliamentary product in much the same way as the word was used in the New Testament book, 'Acts of the Apostles': that is, as 'a narrative of things said and done'.[67]

Legislation in medieval England was a royal facility. The king would consult the barons and attempt to obtain their consent, for legitimacy. The legislation of the Magna Carta, settled by King John and the barons in 1215, embodied seminal ideas of liberty including due process, and represented something of a treaty between king and nobles. It was regarded by Sir Edward Coke, writing about it some four centuries later, as 'but a confirmation or restitution of the Common Law'[68] (although critical historical research would point to the inconstant observance of its provisions and its irrelevance in many respects to the commoner).[69] The legislative powers were very different in scope from what we now associate with parliaments. Enactments did not change the common law. There was no clear distinction between adjudication and legislation. Courts and parliament both originated in the royal council which advised the

---

[64] See Witte, *Law and Protestantism*, pp. 15, 43–4, 182–4; Wieacker, *Private Law*, pp. 143–55.

[65] On France, see Robinson, *European Legal History*, [12.2.1]–[12.2.5], [12.5]; and van Caenegem, *Private Law*, pp. 87–94, for the Continent generally. On the background, see Susan Reynolds, *Kingdoms and Communities in Western Europe, 900–1300* (Oxford: Clarendon Press, 2nd edn 1997), pp. 45–51, 302–19; Alan Harding, *Medieval Law and the Foundations of the State* (Oxford: Oxford University Press, 2002), pp. 186–200.

[66] See Jeffrey Goldsworthy, *The Sovereignty of Parliament: History and Philosophy* (Oxford: Clarendon Press, 1999), pp. 29–32.

[67] See Morris S. Arnold, 'Statutes as Judgments: The Natural Law Theory of Parliamentary Activity in Medieval England' (1977) 126 *University of Pennsylvania Law Review* 329–43, 336.

[68] Sir Edward Coke, 'The First Part of the Institutes of the Laws of England, 1628' in James C. Holt, *Magna Carta and the Idea of Liberty* (New York: John Wiley & Sons, 1972), p. 18.

[69] See Edward Jenks, 'The Myth of Magna Carta' [1902], reprinted in Holt, *Magna Carta*, pp. 22–37.

king.[70] Morris Arnold, who emphasises the innovative nature of legislation in its history, admits as inconclusive the evidence in the thirteenth century that legislation went beyond declaration and was innovative, by reference to the silence of Bracton and other thirteenth-century treatise writers. As late as 1341 in England, Edward revoked one of his earlier enactments, because it was 'prejudicial and contrary to the laws and usages of the realm'.[71]

In the late middle ages, parliamentary acts were not subject to the judges. Like modern notions of parliamentary authority, parliament was assumed to represent the consent of the communities of England. This provided parliament with the legitimacy to make declarations of the law and to give certainty to those declarations (for example, removing doubts about the 1483 accession of King Richard III by enactment in 1485). Around this time, such 'declarations' of already existing laws could be considered fictions in so far as the declarations were used to cloak the innovation; a party could sue in parliament, according to Chief Justice Herle, to make a new law – parliament could make and unmake law.[72]

By the 1530s, and the Reformation of Henry VIII, it became acceptable to credit parliament with the power to dispose of the crown, even on the admission of Sir Thomas More, who steadfastly refused, nonetheless, to accept the power of parliament to terminate the power of the papacy in spiritual matters.[73] Nevertheless, recall the 'divers . . . histories and chronicles' to which Henry VIII appealed in order to ground his Act in Restraint of Appeals, attempting to disguise a radical break within a conservative tradition.[74] History was still very relevant for legitimacy, as the Act in Restraint of Appeals shows, suggesting at least a preference for declaratory legislation, even if just a cloak. In the face of parliamentary imperialism versus his impending Catholic martyrdom, Sir Thomas More's parting public words were that the parliament could do anything except the impossible. This was a stand for universalist natural law against particular state law – in today's terms, a stand for perceived timeless norms against incompatible state legislation (for example, positing abortion and homosexual marriage).[75] The impossible, for this former barrister, parliamentarian, author, diplomat and chancellor, was the attempt to overthrow the papal jurisdiction, although there were many grades of possibility open before this (then seemingly) drastic stage was reached.[76] Possibilities for legislative innovation by consent were unleashed, although even late that century, Richard Hooker records that statute often declared what was already common law.[77]

---

[70] Baker, *English Legal History*, p. 204.   [71] Harding, *Medieval Law*, p. 256.
[72] Goldsworthy, *Sovereignty*, pp. 29–40.
[73] See J. Duncan M. Derrett, 'The Trial of Sir Thomas More' (1964) 79 *English Historical Review* 449–77; Richard Marius, *Thomas More: A Biography* (London: J. M. Bent, 1984), chs. 26, 27.
[74] See pp. 149–50 above.
[75] See e.g. Blake D. Morant, 'Lessons from Thomas More's Dilemma of Conscience: Reconciling the Clash Between a Lawyer's Beliefs and Professional Expectations' (2004) 78 *Saint John's Law Review* 965–1009.   [76] See Goldsworthy, *Sovereignty*, pp. 59, 134.
[77] J. M. Kelly, *A Short History of Western Legal Theory* (Oxford: Oxford University Press, 1992), p. 185, citing Hooker's *Laws of Ecclesiastical Polity*.

Prior to this time, there may have been odd demonstrations of innovation such as the statutes of mortmain (preventing corporations from inheriting land thereby preventing the avoidance of feudal dues) and the creation of new types of estate in land, but the fact that legislators and kings still felt compelled to make reference, as Henry VIII did, to custom and to God, indicates that even the mind-set projecting late medieval or early modern constitutionalism was far from the atheistic, electoral term-driven, goal-justified legislative mentality of today. Statutes in the late medieval period were policies for the judges which were to be 'extended and restricted', reflecting 'the different relationship between legislation and adjudication that prevailed at that time'. Powers of the parliament, courts and King's Council were blurred, each with the capacity to draft and interpret legislation and to adjudicate.[78]

Checks and balances on government power had not, therefore, been espoused in a modern sense. Not quite a modern legislative prototype, at least until the Reformation there was a common law attitude of integrated commitment to the exterior enunciation of positive law, morally referenced to permeating Christian principles on the Space Axis, historically revealed in case law on the Time Axis. That is, there was still a personal, moral aspect to the laws of the community nonetheless posited from outside the community by the council, legislature and judiciary. This process was subject to the interpretation of judges trained in a common law reasoning which was entwined with the reason and custom from the history of the community. This was Sir Edward Coke's 'artificial reason' of the law, which did not just defer to government policy.

Even in the early seventeenth century, parliament was regularly called a court, although a court which could go beyond discovering and interpreting law. As parliament became more associated with reason, and the common law with a reason grounded more in custom, it seems that parliamentary innovation grew in legitimacy. Because of its size and representative qualities, parliament was better able to 'judge' what was best for the welfare of the people.[79] Courts, therefore, were more concerned with *nomos* or custom. Parliament grew into a more *logos*-orientated or rational institution, the rationality of which was political and increasingly associated with limited democracy.

Medieval notions of the created universe and the centrality of religion were not dislodged by the Reformations in one sweep of the sword. Significantly, though, the conception was taking shape that the state was rightfully the law-making monolith. Whereas the Catholic church had shared in government, wielding the 'spiritual sword', state government took over both swords. Reformation governments seized the spiritual sword in one hand and ruled with the secular sword in the other, gradually melding from these two swords one double-edged sword. The *interior*, personal, spiritual, moral allegiance edge of this sword would grow increasingly blunt. The *exterior*, innovative, political edge would grow increasingly sharp. The *past* would become less relevant to law

---

[78] Goldsworthy, *Sovereignty*, pp. 44–5.   [79] See Goldsworthy, *Sovereignty*, pp. 114–20.

as legislation. The vision for the *future* would become increasingly changeable and less rooted in the past. Thomas More's fate was a juncture for these trends. The martyr's execution is to be associated with the incomplete but irreversible severance of legislation from its erstwhile predominating function of declaring the status quo. At the very same time, the state as we know it was arriving.

7.6 Religion, Mammon and the spirit of capitalism

The ultimate, irreducible social authority of the God of our earlier enquiries has changed considerably. No longer was the direct connection between God and the purportedly universal Christian community upheld politically through the Catholic church. Whilst that connection with the Catholic church was to some extent usurped by state monarchies, the authority for law was very much transformed. Consent became important as a strategic device for fostering legitimacy, organised territorially, legitimated by territorial beliefs in ultimate reality and meaning. Less mystery could be tolerated at a political level as law would become more openly instrumental for achieving present goals. Social life, and law, became subject to more earthly strategies for creating and maintaining authority.

Although enquiry into the doctrines of the Last Supper and Christian justification in a book about law and authority may at first seem abstract, recall the insight of Philip Allott about social theory. 'The total social process of every society contains a struggle to control the commanding heights of theory. The history of every society is also a history of that society's theories.'[80] These Reformation theologies well illustrate how legal authority was transformed into an ideology less attuned to Christian mystery, more compatible with material values.

7.6.1 Outgoing God in the Last Supper

About the time of the Reformation, the nature of the eucharist[81] – the Christian communion ritual of the Last Supper – was particularly divisive. The Catholic church regarded this sacrament, undertaken in regular services and central to them, as a re-enactment of Christ's sacrifice. The church's doctrine of 'transubstantiation' held that the bread and wine of the ritual were essentially if not mysteriously transformed into the elements of Christ's body and blood, appearing only outwardly to be bread and wine.

Luther departed from the dogma of transubstantiation, asserting that the sacrifice was a unique event incapable of re-enactment. He believed the eucharistic

---

[80] Philip Allott, *Eunomia: New Order for a New World* (Oxford: Oxford University Press, 1990) [12.41]. See ch. 6, section 6.3, pp. 128–9.

[81] The eucharist is a church sacrament which celebrates the last supper of Christ. There, Christ had broken the bread, saying 'Take, eat; this is My body'; and, taking the cup, said 'Drink from it, all of you. For this is My blood of the new covenant, which is shed for many for the remission of sins.' See Matthew 26: 26–28 (NKJV).

blessing of the bread and wine to result in a real presence which amounted to the 'substance' of the body and blood through grace and faith coexisting in and with the bread and wine. This was the 'consubstantiation' position. The distinction was subtle but politically significant. Consubstantiation regarded the earthly objects of the bread and wine as having received the divine addition of the body and blood; transubstantiation considered a complete, elemental transformation of the bread and wine into body and blood with only the outward appearance of bread and wine. Some, such as Zwingli, denied a transformation altogether, regarding the ritual as purely symbolic.[82] How was this politically significant?

Religious cosmologies make for powerful political statements.[83] Oddly perhaps, from today's perspective, the mysterious ritual of communion was a central symbol of power. Sacraments in general had tremendous authority and significance, prompting some individuals even to eat the vomit of others.[84] The ritual of the eucharist was about getting as close to Christ as was possible in earthly life and seeing divinity manifested on earth. The sacrament was, for Christians:

> both a conduit of power and a representation of the manner in which divine power operated within their world of experience . . . In the late Middle Ages, both theological definitions and popular religious practices placed the eucharist at the very center of religious life and underlined its status as the preeminent locus of divine power within the Christian's world of experience.[85]

The Protestant theology of the eucharist provided a new way of symbolising power. Divine power could not be located in a visible object or institution. This influenced the way ordinary people understood and related to authority. New beliefs about the eucharist operated to undo the intimate, organic ties of ritual and authority which had been so easy for the individual to relate to because they captured personal, moral allegiance. God was understood by the Protestants to be too transcendent to reside in earthly objects and also institutions.[86]

Criticism became more acceptable and the complexity of authority became apparent. Liberty crept further into popular consciousness, not least because the printing press made accessible not only the Bible but also theology in vernacular languages. Personal interpretation and judgement assumed greater

---

[82] See G. R. Elton, *Reformation Europe 1517–1559* (London: Fontana, 1963), pp. 71–3.

[83] Gerald Strauss, 'The Idea of Order in the German Reformation' in *Enacting the Reformation in Germany: Essays on Institution and Reception* (Aldershot: Variorum, 1993), XIV, p. 10. Strauss continues: 'The extent to which their assertions about God's universe are true, or even believed to be true, matters much less than does their utility as legitimizing phrases and enabling clauses for the accomplishment of particular political aims.'

[84] Some medieval priests felt inspired to eat the vomit of a dying man who had just received the sacrament of Last Rites, on the basis that the vomit had been transformed into the body of Christ: see Robert A. Hinde, *Why Gods Persist: A Scientific Approach to Religion* (London, Routledge, 1999), p. 46.

[85] Christopher Elwood, *The Body Broken: The Calvinist Doctrine of the Eucharist and the Symbolization of Power in Sixteenth-century France* (New York: Oxford University Press, 1999), p. 4.   [86] See Elwood, *Body Broken*, ch. 2.

legitimacy.[87] God did not intervene directly in earthly rituals by inhering in objects such as bread and wine. Nor could divine authority be thought, convincingly, to inhere in the institutions of human government. The hand of God could not be claimed, without debate, to buttress human institutions.

7.6.2 Incoming Mammon in the spirit of capitalism

Something pivotal to the evolution of modern globalist authority happened around this time too, in addition to the new significance of the state as the single sword of sovereignty. Theological attitudes towards money and industry were changing. The authority underlying our rhetorical holy Roman empire was ceding to a new, secular authority. This is not to suggest that the change in theology *caused* the increased development of capitalism, which is not of present concern. It is to suggest that the justifications for such activity changed in response to the times, explaining *how* emerging norms and law could become authoritative.

The trend is well illustrated by starting with the medieval Catholic approach to the charging of interest, and comparing it to the emerging Protestant views. Usury provides a salient example of the reach of ideas of the invisible God into visible money and trade. The Old Testament prohibition against usury provided:

> Thou shalt not lend upon usury to thy brother; usury of money, usury of victuals, usury of any thing that is lent upon usury: unto a stranger thou mayest lend upon usury: but unto thy brother thou shalt not lend upon usury: that the LORD thy God may bless thee in all that thou settest thine hand to in the land whither thou goest to possess it.[88]

For the Jews, this stipulation prohibited the charging of interest on money lent to fellow Jews. It allowed, however, the charging of interest to 'a stranger', so long as it was not 'unto thy [Jewish] brother'. Consequently the Jews lent money outside their religion, to 'others' rather than 'brothers'. Medieval Christianity rejected as obnoxious and anachronistic this discrimination against the other, in the universalistic quest to treat the 'other' as the 'brother'.[89] Christianity purported to be a universal religion, transcending the tribalism of Judaism. For Christianity, logically there could be no usury amongst the many different sorts of people who were called as brothers and sisters to follow Christ regardless of race. When members of heathen religions, including Jews, were chosen for loan contracts featuring interest, the usual prohibition of usury did not apply. The heathen had apparently chosen not to be part of the universal family.

There were other theological reasons for the prohibition of usury in addition to the divine, biblical proscription. A merchant was not permitted to demand a

---

[87] See Elwood, *Body Broken*, pp. 4–5, ch. 4.   [88] Deuteronomy 23: 19–20 (KJV).
[89] See Benjamin N. Nelson, *The Idea of Usury: From Tribal Brotherhood to Universal Otherhood* (Princeton: Princeton University Press, 1949), pp. xv–xxi.

greater payment from a person who could not pay the account on time. To do so, the merchant would be trying to sell what he did not own. Time did not belong to the merchant; time belonged to God.[90] Furthermore, profit itself was not endorsed early on: merchants were poorly regarded if they traded for gain as opposed to what was just reward for their efforts,[91] and the canon law condemned ' "shameful" profit (*turpe lucrum*, "filthy lucre")'.[92] Of course, a universal stipulation appears never to be universally obeyed as a matter of factual observation. Exceptions to the law of usury were available. For example, just as self-defence, insanity or provocation do not undermine the universal law against murder, exceptions to usury might occur were a loss to be incurred through lending, or an agreement provided for a financial penalty if the loan was not returned at the agreed time, allowing the lender to receive compensation. A lender holding a pledge could deduct from it expenses for caring for it. The church could lend money for church purposes, such as crusades.[93]

Although usury had been losing its taint since the thirteenth century, it was not until the Lutheran Reformation that usury achieved acceptance, when the Mosaic law was pronounced dead and not binding on the conscience.[94] Spurred on by Reformation doctrines, usury was to become almost thoroughly acceptable within Christian states by the seventeenth century. This was accomplished hand-in-hand with the dramatic spiritualisation of productive labour and greed for gain, or Mammon.[95] The Protestant Reformations boldly dispensed with Mosaic law and made more acceptable the unlimited lust for gain prevalent in all societies.[96] The developing rationalistic economic society was structured not so much on custom or tradition but on the attainment of economic

---

[90] Jacques Le Goff, 'Merchant's Time and Church Time in the Middle Ages' in *Time, Work, & Culture in the Middle Ages*, trans. Arthur Goldhammer (Chicago: University of Chicago Press, 1980), p. 29. Similarly, university teachers were not supposed to charge money for selling knowledge, which only God owned: Jacques Le Goff, *The Birth of Europe*, trans. Janet Lloyd (Oxford: Blackwell Publishing, 2005), p. 121.

[91] Raymond de Roover, 'The Scholastic Attitude Towards Trade and Entrepreneurship' in *Business, Banking and Economic Thought in Late Medieval and Early Modern Europe* (Chicago: University of Chicago Press, 1974), pp. 339–41.

[92] Harold J. Berman, *Law and Revolution: The Formation of the Western Legal Tradition* (Cambridge, MA: Harvard University Press, 1983), pp. 248, 337–8. The canon law is well covered in John Gilchrist, *The Church and Economic Activity in the Middle Ages* (London: Macmillan, 1969).

[93] Malcolm Barber, *The Two Cities: Medieval Europe 1050–1320* (London: Routledge, 1992), p. 76.

[94] Nelson, *Idea of Usury*, p. xix. In Islamic law, the prohibition against usury persists, a loan for purchase of property being disguised as, in effect, a licence to use the property which is owned by the lender.

[95] Scriptural references were used to support this idea. Some examples are: Christ's parable of the talents, where those who gained the greatest return on a money gift were rewarded (Matthew 25: 14–30); Proverbs 22: 29 – 'Do you see a man who excels in his work? He will stand before kings; He will not stand before unknown men' (NKJV); and St Paul's 'If anyone will not work, neither shall he eat' (2 Thessalonians 3: 10 (NKJV)).

[96] See Max Weber, *The Protestant Ethic and the Spirit of Capitalism*, trans. Talcott Parsons (London: Unwin University Books, 1930 reprinted 1971), pp. 17, 19.

profit[97] – with an associated natural law and underlying economic logic. Capitalism has been defined by Max Weber as a 'philosophy of avarice', 'an idea of a duty of the individual toward the increase of his capital, which is assumed as an end in itself'.[98] Seedlings of the spirit of capitalism were to grow and choke the universalistic, traditional societies of the middle ages, in which all aspects of life had been made to fit together naturally in harmony with the universalistic teachings of Catholic Christendom. The calling, or the vocation, of the medieval time, had been thought to come from heaven; but to the Calvinists of the Reformation, the calling became a choice and strenuous pursuit by the individual, according to individual drives.[99] Everyday worldly activity came to assume a religious significance.[100] Individualism was eroding universalist moral and ethical normativity (characterised by the outgoing Catholic church law).

It would be artificial to attribute modern capitalism to Protestant doctrines in a cause-and-effect manner. There had been significant capitalist activity from the tenth century onwards, boosted by the new facilities for commerce provided by Western legal science after the eleventh century. Max Weber's famous thesis that modern capitalism was prompted by Protestant theology has been widely criticised, even though Weber qualified his findings by noting that parallel developments in commerce, finance and industry are relevant.[101] The critiques of Weber do not detract from the value of his argument for our purposes.[102] That there may have been Catholic support for some of the Protestant doctrines about this time (sixteenth and seventeenth centuries), for example by the Jesuits,[103] may simply show that authority in Catholic countries was being justified in similar terms.[104] What is of moment is the doctrine itself, not its extoller – hence my choice of the word 'religion', not 'Protestantism', in this section heading. R. H. Tawney's criticism that religious change was more due to the economic changes, rather than vice versa,[105] simply confirms the important association of social theory with social order and the reaction of both capitalism and Protestantism to the old order. Similarly, the criticism should not concern us that business people may have allied themselves with Puritans

---

[97] See R. H. Tawney, 'Foreword' in Weber, *Protestant Ethic*, p. I(e).

[98] Weber, *Protestant Ethic*, p. 51.   [99] Tawney, 'Foreword', p. 2; Weber, *Protestant Ethic*, p. 160.

[100] Weber, *Protestant Ethic*, p. 80.   [101] See Tawney, 'Foreword', p. 6.

[102] See e.g. Elton, *Reformation Europe*, pp. 312–18, although acknowledging the mass of pamphlets and sermons of the seventeenth century, together with 'so much sympathy' which 'stern Protestantism' had for the 'enterprising and independent mind' (p. 316).

[103] See generally H. R. Robertson, *Aspects of the Rise of Economic Individualism: A Criticism of Max Weber and his School* (Cambridge: Cambridge University Press, 1933).

[104] Catholic countries do not appear to have developed to *quite* the same extent, for they were not as autonomous from government: see S. N. Eisenstadt, 'The Protestant Ethic Thesis in Analytical and Comparative Context', reprinted in Roland Robertson (ed.), *The Sociology of Religion: Selected Readings* (Harmondsworth: Penguin, 1969 reprinted 1972), pp. 309–11.

[105] See R. H. Tawney, *Religion and the Rise of Capitalism: A Historical Study* (Harmondsworth: Penguin, 1938).

because both groups sought freedom from external controls.[106] Justification for social action and authority in terms of the new theology was still sought.[107] Upon this justification, law depended.

Weber's thesis has strong explanatory power from our perspective. Rather than explaining Protestantism as a cause of the Mammon-orientated society, Weber's thesis does very well to elucidate the underlying justifications for state and territorial authorities and the individualism which were taking hold. In this sense, it provides an ample pivot for showing *how* authority was transformed, over succeeding centuries, from God to Mammon as ultimate reality and meaning. So what were some of those doctrines which were so crucial to the transformation in legal authority?

The theological doctrine of predestination ('supralapsarianism'), espoused by John Calvin, a Frenchman who lived in Geneva, encouraged private industry in a novel fashion. That industry supported the emergence of liberalism, utilitarianism and the individualism of the later Enlightenment and nineteenth century – and the economics of the division of labour and specialisation which coincides with globalisation nowadays. The individual fell upon a personal and isolated quest. Satisfaction for an individual that she or he was one of those who had been elected by God at the beginning of time to be saved was a matter of personal self-convincing. An 'implicit trust in Christ' had to be relied upon, together with good works as a sign of election to the saved.[108] Faith had to be proved in worldly activity, and emotional spiritualism was redirected into mundane occupations,[109] or callings (chosen by humans and usually very practical as opposed to, say, the older Catholic calling of the priesthood or the contemplative life). Outward appearances were of heightened social relevance. Salvation was signified (although not demonstrated or earned) by the appearance of economic productivity. Sacraments were relegated to the realm of personal faith.

Economically, the division of labour and specialisation increased. Capitalism received a boon. Production could increase by being undertaken where most efficient,[110] inspired by the perception of a vocation. Conversely, in matters of philosophy and personal determination, there was to be a decrease in specialisation with the passing of time. Humans became more autonomous and

---

[106] See Kurt Samuelsson, *Religion and Economic Action: The Protestant Ethic, the Rise of Capitalism, and the Abuses of Scholarship*, trans. E. Geoffrey French [1957] (Toronto: University of Toronto Press, 1993). Current 'Protestant ethic' literature appears in Lutz Kaelber, Book Review (*Protestantism and Capitalism* by Jere Cohen) (2003) 28 *Canadian Journal of Sociology* 575–81. More polemically, see Rodney Stark, *The Victory of Reason: How Christianity Led to Freedom, Capitalism, and Western Success* (New York: Random House, 2005).

[107] Non-Western cultures have been buttressed by helpful religions to encourage economic success too: Francis Fukuyama, *The End of History and the Last Man* (New York: Simon & Schuster, 1992), pp. 227–9.   [108] Weber, *Protestant Ethic*, pp. 110–13.   [109] Ibid., p. 121.

[110] See Peter F. Beyer, 'Privatization and the Public Influence of Religion in Global Society' in Mike Featherstone (ed.), *Global Culture: Nationalism, Globalization and Modernity* (London: Sage, 1990 reprinted 1996), p. 380, discussing Luhmann.

morally sovereign, and confident of their own abilities to determine personal norms. Every person became a priest unto herself or himself, and a philosopher. Beneficially, by sanctifying the everyday aspects of economic production, the worth was recognised of the masses of previously ignored and mostly oppressed classes outside the royalty, nobility and clergy. In that respect, a new style of self-propelled moral allegiance was possible. A 'new emphasis on public spirit and civic virtue' accompanied parliamentary and judicial rule in England,[111] which suggests that Weber was inaccurate to focus only on the materialistic implications of Protestantism.[112] These institutions, however, tended towards normative absolutism as they sought to monopolise the creation and interpretation of law, discarding the multiplex medieval sources of law.[113] Unfortunately, law, as the guidelines for the exercise of social authority, was destined under this model to be less capable of obtaining personal allegiance and moral authority. Rather, law could become more a device for political coercion at the exterior end of the Space Axis of the Space–Time Matrix – a tool for getting things done. Time was somewhat neglected: life could become more present-minded and disenchanted, although the authority for the new theology came from reinterpreting historical scriptures.

Above all, this was a secularising and rationalising force, 'one of the roots of that disillusioned and pessimistically inclined individualism'.[114] Unmediated personal relationships with God, without community or, at best, with localised communities of the faithful, tended to personalise behaviour in confluence with self-administered judgement.[115] Catholic countries secularised their legal processes too, and their governments were open to legislating in areas once within the competence of the ecclesiastical courts.

7.7 Demystification and globalist jurisprudence

The Protestant Reformations were, according to John Witte, 'the second great human rights movement of the West' following the Papal Revolution. The Protestant doctrine of equality before God and neighbour rendered every person a 'prophet, priest, and king' with corresponding rights in the community. With these rights there were, however, obligations or duties. The sinfulness of humanity meant that law and the protection of the state were required to keep these newly endowed individuals within the natural constraints of family, church and political community.[116] Basic rule of law principles were

---

[111] Harold J. Berman, 'The Origins of Historical Jurisprudence: Coke, Selden, Hale' (1994) 103 *Yale Law Journal* 1651–738, 1722.   [112] See Berman, *Law and Revolution II*, pp. 24–8.

[113] See Strauss, 'Idea of Order', esp. pp. 11–12. The multiple sources of law and normativity of old came to be associated with disorder. Such perceived chaos was thought to contradict St Paul's instruction in 1 Corinthians 14: 40 (NKJV): 'Let all things be done decently and in order.'   [114] Weber, *Protestant Ethic*, pp. 103–5.   [115] Ibid., pp. 106, 222–3.

[116] John Witte Jr, 'Law, Religion, and Human Rights' (1996) 28 *Columbia Human Rights Review* 1–31, 22–4.

encouraged too. Tyranny, at least in the German experience, was constrained by the need for published laws applicable also to the ruler; justice was of increased concern to the perfection of the earthly world; and civil disobedience was permitted in certain circumstances.[117] Other conditional rights to welfare, freedom of marriage, rights to vote, fair trial, self-preservation, religious freedom, proportionality in punishment and privacy can also be identified.[118] Compared to today, Sir John Baker has written that many but certainly not all of today's human rights were recognised and breached no more frequently in renaissance England. Significantly, those rights were embodied in the common law and developed through the people, through precedent, without the uncertainty of modern human rights and the politicisation of the judiciary which tend to undermine the rule of law.[119] Justifications for human or natural rights which existed back then were much less grounded in individualism than they are today.

Amidst the concentration of political and lawmaking authority in territorial slabs, based upon relatively common Western secular innovations, new universalist ideas of authority were emerging. Interior faith popularly became transformed into behaviour to exhibit outwardly towards the exterior end of the Space Axis in obvious worldly activity. Productivity became a new measure of blessedness. It is true to pronounce a secularisation of the spiritual and a spiritualisation of the secular, as Harold Berman does of the Reformations.[120] It is also true to observe the abandonment of a dedicated spiritual power, universally projected. The Two Swords (universalist) spiritual and (particular) secular constitutionalism of the church and the kingdoms was melded into the one double-edged sword of the territorial ruler whose reach was limited by the territorial sphere of containable disruption. The early tendencies of parliamentary legitimacy demonstrated by Henry VIII's embodiment of the 'legislative mentality' entailed, more or less, the vacation of an interior commitment to the role of law as more than a tool for achieving political goals. With this decrease in interior allegiance and the demystification of political institutions, one must welcome the increase in consent and (what we would now regard as) democratic legitimacy. Many non-Western and even Western religious cultures struggle, though, to accept the disenchantment and fluidity of norms generated by the legislative mentality. So may be observed the West's Faustian bargain of increased consent for increased disenchantment.

Yet the Protestant reformers did not choose and could not, of course, have known their role in taking steps towards the modern Western legislative

---

[117] Witte, *Law and Protestantism*, pp. 13, 295–303.

[118] R. H. Helmholz, 'Natural Human Rights: The Perspective of the Ius Commune' (2003) 52 *Catholic University Law Review* 301–25.

[119] Sir John Baker, 'Human Rights and the Rule of Law in Renaissance England' (2004) 2 *Northwestern University Journal of International Human Rights* 3–23, 23. Cf. R. H. Helmholz, 'Natural Law and Human Rights in English Law: From Bracton to Blackstone' (2005) 3 *Ave Maria Law Review* 1–22.   [120] See Berman, *Law and Revolution II*, pp. 64, 187.

mentality which projects itself globally today. Despite Luther's initial, vociferous disparagement of law and lawyers,[121] law for the Protestants was married to ultimate reality and meaning. Heaven on earth was the pursuit of Calvinists and featured in the jurist Eisermann's Lutheran thought.[122] Amidst all of Luther's political ambitions, law was not conceived in his more mature framework to be simply a tool for pursuing social policies, and law was not just made by governments. Law had a transcendent quality. As Luther's jurist, Oldendorp, wrote, 'the study of law is the most important pursuit after God's Word'.[123]

With the demystification of law and political institutions assisted by the Reformations, law's essential potential for achieving a better world has faded from focus. A significant Protestant bequest to legal thought is that there are legislative panaceas for all manner of social ailment, which can be effected through more and more mounds of legislation. Whilst the benefits of legislation and representative democracy are self-evident, a general, globalist jurisprudence must wrestle with the surface rubric of 'universal rights' (which embody perceived timeless aspirations) and 'state sovereignty' (which seeks to administer the needs of the present). Tentative resolutions are explored in chapters 10–13. Alas, two further chapters' worth of excavations must be continued in the interim, before resurfacing in today's terrain.

---

[121] See n. 44 above.
[122] See Witte, *Law and Protestantism*, pp. 12, 150, 172; and Wieacker, *Private Law*, p. 209.
[123] Witte, *Law and Protestantism*, p. 156.

Part 4
A Wholly Mammon Empire?

8

The constricted universalism of the nation-state

A constitutional legacy of the Protestant reformers was the increasingly absolutist, territorial state, aided by the innovative legislative mentality. The universalist legal pluralism of Christendom fractured into states and territories claiming legal monopolies. Generally these monopolies were grounded in the natural rights of people living together in a territorial compact to protect themselves from both within and without. As late as the eighteenth century in France, the divine right of kings to govern still served this function. Out of that repression burst the French Revolution and codified rights universal in aim but national in application. Conventional legal and political theory locates the sovereign authority of the state in the social thought of the English and French Revolutions. International law at those times was universal to the extent that it tended to reflect a system of norms of the lowest common denominator in a schoolyard of states administered by bullies. Theorists continued to explore universal international and territorial authority, constricted by the relativism inherent in competing nation-states determined, like their constituents, to pursue their own economic and political aspirations. Thus the inquisitive child of our Introduction[1] can be told by the adult today that law is obeyed because it comes from the state and it is justified because it brings order to the pursuit of economic needs.

In this chapter, we shall see how the aspirations of the nation-state ascended as a strategy for central authority, and how the 'codification mentality' assisted that purpose. Despite formidable codifiers preceding him – for example, God (via Moses) and Emperor Justinian – Napoleon was to find his people no more adept at accepting his law without expansion, reform, clarification and debate.

8.1 Universalism in a different guise

In the dusk of the Holy Roman Empire and the Christian commonwealth (*respublica Christiana*) purportedly reflected in it, as early as 1598 the duc de Sully had planned a universalistic European League of Princes to override the ideological pretensions of the Holy Roman Empire, and to divide Europe along territorial lines into fifteen equal states with attributes of modern sovereignty.

---

[1] See ch. 1, pp. 1–2 above.

This prototypical League of Nations or European Union, meeting once a year in alternative cities from a list of fifteen, was to be united against 'the Turk, laying down international law, settling disputes, preserving the peace, and punishing transgressors'.[2] In its second edition, over one hundred years after the author's death, it was republished for maximum European effect. It was predicated on establishing an equilibrium of strength and an acknowledgement that 'peace is a function of power', with free trade, pooled sovereignty and joint enforcement being contemplated.[3] The imagined imperial function of a European union can foggily be discerned: common security and conceptions of transgression; and a common ideological or spiritual enemy, then the Ottoman Turk (perhaps parallel to the illiberal nation-state of our times).

The universalist order envisaged in such projects was slow in the coming. It would face increasing gravity from the nation-state and difficulty projecting itself beyond the totalising self-conception of nation-state sovereignty. The international order was to become more orientated to the self-direction of particular states' sovereign wishes before more universalist aims could be pursued in earnest. The system of particular nation-states was projected as a new universalism. The previous Western universalism of our rhetorical holy Roman empire had obtained allegiance through common, moral, religious bonds and faith and the common Latin language, within the universalist political authority of Two Swords legal pluralism. That was the Christian commonwealth. What was, however, emerging was something different – the European public law system (*ius publicum Europaeum*). European public law conceived authority more juridically and politically in equally sovereign European states. Rather than the just cause (*iusta causa*) to unite the Christian empire against the infidel prince or empire, under the emerging European public law a state could be a legitimate enemy (*iustus hostis*) of another state in what might be thought of as a situation of European civil war.[4] Obviously in the days of medieval Christendom, princes fought one another; and the Catholic church would often side with one prince against another. The conception in the seventeenth century was different. Just wars were being justified according to the particular, self-determining will of the emerging nation-state.

In the emerging era of the nation-state under European public law, the sovereign nation-state was its own justification unto itself. As will be seen in coming pages, the underlying authority was to evolve through a complicated, secularising, territorially bound process. Morality was consciously removed from the market in pursuit of free trade, and profound human rights were theoretically developed for economically productive people within the territory.

---

[2] Martin van Creveld, *The Rise and Decline of the State* (Cambridge: Cambridge University Press, 1999), p. 84.

[3] Norman Davies, *Europe: A History* (London: Pimlico, 1997), pp. 662–3.

[4] See Martti Koskenniemi, *The Gentle Civilizer of Nations: The Rise and Fall of International Law 1870–1960* (Cambridge: Cambridge University Press, 2001), pp. 413–37, summarising Carl Schmitt's conceptualisation.

8.2 The secularisation of international law: European public law

In the de-universalising process of the emerging sovereign nation-state, Baron Christian von Wolff (1679–1754) contributed to the humanisation of the naturalistic, idealistic rationalisations of international law, with his concept of 'voluntary law'. He envisaged a supreme world-state, sovereign over individual nations. This he considered a natural order. Such a natural order could be enforced as a matter of Realpolitik by the majority of the civilised (Western) nations, which was deemed to reflect the natural law, in a conservative justification of the status quo: '[t]hus, under the disguise of natural law, positive law triumphs over it'. Law – that is, positive law – was dependent upon states or nations for its moving force. Authority was moving from naturalistic reason to a more earthly, pragmatic positivism: Wolff's work 'can be considered as the first private codification of positive international law, which had the effect of spreading its acceptance and consolidating its rules'.[5] Although representing a shift away from the Christian metaphysical rationality of the natural law tradition, an earthly type of scientific rationality underpinned the ensuing Enlightenment transformation. The latter was a rationality which esteemed the normative power of the individual and the state to govern themselves through a socially contracted will. The universalism of the aspirations of the Enlightenment lay in the very relativism sought to be encouraged. Recognising the political importance of religion in an essentially Christian intellectual and social world, religion was relevant only as a matter of national policy.[6] As Christianity became the province of particular nations, the universalist legal appeal of Christianity had to fail, as the Christian commonwealth ceded to the model of European public law.

Emerich de Vattel (1714–76) recognised the emerging particularity and relativity of claims to legality made by different nations. He acknowledged the positivism, divorced from a universalist rationality or natural law, which could seek to justify international norms. That is, states could assert their wills independently of a higher, unifying universal wisdom or social logic. It was this particular and relative authority of the individual state, supreme though within its own territory, which was ideally to be supervised by an international law which recognised and attempted to reproduce state legal norms at an international level. This represented something of an apology for the status quo. Vattel wrote that 'A dwarf is as much a man as a giant is; a small Republic is no less a sovereign State than the most powerful Kingdom.'[7] Indeed, Article 2 paragraph 1 of

---

[5] See Alfred Verdross and Heribert Franz Koeck, 'Natural Law: The Tradition of Universal Reason and Authority' in R. St J. Macdonald and Douglas M. Johnston (eds.), *The Structure and Process of International Law: Essays in Legal Philosophy Doctrine and Theory* (The Hague: Martinus Nijhoff Publishers, 1983), pp. 36–7.

[6] See Wilhelm G. Grewe, *The Epochs of International Law*, trans. Michael Byers (Berlin: Walter de Gruyter, 2000), p. 288.

[7] E. de Vattel, *The Law of Nations* (Philadelphia: T. & J. W. Johnson & Co., 1849), §18, p. 7.

the United Nations Charter ('The Organization is based on the principle of the sovereign equality of all its Members') recognises Vattel's doctrinal influence.[8] Vattel's ideas reflected a Hobbesian idea of nature: rather than nature being idealised, nature was the actual state 'of men in their presocial isolation, each self-dependent for survival and as yet uninhibited by the bonds of sociality'. Independent states were to obey the laws of nature which were akin to the natural laws of the Hobbesian presocial man in the war of all against all.[9] This idea of nature was heavily imbued with the philosophy of positivism: nature is what exists, as a matter of practice or fact. Vattel developed the view of diplomacy and war as the total social process in international society. State governments represented their own abstract entities in international law and not the individual humans who made up the society, leading to the 'enforced alienation' of the people from international law.[10]

Wholesale international legal positivism was ushered in by Johann Jacob Moser (1701–85), who somewhat immodestly claimed to advance the only realistic approach, recognising only 'treaties and custom as sources of international law'.[11] In his view there was no longer a strong need to ground authority in reason, metaphysics and morality: politics and the cold, hard facts arising from international relations were the alleged source of international law. Yet there had still to be some ideological framework, which no human social system can deny of itself. That framework was fraught with the Enlightenment paradox of universal truth through individual perceptions of it within a territorially defined, economically productive, polity. Perceptions of ultimate reality and meaning were changing, amidst this emergence in the European public law period of what today is known as 'international law'. Indeed, the term 'public international law' was invented shortly after this time by Jeremy Bentham, whom we shall encounter later in this chapter.

8.3 The secularisation of the economy

The gospel opposition between God and Mammon assists the understanding, in stark symbolic terms, of the transformation in legal authority which took place in much of Western Europe around the time of the French Revolution and amongst Enlightenment philosophers. Initially I chose the word 'Mammon' in the phrase 'Wholly Mammon Empire' as a matter of poetic licence when seeking to compare the modern age with the Christendom of the loosely designated Holy Roman Empire. 'Mammon', being the 'devil of covetousness' or 'wealth as an idol'[12] is nonetheless an appropriate term to represent the theoretical

---

[8] Verdross and Koeck, 'Natural Law', p. 38.

[9] See Julius Stone, *Visions of World Order: Between State Power and Human Justice* (Baltimore: The Johns Hopkins University Press, 1984), p. 81.

[10] Philip Allott, *Eunomia: New Order for a New World* (Oxford: Oxford University Press, 1990), [13.105].   [11] Verdross and Koeck, 'Natural Law', p. 39.

[12] *Shorter Oxford English Dictionary* (Oxford: Oxford University Press, 5th edn 2002).

opposite of the authority of Christendom. Christ taught that Mammon was opposed to God.[13] Adopting the insight of Karl Barth,[14] Mammon in the theoretical extreme, or the liberal ideology of freedom of markets, may well be a belief in one type of God or theology as opposed to another type. All belief, for Barth, acknowledges some theology featuring its own god or gods as the object of highest desire and trust. Liberalism is a belief-system – something of a religion. It emerged from Christianity.[15]

Karl Polanyi has famously referred to the 'Great Transformation' of the eighteenth century, concentrating upon England and France.[16] In the outgoing economic system of mercantilism, land had not been a commodity. Rather, it had been part of social organisation, namely a basis for representation and participation in public life, in politics, law and the military. Similarly, labour was part of the general organisation of society, deeply imbued with custom and regulated by guilds. The state intervened to a great extent in the economies of these societies. To 'deregulate' both labour and land would have been to subordinate society itself to the laws of the market. Unthinkable as it was prior to this time, it was to happen. Land and labour were fictitiously ascribed significance as commodities – as being subject to unencumbered purchase and sale.

Social historians have termed this eighteenth-century phenomenon a movement from a moral economy to political economy. In the moral economy, for example, customary *noblesse oblige* had dictated that grain markets were to be regulated so that peasants had access before the larger buyers purchased the grain to resell at a profit.[17] This was a welfare principle preventing, for example, a bulk purchaser from buying more cheaply than a small purchaser, it being against religion and humanity to allow such a thing.[18] Reading his religion and humanity differently, parliamentarian Edmund Burke, despite being famously conservative, sermonised the case of the free market which would triumph.

> The moment that government appears at market, all the principles of market will be subverted . . . We, the people, ought to be made sensible, that it is not in breaking the *laws of commerce*, which are the *laws of nature*, and consequently the *laws of God*, that we are to place our hope of softening the Divine displeasure to remove any calamity under which we suffer . . .[19] [italics added]

---

[13] Matthew 6: 24; Luke 16: 13.   [14] See ch. 3, section 3.1, p. 54 above.

[15] It has been argued that liberalism lacks positive ideals (instead, its ideals are expressed in negative terms such as 'freedom from . . .') because it has been severed from Christianity: see Edward Skidelsky, 'A Liberal Tragedy', *Prospect* (January 2002), 14–15.

[16] See Karl Polanyi, *The Great Transformation* (Boston: Beacon Press, 1944).

[17] See E. P. Thompson, *Customs in Common: Studies in Popular Culture* (New York: The New Press, 1993), chs. 4–5.

[18] See C. J. Kenyon in *R v Rusby*, Peake Add. Cas. 189; (1800) 170 ER 241 at [192], also wishing that Adam Smith had been present to consider the evidence, at [193].

[19] Edmund Burke, cited in Douglas Hay, 'Moral Economy, Political Economy and Law' in Adrian Randall and Andrew Charlesworth (eds.), *Moral Economy and Popular Unrest: Crowds, Conflict and Authority* (Hampshire: Macmillan Press Ltd, 2000), p. 103.

God was not now in the nobility which oversaw welfare initiatives; God had become manifest in Adam Smith's 'invisible hand' which solved the economic problem by matching supply with demand in the liberalising market. The *laws of commerce* were the *laws of nature* which were the *laws of God*. The consequent de-moralisation of the economy represented the institutional separation of politics from the economy, and the objectification of the market. A telling case of this new paradigm in England was *Steel v Houghton*.[20] The majority opinion held that no person had a right at common law to glean or take scraps from the master's field. Although precedent and learned writing (including from William Blackstone) suggested that the poor did have a right to glean under the Jewish law of Leviticus 23: 22, those references were found unconvincing given that such a custom 'would be injurious to the poor themselves'[21] by the new logic.

The liberal economic transformation was a movement from interior to purportedly more objective exterior references on the Space Axis of the Space–Time Matrix. Under the mercantilist and medieval precedents, government had acted in markets for moral (and not so moral) purposes in the economy. Under *laissez-faire* liberalism, the economy was left, where possible, to its own devices. In this Western European transformation led by England, the growth of credit and speculation required a transformed view of the future, on the Time Axis. People had to feel comfortable about their collective capacity to pay and perform their obligations in the future. The new 'image of a secular and historical future' appeared, according to which future generations too would be willing to repay debts including the collective 'National Debt'.[22] This ideology was universalist and imperial – 'the agent of a new world order, a new empire, which would be based not upon power and plunder, but upon reciprocity'.[23] An evaluation of the underlying transformation in authority can be conducted by reference to the French Declaration of the Rights of Man and Citizen and then the Civil Code. The French juristic vision facilitates an appreciation of the revolutionary legal dimensions of liberalism (not so obviously expressed in the earlier liberalised England).

8.4 The French juristic vision

The French Revolution gave the Western world a profound set of norms.[24] A sophisticated concept of rights inspired a codification movement and juristic

---

[20] 1 H.B.L. 51; (1788) 126 ER 32.   [21] Per Lord Loughborough at [53].

[22] J. G. A. Pocock, *Virtue, Commerce, and History: Essays on Political Thought and History, Chiefly in the Eighteenth Century* (Cambridge: Cambridge University Press, 1985), pp. 98–9.

[23] Anthony Pagden, *Lords of All the World: Ideologies of Empire in Spain, Britain and France c.1500–c.1800* (New Haven: Yale University Press, 1995), p. 180.

[24] The reasons for choosing the French over the American experience are fourfold: geographical location; the French Declaration was the product of an indigenous political history as opposed to a colonial reaction; France had the paradigmatic codification experience; and space constraints. This risks unfairness given the Anglo-American influences on the French: see Philip Bobbitt, *The Shield of Achilles: War, Peace and the Course of History* (London: Penguin, 2003), p. 585, referring to Jellinek's research.

discourse, linking law to a modified ultimate reality and meaning of life, popularly perceived. The ensuing Declaration of the Rights of Man and Citizen (the 'French Declaration') relegated God to the position of deistic creator who had set in train the physical laws of nature but who had withdrawn to leave humans in this world with their own laws.[25] Authority was even more demystified and secularised. The significance of the French Declaration is still being felt in the constitutional principles of the twentieth-century universal declarations, as will be seen in chapter 10.

8.4.1 Declaration of the Rights of Man and Citizen

The Enlightenment aim of '*liberté, egalité et fraternité*' was the motto of the revolutionaries in a time of crippling royal taxes, political oppression, and corporatism (privileges were based upon status, not contract). On 26 August 1789, the Declaration of the Rights of Man and Citizen, with its remarkable although not strictly legal authority, was accepted by the representatives of the French people, constituted as a National Assembly. The secular equivalent of All Souls' Day[26] had arrived in France. All were equal in the eyes of God and now the market. Notably, the feminine was not embraced by the text,[27] although there was a drafting ambiguity, for example, in separate articles referring to 'man', 'person', 'citizens' and 'society'. The outmoded privileges of the *ancien régime*, together with the divine right of the monarch, were decapitated, in principle, at the execution of King Louis XVI in 1793. At his trial, the leading political actors had been called upon to justify their stances as a matter of political philosophy, in a forum akin to a modern Western constitutional convention, albeit one with deadly intellect. The revolutionaries were beneficiaries of the legislative mentality – 'the exaltation of positive law and the weakening of all moral restraints on legislative authority'.[28]

Humans took responsibility for the text of the Declaration, which set out the rights of man and citizen in France. It was created 'under the auspices of the Supreme Being', not God by the old name. Individualism was paramount – the fortune of a nation, no less, depended upon its recognition of the 'natural, inalienable and sacred rights of man', according to the Preamble. Although aspiring to universality, these were not the principles of a universe of meaning with an interconnected, preordained plan for everything in it. Rather, they were principles which universalised the 'disconnectedness' of humans from society and nature.[29] The main principles to emerge from the Declaration, which laid

---

[25] See John Toland, 'Christianity Not Mysterious', in Peter Gay (ed.), *Deism: An Anthology* (Princeton: D. van Nostrand Company, Inc., 1968) and that anthology generally.

[26] See ch. 5, section 5.2.2, p. 101 above.

[27] See generally Sara E. Melzer and Leslie W. Rabine (eds.), *Rebel Daughters: Women and the French Revolution* (New York: Oxford University Press, 1992).

[28] See Michael Walzer, *Regicide and Revolution: Speeches at the Trial of Louis XVI* (New York: Columbia University Press, 1992), p. 42.

[29] See generally Thomas D. Barton, 'Troublesome Connections: The Law and Post-Enlightenment Culture' (1998) 47 *Emory Law Journal* 163–236.

the foundation for the twentieth century emergence of human rights, may be summarised.[30]

> *Equality* 'Men are born and remain free and equal in rights. Social distinctions may only be founded on public utility' (article I). Along this line, public taxation 'should be apportioned equally among all citizens according to their capacity to pay' (article XIII). Equality is therefore linked with utility. Utilitarianism as a philosophy is oriented towards exploiting means to obtain ends. A chief measure of utility is in terms of economic productivity.
>
> *Property* 'The aim of all political association is to preserve the natural and imprescriptible rights of man', being 'liberty, property, and security and resistance to oppression' (article II). 'All citizens . . . have the right' to approve the purposes, levels and extent of taxation' (article XIV). 'Property being an inviolable and sacred right, no one may be deprived of it except for an obvious requirement of public necessity, certified by law, and then on condition of a just compensation in advance' (article XVII). The goal of politics is directed firmly to earthly purposes of individuals, and not salvation. Property no longer represents a qualification for political representation.
>
> *Sovereignty* 'The principle of all sovereignty rests essentially in the nation' and 'no body and no individual may exercise authority which does not emanate from the nation expressly' (article III). 'Law is the expression of the general will . . . the same for all, whether it protects or penalizes' (article VI). Whatever universalist, non-territorial constitutional principles may have existed under the church–state combination, those principles were now to be politically limited to the nation as the natural social unit.
>
> *Liberal Freedom* 'Liberty consists in the ability to do whatever does not harm another' (article IV). 'Law may rightfully prohibit only those actions which are injurious to society' (article V). 'No one may be disturbed for his opinions, even in religion, provided that manifestation does not trouble public order' (article X). 'Free communication of thought and opinion is one of the most precious rights of man' allowing '[e]very citizen' to 'speak, write, and print freely, on his own responsibility for abuse of this liberty in cases determined by law' (article XI). Law serves no articulated purpose other than to prevent injury, rather than to guide to virtue or salvation.
>
> *Rule of Law* 'Every man [is] presumed innocent until judged guilty' (article IX). 'No man may be indicted, arrested or detained except in cases determined by law and according to the forms which it has prescribed' (article VII). 'Only strictly necessary punishments may be established by law . . .'

---

[30] See The Declaration of the Rights of Man and Citizen, reprinted in Georges Lefebvre, *The Coming of the French Revolution* (Princeton: Princeton University Press, 1967), p. 221.

and then not by retrospective legislation (article VIII). 'Society has the right to hold accountable every public agent of administration' (article XV). These rule of law notions have a lineage traceable to the English experience of Magna Carta in the thirteenth century and the 1689 Bill of Rights, although in the French Declaration they are clearly articulated in a modern, populist document.

As with a good deal of law, there is hypocrisy and idealism when the reality of the social order is compared with the aspirations of a legal text such as the Declaration of the Rights of Man and Citizen. Advance had nonetheless been made by codifying the chief political ideals of the Enlightenment philosophers. Seeds of logic were scattered across transnational social soils – rocky, weedy and fertile – which could take hold and germinate, in time, as norms which were to prove authoritative in theory, even if often not in practice. Increasing convergence between these basic human rights ideals and social practice was to follow in the succeeding centuries in the West, reflected in both the statutes and case law reasoning which followed in the essentially constitutional areas of property law, freedom of speech and association, sovereignty and rule of law.

What was the nature of this new constitutional authority?

8.4.2 The rational, contracting, productive individual

The French Declaration was born into a time which was, in a new way, future orientated on the Time Axis of the Space–Time Matrix. In implementing their new humanist vision, the French '*philosophes*' of the Enlightenment displayed an obvious learning in the classics, although hostile to most of the achievements of Christian philosophers and theologians. The Jacobins urgently sought to achieve the French future even if by resort to terror in the last decade of eighteenth-century France. The future was to represent a complete break from the past. Time was being abstracted from custom into rationalised, intellectually conceived impositions, reflected in the new calendar, which was decimalised into weeks of ten days.[31] Similarly, the view of spatial relationships was radical: old local differences and customs would be obliterated by new jurisdictions for 'the uniformly correct application of law throughout the nation, subordinating local prejudice, hierarchy and oppression to nationally guaranteed ideals', detracting from the sacredness and personality of everyday society.[32] This universality was, though, qualified. The ambition of this projection of universality was limited to the territorial boundaries of the French nation. This was later unleashed further afield by Napoleon, at the same time as he militarily

---

[31] See Eugen Rosenstock-Huessy, *Out of Revolution: Autobiography of Western Man* [1938] (Providence and Oxford: Berg, 1993), p. 213; Alfred Cobban, *A History of Modern France*, 3 vols. (Harmondsworth: Penguin, 1963), vol. I, p. 225.

[32] Richard T. Ford, 'Law's Territory (A History of Jurisdiction)' (1999) 97 *Michigan Law Review* 843–930, 876–7.

defeated the Holy Roman Empire in 1806 and thereby terminated its Christian universalism. Yet despite containing a universalist moral vision, the French Declaration was more concerned with state and citizen relations.[33]

In this way, the French nation-state projected what might be termed a 'constricted universalism'. Esteem of the nation and the state was the hallmark of the Declaration's authority, legitimating the general will as opposed to the diverse associations of moral and cultural allegiance which had comprised society. Herein a tension is exposed: the tendency towards conflicting associations of tight interior allegiance embodied in the pre-revolutionary estate system of clergy, nobility and the mainly bourgeois Third Estate remainder; versus the tendency towards a political super-association, created afresh with fewer lived references to the past and without strong moral and cultural bonds forged through time, upon which to build a new vision for the future. The political and economic starvation which had historically been suffered by the Third Estate could not be endured by the masses, inspiring a later tendency of rootless futurism. The ideal of this undifferentiated super-collective of functionalised economic beings was 'the complete nation' for the purpose of authority, in the words of the contemporary pamphleteer Abbé Sièyes.[34]

Abolishing privilege and increasing political participation must be a good thing. An associated loss of identity and meaning should also be balanced, though, with such a change to the structure of the normative universe. Technological progress, in the form of the increased division of labour (alienating skill and pride through the repetition of meaningless but consuming tasks) and increased trade, undermined custom and social rank, creating an undifferentiated state.[35] Human associations lose meaning in the face of the increased functionalisation of social life, as humans expose only particular interests to the particular interest groups which comprise their social lives.[36] Economic specialisation also has a counterpart social specialisation. The modern Western human wears many different hats – work, home, hobby, family, church and more – in different, particular, uncommitted social worlds which crash and collide in cosmological confusion in a universe without perceived meaning. This is the antithesis of the universe of meaning in which existed the medieval society following the Papal Revolution.[37]

The 'General Will' as the source of the sovereignty of the nation was, above all, presented as *natural*,[38] as was the individual's right to pursue self-interest. The

---

[33] See Joy Gordon, 'The Concept of Human Rights: The History and Meaning of its Politicization' (1998) 23 *Brooklyn Journal of International Law* 689–791, 729–35.

[34] See Abbé Sièyes, 'What is the Third Estate?' in J. H. Stewart (ed.), *A Documentary Survey of the French Revolution* (New York: MacMillan, 1951).

[35] See James Tully, *Strange Multiplicity: Constitutionalism in an Age of Diversity* (Cambridge University Press, 1995), pp. 67, 81–9.

[36] See Roberto Mangabeira Unger, *Law in Modern Society: Toward a Criticism of Social Theory* (New York: The Free Press, 1976), p. 168.   [37] See ch. 5, section 5.4, pp. 106–11 above.

[38] Philip Allott, *Eunomia: New Order for a New World* (Oxford: Oxford University Press, 1990), [13.33].

aristocratic structure could no longer be justified logically.[39] The logic of equality (in principle) had to overtake the custom and culture of privilege. The French Declaration comprised rational, logical, visionary statements of principle, directed to human government abstracted from human custom. Power was depersonalised. Legal formality increased to give the appearance of neutrality and predictability, as humans pursued their capitalist interests. The 'bugbear of the Enlightenment' – arbitrary governmental action[40] – required the depersonalisation of political power. Government was further objectified, at the exterior end of the Space Axis.

The means for this abstraction of government from individual morality and input was the fiction of the 'social contract'. Natural freedom was limited by the allegedly freely willed renunciation of personal freedom from smaller-scale associations to the state. That renunciation, above all, was a renunciation of life in a more thoroughgoing culture or *nomos* – that is, the rejection of a value-filled, moral universe where virtue and legality were connected in principle and, at least, pretence (which is not to be underestimated for its power to inspire a culture of compliance with norms). The state centredness of this logical although uncustomary enterprise was, however, to retard the development of a truly universal normative enterprise. In the process of depersonalising power, a normative commitment to being unconcerned with normative commitment was set in train.

The French Revolution launched an especially economic form of nationalism or statehood, which proceeded, to use de Tocqueville's words, with similarities to 'a religious revolution'.[41] The French Revolution bequeathed the legacy that political and economic allegiances can be greater than more cultural, interior allegiances. A Jew could be a French citizen if accepting the requirement to work. 'Useful work' qualified one for membership of the nation. The French nation no longer included the unproductive classes of *ancien régime* clergy and nobility, which were akin, as Sièyes wrote, to 'a malignant affliction' which 'saps and torments' the body of a sick man.[42]

Reliance upon production and economic value reflected a different kind of underlying constitutional authority. It was a legitimacy which transcended the post-Reformation parochialism of religion and culture and those interior though powerful moral allegiances. The attitude of the day was contractual and political. Above all, it was tolerant of cultural difference provided that proper tribute was paid to the universalist ethical goal of being a productive member of society. The market-led normativity of Mammon (which, at least where

---

[39] See Niklas Luhmann, *Law as a Social System*, trans. K. A. Ziegert (Oxford: Oxford University Press, 2004), pp. 434–40.

[40] Gianfranco Poggi, *The State: Its Nature, Development and Prospects* (Stanford: Stanford University Press, 1990), p. 75.

[41] Quoted in Philip Allott, *The Health of Nations: Society and Law Beyond the State* (Cambridge: Cambridge University Press, 2002), p. 387.   [42] Sièyes, 'Third Estate', p. 56.

consumers are concerned is extremely exterior on the Space Axis)[43] was becoming the logical good or index of goodness. Historical, Christian-led persecutions of spiritual dissent, with attendant normative conflict and complexity, were condemned by Enlightenment thought, particularly in France. Voltaire (1694–1778) advocated an antique toleration which resembled Ancient Roman logic and procedure.[44] Veneration of the classics was a veneration of Greek philosophy and its conquest of myth by reason. So too did the Enlightenment *philosophes* believe their own projects to be advancing secularisation away from Christian myth.[45] The Enlightenment built and idolised the modern scientific attitude from foundations in René Descartes's proof of existence. His simple yet profound *cogito ergo sum* (I think therefore I am) motif located reality in personal reflection, overcoming all other conceivable doubts about the reality of existence.[46] This attitude, it was hoped, 'would become the prelude, and even the servant, of moral and political improvement'.[47] As Peter Gay has written, to speak of this is 'to speak of a subtle shift of attention: religious institutions, and religious explanations of events were slowly being displaced from the center of life to its periphery'.[48]

The perception of ultimate reality and meaning, and the human relationship to that transcendence, of course changes over time.[49] In the Enlightenment, and embodied in the French Declaration, the ensuing contractarian and economic approach to norms and authority 'prettified the image of God': no longer was God an absolute monarch, but now a 'constitutional ruler bound to save those Christians who had fulfilled their contractual obligations'.[50] With such an altered notion of God, there had to be a change in the nature of law. Law became more than ever an instrument applied by political will to achieve social goals – 'custom and convention became its antithesis'.[51] Although the French Revolution did not follow the instruction manuals of the *philosophes*, the ensuing legal reforms implemented by Napoleon were a lesson from the proud Enlightenment intellectual climate (although at the personal, psychological level, Napoleon perceived himself to be fulfilling biblical prophecy).[52] The legal reforms were characterised by the phenomenon of codes. They possess a Western significance.

---

[43] The market is 'the most impersonal relationship of practical life into which humans can enter with one another because of "its matter-of-factness, its orientation to the commodity and only that"; and on that account it knows nothing about caring'. See Poggi, *The State*, p. 126.

[44] See Peter Gay, *The Enlightenment: An Interpretation/The Rise of Modern Paganism* (New York: W. W. Norton & Company, 1966, reprinted 1977), p. 51.   [45] Ibid., p. 81.

[46] See René Descartes, *A Discourse on Method, Meditations on the First Philosophy, Principles of Philosophy*, trans. John Veitch (London: Everyman, 1997), pp. 25–6, 79–80.

[47] Gay, *The Enlightenment*, p. 82.   [48] Ibid., p. 338.   [49] See pp. 8–10, 53–6 above.

[50] Gay, *The Enlightenment*, p. 354.

[51] Brian Z. Tamanaha, *A General Jurisprudence of Law and Society* (Oxford: Oxford University Press, 2001), p. 91.

[52] Napoleon took it upon himself to reconvene, in Paris, the Grand Sanhedrin of Jews (which last sat in 68–70 CE) with the brief to reconcile Jewish law to French law: David S. Katz and Richard H. Popkin, *Messianic Revolution: Radical Religious Politics to the End of the Second*

8.4.3 The codification mentality

> A code, or not a code – that is the question!
> Whether 'tis better in the law to suffer
> The flaws and defects of numerous practiques,
> Or to take arms against a sea of troubles,
> And, by revising, end them! – To Prune – to change –
> No more! And by a code to say we end
> Abuses, and the thousand natural pests
> That law is heir to: 'tis a consummation
> Devoutly to be wished . . .[53]

This 1830 rendition of Hamlet's soliloquy introduces the problematic of codification: to suffer the complicated nature of law as it had become known through practical cases and decisions, or supposedly to terminate those complications by codifying them. Codification embodied, with practical effect, the theological paradigm shift of the Enlightenment. Deistic thought disclaimed revelation.[54] The human in society 'was free and able to go to perfection by the sovereign power of reason, and reason had found its "natural apotheosis" in the fully rational and therefore legitimately sovereign state'.[55] Reference was made to God as 'the Eternal legislator, Who has endowed the universe with unalterable laws'.[56] Discourse or revelation in the form of case law surrounding these laws was devalued. The public law was made subject to a written constitution. Ultimate power was placed in a representative legislative assembly. Legislative rationality overtook historical, cultural customs. Private law in non-unified states was subjected to codification at a national level, overriding cultural differences,[57] in a futurist vision purportedly freed from the past. An all-encompassing logic sought to reduce the administrative inefficiency of cultural differences by codifying all of the norms in one convenient, expedient place, or by relying upon the natural logic of new, invented laws in purportedly comprehensive codes.[58] Codification of laws in major and minor European states, and the

---

Millennium (New York: Hill & Wang, 1998), pp. 134–7. He had prepared to proclaim an independent Jewish state in Palestine: Franz Kobler, *Napoleon and the Jews* (New York: Schoken Press, 1976), pp. 55–7.

[53] 'Codification' reprinted from *United States Law Intelligencer and Review* (1830) in Charles M. Cook, *The American Codification Movement: A Study of Antebellum Legal Reform* (Westport: Greenwood Press, 1981), p. 111. Written by an American lawyer contemplating codification in its topical period in the US from 1815 to the mid century, it neatly captures the contemporary European issues.   [54] Gay, *The Enlightenment*, p. 376.

[55] Henry E. Strakosch, *State Absolutism and the Rule of Law: The Struggle for the Codification of Civil Law in Austria 1753–1811* (Sydney: Sydney University Press, 1967), p. 121.

[56] Gay, *The Enlightenment*, p. 384.

[57] See Berman, *Faith and Order*, p. 133, regarding north and south France; Csaba Varga, *Codification as a Socio-Historical Phenomenon*, trans. Sándor Eszenyi *et al.* (Budapest: Akadémiai Kiadó, 1991), p. 14.

[58] O. F. Robinson, T. D. Fergus and W. M. Gordon, *European Legal History* (London: Butterworths, 1994), [15.5.8].

overall influence of this mentality of collecting, revising and positing them in one place, facilitated the transition from the corporate government of the old nobility regimes to centralised state governments.[59]

8.4.4 Enlightenment legal science

From the sixteenth century, codification ideas were percolating in England and from the seventeenth century on the Continent.[60] The Enlightenment and ensuing French Revolution contributed a newer, although related, mentality to that of the legislative mentality,[61] which I shall term the 'codification mentality'. The mindset received expression in the philosophical revolution of Descartes in the early seventeenth century. He located human reality in a mode of personal reflection heavily dependent upon logic and intellect.[62] Jurisprudentially:

> A 'good' law in Cartesian thinking is a law which can be logically deduced from a first principle; its 'goodness' is immanent . . . Cartesianism invested every positive law with the absoluteness of law as such. The relative validity of positive law within a moral order of absolute validity had been transformed into the postulate of the absolute validity of every positive law.[63]

Reductionist and hyper-rational, this mentality purported to reduce case law into simpler codes, by the efficient use of words and concepts. As such, much doctrine in the French Civil Code was not new. It was subject to conservative input, reflected in its content.[64] What was radical was the application of the legislative mentality (new rules can be made for society) to customary sources of norms, where those norms were not necessarily inappropriate for society, but were believed to be open to clearer expression in codes. Custom, history and culture were submitted to the pride of mathematical logic, within an ideology that used science for economic production.[65] The aspiration was for rationally deductive codes which would completely cover all interpersonal relations in civil society, universally and not just in Europe.[66]

The Enlightenment favoured 'abstracted rationality over information supplied by the senses';[67] law had to be rationalised rather than just gathered

---

[59] See Strakosch, *State Absolutism*, pp. 9, 14. On Continental experiences generally, see Thomas Glyn Watkin, *An Historical Introduction to Modern Civil Law* (Aldershot: Ashgate, 1999), ch. 7.

[60] See generally Gunther A. Weiss, 'The Enchantment of Codification in the Common-Law World' (2000) 25 *Yale Journal of International Law* 435–532, 471–3 (England) and 451–2 (Continent).   [61] See ch. 7, section 7.5, pp. 157–61 above.

[62] See e.g. Descartes, *Discourse*, p. 87.   [63] Strakosch, *State Absolutism*, p. 116.

[64] See R. C. van Caenegem, *European Law in the Past and the Future: Unity and Diversity over Two Millennia* (Cambridge: Cambridge University Press, 2002), pp. 65–8, discussing the influence of Portalis in J.-L. Halperin, *L'Impossible Code Civil*; Jean Louis Bergel, 'Principal Features and Methods of Codification' (1988) 48 *Louisiana Law Review* 1073–97, 1081.

[65] See Varga, *Codification*, pp. 94–5.

[66] See H. Patrick Glenn, 'The Grounding of Codification' (1998) 31 *U.C. Davis Law Review* 765–82 at 766; van Caenegem, *European Law*, p. 40.

[67] Barton, 'Troublesome Connections', 177. See too Peter G. Stein, 'Roman Law, Common Law, and Civil Law' (1992) 66 *Tulane Law Review* 1591–604, 1595. On codification generally, see

factually and followed. There are two ways to do this. A *deductive* theory of law proceeds by drawing a conclusion from a general proposition (as from a provision in code) applied to a particular circumstance (the case to be decided). An *inductive* theory, on the other hand, proceeds in the case law fashion by drawing a conclusion from the particularistic instances of the law, and applying the conclusion to a particular case by analogy. The inductive approach does not permit of one truth, because 'new extensions to existing rules can be revealed at any time by the courts'.[68] The scholastic method, in which the science of the Western legal tradition originated, was though neither singularly deductive nor singularly inductive: the whole was not derived from the parts (induction) nor were the parts derived from the whole (deduction). The whole was in the parts interacting with each other.[69]

The deductive mindset is characteristic of the operation of civil law codes. The method of classical Roman law was far from such civilian code systems which developed from the eighteenth century. Roman law, being inductive, actually has more in common with English common law, given their inductive emphases on case law, although the common law is more scientifically coherent.[70] The old Roman 'formal' or 'quantitative codification' of Justinian and the medieval initiatives which sought to express complex law in one place must be distinguished from the 'substantive' or 'qualitative codification' sought to be imposed by the codification mentality of the French Revolution. The latter deductive 'illusion of certainty',[71] self-deceptively pretended by modern civil law, proceeds by way of a deductive logic which was not present in Roman law or medieval codes.[72]

In its extreme eighteenth-century ideological form, the codification mentality was a natural law battle against feudal history. Voltaire, for example, saw no baby in the bathwater he sought to throw out. The only way to have good laws was to 'burn the existing ones and make new ones instead', just as London, in his view, had to be incinerated in the Great Fire to make way for wider and straighter streets.[73] French codification aims became more moderate and less naturalistic around 1796, in draft laws which sought to link codification ideals to the national legacy of the past.[74] Yet there was still a general, European decline for

---

R. C. van Caenegem, *An Historical Introduction to Private Law*, trans. D. E. L. Johnston (Cambridge: Cambridge University Press, 1988), ch. 4 and his *Judges, Legislators and Professors: Chapters in European Legal History* (Cambridge: Cambridge University Press, 1987), pp. 39–53, 152–5.   [68] Stein, 'Roman Law', 1596.

[69] See Berman, *Law and Revolution: The Formation of the Western Legal Tradition* (Cambridge, MA: Harvard University Press, 1983), p. 142.

[70] Justinian's *Institutes* contain the famous tripartite division of law into persons, things and actions, although this work comprises a small fraction of the whole *Corpus*, which is for the most part a morass of case discussions.

[71] The belief in 'one right answer to any legal problem' explains why civil law judges now tend not to give dissenting opinions: Stein, 'Roman Law', 1596.

[72] See Barry Nicholas, *An Introduction to Roman Law* (Oxford: Clarendon Press, 1991), p. 43; Bergel, 'Features and Methods', generally; and ch. 6, section 6.2.3, p. 127 above.

[73] See Varga, *Codification*, p. 128.   [74] Ibid., p. 99.

almost two centuries of a historical, culturally based constitutional order. Vanquished by political authority, the new order fostered a new type of individualistic morality, the legislative dictates of which struggled to achieve widespread personal allegiance. Positivism, being the statement of law in writing by the relevant political authority, was bolstered by the legislative power of the sovereign nation-state. French revolutionaries such as Sièyes sought to impose on society novel effects from gathering and doing away with custom, with the associated aspiration of law being freed from lawyers. The connection of lawyers to pre-revolutionary legal science and the nobility motivated the revolutionaries to 'laicise' law (much as communist Eastern European countries initially sought to do away with lawyers on account of their bourgeois normativity).[75]

Montesquieu, famous as an Enlightenment figure seeking universal values and for his praise of the English separation of powers principle (independent legislature, executive and judiciary), at once appreciated the problems of particularity and diversity.[76] Local and national characteristics of a people needed to be taken into account in framing law. He justified his opposition to legislative reform and universal codes on a natural science of variations of senses in hot and cold climates.[77] His recognition of the virtue of the customary, historical nature of a people's laws foreshadowed the stance adopted by 'the Historical School' in Germany.

8.4.5 Rebellion from the Historical School

To understand how un-Roman and un-customary the codification movement was, one of the greatest 'modern' Romanist thinkers, Friedrich Carl von Savigny, assists with the 'Historical School' he founded.[78] With the fall of the Holy Roman Empire in 1806, the Napoleonic wars and oppression and the German liberation and revenge had not dislodged the popular French codes in the Rhine

---

[75] See Csaba Varga, 'Utopias of Rationality in the Development of the Idea of Codification' in F. C. Hutley *et al.* (eds.), *Law and the Future of Society* (Wiesbaden: Franz Steiner Verlag GMBH, 1979), pp. 22, 27–8, 35–6. Cf. Catherine Valcke, 'Comparative History and the Internal View of French, German, and English Private Law' (2006) 19 *Canadian Journal of Law and Jurisprudence* 133–60, 136–44.

[76] See Montesquieu, *Persian Letters*, trans. C. J. Betts [1721] (London: Penguin, 1973 reprinted 1993).

[77] See Montesquieu, *The Spirit of the Laws*, trans. A. Cohler, B. Miller and H. Stone [1750] (Cambridge: Cambridge University Press, 1989).

[78] See generally Hermann Kantorowicz, 'Savigny and the Historical School' (1937) 53 *Law Quarterly Review* 326–43, 342; Peter Stein, *Roman Law in European History* (Cambridge: Cambridge University Press, 1999), pp. 116–18. On Savigny and the Historical School in general, see Franz Wieacker, *A History of Private Law in Europe, With Particular Reference to Germany*, trans. Tony Weir (Oxford: Oxford University Press, 1995), chs. 20–2; Reinhard Zimmermann, 'Savigny's Legacy: Legal History, Comparative Law, and the Emergence of a European Legal Science' (1996) 112 *Law Quarterly Review* 576–605; Joshua Getzler, 'Law, History, and the Social Sciences: Intellectual Traditions of Late Nineteenth- and Early Twentieth-century Europe' (2003) 6 *Current Legal Issues* 215–63, 227–32; Valcke, 'Comparative History', 144–51.

valley, which remained for Savigny as a '*Schandfrieden*' – a peace of disgrace. For many Germans, the codes represented 'an expression of the modern era of economic individualism' and the basis for the codification of German law and the unification of the Reich.[79] For Savigny, though a proud German, the French influence and method became an object of odium (notwithstanding German principles being contained in the code).[80] In opposing A. F. J. Thibaut's call for a German Civil Code, Savigny did not mindlessly adhere to Romanist jurisprudence. By Savigny's own definition of his 'rigorous historical method of jurisprudence':

> Its character does not consist, as some recent opponents have strangely maintained, in an exclusive admiration of its Roman law; nor in desiring the unqualified preservation of any one established system, to which, indeed, it is directly opposed . . . On the contrary, its object is to trace every established system to its root, and thus discover an organic principle, whereby that which still has life may be separated from that which is lifeless and only belongs to history.[81]

There was a place for legislation in Savigny's scheme – it was just not a totalising place. Law could not be separated from its history by legislating a codified legal system, in Savigny's opinion, because the law arises from unintentional developments in that history which reflect the *Volksgeist*, or the spirit of the people. That spirit was not necessarily metaphysical, but rather a 'deposit, or residue, of local behaviour'.[82] Not to be confused with a biological concept, the *Volksgeist* was a cultural tradition, 'almost identical with the country's judges and scholars'.[83] The root of this system, or the organic principle, was Roman jurisprudence. Therefore this was not pure folk law, but the implanted Roman law.[84] The ultimate source of the law had been in the scholarly interpretation and systematisation of the German *ius commune*, which had developed over the centuries out of Justinian's *Corpus* and the canon law of the church.

Eugen Ehrlich's sociology of law, an intensely analytical legal history, aptly exposes the degree to which law, particularly in German territories, had been organic, originating in the interior dimension of the Space Axis. For example, consideration for the family, church, institutions of public welfare and reverence for the dead were non-legislated social forces which gave rise to the duty to make a last will and testament.[85] Employment contracts, agreements with

---

[79] Kantorowicz, 'Savigny', 336.   [80] See van Caenegem, *European Law*, p. 64.

[81] Friedrich Carl von Savigny, *Of the Vocation of Our Age for Legislation and Jurisprudence*, trans. Abraham Hayward [1831] (New York: Arno Press, 1975), p. 137.

[82] Donald R. Kelley, *The Human Measure: Social Thought in the Western Legal Tradition* (Cambridge, MA: Harvard University Press, 1990), p. 245; see too Tamanaha, *General Jurisprudence*, p. 30.   [83] Wieacker, *Private Law*, pp. 305–6, 310.

[84] H. Patrick Glenn, *Legal Traditions of the World: Sustainable Diversity in Law* (Oxford: Oxford University Press, 2nd edn 2004), p. 135.

[85] Eugen Ehrlich, *Fundamental Principles of the Sociology of Law*, trans. Walter L. Moll [1913] (Cambridge, MA: Harvard University Press, 1936), p. 115.

banks, corporate articles of association, contracts of supply and credit contracts – all of these 'bring about the inner order of the group of human beings
that has its being within these economic associations'.[86] These are examples of
Ehrlich's famous notion of 'the living law'. To attempt to codify and legislate
those living laws is to encase them in exterior authority on the Space Axis and
to separate them from a moral, cultural discourse and allegiance.

The failure of the conservative action spearheaded by Savigny had broader
European implications. Ultimate authority now conclusively hailed from
the sovereignty of legislation, a normative facility which had the power to cull
centuries of custom and legal growth in one fell enactment. Law had become
a means to social ends, a tool for getting things done, as Savigny's later oppon-
ent, Rudolf von Jhering, believed it ought. Jeremy Bentham has become
famous for his 'utilitarian' philosophy which embodied that instrumentalist
view of law.

8.4.6 Bentham and the codification mentality

Bentham declared, with some success in France, Spain and the Spanish
Americas, that parliament should 'codify' all of the laws to escape the arbitrariness of the judiciary and the lawyers who constantly offer new explanations of
law. Credited with inventing the very word 'codification', the French Revolution
saw this Englishman distinguished with honorary French citizenship in 1792.[87]
His high exuberance for, and self-propulsion in, this scientific art were matched
only by his total lack of practical experience in the same.[88] Calling for short sentences and commonly understandable language in law, Bentham's own legal
writings bore no obvious witness to his cause.[89] His singular indifference to
the political regimes and history, language and cultural aspects of his clients
illustrates his flawed understanding of the social nature of law.[90] His opposition to rights such as those of the French Declaration was based upon his criticism that such rights simply were not everywhere protected,[91] demonstrating
further lack of insight into the futurist, aspiratory dimension of law on the Time
Axis.

---

[86] Ehrlich, *Fundamental Principles*, p. 46.
[87] Philip Schofield, 'Jeremy Bentham: Legislator of the World' (1998) 51 *Current Legal Problems*
115–47, 118. See too Jeremy Bentham, *Legislator of the World: Writings on Codification, Law,
and Education* (Oxford: Oxford University Press, 1998).
[88] Schofield, 'Jeremy Bentham', 144; Varga, 'Utopias of Rationality', p. 30.
[89] See John Dinwiddy, *Bentham* (Oxford: Oxford University Press, 1989), p. 61.
[90] William Twining, *Globalisation and Legal Theory* (London: Butterworths, 2000), p. 101;
Dinwiddy, *Bentham*, pp. 69–71; cf. Jeremy Bentham, 'Of the Influence of Time and Place in
Matters of Legislation' in John Bowring (ed.), *The Works of Jeremy Bentham* (Edinburgh:
William Tait, 1843), vol. I.
[91] See Jeremy Bentham, 'Nonsense upon Stilts, or Pandora's Box Opened, or the French
Declaration of Rights Prefixed to the Constitution of 1791 Laid Open and Exposed' in Philip
Schofield *et al.* (eds.), *Rights, Representation, and Reform: Nonsense upon Stilts and Other
Writings on the French Revolution* (Oxford: Oxford University Press, 2002).

Jeremy Waldron declares, attempting to refute Savigny and with reliance on Bentham, that the Savignian defenders of historical jurisprudence absurdly associated the codification mentality with natural law and reason.[92] Such a condemnation appears to overlook the fact that the very thing being done through codification was to impose law from the intellect or the logic of an assembled parliament. Old positive law with an historical, cultural discourse was being replaced by a new type of positive law imposed by the state, preoccupied with the new natural law of political rationality.

For Bentham, it was precisely the lack of logic and design behind complicated customs and judge-made common law that provoked his interest in creating certainty through rationally articulated laws in code form. After all, in Bentham's view there was only as much 'genuine reason' in a 'volume of Common Law' as there was 'in a dunghill here and there a grain of corn'.[93] This imposition of Benthamite logic and rationality ignored the organic order which, in Savigny's view, lay behind the volumes of customary and juristic law. Being overlooked by the codifiers, in Savigny's view, was the tangled complexity of doctrines which the Continental *jurist* (not specifically Savigny's contemporary judges whom he did not respect)[94] sought to reconcile within a tradition, giving rise to normative and legal richness. A similar pride could be taken in the English common law with its discourse rich in references to the past which maintained stability whilst accommodating change. Bentham embraced a concept of law which could only acknowledge law as being properly so called if it came from top-down sovereign command, in pursuit of the utilitarian principle of the greatest happiness of the greatest number. The very naturalism of his logical as opposed to customary framework was disguised by his irredeemable positivism.[95]

Although Bentham contemplated reducing custom to neat rules, any attempt to reduce custom to rules is to change the customs through the interpretation of new words.[96] Inducing general rules from cases to codes leads to a process of sifting and discarding material including complexities belonging to a discourse; whilst using that code and deducing the applicable rule from the resultant code creates an added distorting filter. Problems of interpretation and misinterpretation ensue in a situation where 'true meaning' is presumptuously thought to exist on paper in black and white. In fact, many of the legal doctrines arising from the French Revolution such as freedom of contract and property have actually been said to originate not so much in the text of the French Civil Code (that is, the Napoleonic Code) but in the meanings ascribed to those words by

---

[92] See Jeremy Waldron, 'Custom Redeemed by Statute' (1998) 51 *Current Legal Problems* 93–114, 94–5.   [93] Cited from Schofield, 'Jeremy Bentham', 126.

[94] See Kelley, *Human Measure*, p. 244.

[95] See David Lieberman, *The Province of Legislation Determined: Legal Theory in Eighteenth-century Britain* (Cambridge: Cambridge University Press, 1989), pp. 224–32.

[96] Ehrlich, *Fundamental Principles*, ch. 18; Niklas Luhmann, *Law as a Social System*, pp. 241–3.

the nineteenth-century French treatise writers.[97] This represents a type of 'decodification'.[98]

Defeated perhaps by the English affinity for customary law as opposed to abstract sources, such as ancient Roman law,[99] Bentham was unable to achieve acceptance of Roman law in England. He did, however, help to secure the position of the state legislature as the supreme law generating institution in the Western rule of law world. Well within the function of the legislature was the power to obliterate, corrupt and re-declare law which had been established organically over centuries. In this sense there is something of the codification mentality in English law, demonstrated, for example, by the legislative activism in creating 'partial' or 'quasi-codifications'[100] of company, commercial and criminal laws. Similarly, there was, in England, Bentham's constitutional preoccupation with the strong, centralised, sovereign state, entrenched until relatively recently in English legal discourse by the likes of Austin and Dicey.

Perhaps the most benign form of codification was that which originated at this time in the field of public international law. Bentham had tried to graft his strong opinions about codification onto international law. In the tradition of the developing universalistic hope for centralised forms of state co-operation, Bentham detailed international institutions and relations similar in form to the twentieth-century institutions of public international law, although his proposed code was irretrievably idealistic in its quest to be unambiguous, logical and without need of commentary.[101]

The very cosmopolitanism of Bentham, demonstrated by his generous interest in various states of the world and his desire to assist them by offering his services as a codifier to them, make him a significant jurist in the legal history of globalisation. Bentham thought he was addressing the entire field of law as he sought to construct 'the first authentic system of "universal jurisprudence" '.[102] To this extent, codification is perhaps imperial and dangerous, although on another view, when drafted loosely, the exercise of undertaking codification is an activity conducive to the sharing of norms and the reconciliation of complex human behaviour patterns. (This idea will be explored in the case study of international commercial law in chapter 12.)

---

[97] See James Gordley, 'Myths of the French Civil Code' (1994) 42 *American Journal of Comparative Law* 459–505.

[98] See Maria Luisa Murillo, 'The Evolution of Codification in the Civil Law Legal Systems: Towards Decodification and Recodification' (2001) 11 *Journal of Transnational Law and Policy* 163–82, 172–5.

[99] Alan Watson, *The Evolution of Western Private Law* (Baltimore: The Johns Hopkins University Press, expanded edn 2001), p. 258.

[100] R. C. van Caenegem, *Judges, Legislators and Professors: Chapters in European Legal History* (Cambridge: Cambridge University Press, 1987 reprinted 1996), p. 43; see too Varga, *Codification*, pp. 148–9. Common law codifications are formal or quantitative as opposed to the substantive or qualitative civil law codifications: see p. 187 above.

[101] See R. P. Dhokalia, *The Codification of Public International Law* (Manchester: University of Manchester Press, 1970), pp. 38–40.   [102] See Lieberman, *Province of Legislation*, p. 221.

8.5 The struggle for European community

Although Enlightenment ideals and legal science were universal in their aspirations (as was Napoleon), those which we have so far seen were limited in their political expression to territories defined in economic terms. These nation-states were assumed as natural units for Western, if not world, order. Yet there were ideas and initiatives aspiring to a more universal political significance at the level of Europe, in the quest for the world society.

Transcending the nation-state at the more universal level, the Enlightenment influence rendered 'Europe' a term more desirable than 'Christendom'. Publicists of the time appealed for such things as a European parliament, a European confederation and orchestrated initiatives to settle disputes. The Treaty of Utrecht of 1713 provided the last reference to the 'Christian commonwealth', although common norms would continue to subsist. From the 1714 Hispano-Dutch Peace Treaty of Utrecht, 'Europe' had been increasingly appearing in place of 'Christendom'.[103] In 1751, Voltaire noted the common European public law and political principles, and similar religious foundations, whilst in 1796, Edmund Burke wrote that '[n]o European can be a complete exile in any part of Europe'.[104]

The Age of Enlightenment and the French Revolution brought forth, in addition to strong French nationalism, utopian visions of a single European society. Those visions were grounded in the benchmark liberal logic that all men are free and equal and that a realisation of this fact would solve all social ills by allowing men to compete with one another for their betterment. Such thinking also gave way to thoughts of a universal republic governed by French hegemony.[105] These proposals now concentrated upon the nation-state as the desirable polity, featuring amongst other things a prototypical League of Nations and international arbitration as opposed to international government. Transcendent authority was relocated from the traditional God of the heavens to the political compact of the economically defined peoples of the nation-states.

A prototypical European economic community was coercively attempted by Napoleon, in the Milan Decree of 1807: French-occupied countries, and those seeking Napoleon's co-operation such as Russia, Sweden and Denmark, were forbidden from trading with the British.[106] Although the 1815 Declaration against the Trade of Negroes contained historical references to 'the Holy and Indivisible Trinity' and 'all Powers of Christendom', a secular standard now also appeared which was to replace references to Christendom: the 'community of civilised nations'.[107]

The Concert of Europe (the so-called Vienna Congress), born in 1818 of the Napoleonic Wars, provided for consultation amongst Great Britain, Austria,

---

[103] Grew, *Epochs of International Law*, p. 292.   [104] Davies, *Europe*, pp. 7–8.
[105] See Hans A. Schmitt, *The Path to European Union* (Baton Rouge: Louisiana State University Press, 1962), p. 6.   [106] Davies, *Europe*, p. 712.
[107] Grewe, *Epochs of International Law*, p. 289.

Prussia, Russia and France on mutual problems. It also had the ideological purpose of suppressing the extremes of Jacobin-espoused liberty, notably in Germany through the Carlsbad Decrees of 1819 which restricted freedom of expression. The flexibility of the consultative process, which, together with the statesmanship of Metternich achieved a somewhat exaggerated 'century of peace' compared by some to the *pax Romana*, was not ultimately to fall until the outbreak of World War I. The German Customs Union disposed of the economic barriers between the thirty-eight German states, achieving union at about the same time as Italy around 1870, largely driven by nationalism. Despite the Franco-Prussian War of 1870 (which helped to achieve both the Italian and German unions), the League for the Union of Europe, founded in 1869, survived this war and maintained 'a high-minded tenacity that refused to let Europe die in the minds of men', although it was 'far removed from the main stage of political life'.[108]

8.6 Globalist jurisprudence and the Enlightenment

Standing on the platform of the Reformation legislative mentality, the Enlightenment codification mentality boosted to higher levels of disembodied reason the fallacy that law comes from one just one place, the state. In the nineteenth century, not only had codification occurred in the European countries of France, Austria, the Netherlands, Serbia, Italy, Romania, Portugal and Spain, but Latin American countries, Turkey, Egypt and Japan felt its impetus too.[109] Codification thinking, as an adjunct of the nation-state, therefore had some 'global' and not just Western significance.

Reaction to the state centralism of the nineteenth century shares similarities with some of today's anti-globalisation platforms. Norms from one place which are sampled, siphoned, filtered and imposed somewhere else upset interior, regional, cultural affinities, customs and histories. That imperial process also upsets local, cultural visions for the meaning and purpose of life. On the Space–Time Matrix, such a legislative approach to law inhabits the exterior end of the Space Axis and the future, progress-hungry dimension of the Time Axis. References were few to the interior and past dimensions of the Matrix, necessary for a flourishing society with laws believed in rather than just coerced. Codification eschews custom, diversity, regional norms and the historical narratives of peoples which give meaning to law and social life. (In England at that time, custom was also eschewed to some extent by the advent of *stare decisis* – the doctrine of precedent – which enshrined only such custom as was accepted to be law by a judicial hierarchy.)[110] The European experience demonstrates that

---

[108] Schmitt, *Path to European Union*, p. 7.
[109] René Cassin, 'Codification and National Unity' in Bernard Schwartz (ed.), *The Code Napoleon and the Common-Law World* (New York: New York University Press, 1956), pp. 49–50.
[110] H. Patrick Glenn, *On Common Laws* (Oxford: Oxford University Press, 2005), p. 44.

even culturally similar peoples have legitimate objections to being homogenised by the mathematical wisdom of centralised lawmakers. How much more sensitive, then, must regional and purportedly global normative initiatives be to local circumstances.

Internationally, future visions of peace on earth were glimpsed through imagined institutions and new tables of rights – the French Declaration of the Rights of Man and Citizen and the US Bill of Rights – which would ground developments in the twentieth century. God was disappearing from treaty references and as the source of domestic legal authority. In this respect, Napoleon's code 'fell from heaven' like a 'holy book' to safeguard the new bourgeois, free-market order, to be protected from contamination by custom, canon law, natural law and Roman law. All other French civil law was purportedly repealed,[111] removing, on the Time Axis, the allegiance possible from a common history. Napoleon tried to bind the future to the market and his personal will by positive laws.[112]

For all of these exterior, coercive tendencies of law, separated from interior moral allegiance and the allegiance which comes of cultural customs, the Enlightenment contributed an ironic commitment to being uncommitted. That is, one should be committed to a life of questioning and debunking social structures. One could be committed to general 'motherhood' statements of principle, but not unhesitatingly to specific content. In an interconnected world where state boundaries, rivers, seas and oceans provide little insulation or buffer from what is done on the other side, commitment to norms and processes will be essential. Just what norms and processes deserve that commitment are moot. Some suggestions are offered in chapters 9 and 10. In chapter 9, to which we turn, investigation of the nation-state concept will also assist understanding the constricted ability of nation-states to project universalist norms successfully.

[111] See van Caenegem, *European Law*, pp. 68–70.
[112] See Bergel, 'Features and Methods', 1079; Ehrlich, *Fundamental Principles*, p. 433.

9

The incomplete authority of the nation-state

Humans at an individual level are the logical starting place for a social philosophy concerned with the significance of norms and the social conditions for human flourishing. Norms, if they are to be successful, should appeal to the interior dimension of the human on the Space Axis of the Space–Time Matrix; not just decreed from the exterior dimension by state legislation. Interior allegiance requires appealing, amongst other things, to shared culture, language and history – to those instincts and institutions which motivate humans in their collective endeavours. Concerning the political implementation of these instincts and institutions, there can be little doubt, at least for the foreseeable future, that the nation-state is, and is likely to remain, the basic unit of international order, and legally paramount with respect to local societies. To speak of the 'nation-state' then begs a question, if we are to understand the basics of contemporary human ordering: what is the nature of the nation-state, and, by implication, the separate natures of both the nation and the state? Having considered the immediate Western consequences of the French Revolution, it is at this point of our excavation into Western law and authority that the moral and political attachments of greatest socio-legal significance for today can now be traced.

9.1 The cultural foundation of the nation

The 'nation' as a concept has been around for thousands of years. For example, the Fourth Book of Moses, *Numbers*, contains a prophetic reference to Israel amongst the nations.[1] As will become apparent, that idea of the nation is very simple compared with the complexity of nationalism as it erupted in the twentieth century.[2] Rather than applying to an extended tribe, modern nationalism with its fictitious ideas of a scientific racial commonality has been a tendency generated by the industrialisation and then fragmentation of society. Primarily

---

[1] Numbers 23: 9: 'For from the top of the rocks I see him, And from the hills I behold him: There! A people dwelling alone, Not reckoning itself among the nations' (NKJV).

[2] Cf. Aviel Roshwald, *The Endurance of Nationalism: Ancient Roots and Modern Dilemmas* (New York: Cambridge University Press, 2006), asserting a continuity, although acknowledging a distinction, between pre-modern and modern nationalisms (p. 12).

a negative concept, Isaiah Berlin once defined national movements as responses to wounds inflicted on peoples, moving as a twig springs back and whips the face of the person touching the twig.[3]

9.1.1 Language and nation

About the turn of the eighth and ninth centuries, the Venerable Bede had referred to the *gens Anglorum* (English nation).[4] From the ninth to eleventh centuries, there was a history of antagonism between the multiple, parcellised sovereignties of Europe, particularly in Germany, as we saw prior to the Papal Revolution.[5] There was difficulty in giving names to the two Frankish states which comprised what are now France and Germany. Both were 'Frances', carved out of the *regnum Francorum*. The labels 'East' and 'West' did not at the outset evoke national consciousness. Perhaps the greatest contrast between them was in the language: in the West the language was Romance; and in the East, the language was *diutisc*, from which derived the modern German *deutsch*, meaning 'germane or alike'. As Marc Bloch concluded:

> The use of the same language draws men closer together; it brings out the common factors in their mental traditions and creates new ones. But a difference of language makes an even greater impact on untutored minds; it produces a sense of separation which is a source of antagonism in itself. . . . Nothing is more absurd than to confuse language with nationality; but it would be no less foolish to deny its rôle in the crystallization of national consciousness.[6]

An early inkling of English nationalism was noted by a hagiographer, describing the marriage of Henry I (the Norman William the Conqueror's son) to a princess of the ancient dynasty of Wessex.[7] Other than these references, nationalism at that time, as we now consider it, did not exist. What origins there were appear mainly as linguistic commonalities. From the end of the twelfth century, some universities organised 'nations' of students from geographically proximate areas (with some ethnic-based exceptions).[8] In the fourteenth and fifteenth centuries, 'patriotic spirit' was more present than 'nationalism' as such. Certainly there was no such thing as an exclusive national homeland. That concept is a 'modern fantasy'.[9]

Benedict Anderson, in his book *Imagined Communities*, further emphasises the importance of language and its consolidation through print in the

---

[3] See David Miller, 'Crooked Timber or Bent Twig? Isaiah Berlin's Nationalism' (2005) 53 *Political Studies* 100–23, 101; see too Roshwald, *Nationalism*, ch. 3.

[4] R. C. van Caenegem, *An Historical Introduction to Western Constitutional Law* (Cambridge: Cambridge University Press, 1995), p. 13.

[5] Marc Bloch, *Feudal Society*, trans. L. A. Manyon (London: Routlege & Kegan Paul, 1942), p. 433. See too ch. 5, section 5.1, p. 96 above.   [6] Bloch, *Feudal Society*, pp. 434–6.

[7] Ibid., p. 432.

[8] Jacques Le Goff, *The Birth of Europe*, trans. Janet Lloyd (Oxford: Blackwell Publishing, 2005), pp. 175–6.   [9] See Norman Davies, *Europe: A History* (London: Pimlico, 1997), p. 217.

constitution of national identity. What he termed the 'imagined community' of Christianity was maintained to a significant degree by the common language of Latin, which facilitated supranational communication. Print created the possibility for shared simultaneity. Common issues and events could be experienced through a medium of dissemination not confined by parochial languages and word of mouth, enabling reports of emerging common interest to traverse distances in book or pamphlet form. Latin had been a language of bilinguals. New markets also appeared for books in local languages in addition to the universal Latin language. The Protestant Reformations contributed to the undermining of the Latin language and its supranational community of Christendom. Administrative vernaculars became popular in the sixteenth century, consolidating moves towards the decentralisation of universalist high Latin and Roman church culture into parochial, nationalising communities. 'These fellow readers, to whom they were connected through print, formed, in their secular, particular, visible community, the embryo of the nationally imagined community.'[10]

The interior, cultural consciousness of ancient times is a weak form of nationalism. On the Space Axis, nationalism is dependent upon groups becoming aware of other groups exterior to them, and a sense of progress and history is required on the Time Axis of our Space–Time Matrix. Nationalism becomes stronger when peoples, aware of cultural diversity, become more aware of cultural change, inspiring comparisons to other cultures.[11] Allegiance to a national identity is, therefore, a social construct, drawing on mental traditions. Nationality exists in the mind. That accounts for its power, fluidity and at times lethality. '[W]here people define situations as real, they are real in their consequences.'[12] Psychology is arguably the most useful discipline via which to enquire into the concept of the nation.[13]

9.1.2 Industrialisation and nation

Traditionally, as we saw,[14] Western society was in essence status based. People were characteristically born into their social position and rarely ventured beyond their inherited status, subordinated as they were to the hierarchical webs of dependence and reciprocal rights and duties enmeshing kings, lords, knights, serfs, villeins and clergy. There was little scope to 'climb the social

---

[10] See Benedict Anderson, *Imagined Communities: Reflections on the Origin and Spread of Nationalism* (London: Verso, 1991), pp. 37–44.

[11] See John Plamenatz, 'Two Types of Nationalism' in Eugene Kamenka (ed.), *Nationalism: The Nature and Evolution of an Idea* (Canberra: Australian National University Press, 1973), pp. 22–36.

[12] Ray Pahl, 'Are all Communities Communities in the Mind?' (2005) *The Sociological Review* 621–40, 637.

[13] Renier, cited in Davies, *Europe*, p. 381. See too Neil MacCormick, *Questioning Sovereignty: Law, State, and Nation in the European Commonwealth* (Oxford: Oxford University Press, 1999), p. 172.   [14] See ch. 4, section 4.5, p. 88 above.

ladder', so to speak. The movement from status to contract can be associated with emerging social contractarian thought and eventually with the Enlightenment ideology of autonomy, equality and universal brotherhood in reason. This segued with the liberalism of the Industrial Revolution, which spilt through the Western social and ecological landscape in the late eighteenth, early nineteenth centuries.

According to Ernest Gellner, the status-bound relationships of the previous agrarian economy dissipated into 'anonymity, mobility, atomisation . . . [and] the semantic nature of work'. (Semantic work replaced the agrarian reliance upon brawn, and is based upon some degree of literacy and sophistication, typically involving machinery.) Homogeneity (rather than status-dictated differences) became *the* political bond, leading to acceptance in the high culture – the culture used by the bureaucracy. Difference conjured subservient status.[15] To some extent this was borne out by the new British nationalism which, from the 1707 Union, and by means of the promotion of loyal servants, was superimposed upon the prior nationalisms of the English, Welsh, Scots and Irish.[16]

Reactionary nationalism from underclasses may be 'a reaction of peoples who feel culturally at a disadvantage' or inadequate.[17] That disadvantage may be very real and may give rise to the prejudice of a type of 'explanatory nationalism',[18] by which allegedly inherent propensities, for example, to poverty, illness, corruption and laziness, are used by the advantaged to explain the condition of the disadvantaged. The choice of language of the dominating bureaucracy limits social diversity; and competition for power becomes competition also between *kinds* of person.[19] Competition becomes fiercer, and if a culture cannot be imitated to advantage, then those at a disadvantage become even more competitive and demand different criteria of success.[20] Consequently, there can be 'unificatory nationalism', for example, of a nineteenth-century German or Italian type; or 'diaspora nationalism', of the Jewish type.[21] By these means, to adopt a modern term for an old process, 'ethnic cleansing' can occur by gradual attrition and evolution over a thousand years as in France; or quickly and with bloodshed, the Balkans being a modern example.[22] Sometimes there may be no real competition at all, for the disadvantage may be so crippling to a nationally conceived group, even if comprising the majority of a population.[23]

[15] Ernest Gellner, *Nationalism* (London: Phoenix, 1998), pp. 28–30.
[16] See Davies, *Europe*, p. 813.   [17] See Plamenatz, 'Two Types of Nationalism', pp. 27–9.
[18] The term is used in Thomas W. Pogge, *World Poverty and Human Rights: Cosmopolitan Responsibilities and Reforms* (Malden: Polity Press, 2002), pp. 139–44, in the context of developed states deflecting blame from their responsibility for conditions in Third World countries (e.g., by paying military dictatorships who alienate their people's resources).
[19] Gellner, *Nationalism*, pp. 40–2.   [20] Plamenatz, 'Two Types of Nationalism', pp. 32–3.
[21] See Johann P. Arnason, 'Nationalism, Globalization and Modernity' in Mike Featherstone (ed.), *Global Culture: Nationalism, Globalization and Modernity* (London: Sage, 1990 reprinted 1996), pp. 214–15, referring to Gellner, *Nations and Nationalism*.
[22] Gellner, *Nationalism*, pp. 46–7.
[23] For examples, see Amy Chua, *World on Fire: How Exporting Free Market Democracy Breeds Ethnic Hatred and Global Instability* (New York: Anchor Books, 2004).

Religion (a salvationist religion helps more),[24] ethnicity, culture and race are amongst the usual shared attributes which define a nation,[25] in addition to, or perhaps as a corollary of, common language. As opposed to being chosen, these are things which are mostly inherited if not inherent. Potent status complexes are entwined in nationalism as a response to industrialisation. Fears of being socially marginal can lead to nationalistic violence and terrorism.[26]

9.1.3 Race and nation

Racism was not a hallmark of European medievalism. Of course, discrimination on the basis of religious faith in the bold terms of Christian, Jew and heathen had previously been endemic. That discrimination, though, was not racial. It was based less upon physical characteristics and more on habits of worship and social self-ordering. Not until the colonialism of the sixteenth century, spearheaded by the novelty of the Spanish colonial experiences, were racially separatist laws invented to govern churches, schools and guilds.[27] In the nineteenth century, Eurocentric views about the Darwinian, evolutionary nature of civilisation and international law became endemic.[28]

The idea that race was a legitimate basis for community developed primarily in nineteenth-century Europe and the United States, in the natural science of the day. It is most commonly associated with Nazi Germany. The wider West, however, had shared the laboratory of a flawed science issuing from ideology highly convenient to the then contemporary ruling classes. Modern biology suggests that racial similarities at a genetic level are miniscule if not non-existent, debunking the biological evidence of race.[29] St Paul, when he wrote that 'God made from one blood every nation',[30] might also have referred to a common gene pool too. What surface differences exist and have evolved between peoples are perhaps more readily explained by geography.[31] Previous references in this chapter to the mobile European tribalism of medieval Europe undermine the notion of separate, untainted bloodlines. What group cohesion or kinship does exist under such rubric appears to be reducible, again, to

---

[24] Arnason, 'Nationalism, Globalization and Modernity', p. 217.

[25] Lea Brilmayer, 'The Moral Significance of Nationalism' (1995) 71 *Notre Dame Law Review* 7–33, 10.

[26] See Mark Juergensmeyer, *Terror in the Mind of God: The Global Rise of Religious Violence* (Berkeley: University of California Press, 2003), pp. 190–218.

[27] See Martin van Creveld, *The Rise and Decline of the State* (Cambridge: Cambridge University Press, 1999), pp. 300–1.

[28] See Martti Koskenniemi, *The Gentle Civilizer of Nations: The Rise and Fall of International Law 1870–1960* (Cambridge: Cambridge University Press, 2001), pp. 76–8. On the social construction of race, see too Ivan Hannaford, *Race: The History of an Idea* (Washington: The Johns Hopkins University Press, 1996).

[29] See e.g. Joseph L. Graves Jr, *The Emperor's New Clothes: Biological Theories of Race at the Millennium* (New Brunswick: Rutgers University Press, 2001).   [30] Acts 17: 26 (NKJV).

[31] See Jared Diamond, *Guns, Germs, and Steel: The Fates of Human Societies* (New York: W. W. Norton & Company, 1999).

psychology. This is not, however, to deny the social reality of race and, of course, racism, and the socially unequal resource distributions across different peoples.

9.1.4 Retrospection and nation

According to Lea Brilmayer, '[n]ationalism means simply that one identifies with the claims of one's nations and one's conationals, and takes them as one's own'. Typically, these claims are legitimated by reference to such justifications as restoration of land because of wrongful annexation, claims that 'God intended us to have it', or reparations for which land is considered to be the only compensation.[32] Right to territory is the typical claim by nations. The nature of the claim makes it difficult to enter into dialogue with other nations because it is often an absolute claim based upon an absolute moral authority, namely the authority of the national collective and its sacralised history. Such a manifestation of nationalism is primarily cultural and moral, limited in conceptual resources for entering into more logical, political dialogues. Hence nationalism can be regarded as containing, in general, a particularistic moral appeal as opposed to a more general, exterior, political appeal.

These aspects of nationalism can be expressed more strongly. Nations tend to be associated with historical considerations: for example, 'common myths, past glories or defeats, injustices suffered or overcome, grievances nourished and burnished' which, through '[c]ommon language, culture, genealogy and religion project the romanticised past onto the future'. Individuals defining themselves as such are 'likely to want to live among others of the same ethnie', enjoying the same food, music and rhythms of the ancestors.[33] The invention of that tradition, and the investment of national status in a 'tailored discourse' such as 'national history', is not to be ignored.[34] As Eric Hobsbawm has observed, the national movements of the late twentieth century tended to be negative,[35] attempting to shield ethnically self-defined groups from the realities of modern political organisation and responsibility being generated, in dialogue, at a supranational level.

Etymologically, the very word *nation* is rooted in *nature* and the idea of being born (*nasci*, in Latin).[36] This suggests a concept of authority which is grounded more in an intuitive cultural heritage or history rather than in an articulated

---

[32] Brilmayer, 'Moral Significance', 8.

[33] Thomas M. Franck, 'Clan and Superclan: Loyalty, Identity and Community in Law and Practice' (1996) 90 *American Journal of International Law* 359–83, 363.

[34] Eric Hobsbawm, 'Introduction: Inventing Traditions' in Eric Hobsbawm and Terence Ranger (eds.), *The Invention of Tradition* (Cambridge: Cambridge University Press, 1983), p. 14; see too Philip Allott, *The Health of Nations: Society and Law Beyond the State* (Cambridge: Cambridge University Press, 2002), [4.42].

[35] See Eric Hobsbawm, *Nations and Nationalism Since 1780: Programme, Myth, Reality* (Cambridge: Cambridge University Press, 1990), ch. 6.

[36] Gianfranco Poggi, *The State: Its Nature, Development and Prospects* (Stanford: Stanford University Press, 1990), p. 26.

sense of reason or political compact for the future. In the increasingly interconnected, diverse world, such cultural formations had to be open to logical dialogue. Invariably, political autonomy was sought through the vehicle of *the state*.

9.2 Logical aspects of the modern state

In sharp contrast to the shared myths, language and genealogy of the nation or
tribe, the state can be something quite different from the nation. As Thomas
Franck puts it, 'the multicultural *state* reflects quite different social values: a civil
society sharing a preference for the civic virtues of liberty and material well-
being, as well as a desire to associate for protection and security'. The nation-
state is something of an oxymoron: 'there are very few states that consist of a
single nation or ethnie'. Values of the state characteristically do not reflect the
same retrospection as those of the nation. Instead, states substitute for that historical consciousness 'diverse citizens' futurist aspirations'. A state is more likely
self-conceived 'as an invented civil society of persons bound together by ideals,
a constitution and a common enterprise'.[37]

On this view, the state is therefore not the nation. 'While consciousness of
nationality is a comparatively recent development, the structure of the state was
derived from centuries of monarchy and enlightened despotism.'[38] That is not
to say, however, that the states in existence today are of such ancient lineage.
Historical continuity of the states in existence today, as we have seen,[39] has been
surprisingly limited. Most of the older, populous states cannot count their centuries on more than one hand.[40]

The state is a political construct which is more in the nature of a posited,
invented, contracted collectivity rather than being an emanation from the cultural subconscious. It is a rational, logical entity. It is at once more political and
external to the individual's immediate moral references. It is *public*. Rather than
relying upon the cultural status quo, the state tends to rely upon rationally formulated legislation to maintain order, excluding information (and tradition)
perceived to be irrational.[41] The nation, on the other hand, is more of an organic
outgrowth, inspired by affinities such as appearances, religion and culture
including language (although the authenticity of that national exclusiveness –
the inventedness of the traditions – is open to critical psychological enquiry).
On the Space Axis of the Space–Time Matrix, the nation tends to be closer and
more interior to the individual than is the state (although a variant, 'civic
nationalism', places nationalism closer to the state).[42]

---

[37] Franck, 'Clan and Superclan', 361–3.
[38] Hannah Arendt, *The Origins of Totalitarianism* (San Diego: Harcourt Brace & Co., 1948
reprinted 1976), p. 230.   [39] See ch. 6, section 6.4.2, pp. 141–2 above.
[40] See Davies, *Europe*, p. 456.
[41] See H. Patrick Glenn, *Legal Traditions of the World: Sustainable Diversity in Law* (Oxford:
Oxford University Press, 2nd edn 2004), p. 53.
[42] On civic nationalism, see MacCormick, *Questioning Sovereignty*, pp. 170–7.

This space aspect is important and helps to explain the coercion required by the state to enforce its laws. The state is more abstracted from an individual's sense of normative life. To the extent that emotional affinities are not usually inspired by the state, laws of the state cannot be expected to flourish as a moral adjunct of the people. State legislation is triply abstracted and thus distant from the individual. Legislation suffers from the problem that state norms are often posited in compromises (the first abstraction) by delegates who may represent some constituents on some policies but not other policies (the second abstraction), rarely in response to direct legislative mandates from the electoral constituency (a third abstraction). Legislation is therefore not always conducive to framing norms for a people, particularly when the norms are complicated and reliant upon wisdom and sensitivity (as opposed to majoritarian reaction) for their interpretation and implementation. This triple abstraction explains the alienation of state government from the people, on the Space Axis. Individuals are allowed to go about their concerns in the economy, disconnected from their own governance.

Notably, the state's claim to normative authority is based upon its overwhelmingly permeating territorial power. In effect, the state is a corporation without peer in a given territory. It characteristically possesses much greater authority than any other organisation within the territory, arising from its centralised strength and co-ordinated bureaucratic departments. The state's sphere of containable disruption trumps that of all other bodies, being, as it is, vast and as widely dispersed as any sphere of control could be.

9.3 The problematic hyphenation of the nation-state

The moral allegiance felt by some to the nation may assist state authority. A nation-state is a nation governed by the state or a state which seeks to draw upon nationalism to govern. As expressed by Philip Allott, a 'nation organized as a state is thus a nation in which a government conducts the social willing and acting of the society with the authority of the whole of society . . . in which the members of society have taken on a second existence as *citizens*.'[43]

With the aid of nationalism, although not always, the state, in Weber's terms, monopolises legitimate violence and, it may be added, legitimate education.[44] The state can even be defined by the nation, as with Nazi Germany. Indeed, the Pan-German distinction between *Staatsfremde* (aliens of the state) and *Volksfremde* (aliens of the nation) was incorporated into Nazi legislation.[45] In this sense it is true that the relationship between the state and the nation is likely to be constitutionally regulated such that states are used to formulate the national will,[46] in the attempt by the state to capitalise on the moral, subconscious,

---

[43] Philip Allott, *Eunomia: New Order for a New World* (Oxford: Oxford University Press, 1990), [12.61].   [44] Arnason, 'Nationalism, Globalization and Modernity', p. 213.
[45] Arendt, *Totalitarianism*, p. 231.   [46] See Allott, *Eunomia*, [13.68].

normative allegiances inspired by the nation. Similarly, nationalism can be entwined with the state in symbiosis: Anthony Giddens has defined nationalism as 'the cultural sensibility of sovereignty, the concomitant of the co-ordination of administrative power within the bounded nation-state'.[47]

On the Time Axis of the Space–Time Axis, the state tends to be more future oriented.[48] For example, federal states such as the United States, Australia and Canada have reacted with vision against conservative English heritages. They sought a new future. By way of contrast, a more nationally dominated state such as twentieth-century apartheid South Africa, according to Thomas Franck, was more retrospective: there, Afrikaners, Boers and other white settlers imposed a constitutional dictatorship which sought to reserve a narrow notion of a white homeland.[49] Revolution has forced South Africa into more of a state mode. States such as the United States, Australia and Canada have become multi-cultural, or multi-national, given their racial and religious variety. Citizenship is less exclusive than the status of being 'a national'. For all intents and purposes, the French nationalism of the 1789 Revolution is perhaps better considered a form of futurist state movement, accepting as it was of other peoples such as Jews into its aspirations for statehood under the rubric of universal equality. Otherwise, post-revolutionary France can be understood as a national movement which has recognised the requirement for political constitution.[50]

To attempt to comprehend its problematic hyphenation, the theory of the nation-state can be divided into two broad schools.

9.3.1 The Historical-National School

G. W. F. Hegel (1770–1831) rested his philosophy of history upon an attempted synchronisation of the nation and the state. The nation is the biological, organic cement of the state. Hegel's writing on the topic embodied the nationalist view of state political identity. To him, 'the blood tie dictates all personal identity and must determine the contours of communities organized as states, "the absolute power on earth" that demands of persons "absolute obedience, renunciation of personal opinions and reasoning, in fact, complete *absence* of mind" '.[51] The nation lures people into state allegiance. The state can capitalise on the moral power over the individual in community who searches for identity and norms through nationalism, which the state can dictate or at least influence politically. Perceived blood ties (better thought about in this context as shared cultural

---

[47] Anthony Giddens, *The Nation-State and Violence* (Cambridge: Polity Press, 1985), p. 219.

[48] See Philip Bobbitt, *The Shield of Achilles: War, Peace and the Course of History* (London: Penguin, 2003), p. 11.   [49] See Franck, 'Clan and Superclan', 362.

[50] According to Eugene Kamenka, 'nationalism' was a new word in 1798, used in connection with the aim of overthrowing legitimate governments: Eugene Kamenka, 'Political Nationalism – the Evolution of the Idea' in Eugene Kamenka (ed.), *Nationalism: The Nature and Evolution of an Idea*, p. 8, and generally pp. 2–20.

[51] Franck, 'Clan and Superclan', 364, quoting Hegel's *Philosophy of Right*.

characteristics and family) are a moral source of allegiance. On the Space Axis, an exterior, political significance can be imposed more upon the national, interior, collective will, subverting, if it does not inspire, individual determination. Thus Hegel could write that 'the true actuality' of subjectivity is 'the subjectivity which constitutes the concept of the power of the crown and which, as the ideality of the whole state, has not up to this point attained its right or its existence'.[52] For Hegel, the subjectivity of the nation gave rise to a morality perfectly suited to the state and its objective, political social order which was in the process of being realised. High ethical content was required of Hegel's ideal state. It was not just a Hobbesian instrument for imposing positivist law and order – it was 'like the echo of God's footsteps on earth', comprising 'strong private institutions'[53] in a harmonious blend of moral allegiance to the politics of the state, outside the insignificance of the individual taken alone.

This Hegelian model might be termed the Historical-National School of social organisation. Here, there is morality and an interior space orientation in the attraction of nationalism which speaks the language of a selective communal intuition, in the manner of being attracted to a mate. In its racist form, it can be illustrated by the moral allegiance to the cold politics of a dictatorship, for example, that of the Nazi regime. Yet perhaps one can take heart in Hegel's vision from what appears to be a meta-historical reflection on the end or *telos* of the national spirit. He proposes one fulfilled national spirit merging with another national spirit, 'so that we can observe a progression, growth and succession from one national principle to another'.[54] To discover the continuity of this movement of merging nationalisms and the cross-fertilisation of ideas and culture over an extended time scale appears to be the task of his philosophical world history.

Viewed in this way, the nation-state is not an end in itself but a means for the flourishing of humans. The Historical-National School is, then, highly normative in that it idealises the state as a natural culmination of the nation. The value of this model lies in its moral and political dimensions – the interior and exterior authority it attempts to forge with the individual – and the shared historical narratives and visions of the future which cater to the individual's psychological need for meaning and purpose. In Hegel's vision, at least, there is room for interaction amongst nations. Realistically, it is doubtful whether national social ties so strongly conceived can tolerate the idealistic interaction he proposes. The popular modern advocate of Hegel, Francis Fukuyama, touts liberal democracy as the highest stage of human development. Bringing us to the 'end of history', he confesses though that liberal democracy has not yet

[52] Georg Wilhelm Friedrich Hegel, *The Philosophy of Right*, trans. T. M. Knox (Chicago: Encyclopaedia Britannica Inc., 1952 reprinted 1986), [320].

[53] van Creveld, *Rise and Decline*, pp. 195–6, 203.

[54] See Georg Wilhelm Friedrich Hegel, *Lectures on the Philosophy of World History*, trans. H. B. Nesbit (New York: Cambridge University Press, 1975), pp. 80–3; see too his *Philosophy of Right*, [341]–[360].

become universal because of 'the incomplete correspondence between peoples [that is, nations] and states'.[55] In other words, the nation-state is not a theoretically complete concept.

9.3.2 The Contractarian School

For present purposes, the other main theory of the nation-state is the contractarian view. Diverse protagonists of this theory, such as Locke and Aristotle, on Franck's interpretation, separate the state from the nation of Hegel's analysis. The state is a voluntary association for the pursuit of virtue, or the common good, according to Aristotle. People come together in a state structure, the polis, to pursue 'the good' which is the end or *telos* of the polis and public life: '[a] state is an association of similar persons whose aim is the best life possible'.[56] For John Locke (1632–1704), people come together in the state to protect life, liberty and goods.[57] Locke's predecessor Thomas Hobbes (1588–1679) may also be included in this voluntarist school, although for Hobbes the state was a natural imperative to stave off civil war.[58] This theory suggests an interior if not moral foundation for the laws of the state, different from that offered by the Historical-National School, because the moral capacity for free choice has been exercised. Also, that moral allegiance may arise because the state is uniquely placed to protect property.[59]

This view of allegiance may, however, be too simplistic, because the delegation or sacrifice of individual choice to the state can alienate moral choice on that topic for the future, generating the future imposition of political norms in the form of legislation and executive control, abstracted from the individual's moral sphere. We have encountered this in the concept of the 'legislative mentality'[60] and the triple abstraction it creates between personal, interior norms and exterior government on the Space Axis.[61]

9.3.3 Moral and political implications

Can these two models of social allegiance be reconciled or confidently synthesised? From the hyphenated murkiness of the nation-state concept settles the symbiotic relationship between the nation and the state as forces which exert both moral and political pulls of social allegiance. The nation seeks the state, as subconscious ties objectify into a bureaucratic, rational social machine,

---

[55] Francis Fukuyama, *The End of History and the Last Man* (New York: Simon & Schuster, 1992), p. 212.

[56] See Aristotle, *The Politics*, trans. T. A. Sinclair (Harmondsworth: Penguin, reprinted 1992), VII.9, p. 413.

[57] See John Locke, *Two Treatises of Government* [1689] (London: Everyman, 1993 reprinted 1998), ch. 2, p. 117.

[58] See Thomas Hobbes, *Leviathan* (Harmondsworth: Penguin, 1985).

[59] See Allott, *Eunomia*, [16.65]–[16.66].   [60] See ch. 7, section 7.5, pp. 157–61 above.

[61] See section 9.2, p. 203 above.

allowing enemies to be neutralised into mere strangers.[62] Seizures of white-owned land in Zimbabwe under President Mugabe and the unsuccessful Fijian coup of George Speight in 2000 illustrate the failure of nationalism without a principled state. Inversely, the state seeks the nation to authorise and moralise the rational, purposive machinery of the state into a primeval commonality. The failure of civic (as opposed to national or ethnic) ideas of citizenship in colonial Portuguese Angola and Somalia indicates the difficulty of the state project without national authority. The hyphenation of nation and state is therefore a necessary moderating tendency which the words 'nation' and 'state' offer to each other.

At a practical level, as remarked at the outset of this chapter, authority whether conceived nationally or more politically (as the state) will be the basic conceptualisation for social legitimacy in the years to come, despite the challenges globalisation poses. National cultural affinities and the state social contract both rely upon fictions. The very psychological determination of these allegiances suggests that they could be expressed and understood more clearly by alternative means. This might also make their significance more transportable in time, particularly in the face of globalisation. A promising model may draw from Kant's idea for perpetual peace, and Aristotle's idea of friendship.

9.4 Friendship and self-interest as sources of global allegiance

9.4.1 Nation and state as aspects of friendship

In early medieval times, with ancient precedents, 'friendship treaties' created legally enforceable associations amongst rulers and peoples based upon varying degrees of 'kinship, comradeship and lordship'.[63] Aristotle, in *The Nicomachean Ethics*, discussed friendship in profound terms which may be extended to relations across societies today.

Although Aristotle's political theory was said above to correspond to the contractarian, voluntarist, associational choice model of the state, a reconfigured constitutionalism can be drawn from Aristotle's ethics discourse. Consider ideas of nation and state in terms of kinship and comradeship, respectively. Aristotle characterised friendship in these terms: every friendship involves association based upon kindred and comrade models.[64] The nation is a kindred organisation based upon shared commonalities of appearance and culture. The state is a comrade organisation based on politics or choice. Aristotle acknowledged the kindred relationship in the genetic terms that 'parents love

---

[62] Zygmunt Bauman, 'Modernity and Ambivalence' in Featherstone (ed.), *Global Culture*, p. 153.

[63] See Gerd Althoff, '*Amicitiae* [Friendships] as Relationships Between States and Peoples' in Lester K. Little and Barbara H. Rosenwein (eds.), *Debating the Middle Ages: Issues and Readings* (Malden: Blackwell Publishers, 1998).

[64] Aristotle, *The Nicomachean Ethics*, trans. David Ross (Oxford: Oxford University Press, 1925 reprinted 1980), VIII.12, p. 212.

their children as being a part of themselves, and children their parents as having themselves originated from them'. Whilst acknowledging elements of pleasure and utility in the kindred friendship between man and wife, Aristotle tended to equate pleasure and utility more with comrades. Marriage, however, can combine kinship and comradeship – the two theoretical allegiances exerted by the nation and the state – into an institutional loyalty. Children are the culmination of the good purpose. In the context of husband and wife, children are the bond of union: 'for children are a good common to both and what is common holds them together'.[65] Kinship and comradeship, the nation and the state, the Historical-National School and the Contractarian School, are then capable of reconciliation. The key is to arrive at 'the common good'.

Applied to society at all levels from tribe to globe, what can be 'the common good' in inter-associational relationships which are both kindred and comrade based? It would be fruitless to attempt direct subversion of the self-directing (or 'autopoietic') workings of the nation and the state as the two most potent normative tendencies on the globe. How can they be reconciled to produce friendship in a globalised world? How can they be consolidated to minimise the destruction they wrought in the twentieth century? The common good must be common projects similar in the manner of children to Aristotle's husband and wife – projects which do not undermine allegiances which are personal and meaningful, but rather channel these allegiances into greater things. A new approach to education at all levels and communication orientated to an interconnected, world society, including sub-societies, is an appropriate international common project.

A state, or an international or global polity of whatever constitution, cannot be made out of any and every collection of people, as Aristotle would suggest.[66] A vision for global or regional authority must still contain jurisdictional boundaries which cannot stray too far from their natural spheres of containable disruption, which will shift in the ordinary course and as interconnection increases. Education and communication may hold the keys to increasing solidarity as the social face of a love which is beyond the completely personal and self-absorbed sphere of intimacy.[67] The ability to accommodate debate and change (not just a commitment to 'ethnicity or language or some catalogue of shared values') through time is not just the core of any democratic community,[68] it is also at the core of any tradition on its own.[69] Such an approach involving education and dialogue must enhance the potential growth of constitutional structures which would permit multiple allegiances to coexist and flourish.[70]

---

[65] Ibid., VIII.3, VIII.12–13, pp. 195, 214–15.   [66] Aristotle, *Politics*, V.3, p. 304.

[67] On this notion of solidarity, see Roberto Mangabeira Unger, *Law in Modern Society: Toward a Criticism of Social Theory* (New York: The Free Press, 1976), p. 207.

[68] See Jeremy Webber, *Reimagining Canada: Language, Culture, Community, and the Canadian Constitution* (Kingston and Montreal: McGill-Queen's University Press, 1994), p. 223.

[69] See ch. 1, section 1.1.3, pp. 6–7 above.

[70] See Brian Slattery, 'The Paradoxes of National Self-Determination' (1994) 32 *Osgoode Hall Law Journal* 703–33.

9.4.2 The shared self-interest of trade

There remains a prospect less normative than both a commitment to debate and education, for engendering accommodation across traditions. It derives its authority from the utility it brings in a comradeship, social choice setting. The prospect is none other than international free trade. Its international constitutional significance has been explored by Immanuel Kant (1724–1804).

The similarity between nation-states in the international sphere and the individual who stands in the state of nature – in the Hobbesian war of all against all – was noted by Kant in the late eighteenth century. He did not believe that European nation-states had external laws sufficient to maintain order. There had to be some other way of making international law more responsible. His solution was to conceive nation-states in a federation, the only way he could see to invest a common external constraint with *legal* force. Kant's negativity towards the grand figures of international law such as Grotius, Pufendorf and Vattel was a consequence of their writings being used by states to justify military aggression.[71] It is probably as well that Kant did have such a rigid view of law as requiring common external constraint, impervious to the rhetorical and diplomatic power of the writings of the grand figures. It compelled Kant to devise a federal model with some practical compulsion. Underlying it is a comrade-based notion of friendship which generates utility through trade. As a happy incident for our purposes, it is a pluralist conception of supranational order which sees human diversity as a consequence of peace, not a natural cause of conflict.[72]

The model goes something like this. War is absolutely condemned by reason, the highest moral legislative power. Because peace is dependent upon general agreement between the nations, a league is required – a 'pacific federation'. This federation should go further than a peace treaty which is restricted only to specified wars. The proposed federation is for all time. By a series of alliances, this federation should spread, securing the peace and freedom of each new state, one by one. As in the liberal, Hobbesian manner of men in the state of nature renouncing 'their savage and lawless freedom' for the protection of a commonwealth, an international state should develop out of the federation. Unfortunately, 'this is not the will of nations', and as a fallback, what can only be hoped for is 'an enduring and gradually expanding federation likely to prevent war'.[73] International trade then makes its entrance as a concept with potential for greater global peace. Kant observes:

---

[71] Immanuel Kant, 'Perpetual Peace: A Philosophical Sketch' in Hans Reiss (ed.), *Kant: Political Writings*, trans. N. B. Nisbet (Cambridge: Cambridge University Press, 1970, 2nd edn 1991), pp. 102–3.

[72] James Bohman and Matthias Lutz-Bachmann, 'Introduction' in James Bohman and Matthias Lutz-Bachmann (eds.), *Perpetual Peace: Essays on Kant's Cosmopolitan Ideal* (Cambridge, MA: The MIT Press, 1997), p. 6.

[73] Kant, 'Perpetual Peace', pp. 104–5. It can be criticised for impotence: Louis P. Pojman, 'Kant's Perpetual Peace and Cosmopolitanism' (2005) 36 *Journal of Social Philosophy* 62–71, 67.

[N]ature also unites nations . . . and does so by means of their mutual self-interest. For the *spirit of commerce* sooner or later takes hold of every people, and it cannot exist side by side with war. And of all the powers (or means) at the disposal of the power of the state, *financial power* can probably be relied on most. Thus states find themselves compelled to promote the noble cause of peace, though not exactly from motives of morality.[74] [original italics]

Although Kant is cynical of the motive, the motive can be construed within a species of morality. This is because the motive is justified by an inner conviction which directs it, even if that inner conviction is self-interested and coincidental to the broader good it produces. The 'spirit of commerce' is not coerced, and it is potentially of utilitarian benefit to a greater number in society (although this is to apply a consequentialist logic distant from Kant's philosophy). As authority for law goes, it is desirable for its lack of coercion. The difficulty is in maintaining that self-interest within bounds which respect the environment and are not exploitative of humans. This is a tension dealt with in chapter 10. The logical anticipation Kant had for developments in the twentieth century was prophetic, as will become particularly apparent in chapter 11.

A perpetual friendship through trade appears to be a worthwhile and somewhat achievable aim for diverse authorities in globally challenged times. The nation-state, as already noted, will remain the basic authority in the conceivable future. It is possible to reconfigure this apparent fact by reimagining the functions of the nation-state in more helpful theoretical terms. Based upon Aristotle's ideas of the pursuit of common goals through friendship, an aspect of which – comradeship – is orientated towards personal utility such as trade, the Kantian idea of a perpetual peace appears within range of pursuit. There is a popular wisdom which holds that no country with at least one McDonald's outlet goes to war with another country with a McDonald's.[75] It was true until the NATO intervention in the Balkans. Wars between liberal trading democracies, though, are not desired by their constituents.

9.5 On the way to authorities differently conceived

There is nothing 'natural' about the nation or the state. Authorities and allegiances travel through time like ripples on the surface and currents in the

---

74 Kant, 'Perpetual Peace', p. 114. See too, generally, Charles Covell, *Kant and the Law of Peace: A Study in the Philosophy of International Law and International Relations* (London: Macmillan, 1998).

75 See Thomas Friedman, *The Lexus and the Olive Tree: Understanding Globalization* (London: Harper Collins Publishers, 2000), pp. 195–8. Democracies have been known to attack each other. Witness France occupying the Ruhr in 1923 and conflict between India and Pakistan: Bobbitt, *Shield of Achilles*, pp. 266, 780. Huntington asserts that economic growth creates political instability, although his authority is more suggestive of lesser tensions between trading blocs: Samuel Huntington, *The Clash of Civilizations and the Remaking of World Order* (New York: Simon & Schuster, 1996), pp. 218–24.

depths, visible and invisible, kind and unkind, forgotten, remembered and adapted. Westerners strive to find meaning for themselves and for others in an ocean of social constructions, by reference to historical experiences, visions, moral convictions and forms of social organisation. Since Greek philosophy (with Islamic input) met Roman law and the Bible in the twelfth century, Westerners have wandered this Space–Time Matrix with little rest, consciously and unconsciously. Westerners, and those in other cultures too,[76] are not *simply* defined by a sense of nation or statehood, but other associational forms too. In the era of globalisation, never before have there been so many imperatives and norms jostling for attention.[77]

The legal and normative nature of what commonly passes for 'globalisation' remains to be analysed further in some detail. Chief examples include human rights and free trade in the next chapter. In chapters 11 and 12, respectively, case studies of European Union law and international commercial law are offered as paradigmatic examples of legal systems which have responded historically to patterns of interconnection and universalist authority, now recurring with globalisation. The present chapter has been necessary to canvass the conventional, contemporary normative allegiances which formed mainly in the eighteenth and nineteenth centuries. National and state creeds have generated the basic, premier bonds of allegiance which survive today. These larger collectives or spheres have represented a historical movement on the Space Axis in the exterior direction, when compared with the interior ties of allegiance which characterised the Middle Ages and parcellised sovereignty. That is to say, institutions of mainstream law at the hands of the nation-state have become more impersonal and exterior. On the Time Axis, aided by industrialisation, the amalgamation of the nation-state has reduced the future, generally speaking, to a lifetime, rather than inspiring norms programmed for the pursuit of a better place on earth in accordance with a vision.

Globalisation, experienced as the cross-border immigration and emigration of humans, challenges the nation-bond of the nation-state more profoundly than ever before. For the first time in history, a large, industrialised, indigenous population, the whites in Britain, faces the prospect of being an ethnic minority in London by the year 2010, and in England by the end of the twenty-first century.[78] In addition, the political state-bond is challenged more than ever by a resurgence of competing jurisdictions and non-territorial governmental bodies. Members of over 15,000 cultures demand recognition as states in the world-system – an impossibility. An entrenched Western attitude posits that 'every culture worthy of recognition is a nation, and every nation should be

---

[76] See Amartya Sen, *Identity and Violence: The Illusion of Destiny* (New York: W. W. Norton & Co., 2006).

[77] This should not necessarily be of concern: see Thomas M. Franck, *The Empowered Self: Law and Society in the Age of Individualism* (Oxford: Oxford University Press, 1999), ch. 5.

[78] Simon Mann, 'Whites a Minority by End of Century', *Sydney Morning Herald*, 4 September 2000.

recognised as an independent nation state'.[79] Unfortunately that is to suggest that the only defensible autonomous collective of humans is large and technologically advanced enough to hold territory to the exclusion of 'others'. These multifarious identities require reconciliation. They also require protection within the state from the exercise of unfettered political power.[80]

Discourses inspired by globalisation have prompted the pursuit of frameworks for building laws upon complex affinities and nationalities, avoiding the cold formalism and impersonality of the state. In the context of European citizenship, J. H. H. Weiler has suggested, in the face of increasing referents of identity, the concept of *'differentity'*, to unite the different and 'fragmented self of individuals' who comprise states.[81] We have already explored possibilities for peaceful, fruitful diversity, by reference to Aristotle's ideas on friendship and Kant's prescription for perpetual peace through international trade. These possibilities appeal to the human in the interior dimension of the Space Axis of the Space–Time Axis. Good law, authority and legitimacy derive from the respect which is earned in the minds of those to whom the rules are directed. Ideally that will come from more than just a nation-state differently conceived. Required will be more than just a nation of political bonds and not just moral bonds; and more than just a state of moral bonds and not just political bonds. Territorial and national boundaries must not only be physically but also psychologically perforated.

The increasing fragmentation of society, from the medieval universe to the point today of competing worlds crashing and colliding in cosmological confusion, is testament to the ties which bind humans, highly selectively and even contingently, to one another. Although we are too early in our historical period to know with greater surety, social units organised as nation-states, it appears, are eventually to discover greater utility in co-operation rather than annihilation. Perhaps like sleepy, heavy eye-lidded night-walkers absorbed in their own dreams, slowly adapting to the light, the nationalistic state units of world-society collide less frequently with the rise of the United Nations, the European Union, the World Trade Organization and other institutions characteristic of globalisation. To these mixed blessings we now turn.

---

[79] James Tully, *Strange Multiplicity: Constitutionalism in an Age of Diversity* (Cambridge: Cambridge University Press, 1995), p. 8.

[80] See Arendt, *Totalitarianism*, ch. 9.

[81] J. H. H. Weiler, *The Constitution of Europe: 'Do the New Clothes Have an Emperor?' and Other Essays on European Integration* (Cambridge: Cambridge University Press, 1999), p. 329.

10

The return of universalist law: human rights and free trade

One culture's universal human rights can be another culture's universal poison. One person's universal free trade can be another person's unfair trade. One nation-state's tributes to human rights and free trade can be met with jeers of hypocrisy from onlookers. Welcome back to the twentieth century. This chapter considers the bequest of the World Revolution to the major discourses of authority supporting the Western legal tradition today.

At the beginning of the Western legal tradition, the European feudal economy was characterised by dispersed and local markets. Spirituality was for the most part centralised and universalist, under the ultimate reality and meaning extolled by the Catholic church. Today, this eleventh-century dynamic has been inverted. A global economy exists above dispersed spiritual, religious and belief communities.[1] How those particular, dispersed communities and other political units relate to the claims to ultimate reality and meaning extolled by the universalist economy will probably be to future generations a large part of the conventional history of globalisation and law.

Globalisation and law cannot be understood without reference to the entire second millennium. The twentieth-century World Revolution constitutes at once the capstone of an old way of looking at law (which had culminated in state sovereignty) and the lodestar of a potentially globalist legal and ethical tradition coexisting with other legal and ethical traditions. Recurring patterns of Western law and authority are to be found in the pervasive historical tensions between these universalistic and particularistic tendencies. The medieval papacy, we have seen, engaged in almost round robin-like contests for jurisdiction with royal, feudal, manorial, mercatorial and urban legal systems, by reference to common Christian scripts. Reflecting this pattern, emerging universalist ethical and philosophical principles of free trade and human rights now compete with sub-state, state, supra-state and interstate communities. To introduce this latest pattern, our historical chronology resumes in the nineteenth century with key factual developments.

---

[1] Eugen Rosenstock-Huessy, *Out of Revolution: Autobiography of Western Man* (Oxford: Berg, 1993), pp. 495–6.

10.1 The quest for order in the World Revolution

10.1.1 Background interconnections

Economic and social interconnections began to multiply and increase in intensity, in the nineteenth century. The world significance of civil society started to become apparent, although under a shadow. States were approaching the height of their strength, steering not only the Western world but the wider world towards the twentieth-century cataclysm. Despite state power, the international legal significance of civil society, so far as private economic links were concerned, was well illustrated by the formation of the International Telegraph Union in 1865. The communications triumph of the postage stamp arguably overshadowed the victories of Napoleon.[2] Free-trade ideas were advocated with considerable practical effect.[3] Absent government leadership in the later nineteenth century, other private initiatives sought a more public order beyond states. The Institute of International Law was established in 1873. This scholarly community of international lawyers sought to articulate the legal conscience of the civilised world in a Savignian manner.[4] They extolled a universalist but Eurocentric, historical jurisprudence developed by lawyers which they claimed represented the spirit of 'civilised' people.[5] The Inter-parliamentary Union was formed in 1887, and the Nobel Committee too. An International Peace Bureau, located in Berne, operated from 1891, with national branches. A number of individuals made public pacifist comment, advocating the redundancy of war in the face of the economic interests of states.[6] The International Court of Justice arrived in 1900.

More sinister developments were to have catastrophic effects. Outside Europe, colonialism had sought justification in an internally inconsistent, nationally fractured international law discourse. The more (at that time) altruistic but Eurocentric concern for the 'civilising mission' did not stop international lawyers from 'supporting the controversial policies of their native country'. Particularly in Africa, these policies were lethal and morally appalling,[7] not just by today's standards. The competing foreign territorial interests of France, the United Kingdom, Germany and Russia explain, in large measure, the perniciousness of the resulting wars as a matter of economic self-aggrandisement, protection and nationalistic pride. Every major participant entered World War I to protect underlying imperial interests: Austria-Hungary

---

[2] See Martin van Creveld, *The Rise and Decline of the State* (Cambridge: Cambridge University Press, 1999), pp. 382–3.

[3] Martti Koskenniemi, *The Gentle Civilizer of Nations: The Rise and Fall of International Law 1870–1960* (Cambridge: Cambridge University Press, 2001), pp. 58–9; see ch. 2, section 2.1.2, p. 28 above.   [4] See ch. 8, section 8.4.5, pp. 188–9 above.

[5] See Koskenniemi, *Gentle Civilizer*, ch. 1.

[6] See Norman Davies, *Europe: A History* (London: Pimlico, 1997), p. 874.

[7] See Koskenniemi, *Gentle Civilizer*, pp. 155–78.

sought to protect itself against the Pan-Slavic movement; Russia sought to prevent Austro-German dominance in the Balkans; France wished to prevent German expansion; and the UK aimed to prevent Germany from dominating Europe.

10.1.2 The World Wars

Amidst the World Revolution, following World War I, in 1919 the League of Nations was created. The main purposes of the League found in its covenant were the prevention of war, the organisation of peace, the discharge of special duties arising from the peace treaties of 1919–20 and the promotion of international co-operation. Most importantly, article 10 introduced the right of nations to territorial integrity and political independence as fundamental international norms. The United States never joined, and the easy withdrawal of Germany, Japan and Italy, when it suited, reflected a loose association of proud national sovereignties. None of these powers had yielded sovereignty. This, with the lack of focus upon economic matters (aside perhaps from aid programmes in Austria and Hungary) must in large part explain the unchecked, disastrous, global depression of the 1930s. The international economy had malfunctioned at the hands of 'protective tariffs, unfair economic competition, restricted access to raw materials, autarkic governmental policies'.[8] The catastrophe of World War II completed the failure of the League.

An Austrian aristocrat, Count Richard Coudenhove-Kalergi, had founded the Pan-European Union, in 1923. He argued in one of his publications, *Paneuropa*, for a European federation, attracting the support of several prominent politicians. In addition to preventing war and maintaining peace, the emphasis was not on protecting Europe from outsiders but on helping Europe to compete more effectively in the world's economic markets. The logic of this economic and political innovation in the face of the prevailing culture was present in the activity of the smaller Western European states. In 1922, the Belux economic union was formed between Belgium and Luxembourg, with limited practical success. The 1930 Oslo Convention to a limited extent managed to peg tariffs among the Scandinavian states and the Low Countries. The 1932 Ouchy Convention sought to build upon the efforts of the Oslo Convention. The combined effect of these conventions was that the Low Countries had decreased tariffs below the comfort level of the Scandinavian countries, whilst the larger states remained disinterested or indeed vented active hostility, as did the UK.[9]

---

[8] Paul Kennedy, *The Rise and Fall of the Great Powers: Economic Change and Military Conflict from 1500 to 2000* (London: Unwin Hyman, 1988), p. 359. See too Jim Chen, 'Pax Mercatoria: Globalization as a Second Chance at "Peace for our Time"' (2000) 24 *Fordham International Law Journal* 217–51, 226.

[9] See David Urwin, *The Community of Europe: A History of European Integration Since 1945* (London: Longman, 1991), p. 6.

Aristide Briand, the French foreign minister, in September 1929 presented at Geneva a plan for a federal organisation of European states, however no successful encroachments upon the sovereignty of the nation-state ensued. Briand's Memorandum, whilst vague, did make a novel suggestion for a permanent political committee and secretariat. Nonetheless, beyond a rationalisation of customs barriers, no advance was made. Briand's ideas perhaps derived from a French desire to protect itself against Germany: he had been an architect of the 1925 Locarno Pact, the signatories to which (Belgium, the UK, France, Germany and Italy) had guaranteed existing state boundaries and renounced war among themselves. French initiatives appeared to be an attempt to perpetuate the Versailles peace settlement imposed upon Germany after World War I.[10] Lack of support from England and the emergence of the Nazi Party in Germany relegated the Briand Memorandum to insignificance, as economic depression set in and each rise in unemployment triggered new bouts of protectionism.

Individual ideologues of their times had projected their ideas with zeal. Trotsky, at the outbreak of World War I, was writing about 'the United States of Europe' in his socialist dream, *The War and the International*. Later, Mussolini had proposed a pact amongst Britain, France, Germany and Italy.[11] A civil movement, known as the Pan-European movement, was well sponsored and attracted support from important League members, including Mussolini. This movement had exerted no real influence on governmental policy.[12] In the summer of 1940, Hitler's Reichsbank had planned to make the Reichsmark the common currency of an economic union in German-occupied Europe. The Nazis published a journal called *Nation Europa*, appropriating the ideas of a theoretical Europe to an enlarged territory based upon an insanely fictitious racial purity. Ephemeral victories of Nazi Germany were conceived to be in the service of Europe.[13] World War II was then inadvertently to sponsor the emergence of the European Union and the United Nations.

10.1.3 The re-gathering of the European community

Europe had literally worn itself out by the end of World War II. In Washington, a State Department Sub-Committee on European Organization, meeting during 1943 and 1944, on the whole demonstrated a lack of enthusiasm for European union. It was felt by several members of the Sub-Committee that European union did not serve US interests. This was partly on the economic basis that the removal of internal trade barriers amongst European nations might be damaging to American trade. The other main ground for American opposition was the experience of German control of Europe: any power strong

---

[10] Ibid., p. 5.   [11] Davies, *Europe*, pp. 894, 951.
[12] Hans A. Schmitt, *The Path to European Union* (Baton Rouge: Louisiana State University Press, 1962), p. 9.   [13] See Davies, *Europe*, pp. 1007, 1017; Schmitt, *Path to European Union*, p. 9.

enough to unite Europe was a threat to world peace *per se*, jeopardising a refurbished League of Nations (which was to be replaced by the United Nations). Notwithstanding, at this time there was still American support for a European union, on the ground that a united European economy offered attractive market possibilities for the US to exploit, given the predictable increased income and demand for American goods. Political reorganisation was also considered. In particular, the imagined union was to be democratic and expressive of the voluntary wishes of citizens, yet with the retention of national diplomatic entities. In 1944, representatives of many of the resistance movements met in Geneva, issuing a declaration that regarded federation as the only means for European survival, with a federal government responsible to peoples rather than to governments of member states. This federal government was to be possessed of powers similar to those reposed in the federal government of the USA, such as interstate commerce and defence of the continent.[14]

In 1944, the exiled governments of Belgium, the Netherlands and Luxembourg agreed to come together as the Benelux economic unit, although no political arrangements were made. The project was to harmonise the three domestic economies, through the abolition of internal customs duties and the introduction of a joint external tariff on all imports. Complete free trade was still far from being achieved, and by the time the Organization for European Economic Co-operation (OEEC) was established in 1948, the Benelux programme had been stagnant.[15]

In 1946, Winston Churchill, in a speech at Zurich University, announced the prospect of a 'European family' akin to a 'United States of Europe'. One of Churchill's concrete proposals was for this concept to grow around a Franco-German partnership, without the UK.[16] The 1948 Treaty of Brussels called for 'collective self-defense and . . . economic, social and cultural collaboration', the implementation of which was entrusted to a Consultative Council of foreign ministers, a secretariat and a number of committees. This was quickly superseded by the North Atlantic Treaty Organization (NATO). Germany was divided into the communist East and capitalist West, with the need for Western political consolidation becoming apparent. The Western union assumed the mantle of a North Atlantic alliance in the form of NATO with American involvement, pitched defensively against the Eastern countries organised in 1955 under the Warsaw Pact.

Not until America supported the idea could the project of European unity progress. The 'Truman Doctrine' of 1947 involved the US taking over from Britain the provision of assistance to Greece and Turkey. It became apparent that the world balance of power no longer remained in Europe. President

---

[14] See Schmitt, *Path to European Union*, pp. 13–16. On the resistance movements, see Edelgard Mahant, *Birthmarks of Europe: The Origins of the European Community Reconsidered* (Aldershot: Ashgate, 2004), pp. 19–20.   [15] See Urwin, *Community of Europe*, p. 40.
[16] See Schmitt, *Path to European Union*, p. 33.

Truman emphasised the interrelatedness of the democratic world and the connection which the subjugation of European democracy had with the United States: peace was necessary for American security. Protection of American interests – its sphere of containable disruption – had expanded across the Atlantic Ocean. There followed the American Marshall Plan, formally entitled the 'European Recovery Programme', which can be viewed as an early Cold War reaction to the Soviet threat of worldwide communist revolution. Importantly, the Marshall Plan did not deliver untied aid: the proviso was that the recipient states were to co-ordinate economic activities to maximise the benefits from the programme. The permanent organisation charged with administering this mandate, the OEEC, was controlled by the member states, although a decision could not be imposed on a dissenting state. A Council of Ministers comprised one representative from each member state. An elaborate network of agencies developed, liberalising trade with decreasing resort to national veto.[17]

A constitutional prototype had been created for the European Union, the mature features of which are discussed later in chapter 11 as a case study of public law principles relevant to a potential globalist jurisprudence.

10.2 The global hegemony of the USA

The USA was the only country which actually became richer because of World War II, which gave rise to a period which continues to this time, known by some as the *pax Americana*. It countered the fear that 'a postwar slump might follow the decline in US government spending unless new overseas markets were opened up to absorb the products of America's enhanced economic productivity'. The address by the US of this economic problem has coincided with a re-emergent Kantian belief in the Western world that the interests of peace are best served by freedom of international trade. American control of, or access to, crucial materials such as oil, rubber and metal ores demanded by the American military-industrial complex has thereby been facilitated.[18]

As such, America bears 'a very heavy responsibility for the future of humanity – an imperial responsibility' – parallel to that of Rome in the Roman Empire and Greece in the time of Alexander the Great.[19] The hegemonic status of the US in European developments and the quest for order following the world wars warrants some theoretical reflection. Globalisation, as it is commonly thought about in terms of economic interconnections, begins to take its form in large part from the idea of a harmonised Europe and its post-World War II relationship with the US. Characteristic of the broader global landscape is the very great politico-legal significance of the US and the universalist values which it sponsors (although does not always live up to).

---

[17] See Urwin, *Community of Europe*, pp. 15, 22.   [18] See Kennedy, *Rise and Fall*, p. 359.
[19] Philip Allott, 'The True Function of Law in the International Community' (1998) 5 *Indiana Journal of Global Legal Studies* 391–413, 391.

It is instructive to borrow a twentieth-century formulation of sovereignty with Hobbesian overtones, in the attempt to understand the place of the United States in the emerging world society. Carl Schmitt wrote: 'Sovereign is he who decides on the exception ... A jurisprudence concerned with ordinary day-to-day questions has practically no interest in the concept of sovereignty ... What characterizes an exception is principally unlimited authority, which means suspension of the entire existing order.'[20]

Schmitt was asserting that the jurisprudence of everyday lawyers preoccupied with law as rules from cases and statutes has nothing to do with sovereignty. This notion of sovereignty leaves out much of legal value from social processes which coexist below and above the state level. The United States does, however, enjoy a Schmittian notion of sovereignty in its role as a world power or hegemon. The US intervenes at its discretion in international causes (for example, in the Balkans and not in Rwanda). It chooses the economic laws it wishes to follow. (For example, the US expected African nations to pay for unsubsidised AIDS medicines; yet was content, for its own domestic antiterrorist purposes, to order its pharmaceutical companies to produce subsidised anthrax antidote.)[21] US whimsicalness is reminiscent of that of the absolutist monarchies in the seventeenth and eighteenth centuries, guaranteeing, in effect, social stability (at the expense of freedom), without relying necessarily upon law.[22] To be sure, Schmitt's theory may be 'found wanting in respect of those situations in which there is a standing constitutional tradition', as observed by Neil MacCormick.[23] Furthermore, absolutist monarchies have not endured in the West. In the context of an international law which is something less than a 'standing constitutional tradition', in the post-Cold War era the US may be regarded as a global sovereign (subject to some qualifications below). The US continues to decide the exception, periodically, to established world law, for example, in Yugoslavia, Afghanistan, Iraq and some South American countries.[24]

From what we saw of the historical, normative sources of the nation-state, the tendency for humans to ally themselves to their own kin and community of utility[25] should cause no surprise when a state such as the US is seen to act out of self-interest in the international sphere. The US is not, of course, an

---

[20] Carl Schmitt, *The Political Theology of Sovereignty*, trans. George Schwab (Cambridge, MA: MIT Press, 1985), pp. 5, 12.

[21] See Peter Singer, *One World: The Ethics of Globalisation* (Melbourne: Text Publishing, 2nd edn 2004), pp. 80–1, 133, 153.

[22] 'To produce law [the sovereign] need not be based on law': Schmitt, *Political Theology*, p. 13.

[23] Neil MacCormick, *Questioning Sovereignty: Law, State, and Nation in the European Commonwealth* (Oxford: Oxford University Press, 1999), p. 128.

[24] See generally Michael Byers and Georg Nolte (eds.), *United States Hegemony and the Foundations of International Law* (Cambridge: Cambridge University Press, 2003); Michael Ignatieff (ed.), *American Exceptionalism and Human Rights* (Princeton: Princeton University Press, 2005); Philippe Sands, *Lawless World: America and the Making and Breaking of Global Rules from FDR's Atlantic Charter to George W. Bush's Illegal War* (New York: Viking, 2005).

[25] See ch. 9, sections 9.1 and 9.2, pp. 196–203 above.

absolute global sovereign. Its activities are subject to the moral discourse of an emerging world society amongst other societies. That discourse is influential and not clear cut, like any social discourse, and some deference is paid to the moral discourse in a self-conscious way – for example, President George W. Bush's 'war against global terror' and efforts on behalf of 'the free peoples of the world'. To be credible at a moral, interior level on the Space Axis of the Space–Time Matrix, the US, with all of its exterior powers, must affirm human solidarity without reference every time to its own economic and strategic concerns.[26] Visions of that solidarity can be found in some fundamental twentieth-century treaties.

10.3 The preambling quest for human solidarity

On the Time Axis, what has been largely forgotten by most current commentators on this 'globalising' dynamic is the historical significance of four twentieth-century institutions synonymous with globalisation. They were concerned at their establishment to achieve human solidarity and to preserve human dignity and life.

A new moral awareness of world proportions superseded the shifting sands of ineffective international political allegiance and the unsustainable, evidently misplaced domestic nationalisms which had culminated in the World Revolution. Of the purportedly universal moral consciousness, the rallying of regional forces in the name of 'free peoples' and 'fighting evil' has a medieval crusader ring. It harks back to the Christian commonwealth of our rhetorical holy Roman empire. The modern European public law system associated with sovereign states, which had superseded the late medieval Christian commonwealth, is challenged by a new, secular commonwealth. This new commonwealth professes to represent liberalism and democracy, proclaiming notions of human rights, crimes against humanity and free trade. Offences against these universalist principles are considered to warrant collective action in the name of humanity, not a state, for offences against universalist standards. Principles of a 'just war' returned, by which war may only be justified on compelling moral grounds, not as a matter of a state's right.[27] Twentieth-century 'Peace Movements' have acted on behalf of a new commonwealth of humanity, analogous to the previous turn-of-the-millennium Peace Movement acting on behalf of members of the Catholic church.[28]

Nowhere are the aspirations for this new commonwealth better documented than in the preambles to the revolutionary institutions which, after World War II, ensued. A common, painful history and hope for the future are the moral

[26] See Richard Falk, 'Re-framing the Legal Agenda of World Order in the Course of a Turbulent Century' in Likosky (ed.), *Transnational Legal Processes*.

[27] Martin van Creveld, 'On Globalization: The Military Dimension' in Karl-Heinz Ladeur (ed.), *Public Governance in the Age of Globalization* (Aldershot: Ashgate, 2004), pp. 205–6.

[28] See ch. 5, section 5.1, p. 96 above.

lynchpins to the success of these politically established legal endeavours. Four of these institutions are briefly considered by reference to their preambles. Unfortunately the preambles and recitals of legal documents are frequently glossed over in the hurry to exploit operative provisions, to 'get things done' for clients (be they governments, corporations or people) at the expense of someone or something else.

10.3.1 The United Nations

[T]o save succeeding generations from the scourge of war, which twice in our lifetime has brought untold sorrow to mankind, and

to reaffirm faith in fundamental human rights, in the dignity and worth of the human person, in the equal rights of men and women and of nations large and small, and

to establish conditions under which justice and respect for the obligations arising from treaties and other sources of international law can be maintained, and

to promote social progress and better standards of life in larger freedom[29]

In pursuit of these goals, the United Nations (UN), established in 1945, contains codified prohibitions from customary international law in the first two articles of its Charter on aggressive war and the use of force to annex territory belonging to another sovereign. Permeating ideological notions of what is 'civilised', together with the collectivised coercion available from trade sanctions and military force, have compromised the state as a solitary form of government over a territory, unless that state complies with purportedly universal, collective standards of civilisation.

An analogy can be drawn between the medieval papacy and the UN as moral superintendents of the social order, transcending territorial boundaries. For the failures of both supranational organisations politically, some consolation takes place at the level of moral reach. As Martin van Creveld has written of the UN: 'Like the papacy, it is swerving from one financial crisis to another and is forever negotiating with members (formerly princes) who refuse to pay their debts. Like the papacy, its practical impotence is offset in part by the considerable moral authority which it wields.'[30]

The UN's universalist moral imperative is felt in the network of UN committees which project civil, political, cultural and economic rights into the global legal landscape. Unlike the medieval papacy's relatively universal moral and political authority in Europe on the Space Axis, the UN has been politically slow, if not weak, in the face of latter twentieth-century conflicts, for example, in Rwanda, the Balkans and the Ivory Coast. Criticisms of the UN political

---

[29] Preamble, Charter of the United Nations.
[30] van Creveld, *Rise and Decline*, pp. 353, 384. He understates the medieval papacy's political power of excommunication: see ch. 5, section 5.3, pp. 102–3 above.

process abound, including its internal corruption, 'democratic deficit'[31] and lack of permanent representation on the Security Council for countries other than China, France, Russia, the UK and the US. Whilst these issues require debate, disparagement of the UN frequently proceeds according to the UN's perceived impediments to factional goals. References to the UN, particularly in the popular media, rarely recall that the UN was spawned out of bloody revolution and the highest of human aspirations. Cynicism of the institutional culture of the United Nations should not displace respect for the crucial normative significance of this institution in the history, and for the future, of the solidarity of humanity.

10.3.2 International criminal adjudication

The administration of international criminal justice after World War I was morally bankrupt. Armed burglars convicted in the 1920s served more time in prison than the six German officers convicted for war crimes committed in World War I. Those burglars on their release were not received back into their societies amid the national cheer for their return which greeted the war criminals. The plea of 'not guilty' for following orders from superior officers had until that time been persuasive in most war crimes trials.[32]

The Nuremberg and Tokyo Tribunals set a new precedent after World War II. Interests of justice were thought better served through the formality of due process.[33] The undefended summary trial or execution of the vanquished by the victor would have taught no moral lessons. The Nuremberg Charter defined the greatest twentieth-century legal doctrine, 'crimes against humanity', as

> murder, extermination, enslavement, deportation, and other inhumane acts committed against any civilian population, before or during the war, or persecutions on political, racial or religious grounds in execution of or in connection with any crime, within the jurisdiction of the tribunal, whether or not in violation of the domestic law of the country where perpetrated. Leaders, organizers, instigators and accomplices participating in the formulation or execution of a common plan or conspiracy to commit any of the foregoing crimes are responsible for all acts performed by any person in the execution of such plans.[34]

---

[31] See ch. 11, section 11.4, pp. 267–8 below.

[32] Vesselin Popovski, 'The International Criminal Court: A Synthesis of Retributive and Restorative Justice' (2000) 25 *International Relations* 1–10, 2.

[33] Allied justice featured its own inequities. For example, defence counsel were German lawyers without training in adversarial trial procedure. There was allied hypocrisy in relation to the charges of wanton destruction (e.g., Britain had fire-bombed Dresden; the US had used nuclear weapons). The Soviet Union under Stalin was subjecting its vanquished to forced labour. See Geoffrey Robertson, *Crimes Against Humanity: The Struggle for Global Justice* (London: Allen Lane, 1999), pp. 201–2, 206.

[34] Nuremberg Charter article 6(c), extracted in Robertson, *Crimes Against Humanity*, p. 190. See generally Larry May, *Crimes Against Humanity: A Normative Account* (Cambridge: Cambridge University Press, 2005).

By exposing war activities to legal argumentation, individual responsibility during war was established under law. The artificiality of the state was exposed and a 'universal jurisdiction' projected over all human associations. Officers could not hide behind uniforms.

Universal criminal jurisdiction can purportedly be exercised in state tribunals, such as when Adolf Eichmann was abducted from Argentina by the Mossad to face trial in Israel for his role in the Holocaust.[35] A national 'Beth Hamishpath' – 'House of Justice' – risks being undermined by the perception of state bias. One state's house of justice is another state's house of injustice. The state exercise of such jurisdiction also poses the risk of further abductions.

The treaty for the International Criminal Court (ICC), although still to sit in judgment at the time of writing, exercises jurisdiction without obvious national bias over crimes against humanity. The preamble captures its mission:

> <u>Conscious</u> that all peoples are united by common bonds, their cultures pieced together in a shared heritage, and concerned that this delicate mosaic may be shattered at any time,
>
> <u>Mindful</u> that during this century millions of children, women and men have been victims of unimaginable atrocities that deeply shock the conscience of humanity,
>
> <u>Recognizing</u> that such grave crimes threaten the peace, security and well-being of the world[36]

By April 2002, the requisite number of sixty states had signed the treaty. The operational effectiveness of the ICC is threatened by the US refusing to ratify the treaty, for fear of its soldiers being prosecuted. What can be said, given this initiative and the *ad hoc* UN International Criminal Tribunals,[37] is that morality is not simply the preserve of the individual's immediate environs or social spheres where personal relationships exist. Minimal morality as a matter of law is expected of behaviour performed in the service of larger, more exterior, political social collectives such as the state. The particularity of the state is being challenged by the universalism of world moral principles.[38] Curiously, the collective of the 'world' can be closer on the Space Axis to the allegiance of the individual than is the state.[39]

10.3.3 The IMF and World Bank

Two key economic institutions of the global society with continuing world significance are the International Monetary Fund (IMF) and the World Bank. The

---

[35] See generally Hannah Arendt, *Eichmann in Jerusalem: A Report on the Banality of Evil* (Harmondsworth: Penguin, 1997).

[36] Preamble, Rome Statute of the International Criminal Court, 37 ILM 1002 (1998).

[37] See William A. Schabas, *The UN International Criminal Tribunals: The Former Yugoslavia, Rwanda and Sierra Leone* (Cambridge: Cambridge University Press, 2006).

[38] Universal civil jurisdiction over torts and delicts, emanating from a state house of justice, can be seen, for example, in the Alien Tort Claims Act, 28 U.S.C. §1350.

[39] See discussion surrounding n. 70 below.

World Bank (initially called the International Bank for Reconstruction and Development) provides low-interest credit and grants to less-developed countries. The IMF promotes international monetary co-operation and exchange stability, and temporary financial assistance to countries in need. Led by the US and the UK, the charters of both organisations were conceived in 1944 at Bretton Woods, New Hampshire, at the UN Monetary and Financial Conference. Nowadays these institutions are subject to a great deal of criticism. Primarily this is for their attitude to the less-developed countries which these institutions are supposed to serve.[40] Far from being designed to serve the free-market economic dogma which coincides with Western interests at the expense of developing economies, the preambular intentions were different.

The purposes of the Bank are:

(i) To assist in the reconstruction and development of territories of members by facilitating the investment of capital for productive purposes, including the restoration of economies destroyed or disrupted by war, the reconversion of productive facilities to peacetime needs and the encouragement of the development of productive facilities and resources in less developed countries.

     . . .

(v) To conduct its operations with due regard to the effect of international investment on business conditions in the territories of members and, in the immediate postwar years, to assist in bringing about a smooth transition from a wartime to a peacetime economy.[41]

The purposes of the IMF are:

     . . .

(ii) To facilitate the expansion and balanced growth of international trade, and to contribute thereby to the promotion and maintenance of high levels of employment and real income and to the development of the productive resources of all members as primary objectives of economic policy.[42]

The immediate background to the founding of the World Bank and the IMF were the 1930s depression, trade restrictions, discriminatory currency arrangements and unpaid World War I debts regarded as a cause of the Japanese and German aggression facilitated by an absence of collective action.[43] The consequential tasks were collective and threefold: relief and rehabilitation of the

---

[40] The critical literature is voluminous. For the main ideas, see e.g. Joseph Stiglitz, *Globalization and its Discontents* (London: Penguin, 2002); Richard Peet, *Unholy Trinity: The IMF, World Bank, and WTO* (London: Zed Books, 2003).

[41] The International Bank for Reconstruction and Development (now one of five organisations comprising the World Bank) Articles of Agreement, adopted on 22 July 1944, Australian Treaty Series 1947 No. 15.

[42] The International Monetary Fund Articles of Agreement, adopted on 22 July 1944, Australian Treaty Series 1947 No. 11.

[43] Raymond F. Mikesell, *The Bretton Woods Debates: A Memoir* (Princeton: International Section, Department of Economics, Princeton University, 1994), p. 4.

post-World War II world, reconstruction and development, and freeing international markets (which was entrusted to the World Trade Organization).[44] The first fifteen years of the life of the World Bank were dominated by reconstruction efforts shaped by the rise of the Cold War and the need to bolster democracy.[45]

Prevention of another global economic depression was the main province of the IMF. The IMF was to apply pressure to those Member States not contributing their share to global aggregate demand. Loans were to be provided as liquidity injections in economies suffering from economic downturn. There was, therefore, an acceptance back then that markets often did not work well when left only to their own devices.[46] The tension persists.[47]

International organisations, like states and people, move on after they have dealt with tragedy. Free trade, inconsistently with its connotation of equality, produces great inequality and potential instability which could foreseeably betray the birthright given to these Bretton Woods institutions.

10.3.4 The European Communities

. . . Resolved to substitute for age-old rivalries the merging of their essential interests; to create, by establishing an economic community, the basis for a broader and deeper community among peoples long divided by bloody conflicts; and lay the foundations for institutions which will give direction to a destiny henceforward shared[48]

. . . Resolved by thus pooling their resources to preserve and strengthen peace and liberty, and calling upon the other peoples of Europe who share their ideal to join in their efforts[49]

. . . Recalling the historic importance of the ending of the division of the European continent and the need to create firm bases for the construction of the future Europe[50]

The passionate sources of personal moral allegiance which helped to found the European Union were captured in the words of Winston Churchill. In answer to the question 'What is Europe?', he answered in July 1945: 'a rubble heap, a

[44] Edward S. Mason and Robert E. Asher, *The World Bank Since Bretton Woods* (Washington, DC: The Brookings Institute, 1973), pp. 2–3.

[45] Christoper L. Gilbert and David Vines, 'The World Bank: an Overview of Some Major Issues' in Christopher L. Gilbert and David Vines (eds.), *The World Bank: Structure and Policies* (Cambridge: Cambridge University Press, 2000), p. 14.

[46] Stiglitz, *Globalization*, p. 12.

[47] See Mac Darrow, *Between Light and Shadow: The World Bank, the International Monetary Fund and International Human Rights Law* (Oxford: Hart Publishing, 2006); Balakrishnan Rajagopal, *International Law from Below: Development, Social Movements and Third World Resistance* (Cambridge: Cambridge University Press, 2003), ch. 5.

[48] Preamble, Treaty Establishing the European Coal and Steel Community, 18 April 1951.

[49] Preamble, Treaty Establishing the European Economic Community, 25 March 1957.

[50] Preamble, Treaty on European Union, 7 February 1992.

charnel house, a breeding-ground for pestilence and hate'. He appealed in September that year for 'a kind of United States of Europe'. At the privately organised Congress of Europe in 1948, the foundations for moral allegiance received further articulation by Churchill with similar sentiments expressed by other leaders, in terms which sought to replace the necessary national allegiance with allegiance to some other, newer social organism in response to the revolution:

> We must proclaim the mission and the design of a United Europe whose moral conception will win the respect and gratitude of mankind, and whose physical strength will be such that none will dare molest her tranquil sway . . . I hope to see a Europe where men and women of every country will think of being European as belonging to their native land, and wherever they go in this wide domain will truly feel 'Here I am at home'.[51]

This is not economic language, nor is it distantly political. It is a passionate, personal appeal at a nonetheless logical level, to a people recovering from world war in the midst of the World Revolution. Not only does a European moral authority underlie the foundation of the institutions of the EU but the institutions possess a universalist European political authority which has achieved a power comparable to the medieval papacy. There does not, however, appear to be the same confluence between moral and political authority. Forgetful state-nationalism and economic rationalism tend to leaden the loftier aspirations of the EU formulated in response to the past and envisioned for the future.[52]

10.3.5 The community that jurisprudence rebuilds?

Inaugurating memories and purposes are often buried under the dust thrown up by the frenzied pursuit of political and economic goals facilitated by treaties, constitutions and agreements. The exhortations of the political figures who inspired the preambles of these four global legal phenomena face being forgotten in the new time like the cautions uttered by Old Testament prophets. There seems to be some truth in the pregnant conclusion reached by Eugen Rosenstock-Huessy (in his 1938 'autobiography of Western man') that '[i]n the community that common sense rebuilds, after the earthquake, upon the ashes on the slope of Vesuvius, the red wine of life tastes better than anywhere else'.[53] An implicit meaning which may be imbibed from this quote is that when revolutionary times settle into comfort, it is all too easy to become complacent and indulgent. A general, globalist jurisprudence must therefore encourage a normative, historical jurisprudence, to keep alive and to generate, further, the highest human aims and principles to direct the norms of institutions such as the United Nations, International Criminal Court, International Monetary Fund, World Bank and the European Union.

---

[51] See Davies, *Europe*, pp. 1065–6.   [52] See ch. 11 below generally.
[53] Rosenstock-Huessy, *Out of Revolution*, p. 758.

We may now move to examine the principles which accompany these institutions: human rights and free trade.

10.4 Universal human rights

'Human rights', according to former High Court of Australia Chief Justice Sir Gerard Brennan, 'prescribe the minimum conditions in which an individual can live in society with his or her dignity respected'.[54] Human rights discourse seeks universal support by offering some benchmark of normativity which should be able to attract subjective, moral allegiance. Whilst sometimes competing with state law, the universalist principles of human rights and free trade can also provide legitimacy to state law. These discourses rely upon a recurring functional authority by occupying a similar place to traditional Christianity in earlier Western societies.

10.4.1 Patterns of ultimate reality and meaning

Until the seventeenth and eighteenth centuries, God's laws were thought to bind humans unalterably. Nowadays, human, economic and civil rights are, in popular Western consciousness, vying for the functional place of God's laws. The twentieth-century human rights documents represent a continuation of the sorts of universalist, natural law principles characteristic of medieval Christendom,[55] significantly bolstered, as suggested in chapter 8, by the French Declaration of the Rights of Man and Citizen. As apprehended by Friedrich Tenbruck, they build on 'the Creation, the universality of the Children of God and of brotherhood . . . with the chiliastic promise arising in the Middle Ages of the . . . salvation of the Kingdom of God on earth . . .' The 'secular remnants of this Christian theology of history' facilitated ideas 'of an equal and common development of humanity as the fulfilment of history'.[56]

The twentieth-century rights purport to transcend the nation and apply to all of humanity. Human rights evidence the natural laws and natural rights of our time – patterned on a recurring legal need for social theology and now philosophy. Until about the seventeenth century, it was easy to point to God as the crucial normative authority which underlay all other claims to authority. There have been successors, as Johan Galtung has observed:

---

[54] Sir Gerard Brennan, 'Principle and Independence: The Guardians of Freedom' (2000) 74 *Australian Law Journal* 749–59, 755.

[55] See e.g. John Witte Jr, 'Law, Religion, and Human Rights' (1996) 28 *Columbia Human Rights Review* 1–31; Charles J. Reid Jr, 'The Medieval Origins of the Western Natural Rights Tradition: The Achievement of Brian Tierney' (1998) 83 *Cornell Law Review* 437–63.

[56] Friedrich H. Tenbruck, 'The Dream of a Secular Ecumene: The Meaning and Limits of Policies of Development' in Mike Featherstone (ed.), *Global Culture: Nationalism, Globalization and Modernity* (London: Sage, 1990 reprinted 1996), p. 200.

These successors . . . were the king, the state, the people and the state organization (the League of Nations, the United Nations etc.). The state is then constructed in the image of a benevolent, omnipresent, omniscient and omnipotent
king, possibly receiving legitimacy both from the state community and from the
people . . . The state elevates itself through an act of levitation to the transcendental levels of even deciding over omnicide, through weapons of mass destruction, while standing on top of a growing human rights mountain.[57]

Our 'global times', featuring accelerated interconnections amidst perforated
territorial borders, have resulted in a boon to the possibility for certain human
norms to be projected and accepted as universal. This defies the traditional
sphere of containable disruption of the nation-state, such that the nation-state
can appear to be an excuse for privilege in a particular sphere which is unjusti-
fiable on a world scale. These new human rights universalise *humanity* by contesting sovereignty conceived in state, national or territorial terms.[58] This was a
conseqûence of the maniacal horror of the World Revolution which implored a
human, as opposed to national, response.

Human rights received their fundamental codification in the Universal
Declaration of Human Rights (which will at times be referred to as 'the
Universal Declaration'), adopted by the United Nations General Assembly in
1948. Two other documents adopted in 1966 are commonly dealt with in the
context of twentieth-century human rights: the International Covenant on
Civil and Political Rights; and the International Covenant on Economic, Social
and Cultural Rights. Not all of these rights are absolute in the sense of 'covering the field' morally without dispute: some rights can clash 'head-on',[59] for
example where cultural rights might conflict with economic rights. To an
extent there is a difference between 'human rights' and civil, political and social
rights of the covenants, the latter distinguishing between national and alien, for
example, where employment is concerned.[60] The two covenants do, however,
attempt to convert the general language of the Universal Declaration into
legally binding treaties. All of these human rights texts are related. Economic,
social and cultural rights can facilitate the enjoyment of civil and political
rights.[61]

---

[57] Johan Galtung, *Human Rights in Another Key* (Cambridge: Polity Press, 1994), pp. 18–19.

[58] Roland Axtmann, 'Globalization, Europe and the State: Introductory Reflections' in Roland
Axtmann (ed.), *Globalization and Europe: Theoretical and Empirical Investigations* (London:
Pinter, 1998), p. 15.

[59] Alice Tay, 'Human Rights and Human Wrongs' (1999) 21 *Adelaide Law Review* 1–18, 16.

[60] See e.g. Matthew C. R. Craven, *The International Covenant on Economic, Social and
Cultural Rights: A Perspective on its Development* (Oxford: Clarendon Press, 1998),
pp. 172–4, 265–6.

[61] See Abdullahi Ahmed An-Na'im, 'Globalization and Jurisprudence: An Islamic Law
Perspective' (2005) 54 *Emory Law Journal* 25–51, 32; Chen, 'Globalization and its Losers', 161
and sources therein at n. 20; Michael Kirby, 'Human Rights and Economic Development'
(1996) *Australian International Law Journal* 1–14.

10.4.2 From equality of souls (eleventh century) to equality of bodies (twentieth century)

The emanation of human rights from the French Declaration of the Rights of Man and Citizen is easily observed. The universalistic projections of liberty, freedom of speech and thought, and rule of law are developed in the twentieth-century document. There is a similar sense in both the French Declaration and the Universal Declaration that both tables of norms offer an advance over a disturbing past, although more dramatically expressed in the Universal Declaration. The French Declaration posited a vision of equality against a history of corrupt monarchy. For the Universal Declaration, the preamble 'the barbarous acts which have outraged the conscience of all mankind' echoes the institutional preambles to which reference was made above,[62] in response to the despair of world wars. These logical, rational human rights documents are heavily imbued with the futurist dimension of our Space–Time Matrix with a corresponding interior moral urgency and logical impulsion on the Space Axis. Extending the discussion of human rights doctrines commenced with the French Declaration in chapter 8,[63] the following visionary doctrines of universality and social welfare are added by the Universal Declaration.

Universality 'The General Assembly proclaims This Universal Declaration of Human Rights as a common standard of achievement for all peoples and all nations . . .' (Preamble). 'Everyone is entitled to all the rights and freedoms . . . without distinction of any kind, such as race, colour, sex, language, religion, political or other opinion, national or social origin, property, birth or other status' (article 2). 'Everyone has the right to recognition everywhere as a person before the law' (article 6). 'No one shall be arbitrarily deprived of his nationality nor denied the right to change his nationality' (article 15(2)). 'Education shall be directed to the full development of the human personality . . . It shall promote understanding, tolerance and friendship among all nations, racial or religious groups . . .' (article 26(2)). A global civil society, or world society of humans, is clearly contemplated by the Declaration. No nation-state has the moral right to enjoy a sphere of containable disruption impervious to these universal principles.

Social Welfare 'Everyone, as a member of society, has the right to social security and is entitled to realization, through national effort and international cooperation . . . of the economic, social and cultural rights indispensable for his dignity and the free development of his personality' (article 22). 'Everyone has the right to rest and leisure, including reasonable limitation of working hours and periodic holidays with pay' (article 24). 'Everyone has the right to a standard of living adequate for the health

---

[62] See section 10.3, pp. 221–6 above.   [63] See ch. 8, section 8.4.1, pp. 180–1 above.

and well-being of himself and of his family . . . Motherhood and childhood are entitled to special care and assistance' (article 25). 'Everyone has
the right to education' (article 26). These welfare principles moderate the
harshness of liberal capitalism and perhaps have gone some way towards
incorporating the less radical demands of socialism in an effort to avert the
revolutionary threat after World War II.

As a practical matter, human rights under the Universal Declaration are not
'law' in the strict sense of law centrally co-ordinated and enforced by the state
(although human rights have been received as a matter of principle into EU positive law).[64] '[H]uman rights are first and foremost moral rights.'[65] Chiefly, they
animate a jurisdiction for public discourse and recommendation. The United
Nations Human Rights Committee[66] supervises state parties' compliance with
the International Covenant on Civil and Political Rights (ICCPR), through
reporting and petition procedures. Under article 40 of the ICCPR, state parties
are obliged to file, within one year of entry and at five yearly intervals thereafter,
reports with the Committee on their human rights measures. The Committee
reviews submissions in public session, inviting government representatives to
attend and respond to questions. Proceedings are then published in the annual
report to the General Assembly.[67]

The First Optional Protocol to the ICCPR allows for petitions in the form of
written communications from individuals, against states which have ratified the
protocol, to be adjudicated by the Committee. Domestic remedies must first
have been exhausted, under article 2. Communications are invited from the individual and the state party without oral hearings or formal court rules. Opinions
by consensus of the Committee are delivered after considering the written submissions and making a determination in private meeting. Enforcement depends
largely upon publicity by the Committee for the most part.[68] Certain findings,
for example, in France and the Netherlands, have resulted in legislative and
financial measures being taken to afford remedies to claimants.[69]

Conflicting with the old notion that the subjects of international law are
states, individuals may have access to international human rights tribunals.
Non-state actors and international organisations may avail themselves of international norms alongside, if not ahead of, state laws. For example, a person

---

[64] See ch. 11, section 11.2.4, pp. 262–3 below.   [65] Tay, 'Human Rights', 5.
[66] This ICCPR treaty organisation is different from the UN Charter-derived Human Rights
     Council which replaced, in 2006, the Commission on Human Rights.
[67] See Laurence R. Helfer and Anne-Marie Slaughter, 'Toward a Theory of Effective
     Supranational Adjudication' (1997) 107 *Yale Law Journal* 273–391, 338–41.
[68] Helfer and Slaughter, 'Supranational Adjudication', 341–5, 361. The effect of non-government
     organisations has been to assess the conduct of states 'in terms of the binary code legal/illegal
     regardless of any breach of traditional international law obligations': Andrea Bianchi,
     'Globalization of Human Rights: The Role of Non-state Actors' in Gunther Teubner (ed.),
     Global Law Without A State (Brookfield: Dartmouth Publishing Co., 1997), p. 191.
[69] See Rosalyn Higgins, 'Role of Litigation in Implementing Human Rights' (1999) 5 *Australian
     Journal of Human Rights* 4–19, 10.

expressing a minority group sexuality contrary to state law can have recourse to international norms expressed by expert international committees, indirectly bringing about reform of state law.[70] Human rights seminars have even become eligible for inclusion in the mandatory continuing legal education for legal practitioners in Australia and elsewhere. Human rights principles have become a dimension of domestic legal practice, for example, in employment and discrimination law.

Elucidation of human rights abuses has been reliant in large measure on non-state organisations. Enforcement and policy formulation by states and international organisations have been prompted by non-state lobbying, forcing states to justify their conduct and even to intervene in trouble-spots which otherwise they might have ignored (for example, in Kosovo and East Timor). Media can also play a crucial role in this process, exposing atrocities and reporting to obtain political effect. This further illustrates the increasing reliance upon non-state international legal actors, manifesting counter-hegemonic globalisation – what social justice advocates might consider 'good globalisation'. The International Labour Organization and Amnesty International stand as two examples of a trend which features the involvement of non-government organisations (NGOs) in the development of human rights. NGOs increasingly intervene as third parties in the European Court of Human Rights and the inter-American courts of human rights. Some have observer status, for example with the World Trade Organization. Although the activity of NGOs can be traced in some operations to state consent, the NGO can sometimes overcome national interests through limited formal control of the conduct of the NGO by the nation. Instructions of the nation can be vague, open to interpretation and subject to being ignored.[71]

How might we understand, historically, the institutional recognition of the (in principle) equality of all humans? Twentieth-century human rights represent the secular fulfilment of the eleventh century's egalitarianism of all souls. St Odilo of Cluny's advent near the beginning of the Western legal tradition of All Souls' Day in the Catholic church recognised the common quest for all souls to be redeemed, amidst a singular, Christian, European belief system. In this 'Christian democracy', all Christians in the church could pray for the redemption of the departed souls in a ritual without the exclusivity of All Saints' Day the day before, when prayers were offered up only to the chosen few who were in heaven.[72] After the Protestant Reformations and the European wars of religion

---

[70] E.g., see Carl F. Stychin, 'Relatively Universal: Globalisation, Rights Discourse, and the Evolution of Australian Sexual and National Identities' (1998) 18 *Legal Studies* 534–57; Robertson, *Crimes Against Humanity*, pp. 46–7; Henry J. Steiner and Philip Alston, *International Human Rights in Context: Law, Politics, Morals* (Oxford: Oxford University Press, 2nd edn, 2000), pp. 18–53, and pp. 988–1081 regarding common norms and interjurisdictional reasoning concerning issues such as political asylum, torture, environmental degradation and remedies.

[71] See Bianchi, 'Globalization of Human Rights', pp. 186–92.

[72] See ch. 5, section 5.2.2, p. 101 above.

of the seventeenth century and the Westphalian settlement,[73] 'tolerance' as a concept was supposed to moderate Catholic and Protestant reflexes which otherwise impelled them to take steps towards ensuring the salvation of the unorthodox.[74] The French Declaration of the Rights of Man and Citizen recognised freedom of religion and that certain types of humans were equal, dependent upon their conformity to 'the general good', economically defined. More comprehensively, the UN Universal Declaration recognises, amidst the diversity of belief systems, that all humans by virtue simply of their unqualified bodily existence are equal and entitled to rights. Thus we may now speak of the equality of all bodies having been achieved. For reasons given later in this chapter, with this perhaps should come an acceptance, if not a welcoming, of the inequality of souls in larger, more diverse societies which cannot reasonably expect uniform beliefs. That is not, though, to dismiss the significance of religious and ethical traditions for the success of laws.

The presumption to be able to conceive rational principles such as human rights and impose them on perhaps unwilling cultures raises an important issue in the human rights field. Indeed, this is also a burning issue for any attempts to advance a general, globalist jurisprudence.

10.4.3 Cultural relativism: universality versus diversity

Although human rights purport to be a universal appeal at a moral and logical level, they are neither universally accepted nor universally practised.[75] Critical movements, some of which are described below, have objected to human rights as, in effect, plastering over the real structural problems of society, undermining radical change. Others resent human rights, in effect, being parachuted into non-Western territories like unwanted aid being dropped from aeroplanes. Worse still, some think of them as bombs.

Feminist perspectives typically criticise human rights discourse for concentrating upon publicly orientated matters such as the behaviour of government officials, rather than characteristically private, household grievances such as domestic violence.[76] Martha Nussbaum, however, emphasises the need to look critically at cultural inhibitions of what women (and humans generally) can be and do both in advanced and developing countries, in universalist

---

[73] On the religious settlement in the Peace of Westphalia, see ch. 6, section 6.4.1, pp. 139–41 above.

[74] See, for example, John Locke, 'A Letter Concerning Toleration' in Ian Shapiro (ed.), *Two Treatises of Government and a Letter Concerning Toleration* (New Haven: Yale University Press, 2003).

[75] The critical issues are well canvassed in Upendra Baxi, *The Future of Human Rights* (New Delhi: Oxford University Press, 2nd edn, 2006) and William Twining, 'Human Rights: Southern Voices: Francis Deng, Abdullahi An-Na'im, Yash Ghai, and Upendra Baxi' (2006) 11 *Review of Constitutional Studies* 203–80.

[76] On the complexity of these issues (by reference to the Chinese one-child policy, self-employed women and 'honour killings'), see Barbara Stark, 'Women, Globalization, and Law: A Change of World' (2004) 16 *Pace International Law Review* 333–63.

terms.[77] She suggests with vigour the compellability of universal rights, in principle, by any honest cultural standard.

Non-Western cultures may criticise human rights discourse for emphasising individualism compared with, say, Confucian communitarian principles.[78] These are relevant criticisms. The bourgeois individualism reflected by human rights discourse is to some extent inextricable from its most significant origins in the French Declaration of the Rights of Man and Citizen. Another reason for the individualistic emphasis of human rights after World War II was their responsiveness to the oppression then recently suffered by individuals and minorities at the hands of larger collectives, most notoriously the state Nazi party.[79] The logic of human rights is therefore susceptible to the (somewhat obvious) criticism that it is historically and culturally based. Yet this does not discount the prospect of universality. Some of these rights should be quite capable of moral appeal to all cultures. Indeed, human rights standards are being embraced at a regional level, an example being the African Charter of Human and Peoples' Rights of 1981, which cannot be dismissed as a Western imposition.[80] The question may be asked, as Peter Singer does: are certain practices elements of a distinctive culture worth preserving? For example, female genital mutilation may be an aspect of a distinctive culture not worth preserving because this practice disadvantages and marginalises females.[81]

Valuing human rights and the sanctity of individual human life are obviously not exclusively European norms. What today are thought about as 'Western' human rights may actually be as foreign to traditional Western societies as to non-Western societies. Traditional Western societies, in particular those featured in this book in parts 2 and 3, had criminal justice systems in which torture featured prominently at different times. European colonisation of the Americas, Africa, Asia and Australia, not to mention the European fascist and communist dictatorships, are conspicuous on the near horizon skyline of grotesque monuments to inhumanity. Colonial Western powers have at times *opposed* rights.[82] Islamic societies have in some respects been more egalitarian than Christian societies, for example, earlier recognising the separate legal personality of women (although women were not and are not equal to men under sharia law) and being tolerant of other religions, particularly 'People of the Book'.[83]

---

[77] See Martha C. Nussbaum, *Women and Human Development: The Capabilities Approach* (Cambridge: Cambridge University Press, 2000), esp. pp. 6–8 and ch. 1.

[78] Records indicate that Confucius (and Aquinas) were considered in drafting the Universal Declaration: see James A. R. Nafziger, 'The Functions of Religion in the International Legal System' in Mark W. Janis and Carolyn Evans (eds.), *Religion and International Law* (The Hague: Kluwer Law International, 1999), p. 166.

[79] See Sumner B. Twiss, 'History, Human Rights, and Globalization' (2004) 32 *Journal of Religious Ethics* 39–70, 42.   [80] See An-Na'im, 'Globalization and Jurisprudence', 17–18.

[81] See Singer, *One World*, pp. 155–6.

[82] See Twining, 'Human Rights', p. 22, drawing on scholarship of Yash Ghai.

[83] See Abdullahi Ahmed An-Na'im, 'Islam and Human Rights: Beyond the Universality Debate' (2000) 94 *American Society of International Law Proceedings* 95–101, 98.

Human rights may well be a consequence of modernity, not any inherent Western trait. On this view, the West just happened to modernise first, receiving phenomena such as television, modern science, modern industry and modern communications, which would have a similar effect on any culture.[84] For human rights to work universally, all nations and states would have to come as 'equal strangers' to the project of protecting human rights.[85]

Some things may be accessible to most, if not all, cultures. According to John Finnis, there are, in psychology and anthropology, seven forms of human good: life, knowledge, play, aesthetic experience, friendship, practical reasonableness and religion.[86] Although these forms will vary in content across cultures, broadly speaking, they seem to capture universal tendencies. The cross-cultural social practices will, of course, be different, but they will have their functional equivalents falling within these categorical forms of good.

Most cultures can agree that every human being is sacred (although what is taken to constitute a 'human being' can depend upon race, belief, gender and other factors). More difficult is this question: are there things that ought to be done for every human being? This is the question that the cultural relativist will probably answer in the negative. That is, the right to have something done is not the right of *every* human being to have that thing done for her or him. Where the universalist appears to trump the relativist is on the question: are there things that are bad for all humans? Clearly there are. Torture, arbitrary deprivation of property, deprivation of food, rape and ethnic cleansing are, of course, bad for everyone. Less easy is it to find things which are good for all people, although such goods do exist. They take the form of 'motherhood' principles. Affection, co-operation, a place in a community and help in times of trouble are examples.[87] These universal norms may well be addressed differently by various political regimes; a liberal and a socialist might disagree as to the level of help to be given to an individual in trouble.

Satisfactory resolution of these differences in opinion appears to be possible by accepting pluralism about human goods and even about non-core human rights. According to Alice Tay, a former President of the Australian Commonwealth Human Rights and Equal Opportunity Commission, 'The process of identifying, declaring and realising human rights is not unanimous or atemporal. Conflicts do and should arise as we continue our shared discovery of what it means to be

---

[84] Lawrence M. Friedman, 'Borders: On the Emerging Sociology of Transnational Law' (1996) 32 *Stanford Journal of International Law* 65–90, 84–5.

[85] Baxi, *Future of Human Rights*, p. 39.

[86] See John Finnis, *Natural Law and Natural Rights* (Oxford: Clarendon Press, 1980 reprinted 1992), pp. 84–90. For a philosophical attempt to reconcile partiality and diversity to belief in universality, see Joseph Raz, *Value, Respect and Attachment* (Cambridge: Cambridge University Press, 2001); for a theological attempt, in terms of different 'modes' versus common 'cores' of fulfilment, see Frank G. Kirkpatrick, *A Moral Ontology for a Theistic Ethic: Gathering the Nations in Love and Justice* (Aldershot: Ashgate, 2003), esp. p. 72.

[87] See Michael J. Perry, 'Are Human Rights Universal? The Relativist Challenge and Related Matters' (1997) 19 *Human Rights Quarterly* 461–509.

human in an ever-changing world.'[88] Indeed, Amartya Sen suggests that it is the very interactive and dialogical processes of human rights discourse across national boundaries which gives human rights their universal quality.[89] Universality is inadequately contemplated in realist terms. Universality may be considered a process, expressing visionary aspirations.[90] '[U]niversality need not be embodied in a single perspective'; decisions should not be restricted to a single set of institutions or actors to solve problems.[91] This seems to require a complex of competing jurisdictions (even if ultimately a sovereign appellate hierarchy is required for resolution). The manner and spirit of the confrontation of the insider's norms by those of the universalist outsider will be crucial.[92] A new discipline of 'international philosophy'[93] based upon studies of 'global history'[94] might serve the purpose of education into such a discourse. Appreciation of the contingency of cultural concepts, for example, about the nature of God, divine inspiration and other beliefs about ultimate reality and meaning, will be necessary.

In such processes of norm determination, the importance of education must be recognised, reflected in the Universal Declaration of Human Rights. Even if a court or tribunal is foreign to the pedigree of disputants or litigants, judges should be steeped in their own traditions (acknowledging those traditions' own contested meanings) and also minimally learned in other ways, through a well-rounded, empathetic education. At a core, functional, ordering level, it appears important for everyone in society to attempt to appreciate the value of different cultural norms which may in fact be reconcilable with one's own. This would be an 'inclusive universality',[95] although requiring some work to arrive at common denominators. A practical suggestion is offered in the next section.

10.4.4 Reconciling logical and customary norms – a global ethic

A major difficulty with human rights is that, despite being morally understandable, they are logically conceived – they are apprehended by the intellect – with serious lapses in customary observance. Yet the incremental historical acceptance of rights over centuries attests to the logically compulsive power of

[88] Tay, 'Human Rights', 8.

[89] Amartya Sen, 'Elements of a Theory of Human Rights' (2004) 32 *Philosophy & Public Affairs* 315–56, 320.

[90] Eva Brems, *Human Rights: Universality and Diversity* (The Hague: Martinus Nijhoff Publishers, 2001), p. 15.

[91] James Bohman and Matthias Lutz-Bachmann, 'Introduction' in James Bohman and Matthias Lutz-Bachmann (eds.), *Perpetual Peace: Essays on Kant's Cosmopolitan Ideal* (Cambridge, MA: The MIT Press, 1997), p. 15.

[92] Abdullahi Ahmed An-Na'im, 'Problems of Universal Cultural Legitimacy for Human Rights' in Abdullahi Ahmed An-Na'im and Francis M. Deng (eds.), *Human Rights in Africa: Cross-Cultural Perspectives* (Washington: The Brookings Institution, 1990), p. 343.

[93] Philip Allott, *The Health of Nations: Society and Law Beyond the State* (Cambridge: Cambridge University Press, 2002), [5.65].   [94] On this initiative, see ch. 2, section 2.3.4, p. 42 above.

[95] See Brems, *Human Rights*, p. 295.

human rights notions and their potential to be accepted customarily. Consider, for example, advances made in what is now acceptable concerning religious intolerance, slavery, colonialism and sexism.[96]

Especially when economics or Mammon is a major source of authority, it is difficult to say that, no matter what the consequences, a human should not be treated in a particular way. That is, it is difficult to treat humans always as ends in themselves rather than as means to advance some other purpose. For example, take war and capitalist enterprise. Respectively, the humanity of opposing soldiers and employees has to be subordinated to the greater purpose of victory and profit. In the face of the difficulty or 'casuistry' of logical approaches to calculating possible consequences of sacrificing human rights to prevent a greater evil (the consequences of which evils are generally unknown), Finnis suggests that proper judgement should be exercised by respecting human good in one's own existence and in the human lives which might fall into one's 'care and disposal'.[97] Logical and political calculations appear ill suited to the task of upholding human rights.

Universal human rights remain too logical and abstractly political on the Space Axis of the Space–Time Matrix. The commandments of the human rights documents are directed primarily towards state governments. They contemplate strong, central states with vast resources – 'a kind of latter-day god, not only omnipresent, omniscient and omnipotent, but also benevolent, as a welfare state . . . should be'.[98] Taken in isolation, this maintains the state as the normative hub of social life, when what is needed is a more moral appeal to the individual. Proclaiming human rights as the law of the state or as an abstract rights discourse would seem to compound the problem of according responsibility for human rights to something other than one's self or immediate community. Something more personal and cultural is required. Human rights need to engage with people at a deeper cultural and personal level. Abdullahi An-Na'im proposes engagement at a religious level – if not indeed with religions themselves.[99]

To this prospect, a document initially drafted by Hans Küng may make a contribution, entitled 'Towards a Global Ethic (An Initial Declaration)'. Produced by the Council for a Parliament of the World's Religions for religious or ethical peoples, it represents an 'interfaith declaration . . . the result of a two-year consultation among more than two hundred scholars and theologians representing the world's communities of faith'.[100] Contrary to the abstract logic of

[96] Brian Slattery, 'Rights, Communities, and Tradition' (1991) 41 *University of Toronto Law Journal* 447–67, 452.

[97] See Finnis, *Natural Law*, pp. 225–6. Finnis does not regard natural law as rules narrowly conceived by logic; he also admits culture and non-empirical modes of thought into his calculus. See too pp. 3, 94.

[98] Galtung, *Human Rights*, pp. 11–12.

[99] An-Na'im, 'Islam and Human Rights', 95–6; and his 'Universal Cultural Legitimacy'.

[100] See Council for a Parliament of the World's Religions, 'Towards a Global Ethic (An Initial Declaration)' (Chicago, 1993) http://www.cpwr.org/resource/ethic.pdf (viewed 6 January

some human rights in a real-life context where people care little for humans other than those who are familiar, religion for many is a particularly cultural experience which is not necessarily grounded in high-order logic or rationality. That is not to cheapen religion – it may even be to appreciate religion more, because life is so mysterious and complicated that a legitimate way to understand life may be through a belief-system which is itself entwined with mysterious events recollected from history. A more likely way to obtain adherence to abstract rights such as human rights is to put them into the cultural, moral language of different religions. The Global Ethic Initial Declaration seeks to do this. It may be seen as a continuation of the political aspirations of the French Declaration and the Universal Declaration. In addition, it addresses environmental degradation and economic inequality, advancing the unsuccessful attempts of those widely received documents to tap into the moral, cultural sentiments of humans. Such an option was not open to the framers of the Universal Declaration in the latter 1940s, who had to avoid the language and concepts of particular religions, in the important pursuit of ratification amongst diverse cultures.[101] Particular corruptions of religion today, represented primarily by religious fundamentalism and terrorism, demonstrate the need to re-establish the original ethical connections between cultural traditions and the Universal Declaration.

By way of a negotiated consensus (rather than a collection of rules which satisfy the lowest common demominator), the Global Ethic Initial Declaration contains the expression of familiar sentiments in the preamble. Where it departs is by emphasising the interdependence of peoples. Although the Declaration is intrinsically idealistic and it falls short of concrete political projects, its commitment 'to a culture of non-violence, respect, justice and peace' has its target in the most practical place for such a project: the interior space orientation of the Space–Time Matrix. So, alongside the need for political action outside most individuals' immediate influence, individual minds must be targeted to respond to the challenges of the times – through 'meditation, by prayer, or by positive thinking',[102] to change 'the inner orientation, the whole mentality, the "hearts" of people'.[103] This takes the comradeship aspect of logical political pronunciations and seeks to entwine them into a moral, cultural kinship, by reference to the failures of history and a vision for future peace acceptable to diverse cultures. This can be demonstrated in the Initial Declaration text.

On the basis of personal experiences and the burdensome history of our planet we have learned

- that a better global order cannot be created or enforced by laws, prescriptions, and conventions alone;

2007) ('GEID'); and generally Leonard Swidler (ed.), *For All Life: Toward a Universal Declaration of a Global Ethic* (Ashland: White Cloud Press, 1999); William Schweiker, *Theological Ethics and Global Dynamics, in the Time of Many Worlds* (Malden: Blackwell Publishing Ltd, 2004), esp. pp. 14–15.   [101] See Twiss, 'History, Human Rights', 57.
[102] Global Ethic Initial Declaration (GEID), p. 2.   [103] Ibid., p. 6.

- that the realization of peace, justice, and the protection of Earth depends on the insight and readiness of men and women to act justly;
- that action in favor of rights and freedoms presumes a consciousness of responsibility and duty, and that therefore both the minds and hearts of women and men must be addressed;
- that rights without morality cannot long endure, and that *there will be no better global order without a global ethic.*[104] [original italics]

A balance is sought to be struck, on the Time Axis, between '[t]oo many old answers to new challenges'[105] and the 'ancient guidelines for human behavior which are found in the teachings of the religions of the world and which are the condition for a sustainable world order'.[106]

In recognition of the World Revolution, the need is expressed in this new phase of humanity to go beyond guarantees of freedom to 'binding values, convictions, and norms which are valid for all humans . . .'[107] The binding values, to the Western mind, will be familiar. They consolidate several of the Old Testament Ten Commandments and amplify them in empowering rather than prohibitive terms. The fundamental command to treat every human humanely is couched in terms of the golden rule[108] and Kant's categorical imperative: 'What you wish done to yourself, do to others!' This is supported by 'irrevocable directives'. 'You shall not kill' becomes 'Have respect for life!' It follows that animals and plants should receive care.[109] 'You shall not steal' becomes 'Deal honestly and fairly', with the onus on those with property to fulfil the obligation which comes with property, namely a responsibility at the same time for the common good.[110] 'You shall not lie' is expressed in positive terms 'Speak and act truthfully!' The final exhortation worth emphasis avoids specifying a doctrine of sexual immorality such as adultery in the Judeo-Christian tradition. It turns 'You shall not commit sexual immorality' into a prescription to 'Respect and love one another!'[111]

Although the Global Ethic Initial Declaration is inherently idealistic, it targets a vital aspect of human being and becoming. The thoughtful disciplining of individual minds via contextual, educational, moral, cultural prompts is necessary in this regard, before precepts in the Universal Declaration of Human Rights can receive the practical allegiance which they deserve as a matter of political logic. This will require the reinterpretation of religious precepts particularly with respect to the local, political, social and economic circumstances of the communities of believers, not just at the theological level.[112]

---

[104] Ibid., p. 5.   [105] Ibid., p. 3.   [106] Ibid., p. 1.

[107] Ibid., p. 4. This is recognised in Huntington, *Clash of Civilizations*, p. 320.

[108] The 'golden rule' – to love thy neighbour – has equivalents in Islam, Zoroastrianism, Confucius, Buddhism, Hinduism and the New Testament, to name a few beliefs: see H. T. D. Rost, *The Golden Rule: A Universal Ethic* (Welwyn: George Ronald, 1986); Jeffrey Wattles, *The Golden Rule* (Oxford: Oxford University Press, 1996).   [109] See GEID, p. 7.

[110] See Ibid., p. 9.   [111] See Ibid., p. 12.   [112] An-Na'im, 'Islam and Human Rights', 96–7.

Elusive though unanimity about universal human rights across cultures may appear, human rights discourse should still be pursued if suffering and oppression are to be addressed systemically. Disharmony, of course, exists even amongst fellow adherents of a common belief or purpose in the same church, temple, mosque, company meeting, government department or university administration. That is, no community of any size appears insulated from inner conflict when it comes to articulating and interpreting core values. Liberal Muslims, Christians and Jews may have more in common with each other politically than each of these liberal factions has with its fundamentalist counterpart. A truly globalist ethic, which manages to embed human rights in a moral discourse of the equality of all human bodies, may well need to reject, in the political realm, the underlying eleventh-century belief in the equality of all souls subject to the same judgement. The idea of a common heaven, nirvana or paradise available only to particular creeds under particular godheads is a matter which cannot be discussed purely rationally across cultures. The danger is that attempts to project this judgement universally on all souls in different cultures in the present world creates great violence for no apparent practical purpose. Active care for the salvation of another, where it is not wanted, is at the crux of religious intolerance, even though it can be motivated out of love of neighbour.[113] Such unwanted active care for the soul appears unhelpful. That should not, however, deter the pursuit of the considerable commonalities which exist normatively across religious factions and across religions more broadly. It is possible to see 'overlapping consensus'[114] and perhaps even 'overlapping faith' about core elements of a just social order amongst the multifarious communities of belief in the world today. It will be necessary to attempt to harmonise that earthly commitment with the supernatural beliefs of those religions where that supernatural dimension is otherwise in conflict in the minds of some adherents. Abstract, exterior ethical principles espoused by the modern constitutional state, premissed upon tolerance, must find some way of attaching to the interior, cultural norm systems of the associations which make up not just the constitutional state, but the world.[115]

The only way to reconcile logically, politically imposed norms such as human rights with customary or culturally felt laws appears to be to have human rights grow organically within the society. Simple tolerance of differences may not be enough, because that is to maintain a barrier preventing the different practices

---

[113] See Jürgen Habermas, 'Intolerance and Discrimination' (2003) 1 *International Journal of Constitutional Law* 2–12, 7.

[114] On this term, see John Rawls, *Political Liberalism* (New York: Columbia University Press, 1996), lecture IV.

[115] Cf. John Rawls, 'Justice as Fairness: Political not Metaphysical' (1985) 14 *Philosophy and Public Affairs* 223–51, 230. On the application of Rawls's concerns for *international* but not global justice (given the reliance upon state boundaries as natural), see his 'The Law of Peoples' in *The Law of Peoples with 'The Idea of Public Reason Revisited'* (Cambridge, MA: Harvard University Press, 2001); cf. Thomas Pogge, *World Poverty and Human Rights: Cosmopolitan Responsibilities and Reforms* (Cambridge: Polity, 2002), esp. pp. 105–8.

and their people from being accepted. More than simple *tolerance* of the different souls facing different perceived eternal judgements ('tolerance' implying the inferiority of the party being tolerated), an individual's potential to choose a different means of salvation should be *respected*[116] (even if regarded as incorrect). A world civil society, coexisting with other societies, needs to develop as a culture in which plural cultures and values can grow, respectful though of fundamental norms essential for human flourishing. Some possibilities for this growth include interactions through sport, business, civil rights and health rights movements, education and the arts.[117] In that way may otherwise unequal bodies be viewed as equal, when one person can look across the street and see another body of equal value on earth, regardless of appearance, religion, belief or class – or perceived spiritual destiny.[118]

10.5 Free trade

The normative reality of the emerging world society (amongst other societies) appears to be attuned to the pursuit of economic prosperity, overriding, where incompatible, the idealistic statements of human rights principles and ecological awareness. The major economic agreement of the age, the General Agreement on Tariffs and Trade 1994 (GATT), constitutionalised (with powers of rule-generation and adjudication) and expanded the earlier 1947 GATT. That Preamble refers to 'raising standards of living, ensuring full employment and a large and steadily growing volume of real income and effective demand', expanding production and trade.[119] Environmental moderation is a feature of the 1994 reference to the aim of 'optimal use of the world's resources' as opposed to the 1947 objective for the use of the 'full resources of the world'. References to human rights and the calamitous history of the twentieth century are not included. Nonetheless, whilst not explicit, GATT must be viewed in context as a response to the World Revolution. (GATT emerged at Bretton Woods with the IMF and World Bank.)[120] Political leaders chiefly from the US

---

[116] On compassion and hospitality as alternatives, see Martin E. Marty, *When Faiths Collide* (Malden: Blackwell Publishing, 2005), ch. 6; and Conor Gearty, *Can Human Rights Survive?* (Cambridge: Cambridge University Press, 2006), pp. 43–50. On openings for accommodation within traditions, see Paul Knitter (ed.), *The Myth of Religious Superiority: A Multifaith Exploration* (Maryknoll: Orbis Books, 2005).

[117] See Mark Juergensmeyer, *Terror in the Mind of God: The Global Rise of Religious Violence* (Berkeley: University of California Press, 2003), p. 247; Harold J. Berman, 'Faith and Law in a Multicultural World' in Mark Juergensmeyer (ed.), *Religion in Global Civil Society* (New York: Oxford University Press, 2005) and other essays in that collection; and generally, Akbar Ahmed and Brian Forst (eds.), *After Terror: Promoting Dialogue Among Civilizations* (Cambridge: Polity Press, 2005).

[118] Cf. Francesca Klug, *Values for a Godless Age: The Story of the United Kingdom's New Bill of Rights* (London: Penguin Books, 2000). This need not involve abandoning private beliefs that we have souls with different spiritual potentials. *Contra* humans as bodies without souls in Gearty, *Human Rights*, p. 33.   [119] See Preamble, GATT, 1 January 1948, 55 UNTS 194.

[120] See pp. 223–5 above.

were determined to prevent what they saw as mistakes in economic policy during the interwar period. These mistakes included the Great Depression, German reparations and damaging tariffs and trade protection measures choking international trade.[121] They believed free trade would increase productivity and purchasing power for all.[122]

GATT provides 'the common institutional framework for the conduct of trade relations among its Members' in matters relating to agreements annexed to GATT,[123] which include agreements on Agriculture, Textiles and Clothing, Trade-related Investment Measures, Subsidies and Countervailing Measures, and Trade-related Aspects of Intellectual Property Rights.[124] The secularisation of society evident in this economic rationalism is balanced by the installation of sacralising economic ideology, now investigated.

10.5.1 The dogma

The modern economic orthodoxy can be stated by way of natural law principles. They coexist with the human rights natural law already discussed (the interrelationship of which will be discussed in the next section).

Article I of GATT is the 'Most Favoured Nation Treatment' clause, which prevents government import and export regulations from discriminating between the products of other countries: '[A]ny advantage, favour, privilege or immunity granted by any contracting party to any product originating in or destined for any other country shall be accorded immediately and unconditionally to the like product originating in or destined for the territories of all other contracting parties.'[125]

Article III contains a prohibition against treating imports differently from domestically produced products: '[I]nternal taxes and other internal charges, and laws . . . affecting the internal sale . . . of products . . . should not be applied to imported or domestic products so as to afford protection to domestic production.'

In a similar vein, quantitative restrictions such as quotas are prohibited under article XI. Subsidisation of domestic products is sought to be limited under article XVI.

Primarily, these rules are concerned with liberalising trade, establishing equal import access to domestic markets (the 'Most Favoured Nation' doctrine)[126] and reducing tariffs whilst maintaining, in the nation-state, exemptions for national security, health and morals (article XX).

---

[121] See John H. Jackson, *The World Trade Organization: Constitution and Jurisprudence* (London: Pinter, 1998), p. 15.

[122] Paul Kennedy, *The Rise and Fall of the Great Powers: Economic Change and Military Conflict from 1500 to 2000* (London: Unwin Hyman, 1988), pp. 359–60.   [123] Article II.

[124] See Annex 1, GATT.

[125] For origins in the Peace of Westphalia, see ch. 6, section 6.4.1, p. 141 above.

[126] For other historical origins, see ch. 6, section 6.5, p. 142.

Free trade may be understood by seeing what it was not, in the past. The fascisms of Mussolini and Hitler were the subversion of liberal free-trade democracy.[127] As Nietzsche wrote: 'In the market place nobody believes in higher men'[128] – which may go some way to explaining the opposition of dictators of all persuasions to free markets. The market is a mythical leveller of society (although tycoons can breed new family nobilities with market control). The absence of such Romance was the fodder used by Hitler to stir the Nazi reaction to the deteriorating communal bonds of the growing economic and technological society.

Superficially, as suggested in chapter 8, free trade may ironically require a normative commitment to being unconcerned with normative commitment. Such anomie is thought to be preferable to the market control exercised by dictators. The association of liberalism with free markets does, after all, have significant origins in the Enlightenment rejection of excessive authority and arbitrary government. Hirst and Thompson opine that, as national politics shifts the state's attention away from business to leave the market to itself, politics becomes mundane given the centrality of the market to national life.[129] For critical commentators, this is thought to be a major aim of contemporary politics – to leave the market to its own forces and to the experts in economic theology. Yet the perceived decreased normativity of the market does not so consistently fit with the immense increase in commercial legislation throughout the world. Furthermore, the increased volume of legislation, at least in Western jurisdictions, is believed to implement conditions for the desired type of free trade normlessness to allow the market to find its way and to decide social problems. This may be to substitute one type of normativity for a different type of normativity – one which is less socially conscious and historically minded.

Notwithstanding, there is more to liberalism than the ideological predisposition to greed. Adam Smith's eighteenth-century imagery of the 'invisible hand' which co-ordinated market supply with demand was a reference at the time to God's supervision of the market. Similarly, we saw Edmund Burke speak of the laws of the market as God's laws.[130] Liberalism may represent a staunch, disciplined recognition of the intractability of typical moral and religious arguments which ravaged societies before bourgeois revolutions. There is normative value in the proposition that individuals do not have the right to assert that their own conception of the good life is better than that of other individuals. Indeed,

---

[127] See Davies, *Europe*, p. 949.

[128] Friedrich Nietzsche, *Thus Spoke Zarathustra: A Book for None and All*, trans. Walter Kaufman (Harmondsworth: Penguin Books, 1978), p. 286.

[129] Paul Hirst and Grahame Thompson, *Globalization in Question: The International Economy and the Possibilities of Governance* (Cambridge: Polity Press, 2nd edn 1999), pp. 262–3. They further suggest that with the decreasing need for a concerted national 'cultural homogeneity' comes an increased opportunity for 'religious, ethnic and lifestyle pluralism'.

[130] See ch. 8, section 8.3, pp. 177–8 above.

there can be a range of competing conceptions of the good which can contain norms and virtues favoured by liberalism,[131] such as honesty, industriousness and equality. The strength of this sort of liberalism is in its possibility for social pluralism.[132]

By 1998, the IMF 'had programs in no fewer than seventy-five countries with a total of 1.4 billion people; the list began with Albania and ended with Zimbabwe'. The IMF and the World Bank preach and attempt to convert states to an orthodoxy of ending government budget deficits, implementing the privatisation of public assets and the deregulation of markets, with programmes for stable currencies, a relaxed hold on natural resources and opening markets up to foreign capital.[133] The World Bank may be 'to economic development theology what the papacy is to Catholicism, complete with yearly encyclicals'.[134] The dogma has been called a 'golden straitjacket' by Thomas Friedman. The tenets include: private-sector-driven economic growth, low inflation, price stability, decreasing state bureaucracy, balanced budgets if not surpluses, eliminating and lowering tariffs on imported goods, removing restrictions on foreign investment, reduction of quotas and domestic monopolies, increasing exports, privatising state-owned enterprises, deregulating the economy, eliminating government corruption and allowing citizens a choice of pension options.[135] These ideas connect with the so-called 'Washington Consensus' of fiscal austerity, privatisation and market liberalisation. They can be associated with a belief in liberal democracy and rule of law.[136] The economic theology is not without its flawed assumptions. Demand does not always equal supply (for example, in the labour market, where some unemployed persons simply meet with no demand).[137] As the state withdraws from the market, the state is nonetheless required to regulate natural outgrowths of the market such as corporations and monopolies. Also, markets often favour particular ethnic groups which are not the democratic majority, leading to violence against those minorities.[138]

Developed liberal economies of today did not achieve their success through obedience to Washington Consensus principles, which can have deleterious effects on developing countries.[139] The so-called 'East Asian economic miracle' since the 1970s, for example in South Korea, Japan and Malaysia, suggests that

---

[131] Amy Gutmann, 'Undemocratic Education' in Nancy L. Rosenblum (ed.), *Liberalism and the Moral Life* (Cambridge, MA: Harvard University Press, 1989), p. 75.

[132] Nancy L. Rosenblum, 'Introduction' in Rosenblum, *Liberalism*, p. 13.

[133] van Creveld, *Rise and Decline*, p. 376. For critiques, see sources cited in n. 40 above.

[134] M. Holland, quoted in Peet, *Unholy Trinity*, p. 111.

[135] Thomas Friedman, *The Lexus and the Olive Tree: Understanding Globalization* (London: Harper Collins Publishers, 2000), p. 105.

[136] See Boaventura de Sousa Santos, *Toward a New Legal Common Sense: Law, Globalization and Emancipation* (London: Butterworths, 2nd edn 2002), pp. 316ff.

[137] Stiglitz, *Globalization*, pp. 35, 53.

[138] See Amy Chua, *World on Fire: How Exporting Free Market Democracy Breeds Ethnic Hatred and Global Instability* (New York: Anchor Books, 2004).

[139] See Ha-Joon Chang, *Kicking Away the Ladder: Development Strategy in Historical Perspective* (London: Anthem Press, 2002).

high economic growth and human equity can be facilitated by interventionist, communitarian government. As the 'Asian values debate' considers, Western, individualistic human rights may be less effective than Asian values.[140]

Notwithstanding, development as such does appear to lead to increased freedom.[141] How to foster that development is the problem, given that development and exploitation by other countries bears at least some responsibility for the Third World predicament. The 'fair trade' movement warily seeks the benefits of free trade, by easing the impact of development through prices which seek to compensate the producers, with sensitivity to their social and natural environment.[142] The UN's Millennium Development Goals seek to foster 'an open, rule-based, predictable, non-discriminatory trading and financial system', in association with substantial improvements by 2015 in poverty, education, health, gender equality and environmental sustainability.[143] Whether, at present, economic globalisation actually benefits impoverished countries and peoples on the whole is not clear. 'Most likely', according to Peter Singer, 'it has helped some to escape poverty and thrown others deeper into it.'[144] Economic globalisation must be considered with human rights to evaluate the dogma of free trade.

10.5.2 The discourse

The exceptions to the free-trade requirements of GATT lift the dividing wall between international trade and human rights. Exemptions to free trade are broadly contained in article XX of GATT.

> Subject to the requirement that such measures are not applied in a manner which would constitute a means of arbitrary or unjustifiable discrimination between countries where the same conditions prevail . . . nothing in this Agreement shall be construed to prevent the adoption or enforcement by any contracting party of measures:
>
> (a) necessary to protect public morals;
> (b) necessary to protect human, animal or plant life or health; . . .
> (e) relating to the products of prison labour;
> (f) imposed for the protection of national treasures of artistic, historic or archaeological value;
> (g) relating to the conservation of exhaustible natural resources if such measures are made effective in conjunction with restrictions on domestic production or consumption.

---

[140] Rajagopal, *International Law*, pp. 212–16.
[141] See Amartya Sen, *Development as Freedom* (Oxford: Oxford University Press, 1999).
[142] See Alex Nicholls and Charlotte Opal, *Fair Trade: Market-Driven Ethical Consumption* (London: Sage, 2005).
[143] See Jeffrey Sachs, *The End of Poverty: How We Can Make it Happen in Our Lifetime* (London: Penguin, 2005), ch. 11.
[144] Singer, *One World*, p. 100. Amidst a vast literature, see too Pogge, *World Poverty* (much more can relatively easily be done) and Mathias Risse, 'How Does the Global Order Harm the Poor?' (2005) 33 *Philosophy & Public Affairs* 349–76 (identifying the institutional obstacles).

Morality-based examples of trade bans include Israel's ban on the importation of non-kosher meat products, the US government ban on obscene pictures, bans on trade in body organs for valuable consideration, Thailand's ban on the export of Buddha images and sanctions against apartheid South Africa.[145]

A case in point was a controversy surrounding the WTO Government Procurement Agreement 1994 (GPA). This agreement relates to the award of government contracts to foreign suppliers. Under article 23 of the GPA, and overlapping with GATT, exceptions to free trade apply when it may be necessary for a nation-state to protect public morals, human, animal or plant life or health or intellectual property, or products or services of handicapped persons, of philanthropic institutions or of prison labour. Massachusetts, in 1996, enacted legislation 'limiting state agencies from signing new contracts or renewals of contracts with companies doing business with or in Myanmar'. Japan and the EU objected to the Massachusetts legislation on the basis that it discriminated against those states for trading freely with countries with poor human rights records. EU and US diplomacy resulted in an in-principle refinement of policy in relation to economic sanctions targeted against the perpetrators of the human rights breaches.[146] The WTO has not yet had to deal with such issues directly in its jurisprudence.

Refuge for trade discrimination can also be sought under the article XXI Security Exceptions head to use international trade as a weapon against 'bad guys'. The US has resorted to this doctrine at least three times in recent history, directed against Fidel Castro, Iranian and Libyan terrorism, and 'foreign drug kingpins'.[147] In the absence of a UN Security Council resolution, no such power may exist to sanction China for breaches of human rights, now that it is a member of the WTO. There is arguably no national security interest in offshore human rights abuses, and the possibility of economic sanctions as a means of international law enforcement measures is arguably impeded by GATT obligations.[148]

In the absence of GATT tests of the interaction of human rights and free-trade law, ecological analogies must suffice.[149] A related ecological jurisprudence exists in the WTO concerning trade discrimination based upon 'product-related' requirements (namely what product is required) and 'process-related'

---

[145] See Steve Charnovitz, 'The Moral Exception in Trade Policy' (1998) 38 *Virginia Journal of International Trade Law* 689–745, 695–9.

[146] See Christopher McCrudden, 'International Economic Law and the Pursuit of Human Rights: A Framework for Discussion of the Legality of "Selective Purchasing" Laws Under the WTO Government Procurement Agreement' (1999) 2 *Journal of International Economic Law* 3–48, 6. See too, generally, Brooklyn Journal of International Law, 'Symposium: The Universal Declaration of Human Rights at 50 and the Challenge of Global Markets' (1999) 25 *Brooklyn Journal of International Law* 1–183.

[147] Raj Bhala, 'Fighting Bad Guys with International Trade Law' (1997) 31 *U.C. Davis Law Review* 1–122, 3.

[148] See Carlos Manuel Vázquez, 'Trade Sanctions and Human Rights – Past, Present and Future' (2003) 6 *Journal of International Economic Law* 797–839, 804–5.   [149] Ibid., 809, 812.

requirements (how the product is produced). The famous *Tuna/Dolphin* cases considered this distinction.[150] GATT panels held that US bans on imports of tuna caught with drift-nets harmful to dolphins were unlawful under article III of GATT (relating to 'National Treatment on Internal Taxation and Regulation'). Only the characteristics of the products were to be taken into account, not the production processes. Such process-related logic suggests the illegality of discriminating against imports of products created with child labour.

The *Shrimp/Turtle* case,[151] in which the US successfully obtained dispensation to impose bans on the importation of shrimp caught using turtle-unfriendly methods, was successful only because the US used best endeavours to secure multilateral agreement on turtle-friendly techniques for catching shrimp. This process lends itself to dominant powers like the US embracing environmental concerns to advance protection of their own economies.[152] Probably more of a coincidence than a conspiracy, capitalism and big business seem to cope relatively well with ecological regimes. Smaller businesses and developing economies often cannot financially afford to comply with human rights and environmental standards.

The emphasis on free trade by reducing tariffs is fraught with problems at the level of authority. Global free trade has not demonstrated itself to be an ethic superior to state moral and environmental standards.[153] Free trade can also offend the national kinship principle by which one may prefer one's national products. The logic of the international free market not only seeks to displace uncompetitive domestic industries (with some success) but it also overrides the culture of domestic industries such as French filmmaking. It is difficult to imagine these universalist political aspirations of free trade becoming morally attractive to domestic populations. Factory closures in particular industries such as textiles, clothing and footwear (because goods can be produced more cheaply, for example, in Third World sweatshops)[154] can scarcely expect to be greeted cheerily by employees in more-developed countries. In many cases countries, particularly the US, simply refuse to open their markets to certain products and certain countries, to avoid such vote-losing policies.

Despite these myriad tensions, international trade law may be said to be undergoing a 'constitutionalisation' by virtue of the judicial interpretation that is occurring. Traditional concerns of constitutional law are manifest in WTO law, such as the review of power amongst Member States, centralisation of dispute resolution, the borrowing of federal constitutional doctrines such as

---

[150] *Tuna/Dolphin I*, 30 ILM 1594 (1991); *Tuna/Dolphin II*, 33 ILM 839 (1994).

[151] *United States – Import Prohibition of Certain Shrimp and Shrimp Products*, 38 ILM 118 (1999).

[152] See Donald McRae, 'Trade and the Environment: Competition, Cooperation or Confusion?' (2003) 41 *Alberta Law Review* 745–60.   [153] See Singer, *One World*, pp. 71–4.

[154] Developing countries then suffer the dilemma of increased income at the expense of fewer worker protections: see e.g. César A. Rodríguez-Garavito, 'Nike's Law', in Santos and Rodríguez-Garavito (eds.), *Law and Globalization from Below: Toward a Cosmopolitan Legality* (Cambridge: Cambridge University Press, 2005).

proportionality and the competence to hear matters relating to traditionally domestic affairs such as health. Certainly the jurisprudence of the WTO reflects more than just international law. The WTO jurisdiction is one of several competing jurisdictions within a shifting, expanding legal order with an eclectic mix of doctrines from diverse legal systems.[155]

At the moment, human rights and associated ecological rights appear to take a back seat to the universalist norms of economic prosperity believed to be served by free trade. It may be possible in this respect to think of an emerging paradigm of 'trade-related, market-friendly human rights'. Those human rights conducive to trade (such as the right to property and equality before the markets) may be more likely to receive widespread enforcement than are other human rights.[156]

10.6 Globalist jurisprudence, God and Mammon

In this chapter, a number of jurisdictions have been encountered which compete with other jurisdictions. Nation-states have had their spheres of containable disruption challenged. They have been forced to compete with jurisdictions of an emerging world society amongst other societies such as the WTO, and human rights bodies such as the UN Committee on Human Rights. With these new jurisdictions, the individual has alternatives to the nation-state and becomes a subject of what had been the exclusive state preserve of public international law.

There are parallels between the medieval papacy and its universalist Christendom, compared with the natural rights sought to be guaranteed by the UN under the banner of liberal free-trade democracy and human rights. As observed by Eugen Rosenstock-Huessy, '[b]efore the Papal Revolution, no son of a church anywhere had been allowed to denounce the crimes of his bishop or to carry his grievances outside his own diocese'.[157] The Papal Revolution of the late eleventh century had opened up opportunities for discourse and the pursuit of humanity, by offering an alternative to oppressive, particularistic jurisdictions. All souls, by virtue of a common faith, were deemed equal in a community of spiritual believers. The liberties achieved by the church paved the way

---

[155] See generally Deborah Z. Cass, 'The "Constitutionalization" of International Trade Law: Judicial Norm-Generation as the Engine of Constitutional Development in International Trade' (2001) 12 *European Journal of International Law* 39–75. The challenge appears to be for the GATT system to overcome typically national perceptions of its nature as simply 'foreign policy', by strengthening GATT as the 'foreign policy constitution': see Ernst-Ulrich Petersmann, 'Human Rights, Constitutionalism and the World Trade Organization: Challenges for World Trade Organization Jurisprudence and Civil Society' (2006) 19 *Leiden Journal of International Law* 633–67.

[156] See Baxi, *Future of Human Rights*, chs. 8, 9; cf. the recent draft UN code, *Norms on the Responsibilities of Transnational Corporations and other Business Enterprises with Regard to Human Rights* (referred to in ch. 2, section 2.3.3, p. 40).

[157] Rosenstock-Huessy, *Out of Revolution*, p. 518.

for the liberties achieved by individuals in the West.[158] Before the World Revolution of the twentieth century and the emergence of a world-society dynamic, no nationals of a nation-state anywhere could have denounced the crimes of their governmental leaders or carried their grievances outside the country in a way which could attract an authoritative jurisdiction. Nowadays, new jurisdictions allow citizens to take their grievances outside the state territory. All bodies are deemed equal in an emerging world community of secular belief. More than ever, laws do not come only from the state in which one lives.

Spiritual belief and economy are the two key concepts which together explain the deeply historical, constitutional differences between the celestial authority invoked in the Papal Revolution and the terrestrial authority invoked in the World Revolution. Spiritual belief and economy also explain the recurring patterns of universalist authority. As we saw earlier in this book, the economy at the end of the first millennium leading into the Papal Revolution was, like the sovereignty of that time, 'parcellised'.[159] At the end of that first millennium, with limited exceptions, European feudal economies were fixed to the soil and parochial, whilst the spiritual belief of Christianity was broadly universal in Europe. All souls were newly deemed equal in that scheme. The Christian faith permeated. Contrarily, at the end of our second millennium, instead of there being one main spiritual belief, there are 'many sects, many creeds, many races, many ways of education and self-expression' (even in Europe alone). The only widespread universalism today, in the West, appears to be in the market economy[160] and the projected equality of all bodies in human rights and free trade. Rosenstock-Huessy's juxtaposition of the particularistic feudal economies and monotheistic Christian spirituality over today's increasingly monolithic economy and particularistic spiritualities is profound. God and economy are the pivotal authorities which have characterised the Western legal tradition.

Thus there has been an epochal inversion of economy and spiritual belief in the West. Economics now appears at the apex in Western thinking. Crusader-style references by Western politicians to 'evil' and 'free peoples' and the biographies of current political leaders, at least in Australia, the UK and the US, show that Christianity still plays a role in these leaders' and their governments' strategies. These strategies cannot, however, be sold to electorates and the international stage in those terms alone, at least in the West.[161] Christian strategies are no longer express strategies for achieving public authority. They are implicitly interior, moral devices. The prevailing focus upon the market associated with the rule of law, democracy and human rights as the common political discourse would seem to reflect an approaching completion of the secularisation of

---

[158] Ibid., p. 552.   [159] See ch. 4 above.

[160] See Rosenstock-Huessy, *Out of Revolution*, pp. 495–6.

[161] Religious growth is occurring, particularly involving Islam but also Christianity (more so in the Third World): see Philip Jenkins, *The Next Christendom: The Coming of Global Christianity* (Oxford: Oxford University Press, 2002).

religion. Economy and spiritual belief have, in many observable circumstances, 'swapped places', and the market is emerging as the functional equivalent of a god of a universalist, secular religion. Although lacking in the traditional hall-marks of religion at first blush,[162] the *laissez-faire* liberalism of the contemporary economy nonetheless rates as a dominant belief and approaches the level of a religion, in the West. Liberal capitalism contains its share of ethics (read Mill on the freedom of the individual to do anything which does not harm another);[163] ritual (board meetings, corporate regulation compliance); narrative or myth (read Adam Smith on the difference between humans and dogs residing in the capacity of humans to bargain with each other);[164] experience (talk to many business professionals about their education and the historical inevitability of deregulation and low tariffs for prosperity); institutions and society (look skywards in a central business district during the week and downwards on Friday nights to the bars); doctrine (review the jurisprudence of the WTO); and art (observe the consumerism of much art and music). 'Risk management' appears to have overtaken faith as the solace from human fears of the unknown.[165] References to 'market fundamentalism' now abound.

After a relatively brief period of decentralisation into state power, a holy Roman empire of Christian believers has developed characteristics of a noticeably (but not entirely wholly) Mammon empire of cosmopolitan consumers. A crusade has been waged by dominant leaders for a more integrated economy, bringing not only personal prosperity but also the relief of 'the most pressing moral, political and economic issue of the time', namely Third World poverty, the future remedy of which, the evangelists contend, requires further integration.[166] For many of the economically fortunate, the world has become a 'City of Gold', a polity defined by the flow of capital, normatively dominated by capital markets, with states in the background.[167] It is telling that, until now,

---

[162] The indicia which follow are taken from Ninian Smart, *The World's Religions* (Cambridge: Cambridge University Press, 1989), pp. 10–30. Smart admits the possibility of secular religions where he writes of Marxism as 'a new political religion' (p. 549). For 'A Short History of Economics Becoming Religion', see John Ralston Saul, *The Collapse of Globalism and the Reinvention of the World* (Camberwell: Penguin Viking, 2005), ch. 5. For deeper ruminations, see Christoph Deutschmann, 'Capitalism as a Religion? An Unorthodox Analysis of Entrepreneurship' (2001) 4 *European Journal of Social Theory* 387–403 (economics); Werner Hamacher, 'Guilt History: Benjamin's Fragment "Capitalism as Religion"' (2005) 26 *Cardozo Law Review* 887–920 (theology).

[163] See John Stuart Mill, *On Liberty* (1859) (Harmondsworth: Penguin, 1985), pp. 68–9. Harms meriting interference with individual liberty, such as pornography as opposed to art, fair wage as opposed to employer freedom, are the subject of an almost talmudic or scholastic liberal discourse.

[164] See Adam Smith, *An Inquiry into the Nature and Causes of the Wealth of Nations* (Oxford: Clarendon Press, 1976), pp. 25–6.

[165] See Anthony Giddens, 'Risk and Responsibility' (1999) 62 *Modern Law Review* 1–10.

[166] For an orthodox sermon, see *The Economist*, 'The Case for Globalisation' 23 September 2000, 17–18.

[167] See David A. Westbrook, *City of Gold: An Apology for Global Capitalism* (New York: Routledge, 2004).

wars would generally be waged amidst leaders' calls for national sacrifice and belt-tightening. The US 'War on Terror' was inaugurated by calls to march to the shops to stimulate the economy.[168]

There is an emerging perception that people are only rational and fully human when acting within the marketplace, and that the free market is the canonisation of democracy.[169] This perception is increasingly totalising and competes for the ultimate reality and meaning of the modern human. The God of Jews and Christians, to be recalled from chapter 3 of this book as Yahweh – 'I am . . .' – is being reinterpreted by capitalism in the image of industry. Mammon vies for the position of God.

> In a 1998 commercial for IBM's Lotus division that danced across TV screens to the tune of REM's Nietzschean anthem, 'I am Superman,' great throngs of humanity were shown going nobly about their business while a tiny caption asked, 'Who is everywhere?' In the response, IBM identified itself both with the great People and the name of God as revealed to Moses: The words 'I Am' scrawled roughly on a piece of cardboard and held aloft from amid the madding crowd. The questions continued, running down the list from omnipresence to omniscience and omnipotence – 'Who is aware?,' 'Who is powerful?' – while the hallowed scenes of entrepreneurial achievement pulsated by: an American business district, a Chinese garment factory, a microchip assembly room, and, finally, the seat of divine judgment itself, the trading floor of the New York Stock Exchange. 'I can do anything', sang a winsome computer voice.[170]

Karl Marx wrote of 'that single unconscionable freedom – Free Trade' when he observed that '[a]ll that is solid melts into air, all that is holy is profaned'.[171] Unless there is remembrance of the historical constitution of globalisation, the globalisation of the twentieth century may witness the faster home stretch in what has been a slow race by dominant cultures towards a new belief system. Inspired by markets, these beliefs occur within parameters of human meaningfulness traditionally occupied, in the West, by inwardly directed or spiritual religion but now more identifiable as economic religion.

A general, globalist jurisprudence will need to take account of this normative transformation of authority. It will need to evaluate the potential limits of laws and ethics grounded in totalising economic beliefs where once, even in the West, spiritual religious authority had been so important to law. The historical Western importance of spiritual authority to legal order should serve as a reminder to the West about the difficulties other more traditionally religious cultures may have in accepting Western universalist laws – particularly when such Western laws are

---

[168] Aviel Roshwald, *The Endurance of Nationalism: Ancient Roots and Modern Dilemmas* (New York: Cambridge University Press, 2006), p. 300, citing Reich and Lieven.

[169] See Thomas Frank, *One Market Under God: Extreme Capitalism, Market Populism and the End of Economic Democracy* (London: Vintage, 2002), pp. xiii–xv.

[170] Frank, *One Market*, p. 3; management theorists have assumed the mantle of the social theorists in history who defended the aristocracy, the church and the state (p. 179).

[171] Karl Marx, *The Communist Manifesto* (Harmondsworth: Penguin, 1967), p. 82.

seen to defer only to the market and self-interest for authority. On another view, the twentieth-century emphasis on the economic order may reflect, more or less, altruistic concerns of traditional Western religion for the relief of the poor, resulting in some real successes, despite some failures, for Third World liberation.[172] If this may be so, then the economic ambitions will need to be related to the spiritual dimensions of the authority deployed to justify law.

Finally, the West may have achieved the status of a great civilisation for having generated, long after the other major civilisations, its own enduring, albeit secular, religion. If globalisation is to achieve its potential in a legal context, how it is thought about will be crucial. It is not only about perceptions of relentless economics, loss of sovereignty, nor the clash of civilisations as opposed to states. The chief lesson for the normative and inextricably historical dimension of a general, globalist jurisprudence is that the twentieth-century institutions described in this chapter are neither more nor less than forebears responding to technology, world war and economic depression. They set their aspirations as best they could into law, and invested required, novel institutions with authority. These aspirations were not limited, and their legal and institutional achievements were never foreseen to be complacently accepted and unchallenged. That would be to betray their birthright. To keep memories alive and to balance the economic imperatives driving law, a globalist jurisprudence should be mindful that (exterior) theories should not totally replace (interior) stories. Reason alone, or *logos*, cannot create an enduring ethics. Narrative stories and cultural experiences, or *nomoi*, are essential to this aspiration.[173]

The aims of the ten chapters to this point will have been accomplished if the reader has formed three impressions from the story of the Western legal tradition. First, globalisation, for all of its ubiquitous connotations, is also a historical consequence of the attempt to make peace through legal standards. Second, law is a mechanism of historically questionable authority and propositions for social order not constrained by territorial and cultural limits; that is, law in the West has never come from just one place. Third, law is very much dependent upon notions of ultimate reality and meaning for its authority.

These impressions can now be further substantiated in two concentrated case studies of legal communities which exist as jurisdictions in competition with other jurisdictions. The public law example of the European Union will first be considered, followed by the private law example of international commercial law. Whilst not truly global or universal, they do illustrate the aims just described, offering some guidance for models of law in competition with state law. Such models of law and norms are characteristic of what people often mean when they use the word 'globalisation'.

---

[172] See Rajagopal, *International Law*, ch. 4, on the New International Economic Order initiative of the Third World at the Sixth Special Session of the United Nations General Assembly in 1974, seeking a world order of equity and redistribution.

[173] See Robert N. Bellah, 'What is Axial about the Axial Age?' (2005) 46 *European Journal of Sociology* 69–89, 85–6.

Part 5
Competing Jurisdictions Case Studies

11

The twenty-first century European community

A foreigner stands with trepidation at the foot of the volcano of European Union (EU) literature. This volcano regularly erupts and seems to bury so much of what has come before. Some specific purposes warrant and delimit the present case study. A general, globalist jurisprudence must search for the constitutional vocabulary to attempt to understand and foster interactions amongst the various societies comprising the global scene, including civic and international organisations, nation-states and their peoples. This a globalist jurisprudence must seek to do with sensitive deference to a prominent tension of globalisation which has characterised the Western legal tradition: the espousal of universal norms and 'one-size-fits-all' law versus the different norms and laws of particular communities. Some other familiar themes will be advanced too. The regional constitutional construct of the EU proves that law need not be thought to come only from the state, showing a continuity in the West of a legal tradition characterised by competing jurisdictions. Furthermore, the kinship elements of the nation and the comradeship elements of the state are interacting with the fulfilling Kantian prophecy of peace through trade in the creation of new authority.[1]

These developments all take place nowadays amidst some 'benign neglect'[2] of the troubling yet hopeful historical context of Europe. For all of the economic theory which appears to be the raison d'être of the EU in the minds of so many, the proper place of economics must be recalled. According to J. H. H. Weiler, 'Europe began as a political project par excellence served by economic instruments.'[3] French and German elites dutifully sought to overcome the pain of nationalism. The political problem of European security after World War II was to be addressed through economic solutions 'less important than the political

---

[1] See ch. 9, section 9.4, pp. 207–10 above on kinship versus comradeship models of organisation, and peace through the pursuit of self-interest prophesied by Kant.

[2] See Christian Joerges, 'Introduction to the Special Issue: Confronting Memories: European "Bitter Experiences" and the Constitutionalization Process: Constructing Europe in the Shadow of its Pasts' (2005) 6 *German Law Journal* 245–54, 248.

[3] J. H. H. Weiler, 'Epilogue: Europe's Dark Legacy: Reclaiming Nationalism and Patriotism' in Christian Joerges and Navraj Singh Ghaleigh (eds.), *Darker Legacies of Law in Europe: The Shadow of National Socialism and Fascism over Europe and its Legal Traditions* (Oxford: Hart Publishing, 2003), p. 395.

advantages'.[4] To consider the economic purposes of the union paramount is to place the cart before the horse. The correct progression is sought in this chapter, by resuming the narration of Western international law which we left at chapter 10 section 10.1 (pp. 214–18 above).[5]

11.1 The reconstitution of the European community

The founding members of the European Union were Belgium, the Federal Republic of Germany, France, Italy, Luxembourg and the Netherlands. In 1973, Denmark, Ireland and the United Kingdom joined. Greece joined in 1981, then Spain and Portugal in 1986. In 1995, Austria, Finland and Sweden joined, making fifteen Member States. That symbol of medieval sovereignty, a single currency, was introduced as the Euro in twelve Member States in 1999. In May 2004, Cyprus, Malta, the Czech Republic, Hungary, Poland, Slovakia and Slovenia were admitted, plus the former Soviet Union nations of Estonia, Latvia and Lithuania. Bulgaria and Romania were admitted on New Years' Day 2007 (with tough modernisation requirements), bringing the total number of members to twenty-seven. Further growth is planned, inciting much debate.[6] At its heart lies what Philip Allott regards as a European metaphysical crisis of 'our mutual self-knowing, of our consciousness, of our universality and of our particularities, of what we share and what we do not share'.[7] Tracing the evolution of this contemporary European community, with its problems, complements the supranational history and aspirations of the Western legal tradition which have been concerns of this book within the globalisation context.

11.1.1 Background initiatives

Jean Monnet, an ardent integrationist, had stood apart from the idealistic movements and the hopes of political unification for peace, favouring instead the pursuit of union through functional economic means. The Kantian, perpetual peace undertones are apparent. As director of the French Modernization Plan, Monnet saw opportunity in the threat which the rich Ruhr region posed to France for the region's foreseeable enrichment of Germany. Ruhr coal

---

[4] Edelgard Mahant, *Birthmarks of Europe: The Origins of the European Community Reconsidered* (Aldershot: Ashgate, 2004), pp. 123, 134.

[5] In the present context, see too Michael Gehler, 'From Paneurope to the Single Currency: Recent Studies on the History of European Integration' (2006) 15 *Contemporary European History* 273–89 and the books reviewed therein.

[6] See e.g. Antje Wiener, 'Finality vs. Enlargement: Constitutive Practices and Opposing Rationales in the Reconstruction of Europe' in J. H. H. Weiler and Marlene Wind (eds.), *European Constitutionalism Beyond the State* (Cambridge: Cambridge University Press, 2003); Jan Zielonka, *Europe as Empire: The Nature of the Enlarged European Union* (Oxford: Oxford University Press, 2006), ch. 3 and pp. 171–6.

[7] Philip Allott, 'Epilogue: Europe and the Dream of Reason' in Weiler and Wind (eds.), *European Constitutionalism*, p. 206. See too Ian Ward, *A Critical Introduction to European Law* (London: LexisNexis UK, 2003), pp. 272–5.

should be available to French steel mills, the increased output from which could find buyers in German markets. Although an economic strategy was being adopted, these plans 'are best seen as a long-term and transformative strategy for peace among the states of western Europe . . .'[8] Robert Schuman, then the French foreign minister, was approached by Monnet. Monnet's proposal was for a coal and steel community, which was implemented as the 'Schuman Plan'. Whilst the resultant European Coal and Steel Community (ECSC) arising from the 1951 Treaty of Paris did not match the high hopes of supranationalism, it nonetheless created a higher authority, 'a potential nucleus for a European federal system'.[9] Monnet's European Defense Community (EDC), founded in May 1952 on the laurels of the Schuman Plan, was not so successful. The EDC had required the establishment of a supranational political community, the European Political Community, which was not ratified.[10] Both Monnet and Schuman envisaged the European community emerging creatively and gradually.[11]

11.1.2 Treaty establishing the European Community

In 1955, the Benelux countries proposed, to their partners in the ECSC, the establishment of a common market and the joint development of transportation and atomic energy. The ensuing Spaak Report, named after the Belgian Foreign Minister, culminated in the ratification of treaties that would establish a common market and an Atomic Energy Community. Thus emerged in 1957 the two Treaties of Rome creating the European Economic Community (EC) Treaty and the European Atomic Energy Community (Euratom) Treaty, again without Britain. The EEC set out to remove tariffs between Member States and to create common policies in a variety of areas, although the only one which reached fruition was the Common Agricultural Policy.[12] In 1965, the Merger Treaty converged into common institutions the separate institutions created by the three treaties, whilst retaining unanimous or qualified majority voting.

The EC Treaty is the 'basic constitutional charter' of the community.[13] One of the hallmarks of Western constitutionalism is the separation of powers between legislature, executive and judiciary. '[I]nstitutional balance' rather than separation of powers underpins the constitutional structure of the Community,[14]

---

[8] J. H. H. Weiler, *The Constitution of Europe: 'Do the New Clothes Have an Emperor?' and Other Essays on European Integration* (Cambridge: Cambridge University Press, 1999), p. 91.

[9] John Gillingham, *Coal, Steel and the Rebirth of Europe, 1945–55: The Germans and French from Ruhr Conflict to Economic Community* (Cambridge: Cambridge University Press, 1991), p. 297.

[10] For the factual matrix, see Desmond Dinan, *Ever Closer Union: An Introduction to European Integration* (Basingstoke: Palgrave Macmillan, 3rd edn 2005), part 1.

[11] See Ward, *European Law*, pp. 246–7.

[12] The history is well covered in Mahant, *Birthmarks of Europe*, chs. 5 and 6.

[13] See Case 294/83, *Parti Ecologiste 'Les Verts' v. European Parliament* [1986] ECR 1339.

[14] See Koen Lenaerts, 'Some Reflections on the Separation of Powers in the European Community' (1991) 28 *Common Market Law Review* 11–35.

reflected in the executive, legislative and limited judicial powers (for example, in relation to competition) invested in the Commission. Characteristic of the Western legal tradition, the competition amongst, and the sharing of, jurisdictions underlies this new constitutionalism. In addition to its original jurisdiction, under article 234 (ex 177) of the EC Treaty as amended, the European Court of Justice has jurisdiction to give preliminary rulings to courts of Member States on the interpretation of the EC Treaty, acts of EU institutions and statutes of EU bodies established by the Council.[15] Hundreds of references have been made per year since the 1990s.[16] Jurisdictional cross-pollination of ideas and practices has been encouraged. From the French tradition, administrative law has been influential, as have the form and delivery of judgment. German law has offered a very similar notion to the idea of proportionality. The most obvious English influence is the infusion of the principle of precedent, although not to the same extent as in England.[17]

11.1.3 Treaty on European Union

Succeeding the Single European Act (1986), which had increased the use of qualified majority voting, enhanced parliamentary power and further developed the internal market, the Treaty on European Union ('TEU') was a bold document. Signed at Maastricht, the Netherlands, in February 1992, the significant innovations of this treaty were the common foreign and security policy (articles 11–28, ex J)[18] of the TEU as amended and the provisions on co-operation in the field of justice and home affairs (now 'police and judicial co-operation in criminal matters' in articles 29–45, ex K). The 'three pillars' to be fostered by this newly termed 'European Union' consisted of the two pillars of these inter-governmental initiatives, with the third pillar embracing the supranationalism of Euratom, the ECSC (the treaty for which expired in 2002) and the EC. This treaty ventured further than previous EC legal agreements by placing traditional, national areas of jurisdiction within the aspirations if not competence of the European authority.

The aspirations enumerated in the preamble to the TEU, following from earlier treaties,[19] are constitutionally unique. They do not point the way resoundingly: there is much 'feeling in the dark' involved. The historical prompts are clear from the preamble: 'the historical importance of the ending

---

[15] See T. C. Hartley, *The Foundations of European Community Law: An Introduction to the Constitutional and Administrative Law of the European Community* (Oxford: Oxford University Press, 2003), ch. 9.

[16] Laurence R. Helfer and Anne-Marie Slaughter, 'Toward a Theory of Effective Supranational Adjudication' (1997) 107 *Yale Law Journal* 273–391, 310.

[17] See Thijmen Koopmans, 'The Birth of European Law at the CrossRoads of Legal Traditions' (1991) 39 *American Journal of Comparative Law* 493–507.

[18] The articles in the TEU and EC Treaty were renumbered by the Treaty of Amsterdam, 1997, effective May 1999.

[19] On the importance of the EU preambles generally, see ch. 10, section 10.3.4, pp. 225–6 above.

of the division of the European continent'; 'the future of Europe'; the intended 'solidarity between their peoples' being 'deepened' 'while respecting their history, their culture and their traditions'; with 'attachment to the principles of liberty, democracy and respect for human rights and fundamental freedoms and of the rule of law'. These aspirations are conceived with mutating notions of 'democracy' and the 'efficient functioning of the institutions' within 'a single institutional framework'. 'A common foreign and security policy' should exist 'to promote peace, security and progress in Europe and the world'. The secular human rights and free-trade principles permeate the vision of Europe on the Time Axis of the Space–Time Matrix.

11.1.4 Treaty establishing a Constitution for Europe

The Treaty of Nice (2001) had, significantly, featured an increase in the use of qualified majority voting and its reform, in preparation for further enlargement. The Treaty establishing a Constitution for Europe, agreed by the European Council in 2004 but not effectuated, attempts to transform the historical exhortations of the EU Preambles into the language of culture and politics. 'Convinced that, while remaining proud of their own national identities and history, the peoples of Europe are determined to transcend their former divisions and, united ever more closely, to forge a common destiny . . .' the interior customary bonds of nationality are to be transcended by exterior, political reason, on the Space Axis of the Space–Time Matrix. Citizens of the European Member States are asked to remain proud of their nations but to forge a common (political) destiny. This recalls the kinship versus comradeship aspects of relationships. On the Time Axis, the legacy of the Enlightenment is evoked, 'drawing inspiration from the cultural, religious and humanist inheritance of Europe, from which have developed the universal values of the inviolable and inalienable rights of the human person, democracy, equality, freedom and the rule of law'. Bearing in mind that some of the newer Member States suffered the evils of tyranny and war until the last quarter of the twentieth century,[20] the expansion of the EU to poorer states within the community summonses history in an almost Messianic way. The Preamble also exhorts: 'Believing that Europe, reunited after bitter experiences, intends to continue along the path of civilisation, progress and prosperity, for the good of all its inhabitants, including the weakest and most deprived . . .' Bringing Europeans together in this celebration of their diversity of culture and talent might be an achievable agenda were it prescribed for the Eurovision Song Contest. Despite the nobility of the sentiments, it is infinitely more problematic for Europe proper, as we shall later see.

---

[20] See Ian Ward, *European Law*, pp. 220–1; Fabrice Larat, 'Presenting the Past: Political Narratives on European History and the Justification of EU Integration' (2005) 6 *German Law Journal* 274–90, 284.

For present purposes, significant aims of the proposed Constitution are to:

1. repeal the EC Treaty and the TEU, abolishing the EC and re-establishing the EU to take over all activities of the EC;
2. revise the qualified majority voting procedure of the Council of Ministers, taking the 'blocking' power away from some Member States and making the EU more responsive to majority wishes of the EU population;
3. give Member State Parliaments a role in EU affairs with a clearer division of powers; and
4. give the EU separate legal personality to conclude international agreements in certain circumstances.

Clarification rather than innovation predominates.[21] All twenty-seven Member States are required to ratify the Constitution. In 2005, the proposal was defeated in referenda held in the Netherlands and France. The lack of responsiveness of the present and proposed EU to local concerns and democratic input is a common rationalisation for the failure. The EU 'has little or even no appeal to the great majority of the people in Europe'.[22] The failure is also connected to identity and the perception that poorer new members are exploiting the successes of older Member States. (This ignores the effects of leaving poverty on the doorstep, which can result in worse illegal immigration.)[23] A 'period of reflection' was subsequently declared in Brussels.[24]

11.2 EU higher laws

How does the EU attempt to reconcile the universality of its mission with the diversity of its constituency? Four major 'higher law' legal doctrines underlie the 'constitutionalisation' of Europe: direct effect; supremacy; implied powers; and human rights.[25] Two other concepts should be added, these being subsidiarity and the civil society freedoms. Direct effect, supremacy and subsidiarity have historical parallels to the legal pluralism of the Christian commonwealth.

11.2.1 Direct effect

Article 249 (ex 189) EC, regarding regulations and directives issued by the Council and the Commission, provides that:

> A regulation shall have general application. It shall be binding in its entirety and directly applicable in all Member States.

---

[21] See Trevor C. Hartley, *European Union Law in a Global Context* (Cambridge: Cambridge University Press, 2004), pp. xlvi–xlvii.

[22] Alexander Somek, 'Constitutional *Erinnerungsarbeit*: Ambivalence and Translation' (2005) 6 *German Law Journal* 357–70, 366.

[23] On the EU 'politics of exclusion', see Ward, *European Law*, pp. 225–31.

[24] See Commission of the European Communities, 'The Commission's Contribution to the Period of Reflection and Beyond: Plan-D for Democracy, Dialogue and Debate', Brussels, 13 October 2005, COM(2005) 494.   [25] See Weiler, *Constitution of Europe*, pp. 19–25.

A directive shall have general application. It shall be binding, as to the result to be achieved upon each Member State to which it is addressed, but shall leave to the national authorities the choice of form and methods.

The basic thrust of this article is that Treaty provisions can create rights which individuals may rely upon before their domestic courts. As early as 1963, the seminal case of *Van Gend en Loos*[26] established that the EU could not be understood in the same light as other international institutions: the EU constitutes a 'new legal order'. EU Treaties do not simply create rights for Member States as in public international law; rather, rights and duties are conferred and imposed upon individuals as well, in a European society of humans and not just states.[27]

11.2.2 Supremacy

The doctrine of supremacy builds upon the doctrine of direct effect. Whereas direct effect primarily concerns the implementation of EU law domestically in a Member State, the doctrine of supremacy is more concerned with the conflict of laws situation. The ECJ has 'Kompetenz–Kompetenz' in the European legal order such that it is the ECJ which determines which norms come within the sphere of application of EU law. Unlike conventional international treaties, by the doctrine of direct effect and supremacy the EU norm cannot be legislated away by the domestic machinery. Rather, the EU norm will not be regarded merely as part of the 'law of the land' but as part of the 'higher law' of the land.[28] The case of *Costa v ENEL*[29] introduced the doctrine of supremacy, where the precedence of Community law was confirmed according to article 249 (ex 189) EC, the direct effect provision cited above. Irrespective of whether an EU provision comes before or after the national provision, in all cases the national provision must defer to EU law.[30]

Recall the earlier discussion of medieval conflict of laws machinery and Two Swords shared jurisdiction between royal and papal law.[31] The mechanisms for handling conflicts of laws between the EU and Member States are analogous to those mechanisms of the medieval church and king. Medieval papal policy was not conceived to be innovative. In terms of the Time Axis from the Space–Time Matrix, papal legitimacy was historically grounded in scripture and academic commentary, aspiring to reform by reference to biblical vision. For the EU, legitimacy and authority are grounded in a teleological, purposive view of law[32]

---

[26] Case 26/62, *Van Gend en Loos v. Nederlands Administatie de Belastingen* [1963] ECR 1.
[27] Pierre Pescatore, 'The Doctrine of "Direct Effect": An Infant Disease of Community Law' (1983) 8 *European Law Review* 155–77, 158. See too, Ward, *European Law*, pp. 76–80 on 'horizontal direct effect' and 'indirect effect'; and generally Hartley, *Foundations*, ch. 7.
[28] Weiler, *Constitution of Europe*, p. 22.   [29] Case 6/64, [1964] ECR 585.
[30] Case 106/77, *Simmenthal* [1978] ECR 629, cited in Hartley, *Foundations*, pp. 227–8.
[31] See ch. 4, section 4.4.2, pp. 85–8 and ch. 7, section 7.2, pp. 145–6 above.
[32] See Joxerramon Bengoetxea, *The Legal Reasoning of the European Court of Justice: Towards a European Jurisprudence* (Oxford: Clarendon Press, 1993), pp. 251–2, 256–7.

as a tool for achieving the purposes of social justice and material progress, determinable primarily by innovative economic imperatives and social research.

11.2.3 Implied powers

The doctrine of implied powers builds further upon the doctrines of direct effect and supremacy. This doctrine emerged from an ECJ decision concerning the international treaty-making power of the Community with third parties. Although the EC Treaty had not dealt at much length with the external affairs power of the then European Community, the grant of internal competence was held to imply that there was also an external power.[33] Cases dealing with various fact situations have expanded this doctrine, giving rise to criticisms of ECJ judicial activism.[34]

11.2.4 Human rights

The European Court of Human Rights, which has jurisdiction over the European Convention on Human Rights, is not to be confused with the EU human rights initiatives. The European Convention on Human Rights was an initiative of the Council of Europe, which is three years older than the ECSC, with over forty state signatories.[35]

Returning to the EU, whilst there is no bill of rights in the EC Treaty, from 1969 the ECJ asserted that it would review Community measures against the foil of fundamental human rights as demonstrated in the traditions of the Member States. Essentially this came about not by design but as a pragmatic response to a possible German 'rebellion'. The allegiance to fundamental human rights by German lawyers and courts, understandable in light of their national history in the twentieth century, meant that, early on, EU law would have to comply with the human rights standards of the German constitution if EU law were to be applicable in Germany. Somewhat curiously, the ECJ denied that EU law was subject to Member State human rights principles. The ECJ maintained, though, that it was required to protect respect for fundamental rights as part of the general principles of law it applied, which could be inspired by the 'constitutional traditions common to the Member States'.[36] Highly controversial matters such as abortion, thought not to be fundamental to EU law, have been left within the domain of Member States. More recently, the EU resolved to respect the rights guaranteed by the European Convention for

---

[33] Case 22/70, *Commission of the EC v. Council of the EC* [1971] ECR 263, discussed in Weiler, *Constitution of Europe*, pp. 22–3; see generally Hartley, *Foundations*, pp. 106–7, 162–75.

[34] See Ward, *European Law*, pp. 97–101.

[35] See Hartley, *European Union Law*, pp. 3–4, 276–95; on conflicts between the EU and the ECHR, see ch. 17; and generally J. G. Merrills and A. H. Robertson, *Human Rights in Europe* (Manchester: Manchester University Press, 4th edn 2001).

[36] See Hartley, *Foundations*, p. 138, citing *Nold v. Commission*, Case 4/73, [1974] ECR 491.

the Protection of Human Rights and Fundamental Freedoms under article 6 (ex F) TEU.[37]

11.2.5 Subsidiarity

Article 5 (ex 3b) EC uses the term 'subsidiarity', which concerns the relationship between differing levels of authority in society.[38] It derives from the Latin *subsidium*, meaning help or assistance. Participants in an association are to be helped so that they might help themselves, encouraging personal innovation. The immediate source of this notion is to be found in an Encyclical Letter of 1931 by Pope Pius XI, who wrote of it in the context of encouraging smaller groups to perform social functions best undertaken at that level.[39] It has rich origins in pre-national Swiss Protestantism.[40] EU subsidiarity applies when concurrent competences are held by a Member State and the Community.

Three guidelines are used to decide whether EU action in relation to an issue will be justified: it should have transnational aspects; Member State action alone or lack of action by the EU would conflict with the EC Treaty; and action at the EU level should 'produce clear benefits'.[41] Subsidiarity in the EU supports the economic assumption that no single level of organisation appropriately performs all social functions. According to the new incarnation of the doctrine, the best states, like the best firms, are those that reduce transaction costs the most. To reduce these costs, so the argument goes, sovereignty must be transferred to 'sub- and supra-state units' in various fields of juridical competence.[42]

Although of limited legal effect in the EU[43] but of more than symbolic importance,[44] at a global level subsidiarity is a promising doctrine for greater local flexibility, with more systems of norms being recognised with greater possibilities for attracting allegiance. It is an opportunity for the potential accommodation of universality by particular means. It is reflected in the view of Joseph Stiglitz that '[a]ctions the benefits of which accrue largely locally (such as actions related to local pollution) should be conducted at the local level; whilst those that

---

[37] See generally Hartley, *European Union Law*, chs. 15, 16; Weiler, *Constitution of Europe*, ch. 3.

[38] For this principle in pre-modern English and German common law, see ch. 6, pp. 121–2 above.

[39] See John Finnis, *Natural Law and Natural Rights* (Oxford: Clarendon Press, 1980 reprinted 1992), pp. 146, 159, 169. For a detailed background, see Nicholas Aroney, 'Subsidiarity, Federalism and the Best Constitution: Thomas Aquinas on City, Province and Empire' (2007) 26 *Law and Philosophy* 161–228.

[40] Switzerland's counterpart to Luther, Huldrych Zwingli (1484–1531), had launched a significant Protestant trend for local communities to claim the right to control their own affairs: see Norman Davies, *Europe: A History* (London: Pimlico, 1997), p. 488.

[41] EC Treaty: Protocol on the Application of the Principles of Subsidiarity and Proportionality, extracted in Hartley, *European Union Law*, p. 62.

[42] Joel P. Trachtman, '*L'Etat, C'est Nous*: Sovereignty, Economic Integration and Subsidiarity' (1992) 33 *Harvard International Law Journal* 459–73, 468–71.

[43] See Hartley, *European Union Law*, pp. 61–3. For a detailed critique, see Antonio Estella, *The EU Principle of Subsidiarity and its Critique* (Oxford: Oxford University Press, 2002).

[44] See N. W. Barber, 'The Limited Modesty of Subsidiarity' (2005) 11 *European Law Journal* 308–25.

benefit the citizens of an entire country should be undertaken at the national level.' Where impacts are global, 'systems of global governance are essential'.[45]

11.2.6 Civil society freedoms

The general principles of the internal market are to be found in Part three Title III of the EC Treaty as the 'four freedoms': the freedom of movement of workers (chapter 1), goods (chapter 2), services (chapter 3) and capital (chapter 4).

What are the doctrines behind these articles? Non-discrimination requires the equal treatment of persons by public authorities. Proportionality requires the burdens which are imposed not to exceed the public interest to be served by the burdens.[46] In addition, article 28 (ex 30) EC prohibits indirect barriers to trade in the form of quantitative restrictions on imports such as quotas and 'all measures having equivalent effect'.[47]

These notions can be broadly illustrated by the Directive enshrining the mutual recognition of qualifications to practise law in the EU.[48] A fully qualified lawyer in the Member State of origin should be able to practise anywhere in the EU, subject to conditions such as regulation by the domestic profession. For example, an English-trained lawyer may practise French law in France, and vice versa, without further legal education.[49] There has been resistance to such liberal recognition, for example, in Germany.[50] A Member State may require an applicant to pass an aptitude test if there are significant differences between qualifications.[51] Given the technical complexities of particular Member State legal systems, it would still appear more efficient to retain lawyers trained in particular jurisdictions, especially where local knowledge and intuitions can be important, say, for advocacy. Europe is still a long way from being the relatively unified cultural unit it was in the wake of the Papal Revolution, when a man of any city or village might go for education to any school, and become a prelate or an official in any church, court, or university.[52]

11.3 Before and beyond the nation-state: international law as constitutional law

The foregoing discussion of the EU discloses, in Europe at least, a regional movement to something beyond a system of public and private international law. From phoenix-like origins from the ashes of the world wars, growing from

---

[45] Joseph Stiglitz, *Globalization and its Discontents* (London: Penguin, 2002), p. 223.

[46] Case 114/76, *Bela-Muehl* [1977] ECR 1222.

[47] See Case 120/78, *Casis de Dijon* [1979] ECR 649; Cases 267/91 and 268/91, *Keck and Mithouard* [1993] ECR I-6097.   [48] See Council Directive 98/5/EC.

[49] See H. Patrick Glenn, 'Comparative Law and Legal Practice: On Removing the Borders' (2001) 75 *Tulane Law Review* 977–1002, 981. For case discussion, see James Hanlon, *European Community Law* (London: Sweet & Maxwell, 3rd edn 2003), pp. 203–7.

[50] See European Parliament Questions EPQ E-0739/99.

[51] See Council Directive 89/48/EEC.   [52] See ch. 5, section 5.3.1, pp. 104–5 above.

public and private international law and international diplomacy, the EU has emerged as a viable model for channelling once international co-operation through law into a more integrated supranational society. This supranational authority has defused, at least for the time being, the possibility for conflict again approaching the level of the Armageddon of the two world wars. The axial tension between France and Germany appears conclusively alleviated by the EU. In so doing, the nature of traditional state sovereignty symbolised by the Peace of Westphalia[53] has been radically altered in Europe.

Does the membership of (to use a particular example) the United Kingdom in the EU mark the end for English sovereignty? Neil MacCormick has argued that European Community law should not be considered simply in terms of an Austinian theory of law and state 'grounded in the theory of sovereignty as a matter of habitual obedience to state sanctioned commands'.[54] On one view, it might be contended that because the power of the EU organs derives from the delegation of power by the UK Parliament, the UK Parliament is still the ultimate source of authority. As a matter of positive constitutional law, there appears to be nothing to stop the Parliament of the United Kingdom from altering or repealing the European Communities Act (although Parliament's hands are tied, so to speak, such that it cannot interfere with European law without changing the fundamental European Communities Act).[55] On another view, the EU might be considered sovereign because it possesses coercive power over the UK: the UK Parliament is highly unlikely to revoke its membership of the EU unilaterally for the huge economic damage the UK would then suffer. So, whilst the Parliament is free to revisit the enabling act and to recover its full powers by amending the European Communities Act, practically this seems a near impossibility.

Neither of these monocular views of sovereignty should be accepted. As the European Court of Justice has continually held, the EU constitutes a new legal order co-ordinate with that of the Member States.[56] Different legal systems overlap and interact, without requiring subordination or hierarchical inferiority. A single source of sovereignty is an unnecessary if not unreal legal concept in the context of this type of legal pluralism. Potentially incompatible rules exist for recognising the ultimate source of legal authority if, for example, a Member State jurisdiction disagrees with the ECJ. Competing claims for supremacy (notably in German Constitutional Court jurisprudence)[57]

---

[53] See ch. 6, section 6.4.1, pp. 139–41 above.

[54] Neil MacCormick, 'Beyond the Sovereign State' (1993) 56 *Modern Law Review* 1–18, 4.

[55] See Neil MacCormick, *Questioning Sovereignty: Law, State, and Nation in the European Commonwealth* (Oxford: Oxford University Press, 1999), pp. 80–1, 89. This amounts to parliament re-amending its 'rule of recognition', in H. L. A. Hart's terms.

[56] MacCormick, 'Beyond the Sovereign State', 4; see too Ward, *European Law*, pp. 111–29.

[57] See e.g. *Solange II* [1987] 3 CMLR 225; *Brunner v. The European Union Treaty* [1994] 1 CMLR 57 and *The Banana Case* (June 7, 2000) 2 BvL 1/97 discussed in Miriam Aziz, 'Sovereignty Lost, Sovereignty Regained? Some Reflections on the Bundesverfassungsgericht's Bananas Judgment' (2002) 9 *Columbia Journal of European Law* 109–40.

may create co-operation between jurisdictions given the capacity for harm otherwise.[58]

It can be argued that the EU treaties do not deserve the appellation 'constitution' because constitutions address the sovereign power. That is, in the age of constitutional democracy, 'the people' should be addressed, so that government is legitimated by those subject to it.[59] The EU treaties address 'Member States'. This argument is not convincing, affixing to the word 'constitution' an unchanging significance thought to be unique to the modern nation-state. Such a view is historically chauvinist. By that reasoning, the English Tudor and Stuart monarchs did not have a constitution – a derisible contention. Much literature considers the extent to which the EU is an international law construction or a constitution.[60] The answer seems to be that it is both, and something new at that, requiring a new public philosophy.[61] Even were the proposed Constitution to be ratified and effected, the appellation 'constitution' would not make it look less like a treaty or necessarily mean that the EU would then have a constitution in more essentially constitutional terms than it has already.[62]

11.4 Supranationality and the 'democratic deficit'

'Supranational' is the term often used to describe the social location of EU institutions – as it could be used to describe medieval Western papal authority.[63] There are obvious legitimacy problems associated with authority being exercised at the supranational level. Sovereignty and parliamentary democracy, as understood in the greater part of the twentieth century, have effectively been scrambled in the EU.

Citizenship in the European Union is remarkably different from the national models of parliamentary democracy and even federal models such as in Australia, Canada and the United States. State membership of the EU is intended to be dependent upon the pursuit by each Member State of domestic economic performance indicia, such as a specified national inflation rate, price stability

---

[58] N. W. Barber, 'Legal Pluralism and the European Union' (2006) 12 *European Law Journal* 306–29, 323–9.

[59] See Dieter Grimm, 'Does Europe Need a Constitution?' (1995) 1 *European Law Journal* 282–302, 288.

[60] See e.g. Nicholas Aroney, 'Federal Constitutionalism/European Constitutionalism in Comparative Perspective' in G. Leenknegt and E. J. Janse de Jonge (eds.), *Getuigend Staatsrecht: Liber Amicorum A. K. Koekkoek* (Tilburg: Wolf Legal Publishers, 2005) and sources therein.

[61] See Ward, *European Law*, ch. 8.

[62] See Weiler, 'Power of the Word'; Neil Walker, 'Postnational Constitutionalism and the Problem of Translation' in Weiler and Wind (eds.), *European Constitutionalism*, p. 39.

[63] Concerned to demonstrate the 'neo-medievalism' of the European Union enterprise, Zielonka, *Europe as Empire*, is perhaps the best treatise on supranationality. More narrowly, see Peter L. Lindseth, 'The Contradictions of Supranationalism: Administrative Governance and Constitutionalization in European Integration since the 1950s' (2003) 37 *Loyola L.A. Law Review* 363–406; Alexander Somek, 'On Supranationality' (2001) 5 *European Integration online Papers* no. 3 http://eiop.or.at/eiop.

and government deficit levels, under articles 98–130 (ex 102a–109r) EC. In addition, as earlier mentioned, a common foreign and security policy[64] and close co-operation on justice and home affairs are envisaged.[65] Hence the traditional sovereignty of the national parliaments is challenged.

Also challenged is the theory of representation in lawmaking and citizenship, in a twofold manner. First, under article 19 EC, nationality should lose significance in municipal elections for EU positions. In European Parliament elections, the franchise is handed to people with residence but without sworn national allegiance. What is even more radical is that these residents should have the right to stand for election to a municipal government of a Member State to which they have not sworn allegiance.[66] Second, and perhaps more drastic than the change in implication of what it means to be a citizen of a nation-state, is the very practice of political decision-making. As the only European governmental organ which features anything approaching popular participation, the extent of European Parliament power has been 'codecisional' (article 251 (ex 189b) EC) with the Council only in limited areas since the TEU (effective 1993) and in more areas since the Treaties of Amsterdam (effective 1999) and Nice (effective 2003). The Parliament's role includes advisory and supervisory functions, with budgetary, some external affairs and Commission screening powers. After the initiation of legislation by the Commission, Parliament and Council must usually agree upon the final text, with some exceptions as to procedure (assent or consultation) and policy (depending upon treaty powers granted). The Council comprises government delegates of the Member States. Each state is represented by a government minister on the Council. This body also represents the EU to foreign countries. It is only the Council which serves as the forum for the direct expression of national interests.[67] Accountable to governments and not citizens directly, added disfavour is earned by the Council for its secret deliberation process.[68]

The synthetic nature of the EU can be exemplified by the controversy surrounding the so-called 'democratic deficit' which plagues the EU legislative process[69] and other globalist institutions like the WTO and NGOs.[70] 'There is no civic act of the European citizen whereby he or she can influence directly

---

[64] See generally Hartley, *European Union Law*, part IV; Zielonka, *Europe as Empire*, ch. 6.

[65] See section 11.1.3, p. 258 above.

[66] On conceptualisations of European citizenship, see Dora Kostakopoulou, 'Ideas, Norms and European Citizenship: Explaining Institutional Change' (2005) 68 *Modern Law Review* 233–67, 238–43; Ward, *European Law*, 268–72.   [67] See generally Hartley, *Foundations*, ch. 1.

[68] See Stephen S. Sieberson, 'The Proposed European Union Constitution: Will it Eliminate the EU's Democratic Deficit?' (2004) 10 *Columbia Journal of European Law* 173–264, 196–7.

[69] For an overview of associated issues, see MacCormick, *Questioning Sovereignty*, ch. 9.

[70] See e.g. Laurence R. Helfer, 'Constitutional Analogies in the International Legal System' (2003) 37 *Loyola of Los Angeles Law Review* 193–237, 231–7; Alfred C. Aman Jr, *The Democracy Deficit: Taming Globalization through Law Reform* (New York: New York University Press, 2004); Carol C. Gould and Alistair M. Macleod (eds.), 'Democracy and Globalization Special Issue' (2006) 37 *Journal of Social Philosophy* 1–162; Weiler, *Constitution of Europe*, chs. 8 and 10; Zielonka, *Europe as Empire*, ch. 5.

the outcome of any policy choice facing the Community and Union as citizens can when choosing between parties which offer sharply distinct programs.'[71] In the process of EU lawmaking, Member States have been able to delegate traditional state responsibility in some more economic and controversial spheres to 'Eurocrats'. This bureaucratic decision-making is unimpeachable by democratically elected governmental powers.[72] Fatally for the draft European Constitution in the near future, peoples of certain Member States appear to have decided in their referenda that their political participation is not to be 'transcended' in such a fashion. Group and individual political demands arguably need fora for a greater discussion when formulating significant policies.[73] The EU's significant executive level decision-making does not satisfy the populist need for transparency in institutions which resemble domestic manifestations of democracy (however imperfect and idealised that democracy may be).

European supranationality contains both of the idealised tendencies of globalisation: namely of globalised localism (standards of a few nation-state jurisdictions are imposed at a European level, such as fiscal policy); and localised globalism (a nation-state responds uniquely to a universal European initiative such as refusing to adopt the Euro).[74] These tendencies manifest in dialectical, opposing forces of integration and fragmentation – or 'fragmegration'.[75]

Weiler has used the term 'infranationalism' to reflect upon the transformation of Europe to appreciate that 'increasingly large sectors of Community norm generation are done at a meso-level of governance' by 'middle-range officials of the Community and the Member States in combination with a variety of private and semi-public bodies players'.[76] Essentially this is regulation by information, exercised by committees politically powered with knowledge and persuasion.[77] Territorial spheres of containable disruption are being undermined by supranational competence with associated infranational committees and bureaucracies.

If there is to be any solace from the heavy criticism of the supranational democratic deficit, it may lie in a liberal 'process-based' (as opposed to democratic 'input-based') philosophy. It would require power to be controlled through checks and balances so that fairness could be incorporated in the decision-making process, for example through input by interested citizens.[78]

---

[71] Weiler, *Constitution of Europe*, p. 350.　　[72] Somek, 'On Supranationality', 8.

[73] See Vito Breda, 'A European Constitution in a Multinational Europe or a Multinational Constitution for Europe?' (2006) 12 *European Law Journal* 330–44, discussing in the process the rationalist, political ideas of Jürgen Habermas's European patriotism versus Neil MacCormick's more cultural model of nation-state co-operation.

[74] On localised globalism and globalised localism, see ch. 2, section 2.1.4, p. 32 above.

[75] See James N. Rosenau, 'Strong Demand, Huge Supply: Governance in an Emerging Epoch' in Ian Bache and Matthew Flinders (eds.), *Multi-level Governance* (Oxford: Oxford University Press, 2004).　　[76] J. H. H. Weiler, *Constitution of Europe*, p. 98.

[77] See Anne-Marie Slaughter, 'Global Government Networks, Global Information Agencies, and Disaggregated Democracy' (2003) 24 *Michigan Journal of International Law* 1041–75.

[78] See Renaud Dehousse, 'Beyond Representative Democracy: Constitutionalism in a Polycentric Polity' in Weiler and Wind (eds.), *European Constitutionalism*, pp. 155–6.

The quantity and quality of those inputs would be crucial to satisfying complaints about the lack of democracy and public space in the current EU model.[79]

11.5 Political versus cultural community

In 1788, von Martens wrote about the cultural community of Europe.

> The interest which each of the European powers shows in the affairs of all others, as well as the maintenance of a system of balance of power and the similarity of morals in Christian Europe, together with the bonds linking several of them – be it the personality of the same monarch . . . a system of federation . . . common political or religious interest – all this together permits one to look at Europe . . . as a special union of states, which – without having at any time contractually founded a general and positive society – has her own laws, morals and customs, and which in some respects is similar to a nation not yet agreed on a constitution.[80]

That community was not legislated. It was not coerced. Von Martens recognised Europe's interior, cultural compellability. For the future of not just EU law, but law in general in modern times and times of great change, a general, globalist jurisprudence must analyse the nature of legislated, politically imposed norms. Perhaps no greater example of imposed law, especially for the new Eastern Members of the EU, is to be found in the approximately 80,000 regulations comprising the *acquis communautaire* or total body of EU law accumulated to date.[81] Legislation is only one of the utensils in the service of authority, and an often blunt, bludgeoning one at that.

The formal basis of the EU is contractual. The EU was created by means of treaties in a rational and exterior fashion on the Space Axis. Its normativity is fundamentally political and legislated (that is, state-based), which is a problem because it undermines the cultural (nation-based) aspects of authority.[82] There is a historical, moral force behind the institutions if one cares to look at history and the treaty Preambles.[83] For most Europeans, however, an interior, moral compellability may exist only for the economically franchised classes and those able to avail themselves of EU rights law. Notwithstanding, there is a basis for a kinship relationship. With other cultural commonalities, national and legal cross-fertilisation occurred over millennia. Survival of the world wars and the World Revolution are also important cultural commonalities. According to Philip Allott, the true Europe is the Europe of the tribes and also the mind – with its cultural products including religion, philosophy, law, science, literature,

---

[79] See e.g. Ward, *European Law*, pp. 259–68, discussing the approaches of Weiler and Habermas.
[80] G. F. von Martens, *Noveau Recueil de traités* cited in Wilhelm G. Grewe, *The Epochs of International Law* (Berlin: Walter de Gruyter, 2000), p. 291.
[81] See Zielonka, *Europe as Empire*, pp. 25–9.
[82] See generally ch. 9, section 9.3, pp. 203–7 above.
[83] In tabular form, see Larat, 'Presenting the Past', 281–3; and discussion of them in ch. 10, section 10.3, pp. 225–6 below and section 11.1, pp. 256–60 above.

music, fine arts and architecture.[84] Allott is also aware that the EU as a polity has not discovered the historical kinship of its tribes. Until that happens, the national Member States will continue with their potential for pathological national development.[85] It seems that they will require a superabundance of legislation in the meantime.

What cultural appeal can the EU hope to create, to inspire the nationals of Member States to give up, within certain constitutional limits, the priorities arising from the ties of the Member State? There has been an EU programme of attempting to grow an interior culture – to 'invent the traditions' as nations have done historically – integrated with an exterior political logic. Figure the logo of the twelve stars of the EU flag adopted in 1985. The number twelve is historically associated with the twelve apostles, the twelve sons of Jacob, the twelve tables of early Roman law and the labours of Hercules, and also (though not avowedly) with the twelve stars of the Virgin Mary's halo in Revelation 12: 1.[86] Witness, too, EU scholarships, awards, seasonal events (for example, Europe Day on the Schuman Plan anniversary, 9 May), and an anthem, Beethoven's Ode to Joy. Whether such symbolism can actually focus the attention of diverse people into supra-nationhood, or supra-statehood, remains to be seen. It has so far not succeeded. Continued barriers will be supported by the nationalist historiographies which prevail in the schools and popular media of Member States.[87] It will also be difficult in the absence of a single national language, which we saw in chapter 9 was so important to group consciousness.[88]

No simple solutions are on the horizon for the EU. The interior, cultural aspects of community are evidently very difficult to create. The exterior, political aspects of authority are undermined by the democratic deficit. Whether there should, in fact, be any undue alarm about these difficulties is not even clear. Intuitively, there must be something positive about the fact that these difficulties occur at all, given Europe's bloody history. It is as though the family killings have finally stopped (at least in the West) and the surviving elders are able to sit down and plan the children's legacy. Although the voices are raised, the family stays seated at the dinner table. There seems to be more food.

One of the pre-eminent commentators on the EU, J. H. H. Weiler, has compared the constitutional implementation of the EU with the constitutional moment of the Jews at Mt Sinai receiving their law via Moses. Both episodes

---

[84] Philip Allott, 'The European Community is not the True European Community' (1991) 100 *Yale Law Journal* 2485–500, 2496–9.   [85] Allott, *Health of Nations*, [4.85].

[86] See Chris Shore, *Building Europe: The Cultural Politics of European Integration* (London: Routledge, 2000), pp. 47–8, and ch. 2 generally. On the invention of national traditions, see ch. 9, section 9.1.4, p. 201 above.

[87] See Oliver J. Daddow, 'Euroscepticism and the Culture of the Discipline of History' (2006) 32 *Review of International Studies* 309–28; Franz C. Mayer and Jan Palmowski, 'European Identities and the EU – the Ties that Bind the Peoples of Europe' (2004) 42 *Journal of Common Market Studies* 573–98, 580–1.

[88] See ch. 9, section 9.1.1, pp. 197–8 above. See too Philippe van Parijs, 'Europe's Linguistic Challenge' (2004) 45 *European Journal of Sociology* 113–54; Mayer and Palmowski, 'European Identities', 581.

demonstrate that, possibly as with all constitutions, the understanding of constitutional significance comes only after the commitment to the constitution has been made and before interpretation is possible. 'All that the Eternal hath spoken, we will do, and hearken' (Exodus 24: 7).[89] To overcome the trauma – slavery in Egypt or the World Revolution, respectively – a commitment must be made. Then must come the pursuit of understanding. The biblical analogy can be continued. The blood sacrifice of the World Wars must be remembered and recalled regularly when thinking of the emerging EU covenants, just as the spilling of blood gave meaning and sanctity to all of the major biblical covenants, in both the Old and New Testaments.

11.6 The global significance of the EU

The European Union is neither a nation nor a state, yet the reality of its burgeoning legal science, legal system and laws cannot be disputed. Although the EU lacks the religious and theological history of the medieval papacy, the EU is by its simple modernity a far more technologically advanced and industrialised constitution which recognises the global tensions between diversity and universality. The visible achievement has occurred in a remarkably short period of time (although the roots go back for at least a millennium). The medieval papacy evolved differently from the EU, despite the supranational similarities. The papacy required many hundreds of years, if not the first millennium CE, to achieve its legal legitimacy organically and gradually. Between the Papal Revolution and the Protestant Reformations, the papacy, we saw, was able to assert political and moral authority, respectively, at the exterior political and interior moral orientations of the Space Axis of the Space–Time Matrix, through a common biblical narrative and vision of heaven on earth on the Time Axis. The EU is less effective in the moral dimension. It takes its norms from more plural, national spheres, and is governmentally abstracted not only from the citizen to the Member State but also from the Member State to the Union. EU authority is distinctly political as opposed to involving the moral input of individuals in their political processes. The general expansion of executive government power associated with globalisation and modern capitalism may otherwise reflect the progress of the consumer and the regress of the citizen,[90] the progress of appetite and the regress of the mind.[91]

European states formed the basis for the international society of the nineteenth and twentieth centuries, enshrined in the territory-laden world contemplated by the UN Charter and its guarantees of state domestic jurisdiction.[92] The priority of European states in this development is matched by the priority of the European states in now providing an example to the world of co-operation beyond state spheres, made necessary by the World Revolution. The EU may

---

[89] Weiler, *Constitution of Europe*, ch. 1.   [90] Ibid., pp. 333–4.
[91] David A. Westbrook, *City of Gold: An Apology for Global Capitalism* (New York: Routledge, 2004), p. 233.   [92] See article 2(7) of the Charter of the United Nations.

provide a foreboding of legal relations amongst peoples and states in a global context.[93] Freedom of goods, services, labour and capital were part of the EU project long before 'globalisation' became a buzz-word.[94] If globalisation is thought about as 'the process that takes away from individual States the ability to control day-to-day activities within their territories', the EU is 'foremost among a whole pack of international bodies' with a globalising power.[95] Such power is more regional than global. EU law may, though, be considered 'global law' not in the sense of 'universal international norms that prevail globally' (which are relatively rare), but in the globalisation-as-interconnection context of 'a mélange of domestic constitutional and international sources'.[96]

A final matter of global significance worth present note is the public attempt in the EU constitutional documents to come to terms with, if not cope with, the past. That much is apparent from the Preambles to the EU documents and the sorrowful yet hopeful preambles to other post-World War II globalist institutions discussed in chapter 10. The particular German concept of *Vergangenheitsbewältigung* has been applied to European legal history. Not easily translatable, the term represents the effort to face the past, for example to come to terms with Auschwitz.[97] German and French favour for European institutions in their early days reflects this grappling.[98] More widespread grappling with new institutions and their historical origins is a global necessity.

This chapter could only selectively portray the historical, political and legal debates which animate the industry of EU academic discourse. Of necessity we have peered through a keyhole into a large room with many people engaged in noisy conversations. Notwithstanding all of the possible associated and opposing political positions one might strain to understand, a general, globalist jurisprudence might see hope in the EU model of law for its sensitivity to historical and normative considerations. All four dimensions of the Space–Time Matrix are engaged in the academic and public debate. On the Space Axis, the individual has numerous normative systems and jurisdictions vying for allegiance – competing cultures, nations, states, political rationalities and ideals of

---

[93] See e.g. Philip Allott, *The Health of Nations: Society and Law Beyond the State* (Cambridge: Cambridge University Press, 2002), p. xii and his *Eunomia: New Order for a New World* (Oxford: Oxford University Press, 1990), [13.79]; see too Philip Bobbitt, *The Shield of Achilles: War, Peace and the Course of History* (London: Penguin, 2003), p. 638 on 'formally globalizing the European nation-state through a universal international law'.

[94] George Ross, 'European Integration and Globalization' in Roland Axtmann (ed.), *Globalization and Europe: Theoretical and Empirical Investigations* (London: Pinter, 1998), pp. 173–6.

[95] Hartley, *European Union Law*, p. xv; see too Ward, *European Law*, pp. 241–5.

[96] See J. H. H. Weiler, 'On the Power of the Word: Europe's Constitutional Iconography' (2005) 3 *International Journal of Constitutional Law* 173–90, 184.

[97] See Joerges, 'Introduction', 248; his 'Europe a *Großraum*? Shifting Legal Conceptualisations of the Integration Project' in Joerges and Ghaleigh, *Darker Legacies*, pp. 167–8 and also 'Working through "Bitter Experiences" towards Constitutionalisation: A Critique of the Disregard for History in European Constitutional Theory', EUI Working Papers, Law No. 2005/14, European University Institute, 2005. See too Thorsten Keiser, 'Europeanization as a Challenge to Legal History' (2005) 6 *German Law Journal* 473–81, 477–8.

[98] See Mahant, *Birthmarks of Europe*, pp. 10, 53–4.

being European. On the Time Axis, the past dimension is racked by a tormented history which at the same time has sprung from a tradition of social thought alert to the issues associated with attempting to regulate diverse spaces with universal norms. Many visions for the future are available, which the laws may fix upon and attempt to incarnate in the present – visions of peace, economic prosperity, enlargement, charity, and ideals of democracy, statehood and co-operation. In the context of globalisation, there may well be no better microcosm from which to draw lessons about public law as jurisdictions increasingly intersect and interact by evolution and by design.

Amidst these rich orientations to norms, ideas of appropriate legal orders and appropriately ordered laws perhaps stand the greatest prospect of being challenged, evaluated and improved through attempts to reconcile conflicting norms and systems. Law might emerge from that process with richer bearings than law otherwise suffered when it was considered by most to be a tool of an unquestionable sovereign state. In that respect, a general, globalist jurisprudence will do well to be conscious that, in the West, legal concepts have advanced with the times, transforming authority and in turn being transformed, as they did from Aquinas to William of Ockham to Vitoria to Grotius to Hobbes to de Vattel to Bentham; from the Papal Revolution to the Protestant Reformations to the English Revolution to the French Revolution to the World Revolution. At least with that consciousness should come less surprise and an enhanced ability to accommodate change whilst maintaining some stability through law, so conceived.

Again, an irresistible conclusion must be that if widespread satisfaction with a constitution cannot accrue to Europeans who are so comparatively similar, how much more difficult will be the path for closer constitutional relations between the peoples of different continents. A global constitutional document, as one might consider a state constitutional document, is in the realm of science fiction. That is because even just in Europe, everyday authority, or gravity, cannot be found or invented on the Space–Time Matrix in terms more compelling to most people than already exists in their nation-states.

A general, globalist jurisprudence might most realistically concentrate upon the science of the prospects for intermediate forms of normative co-operation across the world and within its normative systems. In the standard textbooks of European Union law, we find something of the traditional public law mainstays with a new constitutional language and method, which can serve a globalist jurisprudence. In the next chapter we shall see something of an emerging Western private law which can serve this enterprise too.

12

International commercial law and private governance

Before retiring to draw conclusions from our Gulliverian travels through the Western legal tradition, a further case study of jurisdictions existing in the same space as other jurisdictions will assist. The *lex mercatoria* – the international commercial law of merchants – is considered. Immediately, the criticism may be levelled that the choice of the *lex mercatoria* suffers from a paradigmatic weakness, despite its existence as a jurisdiction in competition with state commercial law. After all, not all of the commercial world relies upon the distinct *lex mercatoria* and surely commercial laws under various banners are the preserve of societies with a degree of affluence and sophistication. The microeconomic *lex mercatoria* has been chosen, however, because it illustrates the potential for lived (not coerced) law with great historical survival value and supranational success, minimally reliant upon the state. Together with contract law, the *lex mercatoria* also lends itself to contemplation about the extent to which laws can be codified or universalised amidst local diversities. (Deserving of recall in this context are the concerns we saw expressed by the Historical School of jurisprudence in the nineteenth century.) Not only relevant to private relationships, we shall also see that the 'private law' of contract has encroached into the province of the 'public law' of government. Commercial law trends and concerns therefore extend beyond the account of merchants and economics.

12.1 The *lex mercatoria*

12.1.1 Definition

The *lex mercatoria* derives from its customary and spontaneous nature. It is a merchant-driven, historically developed body of law, independent of national law[1] (or at least relegating domestic laws to the bottom of the list of sources), governing the 'international, commercial and financial legal order'.[2]

---

[1] See Berthold Goldman, 'The Applicable Law: General Principles of Law – the *lex mercatoria*' in Julian D. M. Lew (ed.), *Contemporary Problems in International Arbitration* (London: Centre for Commercial Law Studies, Queen Mary College, University of London, 1986), pp. 114–16.

[2] J. H. Dalhuisen, 'Legal Orders and their Manifestation: The Operation of the International Commercial and Financial Legal Order and its Lex Mercatoria' (2006) 24 *Berkeley Journal of*

Substantive tenets of this law can be extracted from a short list expressed by Lord Justice Mustill.

- Contracts should prima facie be enforced according to their terms (*pacta sunt servanda*).
- A contract should be performed in good faith.
- A state entity cannot be permitted to evade the enforcement of its obligations.
- If unforeseen difficulties intervene in the performance of a contract, the parties should negotiate in good faith to overcome them, even if the contract contains no revision clause.
- One party is entitled to treat itself as discharged from its obligations if the other party has committed a breach, but only if the breach is substantial.
- No party can be allowed by its own act to bring about a non-performance of a condition precedent to its own obligation.
- A party that has suffered a breach of contract must take reasonable steps to mitigate its loss.
- A party must act promptly to enforce its rights, on pain of losing them by waiver.
- Failure by one party to respond to a letter written to it by the other is regarded as evidence of assent to its terms.[3]

Jan Dalhuisen expands his definition of the *lex mercatoria* to more universalistic principles of wider application, including procedural fairness, protections against fraud, bribery, market manipulation, money laundering and also fundamental principles of environmental protection.[4] Capitalist if not Western though these notions are, the term 'universal' may be used of them if it is accepted that there can be a 'universe' signified by a particular industrial community, unconstrained by territory.[5]

The modern *lex mercatoria* 'provides a nearly complete potential for the resolution of international conflicts', although national enforcement may be required[6] in the event that customary or peer-based recognition is not accorded

---

International Law 129–91, 132, and his *Dalhuisen on International Commercial, Financial and Trade Law* (Oxford: Hart Publishing, 2nd edn 2004), esp. pp. 193–4, and more generally section 1, part III.

[3] For his 20 principles, see Michael J. Mustill, 'The New Lex Mercatoria: The First Twenty-five Years' (1988) 4 *Arbitration International* 86–119, 91. Klaus Peter Berger proposes 78 rules in *The Creeping Codification of the Lex Mercatoria* (The Hague: Kluwer Law International, 1999), pp. 278–311.   [4] Dalhuisen, *Trade Law*, p. 194.

[5] See Michael Douglas, 'The Lex Mercatoria and the Culture of Transnational Industry' (2006) 13 *University of Miami International and Comparative Law Review* 367–401, 380–1. On the narrowness of these interests serving the 'mercatocracy', see A. Claire Cutler, 'Globalization, the Rule of Law, and the Modern Law Merchant: Medieval or Late Capitalist Associations?' (2001) 8 *Constellations* 480–502, further illustrated in Ronald Charles Wolf, *Trade, Aid, and Arbitrate: The Globalization of Western Law* (Aldershot: Ashgate, 2004) with imperialist momentum. Cf. section 12.4, p. 292 below.

[6] Hans-Joachim Mertens, '*Lex Mercatoria*: A Self-applying System Beyond National Law?' in Gunther Teubner (ed.), *Global Law Without a State* (Brookfield: Dartmouth Publishing Company Limited, 1997), p. 36.

the determination by a party. Typically, domestic concepts of property, security, equity and trusts are relied upon.[7] The qualities of the *lex mercatoria* are said to be its 'universal character', 'informality and speed', 'reliance on commercial custom and practice'[8] (although cost benefit and speed may sometimes be questionable)[9] and 'flexibility and dynamic ability to grow' (if not change quickly).[10] Privacy may also be maintained.

Ideologically, the *lex mercatoria* embodied before its time, and continues to embody, the major modern ethos of free trade, '[e]volving out of the economic theory of perfect competition and philosophical conceptions of free will . . .'[11] This law exists at a relatively interior point on the Space Axis of our Space–Time Matrix, closer to the participants' allegiances rather than further away and imposed. The customary nature of this law profoundly grounds it in a relatively common history and future vision. A brief history of the *lex mercatoria* and the private international law of trade will demonstrate the deeply ingrained and historically evolving and surviving nature of this field of law, even though its continuity and quality of being a system as such is questionable for different periods. The aim is to see how a functioning legal system can evolve and survive with minimal state dependence. This occurs in a system featuring the interior cultural generation of norms which are for the most part successfully objectified, if need be, with political enforcement on the exterior end of the Space Axis.

12.1.2 History

What would now be considered 'transnational' commercial law in the Western tradition can be uncovered in ancient Athens and classical Rome. Those laws were both emporial and customary.[12] The medieval *lex mercatoria* varied in content in different locations, which is to be expected of any customary laws. Of chief importance to the medieval *lex mercatoria* was its reliance upon 'the merchants themselves, who organized international fairs and markets, formed mercantile courts, and established mercantile offices in the new urban communities that were springing up throughout western Europe'.[13] Even outside the

---

7 Dalhuisen, 'Legal Orders', 189–90.

8 Bruce L. Benson, quoted in Berger, *Creeping Codification*, p. 231.

9 Clive M. Schmitthoff, 'Finality of Arbitral Awards and Judicial Review' in Julian D. M. Lew (ed.), *Contemporary Problems in International Arbitration* (London: Centre for Commercial Law Studies, Queen Mary College, University of London, 1986), p. 230.

10 Dalhuisen, 'Legal Orders', 167–8.

11 Leon E. Trakman, *The Law Merchant: The Evolution of Commercial Law* (Littleton: Fred B. Rothman & Co., 1983), p. ix.

12 See C. M. Reed, *Maritime Traders in the Ancient Greek World* (Cambridge: Cambridge University Press, 2003); Dalhuisen, *Trade Law*, pp. 38–47.

13 Harold J. Berman, *Law and Revolution: The Formation of the Western Legal Tradition* (Cambridge, MA: Harvard University Press, 1983) p. 340. See too Susan Reynolds, *Kingdoms and Communities in Western Europe, 900–1300* (Oxford: Clarendon Press, 2nd edn 1997), pp. 57–8; T. F. T. Plucknett, *A Concise History of the Common Law* (London: Butterworths, 1956), p. 23; Albrecht Cordes, 'The Search for a Medieval *Lex Mercatoria*' (2003) *Oxford University Comparative Law Forum* 5 at ouclf.iuscomp.org (viewed 6 January 2007); Mary

independent merchant courts, the English common law of the King's Bench of Edward II sought evidence of customs from merchants. In England, courts of Piepowder (from *pieds poudrés*, referring to the dusty feet of the merchants)[14] were held in fairs and market towns in the thirteenth and fourteenth centuries. They comprised judges who were themselves merchants, who aimed to dispense 'speedy justice to travellers',[15] although subject to review in King's Bench.[16]

Reinforcing the centrality of God to all aspects of social life at this time and the authority of law, the mercantile law was supposed to reflect the canon law. Regardless of the agreement of the merchants, they believed that 'the salvation of their souls depended on the conformity of their practices to a system of law based on the will of God as manifested in reason and conscience'.[17] The religious dimension of the medieval *lex mercatoria* demonstrated the law's highly allied relationship with the belief of the merchants and their capacity to be autonomous generators of their own law. It is an illustration of how central a lived law can be to a society (or at least a subculture) concerned with virtue and reputation,[18] as opposed to the anomie of distantly imposed state law. Despite the interior, cultural allegiance on the Space Axis inspired by the *lex mercatoria*, it also possessed an exterior, political quality. It became increasingly reduced to writing and subject to impartial adjudication with emerging forms of mercantile courts.[19] There was a European universality to this law amidst its diversity, akin to the *ius commune*. Medieval legislation reflected the local customs. 'Each country, it may almost be said each town, had its own variety of Law Merchant, yet all were but varieties of the same species. Everywhere the leading principles and the most important rules were the same, or tended to become the same.'[20]

Merchants spoke different languages and hailed from different cultures. Trust did not, of course, follow automatically. The legal rules of the *lex mercatoria* helped to overcome these differences – to reconcile yet maintain the plurality – by entrenching mercantile custom in uniform codes, seeking those customs which were constant and able to sustain high-level commerce. With the internationalisation of seaborne trade and commerce in the fifteenth and sixteenth centuries, and the opening up of the New World from the Atlantic, there was increased demand for uniform commercial and maritime laws. The prototypical state sovereignty manifesting around that time, we have already seen, had the effect of consolidating the political commonalities amongst provinces into

Elizabeth Basile *et al.*, *Lex Mercatoria and Legal Pluralism: A Late Thirteenth-century Treatise and its Afterlife* (Cambridge, MA: The Ames Foundation, 1998).

[14] O. F. Robinson, T. D. Fergus and W. M. Gordon, *European Legal History* (London: Butterworths, 1994), [6.5.2] (on maritime and guild law sources in Europe in addition, see generally ch. 6).

[15] W. J. V. Windeyer, *Lectures on Legal History* (Sydney: Law Book Co, 1957), p. 176.

[16] J. H. Baker, 'The Law Merchant and the Common Law Before 1700' (1979) 38 *Cambridge Law Journal* 295–322, 306.   [17] Berman, *Law and Revolution*, p. 339.

[18] See Avner Greif, 'On the Political Foundations of the Late Medieval Commercial Revolution: Genoa during the Twelfth and Thirteenth Centuries' (1994) 54 *Journal of Economic History* 271–87.   [19] Berman, *Law and Revolution*, p. 341.

[20] William Mitchell, quoted in Berman, *Law and Revolution*, p. 343.

large, territorial spheres of containable disruption. The relative uniformity of the *lex mercatoria* was undermined by this style of state sovereignty.[21] This was an incident of the monopoly on law and authoritative norms sought by the emerging nation-state.

Debate exists as to the nature of the *lex mercatoria* as a legal system, if indeed it was (or is) a legal system,[22] and there is at least some conflicting evidence.[23] Was it actually a separate system of positive law which was incorporated, for example, into the common law of England? Was it simply a creature of custom which developed within the common law? Was it part of the *ius gentium* (law of nations) which recognised a universal *lex mercatoria*?[24]

It is not so important for our purposes whether, for example, the English common law received the mercantile law principles from an outside system into its own system or whether those norms emanated from its society. Either is allowed by the broad definition of 'law' adopted in this book, being norms which, for one reason or another, achieve authority or receive allegiance. Day-to-day authority is what is vital. Significantly, the authority of the *lex mercatoria* was firmly grounded in the community it served. A cosmopolitan commercial tradition in Europe had given rise to similar issues which were dealt with in similarly principled manners across territorial jurisdictions.[25] Transactional documents reflected uniformity in character and design. Proceedings before *lex mercatoria* tribunals commonly featured oral adjudication, informal testimonies, judicial notice of trade custom together with speedy resolution of the dispute.

12.1.3 The nature of the 'new' *lex mercatoria*

Whilst the *lex mercatoria* has been around for at least 900 years or even longer, back to classical Greek and Roman times, it has undergone, as is to be expected, substantial transformations. It is problematical whether the perceived continuity has survived the disjunctures over time. Clive M. Schmitthoff considered

---

[21] Trakman, *Law Merchant*, pp. 11, 21.

[22] See Stephen E. Sachs, 'From St Ives to Cyberspace: The Modern Distortion of the Medieval "Law Merchant"' (2006) 21 *American University International Law Review* 685–812 and Emily Kadens, 'Order within Law, Variety within Custom: The Character of the Medieval Merchant Law' (2004) 5 *Chicago Journal of International Law* 39–65, suggesting the need for revising the traditional belief in the extent of the systemic and autonomous nature of the *lex mercatoria*.

[23] Charles Donahue Jr, 'Medieval and Early Modern Lex Mercatoria: An Attempt at the Probatio Diabolica' (2004) 5 *Chicago Journal of International Law* 21–37, 34–6.

[24] In the seventeenth century, Serjeant Davies, Sir Edward Coke and Sir Matthew Hale thought the *lex mercatoria* part of the English common law: Baker, 'Law Merchant', 314–16. Lord Mansfield in the eighteenth century acknowledged the transnational, *ius gentium*-like dimensions of mercatorial maritime law: Trakman, *Law Merchant*, pp. 27–8. Blackstone suggested a separate system: Sir William Blackstone, *Commentaries on the Laws of England*, 4 vols. [1783] (New York: Garland Publishing Inc., 1978), vol. I, p. 273.

[25] See Harold J. Berman and Colin Kaufman, 'The Law of International Commercial Transactions (*Lex Mercatoria*)' (1978) 19 *Harvard International Law Journal* 221–77, 224–9.

the new law merchant different, taking its binding force only from being incorporated into national legal systems.[26] The differences between the old and new types include the choices of jurisdiction and law which can govern parties and arbitrators; and modern arbitration can be expensive and time-consuming.[27] It is possible, though, to see 'that the old law merchant of the eleventh to the sixteenth centuries never died but continued to develop, even in the heyday of nationalism, as part of the *jus gentium*'[28] – in the sense of a common legal science with similar principles. Continuing to develop today, such an approach to the *lex mercatoria* is to emphasise general principles of norm generation by, and application of the norms in, industrialised communities of importers and exporters. In these communities, there is a universality to the *lex mercatoria*, generally conceived, although not grounded in dogmatic rules. Whilst many principles of state commercial laws can be found in *lex mercatoria* principles, many of those state laws originate in merchant custom.[29] Therefore national legal systems are not as crucial to the modern *lex mercatoria* as might otherwise be thought.

Further to our earlier introduction of the concept of *lex mercatoria* in section 12.1.1 above, the modern *lex mercatoria* has been described as a body of international legal practice with a system of norms which is open to judicial decisions. These principles exist relatively independently from national laws[30] and public international law, in party autonomy and usage.[31] Nonetheless, there may be elements of *lex mercatoria* in public international law, uniform laws and general principles, rules of international organisations, standard form contracts and arbitral awards.[32] The *lex mercatoria* may refer to the laws of individual states simply 'as a quarry from which to draw the raw materials for generalised rules', within the 'strong family resemblance between laws of developed trading states'.[33] Similar quarries for the *lex mercatoria* exist in scholarly discourse, arbitral awards, and international harmonisation initiatives. As such, the modern *lex mercatoria* bears the quality of being a somewhat loosely organised legal system with practical, local variations, with the internal resources to adapt to change over time whilst

---

[26] Clive M. Schmitthoff, 'Finality', p. 232.

[27] Leon E. Trakman, 'From the Medieval Law Merchant to E-Merchant Law' (2003) 53 *University of Toronto Law Journal* 265–304, 267. At 284–93, other variances such as the different training of judges, regulations created not by custom, and procedural formality can be found between the medieval *lex mercatoria* and its cyberspace variant (for example, in the resolution of domain name disputes).

[28] Berman and Kaufman, 'International Commercial Transactions', 273–4; see too Harold J. Berman and Felix J. Dasser, 'The "New" Law Merchant and the "Old": Sources, Content and Legitimacy' in Thomas E. Carbonneau (ed.), *Lex Mercatoria and Arbitration: A Discussion of the New Law Merchant* (Juris Publishing/Kluwer Law International, rev. edn 1998), p. 64.

[29] See Eugen Ehrlich, *Fundamental Principles of the Sociology of Law*, trans. Walter L. Moll [1913] (Cambridge, MA: Harvard University Press, 1936), p. 366.

[30] Mertens, 'Lex Mercatoria', p. 32.   [31] See Berger, *Creeping Codification*, pp. 39–41.

[32] Roy Goode, 'Usage and Custom in Transnational Commercial Law' (1997) 46 *International & Comparative Law Quarterly* 1–36, 3.   [33] Mustill, 'New *Lex Mercatoria*', 44.

maintaining its general identity borne of the origins of its norms in custom and interior allegiance.

For a general, globalist jurisprudence, concerned to develop concepts which, to use William Twining's concept, 'travel well' across jurisdictions,[34] the exemplary and precedent value of the *lex mercatoria* should be obvious within the universality of the industrialised community it serves.

12.1.4 Codification

The *lex mercatoria* has been subjected to codification initiatives. Codification represents an attempt to simplify laws into a readily understandable and usable form. It is an aid to capitalist relations which seek certainty. Uniformity is also a leveller. With greater uniformity across jurisdictions, finding a way to do something across borders becomes less the preserve of the rich who can afford specialist multi-jurisdictional lawyers.[35] Mystery and uncertainty, which the evolution and interpretation of uncodified norms might otherwise seem to possess in the hands of the legally educated or experienced, are sought to be removed through the normative deforestation of codification. The utility of codification is not without danger to the legal ecosystem. The German historical school of jurisprudence has taught that codification poses threats to a flexible and organic system of norms,[36] with lessons for the *lex mercatoria*. Such initiatives need to avoid the temptation to state in absolutist terms what constitutes the doctrines of the *lex mercatoria*, which evolves like all social systems with references to the past, drawing upon experiences.

Two major codification initiatives are now explored. These initiatives continue the aim of the United Nations Commission on International Trade Law (UNCITRAL) originating in the 1960s. First, *lex mercatoria* developments are being advanced by the International Institute for the Unification of Private Law (*Institut International Pour L'Unification Du Droit Privé*, UNIDROIT), founded in 1926, under the aegis of the League of Nations. It received a more recent impetus in the 1970s, culminating in the Principles of International Contracts 1994 (the UNIDROIT Principles). Secondly, at a European level, the 'Commission on European Contract Law' has been led by Danish law professor Ole Lando (the Lando Commission), to be discussed in the next section. The aim of both of these commissions was, and is, to produce a modern kind of *ius commune* and *lex mercatoria* in code form. Like the historical forms of *ius commune* which developed on the Continent, the initiative is being led by academics, many of whom have practical experience in the field of international commercial arbitration.[37]

---

[34] See William Twining, 'The Province of Jurisprudence Re-examined' in Catherine Dauvergne (ed.), *Jurisprudence for an Interconnected Globe* (Aldershot: Ashgate, 2003), p. 33.

[35] See D. McBarnet, 'Transnational Transactions: Legal Work, Cross-border Commerce and Global Regulation' in Likosky (ed.), *Transnational Legal Processes*, p. 101.

[36] See ch. 8, section 8.4.5, pp. 188–90 above.   [37] Berger, *Creeping Codification*, p. 211.

The UNIDROIT Preamble introduces the purpose of the Principles:

> These Principles set forth general rules for international commercial contracts.
>
> They shall be applied when the parties have agreed that their contract be governed by general principles of law, the *lex mercatoria* or the like.
>
> They may provide a solution to an issue raised when it proves impossible to establish the relevant rule of the applicable law.
>
> They may be used to interpret or supplement international uniform law instruments.
>
> They may serve as a model for national and international legislators.[38]

These principles apply to 'all contracts which are concluded with a view towards the direct or indirect making of profits and which are related to the cross-border movement of goods, currencies, services, technologies or other financial or economic assets, provided that no "typical element of consumer transactions" can be ascertained'.[39]

The UNIDROIT Principles embody the modern *lex mercatoria*, without the hubris of believing law to be only what is written in the code.[40] Rather than being regarded as a field of law ripe for codification in the orthodox sense, Klaus Peter Berger has described these international economic law developments under the rubric of a 'creeping codification' of the *lex mercatoria*. A middle way is sought through the dichotomy of fixed, certain doctrines and the flexible openness of equitable processes[41] – abandoning the now largely discredited Napoleonic ideal of a self-contained code. The UNIDROIT Principles have been applied by the International Chamber of Commerce as governing law and as a supplement or interpretive aid to domestic law and international conventions.[42]

This follows a trend for contracts to refer to common principles of law from a multiplicity of jurisdictions, reflecting the home jurisdictions of the parties to the contract. For example, an article of a contract between Iran and the National Iranian Oil Company of one part, and nine other nations of the other part, has referred to 'the principles of law common to Iran and the several nations in which the other parties to this Agreement are incorporated, and, in the absence of such common principles, by . . . the principles of law recognized by civilized nations in general'. Similarly, for the construction of the English Channel tunnel, principles common to both English and French law were specified, failing which relations were to be governed 'by such general principles of

---

[38] UNIDROIT (ed.), *Principles of International Commercial Contracts* (Rome, 1994).

[39] Berger, *Creeping Codification*, p. 161.

[40] See Gesa Baron, 'Do the UNIDROIT Principles of International Commercial Contracts Form a New *Lex Mercatoria*?' (1999) 15 *Arbitration International* 115–30, 122. Accepting this notion of the *lex mercatoria* as norms which can be gathered, focused upon and subjected to discourse, the indeterminacy otherwise believed by some to inhere in the *lex mercatoria* erodes: cf. Roy Goode, 'Rule, Practice and Pragmatism in Transnational Commercial Law' (2005) 54 *International & Comparative Law Quarterly* 539–62, 552.

[41] See Berger, *Creeping Codification*, pp. 3–6, 228.

[42] See Michael Pryles, 'Application of the *Lex Mercatoria* in International Commercial Arbitration' (2004) 78 *Australian Law Journal* 396–416, 408.

international trade law as have been applied by national and international tribunals'.[43]

In this process, lists of general principles and rules of transnational law are drafted, unifying as well as creating law in the process, just as we have observed of the French Enlightenment codification initiatives.[44] The compilation of these common principles themselves forms the *lex mercatoria*. So the *lex mercatoria*, even with the evolution of 'creeping codification', may be considered a legal system in the historical, Savignian sense because it is 'an *unwritten* framework of values and convictions providing and enriching it with the necessary logical consistency and internal unity', in a pluralistic framework which recognises the role of competing jurisdictions and systems in the Western legal tradition.[45]

12.2 European contract law and codification

The Lando Commission on European Contract Law has been mentioned in the context of the *lex mercatoria*, as part of a codifying initiative. The Lando Principles are intended to be 'a modern European *lex mercatoria*'.[46] The development of the Lando Principles further illustrates the difficulties associated with codification, in the attempt to impose, in the long term, a consolidated, single set of laws over jurisdictions where functionally equivalent laws are already established. A more moderate approach to the induction of European contract law is to be found in the Trento Common Core project.[47] Reliable information is the aim of this project, not the forcing of a uniform contract law or convergence of contract law. Both styles of codification initiative temper the aspirations of a general, globalist jurisprudence by illuminating the difficulties and dangers of attempting to create normative unity from diversity.

12.2.1 Synthetic aspects

The intention behind the Lando Commission has been to contribute to the formation of a new system of European *ius commune*, drawing, like UNIDROIT, upon comparative materials from domestic and international sources such as the American Restatement of the Law of Contracts and the Vienna Sales Conventions. The Lando principles 'constitute a collection of rules

---

[43] See Berger, *Creeping Codification*, pp. 34–5.   [44] See ch. 8, section 8.4.6, pp. 191–2 above.
[45] See Berger, *Creeping Codification*, pp. 28, 38, 91–2; Mark D. Rosen, 'Do Codification and Private International Law Leave Room for a New Law Merchant?' (2004) 5 *Chicago Journal of International Law* 83–90; *contra* Celia Wasserstein Fassberg, '*Lex Mercatoria* – Hoist with its Own Petard' (2004) 5 *Chicago Journal of International Law* 67–82.
[46] Ole Lando and Hugh Beale (eds.), *Principles of European Contract Law – Part I: Performance, Non-performance and Remedies* (Dordrecht: Martinus Nijhoff Publishers, 1995), p. xviii.
[47] See Mauro Bussani and Ugo Mattei (eds.), *The Common Core of European Private Law* (The Hague: Kluwer Law International, 2003). On other European initiatives in context, see the 'Introduction' to Hector L. MacQueen *et al.* (eds.), *Regional Private Laws and Codification in Europe* (Cambridge: Cambridge University Press, 2003).

which are considered by the drafters to form parts of the contract laws of the EU-member states', in the quest for a European Civil Code and the more ambitious project of a European Code of Obligations.[48] This may conflict with the EU constitutional principle of subsidiarity[49] – that is, the notion that smaller networks can better do some things, rather than everything being done at the highest level of organisation. To the extent that the Lando Commission intends to rely upon EU power to reach into domestic European jurisdictions, the principles are more potent than the *lex mercatoria*. Furthermore, if enacted as EU law, not only could the Lando Principles have direct effect upon Member States' domestic jurisdictions, they could also influence the commercial law of non-EU Member States, through the European Free Trade Association (EFTA).[50] In comparison to the *lex mercatoria*, this initiative is therefore an endeavour more rational and exterior than cultural and interior on the Space Axis of the Space–Time Matrix.

Common law systems are closely related, as are civil law systems, and there are examples of cross-system similarities such as between England and Scotland.[51] A common linguistic heritage (for example, of the Nordic countries) or common language (for example, England, Wales and Ireland) will conduce towards similarities.[52] Nevertheless, a European civil code appears unlikely in any present lifetime. 'Because doctrinal and other interests encrust themselves on the competing forms of national, codified rationality, the national codes remain today perhaps the greatest obstacles to further European codification.'[53] The prospect of a European contract code has been compared to renouncing European culinary variety in favour of a McDonald's eating culture.[54] Difficulties in harmonising Continental and English contract law are demonstrable in the English emphasis on individual responsibility as opposed to the French duty to disclose essential information.[55] For example, common law mistake and misrepresentation, duress and undue influence are not treated as defects of consent as in civil law. The common law is more concerned with

---

[48] Berger, *Creeping Codification*, pp. 203–6.

[49] Ewoud Hondius, 'Towards a European Civil Code. General Introduction' in A. S. Hartkamp *et al.* (eds.), *Towards a European Civil Code* (Dordrecht: Martinus Nijhoff Publishers, 2nd edn 1998), p. 12. On subsidiarity, see ch. 11, section 11.2.5, pp. 263–4 above.

[50] Carlos Bollen and Gerard-René De Groot, 'The Sources and Backgrounds of European Legal Systems' in A. S. Hartkamp *et al.* (eds.), *Towards a European Civil Code* (Dordrecht: Martinus Nijhoff Publishers, 1st edn 1994), p. 98.

[51] e.g. the paradigm English common law case of negligence, *Donohue v Stevenson* (1932) AC 562, is common to both jurisdictions.   [52] Hondius, 'European Civil Code', pp. 8–9.

[53] H. Patrick Glenn, 'The Grounding of Codification' (1998) 31 *U.C. Davis Law Review* 765–82, 768.

[54] Ana M. López-Rodriguez, 'Towards a European Civil Code Without a Common European Legal Culture? The Link Between Law, Language and Culture' (2004) 29 *Brooklyn Journal of International Law* 1195–220, 1211 (citing Andre Tunc). The harmonisation issues are well canvassed generally in Mark Van Hoecke and François Ost (eds.), *The Harmonisation of European Private Law* (Oxford: Hart Publishing, 2000).

[55] See Sjef van Erp, 'The Formation of Contracts' in Hartkamp *et al.* (eds.), *European Civil Code* (2nd edn), p. 216.

the unlawful behaviour of the other party.[56] Furthermore, for example, English restitution is limited to the transferor recovering an unfair gain from the transferee, whereas French law ventures more widely and permits recovery by the transferor from a third person who may have received the benefit from the transferee.[57] Considerable doctrinal differences exist amongst different state systems, particularly between common law and civil law traditions.

Moving towards codes, numerous directives have been issued by the European Parliament acting jointly with the Council, the powerful Council on its own and the Commission. Directives have ranged across private law in general, laws against unfair competition, protection of industrial and commercial property, company law, stock-market law, banking law, insurance law and labour law.[58] The fact that the implementation ('form and methods' under article 249) of the directives is left to individual Member States means that the directives cannot be said to form codes.

The obstacles facing a European code are greater than those which were overcome, for example, by conventions such as the 1988 Convention on the International Sale of Goods, or the UNIDROIT Principles. Europe is not a community of like-minded individuals such as merchants, who share a common purpose, namely profit and exchange. Europe comprises, of course, nation-states with all the internal political complexities of modern industrial societies. The necessary Member State parliamentary accessions to international contract principles seem unlikely for some time. European linguistic diversity brings its own difficulties of translation and legal interpretation.[59] So is a codified, universalist European private law possible? Despite the substantial obstacles, legal historian R. C. van Caenegem opines that stranger things have happened.[60]

Conjecture aside, it is vital for legal ideas to circulate, particularly across languages,[61] so that there can be cross-fertilisation of law wherever possible and enhanced discourse about norms, upon which better law depends. Harmonisation of law should perhaps be thought about in musical terms, suggests Patrick Glenn. That is, just as some simultaneously different tones and pitches can produce aesthetic satisfaction, the (commensurable)[62] differences

---

[56] See Madeleine van Rossum, 'Defects of Consent and Capacity in Contract Law' in Hartkamp *et al.* (eds.), *European Civil Code* (1st edn), p. 151.

[57] See William John Swadling, 'Restitution and Unjust Enrichment' in Hartkamp *et al.* (eds.), *European Civil Code* (1st edn), p. 271. For other doctrinal differences, see Reinhard Zimmermann, 'The Civil Law in European Codes' in MacQueen *et al.* (eds.), *Regional Private Laws*.

[58] For a summary, see Peter-Christian Müller-Graff, 'Private Law Unification by Means other than of Codification' in Hartkamp *et al.* (eds.), *European Civil Code* (2nd edn), pp. 83–9.

[59] See López-Rodriguez, 'European Civil Code'.

[60] R. C. van Caenegem, *European Law in the Past and the Future: Unity and Diversity over Two Millennia* (Cambridge: Cambridge University Press, 2002), pp. 33–7; see too his 'The Unification of European Law: A Pipedream?' (2006) 14 *European Review* 33–48.

[61] See Hondius, 'European Civil Code', p. 18.

[62] 'Understanding different legal concepts means recognition of their underlying commensurability. The concepts are different, but capable of explanation in terms of one another': H. Patrick Glenn, 'Conflicting Laws in a Common Market? The NAFTA Experiment'

should rightly be made the focus of understanding and learning[63] in an orchestrated attempt to comprehend legal orders across jurisdictions.

12.2.2 Organic aspects

On the Space–Time Matrix, what are the implications of attempts at uniform codes brought about through legislative re-engineering (as opposed to a more philosophical, discourse-based approach to harmonisation just advocated)? Present state laws on a topic, and their historical evolution, would tend towards redundancy. State laws, which have evolved through cases, legislation and in learned treatises, reflect the culture of the people, even if mainly through their lawyers. In our time, more abstract and exterior (on the Space Axis) implants of legislation, for example, giving domestic effect to EU directives, have been 'fragmented' and 'inserted rather unorganically', sometimes creating 'confusion and uncertainty'.[64] Legislation in the nation-state often seems to operate in this way too, when effecting wholesale innovation.

Against this criticism, it might be argued that participants in routine contracts and exchanges do not pay regard to their position according to black letter law. Indeed, Hein Kötz suggests that a European private law need simply be taught to the lawyers of the future.[65] Laws of restitution, or whether there is a material difference in conduct as a result of a circumstance being analysed either as a defect in consent or as a party's fraud or misrepresentation, are largely matters for framing litigation which is generally avoided by most people. Many people, in commerce at least, are probably guided by their own senses of decency.[66] Jan Smits even suggests that consumer choice of particular commercial laws over others will lead to the convergence of such laws.[67] As with all law and norms throughout the history surveyed in this book, *how* law is thought about is crucial. If law is felt to represent the revelation of a local wisdom, even if delivered by lawyers, maybe this is a good thing. For example, in one local tradition of contract the emphasis on the importance of giving effect to contracts compared with awarding damages for their breach may represent a local moral belief in the sanctity of the promise. For laws and norms to be impelling, humans (if they pause to think about their normative authority) will probably

---

(2001) 76 *Chicago-Kent Law Review* 1789–1819. See too that author's *Legal Traditions of the World: Sustainable Diversity in Law* (Oxford: Oxford University Press, 2nd edn 2004), pp. 44–8; and his 'Are Legal Traditions Incommensurable? (2001) 49 *American Journal of Comparative Law* 133–45.   [63] Glenn, 'Conflicting Laws', 1794.

[64] See Reinhard Zimmermann, 'Roman Law and European Legal Unity' in Hartkamp *et al.* (eds.), *European Civil Code* (2nd edn), pp. 25–6.

[65] See Hein Kötz, *European Contract Law Volume One: Formation, Validity, and Content of Contracts; Contract and Third Parties*, trans. Tony Weir (Oxford: Clarendon Press, 1997), p. vi.

[66] See e.g. Stewart Macaulay, 'Non-Contractual Relations in Business: A Preliminary Study' (1963) 28 *American Sociological Review* 55–67, 61. 'One doesn't run to lawyers if he wants to stay in business because one must behave decently.'

[67] See Jan Smits, *The Making of European Private Law: Towards a Ius Commune Europaeum as a Mixed Legal System* (Antwerp: Intersentia, 2002).

want to feel called by a mixture of history, vision, morality and political objectivity to obey the norms. Imposition does not inspire the conscience. Technical genius calculating the codifications is unlikely to fare better as a matter of allegiance.

Where might the gaze venture for cultural input into the rationalist enterprise of codification? Can the common European experience of Roman law, renaissance humanism, Enlightenment rationalism, Romanticism and democracy be tapped into? There may be a way of attuning European law to an animating force which is of some cultural attraction for the European populace. Reinhard Zimmermann suggests the solution is in the notion of Western legal science, in a process of 're-Europeanization', not simply 'Europeanization'.[68]

We have already seen in some detail in parts 2 and 3 of this book that Continental Europe featured an academic tradition of law which was supranational and recognisable throughout Europe, despite regional variations which did not, though, undermine the common legal grammar. 'Moving with the same cultural tides running through Europe, and moored to an educational and scientific tradition, as well as to a common language [Latin], European legal science, in spite of many differences in detail, remained a unified intellectual world; and the international *communis opinio doctorum* was authoritative for its application and development.'[69] For example, some major features of the development of modern contract occurred by adaptation from the Roman law. Justinian's *Corpus* confused form-bound oral promises and informal consensual contracts in limited circumstances. This was modified by a combination of canon law, international commercial practice and Germanic notions of good faith. Even in the modern German Civil Code (the *Bürgerliches Gesetzbuch* or BGB), many codified rules of ancient Roman law prevail.[70]

The common misconception that English law is isolated from the Romanist method has already been identified.[71] Numerous English authors adopted the systematisation methodology characteristic of Roman law. Zimmermann's plan is 'to design a ius commune Europeaum around the core of the general private law' through reviving Roman law and legal history and integrating it with comparative law and doctrinal scholarship. His aim is to avoid a bureaucratic Europe 'which merely reacts to specific needs and aims at implementing economic policies . . .' as opposed to a law with a spirit which has sprung from the people and their history.[72] The varieties of the *ius commune*, having adopted an admixture of Roman law at the end of the fifteenth century, now have an indigenous quality. Zimmermann's view has been interpreted as an anti-globalisation

---

[68] See Zimmermann, 'Roman Law', pp. 26–7.   [69] Ibid., p. 28.

[70] Ibid., pp. 32–4.   [71] See ch. 6, section 6.2.2, pp. 122–6 above.

[72] Zimmermann, 'Roman Law', p. 39. Zimmermann has been criticised for isolating the uniquely Roman contribution to the origins of Western law: see P. G. Monateri, 'Black Gaius: A Quest for the Multicultural Origins of the "Western Legal Tradition" ' (2000) 51 *Hastings Law Journal* 479–555, 507, 551. Regardless of whether Justinian's Roman law was exclusively Roman or more cosmopolitan in composition, what Zimmermann has described is the possibility for a legal culture grounded in a common, historically practised legal science.

measure which seeks to thwart the growing American domination of jurisprudential techniques.[73] Rather than being anti-globalisation *per se*, it would seem
that Zimmermann is more simply calling for self-consciousness and considered
reflection in the face of the rush to codify and use law as a crude tool for getting
things done,[74] devoid of meaningful authority.

12.3 Contract and private governance

Adjudication of the sorts of commercial laws evaluated above gives rise to some
complex issues concerning the institutional authority of those adjudicating
bodies, and, more generally, the nature of legal authority in competing jurisdictions outside the nation-state. Of less significance to the present enquiry is
the conventional authority exercised by judiciaries in the nation-state or even
the European Court of Justice.[75] Of most interest is the nature of the contractual mechanism for triggering arbitration and the institutionalisation of
authoritative adjudication outside the state.

12.3.1 Arbitration

A number of arbitration institutions exists, with their own procedural rules.
The International Chamber of Commerce in Paris is perhaps the most prestigious. Others include the American Arbitration Association, the London Court
of International Arbitration and the World Bank's International Center for the
Settlement of Investment Disputes. Typically, three arbitrators sit as a panel,
one appointed by each party and a third appointed by the parties jointly.[76]
Commercial arbitration of the *lex mercatoria* has been institutionalised under
the Rules of the International Chamber of Commerce, resorting to *lex mercatoria* concepts and doctrines with expert judges dispensing settlement through
flexible procedures of conciliation or arbitration.[77] Conceptually, modern arbitration centres are reminiscent of the medieval merchant courts. Arbitrators
may be appointed with experience in business, rather than being drawn from
narrow, doctrinal legal backgrounds.[78]

---

[73] See Ugo Mattei, 'The Issue of European Civil Codification and Legal Scholarship: Biases,
Strategies and Developments' (1998) 21 *Hastings International & Comparative Law Review*
883–902, 890.

[74] *Contra* e.g. Wayne R. Barnes, 'Contemplating a Civil Law Paradigm for a Future International
Commercial Code' (2005) 65 *Louisiana Law Review* 677–774, advocating the 'most politically
expedient, and most pragmatic solution' in the presumed expectation of 'increasing the
standards of living of all peoples' through 'reducing obstacles to global trade and commerce'
(773–4).

[75] It is of passing interest to note, though, that state jurisdictions can be 'marketed' and
expressed in contracts as governing law, entitling a party to bring traditional proceedings in
that jurisdiction.

[76] Yves Dezalay and Bryant G. Garth, *Dealing in Virtue: International Commercial Arbitration and
the Construction of a Transnational Legal Order* (Chicago: University of Chicago Press, 1996),
pp. 5–6.   [77] Trakman, *Law Merchant*, p. 42.   [78] See section 12.1.2, p. 277 above.

Criticisms have been levelled at commercial arbitrators for not giving reasoned grounds for awards, for not following rules of evidence and procedure and for lengthiness of proceedings.[79] At least there remains the prospect of nominating, through the contract, an appropriate arbitration association. In addition, the increased publicity accorded arbitral decisions is contributing to the stabilisation of this form of law. Although not binding, arbitral awards can be persuasive precedents.[80] German legal doctrine suggests that courts should refer to these awards when interpreting some international contracts. The German Federal Supreme Court has even held that in some cases where a contract is silent, the dispute must first be sent for arbitration, for so prevalent has arbitration become in trade usage.[81]

There has been a tendency for arbitrators to be appointed increasingly from the US multinational law firms, away from the 'grand old men' who set arbitration precedents on the Continent. Many of them were professors, participating in a process reminiscent of the centuries old German tradition of consulting universities for legal opinions (*Aktendversendung*).[82] This academic input, both through practitioners drawing on MBA educations and also practitioners from within university law schools, has injected outside norms, such as economics and management insights, into juridical and arbitral processes, contributing to the possibilities for self-impelled norms. This legal order displays autonomy and a tendency for a useful universalism in its particular universe of cross-border transactions (although the club atmosphere has drawn scepticism).[83]

Reflecting this type of universalism, high-level arbitration has proved popular where nation-states have had disputes against transnational corporations and large private organisations. Libyan (1971) and Iranian (1950s) nationalisation of oil production created disputes under state contracts. Western arbitration processes proved preferable to formal international legal processes. The perceived neutrality of the adversarial process and an apparent belief in the bona fides of the arbitrators were relied upon to balance the sensitive problem of the public right of sovereignty over national resources with the private rights of a foreign corporation. Promoters of Islamic arbitration have even argued that the *lex mercatoria* is consistent with Islamic law[84] (although others would disagree).[85]

12.3.2 Contractual authority as private government

Contractual arbitration mechanisms conjure a problem of logic: a paradox of self-reference. If a contract creates its own law, and if the validity of the contract

---

[79] Trakman, *Law Merchant*, pp. 57–9.
[80] Abdul F. M. Maniruzzaman, 'The *Lex Mercatoria* and International Contracts: A Challenge for International Commercial Arbitration?' (1999) 14 *American University International Law Review* 657–734, 730.   [81] Berger, *Creeping Codification*, pp. 64, 70.
[82] See ch. 6, section 6.2.1, p. 121 above.
[83] See Dezalay and Garth, *Dealing in Virtue*, pp. 10, 175–9.   [84] Ibid., pp. 68, 85, 90.
[85] See n. 104 below and surrounding text.

is challenged, the contract can be said to be without law (*contrat sans loi*). How may such a contract be binding when it relies for resolution and enforcement upon a mechanism of its own creation? The contract may not refer to a state jurisdiction but only to its own arbitration procedure. That resolution and enforcement mechanism, it follows, might be impugnable. Is the contract therefore invalid? Can it be enforceable outside the state jurisdiction, if the state jurisdiction would deny the contract's existence? This puzzle bears comparison to the liar's paradox, known to the philosophy of logic: if I say I am a liar, not only does anything I say thereafter become dubious, but my very statement that I am a liar may also be a lie.[86]

In order to ground the contractual rules outside the contractual relationship, for example in some third-party adjudication process, there may be reliance upon peer pressure to abide the resolution process and to preserve livelihood. The widespread legal validity of the contractual arbitration process is demonstrated by Berger's statistic that over 90 percent of international arbitral awards receive voluntary compliance, and almost 90 percent of international contracts contain an arbitration clause. This overcomes the paradox of self-reference or 'contracts without law'. In effect, the societal context of the international commercial contract can become a substitute authority by creation of the parties, tending to exclude domestic law, as the parties 'autonomise' their legal relationship.[87] Such privately created law may be enforceable by government although not necessarily requiring that level of coercion.[88]

Vast areas of the law may in fact be 'privatisable', not limited to contract. For example, the International Organization for Standardization's 'ISO 14000' environmental management programme may be expected to influence, in time, not only environmental law but other laws including tort (duties and standards), property (conservation requirements), tax (charitable deductions), information (rights to know), financial (reporting compliance) and trade (GATT recognition).[89] Norms may be embodied in widely adopted contractual terms prepared by industry associations, resulting in what has been called 'competitive lawmaking' or 'molecular federalism'.[90]

---

[86] See Gunther Teubner, ' "Global Bukowina": Legal Pluralism in the World Society' in Teubner (ed.), *Global Law*, p. 17. The notion that contracts could have 'no governing law' or be *contrat sans lois* is foreign to US law: see Symeon C. Symeonides, 'Contracts Subject to Non-State Norms' (2006) 54 *American Journal of Comparative Law* 209–31. Goode believes that contracts cannot constitute a source of law without state law, in 'Rule, Practice and Pragmatism', 547–8. Again, this depends upon the definition of law adopted. If law is thought to obtain its character from state paraphernalia, it is difficult to admit non-state legal possibilities.

[87] Berger, *Creeping Codification*, pp. 111, 162. Nonetheless, domestic legal concepts are still relied upon: see p. 276 above.

[88] See Stephen J. Ware, 'Default Rules from Mandatory Rules: Privatizing Law through Arbitration' (1999) 83 *Minnesota Law Review* 703–54; Gillian K. Hadfield, 'Privatizing Commercial Law: Lessons from ICANN' (2002) 6 *Journal of Small and Emerging Business Law* 257–88.

[89] See Errol E. Meidinger, 'Environmental Certification Systems and US Law: Closer than You May Think' (2001) 31 *Environmental Law Reporter* 10162–79.

[90] David V. Snyder, 'Private Lawmaking' (2003) 64 *Ohio State Law Journal* 371–449, 437–48.

On the Time Axis of the Space–Time Matrix involving disputes between these merchants, we find that the transactional community creates allegiance from the shared history and prospective reward of future deals. On the Space Axis, the externalisation of the resolution and enforcement process in an independent arbitration institution (with prestigious adjudicators) adds perceived political objectivity to the process. These factors combine to ground the contract in the interior, moral consciousness of individuals, by virtue of the personal, contracted creation of the process. Contracting itself can then become for this community a source of law with validity at a global level.[91] (Disputes may though arise, which if taken to court rather than arbitrated independently, *may* result in the state court asserting a politically superior claim to sovereignty over the contract.)[92] Arbitration bodies create an all-important legal discourse which gives meaning to the principles of the *lex mercatoria*, granting 'a true "*opinio juris*" to the practices regularly used in the business world'.[93]

Historically, a rich constitutional lineage underlies contractual authority. Celebrating liberal society, article 1134 of the Napoleonic Code exalts contracts thus: 'contracts legally created have the legal value of statutes for those who entered into them'.[94] Later in the nineteenth century, in the context of the erosion of the doctrine of freedom of contract caused by government intervention, the Scottish philosopher W. G. Miller thought the law should retreat to allow humans 'the power of self-legislation' by 'freedom of contract'.[95] Contracts may be considered a form of private legislation for private government. Regulation by civil society (businesses and individual entrepreneurs) can be distinct from the state, adding to an international commercial law and practice which does not require the state for legitimacy. This is in keeping with the historically demonstrated resilience of the *lex mercatoria* to strict state control (whilst acknowledging the normative mutuality of the state and the *lex mercatoria* as we saw earlier). This law has been described as 'paralegal law' and 'extra-state law', raising understandable concerns (especially in France, somewhat paradoxically given the Napoleonic exaltation of contracts) about the circumvention of the safeguards of domestic legislative and judicial processes.[96] Such

---

91 See Teubner, 'Global Bukowina', pp. 16–18. See too Rodney Bruce Hall and Thomas J. Biersteker (eds.), *The Emergence of Private Authority in Global Governance* (Cambridge: Cambridge University Press, 2004); Christian Joerges *et al.* (eds.), *Transnational Governance and Constitutionalism* (Oxford: Hart Publishing, 2004); Karl-Heinz Ladeur (ed.), *Public Governance in the Age of Globalization* (Aldershot: Ashgate, 2004).

92 See Berger, *Creeping Codification*, p. 43.

93 Bernardo M. Cremades, 'The Impact of International Arbitration on the Development of Business Law' (1983) 31 *American Journal of Comparative Law* 526–34, 526.

94 Cited in Jean-Philippe Robé, 'Multinational Enterprises: The Constitution of a Pluralistic Legal Order' in Teubner (ed.), *Global Law*, p. 58. Roman law also considered the *lex contractus* to be a source of law creation: see Niklas Luhmann, *Law as a Social System*, trans. K. A. Ziegert (Oxford: Oxford University Press, 2004), p. 124 although its Romantic exponent Savigny did not agree.

95 Julius Stone, *Human Law and Human Justice* (Sydney: Maitland Publications Pty Ltd, 1965), p. 87.   96 See Berger, *Creeping Codification*, p. 28.

concerns assume that national domestic legislation and judging comprise the only valid normative model in these commercial circumstances. Assuming a community of roughly equal merchants, it would appear to be more appropriate and in the interests of their self-determination to allow merchants to formulate and apply norms in their own mutually perceived interests.

Private government can be constituted within corporations, especially multinational enterprises. (A literature also considers the state in terms of a firm or corporation 'that specialises in violence and providing protection to a given population'.)[97] Internal legal norms of corporations may be demonstrated by managerial hierarchies overseeing those more junior in the hierarchy carrying out firm policy under threat of sanction, and regularity may be developed across offices for international firms. International codes of practice for a firm may qualify for internal proto-laws. The difficulty with calling these examples 'law' is that mechanisms for compliance are not strenuous and there may be an inability to characterise action as simply 'legal' or 'illegal'. Perhaps the strongest available proof for internal law assuming proto-legal proportions is where different offices contractualise their relationships. For example, the gigantic Union Carbide Corporation contracted with its Indian subsidiary to establish a pesticides plant in Bhopal, effectively making public and international the private legal order.[98] Such proto-law is still reliant, to some extent, upon the external legal system in the event that enforcement might be required. Whether internal or external law, these are authoritative norms being wielded with legal function in a discourse which satisfies historic notions of law.

Private government is as unlikely to exist in isolation as state government is as unlikely to be a normative order unto itself. Regulation has always occurred, although to varying degrees throughout time, by way of competing jurisdictions and normative systems. Globalisation, represented by the accelerating interconnections amongst things that happen in the world, is stimulating this facet of jurisprudence. Arguably this is reflected in a semantic shift from the word *government* to *governance* (suggesting government is not necessarily a public function), and in the new emphasis on *civil society* as distinct from plain *society* (recognising politically determining social units). The rise in the use of the word 'governance' is directly correlated to the rise of the word 'globalisation'.[99] Referring to similarities between the OECD Principles of Corporate

[97] Jean-Jacques Rosa, 'The Competitive State and the Industrial Organization of Nations' in Ladeur (ed.), *Public Governance*, p. 220.

[98] Peter T. Muchlinski, ' "Global Bukowina" Examined: Viewing the Multinational Enterprise as a Transnational Law-making Community' in Teubner (ed.), *Global Law*, pp. 81–4. Diverse national laws may be in operation to the firm's satisfaction in different states, offering different degrees of protection to capital and workers.

[99] Boaventura de Sousa Santos, 'Beyond Neoliberal Governance: The World Social Forum as Subaltern Cosmopolitan Politics and Legality' in Boaventura de Sousa Santos and César A. Rodríguez-Garavito (eds.), *Law and Globalization from Below: Towards a Cosmopolitan Legality* (Cambridge: Cambridge University Press, 2005), p. 31.

Governance and the European Commission's White Paper on Corporate Governance, Philip Allott notes the convergence of 'the governmentalising of the corporation and the corporatising of government'.[100] Not necessarily undemocratic, this phenomenon may represent a move towards 'polycentric networks'[101] or, as earlier mentioned, 'molecular federalism'. Controversies about the 'democratic deficit' agitated in our discussion of EU constitutionalism in chapter 11 still, however, seethe in this context.

12.4 Private authority and globalist jurisprudence

Returning to the international commercial law represented by the *lex mercatoria*, its virtue is in the mutuality of the norms which regulate the internal relationships of its merchant community. This occurs in relative freedom from state coercion. Particularly appropriate in its area, the merchants themselves largely construct their communal law. Concerns of modern consumer law are not relevant, because of the in principle equal bargaining position and professional competence of *lex mercatoria* participants. Theoretically, at least, this relatively autonomous, market law is fair enough to avoid the need for the redistributive effect of state law.[102]

An important qualification should be issued when thinking of international commercial law and arbitration in the context of globalisation and universality. These practices are not universal in the sense that they are everywhere found. In that respect, we earlier confined our notion of 'universality' to a 'universe' of a particular community, unconstrained by territory.[103] Whilst there are for the most part common forms and terms encountered in cross-border trade agreements, there are trade cultures and arbitration systems which are not instantly translatable into the Western style discussed in this chapter.[104] This is a reminder that a general, globalist jurisprudence will need to be sensitive about the extent of its generalisations. Whilst these generalisations can be across territorial borders, they will likely be constrained by other borders – borders, for example, of culture, language and enforceability.

---

[100] Philip Allott, *The Health of Nations: Society and Law Beyond the State* (Cambridge: Cambridge University Press, 2002), [6.2]–[6.4]; see too David Held and Anthony McGrew, *Globalization/Anti-Globalization* (Cambridge: Polity Press, 2002), p. 120.

[101] Karl-Heinz Ladeur, 'Globalization and the Conversion of Democracy to Polycentric Networks: Can Democracy Survive the End of the Nation State' in Ladeur (ed.), *Public Governance*.

[102] See Ehrlich, *Fundamental Principles*, p. 379; Berger, *Creeping Codification*, p. 107.

[103] See section 12.1.1, p. 275 above.

[104] See e.g. Sampson L. Sempasa, 'Obstacles to International Commercial Arbitration in African Countries' (1992) 41 *International & Comparative Law Quarterly* 387–413; M. Sornarajah, 'The UNCITRAL Model Law: A Third World Viewpoint' (1989) 6 *Journal of International Arbitration* 7–20; Maniruzzaman, '*Lex Mercatoria*'; Amr A. Shalakany, 'Arbitration and the Third World: A Plea for Reassessing Bias Under the Specter of Neoliberalism' (2000) 41 *Harvard International Law Journal* 419–68; Charles N. Brower and Jeremy K. Sharpe, 'International Arbitration and the Islamic World: The Third Phase' (2003) 97 *American Journal of International Law* 643–56.

As a strategy for accommodating the current momentum for diverse laws to be centralised, codification is problematic. For a globalist jurisprudence, we must again conclude, with reference to Europe, that if codification is problematic at that level with its comparatively common culture, how much more problematic should codification be 'globally'. Perhaps codification in our time is even more problematic than that in nineteenth-century European states, given the deficiencies of the current method and critique, and the linguistic obstacles (as with the EU project). Zimmermann has, however, argued that the diversity within the territories unified in the nineteenth-century codifications may have been no less difficult to reconcile into a single code than might be the case in Europe today.[105] What can be asserted more confidently is that, with some exceptions, the contemporary European codification debate too infrequently considers the historical commonalities of Western legal science and the cautions of the historical school of jurisprudence. Those cautions, which can be expressed without need for fraught 'national spirit' (*Volksgeist*) terminology,[106] may be more readily understood today as concerns about the 'lived' or cultural, interior dimension to the law, which cannot be imposed by unsympathetic legislation. Economic and efficiency considerations by themselves cannot be expected to deliver the right norms at the right time to preserve social stability and accommodate change in the face of accelerating interconnections.

Meaningful law requires engagement with its people. On the Space Axis, it requires an interior-dimension relationship with the conscience and the culture. As well, meaningful law requires the requisite objectivity in the exterior dimension, with the political power and accountability to ensure that whim does not triumph over principle. On the Time Axis, law requires enough continuity with the past to maintain a character capable of inspiring allegiance, with flexibility to adapt to the challenges of the future pursued in the present. These things the *lex mercatoria* (loosely conceived) possesses.

The *lex mercatoria* demonstrates again that the state is not the only source of law and authoritative norms. Parties to contracts can choose the law they wish to bind their agreements at least some of the time. That law need not be the law of a state exclusively. The parties may never need the norm-generation, adjudication or enforcement of the legislature, judiciary or executive of state government. Such non-state authority is nowadays considered to be 'private' or consensual – a matter of 'governance' instead of 'government'. Such a purported dichotomy between private and public authority appears problematic, if only because Western sovereignty as a matter of theory is based upon a fiction, if not fantasy, of private contracting and associational choice. Classical republican theory in Aristotle premisses the state upon the formation of an association of

---

[105] Reinhard Zimmermann, 'Civil Law', p. 59. The Germanic and Roman ingredients of that intellectual battle suggest the analogy with the quest for a modern European private law is not 'too far-fetched': van Caenegem, *European Law*, pp. 92–4.

[106] See ch. 8, section 8.4.5, p. 189 above.

peoples for some good purpose.[107] Liberal political theory broadly derives from the covenant amongst people for social order by the 'social contract'.[108] Napoleon took Rousseau's *Contrat Social* seriously enough to apply it to the officers of his regiment in the expectation of a commitment to the whole; which was not an individualistic, characteristically liberal notion of the social contract.[109] Private authority so created need not be considered intrinsically individualistic.

This is not to suggest that personal contractual choices are appropriate for certain relationships in society which would unfairly favour the desires or privileges of the few over the many. Societies which transcend the old spheres of state containable disruption call for creative responses not only to traditionally private needs but also public needs, requiring the exploration of all normative options. 'Contractual' or (more neutrally expressed) 'voluntary' assumptions of social responsibility and rights may harbour potential as legal orders which rely less upon coercion and more upon shared values in areas of transnational criminal, human rights, environmental, sport and labour laws. Common goals could include, for example, contractual requirements to submit to a jurisdiction, benchmark standards for indigenous healthcare or lower greenhouse-gas emissions. More radically, this approach lends itself to considerations of liberation and self-government discourses. Whatever potential that private governance as a concept does harbour, the most energetic contemplations and critiques are demanded by the inequality, suffering, unhappiness and hostility in the world.

The inversion of economy and spiritual belief identified by Eugen Rosenstock-Huessy will be recalled.[110] In the West, at the end of the second millennium and beginning of the third, the market vies to be the legitimating authority which God used to occupy in discourse. The life and times of the *lex mercatoria* support this contention. The *lex mercatoria*, for the medieval merchants of the early second millennium, was entwined with their salvation and belief in ultimate reality and meaning.[111] Indeed, a prototypical transnational corporation in the form of the trading empire of the late medieval Italian Messer Francesco Datini carried the personal trading motto 'In the Name of God and of Profit'.[112] Belief in the redemptive potential of commerce may be

---

[107] Aristotle, *The Politics*, trans. T. A. Sinclair (Harmondsworth: Penguin, reprinted 1992), Iii, 1252a1, p. 54.

[108] For variations upon the theme, see Thomas Hobbes, *Leviathan* [1651] (London: Penguin, reprinted 1985), chs. 13, 14; John Locke, *Two Treatises of Government* [1689] (London: Everyman, 1993 reprinted 1998), chs. 8, 9; Jean-Jacques Rousseau, 'The Social Contract' in *The Social Contract and Discourses*, trans. G. H. Cole [1762] (London: Everyman, reprinted 1998), ch. 6.

[109] C. J. Friedrich, 'The Ideological and Philosophical Background' in Bernard Schwartz (ed.), *The Code Napoleon and the Common-Law World* (New York: New York University Press, 1956), p. 8.   [110] See generally ch. 10, section 10.6, pp. 247–51 above.

[111] See section 12.1.2, p. 277 above.

[112] Norman Davies, *Europe: A History* (London: Pimlico, 1997), pp. 442–3.

gaining momentum today. Its authority is now more terrestrial than celestial. Although there is no longer any intrinsic worth assigned to legal texts, such as was accorded to the canon or royal law, a commitment to a process of arbitration and private, 'gentlemanly' resolution of disputes can be observed. In capitalist communities, arbitration salutes time and cost efficiency and the maintenance of a community of good credit and honour. This takes place within a mindset of industrial progress which, according to at least one prominent legal practitioner in the field, espouses a belief in its own redemptive potential for 'peace and of stability' and the 'development of a more harmonious and peaceful world order', through a 'singular sect' of 'international business lawyers' ensconced in a 'family likeness' with 'briefcase', 'laptop computer' and 'the warmth of encounters' amongst 'inseparable travelling companions' aboard 'flights all over the world'.[113]

Whilst the troubles of the world are not solved by the international commercial law used by merchants, as a model for alternative authority their legal norms and systems inspire contemplation of the limits and potential of a general, globalist jurisprudence.

[113] See Robert Badinter, 'Role of the International Lawyer' (1995) 23 *International Business Lawyer* 505–6.

13

Conclusion: what is to be done?

A human being is part of the whole called by us 'universe', a part limited in time and space. We experience ourselves, our thoughts and feelings as something separate from the rest. A kind of optical delusion of consciousness. This delusion is a kind of prison for us, restricting us to our personal desires and to affection for a few persons nearest to us. Our task must be to free ourselves from the prison by widening our circle of compassion to embrace all living creatures and the whole of nature in its beauty. . . . We shall require a substantially new manner of thinking if mankind is to survive.

Albert Einstein[1]

Albert Einstein discovered the relativity of time and space in the midst of the World Revolution. History may one day show that these scientific symbols were necessary for the emergence of human consciousness of globalisation as we know it (just as Newtonian science accompanied the displacement of divine monarchical government by parliamentary government in seventeenth-century England).[2] Globalisation in a novel way demonstrates the universalist dimensions of the local and the particular, and the diverse particular, local impacts of universalist norms. Natural manifestations of space (such as continent or hemisphere) and time (such as day and night) for the first time in human history can no longer stop events in one part of the world from having almost instantaneous implications in another part. Single events may give rise to a variety of interpretations and ramifications across a multiplicity of communities.

'September 11' is a highly relevant demonstration of this global interconnection, as we have already noted. An act directed against two cities of the one nation-state was widely declared to be a terrorist act against the world (at least in the West). Sensibilities across the globe were aroused in a moment of time witnessed almost contemporaneously in the whole of the industrialised world. People varied in their characterisations of this event. For some, the US received its just deserts for interfering in the Middle East. For others, it was an unwarranted act of war against America in which innocent civilians died. There are

[1] Quoted in Kim Zetter, *Simple Kabbalah* (Berkeley: Conari Press, 1999), p. 151.
[2] See ch. 2, section 2.1.1, p. 26 above, referring to Michael Walzer.

many other opinions too. My own impression is that this event can be characterised as one of many rebounding transfers of human misery symptomatic of
the failed communication of norms and authority which ricochet between East
and West.[3] In this respect, Einstein appears correct to have noticed that we
experience 'our thoughts and feelings as something separate from the rest',
whilst still being part of the universe. This deluded separation is a prison. In
Einstein's century, a new manner of thinking was required. The fruits of that
thinking are required in the twenty-first century.

To appreciate the conflicting loyalties and allegiances which different societies
can inspire and demand, and have done in the past, I have suggested in part 1 a
model. The 'Space–Time Matrix' may inform the pursuit of a globalist jurisprudence aiming to understand and construct law and social order meaningfully
today. On the Space Axis, humans tend to feel moral, cultural allegiance to the
requirements of their closer spheres of involvement such as family, community
group, tribe; whilst at the other extreme, typically at the level of state government,
those responses and calls tend to be political, rational and often abstracted from
personal relevance. On the Time Axis, humans will adopt a position for the future
in response to what history means for them. There will be reasons of some historical significance for why someone is perceived to be radical or conservative. To
acknowledge only one or two of these four orientations (interior, exterior, history,
future) on a particular issue is to be imprisoned in a type of ignorance identified
by Einstein. Social harmony requires breaking out of 'personal desires and
affection for a few persons nearest to us' as Einstein has suggested. Social harmony
also requires us to break out of visions of the future which cannot be subjected to
dialogue and formulation by reference to interpretations of history. There is a
need to embrace these four orientations of the Space–Time Matrix all at once –
learning about other versions of the past and future and other people's notions of
personal morality and expectations of political organisations. Meaningful law
and norms at all social levels will need to be sensitive to these commitments.

At all times, I have endeavoured to emphasise the historical circumstances in
which law has attracted allegiance by maintaining rich normative references to
these orientations, and how these allegiances have been dissipated and reconstituted. Understanding this experience will be important if law is to live to its
potential today. Not only will law be more effective when it is believed in rather
than just coerced[4] but it will also be more meaningful. This can be contemplated
by reviewing the recurring patterns of authority which we saw characterise the
second millennium in Europe, before reconsidering the idea of 'globalisation'
with some recommendations for thinking about law now and in the future.

---

[3] On initiatives for intercultural dialogue, see ch. 10, section 10.4.4 pp. 235–40 above.
[4] See Iredell Jenkins, *Social Order and the Limits of Law (A Theoretical Essay)* (Princeton:
  Princeton University Press, 1980), ch. 9. According to H. L. A. Hart, *The Concept of Law*
  (Oxford: Clarendon Press, 2nd edn 1994), pp. 231–2: 'It may well be that any form of legal
  order is at its healthiest when there is a generally diffused sense that it is morally obligatory to
  conform to it.'

13.1 Lions and dragons: revisiting celestial and terrestrial patterns of authority

Laws are often thought to be like a rod with which to beat an errant donkey. Psalmist and pope think otherwise. More precious than gold and sweeter than honey, laws can bring joy and confer reward in their keeping.[5] They can be used to create a social order in which faith, grace and charisma may develop organically.[6] In greater and lesser measure, all of these optimistic and pessimistic ideas of law have received expression in the Western legal tradition considered in this book.

A happy society is one where people live the law gladly, not under threat of punishment but out of a sense of virtue. Self-propulsion[7] or self-direction is a foremost human social ideal. An individual should ideally follow or live the law because the individual feels it appropriate to do so. According to Nietzsche, humans are like lions. The state or lawmaker is something of a dragon which regulates the lions. The lion says 'I will', whilst the dragon has 'thou shalt' written on every scale, sparkling like gold.[8] Something or someone like the dragon saying 'thou shalt' or 'you must do this' does not sit comfortably with a creature like the lion which seeks to be free. Yet laws or dragons of some sort there must be. If self-propelling lions or humans are to be free (although compelled by nature to associate with their species), then the existence of a dragon or regulator of some sort is inherent, whether that dragon be a state, a customary community or the dictatorship of the proletariat.

Globalisation, thought about as the accelerated interconnections amongst things that happen in the world, enlivens old possibilities in some plains for lions to become more self-propelling in the face of less fiery dragons. If globalisation does not make the dragons less fiery, globalisation at least gives the lions some means for sheltering from the dragons' fires in competing jurisdictions. Globalisation *should* pose fewer challenges for legal theory than for other disciplines, not least because the associated normative transformation of the state's normative power (or sphere of containable disruption)[9] evokes strong precedents from Western legal history.

---

[5] Psalm 19.

[6] Pope John Paul II, *Sacrae Disciplinae Legis: Code of Canon Law, Latin–English Edition* (Washington, DC: Canon Law Society of America, 1983), p. xiv.

[7] The expression 'self-propulsion' is used rather than the word 'autonomy' in this context. Autonomy literally conjures independent norm-making at the interior extreme of the Space Axis, which, if it were occurring to a high degree in anyone but a child, would suggest insanity: see Rita L. Atkinson *et al.*, *Hilgard's Introduction to Psychology* (Fort Worth: Harcourt Brace, 12th edn 1996), p. 510. The self-propelling individual of my reckoning does not require the threat of punishment or coercion to behave ethically, but is inspired from a personal philosophical engagement with authoritative norms.

[8] Friedrich Nietzsche, *Thus Spoke Zarathustra: A Book for None and All*, trans. Walter Kaufman (Harmondsworth: Penguin Books, 1978), pp. 26–7. This dragon is symbolically and functionally akin to Thomas Hobbes's state, which he called 'Leviathan' (or Satan's snake, in Isaiah 27: 1).　　[9] See ch. 2, section 2.4, pp. 42–8 above.

13.1.1 The original European community

In medieval Western Europe, there was a dispersal of coercion. In part 2 of this book, we saw that the medieval Catholic church was, particularly from the twelfth century, an autonomous institution, along with other competing institutions such as the manor, crown, feudal demesne and town. Systems of law with modern characteristics, such as feudal law, manorial law, mercatorial law and urban law all comprised viable legal systems which existed alongside, although increasingly subordinate to, royal law and canon law. There was neither need nor place for an across-the-board executive (because authority was not unitary). Neither was there need for such a legislature (law was anyway thought to be uncovered, not created). Matters could sometimes fall before two or more jurisdictions. Conflict between those jurisdictions was generally resolved according to the changing political fortunes of territorial sovereigns and the papacy, in a 'Two Swords' constitutionalism of the spiritual church and secular territorial powers. Oral customs, old Roman law texts and treatises, and emerging indigenous writings from the various systems provided the material for uncovering the law.

Many types of people, including peasants and women, were ignored by the political process. By modern standards, this was a considerable shortcoming. The richness of the society may still be appreciated. Modern state authority commands everybody without much moral impulsion, like computers attached to a central network. Feudal government, on the other hand, radiated moral authority along branches of a tree generally to lesser and lesser lords who kept the smaller branches and leaves to their reciprocal duties – all within a reasonably common cosmology and sense of life's meaning. Moral and political allegiance were inspired by a Christian view of the universe which ritually permeated daily life and social institutions, with a common history and vision for the future preached from the pulpit. To obey law probably came quite naturally to most. Lions they probably were not, but social order at least depended less upon the fire of the dragon's breath.

13.1.2 The rise of the state

Globalisation as a concept is usually opposed to the state. In fact, the state was essential to the interconnection of the second millennium world, at least in Europe. The territorial focal point of the state was inevitably necessary in the process of globalisation, to gather the particularities of so much social diversity and feudal parochialism. Social desire and eventually bureaucratic compulsion to step outside the confines of the everyday life of the individual caught up in the affairs of the local manor, town or church were created. Only then could social distance be more popularly traversed, with parcels of sovereignty in one territory becoming relevant to other territories great distances away. We saw that the broadly defined holy Roman empire had a universalist legal science which could cope with this diversity, facilitating interconnection and the exchange of cultural information. Politically, though, papal universalism was undermined by the sixteenth-century Protestant Reformations, which expelled papal universalism. State sovereignties filled this absence, within their territorial boundaries, arguably without the same moral allegiance.

Following the end of the Thirty Years War in 1648, we saw in part 3 that the Peace of Westphalia was symbolic of the entrenchment of the state system in Europe and the decline of supranational papal power. Final executive power was being established in states, afloat in a functional international order with diplomatic representation and treaties. Contrary to most impressions, this was a direct development in the evolution of globalisation. About 900 parcels of sovereignty in the Habsburg Empire were rationalised into about 300. Generally, this represented the disintegration of religious order in Europe (which was a fragmenting tendency), alongside the movement towards a reduced number of absolutist centres of normative authority (an integrating tendency).

The style of this emerging authority was more political and exterior than moral and interior; more abstract and rational than culturally and spiritually compelling. It was entwined with legislation and the discovered ability of humans to invent authoritative propositions for imposition on a population. The chief mechanism for this was innovative legislation, which openly made law rather than just declared law, from about the sixteenth century. The fiery breath of the dragon was rising in temperature to maintain order, at the very time people became more leonine and individualistic, with emerging freedoms for capital owners which were to explode with the Industrial Revolution.

13.1.3 The economic particularity of the nation-state

Whilst commerce-led cultural interconnection has been a characteristic of world and not just Western history since the most ancient of times, in the eighteenth century it received a boost with the Industrial Revolution and *laissez-faire* economic policies. The emerging separation at that time of the economic and political spheres, leaving the market more to its own devices, in effect *de*-moralised production, and gave rise to the tendencies of a secular and Mammon-influenced universalism in part 4. The effect on productivity was tremendous, illustrated by the hegemonic success of England in the following century as the premier exemplar of this approach to political economy. The profounder sources of what is today termed 'globalisation' are to be found in this era.

At the level of law and social control, the nation-state of the eighteenth century onwards pioneered. A bourgeois phenomenon, it was captured in the French Declaration of the Rights of Man and Citizen. That document contains the codified articulation of the equality of humans, the inviolability of property, national sovereignty as the expression of the general will, the liberal freedom to do whatever does not harm another and basic rule of law principles. It was directed towards economically productive persons everywhere, although practically constricted to France. Nation-state authority was more terrestrial than celestial.

The parliamentary democracies which were to emerge in Western Europe generally attracted allegiance to their centralised, sovereign, nation-states, the lions winning an actual and symbolic influence over the dragon with setbacks on the way. The parliamentary dragon still, though, required brimstone and fiery breath. Parliamentary authority is several times abstracted from the individual in community. First, the individual's authority is abstracted to a parliamentary representative; and secondly, the vote of that representative is abstracted to the decisions and corporate personality of the parliament. Further abstractions occur in executive implementation and judicial interpretation. Political allegiance, if any, often comes at a high cost of moral allegiance.

The state of the eighteenth and nineteenth centuries wore the more obvious guise of a dragon in all realms but that of commerce. In this realm, the civil society of lions has been able to maintain a sense of autonomy, loosely conceived, for almost a millennium through its very own international commercial law, as we saw in chapter 12. The wider world was not so fortunate.

13.1.4 The rise of world society

Baldly stated, the nation-state and its economics facilitated the killing of about 150 million people in conditions of terror associated with the World Revolution of the two world wars. The natural environment did not fare much better. This trauma gave rise to the major international or 'global' treaties of the twentieth century such as those constituting the European Union, the United Nations and the General Agreement on Tariffs and Trade. Chief vehicles of globalisation – computer technology, mass media and jet transportation – are all implicated in the twentieth-century World Revolution.

Akin to the manner in which the social trauma of continental proportions in the late eleventh century established a world society of Christendom, nowadays a world society appears to be developing, with tentative laws although an emerging moral conscience. That is not, however, to suggest a single, all-encompassing society, but rather an alternative society or societies in conversation with other societies at the sub-global level. The major world treaties must not be treated as mere obstacles to, or instruments of, social goals in the present. To endure, this world society must become conscious of its history, its origins, its purposes.[10] Such as it may be, our world society emerged; it was not just created and imposed in the twentieth century. The twentieth century Universal Declaration of Human Rights (in chapter 10) required the eighteenth-century Declaration of the Rights of Man and Citizen (in chapter 8) which required the

---

[10] See Philip Allott, *The Health of Nations: Society and Law Beyond the State* (Cambridge: Cambridge University Press, 2002), ch. 11.

eleventh-century advent of All Souls' Day (in chapter 5), and many intervening developments. All souls had to be equal before all men could be equal before all humans could be equal, in the West.

Is obedience to globalist laws and norms self-propelled, as, for example, feudal law or canon law was part of the medieval psychology? My own sense is that allegiance to different systems comes increasingly naturally for different people,[11] and that the dispassionate, political approach to law is slowly ceding to a more moral approach in some realms even if breaches by state governments continue. Growing global contests between individuals, non-government organisations and the nation-state attest to this. A polarisation seems to be ensuing between those who are open to the idea of world society versus those who cannot see past state sovereignty. Some people are attracted or open to the norms of the world society through, for example, treaties received in principle, although not necessarily as, state law, which provide for human, environmental or free-trade rights. Others may suddenly find themselves allied with the legitimacy of the nation-state. There are progressive and reactionary sensibilities which attach to both positions, depending upon the subject-matter of the contested norms and the particular views of history and visions of the future held by the onlookers.

Such competitions between jurisdictions vividly recall a medieval precedent. They venture further than the competing jurisdictions which underlie federally organised states. They testify to competing systems of norms between territorial societies and societies which exist beyond territorial boundaries. Like a medieval peasant seeking refuge in a town, choosing urban law over manorial law, an individual now might look to international human rights or free-trade law to vindicate a freedom denied by the domestic system of law. Perhaps more people are not now pursuing self-propelled freedom like lions. Maybe there are simply more dragons or lawgivers for the lion to choose from. Either way, the necessary consequence is the articulation of norms and the need to locate oneself meaningfully in the world. Competitions between jurisdictions may well be inherently good,[12] if the jurisdictions are compelled to justify their norms and to reconcile conflict also by reference to other ways of looking at things.

In the West, a new, universalist, secular religious authority increasingly occupies the place once occupied by the Judeo-Christian God in legitimating the laws of competing jurisdictions. These new, universalist norms embody a tension between human rights and free trade. At the same time, the modern

---

[11] Perhaps this is more true in respect of deeper or more fundamental laws such as laws of war and human rights; and less so for venial laws such as motor traffic laws and other collective laws impinging upon individual convenience (e.g., water or waste restrictions).

[12] It is on this basis that I believe the most effective arguments are to be made against European civil codification and tendencies towards centralisation. See e.g. Pierre Legrand, 'Against a European Civil Code' (1997) 60 *Modern Law Review* 44–63, arguing that European 'plurijurality' is under threat from administrative convenience and fear.

incarnations of medieval religious beliefs remain important to the consciousness of the legislators. Occasionally, political leaders give voice to their religious convictions and constituencies. For the most part, though, religious, moralistic inputs into politics are concentrated in politicians' private campaigns for election and later reconstituted publicly into politically safe, rationalistic language and authority.

Before we were able to evaluate the constitutional significance and antecedents of globalisation, we had to arrive at a notion of 'globalisation'. That important notion deserves reflection.

13.2 Revisiting the concept of globalisation

The idea of globalisation we began with was ultimately the idea of globalisation which sustained the enquiry in this book, after exploring more elaborate notions in chapter 2. The relatively simple notion retained was of globalisation as the accelerated interconnections amongst things that happen in the world. Some features accompany this idea of globalisation.

Significantly, globalisation is a *process*. It is not a thing. One may touch globalisation no more than one may touch evolution or entropy. No single description or cause-and-effect phenomenon defines globalisation as such. John Ralston Saul, for example, has promoted the idea that globalisation is dead.[13] What he is talking about when he uses the word globalisation is a very narrow concept of economic globalisation (the 'death' perhaps being just a prematurely pronounced sleep). Of course, there is no monopoly on the meaning of a word such as globalisation. All usages considered, globalisation means much more than just economic rationalism, although it does comprehend Saul's definition of globalisation as a fraction of the total significance of the idea.

I have maintained that globalisation can only be grasped if it is thought about in association with a wide variety of social issues, such as, for example, international trade and capitalism, diverse cultures facing challenge from universalist sources and vice versa, and technology altering the way we relate to space and time. All of these phenomena have demonstrated, since the latter twentieth century, remarkable energies which seem to be related. In this sense, globalisation, whilst having a long historical background as old as merchants and religious proselytisers, appears to be a process which deserves to be recognised and defined by the experiences of the latter half of the twentieth century and beyond into the twenty-first century, spawned by the World Revolution.

If this is world domination, then it is world domination by a dawning consciousness and energised social network and information economy. As we saw in chapter 1 with reference to H. Patrick Glenn's work, a tradition is made up of information.[14] The central place of this information–tradition interchange

---

[13] John Ralston Saul, *The Collapse of Globalism and the Reinvention of the World* (Camberwell: Penguin Viking, 2005).   [14] See ch. 1, section 1.1.3, pp. 6–7 above.

underlying globalisation is captured in Manuel Castells' focal point – 'the informational economy' – for his three-volume foray into the global condition. For Castells, the economy which has emerged since the 1970s is informational because 'the productivity and competitiveness of units or agents in this economy . . . fundamentally depend upon their capacity to generate, process, and apply efficiently knowledge-based information'.[15] Globalisation, then, as the accelerated interconnections amongst things that happen in the world, is essentially about the exploding nexus of alternative traditions and information from those traditions. This information includes all of the logical, cultural, political and moral references which have dynamically interacted to make this era of the West so prone to change in all aspects of human endeavour.

By considering globalisation in these informational terms which emphasise the mobility of tradition, we can comprehend why globalisation can be perceived to represent world domination and be threatening to established cultures. Universalised Western values reflected, for example, in World Bank lending criteria to the Third World, can be characterised on the Time Axis of the Space–Time Matrix as the imposition of a Western economic vision of the future over less industrialised, more conservative visions. On the Space Axis, this would suggest an impersonal, exterior political vision unevenly superimposed on the cultural, moral bonds of an agrarian or traditional society. Information flows and dynamics embodying and reflecting competing norms are therefore important for understanding globalisation. Those flows are uneven, and it is that unevenness which gives rise, understandably, to the fixation by many observers on domination and imperialism as the signal characteristics of globalisation. Globalisation is, however, more than just domination. There are pluralistic and emancipatory tendencies in the process of globalisation too, such as the increasing recognition of marginalised people. Depending upon the universalist values of globalisation chosen for discussion, they are not all intrinsically Western, such as the prohibition, in principle, of murder, rape and torture.

13.3 Some implications for legal education and practice

Earlier I suggested, using Nietzsche's simile, that humans are like lions and the lawmaker (typically the state) is like a dragon. Ideally, the lawmaking dragons should breathe less fire, and humans as leonine creatures should be as free as their endowments would allow them whilst living in a stable social order. To this end, law- and norm-making processes should incorporate references from traditions which appeal to the individual at the moral level and cause the individual to be normatively self-propelled. The turn which globalisation signals, away from the particular norms of the nation-state to more universalist principles,

---

[15] Manuel Castells, *The Information Age: Economy, Society and Culture*, 3 vols. (Malden: Blackwell Publishers, 1997), vol. I, *The Rise of the Network Society*, p. 66.

across traditions, should be watched with optimism. This should be coupled with a willingness to debate the universality of the norms in question by way of philosophically engaging them with the norms allied to one's innermost personal attitudes. How might this be pursued in practice, today?

Much can, and is, being written about legal education and globalisation. Some issues have been touched upon in previous chapters of this book, such as mutual recognition of qualifications from other states and the cosmopolitanism of student populations and subject offerings. A pattern of law generation and maintenance is recurring. Just as we saw a medieval European, universalistic legal science generated by a transportable legal qualification from one of many law schools teaching Roman and canon law, now too we see a common university socialisation of global proportions. A possible 'Americanisation' of legal practice looms. For example, Japan has 'one of the strongest concentrations of Harvard Law School alumni ... mainly in the bureaucratic and financial fields'.[16] It has even been suggested that a reception of American law as *ius commune* is occurring, akin to the European reception of Roman law *ius commune* in the late middle ages.[17] Cases from foreign jurisdictions are cited increasingly in domestic jurisdictions, especially at the appellate level.

All of these local diversities interacting with universalist norms can be focused with clarity into a vision for a socially inclusive approach to legal education and law.

13.3.1 The contingency of law and justice

If a society is to flourish in its ordering and quest for improvement, education in general, and legal education in particular, must rediscover their former, combined moral and political relevance to the psychology of identity. Law as it is taught must be presented in lectures, tutorials and texts in such a way that it is capable of appealing to the individual in all four dimensions of the Space–Time Matrix. Take a very general example of norms of native title law. What is the political significance of those norms? What sorts of moral and cultural problems might individuals have with those norms? What sort of view of history are those norms based upon? What do they mean for the future? By appreciating that different individuals and corporate groups may have very different (and understandable) responses to these questions, the way is opened not only to participating in that discourse but also to learning the complexities of that doctrinal area of law and practising it more effectively. The evolution of this law, and much law in general, is the story of lawyers, academics, legislators, litigants and activists opening the leaves of the law reports and statute-books to different perspectives and allegiances. We have seen this in our discussion of law as a

---

[16] Yves Dezalay and Bryant Garth, 'Law, Lawyers and Social Capital: "Rule of Law" versus Relational Capitalism' (1997) 6 *Social & Legal Studies* 109–41, 129–31.

[17] Wolfgang Wiegand, 'The Reception of American Law in Europe' (1991) 39 *American Journal of Comparative Law* 229–48.

Zenonic paradox of motion. Just as the still snapshot of an arrow in flight does not describe the arrow, law too is always moving. When we try to state the law in the present or reduce law to some simple proposition, we are really seeing something out of its context.

Returning to our proposition in chapter 3 that law does not really exist in the present, and that enquiry into law will do well to include what 'is not' law, the notion of dissent emerges as a philosophical strength.[18] It is crucial to the very notion of a 'general jurisprudence'.[19] Common law legal education underplays dissenting judgments. Fortunately, Continental legal education, at least in Germany, rigorously teaches 'minority views' in the highly influential academic discourse.[20] Alas, common law dissenting judgments tend to be taught as the 'wrong' approach to a legal problem. Law actually comprises the majority and the minority views in a state of flux, sometimes to the point of utter obscurity.[21] Yet from this confusion, a treatment for the current malaise affecting law and contemporary legal education can be proposed. The multiplicity of norms which vie for legal authority, sometimes successfully, at other times in persuasive dissents, can be used to speak to the multiplicity of students with their multiplex allegiances. Dissenting opinions are conducive to dialogue and may even inspire students, in effect calling them by name to see themselves in what they study. History shows that minority views today may be the majority views of tomorrow. This should give some hope to those who feel their norms are unrecognised in the dominant law of the state. To this extent, law may be emancipatory and not just regulatory.[22]

The importance of connecting legal education to the moral, interior orientation of the human is captured by Boaventura de Sousa Santos: 'each great period of intellectual history is characterized by a specific close relationship between subjectivity and knowledge'.[23] Slavery and child labour have been overturned

---

[18] See e.g. Cass R. Sunstein, *Why Societies Need Dissent* (Cambridge, MA: Harvard University Press, 2003); David Daube, 'Dissent in Bible and Talmud' (1971) 59 *California Law Review* 784–94. Dissent is often required and is frequently endemic in the most sacred of texts. The diversity of biblical interpretations and emphases underlying the changing constitutions of society in parts 2, 3 and 4 of this book attest to the revolutionary progress which is built upon dissent.

[19] Jeremy Waldron, *Law and Disagreement* (Oxford: Clarendon Press, 1999), pp. 6–8.

[20] See Stefan Vogenauer, 'An Empire of Light? II: Learning and Lawmaking in Germany Today' (2006) 26 *Oxford Journal of Legal Studies* 627–63.

[21] It can happen that the majority orders of an appellate court can be based upon conflicting statements of principle which in fact amount to dissenting judgments within the majority: see e.g. *Northern Sandblasting v Harris* (1997) 188 CLR 313.

[22] Cf. Boaventura de Sousa Santos, *Toward a New Legal Common Sense: Law, Globalization and Emancipation* (London: Butterworths, 2nd edn 2002), ch. 9; Heidi Libesman, 'Between Modernity and Postmodernity' (2004) 16 *Yale Journal of Law and the Humanities* 413–23, 421–3, critiquing Santos's dismissal of liberal and modern constitutionalism. According to Australian popular music icon, social activist, now politician and law graduate Peter Garrett, 'know that a law degree equips you in ways unimaginable to do anything that really stirs your heart': NSW Young Lawyers, *Debrief* (February 2002).

[23] Boaventura de Sousa Santos, *Toward a New Common Sense: Law, Science and Politics in the Paradigmatic Transition* (New York: Routledge, 1st edn 1995), p. 489.

by views of law born on the fringe,[24] in this dimension of interior, subjective, morally compelled struggle and experience of oppression. Recognition of the historical revelation of justice through social activism, judicial determinations and multidisciplinary academic writings on social values will do better than the pretended knowledge of justice at a particular point in time.[25] That pretension epitomises the common law fetish of modern legal thought and education for majority judgments and statements of what the law 'is'. That fetish is misguided. It is to misunderstand, profoundly, the social construction of justice and law. After all, it is conceivable that some things which many people take for granted today will be harshly judged by future generations. In one thousand years, 'civilised society' might be vegetarian and dismissive of our carnivorous society, as we are dismissive of slavery, child labour, apartheid, the selling of holy relics, trial by ordeal and death sports in the Colosseum. Law in the Western tradition has been alive to (if not animated by) this systemic wisdom. Accommodating change whilst maintaining stability is a paradigmatic feature of the Western legal tradition.

By emphasising the worth of dissenting judgments, minority views and legal history, the space–time approach to legal education appears doctrinally, academically and socially sound. Doctrinally, this approach fulfils the traditional professional requirement to teach law according to a practically, professionally relevant curriculum which survives regular change. Academically, it accords with the more philosophical and educationally liberal curriculum of traditional university educators. The social soundness is an aspect of the academic value. The space–time approach is concerned with forming meaningful relationships with what is being studied, as an aspect of 'liberal education' – which aims to reflect upon the values of the culture[26] and to relate ideas from one subject to another.[27] Such interconnections are occurring more than ever in all areas of society, between cultures, professions, university disciplines and in general ways of thinking.[28] A responsive legal education will recognise these interconnections and promote the development of one's humanity, all too often neglected in legal thought and practice.[29]

Scholarship and practice seem more entwined than ever in responding to the demands of globalisation represented by this interconnection. Academic

---

[24] See Keith Mason, *Constancy and Change: Moral and Religious Values in the Australian Legal System* (Leichhardt: Federation Press, 1990), p. 88.

[25] On this theme, see R. E. Ball, *The Law and the Cloud of the Unknowing* (Ilfracombe: Stockwell, 1976).

[26] See Anthony Bradney, 'Liberalising Legal Education' in Fiona Cownie, *The Law School – Global Issues, Local Questions* (Aldershot: Ashgate Dartmouth, 1999), p. 18.

[27] See Andrew Goldsmith, 'Standing at the Crossroads: Law Schools, Universities, Markets and the Future of Legal Scholarship' in Cownie, *The Law School*, p. 79. See too William Twining, *Law in Context: Enlarging a Discipline* (Oxford: Clarendon Press, 1997), p. 141.

[28] See Adelle Blackett, 'Globalization and its Ambiguities: Implications for Law School Curricular Reform' (1998) 37 *Columbia Journal of Transnational Law* 57–79, 79.

[29] See Harvey M. Weinstein, 'The Integration of Intellect and Feeling in the Study of Law' (1982) 32 *Journal of Legal Education* 87–98, 97.

scholarship cannot be the only place to search for truth in law, just as legal practice or social activism will not be enough.[30] To indulge the theory without the practice[31] is to perpetuate the divisive opposition between interior and cultural allegiances (experience) versus exterior and political allegiances (reason). It is to assume that rationality (*logos*) is superior to culture (*nomos*), and to ignore practical allegiances from historical practices. Returning to the gambit at the very start of this book, purely theoretical, logical enquiry in law is fraught with the dynamic of the child attempting to answer the problems of the world with an untested logic, ignoring the lessons from the adult's practical experience. Each is undesirable in isolation.

13.3.2 Speed as virtue

What might all of this interconnection hold for the future of law, at the level of practice? The accelerated interconnections sprung from the technology and novelty associated with globalisation are particularly relevant to legal education and practice. Electronic precedents, research and knowledge management have prompted Richard Susskind to suggest that the lawyer will become more like a 'legal information engineer'.[32] On this prognosis, the lawyer will work with information like a skilled technician, plucking, grinding and inserting information where, when and how directed, to build the strongest, most convenient argument and document from the materials available. Of critical significance is the value this 'computerisation' of law salutes, namely economic productivity, utilising law and lawyers as economic tools. Productivity will be measured in terms of speed. According to Microsoft chairman, Bill Gates: 'If the 1980s were about quality and the 1990s were about reengineering, then the 2000s will be about velocity. About how quickly the nature of business will change. About how quickly business itself will be transacted. About how information access will alter the lifestyle of consumers and their expectations of business.'[33]

The 'nervous system' or brain of a business will be 'digital'. Lawyers, in the estimation of Gates, will have to work 'seamlessly'[34] with such systems. Deals will need to be completed faster. For private lawyers, more clients will need to be advised in less time to increase profitability. Existence will be deconstructed by the panopticon of the timesheet into 6-minute units which are either chargeable or non-chargeable, rewarded or not rewarded, worthwhile or not worthwhile

---

[30] *Contra* John Gava, 'Scholarship and Community' (1994) 16 *Sydney Law Review* 443–72, esp. 450.

[31] See Christine Parker and Andrew Goldsmith, ' "Failed Sociologists" in the Market Place: Law Schools in Australia' (1998) 25 *Journal of Law & Society* 33–70, 48; O. Weyrauch, 'Legal Practice as Search for Truth' (1985) 35 *Journal of Legal Education* 123–9.

[32] See Richard Susskind, *The Future of Law: Facing the Challenges of Information Technology* (Oxford: Oxford University Press, 1998).

[33] Bill Gates, with Collins Hemingway, *Business @ the Speed of Thought: Using a Digital Nervous System* (New York: Warner Books, 1999), p. xiii.   [34] Ibid., pp. 37, 140.

according to financial return. For public interest lawyers, backlogs will need to be cleared and case turnover increased. Novelty will need to be devoured and fashioned into practical solutions. Economic criteria will be used increasingly to account for the time of any university graduate pursuing probably any career. There will be less time to think. There will be less time to wonder. That is just for the lawyers. For those who require legal services, considerably greater social justice issues lurk beneath.

Aggressive competition will be a hallmark of what Philip Bobbitt calls the 'market-state' which is replacing the nation-state and the predisposition of that prior model to trade wars.[35] Aggressive competition is likely to be more reliant upon speed to meet impatient goals for the production of goods and services – including law – within and across traditional jurisdictions. Humans become pitted against time. Momentously, the economy now claims ownership of time, where time was once believed to be owned by God.[36] It is an article of faith in modern Western societies that money, by one of its definitions, captures and stores time which has been spent on productive work. Generally, money comes at the expense of time.[37] The dependence of advanced capitalist economies on credit means that the receipt of money in the present by way of credit creates a mortgage over the future which must be repaid by working ever-harder and longer hours. For bourgeois and managerial classes, the trend is new on this scale.

Alas, creative thought requires time as an essential nutrient. In an age when speed becomes a prized virtue and the time allowed for thinking decreases, thoughts risk growing reactionary, and instinctively at the service of unquestioned imperatives. Minds face being run into the ground like the bodies of Dickensian factory workers. The lawyer becomes *homo computans*, absorbed in reckoning other people's purposes. Education therefore becomes more important than ever to stimulate the sorts of intuitions and values which might otherwise be difficult to generate independently in the so-called 'real world' of professional practice. Education, however, feels the strain. More law students will need to be produced with less money, a challenge faced in all university disciplines. This poses problems for learning and prac-tising law ethically[38] and meaningfully, let alone living meaningfully and with soul.[39]

---

[35] Philip Bobbitt, *The Shield of Achilles: War, Peace and the Course of History* (London: Penguin, 2003), p. 706.   [36] See ch. 7, section 7.6.2, pp. 163–4 above.

[37] Christoph Deutschmann, 'Capitalism as Religion: An Unorthodox Analysis of Entrepreneurship' (2001) 4 *European Journal of Social Theory* 387–403, 392.

[38] See Patrick Schiltz, 'On Being a Happy, Healthy and Ethical Member of an Unhappy, Unhealthy, and Unethical Profession' (1999) 52 *Vanderbilt Law Review* 871–951, 888, 900, 911 and 949 (in a commercial law firm, 'you *cannot* practice law ethically – unless acting ethically is *habitual* for you', at 911 [original italics]).

[39] On 'time of the essence' society and the loss of soul, see Richard K. Fenn, *The Persistence of Purgatory* (Cambridge: Cambridge University Press, 1995), pp. 177–97.

13.3.3 Time for generalities

Against this surreal confusion between human and machine, wondering and thinking offer the potential to have new ideas and to appreciate what may not at first be apparent. Globalisation, we have seen, is popularly perceived as a dominant set of universalist values such as free trade, global markets and human rights (however reflected or not reflected in practice). In fact, these notions are fraught with complexities as they work themselves out in particular contexts. The particular manifestations are often characterised by long, rich histories and traditions confronted by dominant, universalistic global tendencies which do not respond in typical ways. The confrontations are good for some and bad for others on both the universalist and the differentiated, particular teams.[40] Importantly, these confrontations must be thought about. They must be subjected to discourse and curiosity.

General theorising, rather than just production-line-like concentration upon the particular task for which one has been trained, is essential for understanding what is going on now and for directing the future. We must avoid the admonition in Aldous Huxley's *Brave New World* that 'you won't have time for generalities'.[41] The Chief Justice of the Vermont Supreme Court has been critical of the particularistic proclivities of judges. Judges 'with less time to think broadly, and more responsibility to decide narrowly, are most comfortable when speaking of parts'.[42] Technical excellence directed to a particular doctrinal area will always be important for lawyers attempting to achieve clients' goals and for judges seeking to discern and apply 'the law', but the big picture must not be overlooked. Global and technological challenges open a Pandora's box of legal issues associated with genetics, artificial intelligence, universal norms for different peoples and human disregard, if not contempt, for the natural environment (which will eventually be avenged). Such questions are neither to be answered quickly nor even by reference only to the humanities or the sciences. Certainly, more than just narrow legal doctrine will be required for the education of a profession which must pursue meaningful order amidst all of this change.

The treatment of knowledge as so many units of information on a database, to be imparted to students as quickly as possible, encourages simplicity where there is actually complexity. Insufficient time to reflect duly upon these phenomena induces a satisfaction with simple answers in the face of complex legal,

---

[40] See Immanuel Wallerstein, 'Opening Remarks: Legal Constraints on the Capitalist World-Economy' in Michael Likosky (ed.), *Transnational Legal Processes* (London: Butterworths, 2002).

[41] Aldous Huxley, *Brave New World* [1932] (Essex: Longman Group UK, 1989), p. 2; see too ch. 1, section 1.3, p. 12 above. Resorting with some licence to Huxley, legal training should be 'less rigid than the training imposed upon those whose business is not to reason why, but merely to do and die with a minimum of fuss': Aldous Huxley, *Brave New World Revisited* (London: Triad Grafton Books, 1983), p. 108.

[42] Jeffrey L. Amestoy, 'Uncommon Humanity: Reflections on Judging in a Post-Human Era' (2003) 78 *New York University Law Review* 1581–95, 1586.

philosophical and sociological dynamics. Unfortunately these simple answers may make only for simple people. Education confined only to perceived usefulness, in the chrestomathic style advocated by the codifier Jeremy Bentham, serves only to edify present-minded teachers and the perceived needs of the present. Interconnected societies will not be served well by simple conceptions of globalisation and law, carried as articles of faith by students encouraged in their haste to become professional lawyers and unthoughtfully productive participants in an economy of unquestioned imperatives.

Speed as a cardinal virtue will discourage reflection and, in so doing, the very thing legal practice needs most at this point of time – critical, creative thought, born of the wandering, wondering mind, which can adapt to change and construe those changes meaningfully. Students should be equipped neither solely nor even primarily with technical legal knowledge, which can quickly become redundant. Skills which will last a lifetime of change and time-pressures will better serve the student and society – skills of interpreting legal materials and materials which can become legal materials (which includes any body of writing which can be called into evidence, relied upon to advise any manner of client, or used to understand and to influence the laws of judges and legislators).

If lawyers wish to practise law as a vocation with a significance beyond the immediacy of client interests and remuneration, they will require some basic awareness of a variety of disciplines which all add meaning to law and, not least of all, human life. A consciousness of history will alert that practice to the contingency of the moment.

13.4 The importance of historical consciousness today

In the global context, the major peril besetting law is the ignorance of the symbolism in the major treaties and documents of the emerging world society. That symbolism is historical. It is bound up with the ultimate reality and meaning of life. That symbolism is explicit in general terms in the preambles, as we have seen, to the major European Union and United Nations documents which reflect upon the human tragedy of the World Revolution and the need for a world society existing with other societies. The two world wars and the associated intervening great economic depression are mostly forgotten in the discourse relating to these documents. Yet this revolution was the reason for their birth.

13.4.1 Integrative jurisprudence

The United Nations and the European Union are human devices which reflect, arguably, the greatest ambition glimpsed by humans in modern history – namely, a world society coexisting with, and enabling order to flourish in, other societies. EU and UN constitutional preambles have a religious intensity about them which risks being forgotten if the legal systems they have inspired live only functionally (and not symbolically too) in the minds of their practitioners and subjects. Economic relations are legally established on such a grand scale under these regimes that they have come into adulthood with only infrequent references to the historical circumstances of their important conception. The World Revolution was no historical trifle. It claimed the lives of some 150 million people and scarred their children and environments. Particular cultures, as the associated events have affected them, have turned composites of this figure into their own ritual laments. National remembrance days, civic monuments and holocaust memorials attest to this. Transcending this diversity, at the more universal level, the greatest chance for avoiding such catastrophe in the future is linked to the emerging world society and its laws, and remembrance of the origins of these new institutions of world society such as the EU at the European level and the UN at the world level. In the midst of relying upon technical aspects of these legal systems, the preambles to their treaties should recall the horrors of the World Revolution and inspire the moral allegiance all humans owe to the avoidance of such catastrophe. Just as the blow to the face of the medieval knight reminded him for all time of the service he owed to his sponsor, or as the blood sacrifice reminded Old and New Testament peoples of (and sanctified) social covenants, the preambles must be read and lived in their bloody yet hopeful context.

As a matter of jurisprudence, the historical dimension to this law must be integrated with the exterior, positive law which comes from the state and suprastate law. This is to integrate the positivist school with the historical school. Joining this equation must be the moral and rational justifications which come from both the interior and exterior orientations on the Space Axis (morality being more associated with the interior and rationality with the exterior). This is to bring the natural law school into the equation. Altogether, this is the project of 'integrative jurisprudence' advocated by Harold J. Berman. His examples of the three major schools of legal thought may be adapted to fit the Space–Time Matrix. From the exterior orientation of the Space Axis (corresponding to his use of the positive law school), capital punishment may be legal (or illegal) because the state says so. From the interior dimension of the Space Axis (corresponding to the natural law school), capital punishment may be wrong because it contravenes the sanctity of life, or right, because anybody who murders deserves to die.[43] From the past–future orientation of the Time Axis (corresponding to the historical school), capital punishment might be wrong in certain countries but not other countries; it may be wrong in Germany, given what Germany lived through under Nazism.[44] In a further specific example taken from Germany, Bruce Ackerman has written that the Basic Law interpreted by the German Constitutional Court has become 'a central symbol of the nation's

---

[43] Natural law theory can also issue from the exterior orientation, through the exercise of rationality which might not necessarily attract personal, moral allegiance.

[44] So said the German philosopher Jürgen Habermas, as quoted in the examples taken above from Harold J. Berman, *Faith and Order: The Reconciliation of Law and Religion* (Atlanta: Scholars Press, 1993), p. 301.

break with its Nazi past'.[45] This historical style of argument is perhaps pertinent to raise in the face of any exercise of illiberal trade measures being adopted in Europe. Barriers to free trade are historically associated with national self-aggrandisement, the consequences of which have been horrific. Such argument should comprise the first principles of trade debate and legal interpretation; the interests of consumers or business should be secondary or at least integrated with the important historical considerations.

Finally, a reflection upon the normative complexity of love from an extract of a novel may further illustrate the importance of historical consciousness to law and authority.

13.4.2 Justifying authority: a romantic lesson

George Eliot's novel *The Mill on the Floss*, originally published in 1860, contains a dialogue which highlights the sources of authority which issue from the various orientations of the Space–Time Matrix. Although the dialogue addresses the normative complexity of love, we can use the principles expressed in the dialogue to illustrate the way law is justified. Eliot portrays love in terms of the interior (natural law), exterior (positive law) and past and future (historical) orientations. The dialogue reveals the great normative value of a historical consciousness outside legislation and resolutions, on the one hand, and self-serving morality, on the other.

Maggie has inadvertently left behind her sensitive but deformed suitor, Phillip, finding herself on a boat with her best friend Lucy's suitor, Stephen. Previous chapters have identified an undercurrent of love between the couple now alone on the boat. Maggie and Stephen have drifted too far and must spend the night together. It seems that with all the shame which must follow, the simplest solution for Stephen and Maggie would be to elope and consummate their suppressed love. An emotionally wrenching debate about the circumstance ensues.[46] Says Stephen:

> 'We have proved that it was impossible to keep our resolutions. We have proved that the feeling which draws us towards each other is too strong to be overcome: that natural law surmounts every other; we can't help what it clashes with.'

By these words, Stephen reveals himself as a naturalist, for whom resolutions (analogy: legislation) can be overridden by the convenience of one's personal, idiosyncratic, *interior* moral impulses or sense of reason.[47]

---

[45] Bruce Ackerman, 'The Rise of World Constitutionalism' (1997) 83 *Virginia Law Review* 771–97, 778. See too Michael Schäfer, 'Memory in the Construction of Constitutions' (2002) 15 *Ratio Juris* 403–17 and the German concept of *Vergangenheitsbewältigung* in ch. 11, section 11.6, p. 272 above.

[46] These quotations are taken from George Eliot, *The Mill on the Floss* [1860] (London: Wm Collins, 1952), p. 466.

[47] 'Naturalism in action, striding from declaring reality to prescribing policy, knowing no justice but the purpose of the party in power, is perhaps the greatest threat to the idea of law . . .': Franz Wieacker, *A History of Private Law in Europe, With Particular Reference to Germany* (Oxford: Oxford University Press, 1995), p. 458.

Maggie however follows with an alternative. Says Maggie:

'It is not so, Stephen – I'm quite sure that is wrong. I have tried to think it again and again; but I see, if we judged in that way, there would be a warrant for all treachery and cruelty – we should justify breaking the most sacred ties that can ever be formed on earth. If the past is not to bind us, where can duty lie? We should have no law but the inclination of the moment.'

Maggie is responding with a positivist emphasis on ties being formed or enacted outside oneself, and also with a historical emphasis on the binding value of past action.

Stephen retorts with a further attempt to erode positivism with his naturalism:

'But there are ties that can't be kept by mere resolution,' said Stephen, starting up and walking about again. 'What is outward faithfulness? Would they have thanked us for anything so hollow as constancy without love?'

The narrator then describes the methodology of Maggie:

Maggie did not answer immediately. She was undergoing an inward as well as an outward contest.

In the midst of a crisis, Maggie looks to her own convictions and then outside, implicitly, to other people, to benchmarks. Phillip, Lucy and Stephen all rely upon her.

At last she said, with a passionate assertion of her conviction, as much against herself as against him –
'That seems right – at first; but when I look further, I'm sure it is *not* right. Faithfulness and constancy mean something else besides doing what is easiest and pleasantest to ourselves. They mean renouncing whatever is opposed to the reliance others have in us – whatever would cause misery to those whom the course of our lives has made dependent on us . . .'

Worthy of note are Maggie's interior self-analysis and attention outside herself to her exterior, and her concern with the implications of her historical behaviour towards Phillip, Lucy and Stephen. These initiatives display greater sophistication than is reflected in Stephen's inability to overcome his urges to revoke inconvenient resolutions. Stephen seems to represent the power of natural law to criticise, modify and revoke human laws, by relying upon his interior whims. Maggie is a paragon of the type of legal virtue I have advocated in this book. She comprehends exterior rules and interior impulses, and balances these concepts with the duty she attributes to her past actions which have inspired reliance. Maggie, for our purposes, draws on the paradigm of historical jurisprudence.

The world society is reliant for its survival upon the resolutions by which bodies such as the UN and the EU were established. They should not be undermined by what feels natural in a time of relative peace and prosperity – namely the unrestrained pursuit of trade. As we have learned from Kant in chapter 9, both peace and trade can go together. Nonetheless, when there is conflict between free trade and human rights, it would seem fair to revert as a matter of interpretation to the real historical meaning behind the universalist structures. No matter what the conclusion, references to history would at least keep alive the highest human ideals in the legal order.

This tangential exploration of a similarity between the complexity of legal authority and the norms of love should have shown the benefit of integrating all of the dimensions of human being on the Space–Time Matrix. Interior and exterior allegiances to norms should be spoken and subjected to dialogue. Likewise, visions of the future based upon interpretations of history are articulated and can become common or at least subject to empathy through dialogue. History can remind us that some norms are too important to the future to be overridden by the logical conclusions of parliaments or the moral conclusions of individuals. Thus, law may be thought about as 'the balancing of morality and politics in the light of history; it is the balancing of justice and order in the light of experience'.[48] The future success of Western law depends no less upon the wedding if not reconciliation of the past and the future and the inner and the outer dimensions of authority.

13.5 Is there anything new under the sun?

> Vanity of vanities, all is vanity . . . There is nothing new under the sun . . . There is no remembrance of former things, nor will there be any remembrance of things that are to come by those who will come after.[49]

Recurring patterns of law and authority have featured in this book. With the remembrance of former things, discernment may arrive as to whether there are actually new things under the sun, overcoming the amnesiac presumption that challenges such as globalisation are necessarily novel in all respects. Remembrance can overcome the vanity of forgetfulness, as history can endow, with meaning, the achievement of a phenomenon such as globalisation.

The radical nature of a development can be measured by the lack of its commonality with things past. Constitutionally, it has been shown, globalisation is manifesting significant ancestral traits of the Western legal tradition. Chiefly, we have found that the authority behind law is very much dependent upon prevailing notions of a universal God, or ultimate reality and meaning. By these references, the human becomes orientated on the Space–Time Matrix, generating feelings of interior morality and respect for, or rejection of, exterior political authority, in the context of a sense of historical destiny. Despite the historical patterns, globalisation also represents an encounter with the hitherto unseen worldwide destruction of humans and environment. The periodical suicidal tendencies of human societies are being addressed in an

[48] Harold J. Berman, 'The Origins of Historical Jurisprudence: Coke, Selden, Hale' (1994) 103 *Yale Law Journal* 1651–738, 1731, attributing a definition of law to Coke, Selden and Hale.
[49] Ecclesiastes 1: 2–3, 9, 11 (NKJV).

unprecedented way through dramatically increasing interconnections and unity of response.

A more sophisticated legal science appears to be the principal prospect – a science which might draw upon more and more sources of norms, integrating the technology of ever more complicated legal rules, jurisdictions, discourses of morality and wisdom from historical reflection. In this respect, many of the legal challenges issuing under the trendy modern banner of 'globalisation' may be considered revolutionary in terms of scale, although not necessarily in terms of conception. That is, we have already seen a number of jurisdictions competing within and across given territories and social spheres. What has not been seen until recently is the sheer number of jurisdictions and normative discourses within and across such territories and spheres. The universalist peace which is being pursued is also revolutionary in response to unprecedented destruction. In the twenty-second century, schoolchildren may well consider these matters in their studies of 'the World Revolution' or 'the Global Revolution'. They should not catalogue and recite phenomena associated with these studies like the rote learner does of wars and explorers in the school history curriculum. Permanent insights into the social condition will hopefully be recalled and located in the human quest for peace and good order.

By the twenty-second century, in response to the question 'Why is something law?', the child of our Introduction, full of philosophical wonder, may be answered by the adult in terms different from those we began with. To answer 'Because the state says so' will not do. Perhaps the adult may be humbled to say: 'Now that's a very good question. As globalisation confirms, it is because history, cultural morality and political logic suggest that it is law, although it may not always be law.' Granted, this may all be a bit too serious for a child, even in the twenty-second century. Perhaps this answer might be more appropriate for adolescents in high school social or legal studies. Today, the approach may not be lost on university students and lawyers. The complex answer I have attributed to the adult by way of conclusion may prompt better questions from the enquirer. By asking better questions, better answers may be pursued. In the end, on this the advancement of all thought depends, not least of all legal thinking.

Bibliography

Ackerman, Bruce, 'The Rise of World Constitutionalism' (1997) 83 *Virginia Law Review* 771–97.

Ahmed, Akbar and Forst, Brian, *After Terror: Promoting Dialogue Among Civilizations* (Cambridge: Polity Press, 2005).

Allott, Philip, 'The European Community is Not the True European Community' (1991) 100 *Yale Law Journal* 2485–500.

Eunomia: New Order for a New World (Oxford: Oxford University Press, 1990).

'The True Function of Law in the International Community' (1998) 5 *Indiana Journal of Global Legal Studies* 391–413.

The Health of Nations: Society and Law Beyond the State (Cambridge: Cambridge University Press, 2002).

Epilogue: Europe and the Dream of Reason' in J. H. H. Weiler and Marlene Wind (eds.), *European Constitutionalism Beyond the State* (Cambridge: Cambridge University Press, 2003).

Althoff, Gerd, '*Amicitiae* [Friendships] as Relationships Between States and Peoples' in Lester K. Little and Barbara H. Rosenwein (eds.), *Debating the Middle Ages: Issues and Readings* (Malden: Blackwell Publishers, 1998).

Aman, Alfred C. Jr, *The Democracy Deficit: Taming Globalization through Law Reform* (New York: New York University Press, 2004).

Amestoy, Jeffrey L., 'Uncommon Humanity: Reflections on Judging in a Post-Human Era' (2003) 78 *New York University Law Review* 1581–95.

Anderson, Benedict, *Imagined Communities: Reflections on the Origin and Spread of Nationalism* (London: Verso, 1991).

Anderson, Perry, *Lineages of the Absolutist State* (London: NLB, 1974).

Passages from Antiquity to Feudalism (London: NLB, 1974).

Anghie, Antony, *Imperialism, Sovereignty and the Making of International Law* (Cambridge: Cambridge University Press, 2006).

An-Na'im, Abdullahi Ahmed, 'Problems of Universal Cultural Legitimacy for Human Rights' in Abdullahi Ahmed An-Na'im and Francis M. Deng (eds.), *Human Rights in Africa: Cross-Cultural Perspectives* (Washington, DC: The Brookings Institution, 1990).

'Islam and Human Rights: Beyond the Universality Debate' (2000) 94 *American Society of International Law Proceedings* 95–101.

'Globalization and Jurisprudence: An Islamic Law Perspective' (2005) 54 *Emory Law Journal* 25–51.

Aquinas, St Thomas, *Summa Theologica*, in Anton C. Pegis (ed.), *Introduction to St Thomas Aquinas* (New York: The Modern Library, 1948).

Arendt, Hannah, *The Origins of Totalitarianism* (San Diego: Harcourt Brace & Co., 1948 reprinted 1976).

The Human Condition (Chicago: University of Chicago Press, 1958).

Eichmann in Jerusalem: A Report on the Banality of Evil (Harmondsworth: Penguin, 1997).

Aristotle, *The Nicomachean Ethics*, trans. David Ross (Oxford: Oxford University Press, 1925 reprinted 1980).

The Politics, trans. T. A. Sinclair (Harmondsworth: Penguin, reprinted 1992).

Arnason, Johann P., 'Nationalism, Globalization and Modernity' in Mike Featherstone (ed.), *Global Culture: Nationalism, Globalization and Modernity* (London: Sage, 1990 reprinted 1996).

Arnold, Morris S., 'Statutes as Judgments: The Natural Law Theory of Parliamentary Activity in Medieval England' (1977) 126 *University of Pennsylvania Law Review* 329–43.

Aroney, Nicholas, 'Federal Constitutionalism/European Constitutionalism in Comparative Perspective' in G. Leenknegt and E. J. Janse de Jonge (eds.), *Getuigend Staatsrecht: Liber Amicorum A. K. Koekkoek* (Tilburg: Wolf Legal Publishers, 2005).

'Subsidiarity, Federalism and the Best Constitution: Thomas Aquinas on City, Province and Empire' (2007) 26 *Law and Philosophy* 161–228.

Atkinson, Rita L. *et al.*, *Hilgard's Introduction to Psychology* (Fort Worth, TX: Harcourt Brace, 12th edn 1996).

Augustine, Saint, *Confessions*, trans. R. S. Pine-Coffin (Harmondsworth: Penguin, 1961).

City of God, trans. Henry Bettenson (London: Penguin, 1984).

Austin, John, *The Uses of the Study of Jurisprudence* (London: Weidenfeld & Nicolson, 1954).

Axtmann, Roland, 'Globalization, Europe and the State: Introductory Reflections' in Roland Axtmann (ed.), *Globalization and Europe: Theoretical and Empirical Investigations* (London: Pinter, 1998).

Aziz, Miriam, 'Sovereignty Lost, Sovereignty Regained? Some Reflections on the Bundesverfassungsgericht's Bananas Judgment' (2002) 9 *Columbia Journal of European Law* 109–40.

Backer, Larry Cata, 'Multinational Corporations, Transnational Law: The United Nation's Norms on the Responsibilities of Transnational Corporations as Harbinger of Corporate Responsibility' (2005) 37 *Columbia Human Rights Law Review* 287–389.

Badinter, Robert, 'Role of the International Lawyer' (1995) 23 *International Business Lawyer* 505–6.

Baker, J. H., 'The Law Merchant and the Common Law Before 1700' (1979) 38 *Cambridge Law Journal* 295–322.

'Why the History of English Law Has Not Been Finished' (2000) 59 *Cambridge Law Journal* 62–84.

An Introduction to English Legal History (London: Butterworths, 4th edn 2002).

The Law's Two Bodies: Some Evidential Problems in English Legal History (Cambridge: Cambridge University Press, 2003).

Oxford History of the Laws of England: 1483–1558 (Oxford: Oxford University Press, 2003), vol. VI.

'Human Rights and the Rule of Law in Renaissance England' (2004) 2 *Northwestern University Journal of International Human Rights* 3–23, 23.

Baldwin, James, *Nobody Knows My Name: More Notes of a Native Son* (New York: Vintage International, 1961 reprinted 1993).

Ball, Milner S., *The Word and the Law* (Chicago: University of Chicago Press, 1993).

Ball, R. E., *The Law and the Cloud of the Unknowing* (Ilfracombe: Stockwell, 1976).

Barber, Malcolm, *The Two Cities: Medieval Europe 1050–1320* (London: Routledge, 1992).

Barber, N. W., 'The Limited Modesty of Subsidiarity' (2005) 11 *European Law Journal* 308–25.

'Legal Pluralism and the European Union' (2006) 12 *European Law Journal* 306–29.

Barbero, Alessandro, *Charlemagne: Father of a Continent*, trans. Allan Cameron (Berkeley: University of California Press, 2004).

Barnes, Wayne R., 'Contemplating a Civil Law Paradigm for a Future International Commercial Code' (2005) 65 *Louisiana Law Review* 677–774.

Baron, Gesa, 'Do the UNIDROIT Principles of International Commercial Contracts Form a New *Lex Mercatoria*?' (1999) 15 *Arbitration International* 115–30.

Barth, Karl, 'The Place of Theology' reprinted in Ray S. Anderson (ed.), *Theological Foundations for Ministry: Selected Readings for a Theology of the Church in Ministry* (Edinburgh: T.&T. Clark Ltd, 1979).

Barton, Thomas D., 'Troublesome Connections: The Law and Post-Enlightenment Culture' (1998) 47 *Emory Law Journal* 163–236.

Basile, Mary Elizabeth *et al.*, *Lex Mercatoria and Legal Pluralism: A Late Thirteenth-Century Treatise and its Afterlife* (Cambridge, MA: The Ames Foundation, 1998).

Bauman, Richard, *Human Rights in Ancient Rome* (London: Routledge, 2000).

Bauman, Zygmunt, 'Modernity and Ambivalence' in Mike Featherstone (ed.), *Global Culture: Nationalism, Globalization and Modernity* (London: Sage, 1990 reprinted 1996).

Baxi, Upendra, *The Future of Human Rights* (New Delhi: Oxford University Press, 2nd edn 2006).

Beaulac, Stéphane, *The Power of Language in the Making of International Law: The Word Sovereignty in Bodin and Vattel and the Myth of Westphalia* (Leiden: Martinus Nijhoff Publishers, 2004).

Bellah, Robert N., 'What is Axial About the Axial Age?' (2005) 46 *European Journal of Sociology* 69–89.

Bellomo, Manlio, *The Common Legal Past of Europe 1000–1800*, trans. Lydia G. Cochrane (Washington, DC: Catholic University of America Press, 1995).

Bengoetxea, Joxerramon, *The Legal Reasoning of the European Court of Justice: Towards a European Jurisprudence* (Oxford: Clarendon Press, 1993).

Bentham, Jeremy, 'Of the Influence of Time and Place in Matters of Legislation' in John Bowring (ed.), *The Works of Jeremy Bentham* (Edinburgh: William Tait, 1843), vol. I.

'Nonsense upon Stilts, or Pandora's Box Opened, or the French Declaration of Rights Prefixed to the Constitution of 1791 Laid Open and Exposed' in Philip Schofield *et al.* (eds.), *Rights, Representation, and Reform: Nonsense upon Stilts and Other Writings on the French Revolution* (Oxford: Oxford University Press, 2002).

Legislator of the World: Writings on Codification, Law, and Education (Oxford: Oxford University Press, 1998).

Benton, Lauren, *Law and Colonial Cultures: Legal Regimes in World History, 1400–1900* (Cambridge: Cambridge University Press, 2002).

Bergel, Jean Louis, 'Principal Features and Methods of Codification' (1988) 48 *Louisiana Law Review* 1073–97.

Berger, Klaus Peter, *The Creeping Codification of the Lex Mercatoria* (The Hague: Kluwer Law International, 1999).

Berger, Peter, and Luckmann, Thomas, *The Social Construction of Reality: A Treatise in the Sociology of Knowledge* (Harmondsworth: Penguin, 1966).

Berman, Harold J., *Law and Revolution: The Formation of the Western Legal Tradition* (Cambridge, MA: Harvard University Press, 1983).

  Faith and Order: The Reconciliation of Law and Religion (Atlanta: Scholars Press, 1993).

  'Law and Logos' (1994) 44 *DePaul Law Review* 143–65.

  'The Origins of Historical Jurisprudence: Coke, Selden, Hale' (1994) 103 *Yale Law Journal* 1651–1738.

  'World Law' (1995) 18 *Fordham International Law Journal* 1617–22.

  'The Western Legal Tradition in a Millennial Perspective: Past and Future' (2000) 60 *Louisiana Law Review* 739–63.

  Law and Revolution, II: the Impact of the Protestant Reformations on the Western Legal Tradition (Cambridge, MA: Harvard University Press, 2003).

  'Faith and Law in a Multicultural World' in Mark Juergensmeyer (ed.), *Religion in Global Civil Society* (New York: Oxford University Press, 2005).

Berman, Harold J., and Dasser, Felix J., 'The "New" Law Merchant and the "Old": Sources, Content and Legitimacy' in Thomas E. Carbonneau (ed.), *Lex Mercatoria and Arbitration: A Discussion of the New Law Merchant* (Juris Publishing/Kluwer Law International, rev. edn 1998).

Berman, Harold J., and Kaufman, Colin, 'The Law of International Commercial Transactions (*Lex Mercatoria*) (1978) 19 *Harvard International Law Journal* 221–77.

Berman, Harold J., and Witte, John Jr, 'The Transformation of Western Legal Philosophy in Lutheran Germany' (1989) 62 *Southern California Law Review* 1575–1660.

Berman, Paul Schiff, 'The Globalization of Jurisdiction' (2002) 151 *University of Pennsylvania Law Review* 311–545.

  'From International Law to Law and Globalization' (2005) 43 *Columbia Journal of Transnational Law* 485–556.

  (ed.), *The Globalization of International Law* (Burlington: Ashgate, 2005).

Beyer, Peter F., 'Privatization and the Public Influence of Religion in Global Society' in Mike Featherstone (ed.), *Global Culture: Nationalism, Globalization and Modernity* (London: Sage, 1990 reprinted 1996).

Bhala, Raj, 'Fighting Bad Guys with International Trade Law' (1997) 31 *U.C. Davis Law Review* 1–122.

Bianchi, Andrea, 'Globalization of Human Rights: The Role of Non-state Actors' in Gunther Teubner (ed.), *Global Law Without A State* (Brookfield: Dartmouth Publishing Company, 1997).

Bindoff, S. T., *Tudor England* (Harmondsworth: Penguin, 1964).

Bishop of Cologne, 'The Truce of God' in Norman Cantor (ed.), *The Medieval Reader* (New York: HarperPerennial, 1995).

Black, Antony, *Guilds and Civil Society in European Political Thought from the Twelfth Century to the Present* (London: Methuen, 1984).

Political Thought in Europe, 1250–1450 (Cambridge: Cambridge University Press, 1992).

'Communal Democracy and its History' (1997) 45 *Political Studies* 5–20.

Blackett, Adelle, 'Globalization and its Ambiguities: Implications for Law School Curricular Reform' (1998) 37 *Columbia Journal of Transnational Law* 57–79.

Blackstone, Sir William, *Commentaries on the Laws of England*, 4 vols. [1783] (New York: Garland Publishing Inc., 1978) vols. I, IV.

Blumenthal, Uta-Renate, *The Investiture Controversy: Church and Monarchy from the Ninth to the Twelfth Century* (Philadelphia: University of Pennsylvania Press, 1988).

Bloch, Marc, *Feudal Society*, trans. L. A. Manyon (London: Routlege & Kegan Paul, 1942).

Bobbitt, Philip, *The Shield of Achilles: War, Peace and the Course of History* (London: Penguin, 2003).

Bodin, Jean, *Method for the Easy Comprehension of History*, trans. Beatrice Reynolds [1565] (New York: Columbia University Press, 1945).

On Sovereignty: Four Chapters from *The Six Books of the Commonwealth* [1583], trans. and ed. Julian H. Franklin (Cambridge: Cambridge University Press, 1992).

Bohman, James, and Lutz-Bachmann, Matthias, 'Introduction' in James Bohman and Matthias Lutz-Bachmann (eds.), *Perpetual Peace: Essays on Kant's Cosmopolitan Ideal* (Cambridge, MA: The MIT Press, 1997).

Bollen, Carlos, and De Groot, Gerard-René, 'The Sources and Backgrounds of European Legal Systems' in A. S. Hartkamp *et al.* (eds.), *Towards a European Civil Code* (Dordrecht: Martinus Nijhoff Publishers, 1st edn 1994).

Booth, Ken, 'Security in Anarchy: Utopian Realism, in Theory and Practice' (1991) 67 *International Affairs* 527–45.

Bradney, Anthony, 'Liberalising Legal Education' in Fiona Cownie, *The Law School – Global Issues, Local Questions* (Aldershot: Ashgate Dartmouth, 1999).

Breda, Vito, 'A European Constitution in a Multinational Europe or a Multinational Constitution for Europe?' (2006) 12 *European Law Journal* 330–44.

Brems, Eva, *Human Rights: Universality and Diversity* (The Hague: Martinus Nijhoff Publishers, 2001).

Brennan, Sir Gerard, 'Principle and Independence: The Guardians of Freedom' (2000) 74 *Australian Law Journal* 749–59.

Brilmayer, Lea, 'The Moral Significance of Nationalism' (1995) 71 *Notre Dame Law Review* 7–33.

Brooklyn Journal of International Law, 'Symposium: The Universal Declaration of Human Rights at 50 and the Challenge of Global Markets' (1999) 25 *Brooklyn Journal of International Law* 1–183.

Brower, Charles N., and Sharpe, Jeremy K., 'International Arbitration and the Islamic World: The Third Phase' (2003) 97 *American Journal of International Law* 643–56.

Brown, Michelle P., and Kelly, Richard J. (eds.), *You're History: How People Make the Difference* (London: Continuum Press, 2006).

Brundage, James A., 'The Rise of the Professional Jurist in the Thirteenth Century' (1994) 20 *Syracuse Journal of International Law & Commerce* 185–90.

The Profession and Practice of Medieval Canon Law (Aldershot: Ashgate Variorum, 2004).

Bull, Hedley, *The Anarchical Society: A Study of Order in World Politics* (London: Macmillan, 1977).

'Natural law and International Relations' (1979) 5 *British Journal of International Studies* 171–81.

'Hans Kelsen and International Law' in Richard Tur and William Twining (eds.), *Essays on Kelsen* (Oxford: Clarendon Press, 1986).

Burke, Edmund, *Reflections on the Revolution in France* [1790] (Oxford: Oxford University Press, 1993).

Bussani, Mauro, and Mattei, Ugo (eds.), *The Common Core of European Private Law* (The Hague: Kluwer Law International, 2003).

Byers, Michael, and Nolte, Georg (eds.), *United States Hegemony and the Foundations of International Law* (Cambridge: Cambridge University Press, 2003).

Cantor, Norman F. (ed.), *The Medieval Reader* (New York: HarperPerennial, 1995).

Inventing the Middle Ages: The Lives, Works, and Ideas of the Great Medievalists of the Twentieth Century (New York: Quill William Morrow, 1991).

Caroll, Vic, 'What if . . . free trade had won in 1901', *Sydney Morning Herald*, 5 September 2001.

Cass, Deborah Z., 'The "Constitutionalization" of International Trade Law: Judicial Norm-Generation as the Engine of Constitutional Development in International Trade' (2001) 12 *European Journal of International Law* 39–75.

Cassin, René, 'Codification and National Unity' in Bernard Schwartz (ed.), *The Code Napoleon and the Common-Law World* (New York: New York University Press, 1956).

Castells, Manuel, *The Information Age: Economy, Society and Culture*, 3 vols. (Malden: Blackwell Publishers, 1996).

Cesar, Floriano Jonas, 'Popular Autonomy and Imperial Power in Bartolus of Saxoferrato: An Intrinsic Connection' (2004) 65 *Journal of the History of Ideas* 369–81.

Chadwick, Henry, 'Envoi: On Taking Leave of Antiquity' in John Boardman *et al.*, *The Oxford History of the Classical World* (Oxford: Oxford University Press, 1986).

Chang, Ha-Joon, *Kicking Away the Ladder: Development Strategy in Historical Perspective* (London: Anthem Press, 2002).

Charnovitz, Steve, 'The Moral Exception in Trade Policy' (1998) 38 *Virginia Journal of International Trade Law* 689–745.

Chen, Jim, 'Globalization and its Losers' (2000) 9 *Minnesota Journal of Global Trade* 157–218.

'Pax Mercatoria: Globalization as a Second Chance at "Peace for our Time"' (2000) 24 *Fordham International Law Journal* 217–51.

Cheng, Bin, 'Outer Void Space: The Reason for this Neologism in Space Law' (1999) *Australian International Law Journal* 1–8.

Chua, Amy L., *World on Fire: How Exporting Free Market Democracy Breeds Ethnic Hatred and Global Instability* (New York: Anchor Books, 2004).

Clark, David S., 'The Medieval Origins of Modern Legal Education: Between Church and State' (1987) 35 *American Journal of Comparative Law* 653–719.

Cobban, Alfred, *A History of Modern France*, 3 vols. (Harmondsworth: Penguin, 1963), vol. I.

Cohen, Jean L., 'Whose Sovereignty?: Empire Versus International Law' in Christian Barry and Thomas W. Pogge (eds.), *Global Institutions and Responsibilities: Achieving Global Justice* (Malden: Blackwell Publishing, 2005).

Coke, Sir Edward, 'The First Part of the Institutes of the Laws of England, 1628' in James C. Holt, *Magna Carta and the Idea of Liberty* (New York: John Wiley & Sons, 1972).

Conquest, Robert, *Reflections on a Ravaged Century* (New York: Norton, 2000).

Cook, Charles M., *The American Codification Movement: A Study of Antebellum Legal Reform* (Westport: Greenwood Press, 1981).

Corbett, P. E., *Law and Society in the Relations of States* (New York: Harcourt, Brace and Co., 1951).

Cordes, Albrecht, 'The Search for a Medieval *Lex Mercatoria*' (2003) *Oxford University Comparative Law Forum* 5 at ouclf.iuscomp.org (viewed 6 January 2007).

Cotterrell, Roger, 'Law in Culture' (2004) 17 *Ratio Juris* 1–14.

Council for a Parliament of the World's Religions, 'Towards a Global Ethic (An Initial Declaration)' (Chicago, 1993) cpwr.org/resource/ethic.pdf (viewed 6 January 2007).

Covell, Charles, *Kant and the Law of Peace: A Study in the Philosophy of International Law and International Relations* (London: Macmillan, 1998).

Cover, Robert M., 'The Supreme Court 1982 Term Foreword: *Nomos* and Narrative' (1983) 97 *Harvard Law Review* 4–68.

'Violence and the Word' (1986) 95 *Yale Law Journal* 1601–29.

Cowdrey, H. E. J., *The Cluniacs and the Gregorian Reform* (Oxford: Clarendon Press, 1970).

Pope Gregory VII: 1073–1085 (Oxford: Clarendon Press, 1998).

Craven, Matthew C. R., *The International Covenant on Economic, Social and Cultural Rights: A Perspective on its Development* (Oxford: Clarendon Press, 1998).

Cremades, Bernardo M., 'The Impact of International Arbitration on the Development of Business Law' (1983) 31 *American Journal of Comparative Law* 526–34.

Crystal, David, *English as a Global Language* (Cambridge: Cambridge University Press, 1997).

Cutler, A. Claire, 'Globalization, the Rule of Law, and the Modern Law Merchant: Medieval or Late Capitalist Associations?' (2001) 8 *Constellations* 480–502.

Daddow, Oliver J., 'Euroscepticism and the Culture of the Discipline of History' (2006) 32 *Review of International Studies* 309–28.

Dalhuisen, J. H., *Dalhuisen on International Commercial, Financial and Trade Law* (Oxford: Hart Publishing, 2nd edn 2004).

'Legal Orders and their Manifestation: The Operation of the International Commercial and Financial Legal Order and its Lex Mercatoria' (2006) 24 *Berkeley Journal of International Law* 129–91.

Darrow, Mac, *Between Light and Shadow: The World Bank, the International Monetary Fund and International Human Rights Law* (Oxford: Hart Publishing, 2006).

Daube, David, 'Dissent in Bible and Talmud' (1971) 59 *California Law Review* 784–94.

Daunton, Martin, 'Britain and Globalisation Since 1850: I. Creating a Global Order, 1850–1914' (2006) 16 *Transactions of the Royal Historical Society* 1–38.

Davies, Norman, *Europe: A History* (London: Pimlico, 1997).

Davis, Michael E., and Lee, Ricky J., 'Twenty Years After: The Moon Agreement and its Legal Controversies' (1999) *Australian International Law Journal* 9–33.

Dehousse, Renaud, 'Beyond Representative Democracy: Constitutionalism in a Polycentric Polity' in J. H. H. Weiler and Marlene Wind (eds.), *European Constitutionalism Beyond the State* (Cambridge: Cambridge University Press, 2003).

Dent, Nicholas, 'Logos' in Ted Honderich (ed.), *The Oxford Companion to Philosophy* (Oxford: Oxford University Press, 1995).

de Roover, Raymond, 'The Scholastic Attitude Towards Trade and Entrepreneurship' in *Business, Banking and Economic Thought in Late Medieval and Early Modern Europe* (Chicago: University of Chicago Press, 1974).

Derrett, J. Duncan M., 'The Trial of Sir Thomas More' (1964) 79 *English Historical Review* 449–77.

Derrida, Jacques, 'Force of Law: The "Mystical Foundations of Authority"' (1990) 11 *Cardozo Law Review* 921–1045.

Descartes, René, *A Discourse on Method, Meditations on the First Philosophy, Principles of Philosophy*, trans. John Veitch (London: Everyman, 1997).

Deutschmann, Christoph, 'Capitalism as a Religion? An Unorthodox Analysis of Entrepreneurship' (2001) 4 *European Journal of Social Theory* 387–403.

Dezalay, Yves, and Garth, Bryant G., *Dealing in Virtue: International Commercial Arbitration and the Construction of a Transnational Legal Order* (Chicago: University of Chicago Press, 1996).

'Law, Lawyers and Social Capital: "Rule of Law" versus Relational Capitalism' (1997) 6 *Social & Legal Studies* 109–41.

Dhokalia, R. P., *The Codification of Public International Law* (Manchester: University of Manchester Press, 1970).

Diamond, Jared, *Guns, Germs, and Steel: The Fates of Human Societies* (New York: W. W. Norton & Company, 1999).

Dickinson, John, 'Introduction: The Place of the Policraticus in the Development of Political Thought' in *Policraticus: The Statesman's Book of John of Salisbury* (New York: Russell & Russell, 1963).

Dinan, Desmond, *Ever Closer Union: An Introduction to European Integration* (Basingstoke: Palgrave Macmillan, 3rd edn 2005).

Dinwiddy, John, *Bentham* (Oxford: Oxford University Press, 1989).

Donahue, Charles Jr, '*Ius Commune*, Canon Law, and Common Law in England' (1992) 66 *Tulane Law Review* 1745–80.

'Medieval and Early Modern Lex Mercatoria: An Attempt at the Probatio Diabolica' (2004) 5 *Chicago Journal of International Law* 21–37.

Douglas, Michael, 'The Lex Mercatoria and the Culture of Transnational Industry' (2006) 13 *University of Miami International and Comparative Law Review* 367–401.

Durkheim, Emile, *Suicide: A Study in Sociology*, trans. John A. Spaulding and George Simpson (London: Routledge & Kegan Paul, 1970).

Dworkin, Ronald, *Taking Rights Seriously* (Cambridge, MA: Harvard University Press, 1977).

Law's Empire [1986] (Oxford: Hart Publishing, 1998).

'The Arduous Virtue of Fidelity: Originalism, Scalia, Tribe, and Nerve' (1997) 65 *Fordham Law Review* 1249–68.

Economist, 'The case for globalisation', *The Economist*, 23 September 2000 at 17–18.

Edmunds, June and Turner, Bryan S., 'Global Generations: Social Change in the Twentieth Century' (2005) 56 *British Journal of Sociology* 559–78.

Ehrlich, Eugen, *Fundamental Principles of the Sociology of Law*, trans. Walter L. Moll (Cambridge, MA: Harvard University Press, 1936).

Eisenstadt, S. N., 'The Protestant Ethic Thesis in Analytical and Comparative Context', reprinted in Roland Robertson (ed.), *The Sociology of Religion: Selected Readings* (Harmondsworth: Penguin, 1969 reprinted 1972).

Eliot, George, *The Mill on the Floss* [1860] (London: Wm Collins, 1952).

Elton, G.R., *The Tudor Constitution: Documents and Commentary* (Cambridge: Cambridge University Press, 1960).

Reformation Europe 1517–1559 (London: Fontana, 1963).

Reform and Reformation (London: Edward Arnold, 1977).

English Law in the Sixteenth and Seventeenth Century: Reform in an Age of Change (London: Seldon Society, 1979).

'*Lex Terrae Victrix:* The Triumph of Parliamentary Law in the Sixteenth Century', in D. M. Dean and N. L. Jones (eds.), *The Parliaments of Elizabethan England* (Oxford: Basil Blackwell, 1990).

Elwood, Christopher, *The Body Broken: The Calvinist Doctrine of the Eucharist and the Symbolization of Power in Sixteenth-Century France* (New York, Oxford: Oxford University Press, 1999).

Endicott, Timothy A. O., 'The Conscience of the King: Christopher St German and Thomas More and the Development of English Equity' (1989) 47 *University of Toronto Faculty of Law Review* 549–70.

Estella, Antonio, *The EU Principle of Subsidiarity and its Critique* (Oxford: Oxford University Press, 2002).

Estes, James M., 'The Role of Godly Magistrates in the Church: Melanchthon as Luther's Interpreter and Collaborator' (1998) 67 *Church History* 463–83.

Evans, G. R., *Philosophy and Theology in the Middle Ages* (London: Routlege, 1993).

Eyffinger, Arthur, 'Europe in the Balance: An Appraisal of the Westphalian System' (1998) 45 *Netherlands International Law Review* 161–87.

Falk, Richard, 'Re-framing the Legal Agenda of World Order in the Course of a Turbulent Century' in Michael Likosky (ed.), *Transnational Legal Processes* (London: Butterworths, 2002).

Fassberg, Celia Wasserstein, 'Lex Mercatoria – Hoist with its Own Petard' (2004) 5 *Chicago Journal of International Law* 67–82.

Fenn, Richard K., *The Persistence of Purgatory* (Cambridge: Cambridge University Press, 1995).

Feuerbach, Ludwig, *The Essence of Christianity*, trans. George Eliot [1851] (Amherst: Prometheus Books, 1989).

Field, Lester L., *Liberty, Dominion, and the Two Swords: On the Origins of Western Political Theology (180–398)* (Notre Dame: University of Notre Dame Press, 1998).

Finnis, John, *Natural Law and Natural Rights* (Oxford: Clarendon Press, 1980 reprinted 1992).

Aquinas: Moral, Political, and Legal Theory (Oxford: Oxford University Press, 1998).

Fitzpatrick, Peter, *The Mythology of Modern Law* (London: Routledge, 1992).

Ford, Richard T., 'Law's Territory (A History of Jurisdiction)' (1999) 97 *Michigan Law Review* 843–930.

Foucault, Michel, *Power/Knowledge: Selected Interviews and Other Writings (1972–1977)*, ed. and trans. Colin Gordon *et al.* (New York: Pantheon, 1980).

Franck, Thomas M., 'Clan and Superclan: Loyalty, Identity and Community in Law and Practice' (1996) 90 *American Journal of International Law* 359–83.

Franck, Thomas M., *The Empowered Self: Law and Society in the Age of Individualism* (Oxford: Oxford University Press, 1999).

Frank, Thomas, *One Market Under God: Extreme Capitalism, Market Populism and the End of Economic Democracy* (London: Vintage, 2002).

French, Rebecca R., 'Time in the Law' (2001) 72 *University of Colorado Law Review* 663–748.

Freud, Sigmund, *Civilization and its Discontents*, trans. James Strachey (New York: W. W. Norton & Co. Inc., 1961).

Frey, Bruno S., and Eichenberger, Reiner, *The New Democratic Federalism for Europe: Functional, Overlapping and Competing Jurisdictions* (Northampton: Edward Elgar Publishing, 1999).

Friedman, Jonathan, 'Being in the World: Globalization and Localization' in Mike Featherstone (ed.), *Global Culture: Nationalism, Globalization and Modernity* (London: Sage, 1990 reprinted 1996).

Friedman, Lawrence M., 'Borders: On the Emerging Sociology of Transnational Law' (1996) 32 *Stanford Journal of International Law* 65–90.

Friedman, Thomas, *The Lexus and the Olive Tree: Understanding Globalization* (London: HarperCollins Publishers, 2000).

Friedrich, C. J., 'The Ideological and Philosophical Background' in Bernard Schwartz (ed.), *The Code Napoleon and the Common-Law World* (New York: New York University Press, 1956).

Friedrichs, Jörg, 'The Meaning of New Medievalism' (2001) 7 *European Journal of International Relations* 475–502.

Froude, J. A., *The Divorce of Catherine of Aragon: The Story as Told by the Imperial Ambassadors Resident at the Court of Henry VIII* [1891] (New York: Ams Press, 1970).

Fukuyama, Francis, *The End of History and the Last Man* (New York: Simon & Schuster, 1992).

Gajano, Sofia Boesch, 'The Use and Abuse of Miracles in Early Medieval Culture' in Lester K. Little and Barbara H. Rosenwein (eds.), *Debating the Middle Ages: Issues and Readings* (Malden: Blackwell Publishers, 1998).

Galanter, M., 'Law's Elusive Promise: Learning from Bhopal' in Michael Likosky (ed.), *Transnational Legal Processes* (London: Butterworths, 2002).

Galtung, Johan, *The European Community: A Superpower in the Making* (London: George Allen & Unwin, Ltd, 1973).

　Human Rights in Another Key (Cambridge: Polity Press, 1994).

Garet, Ronald R., 'Meaning and Ending' (1987) 96 *Yale Law Journal* 1801–24.

Gates, Bill, with Hemingway, Collins, *Business @ the Speed of Thought: Using a Digital Nervous System* (New York: Warner Books, 1999).

Gathii, James Thuo, 'Commerce, Conquest and Wartime Confiscation' (2006) 31 *Brooklyn Journal of International Law* 709–39.

Gava, John, 'Scholarship and Community' (1994) 16 *Sydney Law Review* 443–72.

Gay, Peter, *Deism: An Anthology* (Princeton: D. van Nostrand Company, Inc., 1968).

　The Enlightenment: An Interpretation/The Rise of Modern Paganism (New York: W. W. Norton & Co., 1966 reprinted 1977).

Gearty, Conor, *Can Human Rights Survive?* (Cambridge: Cambridge University Press, 2006).

Gehler, Michael, 'From Paneurope to the Single Currency: Recent Studies on the History of European Integration' (2006) 15 *Contemporary European History* 273–89.

Gellner, Ernest, *Nationalism* (London: Phoenix, 1998).

Getzler, Joshua, 'Law, History, and the Social Sciences: Intellectual Traditions of Late Ninteteenth- and Early Twentieth-Century Europe' (2003) 6 *Current Legal Issues* 215–63.

Giddens, *The Nation-State and Violence* (Cambridge: Polity Press, 1985).

   The Consequences of Modernity (Stanford: Polity Press, 1990).

   'Risk and Responsibility' (1999) 62 *Modern Law Review* 1–10.

Gilbert, Christopher L., and Vines, David, 'The World Bank: An Overview of Some Major Issues' in Christopher L. Gilbert and R. David Vines, *The World Bank: Structure and Policies* (Cambridge: Cambridge University Press, 2000).

Gilchrist, John, *The Church and Economic Activity in the Middle Ages* (London: Macmillan, 1969).

Gillingham, John, *Coal, Steel and the Rebirth of Europe, 1945–55: The Germans and French from Ruhr Conflict to Economic Community* (Cambridge: Cambridge University Press, 1991).

Glasberg, Ronald, 'The Evolution of the URAM Concept in the Journal: An Analytic Survey of Key Articles' (1996) 19 *Ultimate Reality and Meaning* 69–77.

Gleick, James, *Chaos: Making a New Science* (New York: Penguin, 1987).

Glenn, H. Patrick, 'Law, Revolution and Rights' in Werner Maihofer and Gerhard Sprenger (eds.), *Revolution and Human Rights, Proceedings of the 14th IVR World Congress, Edinburgh, 1989* (Stuttgart: Franz Steiner Verlag, 1990).

   'The Grounding of Codification' (1998) 31 *U.C. Davis Law Review* 765–82.

   'Are Legal Traditions Incommensurable?' (2001) 49 *American Journal of Comparative Law* 133–45.

   'Conflicting Laws in a Common Market? The NAFTA Experiment' (2001) 76 *Chicago–Kent Law Review* 1789–1819.

   'Comparative Law and Legal Practice: On Removing the Borders' (2001) 75 *Tulane Law Review* 977–1002.

   Legal Traditions of the World: Sustainable Diversity in Law (Oxford: Oxford University Press, 2nd edn 2004).

   On Common Laws (Oxford: Oxford University Press, 2005).

   'Transnational Common Laws' (2006) 29 *Fordham International Law Journal* 457–71.

Goldman, Berthold, 'The Applicable Law: General Principles of Law – the *lex mercatoria*' in Julian D. M. Lew (ed.), *Contemporary Problems in International Arbitration* (London: Centre for Commercial Law Studies, Queen Mary College, University of London, 1986).

Goldman, David B., 'Canon Law Origins of Common Law Defamation, the Hunne Whodunit and Western Legal Science: An Historical Challenge for Modern Lawyers' (1996) 2 *Australian Journal of Legal History* 79–94.

   'Historical Aspects of Globalization and Law' in Catherine Dauvergne (ed.), *Jurisprudence for an Interconnected Globe* (Aldershot: Ashgate, 2003).

Goldsmith, Andrew, 'Standing at the Crossroads: Law Schools, Universities, Markets and the Future of Legal Scholarship' in Fiona Cownie, *The Law School – Global Issues, Local Questions* (Aldershot: Ashgate Dartmouth, 1999).

Goldsworthy, Jeffrey, *The Sovereignty of Parliament: History and Philosophy* (Oxford: Clarendon Press, 1999).

Goode, Roy, 'Usage and Custom in Transnational Commercial Law' (1997) 46 *International & Comparative Law Quarterly* 1–36.

'Rule, Practice and Pragmatism in Transnational Commercial Law' (2005) 54 *International & Comparative Law Quarterly* 539–62, 547–8.

Gordley, James, 'Myths of the French Civil Code' (1994) 42 *American Journal of Comparative Law* 459–505.

Gordon, Joy, 'The Concept of Human Rights: The History and Meaning of its Politicization' (1998) 23 *Brooklyn Journal of International Law* 689–791.

Gould, Carol C., and Macleod, Alistair M., 'Democracy and Globalization Special Issue' (2006) 37 *Journal of Social Philosophy* 1–162.

Gowan, Peter, 'Neoliberal Cosmopolitanism' (2001) 11 *New Left Review* 79–93.

Graves, Joseph L. Jr, *The Emperor's New Clothes: Biological Theories of Race at the Millennium* (Piscataway: Rutgers University Press, 2001).

Green, Leslie, 'General Jurisprudence: A 25th Anniversary Essay' (2005) 25 *Oxford Journal of Legal Studies* 565–80.

Greif, Avner, 'On the Political Foundations of the Late Medieval Commercial Revolution: Genoa during the Twelfth and Thirteenth Centuries' (1994) 54 *Journal of Economic History* 271–87.

Gress, David, *From Plato to NATO: The Idea of the West and its Opponents* (New York: The Free Press, 1998).

Grewe, Wilhelm G., *The Epochs of International Law*, trans. Michael Byers (Berlin: Walter de Gruyter, 2000).

Griffiths, John, 'What is Legal Pluralism?' (1986) 24 *Journal of Legal Pluralism and Unofficial Law* 1–55.

Grimm, Dieter, 'Does Europe Need a Constitution?' (1995) 1 *European Law Journal* 282–302.

Gross, Leo, 'The Peace of Westphalia, 1648–1948' (1948) 42 *American Journal of International Law* 20–41.

Gutmann, Amy, 'Undemocratic Education' in Nancy L. Rosenblum (ed.), *Liberalism and the Moral Life* (Cambridge, MA: Harvard University Press, 1989).

Habermas, Jürgen, 'Intolerance and Discrimination' (2003) 1 *International Journal of Constitutional Law* 2–12.

Hadfield, Gillian K., 'Privatizing Commercial Law: Lessons from ICANN' (2002) 6 *Journal of Small and Emerging Business Law* 257–88.

Hall, Jerome, *Foundations of Jurisprudence* (Indianapolis: Bobbs-Merrill Co., 1973).

Hall, Rodney Bruce, and Biersteker, Thomas J. (eds.), *The Emergence of Private Authority in Global Governance* (Cambridge: Cambridge University Press, 2004).

Hanlon, James, *European Community Law* (London: Sweet & Maxwell, 3rd edn 2003).

Hannaford, Ivan, *Race: The History of an Idea* (Washington: The Johns Hopkins University Press, 1996).

Harding, Alan, *Medieval Law and the Foundations of the State* (Oxford: Oxford University Press, 2002).

Hamacher, Werner, 'Guilt History: Benjamin's Fragment "Capitalism as Religion"' (2005) 26 *Cardozo Law Review* 887–920.

Hart, H. L. A., *The Concept of Law* (Oxford: Clarendon Press, 2nd edn 1994).

Hartley, T. C., *The Foundations of European Community Law: An Introduction to the Constitutional and Administrative Law of the European Community* (Oxford: Oxford University Press, 5th edn 2003).

European Union Law in a Global Context (Cambridge: Cambridge University Press, 2004).

Harvard Law Review Association, 'Note: National Sovereignty of Outer Space' (1961) 74 *Harvard Law Review* 1154–75.

Hay, Douglas, 'Moral Economy, Political Economy and Law' in Adrian Randall and Andrew Charlesworth (eds.), *Moral Economy and Popular Unrest: Crowds, Conflict and Authority* (Hampshire: Macmillan Press Ltd, 2000).

Haskins, Charles Homer, *The Renaissance of the Twelfth Century* (Cambridge, MA: Harvard University Press, 1927 reprinted 1993).

Head, Thomas, 'The Development of the Peace of God in Aquitaine (970–1005)' (1999) 74 *Speculum* 656–86.

Hegel, Georg Wilhelm Friedrich, *The Philosophy of Right*, trans. T. M. Knox (Chicago: Encyclopaedia Britannica Inc., 1952 reprinted 1986).

Lectures on the Philosophy of World History, ed. D. Forbes and H. B. Nesbit (New York: Cambridge University Press, 1975).

Held, David, and McGrew, Anthony, *Globalization/Anti-Globalization* (Cambridge: Polity Press, 2002).

Helfer, Laurence R., 'Constitutional Analogies in the International Legal System' (2003) 37 *Loyola of Los Angeles Law Review* 193–237.

Helfer, Laurence R., and Slaughter, Anne-Marie, 'Toward a Theory of Effective Supranational Adjudication' (1997) 107 *Yale Law Journal* 273–391.

Helmholz, R. H., 'Harold Berman's Accomplishment as a Legal Historian' (1993) 42 *Emory Law Review* 475–96.

'Excommunication in Twelfth Century England' (1994–95) 11 *Journal of Law and Religion* 235–53.

'Excommunication and the Angevin Leap Forward' (1995) 7 *Haskins Society Journal* 133–50.

The ius commune *in England: Four Studies* (Oxford: Oxford University Press, 2001).

'Natural Human Rights: The Perspective of the Ius Commune' (2003) 52 *Catholic University Law Review* 301–25.

The Oxford History of the Laws of England, Volume I: The Canon Law and Ecclesiastical Jurisdiction from 597 to the 1640s (Oxford: Oxford University Press, 2004).

'Natural Law and Human Rights in English Law: From Bracton to Blackstone' (2005) 3 *Ave Maria Law Review* 1–22.

Hetata, Sherif, 'Dollarization, Fragmentation and God' in Fredric Jameson and Masao Miyoshi (eds.), *The Cultures of Globalization* (Durham, NC: Duke University Press, 1998).

Higgins, Rosalyn, 'Role of Litigation in Implementing Human Rights' (1999) 5 *Australian Journal of Human Rights* 4–19.

Hinde, Robert A., *Why Gods Persist: A Scientific Approach to Religion* (London: Routledge, 1999).

Hirst, Paul, and Thompson, Grahame, *Globalization in Question: The International Economy and the Possibilities of Governance* (Cambridge: Polity Press, 2nd edn 1999).

Hobbes, Thomas, *Leviathan* [1651] (London: Penguin, reprinted 1985).

Hobsbawm, Eric, 'Introduction: Inventing Traditions' in Eric Hobsbawm and Terence Ranger (eds.), *The Invention of Tradition* (Cambridge: Cambridge University Press, 1983).

  Nations and Nationalism Since 1780: Programme, Myth, Reality (Cambridge: Cambridge University Press, 1990).

Hoffstadt, Brian M., 'Moving the Heavens: Lunar Mining and the "Common Heritage of Mankind" in the Moon Treaty' (1994) 42 *UCLA Law Review* 575–621.

Hondius, Ewoud, 'Towards a European Civil Code. General Introduction' in A. S. Hartkamp *et al.* (eds.), *Towards a European Civil Code* (Dordrecht: Martinus Nijhoff Publishers, 2nd edn 1998).

Hopkins, A. G. (ed.), *Globalization in World History* (New York: W. W. Norton & Company, 2002).

  Global History: Interactions Between the Universal and the Local (Basingstoke: Palgrave Macmillan, 2006).

Horton, Robin, *Patterns of Thought in Africa and the West: Essays on Magic, Religion and Science* (Cambridge: Cambridge University Press, 1995).

Huntington, Samuel, *The Clash of Civilizations and the Remaking of World Order* (New York: Simon & Schuster, 1996).

Husserl, Edmund, *The Crisis of European Sciences and Transcendental Phenomenology*, trans. David Carr (Evanston: Northwestern University Press, 1970).

Ibbetson, David J., 'Common Lawyers and the Law Before the Civil War' (1988) 8 *Oxford Journal of Legal Studies* 142–53.

Huxley, Aldous, *Brave New World* [1932] (Essex: Longman Group UK, 1989).

  Brave New World Revisited (London: Triad Grafton Press, 1983).

Ignatieff, Michael (ed.), *American Exceptionalism and Human Rights* (Princeton: Princeton University Press, 2005).

Iogna-Prat, Dominique, 'The Dead in the Celestial Bookkeeping of the Cluniac Monks Around the Year 1000' in Lester K. Little and Barbara H. Rosenwein (eds.), *Debating the Middle Ages: Issues and Readings* (Malden: Blackwell Publishers, 1998).

Jackson, John H., *The World Trade Organization: Constitution and Jurisprudence* (London: Pinter, 1998).

Jameson, Fredric, 'Notes on Globalization as a Philosophical Issue' in Fredric Jameson and Masao Miyoshi (eds.), *The Cultures of Globalization* (Durham, NC: Duke University Press, 1998).

Jenkins, Iredell, *Social Order and the Limits of Law (A Theoretical Essay)* (Princeton: Princeton University Press, 1980).

Jenkins, Philip, *The Next Christendom: The Coming of Global Christianity* (Oxford: Oxford University Press, 2002).

Jenks, C. Wilfred, *The Common Law of Mankind* (London: Stevens, 1958).

Jenks, Edward, *Law and Politics in the Middle Ages* (London: John Murray, 1898).

  'The Myth of Magna Carta' [1902], reprinted in James C. Holt, *Magna Carta and the Idea of Liberty* (New York: John Wiley & Sons, 1972).

Joerges, Christian, 'Europe a *Großraum?* Shifting Legal Conceptualisations of the Integration Project' in Christian Joerges and Navraj Singh Ghaleigh (eds.), *Darker Legacies of Law in Europe: The Shadow of National Socialism and Fascism over Europe and its Legal Traditions* (Oxford: Hart Publishing, 2003).

  et al. (eds.), *Transnational Governance and Constitutionalism* (Oxford: Hart Publishing, 2004).

'Introduction to the Special Issue: Confronting Memories: European "Bitter Experiences" and the Constitutionalization Process: Constructing Europe in the Shadow of its Pasts' (2005) 6 *German Law Journal* 245–54.

'Working through "Bitter Experiences" Towards Constitutionalisation: A Critique of the Disregard for History in European Constitutional Theory', EUI Working Papers, Law No. 2005/14, European University Institute, 2005.

John Paul II, *Sacrae Disciplinae Legis: Code of Canon Law, Latin–English Edition* (Washington, DC: Canon Law Society of America, 1983).

John of Salisbury, *Policraticus*, trans. Cary J. Nederman (Cambridge: Cambridge University Press, 1990).

Joyner, Christopher C., 'Legal Implications of the Concept of the Common Heritage of Mankind' (1986) 35 *International and Comparative Law Quarterly* 190–9.

Juergensmeyer, Mark, *Terror in the Mind of God: The Global Rise of Religious Violence* (Berkeley: University of California Press, 2003).

Kadens, Emily, 'Order Within Law, Variety Within Custom: The Character of the Medieval Merchant Law' (2004) 5 *Chicago Journal of International Law* 39–65.

Kaelber, Lutz, Book Review (*Protestantism and Capitalism* by Jere Cohen) (2003) 28 *Canadian Journal of Sociology* 575–81.

Kamenka, Eugene, 'Political Nationalism – the Evolution of the Idea' in Eugene Kamenka (ed.), *Nationalism: The Nature and Evolution of an Idea* (Canberra: Australian National University Press, 1973).

Kant, Immanuel, 'Perpetual Peace: A Philosophical Sketch – Appendix 1: On the Disagreement Between Morals and Politics in Relation to Perpetual Peace' in Hans Reiss (ed.), *Kant: Political Writings*, trans. N. B. Nisbet (Cambridge: Cambridge University Press, 1970, 2nd edn 1991).

Kantorowicz, Ernst, *The King's Two Bodies: A Study in Medieval Political Theology* (New Jersey: Princeton University Press, 1957).

Kantorowicz, Hermann, 'Savigny and the Historical School' (1937) 53 *Law Quarterly Review* 326–43.

Katz, David S., and Popkin, Richard H., *Messianic Revolution: Radical Religious Politics to the End of the Second Millennium* (New York: Hill & Wang, 1998).

Kaveh, Moshe, 'Faith and Science in the Third Millennium' in *Eshkolot: Essays in Honour of Rabbi Ronald Lubofsky* (Melbourne: Hybrid Publishers, 2002).

Keiser, Thorsten, 'Europeanization as a Challenge to Legal History' (2005) 6 *German Law Journal* 473–81.

Kelley, Donald R., *The Human Measure: Social Thought in the Western Legal Tradition* (Cambridge, MA: Harvard University Press, 1990).

Kelly, J. M., *A Short History of Western Legal Theory* (Oxford: Oxford University Press, 1992).

Kennedy, Paul, *The Rise and Fall of the Great Powers: Economic Change and Military Conflict from 1500 to 2000* (London: Unwin Hyman, 1988).

Kercher, Bruce, 'Resistance to Law under Autocracy' (1997) 60 *Modern Law Review* 779–97.

Kerruish, Valerie, *Jurisprudence as Ideology* (London: Routledge, 1991).

Kirby, Michael, 'Human Rights and Economic Development' (1996) *Australian International Law Journal* 1–14.

Kirkpatrick, Frank G., *A Moral Ontology for a Theistic Ethic: Gathering the Nations in Love and Justice* (Aldershot: Ashgate, 2003).

Klug, Francesca, *Values for a Godless Age: The Story of the United Kingdom's New Bill of Rights* (London: Penguin Books, 2000).

Knitter, Paul (ed.), *The Myth of Religious Superiority: A Multifaith Exploration* (Maryknoll: Orbis Books, 2005).

Knowles, David, *The Evolution of Medieval Thought*, 2nd edn by D. E. Luscombe and C. N. L. Brooke (London: Longman, 1988).

Kobler, Franz, *Napoleon and the Jews* (New York: Schoken Press, 1976).

Koopmans, Thijmen, 'The Birth of European Law at the Crossroads of Legal Traditions' (1991) 39 *American Journal of Comparative Law* 493–507.

Korsgaard, Christine, 'Prologue: Excellence and Obligation: A *Very* Concise History of Western Metaphysics 387 BC to 1887 AD' in Christine Korsgaard (ed.), *The Sources of Normativity* (Cambridge: Cambridge University Press, 1996).

Koskenniemi, Martti, *The Gentle Civilizer of Nations: The Rise and Fall of International Law 1870–1960* (Cambridge: Cambridge University Press, 2001).

Kostakopoulou, Dora, 'Ideas, Norms and European Citizenship: Explaining Institutional Change' (2005) 68 *Modern Law Review* 233–67.

Kötz, Hein, *European Contract Law Volume One: Formation, Validity, and Content of Contracts; Contract and Third Parties*, trans. Tony Weir (New York: Clarendon Press, 1997).

Krodel, Gottfried G., 'Review Essay: The Opposition to Roman Law and the Reformation in Germany' (1993/4) 10 *Journal of Law and Religion* 221–66.

Krugman, Paul R., *Pop Internationalism* (Cambridge, MA: MIT Press, 1996).

Krygier, Martin, 'Law as Tradition' (1986) 5 *Law and Philosophy* 137–62.
   'The Traditionality of Statutes' (1988) 1 *Ratio Juris* 20–39.

Kunz, Josef L., 'Pluralism of Legal and Value Systems and International Law' (1955) 49 *American Journal of International Law* 370–6.

Ladeur, Karl-Heinz, 'Globalization and the Conversion of Democracy to Polycentric Networks: Can Democracy Survive the End of the Nation State' in Karl-Heinz Ladeur (ed.), *Public Governance in the Age of Globalization* (Aldershot: Ashgate, 2004).

Landes, Richard, 'The Fear of an Apocalyptic Year 1000: Augustinian Historiography, Medieval and Modern' (2000) 75 *Speculum* 97–145.

Lando, Ole, and Beale, Hugh (eds.), *Principles of European Contract Law – Part I: Performance, Non-performance and Remedies* (Dordrecht: Martinus Nijhoff Publishers, 1995).

Larat, Fabrice, 'Presenting the Past: Political Narratives on European History and the Justification of EU Integration' (2005) 6 *German Law Journal* 274–90.

Lauterpacht, Hersch, *International Law and Human Rights* (London: Stevens & Sons, 1950).
   'The Grotian Tradition in International Law' in R. Falk, F. Krathochwil and S. Mendlovitz (eds.), *International Law: A Contemporary Perspective* (Boulder: Westview Press, 1985).

Lechner, Frank, and Boli, John (eds.), *The Globalization Reader* (Oxford: Blackwell Publishers, 2nd edn 2004).

Lefebvre, Georges, *The Coming of the French Revolution* (Princeton: Princeton University Press, 1967).

Le Goff, Jacques, *Time, Work & Culture in the Middle Ages*, trans. Arthur Goldhammer (Chicago: University of Chicago Press, 1980).

Intellectuals in the Middle Ages, trans. Teresa Lavender Fagan (Cambridge, MA: Blackwell,1993).

The Birth of Europe, trans. Janet Lloyd (Oxford: Blackwell Publishing, 2005).

Legrand, Pierre, 'Against a European Civil Code' (1997) 60 *Modern Law Review* 44–63.

Lenaerts, Koen, 'Some Reflections on the Separation of Powers in the European Community' (1991) 28 *Common Market Law Review* 11–35.

Levack, Brian, *The Civil Lawyers in England 1603–1641* (Oxford: Clarendon Press, 1973).

Lewis, C. S., *The Discarded Image: An Introduction to Medieval and Renaissance Literature* (Cambridge: Cambridge University Press, 1964 reprinted 1994).

Libesman, Heidi, 'Between Modernity and Postmodernity' (2004) 16 *Yale Journal of Law and the Humanities* 413–23.

Likosky, M. B., 'Cultural Imperialism in the Context of Transnational Commercial Collaboration' in Michael Likosky (ed.), *Transnational Legal Processes* (London: Butterworths, 2002).

Lieberman, David, *The Province of Legislation Determined: Legal Theory in Eighteenth-century Britain* (Cambridge: Cambridge University Press, 1989).

Lindseth, Peter L., 'The Contradictions of Supranationalism: Administrative Governance and Constitutionalization in European Integration since the 1950s' (2003) 37 *Loyola LA Law Review* 363–406.

Locke, John, *Two Treatises of Government* [1689] (London: Everyman, 1993 reprinted 1998).

'A Letter Concerning Toleration' in Ian Shapiro (ed.), *Two Treatises of Government and a Letter Concerning Toleration* (New Haven: Yale University Press, 2003).

López-Rodriguez, Ana M., 'Towards a European Civil Code Without a Common European Legal Culture? The Link Between Law, Language and Culture' (2004) 29 *Brooklyn Journal of International Law* 1195–220.

Luhmann, Niklas, *Law as a Social System*, trans. K. A. Ziegert (Oxford: Oxford University Press, 2004).

Lupoi, Maurizio, *The Origins of the European Legal Order*, trans. Adrian Belton (Cambridge: Cambridge University Press, 2000).

Macaulay, Stewart, 'Non-Contractual Relations in Business: A Preliminary Study' (1963) 28 *American Sociological Review* 55–67.

MacCormick, Neil, 'Beyond the Sovereign State' (1993) 56 *Modern Law Review* 1–18.

Questioning Sovereignty: Law, State, and Nation in the European Commonwealth (Oxford: Oxford University Press, 1999).

Machiavelli, Niccolò, *The Prince*, trans. N. H. Thompson (Toronto: Dover Publications, Inc., 1992).

MacIntyre, Alasdair, *After Virtue: A Study in Moral Theory* (London: Duckworth, 1981 2nd edn 1996).

MacQueen, Hector L. *et al.*, 'Introduction' in Hector L. MacQueen *et al.* (eds.), *Regional Private Laws and Codification in Europe* (Cambridge: Cambridge University Press, 2003).

Maddox, Graham, 'The Secular Reformation and the Influence of Machiavelli' (2002) 82 *Journal of Religion* 539–62.

Mahant, Edelgard, *Birthmarks of Europe: The Origins of the European Community Reconsidered* (Aldershot: Ashgate, 2004).

Maine, Sir Henry Sumner, *Ancient Law: Its Connection with the Early History of Society and its Relation to Modern Ideas* [1861] (reprinted Dorset Press, 1986).

Maitland, Frederic William, 'English Law and the Renaissance' in *Select Essays in Anglo-American Legal History*, 3 vols. (London: Wildy & Sons, 1968), vol. I.

Makdisi, Joh A., 'The Islamic Origins of the Common Law' (1999) 77 *North Carolina Law Review* 1635–739.

Mann, Simon, 'Whites a Minority by End of Century', *Sydney Morning Herald* 4 September 2000.

Maniruzzaman, Abdul F. M., 'The Lex Mercatoria and International Contracts: A Challenge for International Commercial Arbitration?' (1999) 14 *American University International Law Review* 657–734.

Marius, Richard, *Thomas More* (London: Wiedenfeld, 1993).

Marty, Martin E., *When Faiths Collide* (Malden: Blackwell Publishing, 2005).

Marx, *The Communist Manifesto* (Harmondsworth: Penguin, 1967).

Mason, Edward S., and Asher, Robert E., *The World Bank Since Bretton Woods* (Washington, DC: The Brookings Institute, 1973).

Mason, Keith, *Constancy and Change: Moral and Religious Values in the Australian Legal System* (Leichhardt: Federation Press, 1990).

Mattei, Ugo, 'The Issue of European Civil Codification and Legal Scholarship: Biases, Strategies and Developments' (1998) 21 *Hastings International & Comparative Law Review* 883–902.

Mautner, Thomas, 'Grotius and the Skeptics' (2005) 66 *Journal of the History of Ideas* 577–601.

May, Larry, *Crimes Against Humanity: A Normative Account* (Cambridge: Cambridge University Press, 2005).

Mayer, Franz C., and Palmowski, Jan, 'European Identities and the EU – the Ties that Bind the Peoples of Europe' (2004) 42 *Journal of Common Market Studies* 573–98.

Mayer, Thomas F., 'Starkey and Melanchthon on Adiaphora: A Critique of W. Gordon Zeeveld' (1980) 11 *Sixteenth Century Journal* 39–49.

Mazlish, Bruce, 'A Tour of Globalization' (1999) 7 *Indiana Journal of Global Legal Studies* 5–16.

Mazlish, Bruce, and Iriye, Akira (eds.), *The Global History Reader* (New York: Routlege, 2005).

McBarnet, D., 'Transnational Transactions: Legal Work, Cross-border Commerce and Global Regulation' in Michael Likosky (ed.), *Transnational Legal Processes* (London: Butterworths, 2002).

McRae, Donald, 'Trade and the Environment: Competition, Cooperation or Confusion?' (2003) 41 *Alberta Law Review* 745–60.

McCrudden, Christopher, 'International Economic Law and the Pursuit of Human Rights: A Framework for Discussion of the Legality of "Selective Purchasing" Laws Under the WTO Government Procurement Agreement' (1999) 2 *Journal of International Economic Law* 3–48.

Meidinger, Errol E., 'Environmental Certification Systems and US Law: Closer Than You May Think' (2001) 31 *Environmental Law Reporter* 10162–79.

Melzer, Sara E., and Rabine, Leslie W. (eds.), *Rebel Daughters: Women and the French Revolution* (New York: Oxford University Press, 1992).

Mennell, Stephen, 'The Globalization of Human Society as a Very Long-term Social Process: Elias's Theory' in Mike Featherstone (ed.), *Global Culture: Nationalism, Globalization and Modernity* (London: Sage, 1990 reprinted 1996).

Merrills, J. G., and Robertson, A. H., *Human Rights in Europe* (Manchester: Manchester University Press, 4th edn 2001).

Merry, Sally Engle, 'Legal Pluralism' (1988) 22 *Law & Society Review* 869–96.

Mertens, Hans-Joachim, '*Lex Mercatoria*: A Self-applying System Beyond National Law?' in Gunther Teubner (ed.), *Global Law Without a State* (Brookfield: Dartmouth Publishing Company Limited, 1997).

Meyer, John W. *et al.*, 'World Society and the Nation-State' in Frank Lechner and John Boli (eds.), *The Globalization Reader* (Oxford: Blackwell Publishers, 2nd edn 2004).

Mikesell, Raymond F., *The Bretton Woods Debates: A Memoir* (Princeton: International Finance Section, Department of Economics, Princeton University, 1994).

Mill, John Stuart, *On Liberty* (1859) (Harmondsworth: Penguin, 1985).

Miller, David, 'Crooked Timber or Bent Twig? Isaiah Berlin's Nationalism' (2005) 53 *Political Studies* 100–23.

Mills, Alex, 'The Private History of International Law' (2006) 55 *International and Comparative Law Quarterly* 1–49.

Mommsen, Theodor, and Krueger, Paul (eds.), *The Digest of Justinian*, trans. Alan Watson (Philadelphia: University of Pennsylvania Press, 1985), vol. I.

Monateri, P. G., 'Black Gaius: A Quest for the Multicultural Origins of the "Western Legal Tradition"' (2000) 51 *Hastings Law Journal* 479–555.

Montesquieu, *Persian Letters*, trans. C. J. Betts [1721] (London: Penguin, 1973 reprinted 1993).

    The Spirit of the Laws, trans. A. Cohler, B. Miller and H. Stone [1750] (Cambridge: Cambridge University Press, 1989).

Moore, Michael E. Hoenicke, 'Demons and the Battle for Souls at Cluny' (2003) 32 *Studies in Religion/Sciences Religieuses* 485–98.

Moore, R. I., *The First European Revolution: 970–1215* (Oxford: Blackwell, 2000).

Morant, Blake D., 'Lessons from Thomas More's Dilemma of Conscience: Reconciling the Clash Between a Lawyer's Beliefs and Professional Expectations' (2004) 78 *Saint John's Law Review* 965–1009.

Mortensen, Reid, 'The Theory Behind Secularisation' (1993) 18 *Bulletin of the Australasian Society of Legal Philosophy* 19–42.

Muchlinski, Peter T., '"Global Bukowina" Examined: Viewing the Multinational Enterprise as a Transnational Law-making Community' in Gunther Teubner (ed.), *Global Law Without a State* (Brookfield: Dartmouth Publishing Company, 1997).

Muldoon, James, *Popes, Lawyers, and Infidels* (Philadelphia: University of Pennsylvania Press, 1979).

    Empire and Order: The Concept of Empire, 800–1800 (New York: St Martin's Press, Inc., 1999).

    'Who Owns the Sea?' in Bernhard Klein (ed.), *Fictions of the Sea: Critical Perspectives on the Ocean in British Literature and Culture* (Aldershot: Ashgate, 2002).

Müller-Graff, Peter-Christian, 'Private Law Unification by Means other than of Codification' in A. S. Hartkamp *et al.* (eds.), *Towards a European Civil Code* (Dordrecht: Martinus Nijhoff Publishers, 2nd edn 1998).

Murillo, Maria Luisa, 'The Evolution of Codification in the Civil Law Legal Systems: Towards Decodification and Recodification' (2001) 11 *Journal of Transnational Law and Policy* 163–82.

Murphy, Cornelius F. Jr, 'The Grotian Vision of World Order' (1982) 76 *American Journal of International Law* 477–98.

Mustill, Michael J., 'The New Lex Mercatoria: The First 25 Years' (1988) 4 *Arbitration International* 86–119.

Nafziger, James A. R., 'The Functions of Religion in the International Legal System' in Mark W. Janis and Carolyn Evans (eds.), *Religion and International Law* (The Hague: Kluwer Law International, 1999).

Nederman, Cary J., 'Private Will, Public Justice: Household, Community and Consent in Marsiglio of Padua's *Defensor Pacis*' (1990) 43 *Western Political Science Quarterly* 699–717.

   'Empire and the Historiography of European Political Thought: Marsiglio of Padua, Nicholas of Cusa, and the Medieval/Modern Divide' (2005) 66 *Journal of the History of Ideas* 1–15.

Nelson, Benjamin N., *The Idea of Usury: From Tribal Brotherhood to Universal Otherhood* (Princeton: Princeton University Press, 1949).

Netanel, Neil Weinstock, 'Cyberspace Self-Governance: A Skeptical View from Democratic Theory' (2000) 88 *California Law Review* 395–498.

Neufeld, H., *The International Protection of Private Creditors from the Treaties of Westphalia to the Congress of Vienna (1648–1815): A Contribution to the History of the Law of Nations* (Leiden: A. W. Sijthoff, 1991).

Nicholas, Barry, *An Introduction to Roman Law* (Oxford: Clarendon Press, 1991).

Nicholls, Alex, and Opal, Charlotte, *Fair Trade: Market-driven Ethical Consumption* (London: Sage, 2005).

Nietzsche, Friedrich, *Thus Spoke Zarathustra: A Book for None and All*, trans. Walter Kaufman (Harmondsworth: Penguin Books, 1978).

NSW Young Lawyers, *Debrief* (February 2002).

Nussbaum, Arthur, *A Concise History of the Law of Nations* (New York: The Macmillan Company, 1947).

Nussbaum, Martha C., 'Kant and Cosmopolitanism' in James Bohman and Matthias Lutz-Bachmann, *Perpetual Peace: Essays on Kant's Cosmopolitan Ideal* (Cambridge, MA: MIT Press, 1997).

   Women and Human Development: The Capabilities Approach (Cambridge: Cambridge University Press, 2000).

   Upheavals of Thought: The Intelligence of Emotions (Cambridge: Cambridge University Press, 2001).

O'Brien, Patrick, 'Historiographical Traditions and Modern Imperatives for the Restoration of Global History' (2006) 1 *Journal of Global History* 3–39.

O'Donovan, Joan Lockwood, *Theology of Law and Authority in the English Reformation* (Atlanta: Scholars Press, 1991).

O'Rourke, Kevin, and Williamson, Jeffrey, 'After Columbus: Explaining the Global Trade Boom, 1500–1800' (March 2001) NBER Working Paper No. W8186.

Ostwald, Martin, *From Popular Sovereignty to the Sovereignty of Law: Law, Society and Politics in Fifth-century Athens* (Berkeley: University of California Press, 1986).

Pagden, Anthony, *Lords of All the World: Ideologies of Empire in Spain, Britain and France c.1500–c.1800* (New Haven: Yale University Press, 1995).

Pahl, Ray, 'Are all Communities Communities in the Mind?' (2005) *The Sociological Review* 621–40.

Parekh, Bikhu, and Berki, R. N. (eds.), *The Morality of Politics* (London: George Allen & Unwin Ltd, 1972).

Parker, Christine, and Goldsmith, Andrew, ' "Failed Sociologists" in the Market Place: Law Schools in Australia' (1998) 25 *Journal of Law & Society* 33–70.

Peet, Richard, *Unholy Trinity: The IMF, World Bank, and WTO* (London: Zed Books, 2003).

Pelikan, Jaroslav, *The Vindication of Tradition: The 1983 Jefferson Lecture in the Humanities* (New Haven: Yale University Press, 1984).

Pennington, K., 'Law, Legislative Authority, and Theories of Government, 1150–1300' in J. H. Burns (ed.), *The Cambridge History of Medieval Political Thought c.350–1450* (Cambridge: Cambridge University Press, 1988).

   The Prince and the Law, 1200–1600: Sovereignty and Rights in the Western Legal Tradition (Berkeley: University of California Press, 1993).

Perry, Michael J., 'Are Human Rights Universal? The Relativist Challenge and Related Matters' (1997) 19 *Human Rights Quarterly* 461–509.

Pescatore, Pierre, 'The Doctrine of "Direct Effect": An Infant Disease of Community Law' (1983) 8 *European Law Review* 155–77.

Petersmann, Ernst-Ulrich, 'Human Rights, Constitutionalism and the World Trade Organization: Challenges for World Trade Organization Jurisprudence and Civil Society' (2006) 19 *Leiden Journal of International Law* 633–67.

Peterson, Daniel J., 'Speaking of God after the Death of God' (2005) 44 *Dialog: A Journal of Theology* 207–26,

Plamenatz, John, 'Two Types of Nationalism' in Eugene Kamenka (ed.), *Nationalism: The Nature and Evolution of an Idea* (Canberra: Australian National University Press, 1973).

Plato, *Theaetetus*, in B. Jowett (ed. and trans.), *The Dialogues of Plato*, 5 vols. (Oxford: Oxford University Press, 1892), vol. IV.

Plucknett, T. F. T., *A Concise History of the Common Law* (London: Butterworths, 1956).

Pocock, J. G. A., *Virtue, Commerce, and History: Essays on Political Thought and History, Chiefly in the Eighteenth Century* (Cambridge: Cambridge University Press, 1985).

   The Machiavellian Moment: Florentine Political Thought and the Republican Tradition (Princeton: Princeton University Press, 2nd edn 2003).

Pogge, Thomas, *World Poverty and Human Rights: Cosmopolitan Responsibilities and Reforms* (Cambridge: Polity, 2002).

Poggi, Gianfranco, *The State: Its Nature, Development and Prospects* (Stanford: Stanford University Press, 1990).

Pojman, Louis P., 'Kant's Perpetual Peace and Cosmopolitanism' (2005) 36 *Journal of Social Philosophy* 62–71.

Polanyi, Karl, *The Great Transformation* (Boston, MA: Beacon Press, 1944).

Polybius, *The Rise of the Roman Empire*, trans. Ian Scott Kilvert (Harmondsworth: Penguin, 1979).

Popovski, Vesselin, 'The International Criminal Court: A Synthesis of Retributive and Restorative Justice' (2000) 25 *International Relations* 1–10.

Posner, Richard, *Law and Legal Theory in England and America* (Oxford: Clarendon Press, 1996).

Post, Gaines, *Studies in Medieval Legal Thought: Public Law and the State 1100–1322* (Princeton: Princeton University Press, 1964).

Pound, Roscoe, *Introduction to the Philosophy of Law* (New Haven: Yale University Press, 1954).

Prest, Wilfred, *The Inns of Court Under Elizabeth I and the Early Stuarts 1590–1640* (London: Longman, 1972).

Pryles, Michael, 'Application of the *Lex Mercatoria* in International Commercial Arbitration' (2004) 78 *Australian Law Journal* 396–416.

Purdy, Jebediah, 'The New Liberal Imperialism: Assessing the Arguments' in Christian Barry and Thomas W. Pogge (eds.), *Global Institutions and Responsibilities: Achieving Global Justice* (Malden: Blackwell Publishing, 2005).

Pureza, José Manuel, 'Defensive and Oppositional Counter-Hegemonic Uses of International Law: From the International Criminal Court to the Common Heritage of Mankind' in Santos and Rodríguez-Garavito (eds.), *Law and Globalization from Below: Towards a Cosmopolitan Legality* (Cambridge: Cambridge University Press, 2005).

Rajagopal, Balakrishnan, *International Law from Below: Development, Social Movements and Third World Resistance* (Cambridge: Cambridge University Press, 2003).

Rana, Harminderpal Singh, 'The "Common Heritage of Mankind" & the Final Frontier: A Revaluation of Values Constituting The International Legal Regime for Outer Space Activities' (1994) 26 *Rutgers Law Journal* 225–50.

Rawls, John, 'Justice as Fairness: Political not Metaphysical' (1985) 14 *Philosophy and Public Affairs* 223–51.

    Political Liberalism (New York: Columbia University Press, 1996).

    The Law of Peoples with 'The Idea of Public Reason Revisited' (Cambridge, MA: Harvard University Press, 2001).

Raz, Joseph, *The Authority of Law: Essays on Law and Morality* (Oxford: Clarendon Press, 1979).

    Value, Respect and Attachment (Cambridge: Cambridge University Press, 2001).

Re, Edward D., 'The Roman Contribution to the Common Law' (1993) 39 *Loyola Law Review* 295–311.

Reed, C. M., *Maritime Traders in the Ancient Greek World* (Cambridge: Cambridge University Press, 2003).

Reid, Charles J. Jr, 'The Medieval Origins of the Western Natural Rights Tradition: The Achievement of Brian Tierney' (1998) 83 *Cornell Law Review* 437–63.

Reid, Charles J. Jr, and Witte, John Jr, 'In the Steps of Gratian: Writing the History of Canon Law in the 1990s' (1999) 48 *Emory Law Journal* 647–88.

Reynolds, Susan, *Kingdoms and Communities in Western Europe, 900–1300* (Oxford: Clarendon Press, 2nd edn 1997).

Risse, Mathias, 'How Does the Global Order Harm the Poor?' (2005) 33 *Philosophy & Public Affairs* 349–76.

Robbins, Sara (ed.), *Law: A Treasury of Art and Literature* (New York: Hugh Levin, 1990).

Robé, Jean-Philippe, 'Multinational Enterprises: The Constitution of a Pluralistic Legal Order' in Gunther Teubner (ed.), *Global Law Without a State* (Brookfield: Dartmouth Publishing Company Limited, 1997).

Roberts, Simon, 'After Government? On Representing Law Without the State' (2005) 68 *Modern Law Review* 1–24.

Robertson, Geoffrey, *Crimes Against Humanity: The Struggle for Global Justice* (London: Allen Lane, 1999).

Robertson, H. R., *Aspects of the Rise of Economic Individualism: A Criticism of Max Weber and his School* (Cambridge: Cambridge University Press, 1933).

Robertson, Roland, 'Mapping the Global Condition: Globalization as the Central Concept' in Mike Featherstone (ed.), *Global Culture: Nationalism, Globalization and Modernity* (London: Sage, 1990 reprinted 1996).

　Globalization: Social Theory and Global Culture (London: Sage Publications, 1992 reprinted 1998).

Robinson, O. F., Fergus, T. D., and Gordon, W. M., *European Legal History* (London: Butterworths, 1994).

Rodríguez-Garavito, César A., 'Nike's Law' in Santos and Rodríguez-Garavito (eds.), *Law and Globalization from Below: Towards a Cosmopolitan Legality* (Cambridge: Cambridge University Press, 2005).

Rosa, Jean-Jacques, 'The Competitive State and the Industrial Organization of Nations' in Karl-Heinz Ladeur (ed.), *Public Governance in the Age of Globalization* (Aldershot: Ashgate, 2004).

Rosen, Mark D., 'Do Codification and Private International Law Leave Room for a New Law Merchant?' (2004) 5 *Chicago Journal of International Law* 83–90.

Rosenau, James N., 'Strong Demand, Huge Supply: Governance in an Emerging Epoch' in Ian Bache and Matthew Flinders (eds.), *Multi-level Governance* (Oxford: Oxford University Press, 2004).

Rosenblum, Nancy L., 'Introduction' in Nancy L. Rosenblum (ed.), *Liberalism and the Moral Life* (Cambridge, MA: Harvard University Press, 1989).

Rosenstock-Huessy, Eugen, *Out of Revolution: Autobiography of Western Man* [1938] (Providence and Oxford: Berg, 1993).

　The Christian Future, or, The Modern Mind Outrun [1946] (New York: Harper Torch, 1966).

　Speech and Reality (Norwich: Argo Books Inc., 1970).

　Practical Knowledge of the Soul, trans. Mark Huessy and Freya von Moltke (Norwich: Argo Books, 1988).

Ross, George, 'European Integration and Globalization' in Roland Axtmann (ed.), *Globalization and Europe: Theoretical and Empirical Investigations* (London: Pinter, 1998).

Rossum, Madeleine van, 'Defects of Consent and Capacity in Contract Law' in A. S. Hartkamp *et al.* (eds.), *Towards a European Civil Code* (Dordrecht: Martinus Nijhoff Publishers, 1st edn 1994).

Rost, H. T. D., *The Golden Rule: A Universal Ethic* (Welwyn: George Ronald, 1986).

Roshwald, Aviel, *The Endurance of Nationalism: Ancient Roots and Modern Dilemmas* (New York: Cambridge University Press, 2006).

Rousseau, Jean-Jacques, *Émile or Treatise on Education*, trans. William H. Payne [1762] (Amherst: Prometheus Books, 2003).

　'The Social Contract' in *The Social Contract and Discourses*, trans. G. H. Cole [1762] (London: Everyman, reprinted 1998).

Ruddy, Francis Stephen, *International Law in the Enlightenment: The Background of Emmerich de Vattel's* Le Droit des Gens (New York: Oceana Publications, 1975).

Sachs, Jeffrey, *The End of Poverty: How We Can Make it Happen in Our Lifetime* (London: Penguin, 2005).

Sachs, Stephen E., 'From St Ives to Cyberspace: The Modern Distortion of the Medieval "Law Merchant"' (2006) 21 *American University International Law Review* 685–812.

Samuelsson, Kurt, *Religion and Economic Action: The Protestant Ethic, the Rise of Capitalism, and the Abuses of Scholarship*, trans. E. Geoffrey French [1957] (Toronto: University of Toronto Press, 1993).

Sands, Philippe, *Lawless World: America and the Making and Breaking of Global Rules from FDR's Atlantic Charter to George W. Bush's Illegal War* (New York: Viking, 2005).

Santos, Boaventura de Sousa, *Toward a New Common Sense: Law, Science and Politics in the Paradigmatic Transition* (New York: Routledge, 1995).

  Toward a New Legal Common Sense: Law, Globalization and Emancipation (London: Butterworths, 2nd edn 2002).

  'Beyond Neoliberal Governance: The World Social Forum as Subaltern Cosmopolitan Politics and Legality' in Boaventura de Sousa Santos and César A. Rodríguez-Garavito (eds.), *Law and Globalization from Below: Towards a Cosmopolitan Legality* (Cambridge: Cambridge University Press, 2005).

Santos, Boaventura de Sousa, and Rodríguez-Garavito, César A., 'Law, Politics, and the Subaltern in Counter-Hegemonic Globalization' in Santos and Rodríguez-Garavito (eds.), *Law and Globalization from Below: Towards a Cosmopolitan Legality* (Cambridge: Cambridge University Press, 2005).

Sassen, Saskia, *Losing Control: Sovereignty in an Age of Globalization* (New York: Columbia University Press, 1996).

Saul, John Ralston, *The Collapse of Globalism and the Reinvention of the World* (Camberwell: Penguin Viking, 2005).

Savigny, Friedrich Karl von, *Of the Vocation of Our Age for Legislation and Jurisprudence* (1831), trans. Abraham Hayward (reprinted New York: Arno Press, 1975).

Scarisbrick, J. J., *Henry VIII* (London: Methuen, 1976).

Schabas, William A., *The UN International Criminal Tribunals: The Former Yugoslavia, Rwanda and Sierra Leone* (Cambridge: Cambridge University Press, 2006).

Schäfer, Michael, 'Memory in the Construction of Constitutions' (2002) 15 *Ratio Juris* 403–17.

Schiltz, Patrick J., 'On Being a Happy, Healthy and Ethical Member of an Unhappy, Unhealthy, and Unethical Profession' (1999) 52 *Vanderbilt Law Review* 871–951.

Schmitt, Carl, *The Political Theology of Sovereignty*, trans. George Schwab (Cambridge, MA: MIT Press, 1985).

Schmitt, Hans A., *The Path to European Union* (Baton Rouge: Louisiana State University Press, 1962).

Schmitthoff, Clive M., 'Finality of Arbitral Awards and Judicial Review' in Julian D. M. Lew (ed.), *Contemporary Problems in International Arbitration* (London: Centre for Commercial Law Studies, Queen Mary College, University of London, 1986).

Schofield, Philip, 'Jeremy Bentham: Legislator of the World' (1998) 51 *Current Legal Problems* 115–47.

Schulz, Fritz, *A History of Roman Legal Science* (London: Oxford University Press, 1967).

Schweiker, William, *Theological Ethics and Global Dynamics, in the Time of Many Worlds* (Malden: Blackwell Publishing Ltd, 2004).

Seipp, David J., 'The Reception of Canon Law and Civil Law in English Common Law Courts Before 1600' (1993) 13 *Oxford Journal of Legal Studies* 388–420.

Seita, Alex Y., 'Globalization and the Convergence of Values' (1997) 30 *Cornell International Law Journal* 429–91.

Sempasa, Sampson L., 'Obstacles to International Commercial Arbitration in African Countries' (1992) 41 *International & Comparative Law Quarterly* 387–413.

Sen, Amartya, *Development as Freedom* (Oxford: Oxford University Press, 1999).
  'Elements of a Theory of Human Rights' (2004) 32 *Philosophy & Public Affairs* 315–56.
  Identity and Violence: The Illusion of Destiny (New York: W. W. Norton & Co., 2006).

Shalakany, Amr A. 'Arbitration and the Third World: A Plea for Reassessing Bias Under the Specter of Neoliberalism' (2000) 41 *Harvard International Law Journal* 419–68.

Shamir, Ronen, 'Corporate Social Responsibility: A Case of Hegemony and Counter-Hegemony' in Boaventura de Sousa Santos and César A. Rodríguez-Garavito (eds.), *Law and Globalization from Below: Towards a Cosmopolitan Legality* (Cambridge: Cambridge University Press, 2005).

Shany, Yuval, *The Competing Jurisdictions of International Courts and Tribunals* (Oxford: Oxford University Press, 2003).

Sherry, Michael, 'Dead or Alive: American Vengeance Goes Global' (2005) 31 *Review of International Studies* 245–63.

Shore, Chris, *Building Europe: The Cultural Politics of European Integration* (London: Routledge, 2000).

Sieberson, Stephen S., 'The Proposed European Union Constitution: Will It Eliminate the EU's Democratic Deficit?' (2004) 10 *Columbia Journal of European Law* 173–264.

Sièyes, Abbé, 'What is the Third Estate?' in J. H. Stewart (ed.), *A Documentary Survey of the French Revolution* (New York: Macmillan, 1951).

Simpson, A. W. B., *Legal Theory and Legal History: Essays on the Common Law* (London: The Hambledon Press, 1987).

Singer, Peter, *One World: The Ethics of Globalisation* (Melbourne: Text Publishing, 2nd edn 2004).

Singer, P. W., 'War, Profits, and the Vacuum of Law: Privatized Military Firms and International Law' (2004) 42 *Columbia Journal of Transnational Law* 521–49.

Skidelsky, Edward, 'A Liberal Tragedy' *Prospect* (January 2002), 14–15.

Skinner, Quentin, *The Foundations of Modern Political Thought*, 2 vols. (Cambridge: Cambridge University Press, 1978).
  'Introduction: The Return of Grand Theory' in Quentin Skinner (ed.), *The Return of Grand Theory in the Human Sciences* (Cambridge: Cambridge University Press, 1985 reprinted 1997).

Skotnicki, Andrew, 'God's Prisoners: Penal Confinement and the Creation of Purgatory' (2006) 22 *Modern Theology* 85–110.

Slattery, Brian, 'Rights, Communities, and Tradition' (1991) 41 *University of Toronto Law Journal* 447–67.
  'The Paradoxes of National Self-Determination' (1994) 32 *Osgoode Hall Law Journal* 703–33.

Slaughter, Anne-Marie, 'Global Government Networks, Global Information Agencies, and Disaggregated Democracy' (2003) 24 *Michigan Journal of International Law* 1041–75.
  A New World Order (Princeton: Princeton University Press, 2004).

Smart, Ninian, *The World's Religions* (Cambridge: Cambridge University Press, 1989).

Smith, Adam, *An Inquiry into the Nature and Causes of the Wealth of Nations* (Oxford: Clarendon Press, 1976).

Smith, Anthony D., 'Towards a Global Culture?' in Mike Featherstone (ed.), *Global Culture: Nationalism, Globalization and Modernity* (London: Sage, 1990 reprinted 1996).

Smits, Jan, *The Making of European Private Law: Towards a Ius Commune Europaeum as a Mixed Legal System* (Antwerp: Intersentia, 2002).

Snyder, David V., 'Private Lawmaking' (2003) 64 *Ohio State Law Journal* 371–449.

Snyder, Francis, 'Governing Globalisation' in Michael Likosky (ed.), *Transnational Legal Processes* (London: Butterworths, 2002).

Somek, Alexander, 'On Supranationality' (2001) 5 *European Integration online Papers* no. 3 http://eiop.or.at/eiop.

   'Constitutional *Erinnerungsarbeit*: Ambivalence and Translation' (2005) 6 *German Law Journal* 357–70.

Sornarajah, M., 'The UNCITRAL Model Law: A Third World Viewpoint' (1989) 6 *Journal of International Arbitration* 7–20.

Southern, R. W., *The Making of the Middle Ages* (New Haven: Yale University Press, 1953).

Spigelman, James J., *Becket and Henry: The Becket Lectures* (Sydney: St Thomas More Society, 2004).

Spruyt, Hendrik, *The Sovereign State and its Competitors: An Analysis of Systems Change* (Princeton: Princeton University Press, 1994).

Stahmer, Harold, 'Introduction' in Eugen Rosenstock–Huessy, *The Christian Future; or, The Modern Mind Outrun* (New York: Harper Torch, 1966).

Stanojevic, Obrad, 'Roman Law and Common Law – A Different View' (1990) 36 *Loyola Law Review* 269–74.

Stark, Barbara, 'Women, Globalization, and Law: A Change of World' (2004) 16 *Pace International Law Review* 333–63.

Stark, Rodney, *The Victory of Reason: How Christianity Led to Freedom, Capitalism, and Western Success* (New York: Random House, 2005).

Stein, Peter G., 'Roman Law, Common Law, and Civil Law' (1992) 66 *Tulane Law Review* 1591–604.

   Roman Law in European History (Cambridge: Cambridge University Press, 1999).

Steiner, Henry J., and Alston, Philip, *International Human Rights in Context: Law, Politics, Morals* (Oxford: Oxford University Press, 2nd edn 2000).

St German, Christopher, *Doctor and Student*, ed. T. F. T. Plucknett and J. L. Barton (London: Selden Society, 1974).

Stiglitz, Joseph, *Globalization and its Discontents* (London: Penguin, 2002).

Stone, Julius, *Human Law and Human Justice* (Sydney: Maitland Publications Pty Ltd, 1965).

   Of Law and Nations: Between Power Politics and Human Hopes (Buffalo: W. S. Hein, 1974).

   Visions of World Order: Between State Power and Human Justice (Baltimore: The Johns Hopkins University Press, 1984).

Strakosch, Henry E., *State Absolutism and the Rule of Law: The Struggle for the Codification of Civil Law in Austria 1753–1811* (Sydney: Sydney University Press, 1967).

Strauss, Gerald, 'The Idea of Order in the German Reformation' in *Enacting the Reformation in Germany: Essays on Institution and Reception* (Aldershot: Variorum, 1993).

Strayer, Joseph R., *Western Europe in the Middle Ages* (New York: Appleton-Century-Crofts Inc., 1955).

    On the Medieval Origins of the Modern State (Princeton: Princeton University Press, 1970).

Susskind, Richard, *The Future of Law: Facing the Challenges of Information Technology* (Oxford: Oxford University Press, 1998).

Stychin, Carl F., 'Relatively Universal: Globalisation, Rights Discourse, and the Evolution of Australian Sexual and National Identities' (1998) 18 *Legal Studies* 534–57.

Sunstein, Cass R., *Why Societies Need Dissent* (Cambridge, MA: Harvard University Press, 2003).

Swadling, William John, 'Restitution and Unjust Enrichment' in A. S. Hartkamp *et al.* (eds.), *Towards a European Civil Code* (Dordrecht: Martinus Nijhoff Publishers, 1st edn 1994).

Swidler, Leonard, 'Toward a Universal Declaration of a Global Ethic' in Leonard Swidler (ed.), *For All Life: Toward a Universal Declaration of a Global Ethic* (Ashland: White Cloud Press, 1999).

Symeonides, Symeon C., 'Contracts Subject to Non-State Norms' (2006) 54 *American Journal of Comparative Law* 209–31.

Tamanaha, Brian Z., *A General Jurisprudence of Law and Society* (Oxford: Oxford University Press, 2001).

    Law as a Means to an End: Threat to the Rule of Law (Cambridge: Cambridge University Press, 2006).

    'The Contemporary Relevance of Legal Positivism' (2007) *Australian Journal of Legal Philosophy* 1–38.

Tawney, R. H., *Religion and the Rise of Capitalism: A Historical Study* (Harmondsworth: Penguin, 1938).

    'Foreword' in Max Weber, *The Protestant Ethic and the Spirit of Capitalism*, trans. Talcott Parsons (London: Unwin University Books, 1930 reprinted 1971).

Tay, Alice, 'Human Rights and Human Wrongs' (1999) 21 *Adelaide Law Review* 1–18.

Tellenbach, Gerd, *Church, State and Christian Society at the Time of the Investiture Contest*, trans. R. F. Bennett (Oxford: Basil Blackwell, 1948).

Tenbruck, Friedrich H., 'The Dream of a Secular Ecumene: The Meaning and Policies of Development' in Mike Featherstone (ed.), *Global Culture: Nationalism, Globalization and Modernity* (London: Sage, 1990 reprinted 1996).

Teschke, Benno, 'Geopolitical Relations in the European Middle Ages: History and Theory' (1998) 52 *International Organization* 325–58.

Teubner, Gunther, ' "Global Bukowina": Legal Pluralism in the World Society' in Gunther Teubner (ed.), *Global Law Without a State* (Brookfield: Dartmouth Publishing Company, 1997).

Thompson, E. P., *Customs in Common* (London: Merlin, 1991).

Tierney, Brian, *Foundations of the Conciliar Theory: The Contribution of the Medieval Canonists From Gratian to the Great Schism* (Cambridge: The University Press, 1955 reprinted 1968).

    The Crisis of Church and State 1050–1300 (NJ: Englewood Cliffs, 1964).

Tierney, Brian, 'The Idea of Natural Rights – Origins and Persistence' (2004) 2 *Northwestern University Journal of International Human Rights* 1–33.

Toland, John, 'Christianity Not Mysterious' in Peter Gay (ed.), *Deism: An Anthology* (Princeton: D. van Nostrand Company, Inc., 1968).

Tolkien, J. R. R., *The Lord of the Rings* [1954] (London: HarperCollins Publishers, 1997).

Toynbee, Arnold, *Civilization on Trial* (Oxford: Oxford University Press, 1948).

Trachtman, Joel P., '*L'Etat, C'est Nous*: Sovereignty, Economic Integration and Subsidiarity' (1992) 33 *Harvard International Law Journal* 459–73.

Trakman, Leon E., *The Law Merchant: The Evolution of Commercial Law* (Littleton: Fred B. Rothman & Co., 1983).

'From the Medieval Law Merchant to E-Merchant Law' (2003) 53 *University of Toronto Law Journal* 265–304, 267.

Tully, James, *Strange Multiplicity: Constitutionalism in an Age of Diversity* (Cambridge: Cambridge University Press, 1995).

Twining, William, 'Globalization and Legal Theory: Some Local Implications' (1996) 49 *Current Legal Problems* 1–42.

Law in Context: Enlarging a Discipline (Oxford: Clarendon Press, 1997).

Globalisation and Legal Theory (London: Butterworths, 2000).

'Reviving General Jurisprudence' in Michael Likosky (ed.), *Transnational Legal Processes* (London: Butterworths, 2002).

'The Province of Jurisprudence Re-examined: Problems of Generalization in a Global Context' in Catherine Dauvergne (ed.), *Jurisprudence for an Interconnected Globe* (Aldershot: Ashgate, 2003).

'A Post-Westphalian Conception of Law' (2003) 37 *Law & Society Review* 199–257.

'Diffusion of Law: A Global Perspective' (2005) 49 *Journal of Legal Pluralism and Unofficial Law* 1–45.

'General Jurisprudence' in Manuel Escamilla and Modesto Savedra (eds.), *Law and Justice in a Global Society* (Granada: International Association for Philosophy of Law and Social Sociology, 2005).

'Social Science and Diffusion of Law' (2005) 32 *Journal of Law and Society* 203–40.

'Glenn on Tradition: An Overview' (2005) 1 *Journal of Comparative Law* 107–15.

'Human Rights: Southern Voices: Francis Deng, Abdullahi An-Na'im, Yash Ghai, and Upendra Baxi' (2006) 11 *Review of Constitutional Studies* 203–80.

'Globalisation and Comparative Law' in David Nelkin and Esin Örücü (eds.), *Comparative Law: A Handbook* (Oxford: Hart Publishing, forthcoming).

Twiss, Sumner B., 'History, Human Rights, and Globalization' (2004) 32 *Journal of Religious Ethics* 39–70.

Tyler, Tom R., Why People Obey the Law (Princeton: Princeton University Press, reprinted 2006).

Ullmann, Walter, 'The Medieval Papal Court as an International Tribunal' (1971) 11 *Virginia Journal of International Law* 356–71.

The Church and the Law in the Earlier Middle Ages: Selected Essays (London: Variorum Reprints, 1975).

Medieval Political Thought (Harmondsworth: Penguin, 1975).

Law and Politics in the Middle Ages (London: Sources of History Ltd, 1975).

'This Realm of England is an Empire' (1979) 30 *Journal of Ecclesiastical History* 175–203.

Unger, Roberto Mangabeira, *Law in Modern Society: Toward a Criticism of Social Theory* (New York: The Free Press, 1976).

UNIDROIT (ed.), *Principles of International Commercial Contracts* (Rome, 1994).

Urwin, David, *The Community of Europe: A History of European Integration Since 1945* (London: Longman, 1991).

Valcke, Catherine, 'Comparative History and the Internal View of French, German, and English Private Law' (2006) 19 *Canadian Journal of Law and Jurisprudence* 133–60.

van Caenegem, R. C., *The Birth of the English Common Law* (Cambridge: Cambridge University Press, 1973).

    Judges, Legislators and Professors: Chapters in European Legal History (Cambridge: Cambridge University Press, 1987 reprinted 1996).

    An Historical Introduction to Private Law, trans. D. E. L. Johnston (Cambridge: Cambridge University Press, 1988).

    An Historical Introduction to Western Constitutional Law (Cambridge: Cambridge University Press, 1995).

    European Law in the Past and the Future: Unity and Diversity over Two Millennia (Cambridge: Cambridge University Press, 2002).

    'The Unification of European Law: A Pipedream?' (2006) 14 *European Review* 33–48.

van Creveld, Martin, *The Rise and Decline of the State* (Cambridge: Cambridge University Press, 1999).

    'On Globalization: The Military Dimension' in Karl-Heinz Ladeur (ed.), *Public Governance in the Age of Globalization* (Aldershot: Ashgate, 2004).

van Erp, Sjef, 'The Formation of Contracts' in A. S. Hartkamp *et al.* (eds.), *Towards a European Civil Code* (Dordrecht: Martinus Nijhoff Publishers, 2nd edn 1998).

Van Hoecke, Mark, and Ost, François (eds.), *The Harmonisation of European Private Law* (Oxford: Hart Publishing, 2000).

Van Parijs, Philippe, 'Europe's Linguistic Challenge' (2004) 45 *European Journal of Sociology* 113–54.

Varga, Csaba, 'Utopias of Rationality in the Development of the Idea of Codification' in F. C. Hutley *et al.* (eds.), *Law and the Future of Society* (Wiesbaden: Franz Steiner Verlag GMBH, 1979).

    Codification as a Socio-Historical Phenomenon, trans. Sándor Eszenyi *et al.* (Budapest: Akadémiai Kiadó, 1991).

Vázquez, Carlos Manuel, 'Trade Sanctions and Human Rights – Past, Present and Future' (2003) 6 *Journal of International Economic Law* 797–839.

Vattel, E. de, *The Law of Nations* (Philadelphia: T. & J. W. Johnson & Co., 1849).

Verdross, Alfred, and Koeck, Heribert Franz, 'Natural Law: The Tradition of Universal Reason and Authority' in R. St J. Macdonald and Douglas M. Johnston (eds.), *The Structure and Process of International Law: Essays in Legal Philosophy Doctrine and Theory* (The Hague: Martinus Nijhoff Publishers, 1983).

Vining, Joseph, *From Newton's Sleep* (Princeton: Princeton University Press, 1995).

Vinogradoff, Paul, *The Collected Papers of Paul Vinogradoff*, 2 vols. (Oxford: Clarendon Press, 1928) vol. II.

Voegelin, Eric, 'The Nature of the Law' in R. Pascal *et al.* (eds.), *The Collected Works of Eric Voegelin*, 34 vols. (Columbia: University of Missouri Press, 1991), vol. XXVII.

Vogenauer, Stefan, 'An Empire of Light? II: Learning and Lawmaking in Germany Today' (2006) 26 *Oxford Journal of Legal Studies* 627–63.

Waldron, Jeremy, 'Custom Redeemed by Statute' (1998) 51 *Current Legal Problems* 93–114.

    Law and Disagreement (Oxford: Clarendon Press, 1999).

Walker, Neil, 'The Idea of Constitutional Pluralism' (2002) 65 *Modern Law Review* 317–59.

    'Postnational Constitutionalism and the Problem of Translation' in J. H. H. Weiler and Marlene Wind (eds.), *European Constitutionalism Beyond the State* (Cambridge: Cambridge University Press, 2003).

Walker, T. A., *History of the Law of Nations* (Cambridge: Cambridge University Press, 1899).

Wallerstein, Immanuel, 'Opening Remarks: Legal Constraints on the Capitalist World-Economy' in Michael Likosky (ed.), *Transnational Legal Processes* (London: Butterworths, 2002).

Walzer, Michael, 'On the Role of Symbolism in Political Thought' (1967) 82 *Political Science Quarterly* 191–204.

    Regicide and Revolution: Speeches at the Trial of Louis XVI (New York: Columbia University Press, 1992).

Ward, Ian, *A Critical Introduction to European Law* (London: LexisNexis UK, 2003).

Ware, Stephen J., 'Default Rules from Mandatory Rules: Privatizing Law Through Arbitration' (1999) 83 *Minnesota Law Review* 703–54.

Watkin, Thomas Glyn, *An Historical Introduction to Modern Civil Law* (Ashgate: Aldershot, 1999).

Watson, Alan, 'Roman Law and English Law: Two Patterns of Legal Development' (1990) 36 *Loyola Law Review* 247–74.

    International Law in Archaic Rome: War and Religion (Baltimore: Johns Hopkins University Press, 1993).

    The Evolution of Western Private Law (Baltimore: Johns Hopkins University Press, expanded edn 2001).

Watt, Horatia Muir, 'Choice of Law in Integrated and Interconnected Markets: A Matter of Political Economy' (2003) 9 *Columbia Journal of European Law* 383–409.

Watt, J. A., 'Spiritual and Temporal Powers' in J. H. Burns (ed.), *The Cambridge History of Medieval Political Thought c.350–c.1450* (Cambridge: Cambridge University Press, 1988).

Wattles, Jeffrey, *The Golden Rule* (Oxford: Oxford University Press, 1996).

Webber, Jeremy, *Reimagining Canada: Language, Culture, Community, and the Canadian Constitution* (Kingston & Montreal: McGill-Queen's University Press, 1994).

    'Beyond Regret: Mabo's Implications for Australian Constitutionalism' in Duncan Ivison *et al.* (eds.), *Political Theory and the Rights of Indigenous Peoples* (Cambridge: Cambridge University Press, 2000).

    'Legal Pluralism and Human Agency' (2006) 44 *Osgoode Hall Law Journal* 167–98.

Weber, Max, *On Law in Economy and Society*, trans. Max Rheinstein and Edward Shils [1925] (New York: Simon & Schuster, 1954).

    The Protestant Ethic and the Spirit of Capitalism, trans. Talcott Parsons [1930] (London: Unwin University Books, 1971).

Weiler, J. H. H., *The Constitution of Europe: 'Do the new clothes have an emperor?' and Other Essays on European Integration* (Cambridge: Cambridge University Press, 1999).

'Epilogue: Europe's Dark Legacy: Reclaiming Nationalism and Patriotism' in Christian Joerges and Navraj Singh Ghaleigh (eds.), *Darker Legacies of Law in Europe: The Shadow of National Socialism and Fascism over Europe and its Legal Traditions* (Oxford: Hart, 2003).

'On the Power of the Word: Europe's Constitutional Iconography' (2005) 3 *International Journal of Constitutional Law* 173–90.

Weinstein, Harvey M., 'The Integration of Intellect and Feeling in the Study of Law' (1982) 32 *Journal of Legal Education* 87–98.

Weiss, Gunther A., 'The Enchantment of Codification in the Common-Law World' (2000) 25 *Yale Journal of International Law* 435–532.

Westbrook, David A., *City of Gold: An Apology for Global Capitalism* (New York: Routledge, 2004).

Weyrauch, O., 'Legal Practice as Search for Truth' (1985) 35 *Journal of Legal Education* 123–9.

Whitman, James Q., *The Legacy of Roman Law in the German Romantic Era: Historical Vision and Legal Change* (Princeton: Princeton University Press, 1990).

Wieacker, Franz, 'Foundations of European Legal Culture' (1990) 38 *American Journal of Comparative Law* 1–29.

A History of Private Law in Europe, With Particular Reference to Germany, trans. Tony Weir (Oxford: Oxford University Press, 1995).

Wiegand, Wolfgang, 'The Reception of American Law in Europe' (1991) 39 *American Journal of Comparative Law* 229–48.

Wiener, Antje, 'Finality vs. Enlargement: Constitutive Practices and Opposing Rationales in the Reconstruction of Europe' in J. H. H. Weiler and Marlene Wind (eds.), *European Constitutionalism Beyond the State* (Cambridge: Cambridge University Press, 2003).

Wiener, Jarrod, *Globalization and the Harmonization of Law* (London: Pinter, 1999).

Wimmer, Andreas, 'Globalizations *Avant la Lettre*: A Comparative View of Isomorphization and Heteromorphization in the Inter-Connecting World' (2001) 43 *Comparative Studies in Society and History* 435–66.

Windeyer, W. J. V., *Lectures on Legal History* (Sydney: Law Book Co., 1957).

Winroth, Anders, *The Making of Gratian's Decretum* (Cambridge: Cambridge University Press, 2000).

Witte, John Jr, 'From Homer to Hegel: Ideas of Law and Culture in the West' (1991) 89 *Michigan Law Review* 1618–36.

'Law, Religion, and Human Rights' (1996) 28 *Columbia Human Rights Review* 1–31.

Law and Protestantism: the Legal Teachings of the Lutheran Reformation (Cambridge: Cambridge University Press, 2002).

Wolf, Ronald Charles, *Trade, Aid, and Arbitrate: The Globalization of Western Law* (Aldershot: Ashgate, 2004).

Wolff, Robert Paul, *In Defence of Anarchism* (New York: Harper, 1976).

Wormald, Patrick, *The Making of English Law: King Alfred to the Twelfth Century* (Oxford: Blackwell, 1999).

Zetter, Kim, *Simple Kabbalah* (Berkeley: Conari Press, 1999).

Zielonka, Jan, *Europe as Empire: The Nature of the Enlarged European Union* (Oxford: Oxford University Press, 2006).

Zimmermann, Reinhard, 'Roman Law and European Legal Unity' in A. S. Hartkamp *et al.* (eds.), *Towards a European Civil Code* (Dordrecht: Martinus Nijhoff Publishers, 2nd edn 1998).

'Savigny's Legacy: Legal History, Comparative Law, and the Emergence of a European Legal Science' (1996) 112 *Law Quarterly Review* 576–605.

'The Civil Law in European Codes' in Hector L. MacQueen *et al.* (eds.), *Regional Private Laws and Codification in Europe* (Cambridge: Cambridge University Press, 2003).

Zolo, Danilo, 'Hans Kelsen: International Peace Through International Law' (1998) 9 *European Journal of International Law* 306–24.

Index